Microsoft® Office Access 2003

ILLUSTRATED, CourseCard Edition

COMPLETE

Lisa Friedrichsen

THOMSON
COURSE TECHNOLOGY™

Australia • Canada • Mexico • Singapore • Spain • United Kingdom • United States

Microsoft® Office Access 2003 - Illustrated Complete, CourseCard Edition

Lisa Friedrichsen

Managing Editor:
Marjorie Hunt

Production Editors:
Daphne Barbas, Pamela Elizian

QA Manuscript Reviewers:
Chris Carvalho, Christian Kunciw,
Maxwell Prior

Product Managers:
Christina Kling Garrett,
Jane Hosie-Bounar

Developmental Editor:
Lisa Ruffolo

Text Designer:
Joseph Lee, Black Fish Design

Associate Product Manager:
Emilie Perreault

Editorial Assistant:
Shana Rosenthal

Composition House:
GEX Publishing Services

The Illustrated Series Vision

Teaching and writing about computer applications can be extremely rewarding and challenging. How do we engage students and keep their interest? How do we teach them skills that they can easily apply on the job? As we set out to write this book, our goals were to develop a textbook that:

- works for a beginning student
- provides varied, flexible, and meaningful exercises and projects to reinforce the skills
- serves as a reference tool
- makes your job as an educator easier, by providing resources above and beyond the textbook to help you teach your course

Our popular, streamlined format is based on advice from instructional designers and customers. This flexible design presents each lesson on a two-page spread, with step-by-step instructions on the left, and screen illustrations on the right. This signature style, coupled with high-caliber content, provides a comprehensive yet manageable introduction to Microsoft Office Access 2003—it is a teaching package for the instructor and a learning experience for the student.

About This Edition

New to this edition is a free, tear-off Access 2003 CourseCard that provides students with a great way to have Access skills at their fingertips!

Acknowledgments

This Access book is dedicated to my students, and all who are using this book to teach and learn about Access. Thank you. Also, thank you to all of the professionals who helped me create this book.

Lisa Friedrichsen
and the Illustrated Team

Preface

Welcome to *Microsoft® Office Access 2003—Illustrated Complete, CourseCard Edition*. Each lesson in this book contains elements pictured to the right.

How is the book organized?

Two units on Windows XP introduce students to basic operating system skills. The book is then organized into 16 units on Access covering creating and using tables, queries, forms, and reports, through advanced database skills including creating data access pages, macros and modules, and managing database objects.

What kinds of assignments are included in the book? At what level of difficulty?

The lessons use MediaLoft, a fictional chain of bookstores, as the case study. The assignments on the light purple pages at the end of each unit increase in difficulty. Data Files and case studies, with many international examples, provide a great variety of interesting and relevant business applications. Assignments include:

- **Concepts Reviews** include multiple choice, matching, and screen identification questions.
- **Skills Reviews** provide additional hands-on, step-by-step reinforcement.
- **Independent Challenges** are case projects requiring critical thinking and application of the unit skills. The Independent Challenges increase in difficulty, with the first one in each unit being the easiest (most step-by-step with detailed instructions). Independent Challenges 2 and 3 become increasingly open-ended, requiring more independent problem solving.
- **E-Quest Independent Challenges** are case projects with a Web focus. E-Quests require the use of the World Wide Web to conduct research to complete the project.
- **Advanced Challenge Exercises** set within the Independent Challenges provide *optional* steps for more advanced students.
- **Visual Workshops** are practical, self-graded capstone projects that require independent problem solving.

Each 2-page spread focuses on a single skill.

Concise text introduces the basic principles in the lesson and integrates a real-world case study.

UNIT
A
Access 2003

Getting Help and Exiting Access

When you are finished working with a database, you need to close all open objects, close the database, and then exit Access. To close an object, click File on the menu bar and then click Close, or click the object's Close button located on the right edge of the menu bar. After you close the objects you have been working with, you close the database and exit Access. As with most programs, if you try to exit Access and have not yet saved changes to open objects, Access prompts you to save your changes. You can use the Access Help system to learn more about the program. You have finished working with the MediaLoft-A database for now. Before exiting Access, though, you want to learn more about the Help system.

STEPS

QUICK TIP
If your Data Files are stored on a floppy disk, do not remove your floppy disk from drive A until you have completely exited Access as instructed in Step 6.

1. **Click the Close button for the MediaLoft-A database, as shown in Figure A-16**
   The MediaLoft-A database is closed, but Access is still running. At this point you can open another database or explore the Help system to learn more about Access.

2. **Click the Type a question for help box, type naming fields, then press [Enter]**
   The Search Results task pane opens, listing potential Help topics that relate to your entry. Using the Help text box is similar to initiating keyword searches via the Office Assistant or using the Answer Wizard. Help menu options and terminology are further explained in Table A-6.

3. **Click About renaming a field in a table (MDB)**
   The Help system opens to the specific page that explains how to rename an existing field in a table. **Glossary terms** are shown as blue hyperlinks. Clicking a blue hyperlink displays a definition.

4. **Click the Show All link in the upper-right corner of the Microsoft Access Help window, then resize the Help window as desired**
   An expanded view of the Help page with all subcategories and definitions appears, as shown in Figure A-17. The Show All link now becomes the Hide All link.

5. **Click the Close button for the Microsoft Office Access Help window**
   You return to the Search Results task pane where you can click another link or initiate another search for information.

6. **Click File on the menu bar, then click Exit**

Clues to Use

Compact on Close
The **Compact on Close** option found on the General tab of the Options dialog box compacts and repairs your database each time you close it. To open the Options dialog box, click Tools on the menu bar, and then click Options. *While the Compact on Close feature works well if your database is stored on your hard drive or on another large storage device, it can cause problems if your Data Files are stored on a floppy disk.* The Compact on Close process creates a temporary file that is just as large as the original database file. This temporary file is used during the compaction process, and is deleted after the procedure successfully finishes. Therefore, if your database file grows larger than half of the available storage space on a floppy disk, the Compact on Close process cannot create the necessary temporary file or successfully compact the database. Such an error might result in a harmless error message or, in the worst case, a corrupt database.

Hints as well as troubleshooting advice, right where you need them—next to the step itself.

Clues to Use boxes provide concise information that either expands on the major lesson skill or describes an independent task that in some way relates to the major lesson skill.

Every lesson features large, full-color representations of what the screen should look like as students complete the numbered steps.

Brightly colored tabs indicate which section of the book you are in.

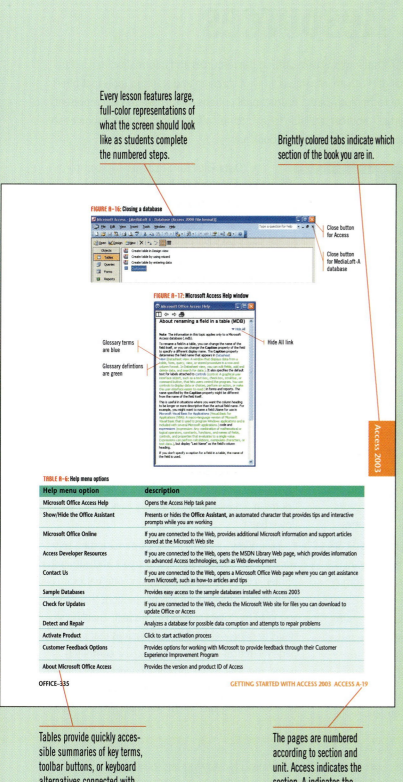

Glossary terms are blue

Glossary definitions are green

Close button for Access

Close button for MediaLoft-A database

Hide All link

Tables provide quickly accessible summaries of key terms, toolbar buttons, or keyboard alternatives connected with the lesson material. Students can refer easily to this information when working on their own projects at a later time.

The pages are numbered according to section and unit. Access indicates the section, A indicates the unit, 19 indicates the page.

What online content solutions are available to accompany this book?

Visit www.course.com for more information on our online content for Illustrated titles. Options include:

MyCourse 2.0

Need a quick, simple tool to help you manage your course? Try MyCourse 2.0, the easiest to use, most flexible syllabus and content management tool available. MyCourse 2.0 offers you brand new content, including Topic Reviews, Extra Case Projects, and Quizzes, to accompany this book.

WebCT

Course Technology and WebCT have partnered to provide you with the highest quality online resources and Web-based tools for your class. Course Technology offers content for this book to help you create your WebCT class, such as a suggested Syllabus, Lecture Notes, Practice Test questions, and more.

Blackboard

Course Technology and Blackboard have also partnered to provide you with the highest quality online resources and Web-based tools for your class. Course Technology offers content for this book to help you create your Blackboard class, such as a suggested Syllabus, Lecture Notes, Practice Test questions, and more.

Is this book Microsoft Office Specialist Certified?

Microsoft Office Access 2003—Illustrated Complete, CourseCard Edition covers the objectives for Microsoft Office Specialist and has received certification approval as courseware for the Microsoft Office Specialist program. See the inside front cover for more information on other Illustrated titles meeting Microsoft Office Specialist certification.

The first page of each unit indicates which objectives in the unit are Microsoft Office Specialist skills. If an objective is set in red, it meets a Microsoft Office Specialist skill. A document in the Review Pack cross-references the skills with the lessons and exercises.

Instructor Resources

The Instructor Resources CD is Course Technology's way of putting the resources and information needed to teach and learn effectively into your hands. With an integrated array of teaching and learning tools that offers you and your students a broad range of technology-based instructional options, we believe this CD represents the highest quality and most cutting edge resources available to instructors today. Many of these resources are available at www.course.com. The resources available with this book are:

• **Data Files for Students**—To complete most of the units in this book, your students will need **Data Files**. Put them on a file server for students to copy. The Data Files are available on the Instructor Resources CD-ROM, in the Review Pack, and can also be downloaded from www.course.com.

Instruct students to use the **Data Files List** located in the Review Pack and on the Instructor Resources CD. This list gives instructions on copying and organizing files.

• **Solutions to Exercises**—Solutions to Exercises contains every file students are asked to create or modify in the lessons and End-of-Unit material. A Help file on the Instructor Resources CD includes information for using the Solution Files. There is also a document outlining the solutions for the End-of-Unit Concepts Review, Skills Review, and Independent Challenges.

• **PowerPoint Presentations**—Each unit has a corresponding PowerPoint presentation that you can use in a lecture, distribute to your students, or customize to suit your course.

• **Instructor's Manual**—Available as an electronic file, the Instructor's Manual is quality-assurance tested and includes unit overviews and detailed lecture topics with teaching tips for each unit.

• **Sample Syllabus**—Prepare and customize your course easily using this sample course outline.

• **Figure Files**—The figures in the text are provided on the Instructor Resources CD to help you illustrate key topics or concepts. You can create traditional overhead transparencies by printing the figure files. Or you can create electronic slide shows by using the figures in a presentation program such as PowerPoint.

• **ExamView**—ExamView is a powerful testing software package that allows you to create and administer printed, computer (LAN-based), and Internet exams. ExamView includes hundreds of questions that correspond to the topics covered in this text, enabling students to generate detailed study guides that include page references for further review. The computer-based and Internet testing components allow students to take exams at their computers, and also save you time by grading each exam automatically.

SAM 2003 Assessment & Training

SAM 2003 helps you energize your class exams and training assignments by allowing students to learn and test important computer skills in an active, hands-on environment.

With SAM 2003 Assessment, you create powerful interactive exams on critical applications such as Word, Access, PowerPoint, Windows, the Internet, and much more. The exams simulate the application environment, allowing your students to demonstrate their knowledge and think through the skills by performing real-world tasks.

Designed to be used with the Illustrated series, SAM 2003 Assessment & Training includes built-in page references so students can create study guides that match the Illustrated textbooks you use in class. Powerful administrative options allow you to schedule exams and assignments, secure your tests, and run reports with almost limitless flexibility.

Contents

ACCESS 2003

Using Forms   C-1

ACCESS 2003

Using Reports   D-1

ACCESS 2003

Modifying the Database Structure   E-1

ACCESS 2003

Creating Multiple Table Queries   F-1

ACCESS 2003

Developing Forms and Subforms   G-1

Read This Before You Begin

Software Information and Required Installation

This book was written and tested using Microsoft Office 2003 - Professional Edition, with a typical installation on Microsoft Windows XP and the most recent Windows XP Service Pack, and with Internet Explorer 6.0 or higher. Some of the exercises in this book assume that your computer is connected to the Internet. If you are not connected to the Internet, see your instructor.

There are several instances where an advanced feature may be installed on first use to complete the exercise. These features, such as the Input Mask Wizard, Find Duplicates Query Wizard, database replication, and the sample Northwind database, are installed the first time you use them. If the sample databases such as Northwind were not originally installed, you will need to run the Office 2003 setup program to install them.

Tips for Students

What Are Data Files?

To complete many of the units in this book, you need to use Data Files. A Data File contains a partially completed database, so that you don't have to type in all the information in the database yourself. Your instructor will either provide you with copies of the Data Files or ask you to make your own copies. Your instructor can also give you instructions on how to organize your files, as well as a complete file listing, or you can find the list and the instructions for organizing your files in the Review Pack.

Why Is My Screen Different from the Book?

Your desktop components and some dialog box options might be different if you are using an operating system other than Windows XP. Depending on your computer hardware and the Display settings on your computer, you may notice the following differences:

- Your screen may look larger or smaller because of your screen resolution (the height and width of your screen).

- Your title bars and dialog boxes may not display file extensions. To display file extensions, click Start on the taskbar, click Control Panel, click Appearance and Themes, then click Folder Options. Click the View tab if necessary, click Hide extensions for known file types to deselect it, then click OK. Your Office dialog boxes and title bars should now display file extensions.

- Access may not display full menus. In order to display full menus, click Tools on the menu bar, click Customize, select the Always show full menus check box on the Options tab, then click Close. This book assumes you are displaying full menus.

Compact on Close?

Important information for Access units if you are using floppy disks

If you are storing your Access databases on floppy disks, *you should **not** use the Compact on Close option* (available from the Tools menu). While the Compact on Close feature works well if your database is stored on your hard drive or on another large storage device, it can cause problems if your database is stored on a floppy when the size of your database is greater than the available free space on the floppy. Here's why: When you close a database with the Compact on Close feature turned on, the process creates a temporary file that is just as large as the original database file. In a successful compact process, this temporary file is deleted after the compact procedure is completed. But if there is not enough available space on your floppy to create this temporary file, the compact process never finishes, which means that your original database is never closed properly. If you do not close an Access database properly before attempting to use it again, you can corrupt it beyond repair. *Therefore, if you use floppies to complete these exercises, please follow the Review Pack guidelines on how to organize your databases or ask your instructor for directions so that you do not run out of room on a floppy disk or corrupt your database.*

Closing a Database Properly

It is extremely important to close your databases properly and exit the Access application before copying, moving, or e-mailing the database file, or before ejecting the Data Files floppy disk from the disk drive. Access database files are inherently multi-user, which means that multiple people can work on the same database file at the same time. To accomplish this capability, Access creates temporary files to keep track of which record you are working on while the database is open. These temporary files must be closed properly before you attempt to copy, move, or e-mail the database or before you eject a floppy that contains the database. If these temporary files do not get closed properly, the database can be corrupted beyond repair.

2000 vs. 2002/2003 File Format

New databases created in Access 2003 default to an Access 2000 file format, which is why "Access 2000 file format" is shown in the database window title bar for the figures in this book. While the Data Files for this book can be opened and used in Access 2000 or Access 2002, the figures in this book present the Access 2003 application, use the Access 2003 menus and toolbars, and highlight the new features of Access 2003 including new smart tags, new error indicators, the ability to easily locate object dependencies, the ability to update properties automatically, a new backup tool, new themes for forms, and improvements to PivotTables and PivotCharts.

Microsoft Jet Database Engine

You may not have the latest version of the Microsoft Jet database engine. To obtain the latest update, follow the prompts in the dialog box that appears when you open a database. (This dialog box will only appear if you do not have the latest version of the Microsoft Jet database engine.)

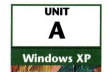

UNIT A
Getting Started with Windows XP

OBJECTIVES

Start Windows and view the desktop
Use the mouse
Start a program
Move and resize windows
Use menus, keyboard shortcuts, and toolbars
Use dialog boxes
Use scroll bars
Use Windows Help and Support Center
Close a program and shut down Windows

If you have a SAM user profile, you may have access to hands-on instruction, practice, and assessment of the skills covered in this unit. Log in to your SAM account and go to your assignments page to see what your instructor has assigned.

Microsoft Windows XP, or simply Windows, is an operating system. An **operating system** is a kind of computer program that controls how a computer carries out basic tasks such as displaying information on your computer screen and running other programs. Windows helps you save and organize the results of your work as **files**, which are electronic collections of data, with each collection having a unique name (called the **filename**). Windows also coordinates the flow of information among the programs, printers, storage devices, and other components of your computer system, as well as among other computers on a network. When you work with Windows, you use **icons**, small pictures intended to be meaningful symbols of the items they represent. You will also use rectangular-shaped work areas known as windows, thus the name of the operating system. This unit introduces you to basic skills that you can use in all Windows programs.

UNIT
A
Windows XP

Starting Windows and Viewing the Desktop

When you turn on your computer, Windows XP automatically starts and the desktop appears (you may be prompted to select your user name and/or enter your password first). The desktop, shown in Figure A-1, is where you can organize all the information and tools you need to accomplish your computer tasks. On the desktop, you can access, store, share, and explore information seamlessly, whether it resides on your computer, a network, or on the **Internet**, a worldwide collection of over 40 million computers linked together to share information. When you start Windows for the first time, the desktop appears with the **default** settings, those preset by the operating system. For example, the default color of the desktop is blue. If any of the default settings have been changed on your computer, your desktop will look different from the one in the figures, but you should be able to locate the items you need. The bar at the bottom of the screen is the **taskbar**, which shows what programs are currently running. You click the **Start button** at the left end of the taskbar to perform such tasks as starting programs, finding and opening files, and accessing Windows Help. The **Quick Launch toolbar** often appears next to the Start button; it contains several buttons you can click to start Internet-related programs quickly, and another that you can click to show the desktop when it is not currently visible. Table A-1 identifies the icons and other elements you see on your desktop. If Windows XP is not currently running on your computer, follow the steps below to start it now.

STEPS

TROUBLE

If a Welcome to Microsoft Windows tour opens, move your mouse pointer over the Next button in the lower-right corner of the dialog box and click the left mouse button once; when you see the Do you want to activate Windows now? dialog box, click the No, remind me every few days option. See your instructor or technical support person for further assistance.

1. **Turn on your computer and monitor**
   When Windows starts, you may see an area where you can click your user name or a Log On to Windows dialog box. If so, continue to Step 2. If not, view Figure A-1, then continue on to the next lesson.

2. **Click the correct user name, if necessary, type your password, then press [Enter]**
   Once the password is accepted, the Windows desktop appears on your screen. See Figure A-1.
   If you don't know your password, see your instructor or technical support person.

Clues to Use

Accessing the Internet from the Desktop

Windows XP provides a seamless connection between your desktop and the Internet with Internet Explorer. Internet Explorer is an example of a **browser**, a program designed to access the **World Wide Web** (also known as the **WWW**, or simply the **Web**). Internet Explorer is included with the Windows XP operating system. You can access it on the Start menu or by clicking its icon if it appears on the desktop or on the Quick Launch toolbar. You can use it to access Web pages and to place Web content such as weather or stock updates on the desktop for instant viewing. This information is updated automatically whenever you connect to the Internet.

FIGURE A-1: Windows desktop

Icons (yours might be different)

Start button

Taskbar

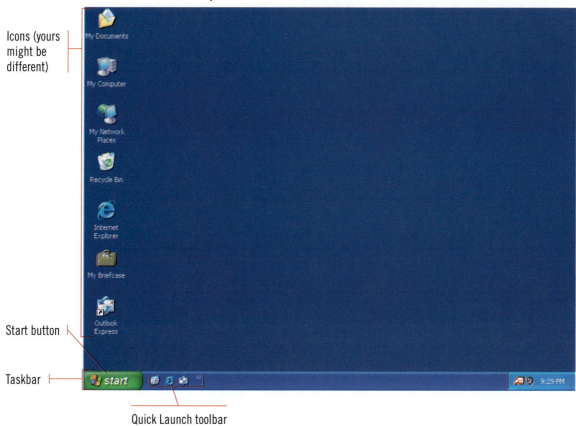

Quick Launch toolbar

TABLE A-1: Elements of a typical Windows desktop

desktop element	icon	allows you to
My Computer		Work with different disk drives, folders, and files on your computer
My Documents folder		Store documents, graphics, video and sound clips, and other files
Internet Explorer		Start the Internet Explorer browser to access the Internet
Recycle Bin		Delete and restore files
My Network Places		Open files and folders on other computers and install network printers
My Briefcase		Synchronize files when you use two computers
Outlook Express		Send and receive e-mail and participate in newsgroups
Start button	start	Start programs, open documents, search for files, and more
Taskbar		Start programs and switch among open programs and files
Quick Launch toolbar		Display the desktop, start Internet Explorer, and start Outlook Express

Using the Mouse

A **mouse** is a handheld **input** or **pointing device** that you use to interact with your computer. Input or pointing devices come in many shapes and sizes; some, like a mouse, are directly attached to your computer with a cable; others function like a TV remote control and allow you to access your computer without being right next to it. Figure A-2 shows examples of common pointing devices. Because the most common pointing device is a mouse, this book uses that term. If you are using a different pointing device, substitute that device whenever you see the term "mouse." When you move the mouse, the **mouse pointer** on the screen moves in the same direction. You use the **mouse buttons** to select icons and commands, which is how you communicate with the computer. Table A-2 shows some common mouse pointer shapes that indicate different activities. Table A-3 lists the five basic mouse actions. Begin by experimenting with the mouse now.

STEPS

1. **Locate the mouse pointer on the desktop, then move the mouse across your desk or mouse pad**

   Watch how the mouse pointer moves on the desktop in response to your movements; practice moving the mouse pointer in circles, then back and forth in straight lines.

2. **Position the mouse pointer over the Recycle Bin icon**

   Positioning the mouse pointer over an item is called **pointing**.

3. **With the pointer over the , press and release the left mouse button**

   Pressing and releasing the left mouse button is called **clicking** (or single-clicking, to distinguish it from double-clicking, which you'll do in Step 7). When you position the mouse pointer over an icon or any item and click, you select that item. When an item is **selected**, it is **highlighted** (shaded differently from other items), and the next action you take will be performed on that item.

4. **With selected, press and hold down the left mouse button, move the mouse down and to the right, then release the mouse button**

   The icon becomes dimmed and moves with the mouse pointer; this is called **dragging**, which you do to move icons and other Windows elements. When you release the mouse button, the item is positioned at the new location (it may "snap" to another location, depending on the settings on your computer).

5. **Position the mouse pointer over the , then press and release the right mouse button**

   Clicking the right mouse button is known as **right-clicking**. Right-clicking an item on the desktop produces a **shortcut menu**, as shown in Figure A-3. This menu lists the commands most commonly used for the item you have clicked. A **command** is a directive that provides access to a program's features.

6. **Click anywhere outside the menu to close the shortcut menu**

7. **Position the mouse pointer over the , then quickly press and release the left mouse button twice**

   Clicking the mouse button twice quickly is known as **double-clicking**; in this case, double-clicking the Recycle Bin icon opens the Recycle Bin window, which displays files that you have deleted.

8. **Click the Close button in the upper-right corner of the Recycle Bin window**

FIGURE A-2: Common pointing devices

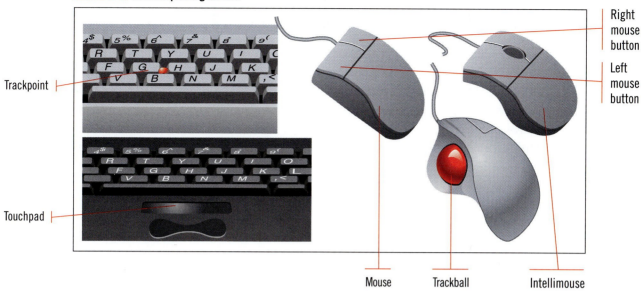

Trackpoint

Touchpad

Right mouse button

Left mouse button

Mouse   Trackball   Intellimouse

FIGURE A-3: Displaying a shortcut menu

Selected icon

Pointer positioned over icon

Shortcut menu

TABLE A-2: Common mouse pointer shapes

shape	used to
⌖	Select items, choose commands, start programs, and work in programs
I	Position mouse pointer for editing or inserting text; called the insertion point or Text Select pointer
⧖	Indicate Windows is busy processing a command
↔	Change the size of a window; appears when mouse pointer is on the border of a window
☝	Select and open Web-based data and other links

TABLE A-3: Basic mouse techniques

technique	what to do
Pointing	Move the mouse to position the mouse pointer over an item on the desktop
Clicking	Press and release the left mouse button
Double-clicking	Press and release the left mouse button twice quickly
Dragging	Point to an item, press and hold the left mouse button, move the mouse to a new location, then release the mouse button
Right-clicking	Point to an item, then press and release the right mouse button

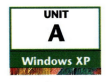
Starting a Program

Clicking the Start button on the taskbar opens the **Start menu**, which lists submenus for a variety of tasks described in Table A-4. As you become familiar with Windows, you might want to customize the Start menu to include additional items that you use most often. Windows XP comes with several built-in programs, called **accessories**. Although not as feature-rich as many programs sold separately, Windows accessories are useful for completing basic tasks. In this lesson, you start a Windows accessory called **WordPad**, which is a word-processing program you can use to create and edit simple documents.

STEPS

1. **Click the Start button on the taskbar**

   The Start menu opens.

2. **Point to All Programs**

   The All Programs submenu opens, listing the programs and categories for programs installed on your computer. WordPad is in the category called Accessories.

QUICK TIP

The left side of the Windows XP Start menu lists programs you've used recently, so the next time you want to open WordPad, most likely it will be handy in this list of recently opened programs.

3. **Point to Accessories**

   The Accessories menu, shown in Figure A-4, contains several programs to help you complete common tasks. You want to start WordPad.

4. **Click WordPad**

   WordPad starts and opens a blank document window, as shown in Figure A-5. Don't worry if your window does not fill the screen; you'll learn how to maximize it in the next lesson. Note that a program button appears on the taskbar and is highlighted, indicating that WordPad is open.

TABLE A-4: Start menu categories

category	description
Default	Displays the name of the current user; different users can customize the Start menu to fit their work habits
Internet Explorer / Outlook Express	The two programs many people use for a browser and e-mail program; you can add programs you use often to this list (called the "pinned items list")
Frequently used programs list	Located below Internet Explorer and Outlook Express, contains the last six programs used on your computer; you can change the number listed
All Programs	Displays a menu of most programs installed on your computer
My Documents, etc.	The five items in this list allow you to quickly access files you've saved in the three folders listed (My Documents, My Pictures, and My Music), as well as access My Computer, which you use to manage files, folders, and drives on your computer; the My Recent Documents list contains the last 15 files that have been opened on your computer
Control Panel / Connect To / Printers and Faxes	Control Panel displays tools for selecting settings on your computer; Connect To lists Internet connections that have been set up on your computer; and Printers and Faxes lists the printers and faxes connected to your computer
Help and Support / Search / Run	Help and Support provides access to Help topics and other support services; Search locates files, folders, computers on your network, and Web pages on the Internet; Run opens a program, file, or Web site by letting you type commands or names in a dialog box
Log Off / Turn Off Computer	End your Windows session; used when you are done using the computer and don't expect to use it again soon

FIGURE A-4: Cascading menus

Arrow indicates submenu

Submenu

Click to open WordPad

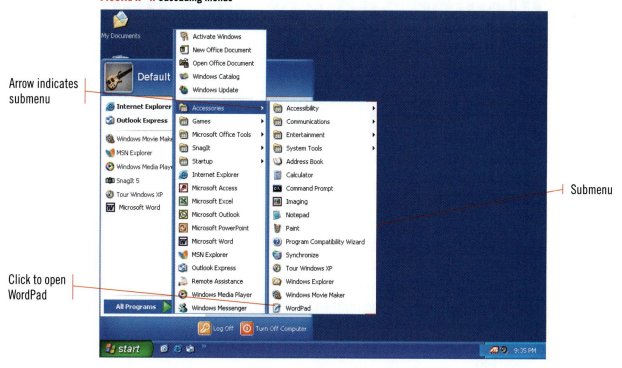

FIGURE A-5: WordPad program window

Document window

Program button indicates open program

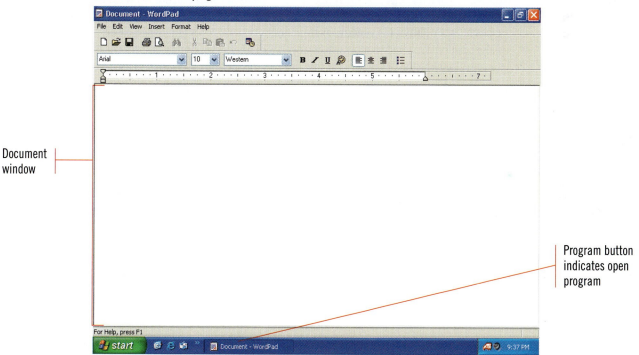

Clues to Use

Customizing the Start Menu

With Windows XP, you can change the way the Start menu looks and behaves by opening the Control Panel (click the Start button and then click Control Panel), switching to Classic view, if necessary, then double-clicking Taskbar and Start Menu. To get the look and feel of the classic Start menu from earlier versions of Windows, click the Start Menu tab and then click the Classic Start menu option

button. You can then click the Customize button to add shortcuts to the Start menu for desired programs and documents, or change the order in which they appear. To preserve the Windows XP look of the Start menu but modify how it behaves, click the Customize button next to the Start menu and select the options you want.

Moving and Resizing Windows

One of the powerful features of Windows is the ability to open more than one window or program at once. This means, however, that the desktop can get cluttered with the various programs and files you are using. You can keep your desktop organized by changing the size of a window or moving it. You can do this by clicking the sizing buttons in the upper-right corner of any window or by dragging a corner or border of any window that does not completely fill the screen. Practice sizing and moving the WordPad window now.

STEPS

1. **If the WordPad window does not already fill the screen, click the Maximize button in the WordPad window**

   When a window is **maximized**, it takes up the whole screen.

2. **Click the Restore button in the WordPad window**

   To **restore** a window is to return it to its previous size, as shown in Figure A-6. The Restore button only appears when a window is maximized.

3. **Position the pointer on the right edge of the WordPad window until the pointer changes to ↔, then drag the border to the right**

   The width of the window increases. You can change the height or width of a window by dragging any of the four sides.

   > **QUICK TIP**
   > You can resize windows by dragging any corner. You can also drag any border to make the window taller, shorter, wider, or narrower.

4. **Position the pointer in the lower-right corner of the WordPad window until the pointer changes to ↘, as shown in Figure A-6, then drag down and to the right**

   The height and width of the window increase proportionally when you drag a corner instead of a side. You can also position a restored window wherever you want on the desktop by dragging its title bar. The **title bar** is the area along the top of the window that displays the filename and program used to create it.

5. **Drag the title bar on the WordPad window up and to the left, as shown in Figure A-6**

   The window is repositioned on the desktop. At times, you might want to close a program window, yet keep the program running and easily accessible. You can accomplish this by minimizing a window.

   > **QUICK TIP**
   > If you have more than one window open and you want to quickly access something on the desktop, you can click the Show Desktop button on the Quick Launch toolbar. All open windows are minimized so the desktop is visible. If your Quick Launch toolbar isn't visible, right-click the taskbar, point to Toolbars, and then click Quick Launch.

6. **In the WordPad window, click the Minimize button**

   When you **minimize** a window, it shrinks to a program button on the taskbar, as shown in Figure A-7. WordPad is still running, but it is out of your way.

7. **Click the WordPad program button on the taskbar to reopen the window**

   The WordPad program window reopens.

8. **Click the Maximize button in the upper-right corner of the WordPad window**

   The window fills the screen.

FIGURE A-6: Restored program window

Title bar ———

Sizing buttons

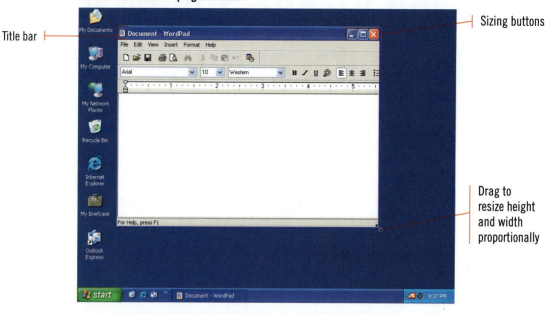

Drag to
resize height
and width
proportionally

FIGURE A-7: Minimized program window

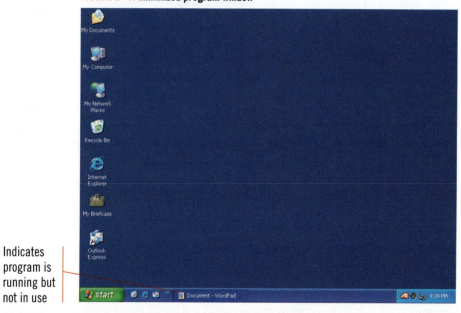

Indicates
program is
running but
not in use

Clues to Use

More about sizing windows

Keep in mind that some programs contain two sets of sizing buttons: one that controls the program window itself and another that controls the window for the file with which you are working. The program sizing buttons are located in the title bar and the file sizing buttons are located below them. See Figure A-8. When you minimize a file window within a program, the file window is reduced to an icon in the lower-left corner of the program window, but the size of the program window remains intact. (*Note:* WordPad does not use a second set of window sizing buttons.)

Also, to see the contents of more than one window at a time, you can open the desired windows, right-click a blank area on the taskbar, and then click either Tile Windows Vertically or Tile Windows

Horizontally. With the former, you see the windows side by side, and with the latter, the windows are stacked one above the other. You can also click Cascade Windows to layer any open windows in the upper-left corner of the desktop, with the title bar of each clearly visible.

FIGURE A-8: Program and file sizing buttons

File window
sizing buttons

Program window
sizing buttons

Using Menus, Keyboard Shortcuts, and Toolbars

A **menu** is a list of commands that you use to accomplish certain tasks. Each Windows program also has its own set of menus, which are located on the **menu bar** under the title bar. The menus organize commands into groups of related tasks. See Table A-5 for a description of items on a typical menu. **Toolbar buttons** offer another method for executing menu commands; instead of clicking the menu and then the menu command, you click the button for the command. A **toolbar** is a set of buttons usually positioned below the menu bar. You will open My Computer, use a menu and toolbar button to change how the contents of the window appear, and then add and remove a toolbar button.

STEPS

TROUBLE

If you don't see the My Computer icon on your desktop, right-click the desktop, click Properties, click the Desktop tab, click the Customize Desktop button, click the My Computer check box, then click OK twice.

1. Minimize WordPad, if necessary, then double-click the My Computer icon 🖥 on the desktop

The My Computer window opens. You now have two windows open: WordPad and My Computer. My Computer is the **active window** (or active program) because it is the one with which you are currently working. WordPad is **inactive** because it is open but you are not working with it.

2. Click View on the menu bar

The View menu appears, listing the View commands, as shown in Figure A-9. On a menu, a **check mark** identifies a feature that is currently enabled or "on." To disable or turn "off" the feature, you click the command again to remove the check mark. A **bullet mark** can also indicate that an option is enabled.

3. Click List

The icons are now listed one after the other rather than as larger icons.

TROUBLE

[Alt][V] means that you should press and hold down the Alt key, press the V key, and then release both simultaneously.

4. Press [Alt][V] to open the View menu, then press [T] to open the Toolbars submenu

The View menu appears again, and then the Toolbars submenu appears, with check marks next to the selected commands. Notice that a letter in each command on the View menu is underlined. These are **keyboard navigation indicators**, indicating that you can press the underlined letter, known as a **keyboard shortcut**, instead of clicking to execute the command.

5. Press [C] to execute the Customize command

The Customize Toolbar dialog box opens. A **dialog box** is a window in which you specify how you want to perform a task; you'll learn more about working in a dialog box shortly. In the Customize Toolbar dialog box, you can add toolbar buttons to the current toolbar, or remove buttons already on the toolbar. The list on the right shows which buttons are currently on the toolbar, and the list on the left shows which buttons are available to add.

6. Click the Home button in the Available toolbar buttons section, then click the Add button (located between the two lists)

As shown in Figure A-10, the Home button is added to the Standard toolbar.

7. Click the Home button in the Current toolbar buttons section, click the Remove button, then click Close on the Customize Toolbar dialog box

The Home button disappears from the Standard toolbar, and the Customize Toolbar dialog box closes.

QUICK TIP

When you rest the pointer over a button without clicking, a ScreenTip often appears with the button's name.

8. On the My Computer toolbar, click the Views button list arrow ▦ ▾, then click Details

Some toolbar buttons have an arrow, which indicates the button contains several choices. Clicking the button shows the choices. The Details view includes a description of each item in the My Computer window.

FIGURE A-9: Opening a menu

Menu bar

Check mark

Bullet

Commands in View menu

Arrow indicates submenu

FIGURE A-10: Customize Toolbar dialog box

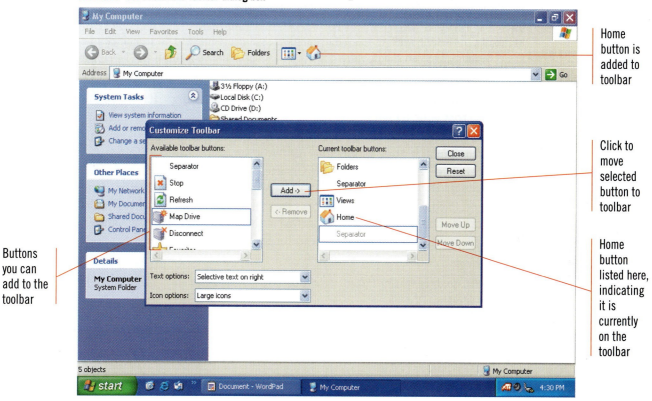

Buttons you can add to the toolbar

Home button is added to toolbar

Click to move selected button to toolbar

Home button listed here, indicating it is currently on the toolbar

TABLE A-5: Typical items on a menu

item	description	example
Dimmed command	Indicates the menu command is not currently available	Recent File
Ellipsis	Indicates that a dialog box will open that allows you to select additional options	Save As...
Triangle	Opens a cascading menu containing an additional list of commands	Toolbars ▶
Keyboard shortcut	Executes a command using the keyboard instead of the mouse	Print... Ctrl+P
Underlined letter	Indicates the letter to press for the keyboard shortcut	Exit

Using Dialog Boxes

A **dialog box** is a window that opens when you choose a menu command that needs more information before the program can carry out the command you selected. Dialog boxes open in other situations as well, such as when you open a program in the Control Panel. See Figure A-11 and Table A-6 for some of the typical elements of a dialog box. 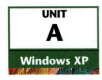 Practice using a dialog box to control your mouse settings.

STEPS

TROUBLE

If you don't see Printers and Other Hardware in the Control Panel window, you are using Classic view, not the default Category view. In the left pane, click Switch to Category view.

1. **In the left side of the My Computer window, click Control Panel; in the Control Panel window, click Printers and Other Hardware, then click the Mouse icon** 🖱

   The Mouse Properties dialog box opens, as shown in Figure A-12. **Properties** are characteristics of a computer element (in this case, the mouse) that you can customize. The options in this dialog box allow you to control the way the mouse buttons are configured, select the types of pointers that appear, choose the speed and behavior of the mouse movement on the screen, and specify what type of mouse you are using. **Tabs** at the top of the dialog box separate these options into related categories.

2. **Click the Pointer Options tab if necessary to make it the frontmost tab**

   This tab contains three options for controlling the way your mouse moves. Under Motion, you can set how fast the pointer moves on the screen in relation to how you move the mouse. You drag a **slider** to specify how fast the pointer moves. Under Snap To is a **check box**, which is a toggle for turning a feature on or off—in this case, for setting whether you want your mouse pointer to move to the default button in dialog boxes. Under Visibility, you can choose three options for easily finding your cursor and keeping it out of the way when you're typing.

3. **Under Motion, drag the slider all the way to the left for Slow, then move the mouse pointer across your screen**

   Notice how slowly the mouse pointer moves. After you select the options you want in a dialog box, you need to click a **command button**, which carries out the options you've selected. The two most common command buttons are OK and Cancel. Clicking OK accepts your changes and closes the dialog box; clicking Cancel leaves the original settings intact and closes the dialog box. The third command button in this dialog box is Apply. Clicking the Apply button accepts the changes you've made and keeps the dialog box open so that you can select additional options. Because you might share this computer with others, you should close the dialog box without making any permanent changes.

QUICK TIP

You can also use the keyboard to carry out commands in a dialog box. Pressing [Enter] is the same as clicking OK; pressing [Esc] is the same as clicking Cancel.

4. **Click Cancel**

   The original settings remain intact, the dialog box closes, and you return to the Printers and Other Hardware window.

FIGURE A-11: Elements of a typical dialog box

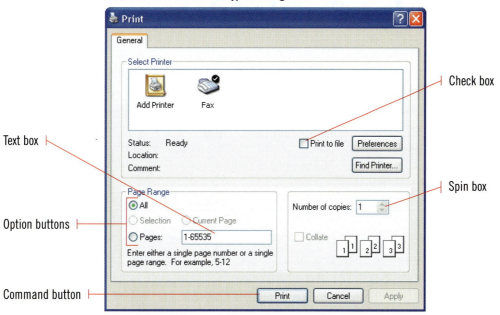

Text box

Option buttons

Command button

Check box

Spin box

FIGURE A-12: Mouse Properties dialog box

Tabs

Slider

TABLE A-6: Typical items in a dialog box

item	description
Tab	A place in a dialog box that organizes related commands and options
Check box	A box that turns an option on (when the box is checked) and off (when it is unchecked)
Command button	A rectangular button with the name of the command on it
List box	A box containing a list of items; to choose an item, click the list arrow, then click the desired item
Option button	A small circle that you click to select a single dialog box option; you cannot select more than one option button in a list
Text box	A box in which you type text
Slider	A shape that you drag to set the degree to which an option is in effect
Spin box	A box with two arrows and a text box; allows you to scroll in numerical increments or type a number

Using Scroll Bars

When you cannot see all of the items available in a window, scroll bars appear on the right and/or bottom edges of the window. **Scroll bars** are the vertical and horizontal bars along the right and bottom edges of a window and contain elements that you click and drag so you can view the additional contents of the window. When you need to scroll only a short distance, you can use the scroll arrows. To scroll the window in larger increments, click in the scroll bar above or below the scroll box. Dragging the scroll box moves you quickly to a new part of the window. See Table A-7 for a summary of the different ways to use scroll bars. With the Control Panel window in Details view, you can use the scroll bars to view all of the items in this window.

STEPS

> **TROUBLE**
>
> Your window might be called Printers and Faxes or something similar, and the Printing link may appear as Troubleshoot printing, but you should still be able to complete the steps.

1. **In the left side of the Printers and Other Hardware window, under Troubleshooters, click Printing**

   The Help and Support Center window opens, which you'll work with further in the next lesson. For now, you'll use the window to practice using the scroll bars.

2. **If the Help and Support Center window fills the screen, click the Restore button 🗗 in the upper-right corner so the scroll bars appear, as shown in Figure A-13**

> **TROUBLE**
>
> If you don't see scroll bars, drag the lower-right corner of the Help and Support Center window up and to the left until scroll bars appear.

3. **Click the down scroll arrow, as shown in Figure A-13**

   Clicking this arrow moves the view down one line.

4. **Click the up scroll arrow in the vertical scroll bar**

   Clicking this arrow moves the view up one line.

5. **Click anywhere in the area below the scroll box in the vertical scroll bar**

   The view moves down one window's height. Similarly, you can click in the scroll bar above the scroll box to move up one window's height. The size of the scroll box changes to reflect how much information does not fit in the window. A larger scroll box indicates that a relatively small amount of the window's contents is not currently visible; you need to scroll only a short distance to see the remaining items. A smaller scroll box indicates that a relatively large amount of information is currently not visible.

6. **Drag the scroll box all the way up to the top of the vertical scroll bar**

   This view shows the items that appear at the top of the window.

7. **In the horizontal scroll bar, click the area to the right of the scroll box**

   The far right edge of the window comes into view. The horizontal scroll bar works the same as the vertical scroll bar.

8. **Click the area to the left of the scroll box in the horizontal scroll bar**

9. **Click the Close button ❌ to close the Help and Support Center window**

   You'll reopen the Help and Support Center window from the Start menu in the next lesson.

FIGURE A-13: Scroll bars

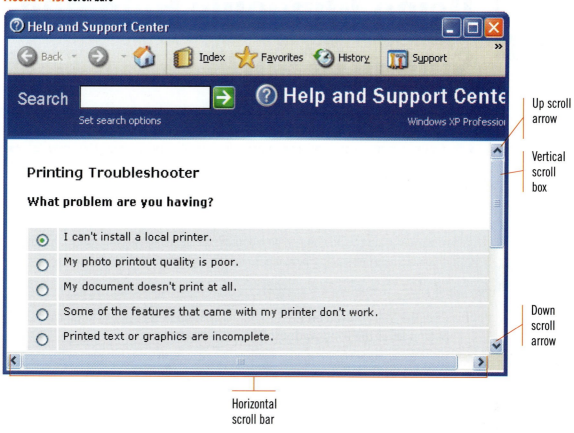

TABLE A-7: Using scroll bars

to	do this
Move down one line	Click the down arrow at the bottom of the vertical scroll bar
Move up one line	Click the up arrow at the top of the vertical scroll bar
Move down one window height	Click in the area below the scroll box in the vertical scroll bar
Move up one window height	Click in the area above the scroll box in the vertical scroll bar
Move up a large distance in the window	Drag the scroll box up in the vertical scroll bar
Move down a large distance in the window	Drag the scroll box down in the vertical scroll bar
Move a short distance side-to-side in a window	Click the left or right arrows in the horizontal scroll bar
Move to the right one window width	Click in the area to the right of the scroll box in the horizontal scroll bar
Move to the left one window width	Click in the area to the left of the scroll box in the horizontal scroll bar
Move left or right a large distance in the window	Drag the scroll box in the horizontal scroll bar

Using Windows Help and Support Center

When you have a question about how to do something in Windows XP, you can usually find the answer with a few clicks of your mouse. The Windows Help and Support Center works like a book stored on your computer, with a table of contents and an index to make finding information easier. Help provides guidance on many Windows features, including detailed steps for completing procedures, definitions of terms, lists of related topics, and search capabilities. You can browse or search for information in the Help and Support Center window, or you can connect to a Microsoft Web site on the Internet for the latest technical support on Windows XP. You can also access **context-sensitive help**, help specifically related to what you are doing, using a variety of methods such as holding your mouse pointer over an item or using the question mark button in a dialog box. In this lesson, you get Help on starting a program. You also get information about the taskbar.

STEPS

1. **Click the Start button on the taskbar, click Help and Support, then click the Maximize button ▣ if the window doesn't fill the screen**

   The Help and Support Center window opens, as shown in Figure A-14. This window has a toolbar at the top of the window, a Search box below where you enter keywords having to do with your question, a left pane where the items matching your keywords are listed, and a right pane where the specific steps for a given item are listed.

2. **Click in the Search text box, type start a program, press [Enter], then view the Help topics displayed in the left pane**

   The left pane contains a selection of topics related to starting a program. The Suggested Topics are the most likely matches for your search text.

> **QUICK TIP**
>
> Scroll down the left pane, if necessary, to view all the topics. You can also click Full-text Search Matches to view more topics containing the search text you typed or Microsoft Knowledge Base for relevant articles from the Microsoft Web site.

3. **Click Start a program**

   Help information for this topic appears in the right pane, as shown in Figure A-15. At the bottom of the text in the right pane, you can click Related Topics to view a list of topics that are related to the current topic. Some Help topics also allow you to view additional information about important words; these words are underlined, indicating that you can click them to display a pop-up window with the additional information.

4. **Click the underlined word taskbar, read the definition, then click anywhere outside the pop-up window to close it**

5. **On the toolbar at the top of the window, click the Index button**

   The Index provides an alphabetical list of all the available Help topics, like an index at the end of a book. You can type a topic in the text box at the top of the pane. You can also scroll down to the topic. In either case, you click the topic you're interested in and the details about that topic appear in the right pane.

> **QUICK TIP**
>
> You can click the Favorites button to view a list of Help pages that you've saved as you search for answers to your questions. You can click the History button to view a list of Help pages that you've viewed during the current Help session.

6. **In the left pane, type tiling windows**

   As you type, the list of topics automatically scrolls to try to match the word or phrase you type.

7. **Double-click tiling windows in the list in the left pane and read the steps and notes in the right pane**

   You can also click the Related Topics link for more information.

8. **Click the Support button on the toolbar**

   Information on the Web sites for Windows XP Help appears in the right pane (a **Web site** is a document or related documents that contain highlighted words, phrases, and graphics that link to other sites on the Internet). To access online support or information, you would click one of the available options in the left pane.

9. **Click the Close button ⊠ in the upper-right corner of the Help and Support Center window**

   The Help and Support Center window closes.

FIGURE A-14: Windows Help and Support Center

Help toolbar

Type keyword or phrase to search for topics

Links for popular Help topics

FIGURE A-15: Viewing a Help topic

Type search text here

Left pane contains list of Help topics matching your search text

Click this topic

Right pane contains information on the topic you select

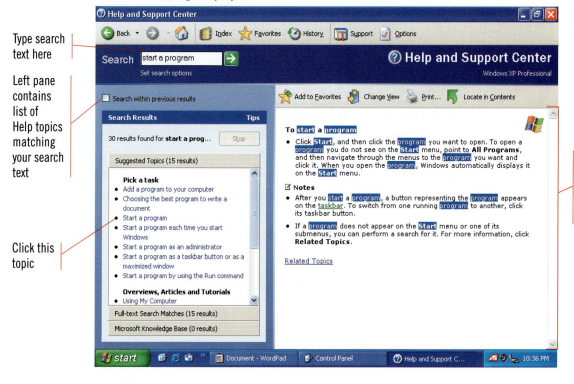

Clues to Use

Other forms of Help

The Help and Support Center offers information on Windows itself, not on all the other programs you can run on your computer. To get help on a specific Windows program, click Help on that program's menu bar. Also, to receive help in a dialog box (whether you are in Windows or another program), click the Help button ? in the upper-right corner of the dialog box; the mouse pointer changes to ?. Click any item in the dialog box that you want to learn more about. If information is available on that item, a pop-up window appears with a brief explanation of the selected feature.

Closing a Program and Shutting Down Windows

When you are finished working on your computer, you need to make sure you shut it down properly. This involves several steps: saving and closing all open files, closing all the open programs and windows, shutting down Windows, and finally, turning off the computer. If you turn off the computer while Windows is running, you could lose important data. To **close** a program, you can click the Close button in the window's upper-right corner or click File on the menu bar and choose either Close or Exit. To shut down Windows after all your files and programs are closed, click Turn Off Computer on the Start menu, then select the desired option in the Turn off computer dialog box, shown in Figure A-16. See Table A-8 for a description of shut down options. ███████ Close all your open files, windows, and programs, then exit Windows.

STEPS

1. **In the Control Panel window, click the Close button ❌ in the upper-right corner of the window**

   The Control Panel window closes.

2. **Click File on the WordPad menu bar, then click Exit**

   If you have made any changes to the open file, you will be asked to save your changes before the program closes. Some programs also give you the option of choosing the Close command on the File menu in order to close the active file but leave the program open, so you can continue to work in it with a different file. Also, if there is a second set of sizing buttons in the window, the Close button on the menu bar will close the active file only, leaving the program open for continued use.

3. **If you see a message asking you to save changes to the document, click No**

   WordPad closes and you return to the desktop.

4. **Click the Start button on the taskbar, then click Turn Off Computer**

   The Turn off computer dialog box opens, as shown in Figure A-16. In this dialog box, you have the option to stand by, turn off the computer, or restart the computer.

5. **If you are working in a lab, click Cancel to leave the computer running; if you are working on your own machine or if your instructor told you to shut down Windows, click Turn Off, then click OK**

6. **If you see the message "It is now safe to turn off your computer," turn off your computer and monitor**

   On some computers, the power shuts off automatically, so you may not see this message.

QUICK TIP

Complete the remaining steps to shut down Windows and your computer only if you have been told to do so by your instructor or technical support person. If you have been told to Log Off instead of exiting Windows, click Log Off instead of Turn Off Computer, and follow the directions from your instructor or technical support person.

FIGURE A-16: Turn off computer dialog box

Click to leave Windows running but reduce computer's power mode

Click to exit Windows and automatically restart it

Click to exit Windows safely and turn off your computer

Click to return to the desktop without taking any action

Clues to Use

The Log Off command

To change users on the same computer quickly, you can choose the Log Off command from the Start menu. When you click this command, you can choose to switch users, so that the current user is logged off and another user can log on, or you can simply log off. Windows XP shuts down partially, stopping at the point where you click your user name. When you or a new user clicks a user name (and enters a password, if necessary), Windows restarts and the desktop appears as usual.

TABLE A-8: Turn off options

Turn off option	function	when to use it
Stand By	Leaves Windows running but on minimal power	When you are finished working with Windows for a short time and plan to return before the end of the day
Turn Off	Exits Windows completely and safely	When you are finished working with Windows and want to shut off your computer for an extended time (such as overnight or longer)
Restart	Exits Windows safely, turns off the computer automatically, and then restarts the computer and Windows	When your programs might have frozen or stopped working correctly

Practice

▼ CONCEPTS REVIEW

Identify each of the items labeled in Figure A-17.

FIGURE A-17

Match each of the statements with the term it describes.

14. Shrinks a window to a button on the taskbar
15. Shows the name of the window or program
16. The taskbar item you first click to start a program
17. Requests more information for you to supply before carrying out command
18. Shows the Start button, Quick Launch toolbar, and any currently open programs
19. An input device that lets you point to and make selections
20. Graphic representation of program

a. dialog box
b. program button
c. taskbar
d. Minimize button
e. icon
f. mouse
g. Start button

Select the best answer from the list of choices.

21. **The term "file" is best defined as**
    a. a set of instructions for a computer to carry out a task.
    c. a collection of icons.
    b. an electronic collection of data.
    d. an international collection of computers.

22. **Which of the following is NOT provided by Windows XP?**
    a. The ability to organize files
    b. Instructions to coordinate the flow of information among the programs, files, printers, storage devices, and other components of your computer system
    c. Programs that allow you to specify the operation of the mouse
    d. Spell checker for your documents

23. **All of the following are examples of using a mouse, EXCEPT**
    a. clicking the Maximize button.
    c. double-clicking to start a program.
    b. pressing [Enter].
    d. dragging the My Computer icon.

24. **The term for moving an item to a new location on the desktop is**
    a. pointing.
    c. dragging.
    b. clicking.
    d. restoring.

25. **The Maximize button is used to**
    a. return a window to its previous size.
    c. scroll slowly through a window.
    b. expand a window to fill the computer screen.
    d. run programs from the Start menu.

26. **What appears if a window contains more information than can be viewed in the window?**
    a. Program icon
    c. Scroll bars
    b. Cascading menu
    d. Check boxes

27. **A window is active when**
    a. you can only see its program button on the taskbar.
    c. it is open and you are currently using it.
    b. its title bar is dimmed.
    d. it is listed in the Programs submenu.

28. **You can exit Windows by**
    a. double-clicking the Control Panel application.
    b. double-clicking the Program Manager control menu box.
    c. clicking File, then clicking Exit.
    d. selecting the Turn Off Computer command from the Start menu.

▼ SKILLS REVIEW

1. **Start Windows and view the desktop.**
    a. Turn on the computer, select your user name, then enter a password, if necessary.
    b. After Windows starts, identify as many items on the desktop as you can, without referring to the lesson material.
    c. Compare your results to Figure A-1.

2. **Use the mouse.**
    a. Double-click the Recycle Bin icon, then click the Restore button if the window fills the screen.
    b. Drag the Recycle Bin window to the upper-right corner of the desktop.
    c. Right-click the title bar of the Recycle Bin, then click Close.

3. **Start a program.**
    a. Click the Start button on the taskbar, then point to All Programs.
    b. Point to Accessories, then click Calculator.
    c. Minimize the Calculator window.

4. **Move and resize windows.**
    a. Drag the Recycle Bin icon to the top of the desktop.
    b. Double-click the My Computer icon to open the My Computer window (if you don't see the My Computer icon, read the Trouble in the lesson on menus and toolbars for how to display it).
    c. Maximize the My Computer window, if it is not already maximized.

d. Restore the window to its previous size.

e. Resize the window until you see the vertical scroll bar.

f. Minimize the My Computer window.

g. Drag the Recycle Bin icon back to its original position.

5. Use menus, keyboard shortcuts, and toolbars.

a. Click the Start button on the taskbar, then click Control Panel.

b. Click View on the menu bar, point to Toolbars, then click Standard Buttons to deselect the option and hide the toolbar.

c. Redisplay the toolbar.

d. Press [Alt][V] to display the View menu, then press [B] to hide the status bar at the bottom of the window.

e. Note the change, then use keyboard shortcuts to change the view back.

f. Click the Up button to view My Computer.

g. Click the Back button to return to the Control Panel.

h. Click View, point to Toolbars, then click Customize.

i. Add a button to the toolbar, remove it, then close the Customize Toolbar dialog box.

6. Use dialog boxes.

a. With the Control Panel in Category view, click Appearance and Themes, click Display, then click the Screen Saver tab.

b. Click the Screen saver list arrow, click any screen saver in the list, then view it in the preview monitor above the list.

c. Click the Appearance tab in the Display Properties dialog box, then click the Effects button.

d. In the Effects dialog box, click the Use large icons check box to select it, click the OK button to close the Effects dialog box, then click OK to close the Display Properties dialog box.

e. Note the change in the icons on the desktop, minimizing windows if necessary.

f. Right-click a blank area on the desktop, click Properties on the shortcut menu, click the Appearance tab, click the Effects button, click the Use large icons check box to deselect it, click OK, click the Screen Saver tab, return the screen saver to its original setting, then click Apply.

g. Click the OK button in the Display Properties dialog box, but leave the Control Panel open and make it the active program.

7. Use scroll bars.

a. In the left side of the Control Panel window, click Switch to Classic View, if necessary, click the Views button on the toolbar, then click Details.

b. Drag the vertical scroll box down all the way.

c. Click anywhere in the area above the vertical scroll box.

d. Click the down scroll arrow until the scroll box is back at the bottom of the scroll bar.

e. Click the right scroll arrow twice.

f. Click in the area to the right of the horizontal scroll box.

g. Drag the horizontal scroll box all the way back to the left.

8. Get Help.

a. Click the Start button on the taskbar, then click Help and Support.

b. Click Windows basics under Pick a Help topic, then click Tips for using Help in the left pane.

c. In the right pane, click Add a Help topic or page to the Help and Support Center Favorites list.

d. Read the topic contents, click Related Topics, click Print a Help topic or page, then read the contents. Leave the Help and Support Center open.

9. Close a program and shut down Windows.

a. Click the Close button to close the Help and Support Center window.

b. Click File on the menu bar, then click Close to close the Control Panel window.

c. Click the Calculator program button on the taskbar to restore the window.

d. Click the Close button in the Calculator window to close the Calculator program.

e. If you are instructed to do so, shut down Windows and turn off your computer.

▼ INDEPENDENT CHALLENGE 1

You can use the Help and Support Center to learn more about Windows XP and explore Help on the Internet.

a. Open the Help and Support Center window and locate help topics on adjusting the double-click speed of your mouse and displaying Web content on your desktop.

If you have a printer, print a Help topic for each subject. Otherwise, write a summary of each topic.

b. Follow these steps below to access help on the Internet. If you don't have Internet access, you can't do this step.

    i. Click a link under "Did you know?" in the right pane of the Help and Support Home page.

    ii. In the left pane of the Microsoft Web page, click Using Windows XP, click How-to Articles, then click any link.

    iii. Read the article, then write a summary of what you find.

    iv. Click the browser's Close button, disconnect from the Internet, and close Help and Support Center.

▼ INDEPENDENT CHALLENGE 2

You can change the format and the actual time of the clock and date on your computer.

a. Open the Control Panel window; in Category view, click Date, Time, Language, and Regional Options; click Regional and Language Options; then click the Customize button under Standards and formats.

b. Click the Time tab, click the Time format list arrow, click H:mm:ss to change the time to show a 24-hour clock, then click the Apply button to view the changes, if any.

c. Click the Date tab, click the Short date format list arrow, click dd-MMM-yy, then click the Apply button.

d. Click the Cancel button twice to close the open dialog boxes.

e. Change the time to one hour later using the Date and Time icon in the Control Panel.

f. Return the settings to the original time and format, then close all open windows.

▼ INDEPENDENT CHALLENGE 3

Calculator is a Windows accessory that you can use to perform calculations.

a. Start the Calculator, click Help on the menu bar, then click Help Topics.

b. Click the Calculator book in the left pane, click Perform a simple calculation to view that help topic, then print it if you have a printer connected.

c. Open the Perform a scientific calculation topic, then view the definition of a number system.

d. Determine how many months you have to work to earn an additional week of vacation if you work for a company that provides one additional day of paid vacation for every 560 hours you work. (*Hint:* Divide 560 by the number of hours you work per month.)

e. Close all open windows.

▼ INDEPENDENT CHALLENGE 4

You can customize many Windows features, including the appearance of the taskbar on the desktop.

a. Right-click the taskbar, then click Lock the Taskbar to uncheck the command, if necessary.

b. Position the pointer over the top border of the taskbar. When the pointer changes shape, drag up an inch.

c. Resize the taskbar back to its original size.

d. Right-click the Start button, then click Properties. Click the Taskbar tab.

e. Click the Help button (a question mark), then click each check box to view the pop-up window describing it.

f. Click the Start Menu tab, then click the Classic Start menu option button and view the change in the preview. (*Note:* Do not click OK.) Click Cancel.

▼ VISUAL WORKSHOP

Use the skills you have learned in this unit to customize your desktop so it looks like the one in Figure A-18. Make sure you include the following:

- Calculator program minimized
- Vertical scroll bar in Control Panel window
- Large icons view in Control Panel window
- Rearranged icons on desktop; your icons may be different. (*Hint*: If the icons snap back to where they were, they are set to be automatically arranged. Right-click a blank area of the desktop, point to Arrange Icons By, then click Auto Arrange to deselect this option.)

Use the Print Screen key to make a copy of the screen, then print it from the Paint program. (To print from the Paint program, click the Start button on the taskbar, point to All Programs, point to Accessories, then click Paint; in the Paint program window, click Edit on the menu bar, then click Paste; click Yes to fit the image on the bitmap, click the Print button on the toolbar, then click Print in the Print dialog box. See your instructor or technical support person for assistance.)

When you have completed this exercise, be sure to return your settings and desktop back to their original arrangement.

FIGURE A-18

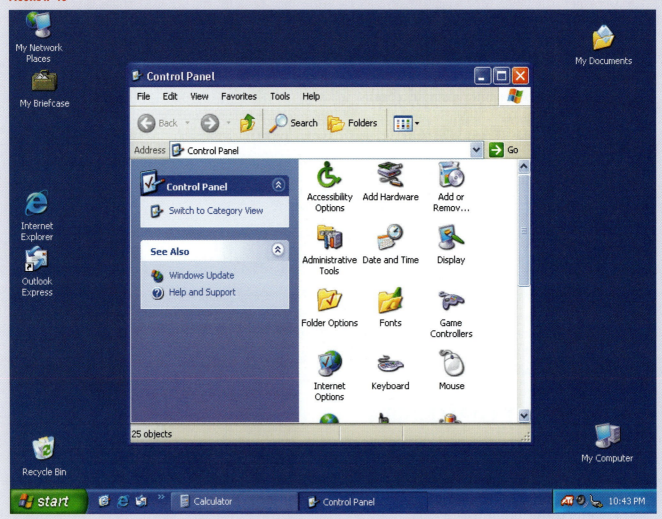

UNIT
B
Windows XP

Working with Programs, Files, and Folders

OBJECTIVES

| Create and save a WordPad document |
| Open, edit, and save an existing Paint file |
| Work with multiple programs |
| Understand file management |
| View files and create folders with My Computer |
| Move and copy files with My Computer |
| Manage files with Windows Explorer |
| Search for files |
| Delete and restore files |

Most of your work on a computer involves using programs to create files. For example, you might use WordPad to create a resumé or Microsoft Excel to create a budget. The resumé and the budget are examples of **files**, electronic collections of data that you create and save on a disk. In this unit, you learn how to work with files and the programs you use to create them. You create new files, open and edit an existing file, and use the Clipboard to copy and paste data from one file to another. You also explore the file management features of Windows XP, using My Computer and Windows Explorer. Finally, you learn how to work more efficiently by managing files directly on your desktop.

Creating and Saving a WordPad Document

As with most programs, when you start WordPad, a new, blank document opens. To create a new file, such as a memo, you simply begin typing. Your work is automatically stored in your computer's random access memory (RAM) until you turn off your computer, at which point anything stored in the computer's RAM is erased. To store your work permanently, you must save your work as a file on a disk. You can save files either on an internal **hard disk**, which is built into your computer, usually the C: drive, or on a removable 3½" **floppy disk**, which you insert into a drive on your computer, usually the A: or B: drive, or on a **CD-ROM** or **Zip disk**, two other kinds of removable storage devices. (Before you can save a file on a floppy disk, the disk must be formatted; see the Appendix, "Formatting a Floppy Disk.") When you name a file, you can use up to 255 characters, including spaces and punctuation, using either upper- or lowercase letters. ▓▓ In this lesson, you start WordPad and create a file that contains the text shown in Figure B-1 and save the file to the drive and folder where your Project Files are stored.

STEPS

QUICK TIP

If you make a mistake, press [Backspace] to delete the character to the left of the insertion point.

1. **Click the Start button on the taskbar, point to All Programs, point to Accessories, click WordPad, then click the Maximize button** 🔲 **if the window does not fill your screen**
   The WordPad program window opens. The blinking insertion point indicates where the text you type will appear.

2. **CType Memo, then press [Enter] to move the insertion point to the next line**

3. **Press [Enter] again, then type the remaining text shown in Figure B-1, pressing [Enter] at the end of each line**

4. **Click File on the menu bar, then click Save As**
   The Save As dialog box opens, as shown in Figure B-2. In this dialog box, you specify where you want your file saved and give your document a name.

TROUBLE

This unit assumes that you are using the A: drive for your Project Files. If not, substitute the correct drive when you are instructed to use the 3 1/2 Floppy (A:) drive. See your instructor or technical support person for help.

5. **Click the Save in list arrow, then click 3½ Floppy (A:), or whichever drive contains your Project Files**
   The drive containing your Project Files is now active, meaning that the contents of the drive appear in the Save in dialog box and that the file will now be saved in this drive.

6. **Click in the File name text box, type Memo, then click the Save button**
   Your memo is now saved as a WordPad file with the name "Memo" on your Project Disk. The WordPad title bar contains the name of the file. Now you can **format** the text, which changes its appearance to make it more readable or attractive.

QUICK TIP

You can double-click to select a word or triple-click to select a paragraph.

7. **Click to the left of the word Memo, drag the mouse to the right to highlight the word, then release the mouse button**
   Now the text is highlighted, indicating that it is **selected**. This means that any action you make will be performed on the highlighted text.

8. **Click the Center button** 🔳 **on the Formatting toolbar, then click the Bold button** 🅱 **on the Formatting toolbar**
   The text is centered and bold.

9. **Click the Font Size list arrow** `10 ▾`**, click 16 in the list, then click the Save button** 💾
   A **font** is a set of letters and numbers sharing a particular shape of type. The **font size** is measured in points; one **point** is 1/72 of an inch in height.

FIGURE B-1: Text to enter in WordPad

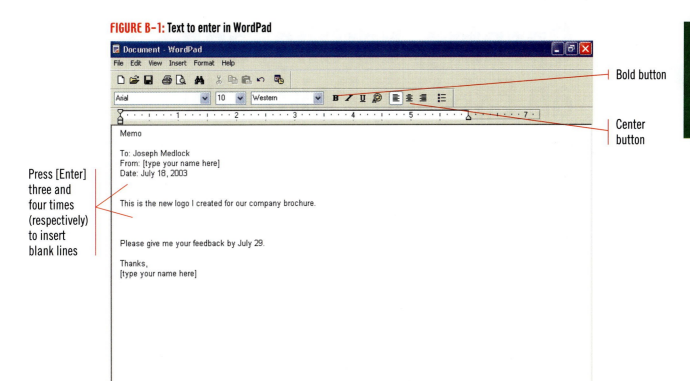

Bold button

Center button

Press [Enter] three and four times (respectively) to insert blank lines

FIGURE B-2: Save As dialog box

Click to select the location in which to save the file

Type new filename here

Opening, Editing, and Saving an Existing Paint File

Sometimes you create files from scratch, as you did in the previous lesson, but often you may want to work with a file you or someone else has already created. To do so, you need to open the file. Once you open a file, you can **edit** it, or make changes to it, such as adding or deleting text or changing the formatting. After editing a file, you can save it with the same filename, which means that you no longer will have the file in its original form, or you can save it with a different filename, so that the original file remains unchanged. In this lesson, you use Paint (a graphics program that comes with Windows XP) to open a file, edit it by changing a color, and then save the file with a new filename to leave the original file unchanged.

STEPS

1. **Click the Start button on the taskbar, point to All Programs, point to Accessories, click Paint, then click the Maximize button** ☐ **if the window doesn't fill the screen**

   The Paint program opens with a blank work area. If you wanted to create a file from scratch, you would begin working now. However, you want to open an existing file, located on your Project Disk.

2. **Click File on the menu bar, then click Open**

   The Open dialog box works similarly to the Save As dialog box that you used in the previous lesson.

3. **Click the Look in list arrow, then click 3½ Floppy (A:)**

   The Paint files on your Project Disk are listed in the Open dialog box, as shown in Figure B-3.

   > **QUICK TIP**
   > You can also open a file by double-clicking it in the Open dialog box.

4. **Click Win B-1 in the list of files, and then click the Open button**

   The Open dialog box closes and the file named Win B-1 opens. Before you change this file, you should save it with a new filename, so that the original file is unchanged.

5. **Click File on the menu bar, then click Save As**

6. **Make sure 3½ Floppy (A:) appears in the Save in text box, select the text Win B-1 in the File name text box, type Logo, click the Save as type list arrow, click 256 Color Bitmap, then click the Save button**

   The Logo file appears in the Paint window, as shown in Figure B-4. Because you saved the file with a new name, you can edit it without changing the original file. You saved the file as a 256 Color Bitmap to conserve space on your floppy disk. You will now modify the logo by using buttons in the **Tool Box**, a toolbar of drawing tools, and the **Color Box**, a palette of colors from which you can choose.

7. **Click the Fill With Color button** ▣ **in the Tool Box, then click the Light blue color box, which is the fourth from the right in the bottom row**

   Notice how clicking a button in the Tool Box changes the mouse pointer. Now when you click an area in the image, it will be filled with the color you selected in the Color Box. See Table B-1 for a description of the tools in the Tool Box.

8. **Move the pointer into the white area that represents the sky until the pointer changes to** 🖌️, **then click**

   The sky is now blue.

9. **Click File on the menu bar, then click Save**

   The change you made is saved to disk, using the same Logo filename.

FIGURE B-3: Open dialog box

List of files

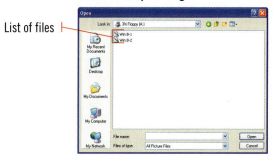

FIGURE B-4: Paint file saved with new filename

Name of file
appears in
title bar

Tool Box

Sky area to
fill with
light blue

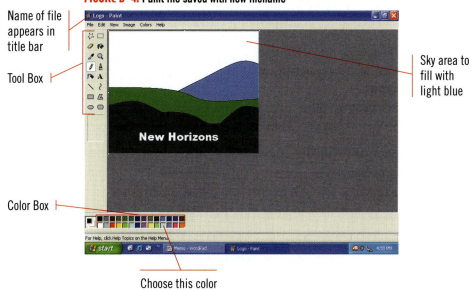

Color Box

Choose this color

TABLE B-1: Paint Tool Box buttons

tool		description
	Free-Form Select button	Selects a free-form section of the picture to move, copy, or edit
	Select button	Selects a rectangular section of the picture to move, copy, or edit
	Eraser button	Erases a portion of the picture using the selected eraser size and foreground color
	Fill With Color button	Fills a closed shape or area with the current drawing color
	Pick Color button	Picks up a color from the picture to use for drawing
	Magnifier button	Changes the magnification; lists magnifications under the toolbar
	Pencil button	Draws a free-form line one pixel wide
	Ellipse button	Draws an ellipse with the selected fill style; hold down [Shift] to draw a circle
	Brush button	Draws using a brush with the selected shape and size
	Airbrush button	Produces a circular spray of dots
	Text button	Inserts text into the picture
	Line button	Draws a straight line with the selected width and foreground color
	Curve button	Draws a wavy line with the selected width and foreground color
	Rectangle button	Draws a rectangle with the selected fill style; hold down [Shift] to draw a square
	Polygon button	Draws polygons from connected straight-line segments
	Rounded Rectangle button	Draws rectangles with rounded corners using the selected fill style; hold down [Shift] to draw a rounded square

Working with Multiple Programs

A powerful feature of Windows is its capability to run more than one program at a time. For example, you might be working with a document in WordPad and want to search the Internet to find the answer to a question. You can start your **browser**, a program designed to access information on the Internet, without closing WordPad. When you find the information, you can leave your browser open and switch back to WordPad. Each open program is represented by a program button on the taskbar that you click to switch between programs. You can also copy data from one file to another (whether or not the files were created with the same Windows program) using the Clipboard, an area of memory on your computer's hard drive, and the Cut, Copy, and Paste commands. See Table B-2 for a description of these commands. In this lesson, you copy the logo graphic you worked with in the previous lesson into the memo you created in WordPad.

STEPS

1. **Click Edit on the menu bar, then click Select All to select the entire picture**
   A dotted rectangle surrounds the picture, indicating it is selected, as shown in Figure B-5.

2. **Click Edit on the menu bar, then click Copy**
   The logo is copied to the Clipboard. When you **copy** an object onto the Clipboard, the object remains in its original location and is also available to be pasted into another location.

QUICK TIP

To switch between programs using the keyboard, press and hold down [Alt], press [Tab] until you select the program you want, then release [Alt].

3. **Click the WordPad program button on the taskbar**
   WordPad becomes the active program.

4. **Click in the first line below the line that ends "for our company brochure."**
   The insertion point indicates where the logo will be pasted.

5. **Click the Paste button 📋 on the WordPad toolbar**
   The contents of the Clipboard, in this case the logo, are pasted into the WordPad file, as shown in Figure B-6.

6. **Click the WordPad Close button; click Yes to save changes**
   Your WordPad document and the WordPad program close. Paint is now the active program.

7. **Click the Paint Close button; if you are prompted to save changes, click Yes**
   Your Paint document and the Paint program close. You return to the desktop.

Clues to Use

Other Programs that Come with Windows XP

WordPad and Paint are just two of many programs that come with Windows XP. From the All Programs menu on the Start menu, you can access everything from games and entertainment programs to powerful communications software and disk maintenance programs without installing anything other than Windows XP. For example, from the Accessories menu, you can open a simple calculator; start Windows Movie Maker to create, edit, and share movie files; and use the Address Book to keep track of your contacts. From the Communications submenu, you can use NetMeeting to set up a voice and/or video conference over the Internet, or use the Remote Desktop Connection to allow another person to access your computer for diagnosing and solving computer problems. Several other menus and submenus display programs and tools that come with Windows XP. You can get a brief description of each by holding your mouse pointer over the name of the program in the menu. You might have to install some of these programs from the Windows CD if they don't appear on the menus.

FIGURE B-5: Selecting the logo to copy and paste into the Memo file

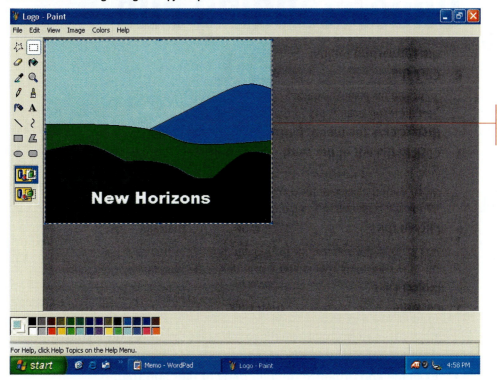

Dotted line indicates selected area

FIGURE B-6: Memo with pasted logo

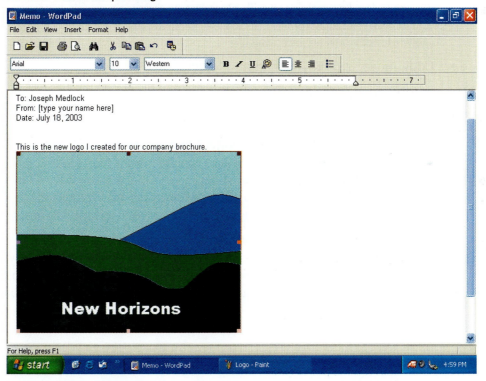

TABLE B-2: Overview of cutting, copying, and pasting

toolbar button	function	keyboard shortcut
✂ Cut	Removes selected information from a file and places it on the Clipboard	[Ctrl][X]
📋 Copy	Places a copy of the selected information on the Clipboard, leaving the file intact	[Ctrl][C]
📋 Paste	Inserts whatever is currently on the Clipboard into another location within the same file or into another file (depending on where you place the insertion point)	[Ctrl][V]

Understanding File Management

After you have created and saved numerous files, the process of organizing and keeping track of all of your files (referred to as **file management**) can be a challenge. Fortunately, Windows provides tools to keep everything organized so you can easily locate the files you need, move files to new locations, and delete files you no longer need. There are two main tools for managing your files: My Computer and Windows Explorer. In this lesson, you preview the ways you can use My Computer and Windows Explorer to manage your files.

DETAILS

Windows XP gives you the ability to:

- **Create folders in which you can save and organize your files**

  Folders are areas on a floppy disk (or other removable storage medium) or hard disk that help you organize your files, just as folders in a filing cabinet help you store and organize your papers. For example, you might create a folder for your work documents and another folder for your personal files. Folders can also contain other folders, which creates a more complex structure of folders and files, called a **file hierarchy**. See Figure B-7 for an example of how files can be organized.

- **Examine and organize the hierarchy of files and folders**

  You can use either My Computer or Windows Explorer to see and manipulate the overall structure of your files and folders. By examining your file hierarchy with these tools, you can better organize the contents of your computer and adjust the hierarchy to meet your needs. Figures B-8 and B-9 illustrate how My Computer and Windows Explorer list folders and files.

- **Copy, move, and rename files and folders**

  If you decide that a file belongs in a different folder, you can move it to another folder. You can also rename a file if you decide a different name is more descriptive. If you want to keep a copy of a file in more than one folder, you can copy it to new folders.

- **Delete files and folders you no longer need and restore files you delete accidentally**

  Deleting files and folders you are sure you don't need frees up disk space and keeps your file hierarchy more organized. The **Recycle Bin**, a space on your computer's hard disk that stores deleted files, allows you to restore files you deleted by accident. To free up disk space, you should occasionally check to make sure you don't need the contents of the Recycle Bin and then delete the files permanently from your hard drive.

- **Locate files quickly with the Windows XP Search feature**

  As you create more files and folders, you may forget where you placed a certain file or you may forget what name you used when you saved a file. With Search, you can locate files by providing only partial names or other facts you know about the file, such as the file type (for example, a WordPad document or a Paint graphic) or the date the file was created or modified.

- **Use shortcuts**

  If a file or folder you use often is located several levels down in your file hierarchy (in a folder within a folder, within a folder), it might take you several steps to access it. To save time accessing the files and programs you use frequently, you can create shortcuts to them. A **shortcut** is a link that gives you quick access to a particular file, folder, or program.

QUICK TIP

To browse My Computer using multiple windows, click Tools on the menu bar, and then click Folder Options. In the Folder Options dialog box, click the General tab, and then under Browse Folders, click the Open each folder in its own window option button. Each time you open a new folder, a new window opens, leaving the previous folder's window open so that you can view both at the same time.

FIGURE B-7: Sample file hierarchy

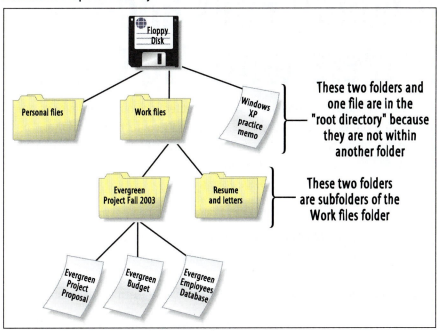

These two folders and one file are in the "root directory" because they are not within another folder

These two folders are subfolders of the Work files folder

FIGURE B-8: Evergreen Project folder shown in My Computer

Tasks related to selected object appear here

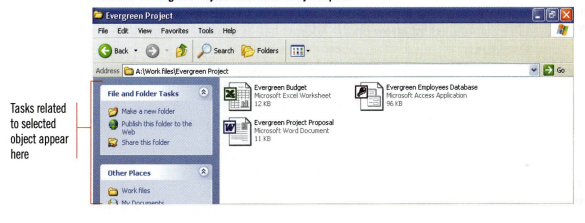

FIGURE B-9: Evergreen Project folder shown in Windows Explorer

File hierarchy is visible; the selected folder's contents appear in the right pane

Viewing Files and Creating Folders with My Computer

My Computer shows the contents of your computer, including files, folders, programs, disk drives, and printers. You can click the icons to view that object's contents or properties. You use the My Computer Explorer Bar, menu bar, and toolbar to manage your files. See Table B-3 for a description of the toolbar buttons. 🎨🎨 In this lesson, you use My Computer to look at your computer's file hierarchy, then you create two new folders on your Project Disk.

STEPS

TROUBLE

If you do not see My Computer, click the Start button, and click My Computer. If you do not see the toolbar, click View, point to Toolbars, and click Standard Buttons. If you do not see Address bar, click View, point to Toolbar, and click Address Bar.

1. **Double-click the My Computer icon 🖥 on your desktop, then click the Maximize button ▫ if the My Computer window does not fill the screen**

   My Computer displays the contents of your computer, as shown in Figure B-10. The left pane, called the **Explorer Bar**, displays tasks related to whatever is selected in the right pane.

2. **Make sure your Project Disk is in the floppy disk drive, then double-click the 3½ Floppy (A:) icon**

   The contents of your Project Disk appear in the window. Each file is represented by an icon, which varies in appearance depending on the program that was used to create the file. If Microsoft Word is installed on your computer, the Word icon appears for the WordPad files; if not, the WordPad icon appears.

TROUBLE

If you are in a lab you may not have access to the My Documents folder. See your instructor for assistance.

3. **Click the Address list arrow on the Address bar, as shown in Figure B-10, then click My Documents**

   The window changes to show the contents of the My Documents folder on your computer's hard drive. The Address bar allows you to open and view a drive, folder, or even a Web page. You can also type in the Address bar to go to a different drive, folder, or Web page. For example, typing "C:\" will display the contents of your C: drive, and typing "http://www.microsoft.com" opens Microsoft's Web site if your computer is connected to the Internet.

QUICK TIP

You can click the list arrow next to the Back or Forward buttons to quickly view locations you've viewed recently.

4. **Click the Back button ◀ on the Standard Buttons toolbar**

   The Back button displays the previous location, in this case, your Project Disk.

5. **Click the Views button list arrow 🎛▾ on the Standard Buttons toolbar, then click Details**

   Details view shows not only the files and folders, but also the sizes of the files, the types of files, folders, or drives and the date the files were last modified.

6. **In the File and Folder Tasks pane, click Make a new folder**

   A new folder called "New Folder" is created on your Project Disk, as shown in Figure B-11. You can also create a new folder by right-clicking in the blank area of the My Computer window, clicking New, then clicking Folder.

QUICK TIP

You can also rename a folder or file by pressing [F2], typing the new name, then pressing [Enter].

7. **If necessary, click to select the folder, then click Rename this folder in the File and Folder Tasks pane; type Windows XP Practice, then press [Enter]**

   Choosing descriptive names for your folders helps you remember their contents.

8. **Double-click the Windows XP Practice folder, repeat Steps 6 and 7 to create a new folder in the Windows XP Practice folder, name the folder Brochure, then press [Enter]**

9. **Click the Up button 🔼 to return to the root directory of your Project Disk**

FIGURE B-10: My Computer window

Menu bar

Address bar

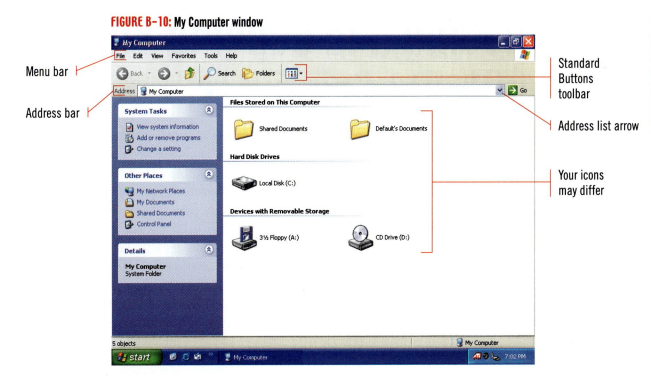

Standard Buttons toolbar

Address list arrow

Your icons may differ

FIGURE B-11: Creating a new folder

Back button

Folder is located on the A: drive

You'll rename the new folder; yours might appear selected

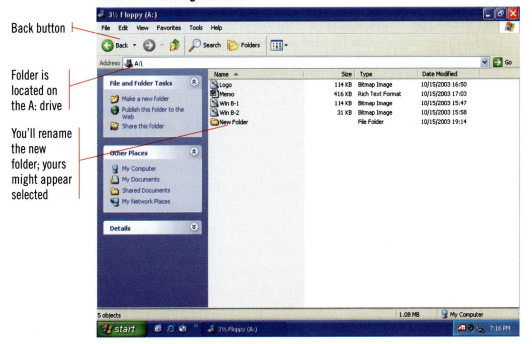

TABLE B-3: Buttons on the Standard Buttons toolbar in My Computer

button	function
Back button	Moves back one location in the list of locations you have recently viewed
Forward button	Moves forward one location in the list of locations you have recently viewed
Up button	Moves up one level in the file hierarchy
Search button	Opens the Search Companion task pane, where you can choose from various options to search for files, computers, Web pages, or people on the Internet
Folders button	Opens the Folders task pane, where you can easily view and manage your computer's file hierarchy
Views button	Lists the contents of My Computer using different views

Moving and Copying Files with My Computer

You can move a file or folder from one location to another using a variety of methods in My Computer. If the file or folder and the location to which you want to move it are both visible, you can simply drag the item from one location to another. You can also use the Cut, Copy, and Paste commands on the Edit menu, or right-click a file or folder and click the appropriate option on the menu that appears. Perhaps the most powerful file management tool in My Computer is the Common Tasks pane. When you select any item in My Computer, the Common Tasks pane changes to the File and Folder Tasks pane, listing tasks you can typically perform with the selected item. For example, if you select a file, the options in the Files and Folders task pane include "Rename this file," "Move this file," and "Delete this file," among many others. If you select a folder, file management tasks for folders appear. If you select more than one object, tasks appear that relate to manipulating multiple objects. You can also right-click any file or folder and choose the Send To command to "send" it to another location – most often a floppy disk or other removable storage medium. This **backs up** the files, making copies of them in case you have computer trouble (which can cause you to lose files from your hard disk). In this lesson, you move your files into the folder you created in the last lesson.

STEPS

1. **Click the Win B-1 file, hold down the mouse button and drag the file onto the Windows XP Practice folder, as shown in Figure B-12, then release the mouse button**
   Win B-1 is moved into the Windows XP Practice folder.

2. **Double-click the Windows XP Practice folder and confirm that the folder contains the Win B-1 file as well as the Brochure folder**

3. **Click the Up button 📁 on the Standard Buttons toolbar, as shown in Figure B-12**
   You return to the root directory of your Project Disk. The Up button shows the next level up in the folder hierarchy.

4. **Click the Logo file, press and hold down [Shift], then click the Memo file**
   Both files are selected. Table B-4 describes methods for selecting multiple objects.

5. **Click Move the selected items in the File and Folder Tasks pane**
   The filenames turn gray, and the Move Items dialog box opens, as shown in Figure B-13.

6. **Click the plus sign next to My Computer if you do not see 3½ Floppy (A:) listed, click the 3½ Floppy (A:) drive, click the Windows XP Practice folder, click the Brochure folder, then click Move**
   The two files are moved to the Brochure folder. Only the Windows XP Practice folder and the Win B-2 file remain in the root directory.

7. **Click the Close button in the 3½ Floppy (A:) (My Computer) window**

FIGURE B-12: Dragging a file from one folder to another

Up button

Common
Tasks pane

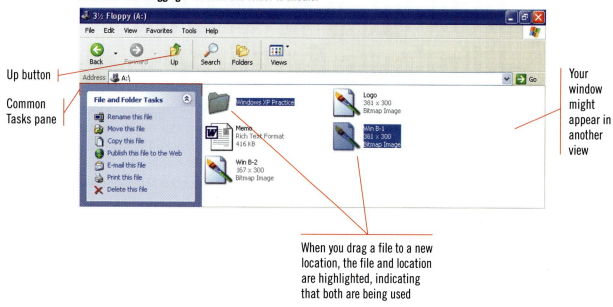

Your
window
might
appear in
another
view

When you drag a file to a new
location, the file and location
are highlighted, indicating
that both are being used

FIGURE B-13: Moving files

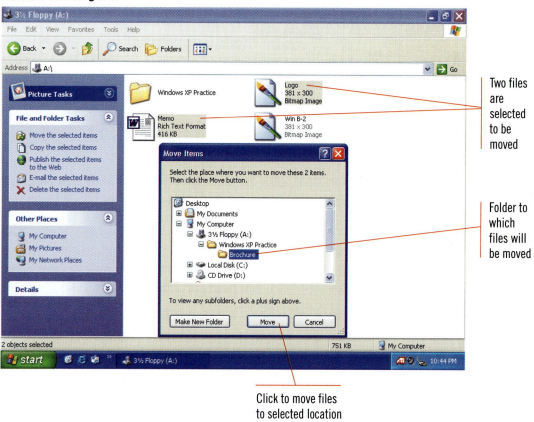

Two files
are
selected
to be
moved

Folder to
which
files will
be moved

Click to move files
to selected location

TABLE B-4: Techniques for selecting multiple files and folders

to select	do this
Individual objects not grouped together	Click the first object you want to select, then press and hold down [Ctrl] as you click each additional object you want to add to the selection
Objects grouped together	Click the first object you want to select, then press and hold down [Shift] as you click the last object in the list of objects you want to select; all the objects listed between the first and last objects are selected

UNIT B
Windows XP

Managing Files with Windows Explorer

As with My Computer, you can use Windows Explorer to copy, move, delete, and rename files and folders. However, in their default settings, My Computer and Windows Explorer look a little different and work in slightly different ways. In My Computer, the Explorer Bar displays the File and Folder Tasks pane when you select files or folders. In Windows Explorer, the Explorer Bar displays the Folders pane, which allows you to see and manipulate the overall structure of the contents of your computer or network while you work with individual files and folders within that structure. This allows you to work with more than one computer, folder, or file at once. Note that you can change the view in My Computer to show the Folders pane, and in Windows Explorer to view the File and Folder Tasks pane. In this lesson, you copy a folder from your Project Disk into the My Documents folder on your hard disk and then rename the folder.

STEPS

> **TROUBLE**
> If you do not see the toolbar, click View on the menu bar, point to Toolbars, then click Standard Buttons. If you do not see the Address bar, click View, point to Toolbars, then click Address Bar.

1. **Click the Start button, point to All Programs, point to Accessories, click Windows Explorer, then maximize the window if necessary**

   Windows Explorer opens, as shown in Figure B-14. The Folders pane on the left displays the drives and folders on your computer in a hierarchy. The right pane displays the contents of whatever drive or folder is currently selected in the Folders pane. Each pane has its own set of scroll bars, so that scrolling in one pane won't affect the other.

2. **Click View on the menu bar, then click Details if it is not already selected**

   Remember that a bullet point or check mark next to a command on the menu indicates that it's selected.

> **TROUBLE**
> If you cannot see the A: drive, you may have to click the plus sign (+) next to My Computer to view the available drives on your computer.

3. **In the Folders pane, scroll to and click 3½ Floppy (A:)**

   The contents of your Project Disk appear in the right pane.

4. **In the Folders pane, click the plus sign (+) next to 3½ Floppy (A:), if necessary**

   You click the plus sign (+) or minus sign (-) next to any item in the left pane to show or hide the different levels of the file hierarchy, so that you don't always have to look at the entire structure of your computer or network. A plus sign (+) next to an item indicates there are additional folders within that object. A minus sign (-) indicates the next level of the hierarchy is shown. Clicking the + displays (or "expands") the next level; clicking the – hides (or "collapses") it. When neither a + nor a – appears next to an icon, it means that the object does not have any folders in it, although it may have files.

5. **In the Folders pane, click the Windows XP Practice folder**

   The contents of the Windows XP Practice folder appear in the right pane, as shown in Figure B-15. Double-clicking an item in the Folders pane that has a + next to it displays its contents in the right pane and also expands the next level in the Folders pane.

> **TROUBLE**
> If you are working in a lab setting, you may not be able to add items to your My Documents folder. Skip, but read carefully, Steps 6, 7, and 8 if you are unable to complete them.

6. **In the Folders pane, drag the Windows XP Practice folder on top of the My Documents folder, then release the mouse button**

   When you drag files or folders from one drive to a different drive, they are copied rather than moved.

7. **In the Folders pane, click the My Documents folder**

   The Windows XP Practice folder should now appear in the list of folders in the right pane. You may have to scroll to see it. Now you should rename the folder so you can distinguish the original folder from the copy.

8. **Right-click the Windows XP Practice folder in the right pane, click Rename in the shortcut menu, type Windows XP Copy, then press [Enter]**

FIGURE B-14: Windows Explorer window

Left pane, known as the Folders list or the Explorer Bar

Your list of devices, folders, and files will differ

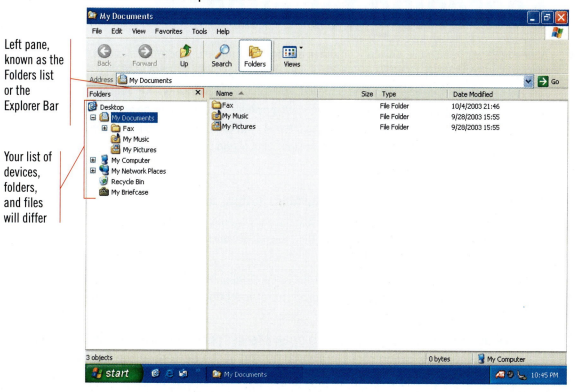

FIGURE B-15: Contents of Windows XP Practice folder

Windows XP Practice folder selected in left pane

Contents of Windows XP Practice folder appear in right pane

Your window might appear in a different view

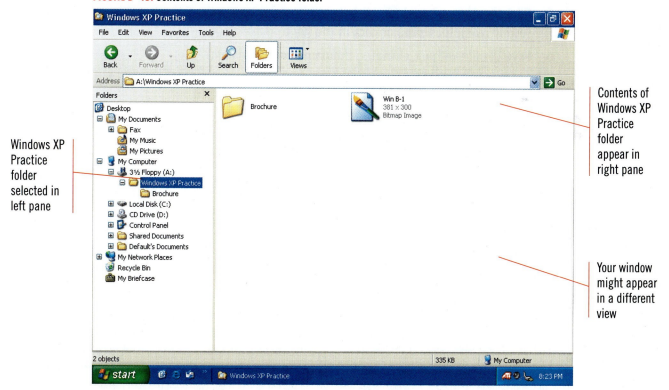

Searching for Files

After you've worked a while on your computer, saving, deleting, and modifying files and folders, you may forget where you've saved an item or what you named it. Or, you may want to send an e-mail to someone, but you can't remember how the name is spelled. You can use the **Windows XP Search** feature to quickly find any kind of object, from a Word document or a movie file to a computer on your network or a person in your address book. If you're connected to the Internet, you can use Search to locate Web pages and people on the Internet. In this lesson, you search for a file on your Project Disk.

STEPS

QUICK TIP

You can also start the Search Companion by clicking the Start button and then clicking Search. To change the way the Search tool works (such as whether the animated dog appears), click Change preferences at the bottom of the Search Companion pane.

1. **Click the Search button 🔍 on the Standard Buttons toolbar**

   The Explorer Bar changes to display the Search Companion pane, as shown in Figure B-16. Let's assume you can't remember where you placed the Logo file you created earlier. You know that it is a picture file and that it is somewhere on your floppy disk.

2. **In the Search Companion pane, click Pictures, music, or video; in the list that appears, click the Pictures and Photos check box, then type Logo in the All or part of the file name text box, as shown in Figure B-17**

3. **Click Use advanced search options to open a larger pane, click the Look in list arrow, click 3½ Floppy (A:), then click the Search button at the bottom of the Search Companion pane**

   The search results are displayed in the right pane and options for further searching are displayed in the Search Companion pane.

4. **Click the Logo icon in the right pane, click File on the menu bar, point to Open With, and then click Paint**

TROUBLE

If you don't like the way your clouds look, click Edit on the menu bar, click Undo, then repeat Step 5.

5. **Click the Airbrush tool 🖌, click the white color box in the Color box (the first one in the second row), then drag or click in the sky to make clouds**

6. **Save the file without changing the name and close Paint**

Clues to Use

Accessing files, folders, programs, and drives you use often

As you continue to use your computer, you will probably find that you use certain files, folders, programs, and disk drives almost every day. You can create a **shortcut**, an icon that represents an object stored somewhere else, and place it on the desktop. From the desktop, you double-click the shortcut to open the item, whether it's a file, folder, program, or disk drive. To create a shortcut on the desktop, view the object in My Computer or Windows Explorer, size the window so you can see both the object and part of the desktop at the same time, use the *right* mouse button to drag the object to the desktop, and then click Create Shortcuts Here. To delete the shortcut, select it and press [Delete]. The original file, folder, or program will not be affected. To **pin** a program to the Start menu, which places it conveniently at the top of the left side of the menu, open the Start menu as far as needed to view the program you want to pin, right-click the program name, and then click Pin to Start menu. To remove it, right-click it in its new position and then click Unpin from Start menu.

FIGURE B-16: Getting ready to search

Search button

Search Companion pane

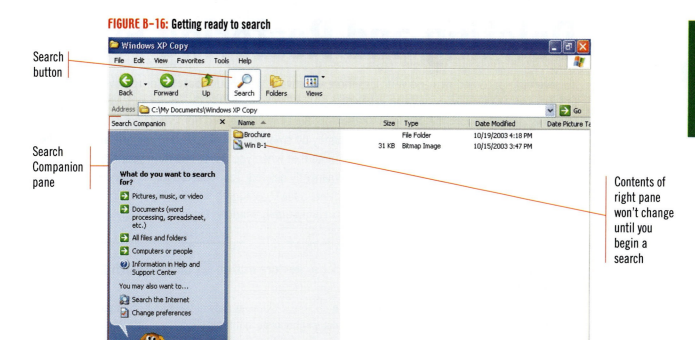

Contents of right pane won't change until you begin a search

FIGURE B-17: Specifying search options

Select this check box

Enter search text here

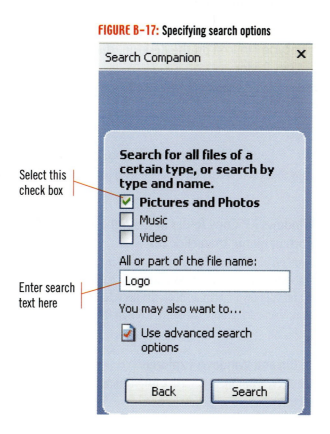

Deleting and Restoring Files

To save disk space and manage your files more effectively, you should **delete** (or remove) files you no longer need. There are many ways to delete files and folders from the My Computer and Windows Explorer windows, as well as from the Windows XP desktop. Because files deleted from your hard disk are stored in the Recycle Bin until you remove them permanently by emptying the Recycle Bin, you can restore any files you might have deleted accidentally. However, note that when you delete files from your floppy disk, they are not stored in the Recycle Bin – they are permanently deleted. See Table B-5 for an overview of deleting and restoring files. In this lesson, you delete a file by dragging it to the Recycle Bin, you restore it, and then you delete a folder by using the Delete command in Windows Explorer.

STEPS

1. **Click the Folders button 📁, then click the Restore button 🗗 on the Search Results (Windows Explorer) title bar**

   You should be able to see the Recycle Bin icon on your desktop, as shown in Figure B-18. If you can't see the Recycle Bin, resize or move the Windows Explorer window until it is visible.

2. **If necessary, select the Windows XP Copy folder in the left pane of Windows Explorer**

QUICK TIP

If you are unable to delete the file, it might be because your Recycle Bin is full or the properties have been changed so that files are deleted right away. See your instructor or technical support person for assistance.

3. **Drag the Windows XP Copy folder from the left pane to the Recycle Bin on the desktop, as shown in Figure B-18, then click Yes to confirm the deletion, if necessary**

   The folder no longer appears in Windows Explorer because you have moved it to the Recycle Bin.

4. **Double-click the Recycle Bin icon on the desktop, then scroll if necessary until you can see the Windows XP Copy folder**

   The Recycle Bin window opens, as shown in Figure B-19. Depending on the number of files already deleted on your computer, your window might look different.

TROUBLE

If the Recycle Bin window blocks your view of Windows Explorer, minimize the Recycle Bin window. You might need to scroll the right pane to find the restored folder in Windows Explorer.

5. **Click the Windows XP Copy folder, then click Restore this item in the Recycle Bin Tasks pane**

   The Windows XP Copy folder is restored and should now appear in the Windows Explorer window.

6. **Right-click the Windows XP Copy folder in the right pane of Windows Explorer, click Delete on the shortcut menu, then click Yes**

   When you are sure you no longer need files you've moved into the Recycle Bin, you can empty the Recycle Bin. You won't do this now, in case you are working on a computer that you share with other people. But when you're working on your own machine, open the Recycle Bin window, verify that you don't need any of the files or folders in it, then click Empty the Recycle Bin in the Recycle Bin Tasks pane.

7. **Close the Recycle Bin and Windows Explorer**

   If you minimized the Recycle Bin in Step 5, click its program button to open the Recycle Bin window, and then click the Close button.

FIGURE B-18: Dragging a folder to delete it

Your desktop background and icons might differ

Drag the folder here

Folder located in the My Documents folder

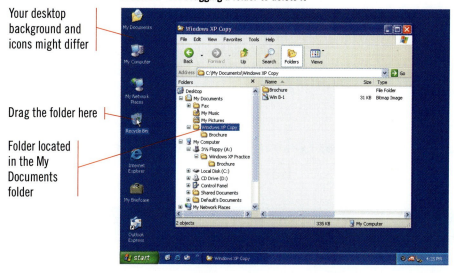

FIGURE B-19: Recycle Bin window

Deleted folder

The buttons on your toolbar might differ

You may see more files and folders, and they may be displayed in a different view

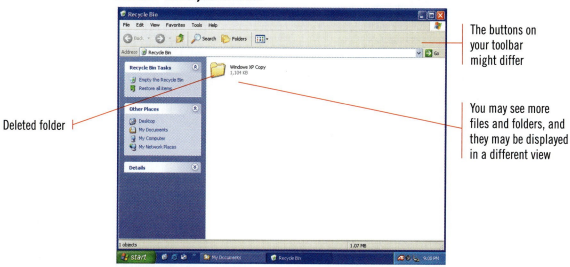

TABLE B-5: Methods for deleting and restoring files

ways to delete a file	ways to restore a file from the Recycle Bin
If File and Folder Tasks pane is open, click the file, then click Delete this file	Click Edit, then click Undo Delete
Select the file, then press [Delete]	Select the file in the Recycle Bin window, then click Restore this file
Right-click the file, then click Delete on the shortcut menu	Right-click the file in the Recycle Bin window, then click Restore
Drag the file to the Recycle Bin	Drag the file from the Recycle Bin to any other location

Clues to Use

Customizing your Recycle Bin

You can set your Recycle Bin according to how you like to delete and restore files. For example, if you do not want files to go to the Recycle Bin but rather want them to be immediately and permanently deleted, right-click the Recycle Bin, click Properties, then click the Do Not Move Files to the Recycle Bin check box. If you find that the Recycle Bin fills up too fast and you are not ready to delete the files permanently, you can increase the amount of disk space devoted to the Recycle Bin by moving the Maximum Size of Recycle Bin slider to the right. This, of course, reduces the amount of disk space you have available for other things. Also, you can choose not to have the Confirm File Delete dialog box open when you send files to the Recycle Bin. See your instructor or technical support person before changing any of the Recycle Bin settings.

Practice

▼ CONCEPTS REVIEW

Label each of the elements of the Windows Explorer window shown in Figure B-20.

FIGURE B-20

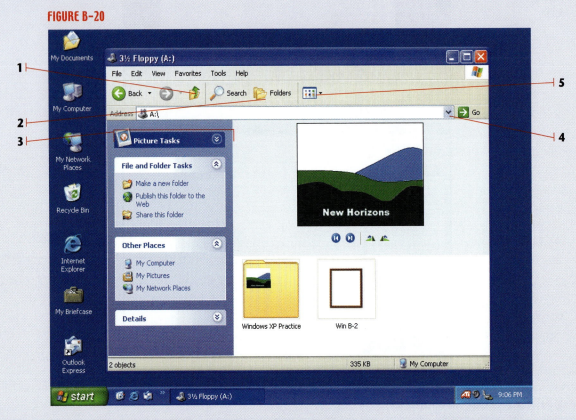

Match each of the statements with the term it describes.

6. Electronic collections of data
7. Your computer's temporary storage area
8. Temporary location of information you wish to paste into another location
9. Storage areas on your hard drive for files, folders, and programs
10. Structure of files and folders

a. RAM
b. Folders
c. Files
d. File hierarchy
e. Clipboard

Select the best answer from the list of choices.

11. To prepare a floppy disk to save your files, you must first make sure
  a. files are copied to the disk.
  b. the disk is formatted.
  c. all the files that might be on the disk are erased.
  d. the files are on the Clipboard.

12. You can use My Computer to
  a. create a drawing of your computer.
  b. view the contents of a folder.
  c. change the appearance of your desktop.
  d. add text to a WordPad file.

13. Which of the following best describes WordPad?
  a. A program for organizing files
  b. A program for performing financial analysis
  c. A program for creating basic text documents
  d. A program for creating graphics

14. **Which of the following is NOT a way to move a file from one folder to another?**
    a. Open the file and drag its program window to the new folder.
    b. In My Computer or Windows Explorer, drag the selected file to the new folder.
    c. Use the Move this file command in the File and Folder Tasks pane.
    d. Use the [Ctrl][X] and [Ctrl][V] keyboard shortcuts while in the My Computer or the Windows Explorer window.

15. **In which of the following can you, by default, view the hierarchy of drives, folders, and files in a split pane window?**
    a. Windows Explorer
    c. My Computer
    b. All Programs
    d. WordPad

16. **To restore files that you have sent to the Recycle Bin,**
    a. click File, then click Empty Recycle Bin.
    c. click File, then click Undo.
    b. click Edit, then click Undo Delete.
    d. You cannot retrieve files sent to the Recycle Bin.

17. **To select files that are not grouped together, select the first file, then**
    a. press [Shift] while selecting the second file.
    c. press [Ctrl] while selecting the second file.
    b. press [Alt] while selecting the second file.
    d. click the second file.

18. **Pressing [Backspace]**
    a. deletes the character to the right of the cursor.
    c. moves the insertion point one character to the right.
    b. deletes the character to the left of the cursor.
    d. deletes all text to the left of the cursor.

19. **The size of a font is measured in**
    a. centimeters.
    c. places.
    b. points.
    d. millimeters.

20. **The Back button on the My Computer toolbar**
    a. starts the last program you used.
    c. backs up the currently selected file.
    b. displays the next level of the file hierarchy.
    d. displays the last location you visited.

▼ SKILLS REVIEW

1. **Create and save a WordPad file.**
   a. Start Windows, then start WordPad.
   b. Type **My Drawing Ability**, then press [Enter] three times.
   c. Save the document as **Drawing Ability** to your Project Disk, but do not close it.

2. **Open, edit, and save an existing Paint file.**
   a. Start Paint and open the file Win B-2 on your Project Disk.
   b. Save the picture with the filename **First Unique Art** as a 256-color bitmap file to your Project Disk.
   c. Inside the picture frame, use [Shift] with the Ellipse tool to create a circle, fill it with purple, switch to yellow, then use [Shift] with the Rectangle tool to place a square inside the circle. Fill the square with yellow.
   d. Save the file, but do not close it. (Click Yes, if necessary to replace the file.)

3. **Work with multiple programs.**
   a. Select the entire graphic and copy it to the Clipboard, then switch to WordPad.
   b. Place the insertion point in the last blank line, paste the graphic into your document, then deselect the graphic.
   c. Save the changes to your WordPad document. Switch to Paint.
   d. Using the Fill With Color tool, change the color of a filled area of your graphic.
   e. Save the revised graphic with the new name **Second Unique Art** as a 256-color bitmap on your Project Disk.
   f. Select the entire graphic and copy it to the Clipboard.
   g. Switch to WordPad, move the insertion point to the line below the graphic by clicking below the graphic and pressing [Enter], type **This is another version of my graphic:** below the first picture, then press [Enter].
   h. Paste the second graphic under the text you just typed.
   i. Save the changed WordPad document as **Two Drawing Examples** to your Project Disk. Close Paint and WordPad.

4. **View files and create folders with My Computer.**
   a. Open My Computer. Double-click the drive that contains your Project Disk.
   b. Create a new folder on your Project Disk by clicking File, pointing to New, then clicking Folder, and name the new folder **Review**.
   c. Open the folder to display its contents (it is empty).
   d. Use the Address bar to view the My Documents folder.
   e. Create a folder in the My Documents folder called **Temporary**, then use the Back button to view the Review folder.
   f. Create two new folders in the Review folder, one named **Documents** and the other named **Artwork**.
   g. Click the Forward button as many times as necessary to view the contents of the My Documents folder.
   h. Change the view to Details if necessary.

5. **Move and copy files with My Computer.**
   a. Use the Address bar to view your Project Disk. Switch to Details view, if necessary.
   b. Press the [Shift] key while selecting First Unique Art and Second Unique Art, then cut and paste them into the Artwork folder.
   c. Use the Back button to view the contents of Project Disk.
   d. Select the two WordPad files, Drawing Ability and Two Drawing Examples, then move them into the Review folder.
   e. Open the Review folder, select the two WordPad files again, move them into the Documents folder, then close My Computer.

6. **Manage files with Windows Explorer.**
   a. Open Windows Explorer and view the contents of the Artwork folder in the right pane.
   b. Select the two Paint files.
   c. Drag the two Paint files from the Artwork folder to the Temporary folder in the My Documents folder to copy – not move – them.
   d. View the contents of the Documents folder in the right pane, then select the two WordPad files.
   e. Repeat Step c to copy the files to the Temporary folder in the My Documents folder.
   f. View the contents of the Temporary folder in the right pane to verify that the four files are there.

7. **Search for files.**
   a. Open the Search companion from Windows Explorer.
   b. Search for the First Unique Art file on your Project Disk.
   c. Close the Search Results window.

8. **Delete and restore files and folders.**
   a. If necessary, open and resize the Windows Explorer window so you can see the Recycle Bin icon on the desktop, then scroll in Windows Explorer so you can see the Temporary folder in the left pane.
   b. Delete the Temporary folder from the My Documents folder by dragging it to the Recycle Bin.
   c. Click Yes to confirm the deletion, if necessary.
   d. **Open the Recycle Bin, restore the Temporary folder and its files to your hard disk, and then close the Recycle Bin.** (*Note*: If your Recycle Bin is empty, your computer is set to automatically delete items in the Recycle Bin.)
   e. Delete the Temporary folder again by clicking to select it and then pressing [Delete]. Click Yes to confirm the deletion.

▼ INDEPENDENT CHALLENGE 1

You have decided to start a bakery business and you want to use Windows XP to create and organize the files for the business.

   a. Create two new folders on your Project Disk, one named **Advertising** and one named **Customers**.
   b. Use WordPad to create a letter inviting new customers to the open house for the new bakery, then save it as **Open House Letter** in the Customers folder.
   c. Use WordPad to create a new document that lists five tasks that need to get done before the business opens (such as purchasing equipment, decorating the interior, and ordering supplies), then save it as **Business Plan** to your Project Disk, but don't place it in a folder.

▼ INDEPENDENT CHALLENGE 1 (CONTINUED)

d. Use Paint to create a simple logo for the bakery, save it as a 256-color bitmap named **Bakery Logo**, then place it in the Advertising folder.

e. Print the three files.

▼ INDEPENDENT CHALLENGE 2

To complete this Independent Challenge, you will need a second formatted, blank floppy disk. Write **IC2** on the disk label, then complete the steps below. Follow the guidelines listed here to create the file hierarchy shown in Figure B-21.

a. In the My Documents folder on your hard drive, create one folder named IC2 and a second named Project Disk 1.

b. Copy the contents of your first Project Disk into the new Project Disk 1 folder. This will give you access to your files as you complete these steps.

c. Place your blank IC2 disk into the floppy drive.

d. Start WordPad, then create a new file that contains a list of things to get done. Save the file as **To Do List** to your IC2 Disk.

e. Start My Computer and copy the To Do List from your IC2 Disk to the IC2 folder and rename the file in the IC2 folder **Important List**.

f. Copy the Open House Letter file from your Project Disk 1 folder to the IC2 folder. Rename the file **Article**.

g. Copy the Memo file from your Project Disk 1 folder to the IC2 folder in the My Documents folder and rename it **Article Two**.

h. Copy the Logo file from your Project Disk 1 folder to the IC2 folder and rename the file **Sample Logo**.

i. Move the files into the folders shown in Figure B-21.

j. Copy the IC2 folder to your IC2 Disk, then delete the Project Disk 1 and IC2 folders from the My Documents folder.

FIGURE B-21

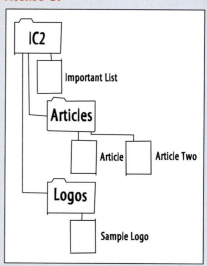

▼ INDEPENDENT CHALLENGE 3

With Windows XP, you can access the Web from My Computer and Windows Explorer, allowing you to search for information located not only on your computer or network but also on any computer on the Internet.

a. Start Windows Explorer, then click in the Address bar so the current location is selected, type **www.microsoft.com**, then press [Enter].

b. Connect to the Internet if necessary. The Microsoft Web page appears in the right pane of Windows Explorer.

c. Click in the Address bar, then type **www.course.com**, press [Enter], and then wait a moment while the Course Technology Web page opens.

d. Make sure your Project Disk is in the floppy disk drive, then click 3½ Floppy (A:) in the left pane.

e. Click the Back button list arrow, then click Microsoft's home page.

f. Capture a picture of your desktop by pressing [Print Screen] (usually located on the upper-right side of your keyboard). This stores the picture on the Clipboard. Open the Paint program, paste the contents of the Clipboard into the drawing window, clicking No if asked to enlarge the Bitmap, then print the picture.

g. Close Paint without saving your changes.

h. Close Windows Explorer, then disconnect from the Internet if necessary.

▼ INDEPENDENT CHALLENGE 4

Open Windows Explorer, make sure you can see the drive that contains your Project Disk listed in the left pane, use the right mouse button to drag the drive to a blank area on the desktop, then click Create Shortcuts Here. Then capture a picture of your desktop showing the new shortcut: press [Print Screen], located on the upper-right side of your keyboard. Then open the Paint program and paste the contents of the Clipboard into the drawing window. Print the screen, close Paint without saving your changes, then delete the shortcut when you are finished.

▼ VISUAL WORKSHOP

Recreate the screen shown in Figure B-22, which shows the Search Results window with the Memo file listed, one shortcut on the desktop, and one open (but minimized) file. Press [Print Screen] to make a copy of the screen, (a copy of the screen is placed on the Clipboard), open Paint, click Paste to paste the screen picture into Paint, then print the Paint file. Close Paint without saving your changes, and then return your desktop to its original state. Your desktop might have different icons and a different background.

FIGURE B-22

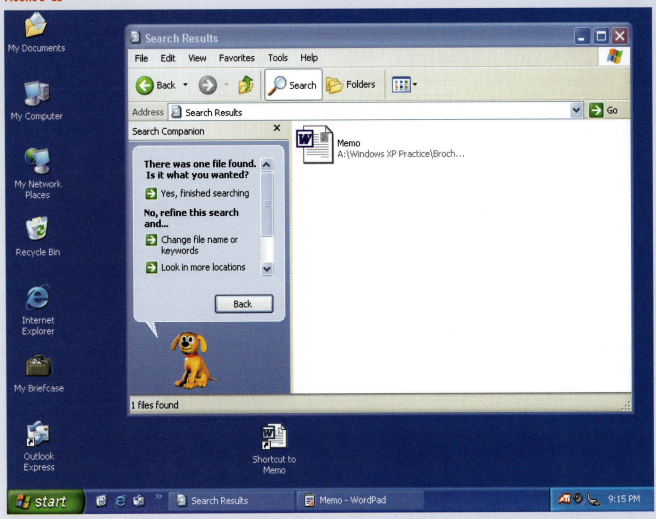

Formatting a Floppy Disk

A **disk** is a device on which you can store electronic data. Disks come in a variety of sizes and have varying storage capacities. Your computer's **hard disk**, one of its internal devices, can store large amounts of data. **Floppy disks**, on the other hand, are smaller, inexpensive, and portable. Most floppy disks that you buy today are 3 ½-inch disks (the diameter of the inside, circular part of the disk) and are already formatted. Check the package that your disk came in for the word "formatted" or "pre-formatted;" such disks do not require further formatting. If your package says "unformatted," then you should follow the steps in this appendix. In this appendix, you will prepare a floppy disk for use.

Formatting a Floppy Disk

In order for an operating system to be able to store data on a disk, the disk must be formatted. **Formatting** prepares a disk so it can store information. Usually, floppy disks are formatted when you buy them, but if not, you can format them yourself using Windows XP. To complete the following steps, you need a blank floppy disk or a disk containing data you no longer need. Do not use your Project Disk for this lesson, as all information on the disk will be erased.

STEPS

TROUBLE

This appendix assumes that the drive that will contain your floppy disks is drive A. If not, substitute the correct drive when you are instructed to use the 3 ½ Floppy (A:) drive.

1. **Start your computer and Windows XP if necessary, then place a 3 ½-inch floppy disk in drive A**

2. **Double-click the My Computer icon 🖳 on the desktop**

   My Computer opens, as shown in Figure AP-1. This window lists all the drives and printers that you can use on your computer. Because computers have different drives, printers, programs, and other devices installed, your window will probably look different.

3. **Right-click the 3 ½ Floppy (A:) icon**

   When you click with the right mouse button, a shortcut menu of commands that apply to the item you right-clicked appears. Because you right-clicked a drive, the Format command is available.

TROUBLE

Windows cannot format a disk if it is write-protected; therefore, you may need to slide the write-protect tab over until it clicks to continue. See Figure AP-3 to locate the write-protect tab on your disk.

4. **Click Format on the shortcut menu**

   The Format dialog box opens, as shown in Figure AP-2. In this dialog box, you specify the capacity of the disk you are formatting, the File system, the Allocation unit size, the kind of formatting you want to do, and if you want, a volume label. You are doing a standard format, so you will accept the default settings.

5. **Click Start, then, when you are warned that formatting will erase all data on the disk, click OK to continue**

   Windows formats your disk. After the formatting is complete, you might see a summary about the size of the disk.

6. **Click OK when the message telling you that the format is complete appears, then click Close in the Format dialog box**

QUICK TIP

Once a disk is formatted, you do not need to format it again. However, some people use the Quick Format option to erase the contents of a disk quickly, rather than having to select the files and then delete them.

7. **Click the Close button ❌ in the My Computer window**

   My Computer closes and you return to the desktop.

FIGURE AP-1: My Computer window

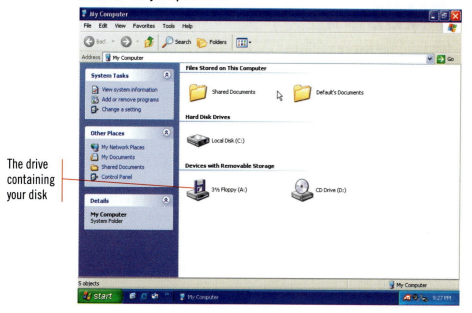

The drive containing your disk

FIGURE AP-2: Format dialog box

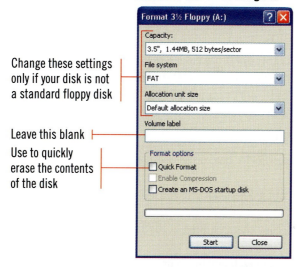

Change these settings only if your disk is not a standard floppy disk

Leave this blank

Use to quickly erase the contents of the disk

FIGURE AP-3: Write-protect tab

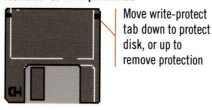

Move write-protect tab down to protect disk, or up to remove protection

3.5" disk

Clues to Use

More about disks

Disks are sometimes called **drives**, but this term really refers to the name by which the operating system recognizes the disk (or a portion of the disk). The operating system typically assigns a drive letter to a drive (which you can reassign if you want). For example, on most computers the hard disk is identified by the letter "C" and the floppy drive by the letter "A." The amount of information a disk can hold is called its capacity, usually measured in megabytes (MB). The most common floppy disk **capacity** is 1.44 MB. Computers also come with other disk drives, such as a **CD drives** and **Zip drives**. Such drives handle CDs and Zip disks, respectively. Both are portable like floppy disks, but they can contain far more data than floppy disks.

Data Files

Read the following information carefully!

It is very important to organize and keep track of the files you need for this book.

1. **Find out from your instructor the location of the Data Files you need and the location where you will store your files.**

   - To complete many of the units in this book, you need to use Data Files. Your instructor will either provide you with a copy of the Data Files or ask you to make your own copy.
   - If you need to make a copy of the Data Files, you will need to copy a set of files from a file server, stand-alone computer, or the Web to the drive and folder where you will be storing your Data Files.
   - Your instructor will tell you which computer, drive letter, and folders contain the files you need, and where you will store your files.
   - You can also download the files by going to www.course.com. A copy of a Data Files list is provided on the Review Pack for this book or may be provided by your instructor.

2. **Copy and organize your Data Files.**

   ### Floppy disk users

   - If you are using floppy disks to store your Data Files, the Data Files List shows which files you'll need to copy onto your disk(s).
   - Unless noted in the Data Files List, you will need one formatted, high-density disk for each unit. For each unit you are assigned, copy the files listed in the **Data File Supplied column** onto one disk.
   - Make sure you label each disk clearly with the unit name (e.g., Word Unit A).
   - When working through the unit, save all your files to this disk.

   ### Users storing files in other locations

   - If you are using a zip drive, network folder, hard drive, or other storage device, use the Data Files List to organize your files.
   - Create a subfolder for each unit in the location where you are storing your files, and name it according to the unit title (e.g., Word Unit A).
   - For each unit you are assigned, copy the files listed in the **Data File Supplied column** into that unit's folder.
   - Store the files you modify or create for each unit in the unit folder.

3. **Find and keep track of your Data Files and completed files.**

   - Use the **Data File Supplied column** to make sure you have the files you need before starting the unit or exercise indicated in the **Unit and Location column**.
   - Use the **Student Saves File As column** to find out the filename you use when saving your changes to a Data File that was provided.
   - Use the **Student Creates File column** to find out the filename you use when saving a file you create new for the exercise.

Getting Started with Access 2003

OBJECTIVES

Understand relational databases
Learn database terminology
Start Access and open a database
Work with the database window
Navigate records
Enter records
Edit records
Preview and print a datasheet
Get Help and exit Access

In this unit, you will learn the purpose, advantages, and terminology of Microsoft Office Access 2003, a relational database software program. You will learn how to use the different elements of the Access window and how to get help. You'll navigate a database, enter and update data, and preview and print data. Kelsey Lang is a marketing manager at MediaLoft, a nationwide chain of bookstore cafés that offers customers the opportunity to purchase books, music, and movies while enjoying a variety of coffees, teas, and freshly baked desserts. Recently, MediaLoft switched to Access for storing and maintaining customer information. You use Access to help Kelsey maintain this valuable information for MediaLoft.

Understanding Relational Databases

Microsoft Access 2003 is a database software program that runs on the Windows operating system. **Relational database software** is used to manage data that can be organized into lists of related information, such as customers, products, vendors, employees, projects, or sales. Many small companies record customer, inventory, and sales information in a spreadsheet program such as Microsoft Excel. While using this electronic format is more productive than using a paper-based system, Excel still lacks many of the database advantages provided by Access. See Table A-1 for a comparison of the two programs. Kelsey asks you to review the advantages of database software over manual and spreadsheet systems.

DETAILS

The advantages of using Access include:

- **Duplicate data is minimized**

  If your database consists of customer, product, and sales data, a paper-based or spreadsheet system would require that you record all of the customer, sales, and product information on index cards as shown in Figure A-1 or in spreadsheet rows as shown in Figure A-2. Both systems duplicate product and customer data each time a sale is made. With Access, however, you enter data about customers or products only once even though it may be related to many sales transactions. Using a relational database eliminates the time-consuming and error-prone process of entering duplicate data.

- **Information is more accurate**

  Because duplicate data is minimized, information in a relational database is more accurate, reliable, and consistent. Data is also easier to maintain because a change in a customer's address, for example, is updated only once rather than each time the customer makes a purchase.

- **Data entry is faster and easier**

  Using a relational database program such as Access, you can create on-screen data entry forms that make data entry easier, faster, and more accurate.

- **Information can be viewed and sorted in multiple ways**

  A manual system or spreadsheet allows you to sort information in only one order at a time. In contrast, Access allows you to view or sort the information in multiple ways in different but simultaneous views. For example, you may want to sort customers in alphabetical order in one window while sorting them according to the value of their total purchases in another. Also, you can save any presentation of data and quickly redisplay it later.

- **Information is more secure**

  You can protect an Access database with a password so only those users with appropriate security clearances can open it. Access databases can be further secured by granting different database capabilities to different users.

- **Information can be shared among several users**

  Access databases are inherently multiuser. More than one person can be entering, updating, and using the database at the same time.

- **Information retrieval is faster and easier**

  With Access you can quickly find, display, and print subsets of information that present or analyze various aspects of the database. Once you create a particular view of the data, you can save and redisplay it.

FIGURE A-1: Using a manual system to record sales data

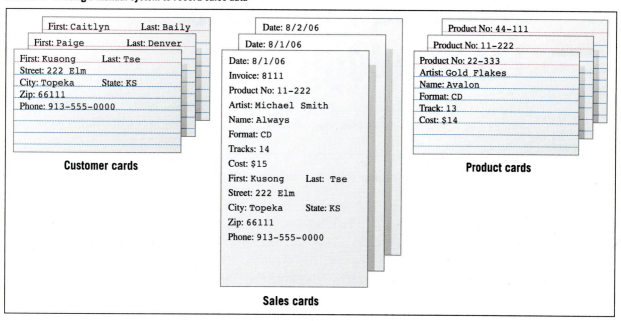

Customer cards

Sales cards

Product cards

FIGURE A-2: Using a spreadsheet to record sales data

	A	B	C	D	E	F	G	H	I	J	K	L	M	N	O	P
1	Cust No	First	Last	Street	City	State	Zip	Phone	Date	Invoice	Product No	Artist	Name	Format	Tracks	Cost
2	1	Kusong	Tse	222 Elm	Topeka	KS	66111	913-555-0000	8/1/2006	8111	11-222	Michael Smith	Always	CD	14	15
3	2	Paige	Denver	400 Oak	Lenexa	MO	60023	816-555-8877	8/1/2006	8112	11-222	Michael Smith	Always	CD	14	15
4	1	Kusong	Tse	222 Elm	Topeka	KS	66111	913-555-0000	8/2/2006	8113	22-333	Gold Flakes	Avalon	CD	13	14
5	3	Caitlyn	Baily	111 Ash	Ames	IA	50010	515-555-3333	8/3/2006	8114	22-333	Gold Flakes	Avalon	CD	13	14
6	2	Paige	Denver	400 Oak	Lenexa	MO	60023	816-555-8877	8/4/2006	8115	44-1111	Lungwort	Sounds	CD	15	13
7	3	Caitlyn	Baily	111 Ash	Ames	IA	50010	515-555-3333	8/4/2006	8116	44-1111	Lungwort	Sounds	CD	15	13
8	4	Max	Royal	500 Pine	Manilla	NE	55123	827-555-4422	8/5/2006	8117	44-1111	Lungwort	Sounds	CD	15	13
9																

Duplicate customer data is entered each time an existing customer makes an additional purchase

Duplicate product data is entered each time the same product is sold more than once

TABLE A-1: Comparing Excel to Access

feature	Excel	Access
Layout	Provides a natural tabular layout for easy data entry	Provides a natural tabular layout as well as the ability to create customized data entry screens
Storage	Limited to approximately 65,000 records per sheet	Stores any number of records up to 2 GB
Linked tables	Manages single lists of information	Allows links between lists of information to reduce data redundancy
Reporting	Limited to the current spreadsheet arrangement of data	Creates and saves multiple presentations of data
Security	Limited to file security options such as marking the file "read-only" or protecting a range of cells	Allows users to access only the records and fields they need
Multiuser capabilities	Does not easily allow multiple users to simultaneously enter and update data	Allows multiple users to simultaneously enter and update data
Data entry	Provides limited data entry screens	Provides the ability to create extensive data entry screens called forms

UNIT A
Access 2003

Learning Database Terminology

To be successful with Access, you need to understand basic database terminology. Before you start working with Access, Kelsey asks you to review the terms and concepts that define a database.

DETAILS

You should become familiar with the following database terminology:

Database
table
Record
Field

- The smallest unit of data organization is called a field. A **field** consists of a specific category of data such as a customer's name, city, state, or phone number. A group of related fields that describe a person, place, or thing is called a **record**. A **key field** is a field that contains unique information for each record, such as a Social Security number for an employee or a customer number for a customer. A collection of records for a single subject, such as all of the customer records, is called a **table**. A collection of tables associated with a general topic (for example, sales of products to customers) is called a **database**.

- An Access database is a **relational database**, in which more than one table, such as the Customers, Sales, and Products tables, may be linked together. The term "relational database" describes a database in which two tables are linked (related) by a common field. For example, in Figure A-3, the Customers and Sales tables are related by the common Cust No field. The Products and Sales tables are related by the common Product No field. Through these relationships a relational database can minimize redundant data and present information from more than one table in a single view. For example, if you want to show the First and Last fields from the Customers table as well as the Product No and Date fields from the Sales table in a single view, the common Cust No field identifies which Sales table records are connected with each record in the Customers table.

- The parts of an Access database that help you enter, view, and manage the data are **tables**, **queries**, **forms**, **reports**, **pages**, **macros**, and **modules**, which are collectively called the database **objects**. They are summarized in Table A-2. Tables are the most important type of **object** in the database because they physically store all of the data within the database. The other objects make it easier to view, modify, or report the data.

- Data can be entered and edited in four objects: tables, queries, forms, and pages. The relationships among tables, queries, forms, and reports are shown in Figure A-4. Regardless of how the data is entered, it is stored in a table object. Furthermore, data can be printed from a table, query, form, page, or report object. The macro and module objects provide additional database productivity and automation features. All of the objects (except for page objects, which create Web pages) are stored in one **Access database file**. In general, however, the phrase "the database" refers only to the data and not the rest of the objects that may be part of an Access database file.

FIGURE A-3: Using Access to organize sales data

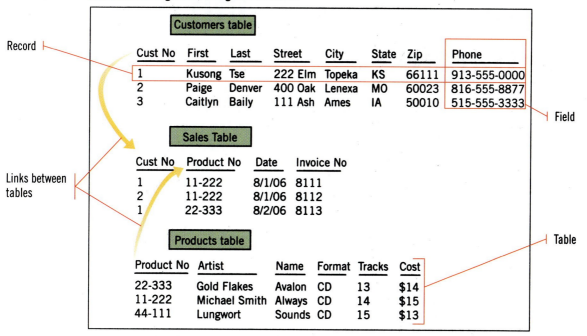

FIGURE A-4: Relationships among Access objects

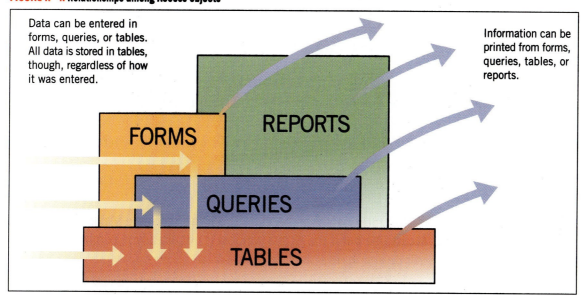

Data can be entered in forms, queries, or tables. All data is stored in tables, though, regardless of how it was entered.

Information can be printed from forms, queries, tables, or reports.

TABLE A-2: Access objects and their purpose

object	purpose
Table	Contains all of the raw data within the database in a spreadsheet-like view; tables are linked with a common field to minimize data redundancy
Query	Provides a spreadsheet-like view of the data similar to tables, but allows the user to select a subset of fields or records from one or more tables; queries are created when a user has a question about the data in the database
Form	Provides an easy-to-use data entry screen which often shows only one record at a time
Report	Provides a professional printout of data that may contain enhancements such as headers, footers, graphics, and calculations on groups of records
Page	Creates dynamic Web pages that interact with an Access database; also called Data Access Page
Macro	Stores a set of keystrokes or commands, such as the commands to display a particular toolbar when a form opens
Module	Stores Visual Basic for Applications programming code that extends the functions and automated processes of Access

Starting Access and Opening a Database

You can start Access 2003 and open a database in a variety of ways. You can start Access by using the menus found when you click the Start button on the taskbar, or if an Access icon is located on the Windows desktop, you can start Access from that shortcut as well. To open a specific database within Access, click the Open button on the Database toolbar or use the Open portion of the Getting Started task pane. You can also open a specific database within Access by opening the database file from My Computer or Windows Explorer. You start Access and open the MediaLoft-A.mdb database.

STEPS

1. **Click the Start button 🏁start on the taskbar**

   The Start button is the first item on the taskbar, and is usually located in the lower-left corner of your screen. You can use the Start menu to start any program on your computer.

2. **Point to All Programs, then point to Microsoft Office**

   Access is generally located on the Microsoft Office submenu of the All Programs menu. All the programs stored on your computer can be found on the All Programs menu or one of its submenus.

TROUBLE
If Microsoft Access is not located on the Microsoft Office submenu, look for it on the Start or All Programs menu.

3. **Click Microsoft Office Access 2003**

   Access opens and displays a task pane on the right, from which you can open an existing file or create a new database.

TROUBLE
If the task pane does not appear on the right side of your screen, click File on the menu bar, then click New.

4. **Click the More link in the Open section of the task pane**

   The Open dialog box opens, as shown in Figure A-5. Depending on the databases and folders stored on your computer, your dialog box might look different.

5. **Click the Look in list arrow, then navigate to the drive and folder where your Data Files are stored**

   When you navigate to the correct folder, a list of the Microsoft Access database files in that folder appears in the Open dialog box.

6. **Click the MediaLoft-A.mdb database file, click Open, then click the Maximize button on the Microsoft Access title bar if the Access window is not already maximized**

   The MediaLoft-A.mdb database opens as shown in Figure A-6.

FIGURE A-5: Open dialog box

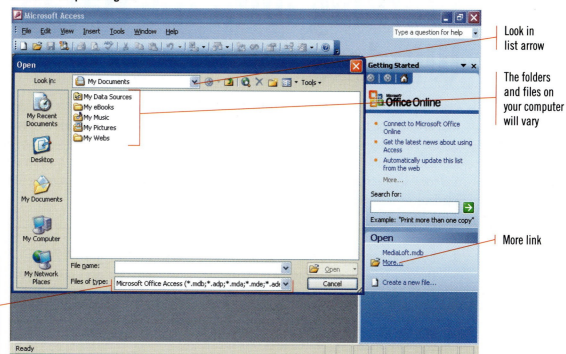

Look in list arrow

The folders and files on your computer will vary

More link

Whether the file extensions are displayed is determined by a Folder Option setting within Windows Explorer

FIGURE A-6: MediaLoft-A database

Microsoft Access title bar

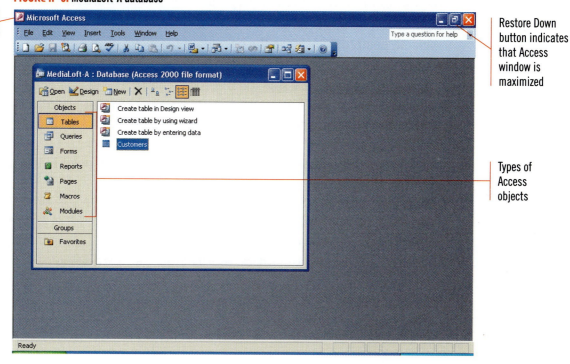

Restore Down button indicates that Access window is maximized

Types of Access objects

Clues to Use

Personalized toolbars and menus in Access 2003

All of the applications within Office 2003 support **personalized toolbars** and **personalized menus** to some extent. "Personalized" means that the toolbars and menus modify themselves to reflect those features that you use most often. To view, modify, or reset the toolbar and menu options, click Tools on the menu bar, and then click Customize. On the Options tab you can reset usage data, eliminate the delay when displaying full menus, and change other toolbar and menu bar characteristics.

Working with the Database Window

When you start Access and open a database, the **database window** displays familiar Windows elements such as a title bar, menu bar, and toolbar. Specific to Access, however, is the **Objects bar**, which displays the buttons for the seven Access objects. Also, the **Groups bar** below the Objects bar displays folders that contain shortcuts to commonly used objects. Clicking the **Objects button** or **Groups button** alternatively expands and collapses that section of the database window. 🎨 You are ready to explore the MediaLoft-A database interface.

STEPS

1. **Examine each of the Access window elements shown in Figure A-7**

    The Objects bar on the left side of the database window displays the seven object types. The other elements of the database window are summarized in Table A-3. Because the Tables object button is selected, the single table object, Customers, is displayed within the database window. In addition, the database window displays three "Create table..." shortcuts that help you create new table objects. The database window toolbar also presents buttons that help you work with table objects.

2. **Click File on the menu bar**

    The File menu contains commands for opening a new or existing database, saving data in a variety of formats, and printing. The menu commands vary depending on which window or database object is currently in use.

> **QUICK TIP**
> Double-click a menu name to quickly display the full menu.

3. **Point to Edit on the menu bar, point to View, point to Insert, point to Tools, point to Window, point to Help, move the pointer off the menu, then press [Esc] twice**

    All menus close when you press [Esc]. Pressing [Esc] a second time deselects the menu bar.

4. **Point to the New button 🗋 on the Database toolbar**

    When you point to a toolbar button, a descriptive **ScreenTip** automatically appears. The buttons on the toolbars represent the most common Access features. Toolbar buttons change just as menu options change depending on which window and database object are currently in use.

5. **Point to the Open button 📂 on the Database toolbar, then point to the Save button 💾 on the Database toolbar**

    Sometimes toolbar buttons or menu options are dimmed, which means they are not currently available. For example, the Save button 💾 is dimmed because you have not made any changes that need to be saved.

6. **Click Queries on the Objects bar**

    A list of previously created queries is displayed in the database window as shown in Figure A-8. Two shortcuts to create new queries are also displayed.

7. **Click Forms on the Objects bar, then click Reports on the Objects bar**

    The MediaLoft-A database contains the Customers table, three queries, one form, and three reports.

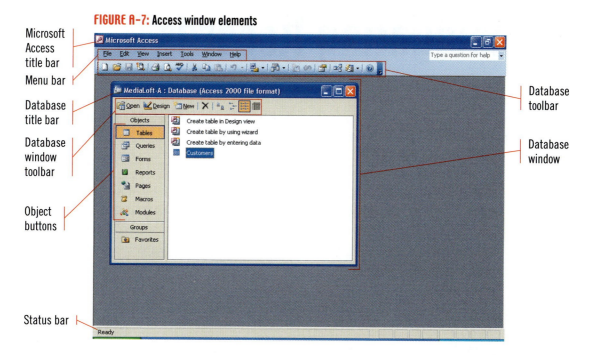

FIGURE A-7: Access window elements

Microsoft Access title bar

Menu bar

Database title bar

Database window toolbar

Object buttons

Status bar

Database toolbar

Database window

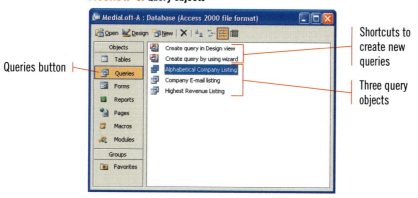

FIGURE A-8: Query objects

Queries button

Shortcuts to create new queries

Three query objects

TABLE A-3: Elements of the database window

element	description
Title bar	Contains the program name (Microsoft Office Access 2003) or filename (MediaLoft-A)
Menu bar	Contains menu options appropriate for the current view of the database
Database toolbar	Contains buttons for common tasks that affect the entire database (e.g., New, Open, or Relationships) or are common to all database objects (e.g., Print, Copy, or Spelling)
Database window	Presents the objects and shortcuts within the open database
Database window toolbar	Contains buttons used to open, modify, create, delete, or view objects
Object buttons	Provide access to the different types of objects stored within the database
Status bar	Displays messages regarding the current database operation

Clues to Use

Viewing objects

You can change the way you view the objects in the database window by clicking the last four buttons on the database window toolbar. You can view the objects as Large Icons, Small Icons, in a List (default view), and with Details. The Details view shows a description of the object, as well as the date the object was last modified and the date it was originally created.

Navigating Records

Your skill in navigating the fields and records of a database helps you productively find, enter, and update data. You use either mouse or keystroke techniques to navigate the data in the table's **datasheet**, a spreadsheet-like grid that displays fields as columns and records as rows. You open the Customers table and practice your record navigation skills.

STEPS

QUICK TIP

You can also select an object and click the Open button 📂 on the database window toolbar to open the object.

1. **Click Tables on the Objects bar, then double-click Customers in the database window**

   The datasheet for the Customers table opens, as shown in Figure A-9. The datasheet contains 27 customer records with 13 fields of information for each record. **Field names** are listed at the top of each column. The number of the selected record in the datasheet is displayed in the **Specific Record box** (also called the **record number box**) at the bottom of the datasheet window. Depending on the size of your monitor and your display properties, you may see a different number of fields. To view more fields, scroll to the right.

2. **Press [Tab] to move to Sprint Systems**

   Sprint Systems is selected in the second field, Company, of the first record.

3. **Press [Enter]**

   The focus moves to Aaron in the third column, the field named First. Pressing either [Tab] or [Enter] moves the focus to the next field. The **focus** refers to which field would be edited if you started typing.

4. **Press [↓]**

   The focus moves to Jacob in the second record. The **current record symbol** in the **record selector box** also identifies which record you are navigating. The Next Record and Previous Record **navigation buttons** in the lower-left corner of the datasheet can also be used to navigate the datasheet.

TROUBLE

If [Ctrl][End] doesn't move the focus to the last field of the last record, you are probably working in Edit mode. Press [Tab] to return to Navigation mode, and then press [Ctrl][End].

5. **Press [Ctrl][End]**

   The focus moves to $6,790.33 in the last field, named YTDSales, of the last record. You can also use the Last Record navigation button to move to the last record.

6. **Press [Ctrl][Home]**

   The focus moves to 1 in the field named ID of the first record. You can also use the First Record navigation button to move to the first record. A complete list of navigation keystrokes to move the focus between fields and records is shown in Table A-4.

FIGURE A-9: Customers datasheet

FIGURE A-9: Customers datasheet

Field names

Current record symbol

Focus

Record selector box

Records

First Record button

ID	Company	First	Last	Street	City	State	Zip
1	Sprint Systems	Aaron	Clark	111 Ash St.	Kansas City	MO	66888-111
2	KGSM	Jacob	Douglas	222 Elm St.	Kansas City	MO	66888-222
3	JCCC	Douglas	Scott	333 Oak Dr.	Kansas City	KS	66777-444
4	Oliver's Salon	Ann	Thomas	444 Apple St.	Kansas City	KS	66777-333
5	Podiatry Surgery Center	Todd	Vandenburg	555 Birch St.	Lenexa	KS	66661-003
6	Mohs Surgery Center	Glenn	Cho	666 Pine St.	Kansas City	MO	66886-333
7	American Diabetes Center	Sandie	Burik	777 Mulberry Way	Overland Park	KS	66555-222
8	Hallmark Company	Kristen	Chung	888 Fountain Dr.	Mission Hills	KS	66222-333
9	Aaron Rents	Tom	Cinotto	999 Riverside Dr.	Shawnee	KS	66111-888
10	IBM	Daniel	Arno	123 Wrigley Field	Overland Park	KS	66333-222
11	Motorola Corporation	Mark	Espindola	234 Wedd St.	Overland Park	KS	66333-998i
12	PFS Investments	David	Duarte	987 Front St.	Gladstone	MO	60011-222
13	Hill Pet Foods	Molly	Wu	6788 Pine St.	Independence	MO	60222-333
14	LabOne	Claire	Dodge	6789 Canyon Pl.	Raytown	MO	60124-222
15	ABC Electricity	Brett	Morgan	987 Lincolnway	Lenexa	KS	66444-444
16	Health Midwest Clinic	Jane	Eagan	201 Jackson St.	Overland Park	KS	66332-999
17	Cerner Industries	Fritz	Bradley	887 Winger Rd.	Shawnee	KS	66111-888
18	EBC	Carl	Salter	444 Metcalf	Overland Park	KS	66111-777
19	Royals	Peg	Fox	554 Stadium Ln.	Raytown	MO	60124-111
20	St. Luke's Hospital	Amanda	Summer	667 Birdie Ln.	Kansas City	MO	66888-555

Record: 1 of 27

Previous Record button

Specific Record box

Next Record button

Last Record button

New Record button

Total number of records

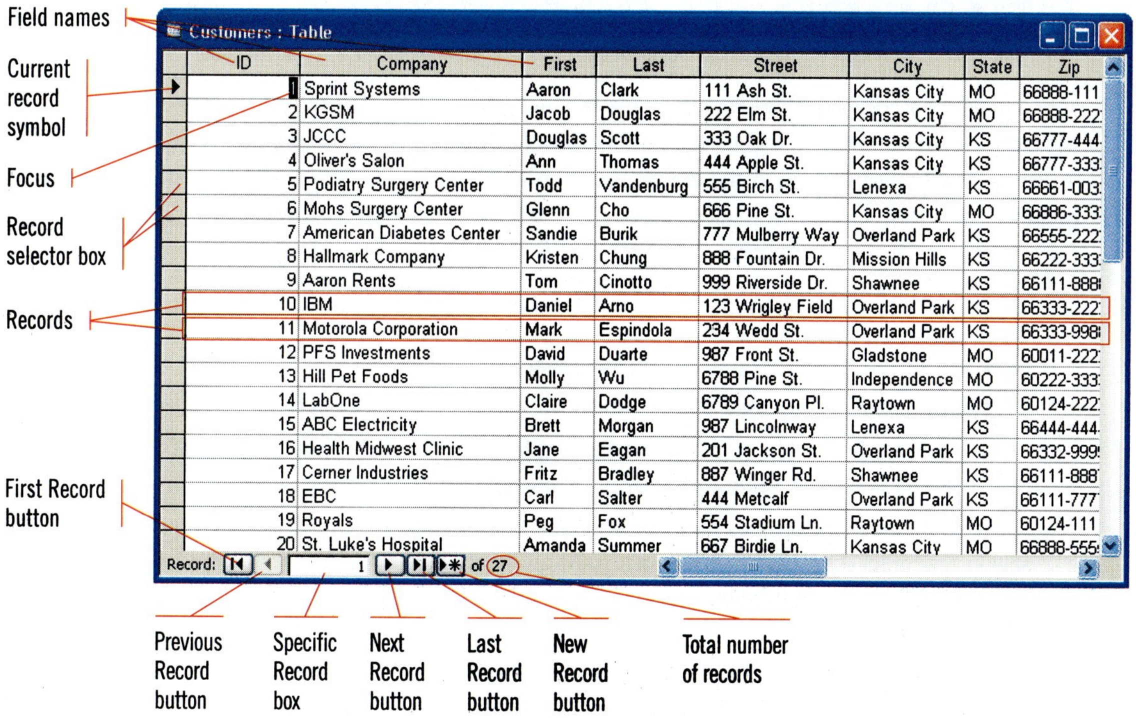

TABLE A-4: Navigation mode keyboard shortcuts

shortcut key	moves to the
[Tab], [Enter], or [→]	Next field of the current record
[Shift][Tab] or [←]	Previous field of the current record
[Home]	First field of the current record
[End]	Last field of the current record
[Ctrl][Home]	First field of the first record
[Ctrl][End]	Last field of the last record
[↑]	Current field of the previous record
[↓]	Current field of the next record
[Ctrl] [↑]	Current field of the first record
[Ctrl] [↓]	Current field of the last record
[F5]	Specific record entered in the Specific Record box

Clues to Use

Changing to Edit mode

If you navigate to another area of the datasheet by clicking with the mouse pointer instead of pressing [Tab] or [Enter], you change from **Navigation mode** to Edit mode. In **Edit mode**, Access assumes that you are trying to make changes to the current field value, so keystrokes such as [Ctrl][End], [Ctrl][Home], [←] and [→] move the insertion point *within* the field. To return to Navigation mode, press [Tab] or [Enter] (thus moving the focus to the next field), or press [↓] or [↑] (thus moving the focus to a different record).

Entering Records

Your ability to add new records into a database is a fundamental skill. You can add a new record by clicking the New Record button ▶* on the Table Datasheet toolbar or by clicking the New Record navigation button. A new record is always added at the end of the datasheet. You can rearrange the order of the records in a datasheet by sorting them, which you will learn later. 🎨 Kelsey asks you to add two new records to the Customers table. First, you maximize the datasheet window to make the working area as large as possible.

STEPS

1. **Click the Maximize button for the Customers table**

   Maximizing both the Access and datasheet windows displays as many fields and records on the screen as possible.

2. **Click the New Record button ▶* on the Table Datasheet toolbar, then press [Tab] to move through the ID field and into the Company field**

   The ID field is an **AutoNumber** field. Each time you add a record, Access automatically displays the next available integer in an AutoNumber field when you start entering data in that record. You cannot type into an AutoNumber field. The AutoNumber field logs how many records have been added to the datasheet since the creation of the table. It does not tell you how many records are currently in the table because Access does not reuse an AutoNumber value that was assigned to a record that has been deleted.

3. **Type CIO, press [Tab], type Taylor, press [Tab], type McKinsey, press [Tab], type 420 Locust St., press [Tab], type Lenexa, press [Tab], type KS, press [Tab], type 661118899, press [Tab], type 9135551189, press [Tab], type 9135551889, press [Tab], type 9/6/69, press [Tab], type taylor@cio.com, press [Tab], type 5433.22, then press [Enter]**

   The value of 28 is automatically entered in the ID field for this record. Notice that the navigation buttons indicate that you are now working on record 29 of 29.

QUICK TIP
You do not need to type the dashes or parentheses in the Zip, Phone, or Fax fields nor the dollar sign or comma in the YTDSales field. These symbols are automatically inserted for these fields. You will learn how to create fields in Unit B.

4. **Enter the new record for Cooper Michaels shown below**

in field:	type:	in field:	type:
ID	[Tab]	Zip	655554444
Company	Four Winds	Phone	9135551212
First	Cooper	Fax	9135552889
Last	Michaels	Birthdate	8/20/1968
Street	500 Sunset Blvd.	Email	coop@4winds.com
City	Manhattan	YTDSales	5998.33
State	KS		

5. **Press [Tab], then compare your updated datasheet with Figure A-10**

   An AutoNumber field displays (AutoNumber) until you start entering data in another field of that record.

FIGURE A-10: Customers table with two new records

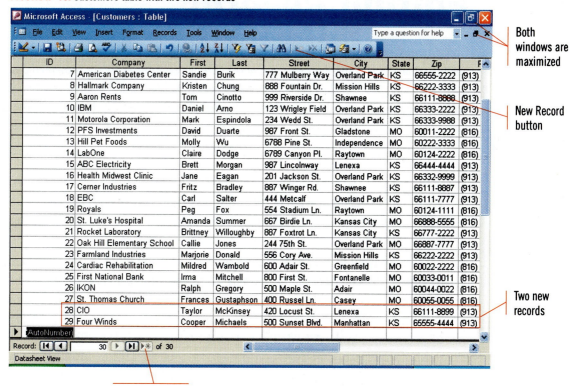

Both windows are maximized

New Record button

Two new records

New Record button

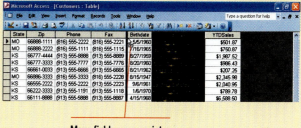

Editing Records

Updating existing information is another critical task. To change the contents of an existing record, click the field you want to change, then type the new information. You can delete unwanted data by clicking the field and using [Backspace] or [Delete] to delete text to the left or right of the insertion point. Other data entry keystrokes are summarized in Table A-5. Kelsey asks you to make some corrections to the datasheet of the Customers table. You start by correcting an error in the Street field of the first record.

STEPS

1. **Press [Ctrl][Home] to move to the first record, click to the right of 111 Ash St. in the Street field, press [Backspace] three times to delete St., then type Dr.**

   When you are editing a record, the **edit record symbol**, which looks like a small pencil, appears in the record selector box to the left of the current record, as shown in Figure A-12.

2. **Click to the right of Hallmark in the Company field in record 8, press [Spacebar], type Cards to change the entry to Hallmark Cards Company, then press [↓] to move to the next record**

   Access automatically saves new records and edits to existing data as soon as you move to another record or close the datasheet.

3. **Click Shawnee in the City field for record 17, then press [Ctrl]['']**

   Pressing [Ctrl]['] inserts the data from the same field in the previous record so the entry changes from "Shawnee" to "Overland Park".

4. **Click to the left of EBC in the Company field for record 18, press [Delete] to remove the E, press [Tab] to move to the next field, then type Doug**

   "EBC" becomes "BC" in the Company field, and "Doug" replaces "Carl" in the First field. Notice the edit record symbol in the record selector box to the left of record 18. Because you are still editing this record, you can undo the changes using [Esc].

5. **Press [Esc]**

   The Doug entry changes back to Carl. Pressing [Esc] once removes the current field's editing changes.

6. **Press [Esc] again**

   Pressing [Esc] a second time removes all changes made to the record you are currently editing. The Company entry is restored to EBC. The ability to use [Esc] in Edit mode to remove data entry changes depends on whether you are still editing the record (as evidenced by the edit record symbol to the left of the record). Once you move to another record, the changes are saved, and you return to Navigation mode. In Navigation mode you can no longer use [Esc] to remove editing changes, but you can click the **Undo button** on the Table Datasheet toolbar to undo the last change you made.

7. **Press [↓] to move to Peg in the First field of record 19, type Peggy, press [↓] to move to record 20, then press [Esc]**

   Because you are no longer editing record 19, [Esc] has no effect on the last change.

QUICK TIP
The ScreenTip for the Undo button displays the action you can undo.

8. **Click the Undo button on the Table Datasheet toolbar**

   You undo the last edit and Peggy is changed back to Peg. Some areas of Access allow you to undo multiple actions, but a datasheet allows you to undo only your last action.

9. **Click anywhere in the ABC Electricity (ID 15) record, click the Delete Record button on the Table Datasheet toolbar, then click Yes**

   The message warns that you cannot undo a record deletion operation. Notice that the Undo button is dimmed, indicating that it cannot be used at this time.

FIGURE A-12: Editing a record

Undo button →

Edit symbol →

Delete Record button →

Insertion point →

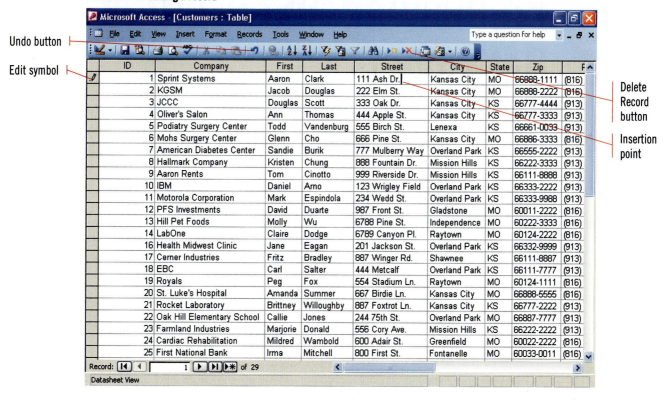

TABLE A-5: Edit mode keyboard shortcuts

editing keystroke	action
[Backspace]	Deletes one character to the left of the insertion point
[Delete]	Deletes one character to the right of the insertion point
[F2]	Switches between Edit and Navigation mode
[Esc]	Undoes the change to the current field
[Esc][Esc]	Undoes all changes to the current record
[F7]	Starts the spell check feature
[Ctrl][']	Inserts the value from the same field in the previous record into the current field
[Ctrl][;]	Inserts the current date in a Date field

Clues to Use

Resizing datasheet columns

You can resize the width of a field in a datasheet by dragging the thin black line that separates the field names to the left or right. The mouse pointer changes to ╫ as you make the field wider or narrower. Release the mouse button when you have resized the field. To adjust the column width to accommodate the widest entry in the field, double-click the thin black line that separates the field names.

Previewing and Printing a Datasheet

Previewing a datasheet shows you how the data will appear on a physical piece of paper before you send it to the printer. Previewing is important because it allows you to see and make printing adjustments, such as changing the margins or page orientation, before printing it. You decide to preview and print the datasheet.

STEPS

QUICK TIP

If you want your name to appear on the printout, enter your name as a new customer in the datasheet before printing.

1. **Click the Print Preview button on the Table Datasheet toolbar**

   The datasheet appears as a miniature page in the Print Preview window, as shown in Figure A-14. The Print Preview toolbar provides options for printing, viewing more than one page, and sending the information to Word or Excel.

2. **Click the pointer on the field names of the datasheet to zoom in**

   By magnifying the top of the printout, you see that Customers, the name of the table, is positioned in the center of the header. Today's date is positioned in the right section of the header.

3. **Scroll down to view the bottom of the page**

   The word "Page" and the current page number are positioned in the center of the footer.

4. **Click the Two Pages button on the Print Preview toolbar**

   The navigation buttons in the lower-left corner are dimmed, indicating that there are no more pages to navigate—the entire printout fits on two pages. To change printing options, use the Page Setup dialog box.

5. **Click the Setup button on the Print Preview toolbar**

   The Page Setup dialog box opens, as shown in Figure A-15. This dialog box provides options for changing margins, removing the print headings (the header and footer), and changing page orientation from portrait (default) to landscape on the Page tab.

6. **Double-click 1 in the Top text box, type 2, then click OK**

   The datasheet now has a two-inch top margin as shown in the Print Preview window.

7. **Click the Print button on the Print Preview toolbar, click File on the menu bar, then click Close**

   Closing the Print Preview window takes you back to the database window.

Clues to Use

Hiding fields

Sometimes you may not want all the fields of a datasheet to appear on the printout. To temporarily hide a field, click anywhere in the field, click Format on the datasheet menu bar, and then click Hide Columns. To redisplay the column, click Format, then click Unhide Columns. The Unhide Columns dialog box, shown in Figure A-13, opens. The unchecked boxes indicate which columns are currently hidden.

FIGURE A-13: Unhide Columns dialog box

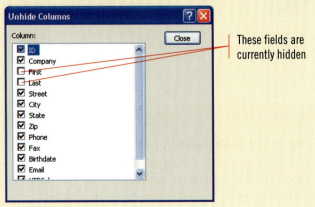

These fields are currently hidden

FIGURE A-14: Datasheet in print preview (portrait orientation)

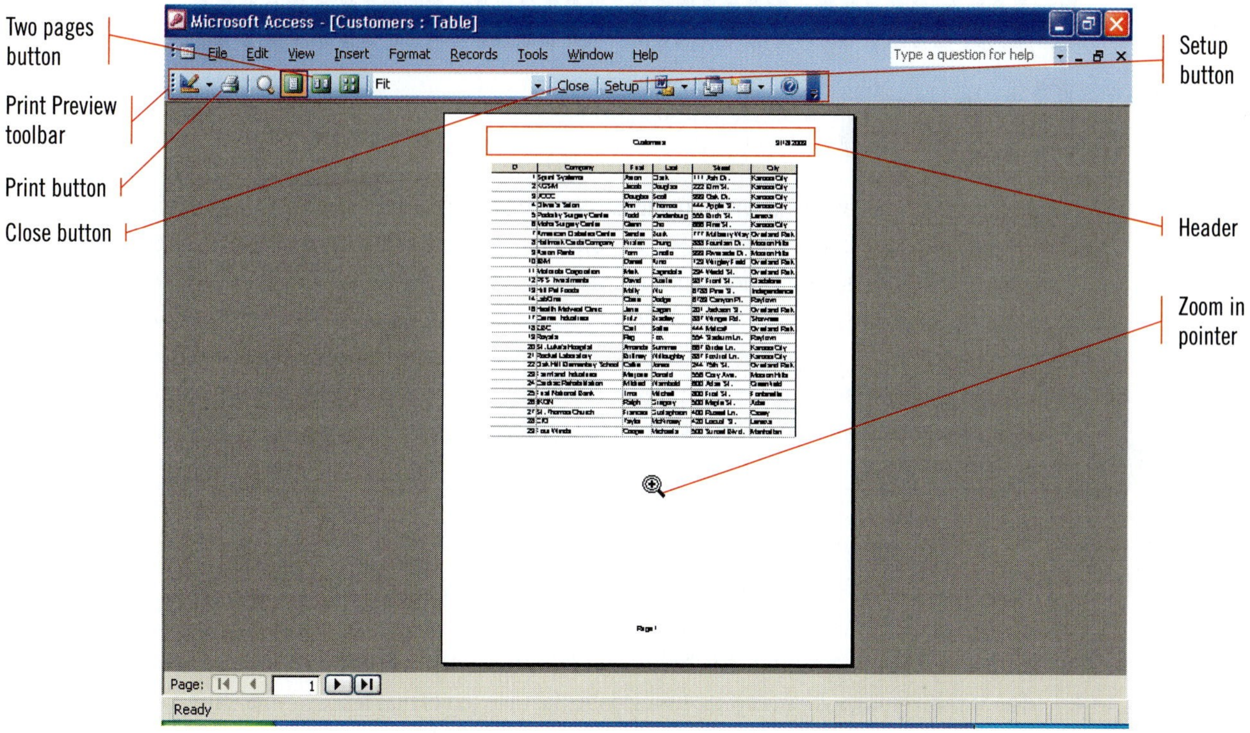

Two pages button

Print Preview toolbar

Print button

Close button

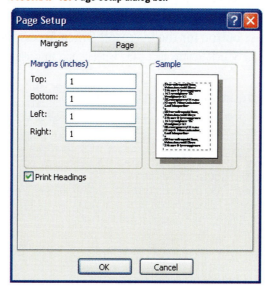

Setup button

Header

Zoom in pointer

FIGURE A-15: Page Setup dialog box

Page Setup

Margins | Page

Margins (inches)

Top: 1

Bottom: 1

Left: 1

Right: 1

Sample

☑ Print Headings

OK | Cancel

Getting Help and Exiting Access

When you are finished working with a database, you need to close all open objects, close the database, and then exit Access. To close an object, click File on the menu bar and then click Close, or click the object's Close button ☒ located on the right edge of the menu bar. After you close the objects you have been working with, you close the database and exit Access. As with most programs, if you try to exit Access and have not yet saved changes to open objects, Access prompts you to save your changes. You can use the Access Help system to learn more about the program. 🎨 You have finished working with the MediaLoft-A database for now. Before exiting Access, though, you want to learn more about the Help system.

STEPS

QUICK TIP

If your Data Files are stored on a floppy disk, do not remove your floppy disk from drive A until you have completely exited Access as instructed in Step 6.

1. **Click the Close button for the MediaLoft-A database, as shown in Figure A-16**

   The MediaLoft-A database is closed, but Access is still running. At this point you can open another database or explore the Help system to learn more about Access.

2. **Click the Type a question for help box, type naming fields, then press [Enter]**

   The Search Results task pane opens, listing potential Help topics that relate to your entry. Using the Help text box is similar to initiating keyword searches via the Office Assistant or using the Answer Wizard. Help menu options and terminology are further explained in Table A-6.

3. **Click About renaming a field in a table (MDB)**

   The Help system opens to the specific page that explains how to rename an existing field in a table. **Glossary terms** are shown as blue hyperlinks. Clicking a blue hyperlink displays a definition.

4. **Click the Show All link in the upper-right corner of the Microsoft Access Help window, then resize the Help window as desired**

   An expanded view of the Help page with all subcategories and definitions appears, as shown in Figure A-17. The Show All link now becomes the Hide All link.

5. **Click the Close button for the Microsoft Office Access Help window**

   You return to the Search Results task pane where you can click another link or initiate another search for information.

6. **Click File on the menu bar, then click Exit**

Clues to Use

Compact on Close

The **Compact on Close** option found on the General tab of the Options dialog box compacts and repairs your database each time you close it. To open the Options dialog box, click Tools on the menu bar, and then click Options. *While the Compact on Close feature works well if your database is stored on your hard drive or on another large storage device, it can cause problems if your Data Files are stored on a floppy disk.* The Compact on Close process creates a temporary file that is just as large as the original database file. This temporary file is used during the compaction process, and is deleted after the procedure successfully finishes. Therefore, if your database file grows larger than half of the available storage space on a floppy disk, the Compact on Close process cannot create the necessary temporary file or successfully compact the database. Such an error might result in a harmless error message or, in the worst case, a corrupt database.

FIGURE A-16: Closing a database

Close button for Access

Close button for MediaLoft-A database

FIGURE A-17: Microsoft Access Help window

Glossary terms are blue

Glossary defintions are green

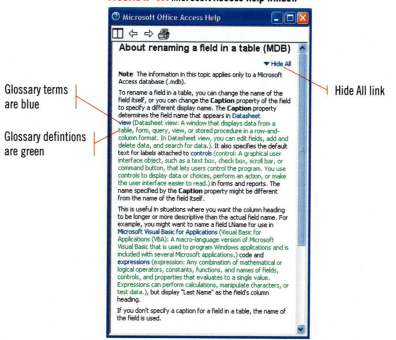

Hide All link

TABLE A-6: Help menu options

Help menu option	description
Microsoft Office Access Help	Opens the Access Help task pane
Show/Hide the Office Assistant	Presents or hides the **Office Assistant**, an automated character that provides tips and interactive prompts while you are working
Microsoft Office Online	If you are connected to the Web, provides additional Microsoft information and support articles stored at the Microsoft Web site
Access Developer Resources	If you are connected to the Web, opens the MSDN Library Web page, which provides information on advanced Access technologies, such as Web development
Contact Us	If you are connected to the Web, opens a Microsoft Office Web page where you can get assistance from Microsoft, such as how-to articles and tips
Sample Databases	Provides easy access to the sample databases installed with Access 2003
Check for Updates	If you are connected to the Web, checks the Microsoft Web site for files you can download to update Office or Access
Detect and Repair	Analyzes a database for possible data corruption and attempts to repair problems
Activate Product	Click to start activation process
Customer Feedback Options	Provides options for working with Microsoft to provide feedback through their Customer Experience Improvement Program
About Microsoft Office Access	Provides the version and product ID of Access

Practice

▼ CONCEPTS REVIEW

Label each element of the Access window shown in Figure A-18.

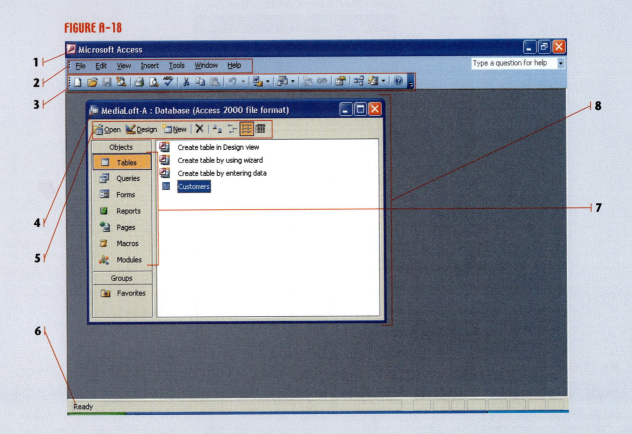

Match each term with the statement that best describes it.

9. **Objects**
10. **Table**
11. **Record**
12. **Field**
13. **Datasheet**
14. **Form**
15. **Compact on Close**

a. A group of related fields, such as all of the demographic information for one customer

b. A collection of records for a single subject, such as all the customer records

c. A category of information in a table, such as a customer's name, city, or state

d. A spreadsheet-like grid that displays fields as columns and records as rows

e. A process that shrinks and repairs a database

f. An Access object that provides an easy-to-use data entry screen

g. Seven types of these are contained in an Access database and are used to enter, enhance, and use the data within the database

Select the best answer from the list of choices.

16. **Which of the following is *not* a typical benefit of relational databases?**
    a. Easier data entry
    b. Faster information retrieval
    c. Minimized duplicate data entry
    d. Automatic trend analysis

17. **Which of the following is *not* an advantage of managing data with a relational database versus a spreadsheet?**
    a. Doesn't require planning before data is entered
    b. Allows links between lists of information
    c. Provides greater security
    d. Allows multiple users to enter data simultaneously

18. **The object that holds all of the data within an Access database is the:**
    a. Query.
    b. Table.
    c. Form.
    d. Report.

19. **The object that creates a dynamic Web page is the:**
    a. Table.
    b. Form.
    c. Page.
    d. Report.

20. **What displays messages regarding the current database operation?**
    a. Status bar
    b. Title bar
    c. Database toolbar
    d. Object buttons

▼ SKILLS REVIEW

1. **Understand relational databases.**
   a. Identify five advantages of managing database information in Access versus using a spreadsheet.
   b. Explain how a relational database organizes data to minimize redundant information. Use an example involving a database with two related tables, Customers and Sales, to make your explanation.

2. **Learn database terminology.**
   a. Explain the relationship between a field, a record, a table, and a database.
   b. Identify the seven objects of an Access database, and explain the main purpose of each.
   c. Which object of an Access database is most important? Why?

3. **Start Access and open a database.**
   a. Click the Start button, point to All Programs, point to Microsoft Office, then click Microsoft Office Access 2003.
   b. Open the **Recycle-A.mdb** database from the drive and folder where your Data Files are stored.
   c. Identify the following elements on a printout. (*Hint*: To create a printout of the Recycle-A database window, press [Print Screen] to capture an image of the window to the Windows Clipboard. Start any word processing program, then click the Paste button to paste the image stored on the Clipboard into the document. Print the document that now contains a picture of the opening database window, and identify the elements on the printout.)
      • Microsoft Access title bar
      • Database toolbar
      • Database window
      • Menu bar
      • Database title bar
      • Object buttons
      • Database window toolbar
      • Status bar

4. **Work with the database window.**
   a. Maximize both the Access window and the Recycle-A database window.
   b. Click each of the Object buttons on the Objects bar, then write down the object names of each type that exists in the Recycle-A database.

5. **Navigate records.**
   a. Open the Clubs table datasheet.
   b. Press [Tab] or [Enter] to move through the fields of the first record.
   c. Press [Ctrl][End] to move to the last field of the last record.
   d. Press [Ctrl][Home] to move to the first field of the first record.
   e. Click the Last Record navigation button to quickly move to the Oak Hill Patriots record.

6. Enter records.

a. In the Clubs table, click the New Record button, then add the following two records:

Club Number	Name	Street	City	State	Zip	Phone	FName	LName
8	EBC Angels	10100 Metcalf	Overland Park	KS	66001	555-333-7711	Steve	Earhart
9	Zoopers	111 Holmes	Kansas City	MO	65001	555-333-8811	Jim	Wheeling

b. Move the Club Number field from the first column of the datasheet to the last column.

7. Edit records.

a. Change the Name field in the first record from Jaycees to **JC Club**.

b. Change the Name field in the second record from Boy Scouts #11 to **Oxford Cub Scouts**.

c. Change the FName field in the record for the Lions club from Cory to **Clayton**.

d. Enter a new record using fictitious but realistic entries for the Name, Street, City, State, Zip, and Phone fields. Enter your name for the FName and LName fields and **99** as the Club Number entry.

e. Resize the datasheet columns so that all field entries are visible.

f. Delete the record for Club Number 3.

8. Preview and print a datasheet.

a. Preview the Clubs table datasheet.

b. Use the Page Setup option on the File menu to change the page orientation from portrait to landscape.

c. Print the Clubs table datasheet.

9. Get Help and exit Access.

a. Close the Clubs table, saving the changes.

b. Close the **Recycle-A.mdb** database, but leave Access running.

c. Search for Help topics by entering the keyword **subdatasheet** into the Type a question for help box. Click the link for the About subdatasheets option.

d. Click the Show All link to display all of the glossary terms, then click the Print button on the Help window toolbar to print that page.

e. Close the Microsoft Office Access Help window.

f. Exit Access.

▼ INDEPENDENT CHALLENGE 1

Twelve examples of database tables are given below.

- Telephone directory
- College course offerings
- Restaurant menu
- Cookbook
- Movie listing
- Islands of the Caribbean
- Encyclopedia
- Shopping catalog
- Product inventory
- Party guest list
- Members of the House of Representatives
- Ancient wonders of the world

For each example, write a brief answer for the following.

a. What field names would you expect to find in each table?

b. Provide an example of two possible records for each table.

▼ INDEPENDENT CHALLENGE 2

You are working with several civic groups to coordinate a community-wide cleanup effort. You have started a database called Recycle-A that tracks the clubs, their trash deposits, and the trash collection centers that are participating.

a. Start Access, then open the **Recycle-A.mdb** database from the drive and folder where your Data Files are stored.

b. Open each table's datasheet, and write down the number of records and fields in each of the tables.

c. In the Centers table datasheet, modify the ContactFirst and ContactLast names for Center Number 1 to be your name.

d. Preview the Centers table datasheet, use the Page Setup options to change the left and right margins to 0.5", and also change the page orientation to landscape. The printout should now fit on one page. Print the Centers table datasheet, then close it.

Advanced Challenge Exercise

■ Open the datasheet for the Clubs table. Click the expand button to the left of each record and count the records in each subdatasheet that appears. (*Hint*: To quickly count the records in a subdatasheet, click within the subdatasheet and then view the total number of records displayed to the right of the navigation buttons in the lower-left corner of the datasheet.) How many total records are in the subdatasheets, and what does this tell you about the relationship between the Clubs and Deposits tables? (*Hint*: How many records did you originally find in the Deposits table from Step b?)

■ Close the datasheet for the Clubs table. Open the datasheet for the Centers table. An expand button appears as a small plus sign to the left of the Name field for each record. Click the expand button to the left of each of the records in the Centers datasheet. A subdatasheet for each center appears. Count the records in each subdatasheet. How many total records are in the subdatasheets, and what does this tell you about the relationship between the Centers and Deposits tables?

e. Close the Centers table, close **Recycle-A.mdb**, then exit Access.

▼ INDEPENDENT CHALLENGE 3

You are working with several civic groups to coordinate a community-wide cleanup effort. You have started a database called Recycle-A that tracks the clubs, their trash deposits, and the trash centers that are participating.

a. Start Access and open the **Recycle-A.mdb** database from the drive and folder where your Data Files are stored.

b. Add the following records to the Clubs table:

Name	Street	City	State	Zip	Phone	FName	LName	Club Number
Take Pride	222 Lincoln Way	Olathe	KS	66001	555-888-2211	Franklin	Rivers	10
Cub Scouts #321	333 Ward Pkwy.	Kansas City	MO	65002	555-777-8800	Jacob	Tamar	11

c. Edit the Lions record 4 in the Clubs table. The Street value should be **444 Maple Way**, the City value should be **Shawnee**, and the Zip value should be **68777**.

d. If you haven't entered a record containing your own name in the FName and LName fields, enter this record using **99** as the Club Number.

e. Print the datasheet in landscape orientation.

f. Close the Clubs table.

Advanced Challenge Exercise

■ Click the Queries button, then open the datasheet for the Deposits by Club query by double-clicking it.

■ Click File on the menu bar, click Print, then enter **1** in the From and To boxes to print only the first page. Click OK in the Print dialog box. On the printout, identify which table supplied the three fields in the datasheet. Close the Deposits by Club query.

g. Close the **Recycle-A.mdb** database, then exit Access.

▼ INDEPENDENT CHALLENGE 4

The World Wide Web can be used to research information about almost any topic. In this exercise, you go to Microsoft's Web site for Access, and explore what's new about Access 2003.

a. Connect to the Internet, and use your browser to go to the www.microsoft.com/access Web page.

b. Web sites change often, but you can probably find a link that provides a tour of Access 2003, or an introduction to Access 2003. Click that link and follow the tour or introduction. Based on what you learned, describe two new features or capabilities that you discovered about Access 2003.

c. Go back to the www.microsoft.com/access or www.microsoft.com/office Web page, then click the appropriate hyperlinks to find out how Office 2003 suites are organized. You might find this information within a pricing or ordering link. Find the Web page that describes what is included in the various Office 2003 suites and print it. On the printout, identify which suites include Access.

▼ VISUAL WORKSHOP

Open the **Recycle-A.mdb** database from the drive and folder where your Data Files are stored, then open the Centers table datasheet. Modify the records in the existing Centers table to reflect the changes shown in Figure A-19. The fields have been reorganized, the Name field for the fourth record has changed, and a new record has been added. If you have not entered your own first and last names in the ContactFirst and ContactLast fields of the first record, do so now. Print the datasheet in landscape orientation, close the Centers table, close the **Recycle-A.mdb** database, then exit Access.

FIGURE A-19

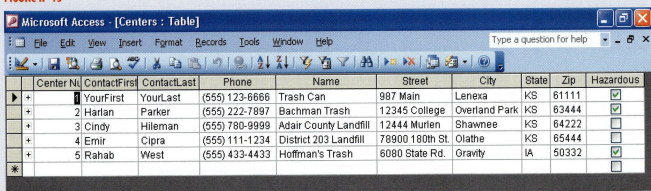

Using Tables and Queries

OBJECTIVES

Organize fields
Plan related tables
Create a table
Modify a table
Format a datasheet
Understand sorting, filtering, and finding
Sort records and find data
Filter records
Create a query
Modify a query

If you have a SAM user profile, you may have access to hands-on instruction, practice, and assessment of the skills covered in this unit. Log in to your SAM account and go to your assignments page to see what your instructor has assigned.

Now that you are familiar with some basic Access terminology and features, you are ready to plan and build your own database. You start by creating tables that store data. Once the tables are created and the data is entered, you use several techniques for finding specific information in the database, including sorting, filtering, and building queries. Kelsey Lang, a marketing manager at MediaLoft, wants you to build a database to track information about MediaLoft's music inventory. You use the database to find, analyze, and report information about MediaLoft's products.

Organizing Fields

Before you build a database in Access, it's wise to carefully plan the fields and tables to avoid rework necessary to later fix a poorly constructed database. To plan a database, start by identifying and organizing the individual fields that the database will store. Each field needs to have a descriptive name and an appropriate data type. The **data type** defines the kind of data that can be stored in each field, such as text, numbers, or dates. Table B-1 lists the data types available within Access. Before you build the new MediaLoft database, you plan its fields.

DETAILS

To organize the fields of a database:

- **Design the reports that you want the database to produce**

    Designing or sketching the reports that you want the database to produce helps you identify the fields that the database should store. In this case, you want to be able to print inventory reports that list MediaLoft's music products by artist, title, and price.

- **Collect the raw data that is required to produce the reports**

    To produce reports, you need **raw data**, the individual pieces of information entered into each field. The raw data for the reports might be in one or multiple locations, including index cards, paper reports, or computer files, such as word processing documents, spreadsheets, or accounting system files. Or, your reports may require you to start collecting fields of information that have not been recorded in the past.

- **Identify a name and data type for each field**

    Based on the reports you design and the raw data you collect, identify the field name and data type for each field that you want the database to contain, as shown in Figure B-1. Be sure to break down and assign each piece of data to its own field. For example, if you were designing a table to hold information about customers, separate the customer address into several fields such as Street, City, State, Zip, and Country in order to make the data easy to find, sort, and merge. Apply the same rule of thumb to a person's name. In most cases, you will want to break names into several fields such as First, Middle, Last, and Title in order to easily find, sort, and merge any part of a person's name.

    Properly defining the data type for each field helps you maintain data consistency and accuracy. For example, a field with a Currency data type will *not* accept a text entry.

Clues to Use

Choosing between the Text and Number data type

When assigning data types, avoid choosing the Number data type for a Telephone or Zip Code field. Although these fields generally contain only numeric entries, they should still be Text data types. For example, suppose you want to enter 1-800-BUY-BOOK in a telephone number field. This would not be possible if the field were designated as a Number data type. Also, when you sort fields such as Telephone or Zip Code, you want them to sort alphabetically, like Text fields, rather than in numeric order. For example, consider the zip codes of 60011 and 50011-8888. If the Zip Code field is designated as a Number data type, the data is interpreted incorrectly as the values 60,011 and 500,118,888, and sorted in that order. Given a Text data type, the zip codes are sorted based on the value of the first character, so 50011-8888 would come before 60011. Also, a Zip Code entry of 01234 would be stored as 1234 if stored as a number (leading zeros are insignificant when evaluated as numbers and are therefore dropped), making the field value incorrect.

FIGURE B-1: Initial design of fields and data types

Field Name	Data Type
RecordingID	AutoNumber
Title	Text
ArtistFirst	Text
ArtistLast	Text
Group	Text
Tracks	Number
Wholesale	Currency
Retail	Currency

TABLE B-1: Data types

data type	description of data	size
Text	Text information or combinations of text and numbers, such as a street address, name, or phone number	Up to 255 characters
Memo	Lengthy text such as comments or notes	Up to 65,535 characters
Number	Numeric information such as quantities	Several sizes available to store numbers with varying degrees of precision
Date/Time	Dates and times	Size controlled by Access to accommodate dates and times across thousands of years (for example, 1/1/1850 and 1/1/2150 are valid dates)
Currency	Monetary values	Size controlled by Access; accommodates up to 15 digits to the left of the decimal point and 4 digits to the right
AutoNumber	Integers assigned by Access to sequentially order each record added to a table	Size controlled by Access
Yes/No	Only one of two values stored (Yes/No, On/Off, True/False)	Size controlled by Access
OLE Object	Objects and files linked or embedded (OLE) that are created in other programs, such as pictures, sound clips, documents, or spreadsheets	Up to 1 GB
Hyperlink	Web and e-mail addresses	Size controlled by Access
Lookup Wizard	Not a data type, but a wizard that helps link the current table to another table or list	Size controlled through the choices made in the Lookup Wizard

Planning Related Tables

Tables are the most important objects in a database because they store all of the raw data. Each table should contain fields that describe only one subject. A table that repeats data in the same field of several records suggests that the table represents more than one subject. If you see repeated data in the fields of several records, you should consider separating the repeating fields into a second table that has a one-to-many relationship with the original table. A **one-to-many relationship** means that a single record in the "one" table is related to many records in the "many" table. For example, in a database that tracks music products, one artist may have many products for sale, such as different recordings. If you separate the fields that describe the artists and products into two tables—one for artists and another for products—you can create a one-to-many relationship between the tables by establishing a common field used to link the tables together. This organization of data allows you to enter the record that describes the artist only once, yet link it to many records that describe that artist's recordings. ![] Now that you have organized the fields, you plan the tables for the new MediaLoft database.

DETAILS

To plan the tables of a database:

- **Separate the fields into specific subject areas**

  For example, if your database manages the sale of products to customers, you should create separate Customers, Sales, and Inventory tables. For the new MediaLoft database, you need to create at least one table to store the fields that you previously identified. At this point, you may not yet see the need for more than one table.

- **Create sample records and examine the entries to determine if more tables are needed**

  Enter several records into the table and examine each field to see if they repeat data from other records, as shown in Figure B-2. If you see repeated data, the fields that contain the redundant information may need to be separated into another table. The two tables will later be linked in a one-to-many relationship.

- **Identify a primary key field for each table**

  A **primary key field** is a field that contains unique information for each record. For example, you could use the Employee Number field as the primary key field for a table that stores information about employees. Usually it is not a good idea to use a name field for a primary key field because two people could have the same name. The primary key field has two roles—it uniquely identifies each record in that table, and it is also used on the "one" side of a one-to-many relationship between two tables. For the new MediaLoft database, RecordingID will serve as the primary key field for the Inventory table and ArtistID will be the primary key field for the Artists table.

- **Identify a common field to link the tables in a one-to-many relationship**

  Once the tables are designed, a common field must be established to link the tables together. The common field is usually the primary key field in the table on the "one" side of a one-to-many relationship. The common field is called the **foreign key field** in the table on the "many" side of a one-to-many relationship. For the new MediaLoft database, one artist may offer many music products. Therefore, the ArtistID field (the primary key field in the Artists table, the "one" side of this relationship) is added to the Inventory table (the "many" side of this relationship) to serve as the common field to link the two tables together. In this situation, the ArtistID field in the Inventory table is called the foreign key field. Figure B-3 shows the final design for the first two tables of the new MediaLoft database. To see the relationships between tables for any existing database, click the Relationships button ![].

  Remember, the benefit of separating the fields into two tables is that it minimizes redundant data entries. In this case, you will enter the data that describes each artist in a record in the Artists table. Through the one-to-many relationship to the Inventory table, that artist record in the Artists table will be linked to many records in the Inventory table. Minimizing redundant data helps you increase the accuracy, consistency, efficiency, reliability, and overall value of data. Because the tables are connected in a relational database, you may view and organize the fields of multiple tables in any organization by using queries, forms, reports, and Web pages.

FIGURE B-2: Examining records for repeated data

RecordingID	Title	ArtistFirst	ArtistLast	Group	Tracks	Wholesale	Retail
1	Autumn	George	Walters	Justice	7	$5.00	$15.00
2	Summer	George	Walters	Justice	15	$7.00	$12.00
3	Spring	George	Walters	Justice	11	$7.00	$15.00
4	Winter	George	Walters	Justice	10	$6.00	$15.00
5	KG Live	Kenny	George	KG	11	$5.00	$14.00
6	Skyline Firedance	Kenny	George	KG	10	$14.00	$18.00
7	Sacred Road	David	Lantz	Lantz Orchestra	12	$6.00	$17.00
8	Heartsounds	David	Lantz	Lantz Orchestra	14	$7.00	$17.00
9	Handel's Messiah	Leonard	Bernard	Leonard Bernard	11	$6.00	$12.00
10	Favorite Overtures	Leonard	Bernard	Leonard Bernard	5	$10.00	$15.00

Using only one table, some fields contain redundant data in multiple records

FIGURE B-3: Final design for the first two tables

ArtistID is the primary key field in the Artists table

ArtistID is the foreign key field in the Inventory table

Using two tables, fields that describe the artist are separated from the fields that describe the products

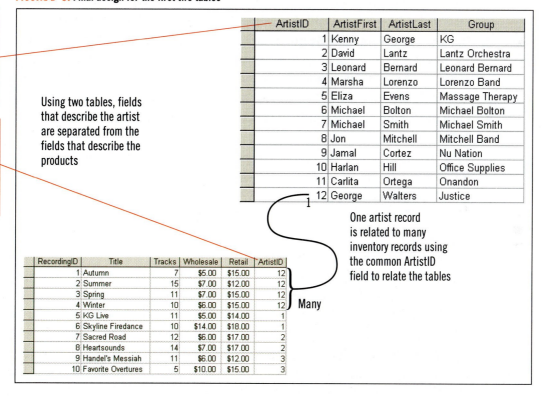

ArtistID	ArtistFirst	ArtistLast	Group
1	Kenny	George	KG
2	David	Lantz	Lantz Orchestra
3	Leonard	Bernard	Leonard Bernard
4	Marsha	Lorenzo	Lorenzo Band
5	Eliza	Evens	Massage Therapy
6	Michael	Bolton	Michael Bolton
7	Michael	Smith	Michael Smith
8	Jon	Mitchell	Mitchell Band
9	Jamal	Cortez	Nu Nation
10	Harlan	Hill	Office Supplies
11	Carlita	Ortega	Onandon
12	George	Walters	Justice

One artist record is related to many inventory records using the common ArtistID field to relate the tables

RecordingID	Title	Tracks	Wholesale	Retail	ArtistID
1	Autumn	7	$5.00	$15.00	12
2	Summer	15	$7.00	$12.00	12
3	Spring	11	$7.00	$15.00	12
4	Winter	10	$6.00	$15.00	12
5	KG Live	11	$5.00	$14.00	1
6	Skyline Firedance	10	$14.00	$18.00	1
7	Sacred Road	12	$6.00	$17.00	2
8	Heartsounds	14	$7.00	$17.00	2
9	Handel's Messiah	11	$6.00	$12.00	3
10	Favorite Overtures	5	$10.00	$15.00	3

UNIT B
Access 2003

Creating a Table

After you plan the structure of the database, your next step is to create the actual database file and the first table object. The database file contains the tables and any other objects that you create to view and work with the data such as queries, forms, and reports. Access offers several methods for creating the database and the first table. For example, you can create a sample database (complete with sample table, query, form, and report objects) using the **Database Wizard**. Or, you could create a blank database and build the objects from scratch. To build your first table, you could import a table from another data source such as a spreadsheet, or use the Access **Table Wizard**. The Table Wizard provides interactive help to create the field names and data types for each field. ▰▰▰ You are ready to create the new MediaLoft database and Inventory table. You use the Table Wizard to create the Inventory table.

STEPS

TROUBLE
If the task pane does not appear in the Access window, click File on the menu bar, then click New.

1. **Start Access, click the Create a new file link near the bottom of the Getting Started task pane, then click the Blank database link in the New File task pane as shown in Figure B-4**
   The File New Database dialog box opens.

2. **Type MediaLoft in the File name text box, click the Save in list arrow, navigate to the drive and folder where your Data Files are stored, then click Create**
   The MediaLoft.mdb database file is created and saved where your Data Files are stored. There are many ways to create the first table in the database, but the Table Wizard offers an efficient and easy way to get started.

TROUBLE
If the Create table by using wizard option does not appear in the database window, click Tools on the menu bar, then click Options. On the View tab, make sure that the New object shortcuts check box is selected, then click OK.

3. **Double-click Create table by using wizard in the MediaLoft database window**
   The Table Wizard dialog box opens. The Table Wizard offers 25 business and 20 personal sample tables from which you can select sample fields. The Recordings table in the Personal database category most closely matches the fields you want to include in the Inventory table.

4. **Click the Personal option button, then scroll down and click Recordings in the Sample Tables list box**
   The Table Wizard offers several sample fields for the Recordings table from which you can choose for your new table.

5. **Click RecordingID in the Sample Fields list, click the Select Single Field button > , click RecordingTitle, click > , click RecordingArtistID, click > , click NumberofTracks, click > , click PurchasePrice, click > **
   Your Table Wizard dialog box should look like Figure B-5.

6. **Click Next, type Inventory, click the No, I'll set the primary key option button, then click Next**
   The next dialog box asks questions about the primary key field. You want the RecordingID field to be the primary key field with an AutoNumber data type so that Access consecutively numbers each new record automatically. Therefore, you don't need to change the default settings that already specify these options.

TROUBLE
If you are in Table Datasheet View, click the Design View button 🔲 on the Table Datasheet toolbar.

7. **Click Next, click the Modify the table design option button, then click Finish**
   The table opens in Design View, shown in Figure B-6, which allows you to add, delete, or modify the fields in the table. The **key symbol** indicates that the RecordingID field has been designated as the primary key field.

FIGURE B-4: New File task pane

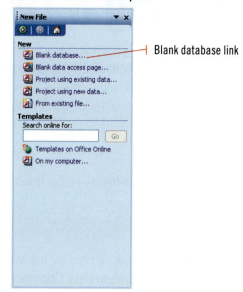

Blank database link

FIGURE B-5: Table Wizard

Sample fields for
Recordings table

Personal category

Recordings table

Select Single
Field button

Fields selected
for the new table

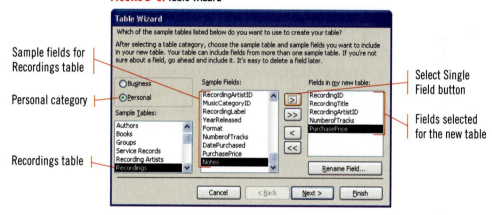

FIGURE B-6: Inventory table in Design View

Inventory table

Key field symbol

Field names

Data types

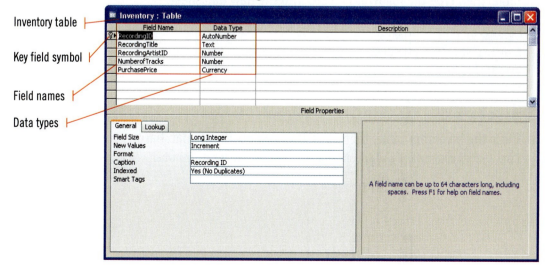

Access 2003

Modifying a Table

Each database object has a **Design View** in which you can modify its structure. The Design View of a table allows you to add or delete fields, add field descriptions, or change other field properties. Field **properties** are additional characteristics of a field such as its size or default value. Using the Table Wizard, you were able to create the Inventory table very quickly. Now in Design View you modify the fields to meet your specific needs.

STEPS

1. **In Design View of the Inventory table, double-click the PurchasePrice field name to select it, then type Wholesale**

   With the Wholesale field clearly named, you need to add another Currency field named Retail to store retail price data.

2. **Click the blank Field Name cell below the Wholesale field, type Retail, press [Tab], click the Data Type list arrow, then click Currency**

   The new field is added to the Inventory table, as shown in Figure B-7. Field names can include any combination of letters, numbers, and spaces, up to 64 characters. The only special characters that are not allowed are the period (.), exclamation point (!), accent grave (`), and square brackets [ ]. Field descriptions are optional, but they help to further identify the field. At this point, you decide to shorten the names of three existing fields.

3. **Double-click RecordingTitle to select it, type Title, double-click RecordingArtistID, type ArtistID, double-click NumberofTracks, then type Tracks**

   You also want to move the ArtistID field to the end of the field list.

4. **Click the row selector button to the left of the ArtistID field to select the entire row, then drag the row selector button to just below the Retail field**

   The black triangle in the row selector button helps you see which field is currently selected. The **Field Properties pane** in the lower half of Table Design View shows you the properties for the currently selected field. The **Caption** property contains the default label for the field when it is displayed in a datasheet or on a form. Without a Caption property, fields are labeled with their field name. The caption that the Table Wizard automatically created for the Wholesale field is "Purchase Price", which is no longer appropriate. Therefore, you decide to delete the Caption property for the Wholesale field.

5. **Click the Wholesale field, then delete Purchase Price in the Caption property**

   Table Design View of the Inventory table should look like Figure B-8. Other field properties, such as **Field Size**, restrict the amount or type of data that can be entered in the field and are helpful in reducing typing errors.

6. **Click the Datasheet View button 📄 on the Table Design toolbar, click Yes to save the table, then type the following record into the new datasheet:**

in field:	type:
Recording ID	[Tab]
Recording Title	Lift Us Up
Number of Tracks	15
Wholesale	20
Retail	25
Recording Artist ID	12

7. **Close the Inventory table, then close the MediaLoft.mdb database**

   Data is saved automatically, so you are not prompted to save the record when you closed the datasheet.

FIGURE B-7: Modifying the Inventory table

Wholesale field

Retail field is created with a Currency data type

Field Properties pane

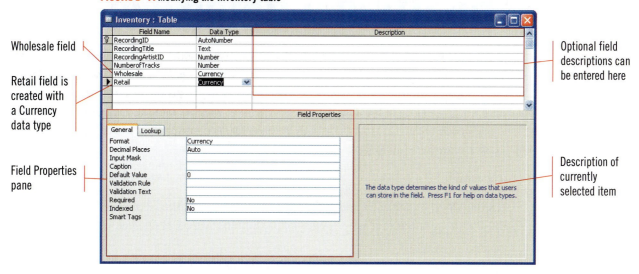

Optional field descriptions can be entered here

Description of currently selected item

FIGURE B-8: Final Table Design View of the Inventory table

Title field has been renamed

Tracks field has been renamed

Wholesale field is selected

Row selector button for ArtistID field

ArtistID field has been renamed and moved

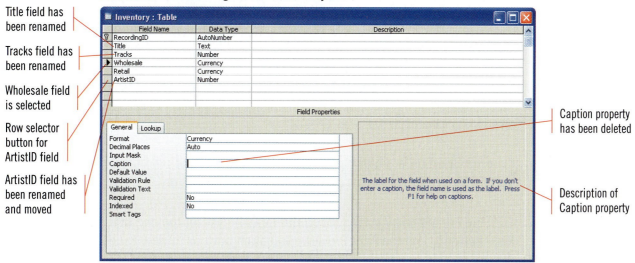

Caption property has been deleted

Description of Caption property

Clues to Use

Learning about field properties

Properties are the characteristics that define the field. Two properties are required for every field: Field Name and Data Type. Many other properties, such as Field Size, Format, Caption, and Default Value, are defined in the Field Properties pane in the lower half of Table Design View. As you add more property entries, you are generally restricting the amount or type of data that can be entered in the field, which in turn increases data entry accuracy. For example, you might change the Field Size property for a State field to 2 in order to eliminate an incorrect entry such as FLL. Field properties change depending on the data type of the selected field. For example, there is no Field Size property for date fields, because Access controls the size of fields with a Date/Time data type.

Formatting a Datasheet

After the database has been designed, the tables have been built, and the data has been entered, you often create printouts. Although the report object is most often used to create professional printouts, you can print data as displayed by a datasheet as well. In a datasheet, you can change the fonts, colors, and gridlines to enhance the appearance of the information. After working with the Table Wizard, you finished building the MediaLoft database to include both the Inventory and Artists tables and entered several records in both tables. Now you want to format and print the Inventory datasheet.

STEPS

1. Click the Open button 🖼 on the Database toolbar, select the MediaLoft-B.mdb database from the drive and folder where your Data Files are stored, then click Open

2. Click the Inventory table in the MediaLoft-B database window, then click the Open button 🖾 on the database window toolbar

   The Inventory table contains 62 records, as shown in Figure B-9. When you format a datasheet, every record in the datasheet is formatted the same way. You use the options on the Format menu to format a datasheet.

3. Click Format on the menu bar, click Font, scroll and click Comic Sans MS in the Font list, then click OK

   Comic Sans MS is an informal font that simulates handwritten text, but is still very readable. Formatting options for a datasheet are also found on the Formatting (Datasheet) toolbar. By default, the Formatting (Datasheet) toolbar does not appear in Datasheet View, but toolbars are easily turned on and off using the View menu.

4. Click View on the menu bar, point to Toolbars, then click Formatting (Datasheet)

   The Formatting (Datasheet) toolbar contains the most common formatting options for changing the font, colors, and gridlines of the datasheet.

5. Click the Line/Border Color button list arrow 🖋, click the red box, click the Gridlines button list arrow 🖩, then click the Gridlines: Horizontal box

6. Click the Print Preview button 🔍 on the Table Datasheet toolbar, then click the Next Page button ▶ in the Print Preview navigation buttons to view Page 2

   The First Page ⏮ and Previous Page ◀ buttons are dimmed if you are viewing the first page of the datasheet. The Next Page ▶ and Last Page ⏭ buttons are dimmed if you are viewing the last page of the datasheet. By default, the table name and current date print in the datasheet header, and the page number prints in the datasheet footer as shown in Figure B-10.

7. Click the Close button [Close] for the preview window, click the Close button on the datasheet, then click No when asked to save the changes to the layout of the table

   All data entries and edits are automatically saved as you move between records or close a datasheet. Therefore, you are never prompted as to whether you want to save data. Access does prompt you as to whether you want to save structural or formatting changes, though.

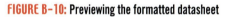

	RecordingID	Title	Tracks	Wholesale	Retail	ArtistID
▶	1	Autumn	7	$5.00	$15.00	12
	2	Summer	15	$7.00	$12.00	12
	3	Spring	11	$7.00	$15.00	12
	4	Winter	10	$6.00	$15.00	12
	5	KG Live	11	$5.00	$14.00	1
	6	Skyline Firedance	10	$14.00	$18.00	1
	7	Sacred Road	12	$6.00	$17.00	2
	8	Heartsounds	14	$7.00	$17.00	2
	9	Handel's Messiah	11	$6.00	$12.00	3
	10	Favorite Overtures	5	$10.00	$15.00	3
	11	Mariah Carey	11	$5.00	$12.00	4
	12	Live with Mariah	9	$5.00	$13.00	4
	13	Daydream	12	$6.00	$13.00	4
	14	Watermark	12	$8.00	$13.00	5
	15	Time and Love	10	$6.00	$12.00	6
	16	I'll Lead You Home	14	$7.00	$12.00	7
	17	Blue	10	$10.00	$15.00	8
	18	God's Property	13	$5.00	$14.00	9
	19	Tribute	10	$5.00	$12.00	10
	20	Union	14	$8.00	$12.00	11

Record: ⏮ ◀ | 1 | ▶ ⏭ ▶* of 62 ————— 62 records

FIGURE B-10: Previewing the formatted datasheet

Table name

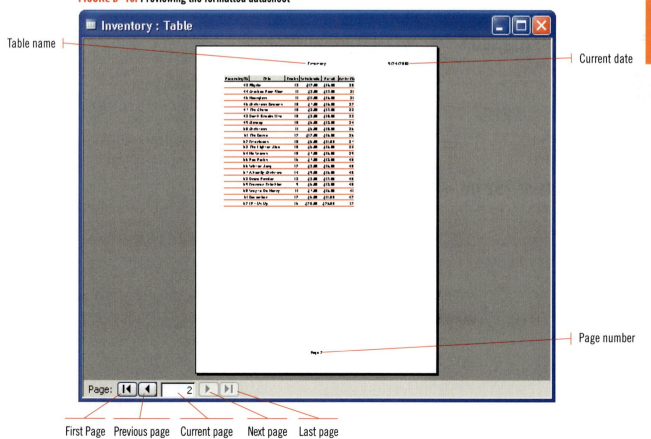

Current date

Page number

Page: ⏮ ◀ | 2 | ▶ ⏭

First Page   Previous page   Current page   Next page   Last page

Access 2003

Understanding Sorting, Filtering, and Finding

The records of a datasheet are automatically sorted according to the data in the primary key field. Often, however, you may want to view or print records in a different sort order, or you may want to display a subset of the records, such as those with the same artist or those less than a certain retail price. Access makes it easy to sort records, find data, and filter a datasheet by using buttons on the Table Datasheet toolbar, summarized in Table B-2. You study the sort, filter, and find features to better learn how to find and retrieve information.

DETAILS

- **Sorting** refers to reorganizing the records in either ascending or descending order based on the contents of a field. In ascending order, Text fields sort from A to Z, Number and Currency fields sort from the lowest to the highest value, and Date/Time fields sort from the oldest date to the date furthest into the future. In Figure B-11 the Inventory table is sorted in descending order based on the values in the Retail field.

- **Filtering** means temporarily isolating a subset of records, as shown in Figure B-12. For example, by using a filter, you can list all records with a value greater than 15 in the Retail field. To redisplay all of the records in the datasheet, click the Remove Filter button. The filtered subset can be formatted and printed just like the entire datasheet.

- **Finding** refers to locating a specific piece of data, such as "Light". The Find and Replace dialog box is shown in Figure B-13. The options in this dialog box are summarized below.

  - **Find What:** Provides a text box for your search criteria. The search criteria might be Amy, Beatles, or Capitol Records.
  - **Look In:** Determines whether Access looks for the search criteria in the current field or in the entire datasheet.
  - **Match:** Determines whether the search criteria must exactly match the contents of the whole field, any part of the field, or the start of the field.
  - **Search:** Allows you to search the entire datasheet (All) or just those records before (Up) or after (Down) the current record.
  - **Match Case:** Determines whether the search criteria are case sensitive (e.g., TX versus Tx or tx).
  - **Search Fields As Formatted:** Determines whether the search criteria are compared to the actual value of the field or the formatted appearance of the value (e.g., 10 versus $10.00).
  - **Replace tab:** Provides a Replace With text box for you to specify replacement text. For example, you can find every occurrence of Corp and replace it with Corporation.

Clues to Use

Using wildcards

Wildcards are symbols you use as substitutes for characters to locate data that matches your criteria. Access uses these wildcards: the **asterisk (*)** represents any group of characters, the **question mark (?)** stands for any single character, and the **pound sign (#)** stands for a single number digit. For example, to find any word beginning with S, type s* in the Find What text box. Wildcards may be used in criteria used to find, filter, or query information. Filters and queries are covered later in this unit.

FIGURE B-11: Descending sort order based on the Retail field

Records are sorted in descending order based on the Retail field

FIGURE B-12: Records filtered for values >15 in the Retail field

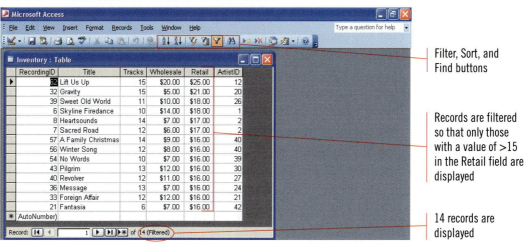

Filter, Sort, and Find buttons

Records are filtered so that only those with a value of >15 in the Retail field are displayed

14 records are displayed

FIGURE B-13: Find and Replace dialog box

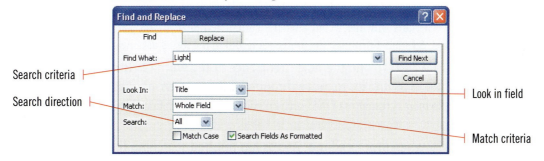

Search criteria

Search direction

Look in field

Match criteria

TABLE B-2: Sort, Filter, and Find buttons

name	button	purpose
Sort Ascending	A↓	Sorts records based on the selected field in ascending order (0 to 9, A to Z)
Sort Descending	Z↓	Sorts records based on the selected field in descending order (Z to A, 9 to 0)
Filter By Selection	▽	Filters records based on selected data and hides records that do not match
Filter By Form	▽	Filters records based on more than one selection criteria by using the Filter by Form window
Apply Filter or Remove Filter	▽	Applies or removes the filter
Find	🔍	Searches for a string of characters in the current field or all fields

Sorting Records and Finding Data

The sort and find features are powerful tools that help you work more efficiently whether you are working with data in a datasheet or viewing it through a form.  You want to create several different printouts of the Inventory datasheet to satisfy various MediaLoft departments. The Marketing Department wants the records sorted by Title. The Accounting Department wants the records sorted from the highest retail price to the lowest.

1. **Double-click the Inventory table to open its datasheet, click any value in the Title field, then click the Sort Ascending button 🔼 on the Table Datasheet toolbar**

   The records are sorted in ascending order by the values in the Title field, as shown in Figure B-14.

2. **Click any value in the Retail field, then click the Sort Descending button 🔽 on the Table Datasheet toolbar**

   The products that sell for the highest retail price are listed first. If you printed the datasheet now, the records would be listed in the current sort order on the printout. Kelsey also asks you to find the titles that may be hot sellers during the Christmas season. Access lets you find all records based on search criteria.

3. **Click any value in the Title field, then click the Find button 🔍 on the Table Datasheet toolbar**

   The Find and Replace dialog box opens with Title selected as the Look In field.

4. **Type Christmas in the Find What text box, click the Match list arrow, then click Any Part of Field, as shown in Figure B-15**

   "Christmas" is the search criteria. Access finds all occurrences of the word Christmas in the Title field, whether it is the first, middle, or last part of the title.

5. **Click Find Next, then drag the title bar of the Find and Replace dialog box up and to the right to better view the datasheet**

   The search starts with the record after the current record so if you started the search at the top of the datasheet, A Family Christmas, the thirteenth record in the sorted datasheet, is the first title found.

6. **Click Find Next to find the next occurrence of the word Christmas, then click Find Next as many times as it takes to move through all the records**

   When no more occurrences of the search criteria Christmas are found, Access provides a dialog box that tells you that no more matching records can be found.

7. **Click OK when prompted that Access has finished searching the records, then click Cancel to close the Find and Replace dialog box**

   If you close a datasheet without saving the layout changes, the records return to the original sort order based on the values in the primary key field. If you close a datasheet and save layout changes, the last sort order is saved.

Records are sorted ascending by title

RecordingID	Title	Tracks	Wholesale	Retail	ArtistID
28	A Christmas Album	11	$10.00	$15.00	17
57	A Family Christmas	14	$9.00	$16.00	40
34	A Winter's Solstice	10	$8.00	$13.00	22
41	Abigail Road	14	$10.00	$15.00	28
1	Autumn	7	$5.00	$15.00	12
42	Best Songs Ever	10	$7.00	$15.00	29
17	Blue	10	$10.00	$15.00	8
50	Christmas	11	$6.00	$10.00	35
46	Christmas Dreams	10	$7.00	$15.00	32
49	Closeup	10	$5.00	$13.00	34
23	Come Walk With M	10	$6.00	$12.00	14
27	Cosmic Thing	10	$10.00	$15.00	17
44	Cracked Rear View	11	$8.00	$12.00	31
37	Creepy Crawlers	10	$5.00	$11.00	25
13	Daydream	12	$6.00	$13.00	4
35	Decade	10	$9.00	$15.00	23
61	December	12	$5.00	$11.00	42
21	Fantasia	6	$7.00	$16.00	42

Record: 1 of 62

FIGURE B-15: Christmas is the search criterion for the Title field

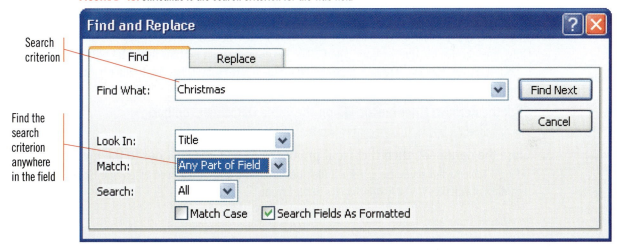

Search criterion

Find the search criterion anywhere in the field

Clues to Use

Using more than one sort field

You may want to apply more than one sort field to a datasheet. For example, the telephone book sorts records by last name (**primary sort field**) and when ties occur on the last name (for example, two or more Johnson entries), the entries are further sorted by the first name (**secondary sort field**). You may sort by more than one field in a datasheet by selecting more than one field name (by dragging through the field name row) before clicking a sort button. Using this method, though, the sort fields must be positioned beside one another. The leftmost field is the primary sort field, the field to its right is the secondary sort field, and so forth. If you want to sort a datasheet by fields that are not positioned next to one another, use a query, which is covered later in this unit.

Access 2003

Filtering Records

Filtering the datasheet temporarily displays only those records that match given criteria. **Criteria** are rules or limiting conditions you set. For example, you may want to show only those records where the Title field contains the word "Christmas" or where the Wholesale field is less than $10. Once you have filtered the records in a datasheet or form, you can sort or find data within the subset of records just as if you were working with all of the records. The Marketing Department asks you for a listing of titles that contain the word "Christmas" with a retail price of 15 or more. You filter the records to provide this information.

STEPS

1. **Double-click the word Christmas in the Title field for RecordingID 28, then click the Filter By Selection button 🌾 on the Table Datasheet toolbar**

   Four records are selected, as shown in Figure B-16. Filter By Selection is a fast and easy way to filter the records for an exact match (in this case, where the Title field contains a word that is *equal to* Christmas). To filter for comparative data and to specify more complex criteria including **comparison operators** (for example, where Retail is *equal to or greater than* 15), you must use the Filter By Form feature. See Table B-3 for more information about comparison operators.

   QUICK TIP

   If criteria become lengthy, you can widen a column to display the entire criteria entry by dragging the right edge of the column to the right. If you need to clear previous criteria, click the Clear Grid button ✖.

2. **Click the Filter By Form button 🔳 on the Table Datasheet toolbar, click the Retail criteria cell, then type >=15**

   The Filter by Form window is shown in Figure B-17. The previous Filter By Selection criteria that you initiated directly on the datasheet, Like "*Christmas*", in the Title field, is still in the grid. Access distinguishes between text and numeric entries by placing quotation marks around text entries. Access also inserts the operator Like and wildcard asterisks in the "*Christmas*" criteria to help you find Christmas in any location of the Title field. Filter By Form is more powerful than Filter By Selection because it allows you to enter criteria for more than one field so that *both* criteria must be true to show the record in the resulting datasheet.

3. **Click the Apply Filter button 🔽 on the Table Datasheet toolbar**

   Only three records are true for both criteria. The record navigation buttons in the lower-left corner of the datasheet display how many records were chosen for the filtered subset. The Apply Filter button becomes the Remove Filter button after a filter is applied.

   QUICK TIP

   Be sure to remove existing filters before applying a new filter or you will apply a filter to the current subset of records instead of applying the filter to the entire datasheet.

4. **Click the Remove Filter button 🔽 on the Table Datasheet toolbar**

   The datasheet redisplays all 62 records when the filter is removed.

5. **Close the datasheet, then click No if prompted to save the changes to the Inventory table**

   Saving a table layout saves the last sort order, but filters are always removed when you close a datasheet, regardless of whether you save the changes to the layout.

FIGURE B-16: Inventory datasheet filtered for Christmas in the Title field

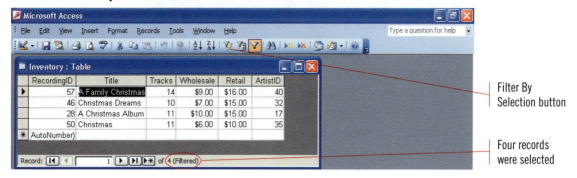

Filter By
Selection button

Four records
were selected

FIGURE B-17: Filter by Form window

Clear Grid
button

* wildcards
used to find
Christmas
anywhere in
Title field

Apply Filter
button

Greater than or
equal to 15

TABLE B-3: Comparison operators

operator	description	expression	meaning
>	Greater than	>500	Numbers greater than 500
>=	Greater than or equal to	>=500	Numbers greater than or equal to 500
<	Less than	<"Braveheart"	Names from A to Braveheart, but not Braveheart
<=	Less than or equal to	<="Bridgewater"	Names from A through, and including, Bridgewater
<>	Not equal to	<>"Fontanelle"	Any name except for Fontanelle

Clues to Use

Searching for blank fields

Is Null and **Is Not Null** are two other types of common criteria. Is Null criteria finds all records where no entry has been made in the field. Is Not Null finds all records where there is any entry in the field, even if the entry is 0. Primary key fields cannot have a null entry.

Creating a Query

A **query** is a database object that creates a datasheet of selected fields and records from one or more tables. You can edit, navigate, sort, find, and filter a query's datasheet just like a table's datasheet. A query is similar to a filter, but much more powerful. For example, a query is a saved object within the database. Filtering creates only a temporary view of the data. Table B-4 compares queries and filters. ■■■ You use the Simple Query Wizard to build a query to display information from both the Inventory and Artists tables in one datasheet.

STEPS

1. **Click Queries on the Objects bar, then double-click Create query by using wizard**
    The Simple Query Wizard dialog box opens asking you to select the fields that you want to view.

2. **Double-click ArtistFirst, double-click ArtistLast, double-click Group, click the Tables/Queries list arrow, click Table:Inventory, double-click Title, then double-click Retail**
    The Simple Query Wizard dialog box should look like Figure B-18.

3. **Click Next, click Next to accept the Detail option, type Product List for the query title, then click Finish**
    The Product List query's datasheet opens with 62 records, each with the five fields of information you requested, as shown in Figure B-19. You can use a query datasheet to edit or add information.

4. **Double-click Kenny in the ArtistFirst cell for the first record, type Kenneth, then press [↓]**
    Editing data through a query datasheet changes the data in the underlying table just as if you were working directly in the table's datasheet. In this case, Kenny changed to Kenneth in the second record as well as the first because this artist's first name is stored only once in the Artists table, but it is selected for this datasheet twice because this artist is related to two records in the Inventory table (via the common ArtistID field). A query is sometimes called a **logical view** of the data because it is not a copy of the data, but rather, a selected view of data from the underlying tables.

5. **Click the Design View button ☒ on the Query Datasheet toolbar**
    The Query Design View opens, showing you **field lists** for the Inventory and Artists tables in the upper portion of the window, and the fields you have requested for this query in the **query design grid** (also called the **query grid**) in the lower portion of the window.

6. **Click the Criteria cell for the Group field, then type Justice as shown in Figure B-20**
    Query Design View is used to add, delete, or change the order of fields, sort the records, or add criteria to limit the number of records shown in the resulting datasheet. Any change made in Query Design View is saved with the query object.

7. **Click the Datasheet View button ☐ on the Query Design toolbar**
    The resulting datasheet has five records that match the Justice criteria in the Group field. To save this query with a more descriptive name than the one currently displayed in the query title bar, use the Save As command on the File menu.

8. **Click File on the menu bar, click Save As, type Justice Titles in the Save Query text box, click OK, then close the query datasheet**
    Both the original Product List and the modified Justice Titles queries are saved in this database. You can double-click a query to reopen it in Query Datasheet View.

FIGURE B-18: Simple Query Wizard

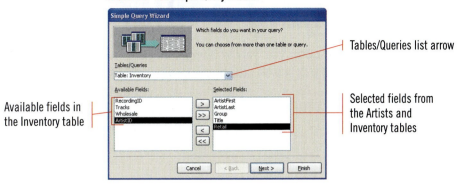

Tables/Queries list arrow

Available fields in the Inventory table

Selected fields from the Artists and Inventory tables

FIGURE B-19: Product List datasheet

Design View button

62 records

FIGURE B-20: Query Design View

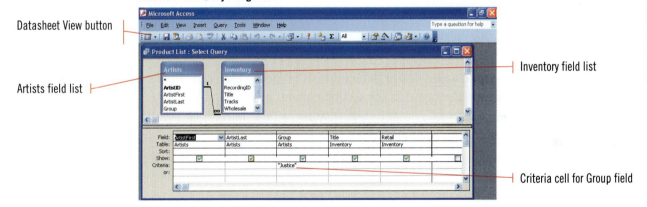

Datasheet View button

Artists field list

Inventory field list

Criteria cell for Group field

TABLE B-4: Queries versus filters

characteristics	filters	queries
Are saved as an object in the database	No	Yes
Can be used to select a subset of records in a datasheet	Yes	Yes
Can be used to select a subset of fields in a datasheet	No	Yes
Its resulting datasheet can be used to enter and edit data	Yes	Yes
Its resulting datasheet can be used to sort, filter, and find records	Yes	Yes
Is commonly used as the source of data for a form or report	No	Yes
Can calculate sums, averages, counts, and other types of summary statistics across records	No	Yes
Can be used to create calculated fields	No	Yes

Modifying a Query

To modify an existing query, you work in **Query Design View**. The upper portion of Query Design View displays the field lists for each table used by the query. The lower portion of Query Design View displays the query grid where you add or change the fields displayed by the query, add criteria to determine which records will be selected, define sort orders, and build calculated fields. To delete or move a field in the query grid, you select it by clicking its field selector. The **field selector** is the thin gray bar above each field in the query grid. You want to modify the Justice Titles query in a variety of ways. You use Query Design View to make the changes and then print the resulting datasheet.

STEPS

1. **Click the Justice Titles query in the MediaLoft-B database window, then click the Design button on the database window toolbar**

   Query Design View opens, displaying the fields and criteria for the Justice Titles query. To add fields to the query, drag the fields from their field list to the position in the query design grid where you want them to appear on the datasheet.

2. **Drag the Tracks field from the Inventory field list to the Retail Field cell in the query design grid, double-click the Wholesale field in the Inventory field list, then scroll to the right in the query grid**

   The Tracks field is added to the query design grid between the Title and Retail fields. Double-clicking a field adds it to the next available column in the grid, as shown in Figure B-21. You can also delete fields in the existing query grid.

3. **Scroll to the left in the query grid, click the field selector for the ArtistFirst field, then press [Delete]**

   Deleting a field from Query Design View does not affect the data stored in the underlying table. Deleting a field from a query only means that this field is not displayed on the datasheet for this query. To move fields, drag the field selector.

4. **Click the field selector for the ArtistLast field to select it, then drag the field selector for the ArtistLast field to the second column position in the query design grid**

   Now that the fields are rearranged in the datasheet as shown in Figure B-22, you're ready to set the sort orders.

5. **Click the Sort cell for the Group field, click the Sort list arrow, click Ascending, click the Sort cell for the Title field, click the Sort list arrow, click Ascending, then click the Datasheet View button on the Query Design toolbar to view the resulting datasheet**

   Because the only value in the Group field is Justice, the secondary sort field, Title, is used to determine the order of the records. If you add another Group to this datasheet, however, both sort fields are used to determine the order of the records.

6. **Click the Design View button on the Query Datasheet toolbar, click the or Criteria cell below "Justice", then type Clownfish**

   The row into which query criteria is entered is extremely important. Criteria entered on the same row must *both* be true for a record to be selected. Criteria entered on different rows are evaluated separately; a record need only be true for *one* row of criteria in order to be selected for the resulting datasheet.

7. **Click**

   The final datasheet is shown in Figure B-23. Seven records matched the criterion entered in the query grid. Also note that the Group field is used as the primary sort order—the Clownfish records sorted before the Justice records. The values in the Title field were used as the secondary sort order. You can specify as many sort orders as you desire in Query Design View, but they are always evaluated from left to right.

8. **Click the Print button, close the datasheet without saving changes, close the MediaLoft-B.mdb database, then exit Access**

FIGURE B-21: Tracks field added to query grid

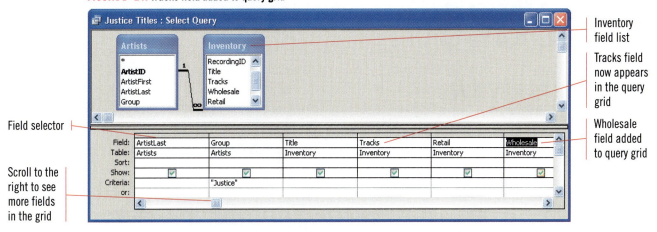

Inventory field list

Tracks field now appears in the query grid

Wholesale field added to query grid

Field selector

Scroll to the right to see more fields in the grid

FIGURE B-22: New field arrangement

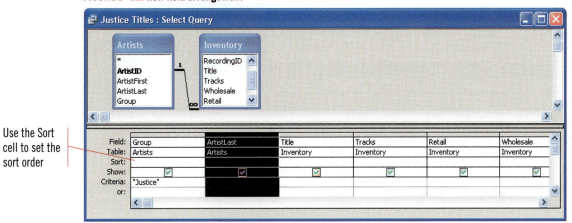

Use the Sort cell to set the sort order

FIGURE B-23: Final datasheet

Primary sort

Records must match the criteria entered in the query gird

Secondary sort

Clues to Use

Understanding And and Or criteria

Criteria placed on different rows of the query design grid are called **Or criteria**. In other words, a record may be true for one row *or* another row in order for it to be displayed on the resulting datasheet. Placing additional criteria in the *same* row, however, creates **And criteria**. In other words, records must meet the criteria for one criterion *and* all other criteria entered on one row in order to be chosen for that datasheet. As you add additional rows of criteria (Or criteria) to the query design grid, you increase the number of records displayed on the resulting datasheet because the record needs to be true for the criteria in only *one* of the rows to be displayed on the datasheet for that query.

Practice

▼ CONCEPTS REVIEW

Label each element of the Access window shown in Figure B-24.

FIGURE B-24

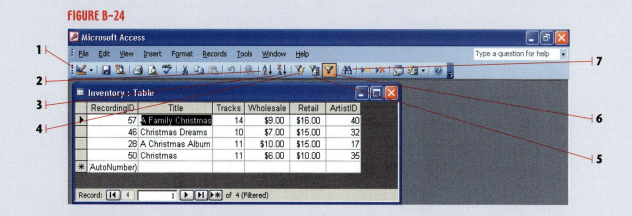

Match each term with the statement that best describes it.

8. Primary key
9. Table Wizard
10. Filter
11. Data type
12. Query
13. AutoNumber
14. One-to-many relationship
15. Foreign key

a. Determines what type of data can be stored in each field
b. Provides interactive help to create the field names and data types for each field in a new table
c. Creates a datasheet of selected fields and records from one or more tables
d. Contains unique information for each record
e. Creates a temporary subset of records
f. Links two tables together
g. Serves as the common field in the "many" table in a one-to-many relationship
h. Inserts a sequential integer as the field value for each new record

Select the best answer from the list of choices.

16. **Which data type would be best for a field that stores Web addresses?**
    a. Text
    b. Memo
    c. OLE
    d. Hyperlink

17. **Which data type would be best for a field that stores telephone numbers?**
    a. Text
    b. Number
    c. OLE
    d. Hyperlink

18. **Which data type would be best for a field that stores birth dates?**
    a. Text
    b. Number
    c. AutoNumber
    d. Date/Time

19. Sorting refers to:
   a. Reorganizing the records in either ascending or descending order.
   b. Selecting a subset of fields and/or records to view as a datasheet from one or more tables.
   c. Displaying only those records that meet certain criteria.
   d. Using Or and And criteria in the query design grid.

20. Each of the following is true about a filter, *except*:
   a. It creates a temporary datasheet of records that match criteria.
   b. The resulting datasheet can be sorted.
   c. The resulting datasheet includes all fields.
   d. A filter is automatically saved as an object in the database.

▼ SKILLS REVIEW

1. Organize fields.
   a. Organize the fields of a database that contains the names and addresses of physicians and clinics. You might use a telephone book to gather information.
   b. On paper, write down the field names in one column and the data types for each field in the second column.

2. Plan related tables.
   a. Organize the fields into two tables: Clinics and Physicians. Identify a primary key field for each table.
   b. Determine how the tables will be related in a one-to-many relationship.
   c. Identify a primary key field for both tables.
   d. Add the foreign key field to the "many" table.

3. Create a table.
   a. Start Access and use the Blank database option to create a database. Save the file as **Medical Directory.mdb** in the drive and folder where your Data Files are stored.
   b. Use the Table Wizard to create a new table. Use the Contacts sample table found in the Business database category.
   c. Choose sample fields in the following order: ContactID, FirstName, LastName, Title.
   d. Name the table **Physicians**, and select the No, I'll set the primary key field option button.
   e. Accept the default options for the primary key field.
   f. Click the Modify the table design option button, then click Finish.

4. Modify a table.
   a. In the first available blank row, add a new field called **ClinicNo** with a Number data type.
   b. Change the Field Size property of the Title field from 50 to **4**.
   c. Add the field description **M.D. or D.O.** to the Title field.
   d. Save the Physicians table, display its datasheet, and enter one record using your own information in the name fields. Remember that the ContactID field is specified with an AutoNumber data type so Access automatically enters a value in that field as you add the record. Enter **1** for the ClinicNo value.
   e. Preview then print the datasheet.
   f. Close the Physicians table and the Medical Directory.mdb database.

5. Format a datasheet.

    a. Open the **Medical Directory-B.mdb** database from the drive and folder where your Data Files are stored. Open the Physicians table datasheet.

    b. Change the font of the datasheet to Arial Narrow, and the font size to **9**.

    c. Change the gridline color to black, and remove the vertical gridlines.

    d. Change the values for the First and Last fields of the first record to your own name, then preview and print the datasheet. Close the Physicians datasheet without saving the formatting changes.

6. Understand sorting, filtering, and finding.

    a. On a sheet of paper, identify three ways that you might want to sort a list of addresses. Be sure to specify both the field you would sort on and the sort order (ascending or descending).

    b. On a sheet of paper, identify three ways that you might want to filter a list of addresses. Be sure to specify both the field you would filter on and the criteria that you would use.

7. Sort records and find data.

    a. Open the Physicians datasheet, sort the records in ascending order on the Last field, then list the first two last names on paper.

    b. Sort the Physicians records in descending order on the ClinicNo field, then list the first two entries in the Last field on paper.

    c. Find the records in which the Title field contains D.O. Write down how many records you found.

8. Filter records.

    a. In the Physicians datasheet, filter the records for all physicians with a last name that starts with the letter "B". (*Hint*: Select only the letter B for an entry that starts with "B" in the Last field, then click the Filter By Selection button).

    b. Filter the records for all physicians with a last name that starts with the letter "B" as well as those with a title of D.O. Change "Baskets" in the Last field to your own last name, then print the datasheet.

    c. Close the Physicians datasheet without saving changes.

9. Create a query.

    a. Use the Query Wizard to create a new query with the following fields: First and Last (from the Physicians table), ClinicName, City, State, Zip, and Phone (from the Clinics table).

    b. Name the query **Clinics in Missouri**, then view the datasheet.

    c. In Query Design View, add the criterion **MO** to the State field, then view and print the datasheet.

10. Modify a query.

    a. Modify the Clinics in Missouri query to include only those doctors in Kansas City, Missouri. (*Hint*: Both criteria entries must be in the same row of the query grid, but in different columns.)

    b. Save the query with the name **Clinics in Kansas City Missouri.** Print the query results, then close the query datasheet.

    c. Modify the Clinics in Kansas City Missouri query so that the ClinicName field is the First field in the datasheet.

    d. Sort the records in ascending order on the ClinicName field, then in ascending order on the Last field.

    e. Print and save the sorted datasheet, then close the datasheet.

    f. Close the **Medical Directory-B.mdb** database, then exit Access.

▼ INDEPENDENT CHALLENGE 1

You want to start a database to track your personal movie collection.

a. Start Access and create a new database called **Movies.mdb** in the drive and folder where your Data Files are stored.

b. Using the Table Wizard, create a table based on the Video Collection sample table in the Personal category with the following fields: MovieTitle, YearReleased, Rating, Length, DateAcquired, PurchasePrice.

c. Enter the name **Collection** for the table and allow Access to set a primary key field.

d. Modify the Collection table in Design View with the following changes:

- Delete the Rating Field. (*Hint*: Use the Delete Rows button on the Table Design toolbar.)
- Rename the YearReleased field to **Year**, and the DateAcquired field to **PurchaseDate**.
- Give the Length field a Number data type.
- Add a field between Year and Length called **PersonalRating** with a Number data type.
- In the Description of the PersonalRating field, enter: **My personal rating from 1 (bad) to 10 (great)**.
- Add a field between the PersonalRating and Length fields called **Rated** with a Text data type.
- In the Description of the Rated field, enter: **G, PG, PG-13, R**.
- Change the Field Size property of the Rated field to **5**.
- Add a field between the Rated and Length called **Format** with a Text data type.
- In the Description of the Format field, enter: **VCR, DVD**.

e. Save the Collection table, and then open it in Datasheet View.

f. Enter five records with sample data, then preview the datasheet. Use the Setup button to change the page orientation to landscape.

g. If the printout spans two pages, return to Datasheet View, narrow the columns, and then preview the datasheet again. When you have narrowed the columns or formatted the data so that it prints on a single piece of paper, print the datasheet, close the Collection table, close the **Movies.mdb** database, then exit Access.

▼ INDEPENDENT CHALLENGE 2

You work for a marketing company that sells medical supplies to doctors' offices.

a. Start Access and open the **Medical Directory-B.mdb** database from the drive and folder where your Data Files are stored, then open the Clinics table datasheet.

b. Filter the records to find all clinics in the city of **Grandview**, modify column widths so that all data is visible, edit the Grandview entry for Cancer Specialists to the name of your hometown, then preview and print the datasheet in landscape orientation.

c. Remove the filter, sort the records in ascending order by Zip, then change the cell color to silver. (*Hint*: Use the Fill/Back Color button on the Formatting toolbar.) Change the font style to bold, then print the datasheet in landscape orientation.

d. Close the Clinics datasheet without saving the changes.

e. Using the Query Wizard, create a query with the following fields: First and Last from the Physicians table and Phone from the Clinics table.

f. Name the query **Telephone List**. Sort the records in ascending order by last name, then print the datasheet. Close the query without saving the changes.

g. In Query Design View of the Telephone List query, delete the First field, then add the Title field between the existing Last and Phone fields. Add an ascending sort order to the Phone field. Save, view, and print the datasheet.

▼ INDEPENDENT CHALLENGE 2 (CONTINUED)

Advanced Challenge Exercise

- In Query Design View of the Telephone List query, add the Address2 field to the fourth column.
- Add criteria so that only those records where there is no entry in the Address2 field are displayed on the resulting datasheet. (*Hint*: Use **Is Null** criteria for the Address2 field.)
- View the datasheet, then print and close the Telephone List query without saving the changes.

h. Close the **Medical Directory-B.mdb** database, then exit Access.

▼ INDEPENDENT CHALLENGE 3

You want to create a database to keep track of your personal contacts.

a. Start Access and create a new database called **People.mdb** in the drive and folder where your Data Files are stored.

b. Using the Table Wizard, create a table based on the Addresses sample table in the Personal category with the following fields: FirstName, LastName, SpouseName, Address, City, StateOrProvince, PostalCode, EmailAddress, HomePhone, Birthdate.

c. Name the table **Contacts**, allow Access to set the primary key field, and choose the Enter data directly into the table option in the last Table Wizard dialog box.

d. Enter at least five records into the table, making sure that two people have the same last name. Use your name in the First Name and Last Name fields of one of the records. Note that the ContactsID field has an AutoNumber data type.

e. Sort the records in ascending order by last name, then save and close the Contacts datasheet.

f. Using the Query Wizard, create a query with the following fields: LastName, FirstName, Birthdate. Name the query **Birthday List**.

g. In Query Design View, sort the records in ascending order by LastName and then by FirstName.

h. Save the query as **Sorted Birthday List**, then view the query. Change the Birthdate value to **1/6/71** for your record.

i. Modify the datasheet by making font and color changes, print it, then close it without saving it.

Advanced Challenge Exercise

- Open the datasheet for the Contacts table and observe the Birthdate value for your record. On a piece of paper, explain why the 1/6/71 value appears in the datasheet for the table when you entered this date while working with the datasheet of the Sorted Birthday List query.
- On paper, explain why the 1/6/71 value was saved even though you closed the query without saving the layout changes.

j. Close the Contacts table, close the **People.mdb** database, then exit Access.

▼ INDEPENDENT CHALLENGE 4

You are on the staff of an economic development team whose goal is to encourage tourism in the Baltic Sea region. You have created an Access database called Baltic-B.mdb to track important fields of information on the countries in that region, and use the Internet to find information about the area.

FIGURE B-25

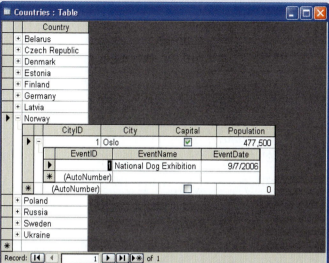

a. Start Access and open the **Baltic-B.mdb** database from the drive and folder where your Data Files are stored.

b. Open the Countries table datasheet, then click the expand button to the left of Norway as well as to the left of Oslo using Figure B-25 as a guide.

c. This arrangement of data shows you how events are tracked by city, and how cities are tracked by country in the Baltic-B database.

d. Create a query that selects the City, Population, Country, and Capital fields from the Cities table. Show details, name the query **City Info**, then display, print, and close the datasheet.

e. Create a query with the City and Country fields from the Cities table, and the EventName and EventDate fields from the Events table. Show details, name the query **List of Events**, then display, print, and close it.

Advanced Challenge Exercise

- Connect to the Internet, then go your favorite search engine to conduct some research for the database. Your goal is to enter at least one city record (the country's capital city) for each country. Be sure to enter the Population data for that particular city, rather than for the entire country. You can enter the data by expanding the country record sub-datasheets as shown for Norway in Figure B-25, or by entering the records directly into the Cities datasheet.
- Return to the search engine, and research upcoming tourist events for Oslo, Norway. Enter three more events for Oslo into the database. You can enter the data into the Event subdatasheet shown in Figure B-25, or enter the records directly into the Events datasheet by opening the Events table datasheet. If you enter the records into the Events datasheet, remember that the CityID field value for Oslo is 1.
- Reopen, then print and close the **City Info** and **List of Event** datasheets.

f. Close the **Baltic-B.mdb** database, then exit Access.

▼ VISUAL WORKSHOP

Open the **MediaLoft-B.mdb** database from the drive and folder where your Data Files are stored. Create a query based on the Inventory and Artists tables that displays the datasheet shown in Figure B-26. Name the query **Most Tracks**. Filter the query for only those records with a value of 15 or greater in the Tracks field, and sort the query by the Group field.

FIGURE B-26

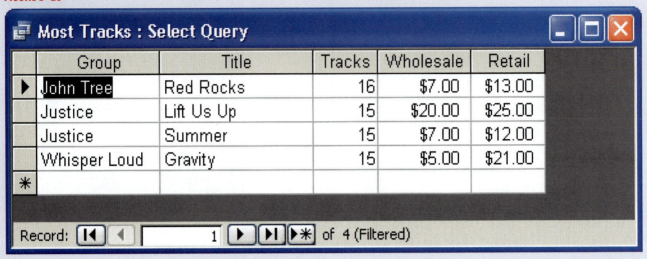

UNIT
C
Access 2003

Using Forms

OBJECTIVES

Plan a form
Create a form
Move and resize controls
Modify labels
Use text boxes for calculations
Modify tab order
Enter, edit, and print records
Insert an image

If you have a SAM user profile, you may have access to hands-on instruction, practice, and assessment of the skills covered in this unit. Log in to your SAM account and go to your assignments page to see what your instructor has assigned.

Forms are the primary type of Access object used to enter and edit data. Although the datasheet view of a table or a query object can also be used to navigate, enter, and edit data, some fields for one record are sometimes not visible unless you scroll left or right. A form solves that problem by allowing you to design the layout of fields on the screen in any arrangement. A form also supports graphical elements such as pictures, buttons, and tabs, which make the form's data easy to understand and use. Kelsey Lang, the marketing manager for MediaLoft, asks you to create forms to make information easier to access, enter, and update in the MediaLoft database.

Planning a Form

Properly organized and well-designed forms make a tremendous difference in the productivity of the end user. Forms are often built to match a **source document** (for example, a paper employment application or a medical history form) to facilitate fast and accurate data entry. Now, however, it is becoming more common to type data directly into the database rather than first recording it on paper. Therefore, form design considerations, such as clearly labeled fields and appropriate formatting, are extremely important. Other form design considerations include how the user tabs from field to field, and what type of control is used. A **control** is an element placed on the form to display or describe data. See Table C-1 for more information on form controls. Before you create a form, you plan the form on paper to share your plans with Kelsey.

Consider the following form design tasks to plan a form:

- **Gather the source documents used to design your form**

  Find all existing source documents (if building the form to match an existing process) and sketch the Access form on paper. This helps you make sure that you identify every control, including fields, text, and graphics that you want the form to display.

- **Determine the best type of control to use for each item on the form**

  Figures C-1 and C-2 show examples of several controls. **Bound controls** display data from the underlying record source and are also used to edit and enter data. **Unbound controls** do not change from record to record and exist only to clarify and enhance the appearance of the form.

- **Determine the underlying record source**

  The **record source** supplies the data that is presented by the bound controls on the form. The record source may be either the fields and records of a single table, or those selected by a query. The record source is also called the **recordset**.

- **Name the form**

  Name your form with its specific purpose, such as "Artist Entry Form".

FIGURE C-1: Form controls

Tab control

Text box

Label

Combo box

Check box

Option button

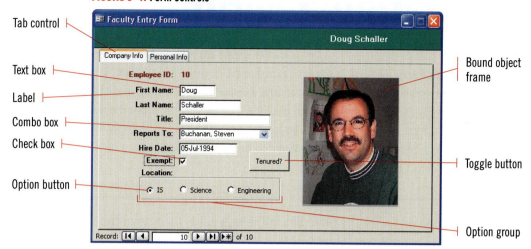

Bound object frame

Toggle button

Option group

FIGURE C-2: Form controls

Unbound object frame

List box

Rectangle

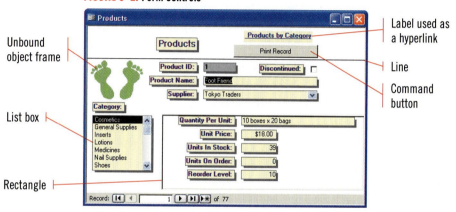

Label used as a hyperlink

Line

Command button

TABLE C-1: Form controls

name	used to	bound	unbound
Label	Provide consistent descriptive text as you navigate from record to record; the label is the most common type of unbound control and can also be used as a hyperlink to another database object, external file, or Web page		x
Text box	Display, edit, or enter data for each record from an underlying record source; the text box is the most common type of bound control	x	
List box	Display a list of possible data entries	x	
Combo box	Display a list of possible data entries for a field, and provide a text box for an entry from the keyboard; combines the list box and text box controls	x	
Tab control	Create a three-dimensional aspect to a form		x
Check box	Display "yes" or "no" answers for a field; if the box is checked, it means "yes"	x	
Toggle button	Display "yes" or "no" answers for a field; if the button is pressed, it means "yes"	x	
Option button	Display a choice for a field	x	
Option group	Display and organize choices (usually presented as option buttons) for a field	x	
Bound object frame	Display data stored by an OLE (Object Linking and Embedding) field, such as a picture	x	
Unbound object frame	Display a picture or clip art image that doesn't change from record to record		x
Line and Rectangle	Draw lines and rectangles on the form		x
Command button	Provide an easy way to initiate a command or run a macro		x

Creating a Form

There are many ways to create a form. You can create a form from scratch using **Form Design View**, or you can use the **Form Wizard** to provide guided steps for developing a form. The Form Wizard prompts you to select the record source for the form, choose a layout, choose a style, and title the form. The Form Wizard is an easy way to create an initial version of a form. Table C-2 summarizes the ways to create a form. No matter what technique is used to create a form, you use Form Design View to modify an existing form object. You decide to use the Form Wizard to build an initial version of your first form in the MediaLoft database, the Artists Entry Form.

STEPS

1. **Start Access, click the More link in the task pane, then open the MediaLoft-C.mdb database from the drive and folder where your Data Files are stored**

QUICK TIP
To access additional form wizards and AutoForms, click the New button 🔳 on the database window toolbar.

2. **Click Forms on the Objects bar in the MediaLoft-C database window, then double-click Create form by using wizard in the database window**

   The Form Wizard dialog box opens, prompting you to identify the record source for the form. The Artists table will serve as the record source for this form.

3. **Click the Select All Fields button >>**

   At this point, you could select more fields from other table or query objects if you wanted to add other fields to the form. In this case, you'll base the new form only on the fields of the Artists table.

4. **Click Next, click the Columnar layout option button, click Next, click the Standard style, click Next, type Artists Entry Form as the title for the form, then click Finish**

   The Artists Entry Form opens in **Form View**, as shown in Figure C-3. Descriptive labels appear in the first column, and text boxes that display data from the underlying record source appear in the second column. You can enter, edit, find, sort, and filter records using a form. The sort, filter, and find features work the same way in a form as they do in a datasheet.

QUICK TIP
Always click in a text box to identify which field you want to sort or filter before clicking the sort or filter buttons.

5. **Click KG in the Group text box, click the Sort Ascending button ᴬⱽ on the Form View toolbar, then click the Next Record button ▶ four times to move to the fifth record**

   Numbers sort before letters in a Text field so the group 4 Him appears before the group Ant Farm. The group Campfire is displayed in the fifth record. Information about the current record number and total number of records appears by the Record navigation buttons.

6. **Click the Last Record button ▶|**

   The group Youngsters is the last record when the records are sorted in ascending order by the Group field.

7. **Close the Artists Entry Form**

   The last sort order is automatically saved when you close a form. Filters are automatically removed when you close a form just as they are for a datasheet.

FIGURE C-3: New form open in Form View

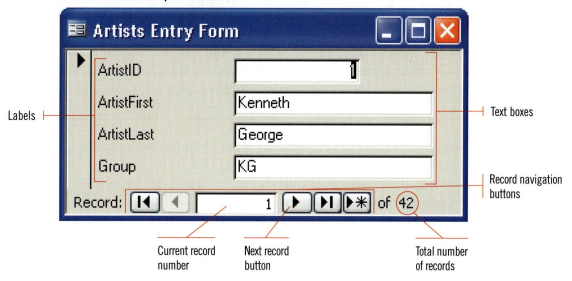

Labels → ArtistID / ArtistFirst / ArtistLast / Group

Text boxes →

Record navigation buttons →

Current record number

Next record button

Total number of records

TABLE C-2: Form creation techniques

technique	description
Form Design View	Provides a layout screen in which the form developer has complete control over the data, layout, and formatting choices that the form will display. Because Form Design View is the most powerful and flexible technique used to create a form, it is also the most complex. Form Design View is also used to modify existing forms, regardless of how they were created.
Form Wizard	Provides a guided series of steps to create a form. Prompts for record source, layout, style, and title.
AutoForm	Instantly creates a form that displays all the fields in the chosen record source. The five different AutoForm options (Columnar, Tabular, Datasheet, PivotTable, and PivotChart) correspond to five different form layouts in the New Form dialog box.
Chart Wizard	Provides a guided series of steps to create a graphical arrangement of data in the form of a business chart such as a bar, column, line, or pie chart that is placed on a form.
PivotTable Wizard	Provides a guided series of steps to create a summarized arrangement of data in a form called a PivotTable. Fields used for the column and row headings determine how the data is grouped and summarized.

Access 2003

Clues to Use

Using the AutoForm button

You can quickly create a form by clicking a table or query object in the database window, then clicking the New Object: AutoForm button on the Database toolbar. The New Object: AutoForm button offers no prompts or dialog boxes; it instantly creates a new form that contains all the fields in the selected table or query.

UNIT
C

Access 2003

Moving and Resizing Controls

After you create a form, you can work in Form Design View to modify the size, location, and appearance of existing controls. Form Design View also allows you to add or delete controls. You decide to move and resize the controls on the Artists Entry Form to improve the layout.

STEPS

QUICK TIP

Another way to open an object in Design View is to right-click it, then click Design View on the shortcut menu.

1. **Click the Artists Entry Form, click the Design button on the database window toolbar, then resize the form as shown in Figure C-4**

   In Form Design View, several elements that help you design the form may automatically appear. The **Toolbox toolbar** contains buttons that help you to add controls to the form. The **field list** contains the fields in the record source (in this case, the Artists table). You can drag fields out of the field list to add them to the form. The vertical and horizontal **rulers** help you position controls on the form. If you are not working with the Toolbox or the field list, you can toggle them off to unclutter your screen.

2. **If the Toolbox toolbar is visible, click the Toolbox button on the Form Design toolbar to toggle it off, and if the field list is visible, click the Field List button on the Form Design toolbar to toggle it off**

   Before moving, resizing, deleting, or otherwise modifying a control, you must select it.

TROUBLE

Be sure to select the ArtistLast label on the left, and not the ArtistLast text box on the right.

3. **Click the ArtistLast label, then press [Delete]**

   Deleting a control on a form does not delete or modify data; deleting a control only removes it from this form.

4. **Click the ArtistLast text box to select it, then drag it to the right of the ArtistFirst text box using the as shown in Figure C-5**

   The form automatically widens to accommodate the new position for the ArtistLast text box. **Sizing handles**, small black boxes, appear in the corners and edges of a selected control. When you work with controls, the mouse pointer shape is very important. Pointer shapes are summarized in Table C-3. You can move controls using the keyboard as well.

QUICK TIP

You can resize controls one **pixel** (picture element) at a time by pressing [Shift] and an arrow key.

5. **Click the Group text box to select it, then press and hold [Ctrl] while pressing [↑] enough times to position the Group label and text box under the ArtistFirst label and ArtistFirst text box**

   The Group label is associated with the Group text box so it automatically moves as you reposition the Group text box. Use the mouse pointer to move a single control.

QUICK TIP

If you make a mistake, click the Undo button and try again. In Form Design View, you can undo up to 20 actions.

6. **Click the 0.5" mark on the horizontal ruler to select all of the labels, then drag to the right the middle sizing handle on the left edge of any selected control using the ↔ pointer**

   Because three labels are selected, all three labels are resized at the same time. Narrowing the width of the labels pulls them closer to the text boxes that they describe.

7. **Click the Form View button on the Form Design toolbar, then resize the final form as shown in Figure C-6**

   Moving and resizing controls requires great concentration and mouse control. Don't worry if your screen doesn't precisely match the figure, but do make sure that you understand how to use the move and resize mouse pointers in Form Design View. Precision and accuracy naturally develop with practice, but even experienced form designers regularly rely on the Undo button .

FIGURE C-4: Form Design View of Artists Entry Form

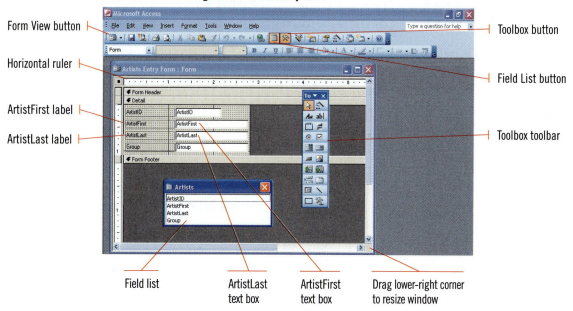

Form View button

Horizontal ruler

ArtistFirst label

ArtistLast label

Toolbox button

Field List button

Toolbox toolbar

Field list

ArtistLast text box

ArtistFirst text box

Drag lower-right corner to resize window

FIGURE C-5: Modifying controls in Form Design View

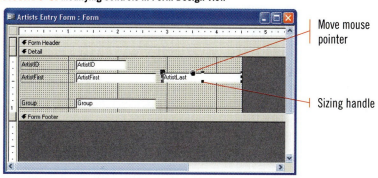

Move mouse pointer

Sizing handle

Access 2003

FIGURE C-6: Form View of modified Artists Entry Form

Text box has been moved

Labels are resized

TABLE C-3: Form Design View mouse pointer shapes

shape	when does this shape appear?	action
↖	When you point to any unselected control on the form (the default mouse pointer)	Single-clicking with this mouse pointer *selects* a control
✋	When you point to the edge of a selected control (but not when you are pointing to a sizing handle)	Dragging this mouse pointer *moves all selected controls*
☝	When you point to the larger sizing handle in the upper-left corner of a selected control	Dragging this mouse pointer *moves only the single control* where the pointer is currently positioned, not other controls that may also be selected
↔↕↗↘	When you point to any sizing handle (except the larger one in the upper-left corner)	Dragging this mouse pointer *resizes* the control

Modifying Labels

When you create a form with the Form Wizard, it places a label to the left of each text box that displays the name of the field. Often, you'll want to modify those labels to be more descriptive or user friendly. You can modify a label control by directly editing it in Form Design View, or you can use the property sheet to modify a control. The **property sheet** is a comprehensive listing of all **properties** (characteristics) for the selected control. You decide to modify the labels of the Artists Entry Form to be more descriptive.

STEPS

TROUBLE

Be sure to modify the ArtistFirst *label* and not the ArtistFirst *text box*.

1. **Click the Design View button on the Form View toolbar, click anywhere on the form to deselect the three labels, click the ArtistFirst label, double-click the ArtistFirst text to select it, type Artist Name, then press [Enter]**

   Directly editing labels in Form Design View is tricky because you must single-click the label to select it, then double-click the text within the label to edit the text. If you double-click the edge of the label, you will open its property sheet, which provides another way to modify label text.

TROUBLE

Be sure to modify the ArtistID *label* and not the ArtistID *text box*.

2. **Click the ArtistID label, click the Properties button on the Form Design toolbar, then click the Format tab, as shown in Figure C-7**

   The title bar of the property sheet indicates what type of control is currently selected (in this case, a label). The **Caption** property on the Format tab controls the text displayed by the label.

3. **Click between the t and I in the Caption property, press [Spacebar] to modify the entry to be Artist ID, then click to close the property sheet**

   Don't be overwhelmed by the number of properties available for each control on the form. Over time, you may want to learn about most of these properties, but in the beginning you'll be able to make most property changes through menu and toolbar options rather than by accessing the property sheet itself. For example, to right-align the labels you could modify the Text Align property in the property sheet for each label, or use the Align Right button on the Formatting (Form/Report) toolbar. To right-align all three labels at the same time, you need to select all three controls.

QUICK TIP

To discard all changes that you have made in Form Design View and return to the last saved copy, click File on the menu bar, then click Revert.

4. **Press and hold [Shift] while clicking the Artist Name and Group labels to add them to the selection, then click the Align Right button on the Formatting (Form/Report) toolbar**

   Now all three labels are positioned closer to the text boxes they describe as shown in Figure C-8. See Table C-4 for a list of techniques to quickly select several controls so that you can apply alignment and formatting changes to more than one control simultaneously.

5. **Click the Save button on the Form Design toolbar, then click the Form View button on the Form Design toolbar to view the changes in Form View**

   The labels are more descriptive and positioned closer to the text boxes they describe.

6. **Close the Artists Entry Form**

FIGURE C-7: Modifying a label using its property sheet

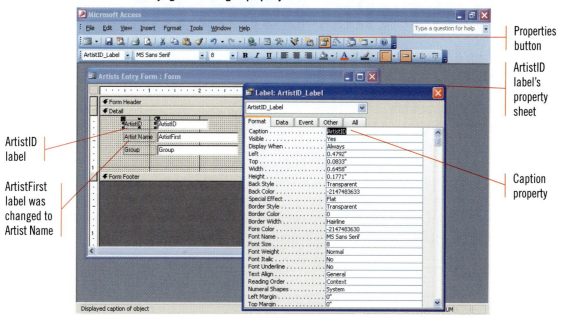

Properties button

ArtistID label's property sheet

ArtistID label

ArtistFirst label was changed to Artist Name

Caption property

FIGURE C-8: Right-aligning labels

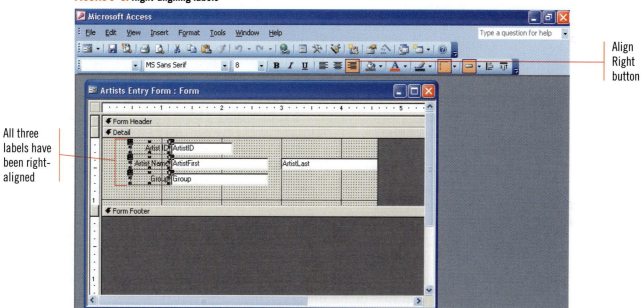

Align Right button

All three labels have been right-aligned

TABLE C-4: Selecting more than one control

technique	description
Click, [Shift]+click	Click a control, then press and hold [Shift] while clicking other controls; each one is selected
Drag a selection box	Drag a selection box (an outline box you create by dragging the pointer in Form Design View); every control that is in or is touched by the edges of the box is selected
Click in the ruler	Click in either the horizontal or vertical ruler to select all controls that intersect the selection line
Drag in the ruler	Drag through either the horizontal or vertical ruler to select all controls that intersect the selection line as it is dragged through the ruler

Using Text Boxes for Calculations

Text boxes are generally used to display data from underlying fields and are therefore *bound* to those fields. The name that appears in a text box control in Form Design View identifies the field to which the text box is bound. A text box control can also display a calculation. To create a calculation in a text box, you enter an **expression**, an equal sign, and a combination of symbols that calculates a result. For example, you could use a text box to store a numeric calculation that determines a commission. Or, you could use a text box to concatenate the values of two Text fields such as FirstName and LastName. You want to add a text box to the Item Entry Form to calculate the difference between the Retail and Wholesale values. You will work in Form Design View to accomplish this.

STEPS

TROUBLE
If the Toolbox is not visible, click to toggle it on. Also, the Toolbox might be docked on the edge of your screen. Drag it to a convenient location.

1. **Click the Item Entry Form in the database window, then click the Design button on the database window toolbar**

   The Item Entry Form opens in Form Design View where you can add, delete, or modify controls. To add a new text box control you will use the Toolbox toolbar.

2. **Click the Text Box button on the Toolbox toolbar, then click just below the Wholesale text box on the form**

   Adding a new text box automatically adds a new label to the left of the text box, too. The number in the default caption of the label depends on how many controls you have previously added to the form. First you will create the expression in the **calculated control** and then you will modify the label.

3. **Click Unbound in the new text box, type =[Retail]-[Wholesale], press [Enter], then widen the text box as necessary to see the entire expression as shown in Figure C-9**

   All expressions entered into a text box start with an equal sign (=). When referencing a field name within an expression, square brackets surround the field name. In an expression, you must type the field name exactly as it was created in Table Design View, but you do not need to worry about capitalization.

TROUBLE
If your calculated control did not work, delete it, then repeat Steps 2 through 4.

4. **Click the Text18: label to select the label control, double-click the Text18: text to select the text, type Profit as the new caption, press [Enter], then click the Form View button to view the changes**

   The Profit text box for the first record correctly calculates the value of 4 ($18-$14) as shown in Form View in Figure C-10. Because this value represents money, you want to format it like the values in the Retail and Wholesale fields. Text boxes can be formatted in Form View using the Formatting toolbar or the property sheet.

QUICK TIP
If the Formatting (Form/Report) toolbar is not visible, right-click any visible toolbar and click Formatting (Form/Report).

5. **Click 4 in the Profit text box, click the Align Right button on the Formatting (Form/Report) toolbar, click View on the menu bar, then click Properties**

   Monetary values such as those in the calculated Profit field should be right-aligned and displayed with a currency format. You can give the values a currency format by modifying the Format property in the property sheet.

6. **Click the Format tab in the property sheet if it is not already selected, click the Format list arrow, then scroll and click Currency**

   A short description of the selected property appears in the status bar. While you can format text boxes in Form View, you can only make some modifications to controls, such as moving, deleting, or adding them, in Form Design View. Also, you can modify labels only in Form Design View.

7. **Click , then click the Properties button to close the property sheet**

   Your last task is to move and resize the new controls to best match the existing layout of the form.

8. **Use the pointer to move the new label and text box and the ↔ pointer to resize the controls directly under the Wholesale label and text box, click the Save button , then click**

   The final form is shown in Figure C-11.

FIGURE C-9: Adding a text box to calculate a value

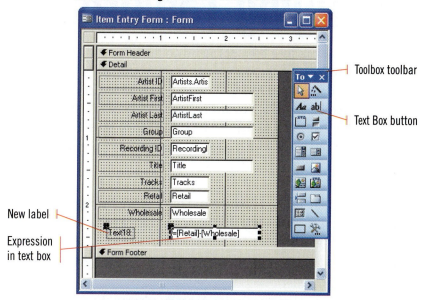

Toolbox toolbar

Text Box button

New label

Expression in text box

FIGURE C-10: Displaying a calculation in Form View

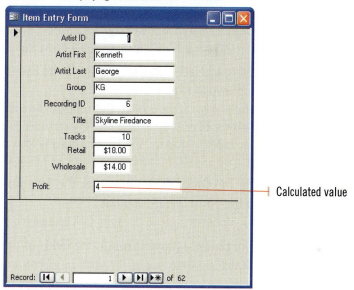

Calculated value

FIGURE C-11: Revised Item Entry Form

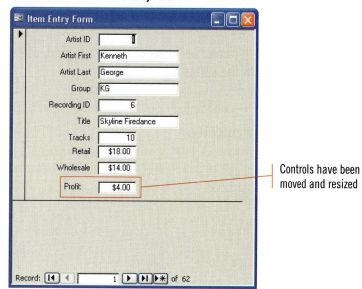

Controls have been moved and resized

Modifying Tab Order

Once all of the controls have been positioned on the form, you'll want to check the tab order. The **tab order** is the order in which the focus moves as you press [Tab] in Form View. **Focus** refers to which field would be edited if you started typing. Generally, you want the focus to move from the top to the bottom through each consecutive bound control on the form. Unbound controls such as labels and lines cannot have the focus in Form View because they are not used to enter or edit data. ▰▰▰▰▰ You check the tab order of the Item Entry Form, then change the tab order as necessary in Form Design View.

STEPS

TROUBLE

If you press [Tab] 10 times, you will move to the first field of the second record. Press [Shift]+[Tab] to tab backward or click the Previous Record button to return to the first record.

1. **Press [Tab] nine times, watching the focus move through the bound controls of the form**
   Currently, focus moves to the Wholesale field before the Retail field. You want to switch the tab order for those two controls.

2. **Click the Design View button ⬔ on the Form View toolbar, click View on the menu bar, then click Tab Order**
   The Tab Order dialog box allows you to change the tab order of controls in three sections: Form Header, Detail, and Form Footer. You can expand these sections in Form Design View by dragging the bottom edge of a section down to open it. Right now, all of the controls are positioned in the form's Detail section. See Table C-5 for more information on form sections. To change the tab order, drag the **row selector**, positioned to the left of the field name, up or down. A black line shows you the new placement of the field in the list.

QUICK TIP

Click the Auto Order button in the Tab Order dialog box to automatically set a left-to-right, top-to-bottom tab order.

3. **Click the Retail row selector in the Custom Order list, drag it up and position it just above Wholesale as shown in Figure C-12**
   Text18 represents the name of the text box that contains the profit calculation. (The number represents the number of controls you have added to the form). If you wanted to give the text box a more descriptive name, you could change its Name property. The **Name property** for a text box is analogous to the Caption property for a label.

QUICK TIP

In Form Design View, press [Ctrl][.] to switch to Form View. In Form View, press [Ctrl][,] to switch to Form Design View.

4. **Click OK in the Tab Order dialog box, click the Save button ⬔, then click the Form View button ⬔ on the Form Design toolbar**
   Although nothing visibly changes on the form, the tab order is different.

5. **Press [Enter] 10 times to move through the fields of the form with the new tab order**
   Both [Tab] and [Enter] move the focus to the next bound control of a form.

6. **Continue pressing [Enter] until you reach the Retail value of the second record, type 20, then press [Enter]**
   Changing the value in either the Retail or the Wholesale fields automatically recalculates the value in the Profit field as shown in Figure C-13.

7. **Press [Enter] to move the focus to the Profit field, attempt to type any value, and observe the message in the status bar**
   Even though the calculated control can receive the focus, its value cannot be directly edited in Form View. As the message in the status bar indicates, its value is bound to the expression [Retail]-[Wholesale].

8. **Close the Item Entry Form**

FIGURE C-12: Changing tab order

Drag the row selector for Retail above Wholesale

Click to set a left-to-right, top-to-bottom tab order

FIGURE C-13: Profit field automatically recalculates

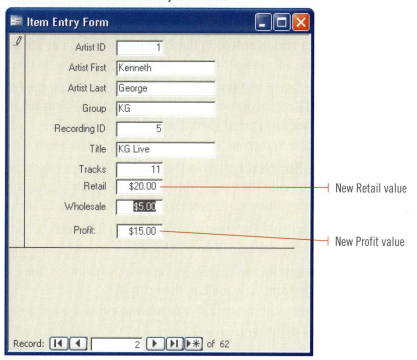

New Retail value

New Profit value

TABLE C-5: Form sections

section	description
Form Header	Controls placed in the Form Header section print only once at the top of the printout; by default, this section is closed in Form Design View
Detail	Controls placed in the Detail section appear in Form View and print once for every record in the underlying table or query object; all controls created by the Form Wizard are placed in this section
Form Footer	Controls placed in the Form Footer section print only once at the end of the printout; by default, this section is closed in Form Design View

Entering, Editing, and Printing Records

You use a form to quickly find, enter, or edit records in the underlying record source. You can also print a form, but printing all records in a form layout produces a very long printout because of the vertical orientation of the fields. To print only a single record in a form, you use the Selected Record option in the Print dialog box. You are ready to use the Artists Entry Form to add new information to the MediaLoft database.

STEPS

QUICK TIP
The New Record button is also located in the navigation buttons at the bottom of the form.

1. **Double-click the Artists Entry Form to open it in Form View, then click the New Record button [icon] on the Form View toolbar**

   A new, blank record is displayed. The Artist ID field is an AutoNumber field that automatically increments when you begin to enter data. The Specific Record box indicates the current record number.

2. **Press [Tab] to move the focus to the Artist Name text box, type your first name, press [Tab], type your last name, press [Tab] to move the focus to the Group text box, then type Snowboards**

   Data is automatically saved as you work in a form so you do not need to worry about saving data.

TROUBLE
The Print button [icon] on the Form View toolbar prints *all* records.

3. **Click File on the menu bar, click Print to open the Print dialog box, click the Selected Record(s) option button in the Print Range section as shown in Figure C-14, then click OK**

   Forms are also often used to find, edit, or delete existing records in the database.

QUICK TIP
Drag the title bar of the Find and Replace dialog box if it covers the Artists Entry Form.

4. **Click the Group text box, click the Find button [icon] on the Form View toolbar to open the Find and Replace dialog box, type Mitchell in the Find What text box, click the Match list arrow, click Any Part of Field, then click Find Next**

   A matching record appears behind the Find and Replace dialog box, as shown in Figure C-15.

5. **Click the Find Next button in the Find and Replace dialog box to find the next occurrence of an artist with the word "Mitchell" in the group name, then click OK**

   Once you find the record you need to change, you can edit data using a form.

6. **Edit the Mitchell Band entry to be Mitchell Brothers**

   Besides editing data using a form, it's also easy to delete records using a form.

7. **Click the Last Record button [icon] in the navigation buttons, click the Delete Record button [icon] on the Form View toolbar, then click Yes**

   As the confirmation message indicates, you cannot undo the deletion of a record.

8. **Close the Artists Entry Form**

FIGURE C-14: Printing a selected record of a form

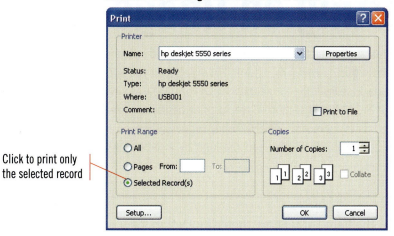

Click to print only
the selected record

FIGURE C-15: Finding data in a form

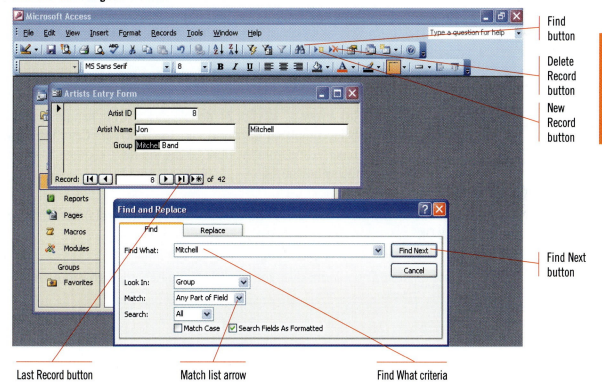

Find
button

Delete
Record
button

New
Record
button

Find Next
button

Last Record button   Match list arrow   Find What criteria

Inserting an Image

Graphic images, such as pictures, logos, or clip art, can add style and professionalism to a form. The form section in which they are placed is significant. For example, if you add a company logo to the Form Header section, the image appears at the top of the form in Form View as well as at the top of a printout. If you add the same image to the Detail section, it would print beside each record in a printout because the Detail section is printed for every record. Kelsey suggests that you add the MediaLoft logo and a descriptive title to the top of the form. You add the logo by inserting an unbound image control in the Form Header section.

STEPS

1. **Right-click the Item Entry Form, then click Design View on the shortcut menu**
   The Item Entry Form opens in Design View.

2. **Maximize the form, then drag the top edge of the Detail section down about 1" to open the Form Header section**
   The Form Header section opens so that you can add controls to that section.

3. **Click the Image button ▨ on the Toolbox toolbar, click in the Form Header section, click the Look in list arrow, navigate to the drive and folder where your Data Files are stored, click Smallmedia.bmp, then click OK**
   The MediaLoft logo is inserted into the Form Header in an image control, as shown in Figure C-16. Table C-6 summarizes other types of multimedia controls that may be added to a form using the Toolbox toolbar. Placing a title in the Form Header section adds a finishing touch to the form.

4. **Click the Label button ▨ on the Toolbox toolbar, click to the right of the MediaLoft logo in the Form Header section, type MediaLoft Music, then press [Enter]**
   Labels can be formatted to enhance their appearance on the form.

5. **Click the Font Size list arrow ⬚, click 24, double-click a sizing handle so that the MediaLoft Music label is completely displayed, click the Font/Fore Color list arrow ▨, click the dark blue box (second from the right on the top row), click the Save button ▨, then click the Form View button ▨**
   The final form is shown in Figure C-17.

6. **Click File on the menu bar, click Print, click the Selected Record(s) option button, then click OK**
   The first record as displayed by the Item Entry Form is sent to the printer.

7. **Close the Item Entry Form, close the MediaLoft-C database, then exit Access**

FIGURE C-16: Adding an image to the Form Header section

Smallmedia.bmp file, MediaLoft's logo

Drag top edge of Detail section down to open the Form Header section

Label button

Image button

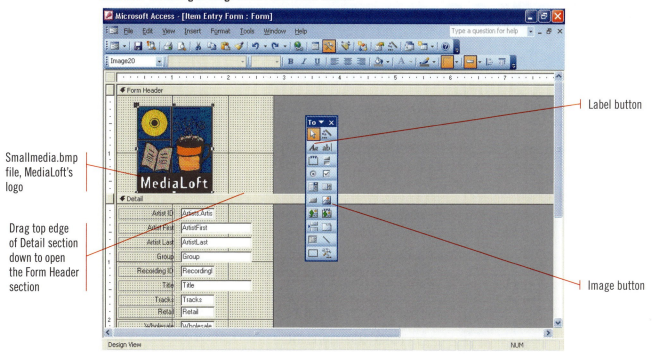

FIGURE C-17: Final Item Entry Form

Font Size list arrow

Form Header section

Form Detail section

Font/Fore Color button and list arrow

Label is 24 points, dark blue

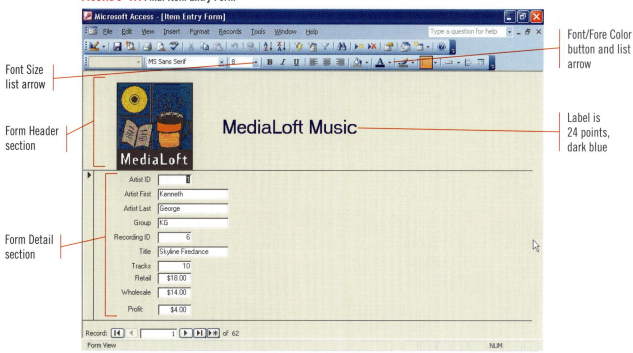

TABLE C-6: Multimedia controls

control	button	description
Image		Adds a single piece of clip art, a photo, or a logo to a form
Unbound object frame		Adds a sound clip, a movie clip, a document, or other type of unbound data (data that isn't stored in a table of the database) to a form
Bound object frame		Displays the contents of a field with an **OLE Object** (object linking and embedding) data type; an OLE Object field might contain pictures, sound clips, documents, or other data created by other software applications

Practice

▼ CONCEPTS REVIEW

Label each element of the Form View shown in Figure C-18.

FIGURE C-18

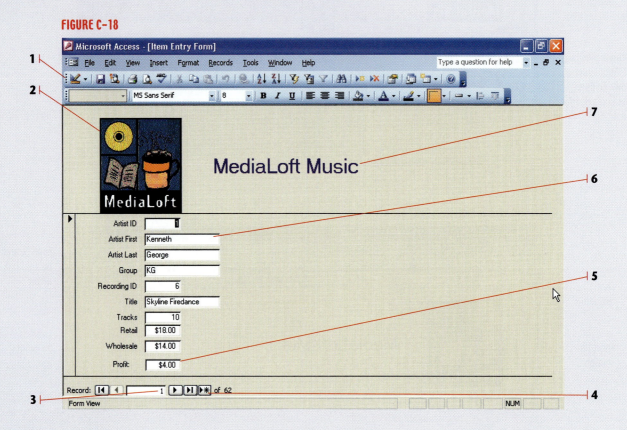

Match each term with the statement that best describes it.

8. **Bound control**
9. **Calculated control**
10. **Detail section**
11. **Form**
12. **Sizing handles**
13. **Tab order**

a. An Access database object that allows you to arrange the fields of a record in any layout and is used to enter, edit, and delete records

b. Used on a form to display data from a field

c. Squares that appear in the corners and edges of the selected control

d. The way in which the focus moves from one bound control to the next in Form View

e. Created by entering an expression in a text box

f. Controls placed here print once for every record in the underlying record source

Select the best answer from the list of choices.

14. **Every element on a form is called a(n):**
    a. Property.
    b. Attribute.
    c. Tool.
    d. Control.

15. **The mouse pointer that could be used to resize a control is:**
    a. ✛
    b. ↔
    c. ☜
    d. ✋

16. **The most common bound control is the:**
    a. List box.
    b. Check box.
    c. Combo box.
    d. Text box.

17. **The most common unbound control is the:**
    a. Label.
    b. Command Button.
    c. Line.
    d. Image.

18. **Form _____ View is used to move or resize form controls.**
    a. Control
    b. Design
    c. Preview
    d. Datasheet

19. **The _____ control is commonly used to display data on a form from a field with a Yes/No data type.**
    a. Check box
    b. Boolean
    c. Text box
    d. Combo box

20. **The _____ Object Frame control is used to display data from a field with an OLE Object data type.**
    a. Bound
    b. Caption
    c. Unbound
    d. Target

▼ SKILLS REVIEW

1. Plan a form.

a. Plan a form to use for entering business contacts by looking at several business cards.

b. Sketch the form.

c. Determine what type of control you will use for each bound field.

d. Identify the labels you would like to display on the form.

2. Create a form.

a. Start Access and open the **Membership-C.mdb** database from the drive and folder where your Data Files are stored.

b. Click the Forms button in the Membership-C database window, then double-click the Create form by using wizard option.

c. Base the form on the Contacts table, and include all of the fields.

d. Use a Columnar layout, a Standard style, title the form **Contact Entry Form**, and display the form in Form View.

3. Move and resize controls.

a. Open and maximize Form Design View for the Contact Entry Form.

FIGURE C-19

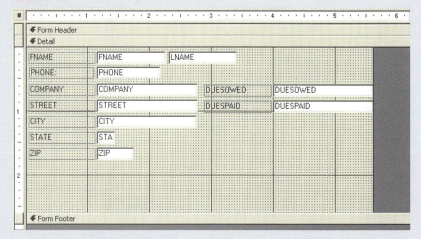

b. Delete the LNAME label, then move the LNAME text box to the right of the FNAME text box.

c. Move the DUESOWED and DUESPAID text boxes and corresponding labels to the right of the COMPANY and STREET text boxes.

d. Resize the CITY text box to be the same width as the COMPANY and STREET text boxes.

e. Move the PHONE text box and corresponding label between the FNAME and COMPANY controls. The resulting form should look similar to Figure C-19.

4. Modify labels.

a. Right-align all of the labels. Be careful to right-align only the labels, and not the text boxes.

b. Edit the caption of the FNAME label to **NAME**, the DUESOWED label to **DUES OWED**, and the DUESPAID label to **DUES PAID**. Be careful to modify the labels and not the text boxes.

5. Use text boxes for calculations.

a. Add a new text box below the DUESPAID text box.

b. Type the expression **=[DUESOWED]-[DUESPAID]** in the new unbound text box. (*Hint*: Remember that you must use the *exact field names* surrounded by square brackets in a calculated expression.)

c. In the property sheet for the new calculated control, change the Format property to Currency.

d. Right-align the new calculated control.

e. Change the accompanying label for the new calculated control to **BALANCE**.

f. Move and resize the new calculated control and label so that they are aligned beneath the DUESOWED and DUESPAID controls.

6. Modify tab order.

  a. Change the tab order so that pressing [Tab] moves the focus through the text boxes in the following order: FNAME, LNAME, PHONE, COMPANY, STREET, CITY, STATE, ZIP, DUESOWED, DUESPAID, Text20 (Text20 represents the text box with the calculated control).

  b. Save your changes, open the form in Form View, then test the new tab order.

7. Enter, edit, and print records.

  a. Use the Contact Entry Form to enter the following new records:

	FIRST NAME	LAST NAME	PHONE	COMPANY	STREET
Record 1	Your first name	Your last name	555-223-1166	Cummins Construction	1515 Maple St.
Record 2	Sena	Tsao	555-777-2277	Magpie Industries	1010 Green St.

	CITY	STATE	ZIP	DUES OWED	DUES PAID
1 continued	Greely	CO	77888-1111	$50.00	$25.00
2 continued	Alva	CO	77889-3333	$50.00	$50.00

  b. Find the record with your name, and print only that record.

  c. Find the Lois Grayson record, enter **IBM** in the COMPANY text box, then change Barnes in the STREET field to **Washington**.

  d. Filter for all records with a ZIP that starts with 64145. (*Hint*: Use Filter By Form with a filter criteria entry of 64145*.)

  e. Sort the filtered 64145 zip code records in ascending order by LAST NAME, change the COMPANY name for this record to **Your Last Name Industries**, then print only this record.

8. Insert an image.

  a. In Form Design View, expand the Form Header section by about 1".

  b. Use the Image control to insert the **Hand.bmp** file in the left side of the Form Header. (*Hint*: The Hand.bmp file is on the drive and folder where your Data Files are stored.)

  c. Centered and below the image, add the label **MEMBERSHIP INFORMATION** in a 24-point font. Be sure to resize the label so that all of the text is visible.

  d. Below the MEMBERSHIP INFORMATION label, add your name as a label.

  e. View the form in Form View, then sort the records in descending order based on the COMPANY values.

  f. Print only the first record.

  g. Save and close the form, close the database, then exit Access.

▼ INDEPENDENT CHALLENGE 1

As the office manager of a cardiology clinic, you need to create a data entry form for new patients.

a. Start Access, then open the **Clinic-C.mdb** database from the drive and folder where your Data Files are stored.

b. Using the Form Wizard, create a form that includes all the fields in the Outcomes Data table, using the Columnar layout and Standard style. Title the form **Medical Chart Information**.

c. Move the four text boxes in the second column down to make room to move the three text boxes at the bottom of the first column (Dietary Cholesterol, Chol, and HDL) to the top of the second column.

d. Drag the top of the Form Footer up to close up the empty space at the bottom of the form.

e. Right-align all labels so that they are closer to the text boxes they describe.

f. Resize the MR# text box to be the same size as the Date text box. Resize all other text boxes to be the same size as the Height text box. (*Hint*: Select several text boxes to resize at the same time, then use the Format, Size, To Narrowest menu option to automatically size the selected text boxes to the narrowest text box.)

g. Add a label with your name to the Form Header, then save the form and display it in Form View.

h. In Form View, check the tab order to make sure it works in a top-to-bottom order for both columns. Modify the tab order as needed.

i. Sort the records in ascending order based on the Height field, then print the first record.

Advanced Challenge Exercise

- In Form Design View, add an Image control to the Form Header. Use the Insert Picture dialog box to search for and find an appropriate piece of clip art to insert on the form. One folder to explore for available clip art images is C:\Program Files\Microsoft Office\media. (*Hint*: If you are having trouble finding an appropriate piece of medical clip art on your computer, use either the Medical.bmp or Medstaff.bmp images provided in your Data Files.)

- To resize the image to fit within the form, open its property sheet. Click the Format tab, click the Size Mode property, and press F1 to read the Microsoft Access Help page about this property. After reading about the property in Help, close Help and change the Size Mode property of the image to Zoom.

j. Save and display the Medical Chart Information in Form View as shown in Figure C-20, sort the records in ascending order on the Weight field, then print the first record.

k. Close the form, close the database, then exit Access.

FIGURE C-20

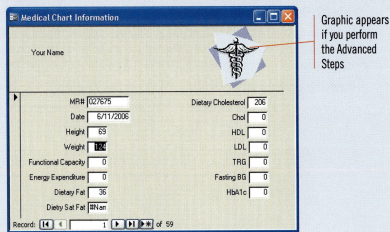

Graphic appears if you perform the Advanced Steps

▼ INDEPENDENT CHALLENGE 2

As office manager of a cardiology clinic, you want to build a form that quickly calculates a height-to-weight ratio value based on information in the Outcomes Data table.

- **a.** Start Access, then open the **Clinic-C.mdb** database from the drive and folder where your Data Files are stored.
- **b.** Using the Form Wizard, create a form based on the Outcomes Data table with only the following fields: MR#, Date, Height, and Weight.
- **c.** Use the Columnar layout and Standard style, and name the form **Height to Weight Ratio Form**.
- **d.** In Design View, use the Text Box button to add a text box and accompanying label below the Weight text box.
- **e.** Enter the expression **=[Height]/[Weight]** in the unbound text box.
- **f.** Modify the new label from Text6: to **Ratio**.
- **g.** Resize the Ratio label so that it is closer to the calculated expression control, then right-align all of the labels. Resize the Weight and calculated text boxes to be the same width as the Height text box.
- **h.** Change the Format property of the calculated control to **Fixed**, and the Decimal Places property to **2**.
- **i.** Open the Form Header section about **0.5"**, then add a label to that section that displays your name. Modify the MR# label to be **Medical Record #**.
- **j.** Save and view the form in Form View, then print only the record with the Medical Record # of 017771.
- **k.** Sort the records in descending order by Height, change the value in the Weight field to **200**, press [Tab], then print only this record.

Advanced Challenge Exercise

- ■ Open the Height to Weight Ratio Form in Form Design View, then open the field list.
- ■ Drag the Chol, HDL, and LDL fields from the field list to the right of the Height, Weight, and Ratio text boxes.
- ■ Move the new labels and text boxes as necessary so that all of the controls on the form are clearly presented. (*Hint*: Once the controls are moved so that they are not touching, you can align the top edges of controls in a row by selecting the controls, then choosing the Format, Align, Top menu option.)

- **l.** Save and display the form in Form View. Find the record for Medical Record # 058231, then print only that record.
- **m.** Close the Height to Weight Ratio Form, close the Clinic-C database, then exit Access.

▼ INDEPENDENT CHALLENGE 3

As office manager of a cardiology clinic, you want to build a form to enter new insurance information.

    a. Open the **Clinic-C.mdb** database from the drive and folder where your Data Files are stored.

    b. Using the Form Wizard, create a form based on all of the fields in the Insurance Company Information table. Use the Columnar layout, Standard style, and accept **Insurance Company Information** as the title.

    c. In Form Design View, change the Insurance Company Name label to **Insurance Company**. Be sure to modify the Insurance Company Name label, and not the text box.

    d. Resize the State text box so that it is the same size as the City text box.

    e. Expand the Form Header section, then add the graphic image **Medical.bmp** to the left side of the Form Header section. The Medical.bmp file is in the drive and folder where your Data Files are stored.

    f. Add a label **Insurance Entry Form** and another for your name to the right of the medical clip art in the Form Header section.

    g. Increase the size of the Insurance Entry Form label to 18 points. Resize the label to display the entire caption.

    h. Switch to Form View, then find the record for the Cigna Insurance Company. Change Sherman in the City field to **Bridgewater**, then print this record.

Advanced Challenge Exercise

    ■ Filter for all records with a State entry of KS. Preview the filtered records, then use the Setup button to modify the top and bottom margins of the printout so that it fits on one page.

    ■ In Form Design View, drag the medical clip art image to the Detail section, then redisplay the form in Form View and preview it again. Notice how the printout differs when you place the image in the Detail section versus the Form Header section.

    ■ If the printout fits on one page (the records should still be filtered for KS), print it. If not, continue modifying the margins or work in Form Design View to make the form small enough so that this filtered printout fits on one page, then print the page.

    i. Save and close the Insurance Company Information Form, close the Clinic-C database, then exit Access.

▼ INDEPENDENT CHALLENGE 4

You are on the staff of an economic development team whose goal is to encourage tourism in the Baltic Sea region. You have created an Access database called Baltic-C.mdb to track important fields of information for the countries in that region, and will use the Internet to find information about the area and enter it into existing forms.

   a. Start Access and open the **Baltic-C.mdb** database from the drive and folder where your Data Files are stored.

   b. Connect to the Internet, then go to any general search engine to conduct research for your database. Your goal is to find information for at least one new city record for each country.

   c. Open the Countries form. You can enter the data you found on the Internet for each city by using the City fields shown in Figure C-21. This arrangement of data organizes cities within countries using a main form/subform arrangement. The main form contains a single text box bound to the Country field. The subform presents a datasheet of four City fields. Be sure to enter the Population data for that particular city, rather than for the entire country. CityID is an AutoNumber field, so it automatically increments as you enter the City, Capital, and Population data.

FIGURE C-21

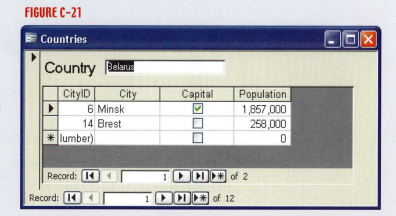

   d. After you have entered one new city for each country, print the record for Sweden.

   e. Close the Countries form, then open the Countries table datasheet. Click all of the expand buttons to the left of each Country record to show the city records that you just entered through the Countries form. Close the Countries table.

   f. Open the Cities form and find the Oslo, Norway, record shown in Figure C-22. This form shows another main form/subform arrangement. The main form contains fields that describe the city, and the subform contains a datasheet with fields that describe the events for that city.

FIGURE C-22

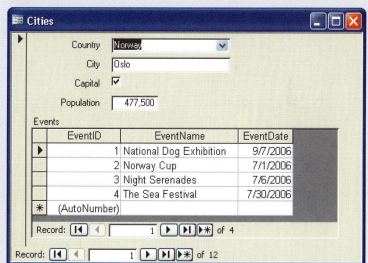

   g. Return to the search engine, and research upcoming tourist events for Copenhagen, Denmark.

   h. In the Cities form, find the Copenhagen record, then enter three events for Copenhagen. EventID is an AutoNumber field, so it automatically increments as you enter the EventName and EventDate information.

   i. Print the Copenhagen record, close the Cities form, close the Baltic-C database, then exit Access.

▼ VISUAL WORKSHOP

Open the **Clinic-C.mdb** database, then use the Form Wizard to create the form based on the Demographics table, as shown in Figure C-23. Notice that the label **Patient Form** is 24 points and has been placed in the Form Header section. The clip art, **Medstaff.bmp**, can be found in the drive and folder where your Data Files are stored. The image has been placed on the right side of the Detail section, and many controls were moved and resized. Also notice that the labels are right-aligned. To change the background color of the Detail section to white, double-click the Detail section bar in Form Design View, then modify the Back Color property on the Format tab of the property sheet to **16777215**, the value that corresponds to white. Enter your own name and gender for the first record, then print it.

FIGURE C-23

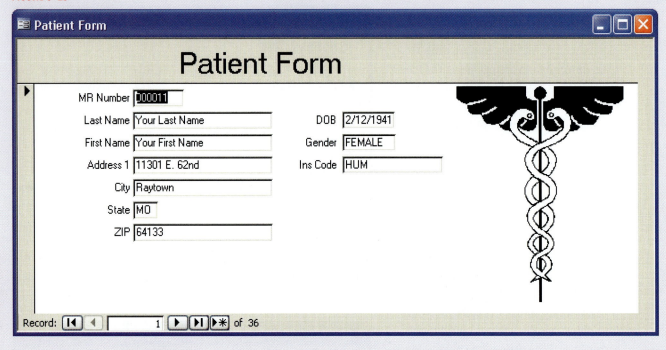

UNIT
D
Access 2003

Using Reports

OBJECTIVES

Plan a report
Create a report
Use group sections
Change the sort order
Add a calculation
Align controls
Format controls
Change page layout

If you have a SAM user profile, you may have access to hands-on instruction, practice, and assessment of the skills covered in this unit. Log in to your SAM account and go to your assignments page to see what your instructor has assigned.

A **report** is an Access object used to create professional printouts. Although you can print a datasheet or form, reports are the primary object used to create professional printouts because reports provide many more printing options. For example, a report may include formatting embellishments such as multiple fonts and colors, extra graphical elements such as clip art and lines, and multiple headers and footers. Reports are also very powerful analysis tools. A report can calculate subtotals, averages, counts, or other statistics for groups of records. You cannot enter or edit data through a report. Kelsey Lang, a marketing manager at MediaLoft, wants you to produce some reports to distribute to MediaLoft employees.

Planning a Report

Hard copy reports are often the primary tool used to communicate database information at internal meetings or with customers. Time spent planning your report not only increases your productivity but also ensures that the report meets its intended objectives. Creating a report is similar to creating a form, in that you work with bound, unbound, and calculated controls in Report Design View just as you do in Form Design View. Reports, however, have more sections than forms. A **section** determines how often and where controls placed within that section print in the final report. See Table D-1 for more information on report sections. Kelsey asks you to create a report that summarizes inventory items within each music category.

DETAILS

Use the following guidelines to plan a new report:

- **Determine the information (the fields and records) that the report will show**

  You can base a report on a table, but usually you create a query to gather the specific fields from one or more tables upon which the report is based. If you base the report on a query, you can also set criteria within the query to limit the number of records displayed by the report.

- **Determine how the fields should be organized on the report**

  Most reports display fields in a horizontal layout across the page, but you can arrange them any way you want. Just as in forms, bound text box controls are used on a report to display the data stored in the underlying fields. These text boxes are generally placed in the report **Detail section**. The Detail section of a report is always visible in Report Design View.

- **Determine how the records should be grouped and sorted within the report**

  In an Access report, **grouping** means to sort records in a particular order *plus* provide a section before each group of records called the Group Header section and a section after the group of records called the Group Footer section. The **Group Header** section usually introduces the upcoming group of records. The **Group Footer** section is most often used to calculate statistics such as subtotals for the group of records it follows. Group Header and Footer sections are created by choices made when initially creating the report using the Report Wizard, or by specifying a Yes value to these field properties in the Sorting and Grouping dialog box in Report Design View. To view or edit the grouping and sorting orders for any report, click the Sorting and Grouping button on the Report Design toolbar. In Figure D-1, the field used to group the records is the Category field. Therefore, the Group Header section for this report is called the Category Header section and the Group Footer section is called the Category Footer section.

- **Identify any other descriptive information that should be placed at the beginning or end of the report, or at the top or bottom of each page**

  You use the **Report Header**, **Report Footer**, **Page Header**, and **Page Footer** sections to add information that you want to print on every page, or at the beginning or end of the report. For example, you might add a text box that contains an expression to display the current date in the Page Header section, or you might add a text box that contains an expression to display the current page number in the Page Footer section. The Report Header and Report Footer sections of a report can be opened using the Report Header/Footer option on the View menu in Report Design View.

- **Identify a meaningful title for the report**

  The title should clearly identify the purpose of the report. The title is created with a label control placed in the Report Header section.

  The sketch of your first report is shown in Figure D-1.

FIGURE D-1: Sketch of the Inventory Report

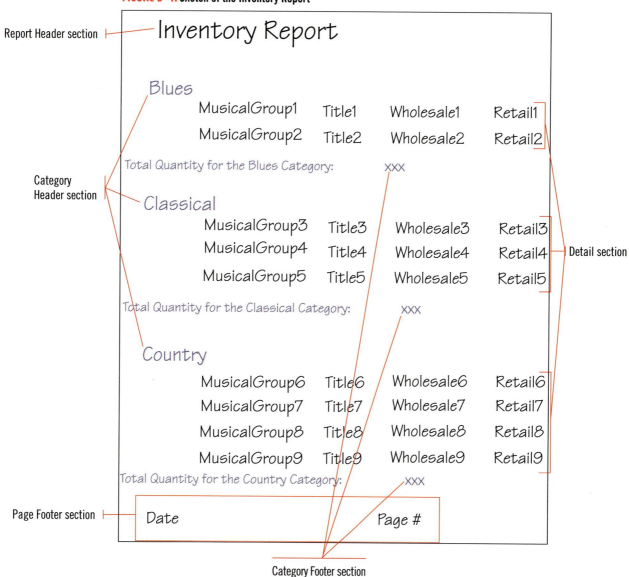

TABLE D-1: Report sections

section	where does this section print?	which controls are most commonly placed in this section?
Report Header	At the top of the first page of the report	Label controls containing the report title; can also include clip art, a logo image, or a line separating the title from the rest of the report
Page Header	At the top of every page (but below the Report Header on page one)	Text box controls containing a page number or date expression
Group Header	Before every group of records	Text box controls for the field by which the records are grouped
Detail	Once for every record	Text box controls for the rest of the fields in the recordset (the table or query upon which the report is built)
Group Footer	After every group of records	Text box controls containing calculated expressions, such as subtotals or counts, for the records in that group
Page Footer	At the bottom of every page	Text box controls containing a page number or date expression
Report Footer	At the end of the entire report	Text box controls containing expressions such as grand totals or counts that calculate a value for all of the records in the report

Access 2003

UNIT
D
Access 2003

Creating a Report

You can create reports in Access in Report Design View, or you can use the Report Wizard to help you get started. The **Report Wizard** asks questions that guide you through the initial development of the report, similar to the Form Wizard. Your responses to the Report Wizard determine the record source, style, and lay-out of the report. The Report Wizard also helps you determine how the records will be sorted, grouped, and analyzed. Another way to quickly create a report is by selecting a table or query, clicking the New Object list arrow ⬚ ▾ on the Database toolbar, and then clicking AutoReport. ░░░ You use the Report Wizard to create the Inventory Report that you previously sketched.

STEPS

1. **Start Access, click the More link in the Open section of the Getting Started task pane, then open the MediaLoft-D.mdb database from the drive and folder where your Data Files are stored**

   This database contains the Inventory and Artists tables.

2. **Click Reports on the Objects bar in the MediaLoft-D database window, then double-click Create report by using wizard**

   The Report Wizard dialog box opens and prompts you to select the fields you want on the report. You can select fields from one or more tables or queries. You need the MusicalGroup field from the Artists table and the Category, Title, Wholesale, and Retail fields from the Inventory table. These fields have been previously selected in the Inventory Items query.

3. **Click the Tables/Queries list arrow, click Query: Inventory Items, then click the Select All Fields button ⟩⟩**

   The five fields are selected and the first dialog box of the Report Wizard should look like Figure D-2.

4. **Click Next**

   The next question asks how you want to view your data. Your response determines how the records will be grouped. Viewing the data "by Artists" makes the MusicalGroup field the grouping field as shown in the sample. Because you want to use Category as the grouping field, you select the "by Inventory" option.

TROUBLE

Click Back to review previous dialog boxes within a wizard.

5. **Click by Inventory, click Next, click Category, click the Select Single field button ⟩ to select Category as the grouping field, then click Next**

   You can use the Report Wizard to specify up to four sort fields in either an ascending or descending sort order for each field. For now, you decide not to choose any sort fields and to finish the steps of the Report Wizard.

6. **Click Next, accept the Stepped layout and Portrait orientation, click Next, click Corporate for the style, click Next, then type Inventory Report for the report title**

7. **Verify that the Preview the report option button is selected, click Finish, then maximize the Inventory Report**

   The Inventory Report opens in Print Preview, as shown in Figure D-3. Notice that the records are grouped by Category.

FIGURE D-2: Report Wizard dialog box

Base the report on the Inventory Items query

Select All Fields button

Fields selected for the report

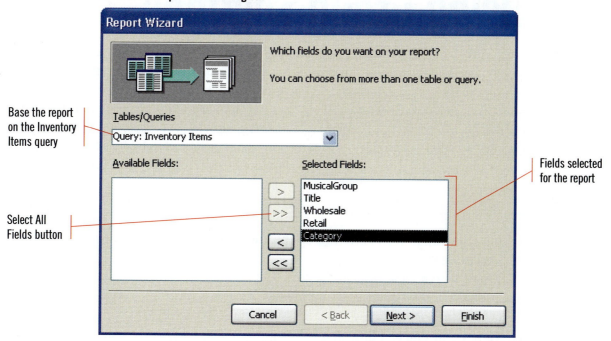

FIGURE D-3: Inventory Report in Print Preview

Report Header section

Page Header section

Category Header section

Detail section

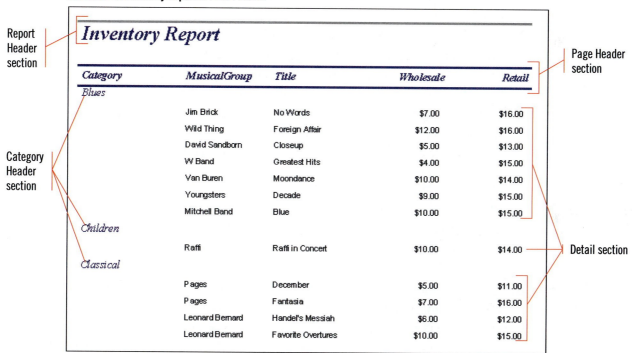

Clues to Use

Why reports should be based on queries

The first dialog box of the Report Wizard asks you to select the fields you want to see on the report. Your choices determine the value of the report's **Record Source** property, which identifies the **recordset** (fields and records) passed to the report. You can modify the Record Source property of any report, thus changing the recordset that is passed to the report. If you choose the fields from a single query (versus selecting fields from different tables), however, the recordset is already defined as a query object, which makes it very easy to modify. For example, you may want to add more fields to the report at a later time. If your report is based on a query, simply open the query used as the report's recordset in Query Design View and add the field to the query grid. The new field will automatically be made available to the report as well.

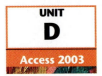

Using Group Sections

Grouping means to sort records in a particular order *plus* provide a section before and after each group, the Group Header and Group Footer. The Group Header and Group Footer sections take the name of the field by which you are grouping the records. If grouping records by the State field, for example, the sections would be called the State Header and State Footer sections. You can create groups on a report through the Report Wizard, or you can change an existing report's grouping fields in Report Design View. The Inventory Report is grouped by the Category field. The name of each category appears in the Category Header section before each group of records within that category. You will open the Category Footer section and add the controls needed to count the number of items within each category.

STEPS

TROUBLE

If the Field List button 📄 or Properties button 📄 on the Report Design toolbar are selected, click them to toggle these windows off for now.

1. **Click the Design View button 🖉 on the Print Preview toolbar to switch to Report Design View**

   Report Design View shows you the sections of the report as well as the controls within each section. Report Design View is where you make all structural changes to a report object including making changes to grouping fields.

2. **Click the Sorting and Grouping button 📑 on the Report Design toolbar, click the Group Footer text box, click the Group Footer list arrow, then click Yes**

   Specifying Yes for the Group Footer property as shown in Figure D-4 opens that section of the report in Report Design View.

TROUBLE

To resize a floating toolbar, drag its edge. To move a floating toolbar, drag its title bar. If your Toolbox toolbar is docked to a side of the screen, you can move it by dragging its topmost or leftmost edge.

3. **Click 📑 to close the Sorting and Grouping dialog box, then click the Toolbox button 🛠 on the Report Design toolbar to toggle it on if it is not already visible**

   You can add a calculated control to count the number of records in each group by placing a text box in the Category Footer section and entering an expression that counts the records into the text box.

4. **Click the Text Box button ab on the Toolbox toolbar, then click in the Category Footer section directly below the Title text box**

   Your screen should look like Figure D-5. When adding a new text box to the report, a new label is also automatically added to the left of the text box. You want to modify the Text16 label to be more descriptive of the information it identifies.

TROUBLE

If you double-click the edge of the label, you open the control's property sheet. Close the property sheet, then double-click Text16 to select it.

5. **Click the Text16: label in the Category Footer section to select the label, double-click Text16 to select the text within the label, type Count, then press [Enter]**

   With the label modified, your next task is to enter the expression that counts the number of items in each category.

6. **Click the Unbound text box control in the Category Footer section to select the text box, click Unbound within the text box, type =Count([Title]), then press [Enter]**

   Expressions start with an equal sign and each character including the parentheses must be entered exactly as shown. Field names used in expressions are not case sensitive but must be surrounded by [square brackets] and match the exact name of the field as defined in Table Design View. This expression counts the number of items in the Title field. Additional information on expressions is covered later in this unit.

TROUBLE

If you see #Error on the report, return to Report Design View, edit the expression in the new text box as shown in Step 6, then preview the report again.

7. **Click the Print Preview button 🔍 on the Report Design toolbar**

   Each group of records is followed by a Group Footer that identifies how many titles are in each category as shown in Figure D-6.

8. **Click the Close button on the Print Preview toolbar, click the Save button, then close the Inventory Report**

FIGURE D-4: Sorting and Grouping dialog box

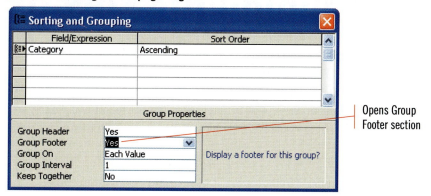

Opens Group Footer section

FIGURE D-5: Inventory Report in Report Design View

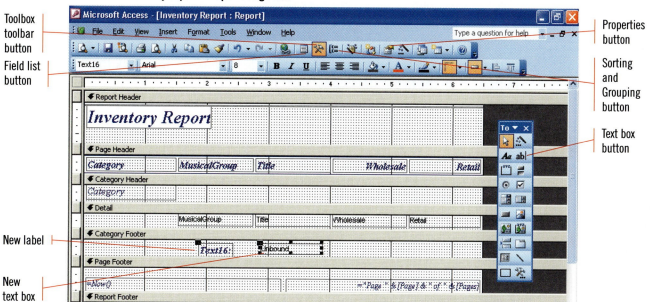

Toolbox toolbar button

Field list button

New label

New text box

Properties button

Sorting and Grouping button

Text box button

FIGURE D-6: Adding a calculation in the Category Footer section

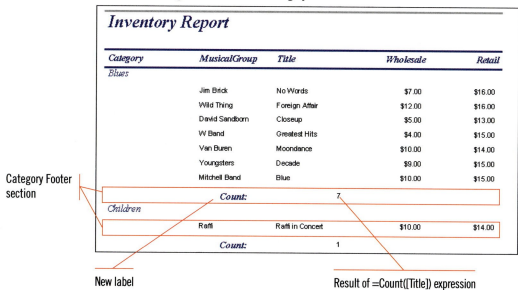

Category Footer section

New label

Result of =Count([Title]) expression

Access 2003

Changing the Sort Order

The grouping field acts as a primary sort field, but you can define additional sort fields within each group. The Report Wizard prompts you for group and sort information at the time you create the report, but you can change the group and sort orders on an existing report by using the Sorting and Grouping dialog box in Report Design View. After reviewing the report with Kelsey, you decide to modify the Inventory Report so that the Detail records are sorted in ascending order by the value in the MusicalGroup field.

STEPS

1. **Right-click the Inventory Report, then click Design View**

   The Inventory Report opens in Report Design View.

2. **Click the Sorting and Grouping button on the Report Design toolbar, click the Field/Expression text box in the second row, click the Field/Expression list arrow, then click MusicalGroup as shown in Figure D-7**

   Both the Group Header and Group Footer property values for the MusicalGroup field are set to No, which indicates that the MusicalGroup field is providing a sort order only.

3. **Click to toggle the Sorting and Grouping dialog box off, then click the Print Preview button on the Report Design toolbar**

   Part of the report is shown in Print Preview, as shown in Figure D-8. You can use the buttons on the Print Preview toolbar to view more of the report.

QUICK TIP

The grid expands to a maximum of 4 x 5 pages if you keep dragging to expand it.

4. **Click the One Page button on the Print Preview toolbar to view one miniature page, click the Two Pages button to view two pages, click the Multiple Pages button, point to 1 x 3 Pages as shown in Figure D-9, then click the 1 x 3 Pages option**

   The Print Preview window displays the three pages of the report. You can click the Zoom pointers and to change the zoom magnification.

QUICK TIP

You can also type a number into the Fit text box to zoom at a specific percent.

5. **Point to the last count on the last page of the report with the pointer, click to read the number 5 in the last Category Footer of the report, then click again to view all three pages of the report in the Preview window**

   To zoom the preview to a specific percentage, click the Zoom list arrow `100%` on the Print Preview toolbar, then click a percentage. The Fit option automatically adjusts the preview to display all pages in the report.

6. **Close the Inventory Report, then click Yes when prompted to save it**

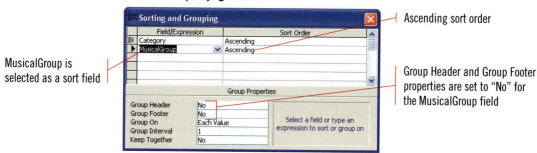

MusicalGroup is selected as a sort field

Ascending sort order

Group Header and Group Footer properties are set to "No" for the MusicalGroup field

FIGURE D-8: Inventory Report sorted by MusicalGroup

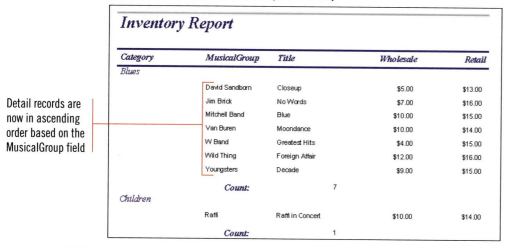

Detail records are now in ascending order based on the MusicalGroup field

FIGURE D-9: Two Page Print Preview

One Page button

Two Pages button

Multiple Pages button

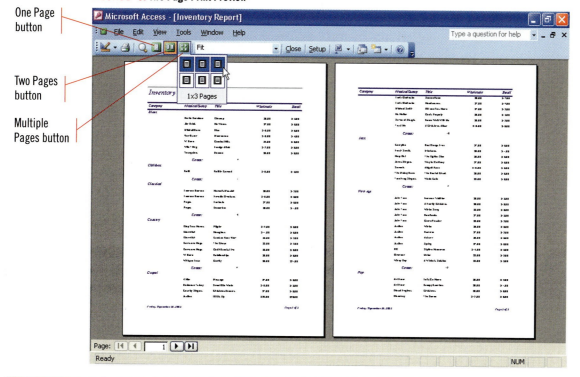

Clues to Use

Adding a field to a report

To add a new field to a report, click the Field List button [image] on the Report Design toolbar, then drag the field from the field list to the appropriate position on the report in Report Design View. This action creates both a label that displays the field name and a text box that displays the value of the field on the resulting report.

Access 2003

Adding a Calculation

In a report, you create a **calculation** by entering an expression into an unbound text box. When a report is previewed or printed, the expression is evaluated and the resulting calculation is placed on the report. An **expression** is a combination of field names, operators (such as +, –, /, and *), and functions that result in a single value. A **function** is a built-in formula such as Sum or Count that helps you quickly create a calculation. See Table D-2 for examples of common expressions that use Access functions. Notice that every expression starts with an equal sign, and when it uses a function, the arguments for the function are placed in parentheses. **Arguments** are the pieces of information that the function needs to create the final answer. When an argument is a field name, the field name must be surrounded by square brackets. Kelsey asks you to add another calculation to the Inventory Report to show the average Retail value for each category of items.

STEPS

1. **Right-click the Inventory Report, click Design View, click the Text Box button** ![ab] **on the Toolbox toolbar, then click in the Category Footer section just below the Retail text box**

   Adding a new text box automatically adds a new label as well. You will modify the label to better describe the value that will be calculated by the text box. (*Note:* If you wanted to add only a descriptive label to the report, you would use the Label button ![Aa] on the Toolbox toolbar.)

TROUBLE

Depending on your activity in Report Design View, you may get a different number in the Text##: label. The number corresponds to the number of controls that have been added to this report.

2. **Click the new Text18: label to select the label, double-click Text18 to select the text within the label, type Average, then press [Enter]**

   Now that the label displays descriptive text, you will enter the appropriate expression in the text box to calculate the average Retail value for each group of records.

3. **Click the new Unbound text box control in the Category Footer section to select the text box, click Unbound within the text box, type =Avg([Retail]), then press [Enter]**

   You used the Avg function to create the expression to average the values in the Retail field as shown in Figure D-10.

4. **Click the Print Preview button** ![preview] **on the Report Design toolbar, then click** ![zoom] **to zoom in on the report as shown in Figure D-11**

   The average Retail value calculation is correct, but is not formatted to look like a monetary value.

QUICK TIP

You can also double-click a control to open its property sheet.

5. **Click the Design View button** ![design] **on the Print Preview toolbar, click the =Avg([Retail]) text box to select it, click the Properties button** ![props] **on the Report Design toolbar to open the property sheet for the text box, click the Format tab, click the Format list arrow, then scroll and click Currency**

   The **property sheet** is a list of all of the characteristics of the selected control that you can modify. In this case, you modified the Format property, which changes the way the resulting calculation will appear on the report.

6. **Click** ![props] **to toggle off the property sheet, click the Save button** ![save] **on the Report Design toolbar, then click** ![preview] **to preview the report again**

   When you save a report object, you are saving the report definition, not the data displayed by the report. The data that the report displays was automatically saved when it was previously entered into the database. Once a report object is saved, it always shows the most up-to-date data when you preview or print the report. The average Retail calculation is now formatted with the Currency format, so it matches the values shown in the Retail field, which has a Currency data type.

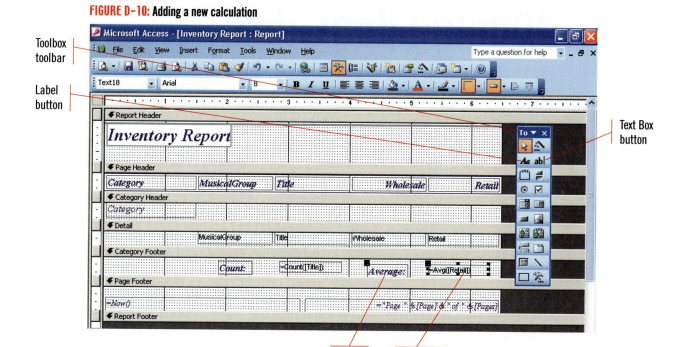

FIGURE D-10: Adding a new calculation

Toolbox toolbar

Label button

Text Box button

New label   New text box

FIGURE D-11: Previewing the new calculation

Result of =Avg([Retail]) expression

New label

TABLE D-2: Sample Access expressions

sample expression	description
=[Price]*1.05	Multiplies the Price field by 1.05 (adds 5% to the Price field)
=[Subtotal]+[Shipping]	Adds the value of the Subtotal field to the value of the Shipping field
=Avg([Freight])	Uses the **Avg** function to display an average of the values in the Freight field
=Date()	Uses the **Date** function to display the current date in the form of mm-dd-yy
="Page "&[Page]	Displays the word Page, a space, and the result of the [**Page**] field, an Access field that contains the current page number
=[FirstName]& " "&[LastName]	Displays the value of the FirstName and LastName fields in one control separated by a space
=Left([ProductNumber],2)	Uses the **Left** function to display the first two characters in the ProductNumber field

Aligning Controls

Once the information that you want to present has been added to the appropriate section of a report, you may also want to align the data on the report. Aligning controls in precise columns and rows makes the information easier to read. There are two different types of **alignment** commands: you can left-, right-, or center-align a control *within its own border* using the Alignment buttons on the Formatting (Form/Report) toolbar, or you can align the edges of controls *with respect to one another* using the Align command on the Format menu. You decide to align the controls in the Category Footer section to improve the readability of the report.

STEPS

QUICK TIP

You can drag through the horizontal ruler to select all controls that intersect with the selection line.

1. **Click the Design View button ☑ on the Print Preview toolbar, then click in the vertical ruler to the left of the Count label in the Category Footer section**

   When you click a ruler, a selection line crosses the report at that point. In this case, the selection line touched all four controls in the Category Footer section as shown in Figure D-12. All four controls are now selected.

2. **Click the Align Right button ☰ on the Formatting (Form/Report) toolbar**

   Now the information displayed by these controls is right-aligned within the border of each control. In addition to aligning the information *within* the controls, you want to align the controls *with respect to each other*.

QUICK TIP

If you make a mistake, click the Undo button ↻.

3. **With the four controls still selected, click Format on the menu bar, point to Align, then click Bottom**

   Now the bottom edges of the four controls are aligned with respect to one another. You can also align controls in different sections with respect to one another to form perfect columns.

4. **Click the Retail text box in the Detail section, press and hold [Shift], click the =Avg([Retail]) text box in the Category Footer section, click Format on the menu bar, point to Align, then click Right**

   The right edges of the Retail text box and =Avg([Retail]) text box are now aligned with respect to each other so they will form a perfect column on the report.

5. **Click the Save button 🖫, click the Print Preview button 🔍, then scroll and zoom so that your report looks similar to Figure D-13**

FIGURE D-12: Selecting multiple controls

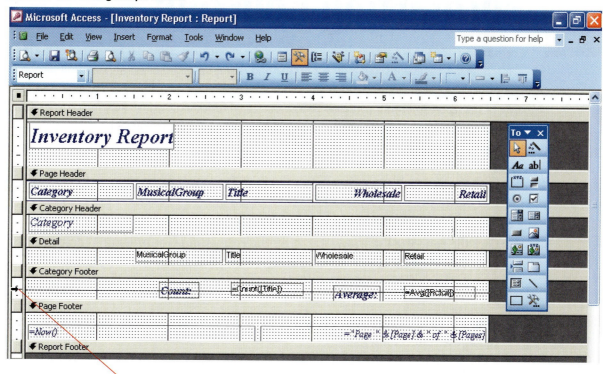

Click in the vertical ruler to select all controls in that section

FIGURE D-13: Controls are aligned

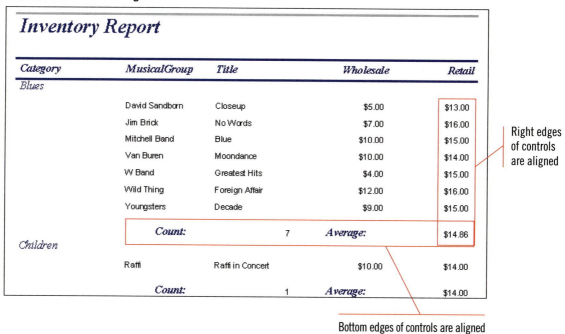

Right edges of controls are aligned

Bottom edges of controls are aligned

Clues to Use

Precisely moving and resizing controls

You can move and resize controls using the mouse, but precise movements are often easier to accomplish using the keyboard. Pressing the arrow keys while holding [Ctrl] moves selected controls one **pixel** (picture element) at a time in the direction of the arrow. Pressing the arrow keys while holding [Shift] resizes selected controls one pixel at a time.

Formatting Controls

Formatting refers to enhancing the appearance of the information. Table D-3 lists several of the most popular formatting commands found on the Formatting (Form/Report) toolbar. Although the Report Wizard automatically applies many formatting embellishments to a report, you often want to improve the appearance of the report to fit your particular needs. ▨▨▨ In reviewing the Inventory Report with Kelsey, you decide to format the category names on the report to make it more prominent.

STEPS

1. **Click the Design View button 🖉 on the Print Preview toolbar, then click the Category text box in the Category Header section**

   Before you can format any control, it must be selected.

2. **Click the Font Size list arrow ⎮11 ▾⎮ on the Formatting (Form/Report) toolbar, click 12, then click the Bold button B on the Formatting (Form/Report) toolbar**

   Increasing the font size and applying bold are common ways to make information more visible on a report. You can also change the colors of the control.

   QUICK TIP

   When the color on the Fill/Back Color 🪣, Font/Fore Color A, or Line/Border Color 🖉 button displays the color you want, you simply click the button to apply that color.

3. **With the Category text box still selected, click the Font/Fore Color button A to select red as the font color**

   Many buttons on the Formatting (Form/Report) toolbar include a list arrow that you can click to reveal a list of formatting choices. When you click the color list arrow, a palette of available colors is displayed.

4. **With the Category text box still selected, click the Fill/Back Color list arrow 🪣 ▾, then click the light gray color (fourth row, last column on the right) as shown in Figure D-14**

   Be careful about relying too heavily on color formatting. Background shades often become solid black boxes when printed on a black-and-white printer or fax machine. Fortunately, Access allows you to undo up to your 20 most recent actions in Report Design View.

   QUICK TIP

   The quick keystroke for Undo is [Ctrl][Z]. The quick keystroke for Redo is [Ctrl][Y].

5. **With the Category text box still selected, click the Undo button ↶ on the Report Design toolbar to remove the background color, click ↶ to remove the font color, then click the Redo button ↷ to redo the font color**

   If you undo more actions than desired, use the Redo command on the Edit menu to redo the last undone action. The Redo menu command changes depending on the last undone action, and it can be used to redo up to 20 undone actions.

6. **Click the Line/Border Color list arrow 🖉 ▾, click the dark blue color (first row, second to last column), then click the Print Preview button 🔍**

   The screen should look like Figure D-15.

   QUICK TIP

   If you want your name on the printout, switch to Report Design View and add your name as a label to the Page Header section.

7. **Click File on the menu bar, click Print, type 1 in the From text box, type 1 in the To text box, then click OK**

8. **Close the Inventory Report, then click Yes when prompted to save it**

FIGURE D-14: Formatting a report

Formatting toolbar

Category text box is selected

Fill/Back Color button

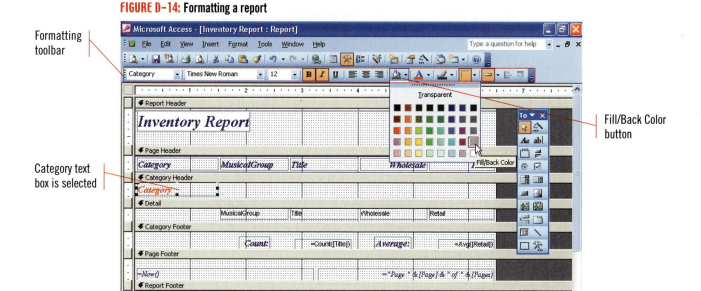

FIGURE D-15: Formatted Inventory Report

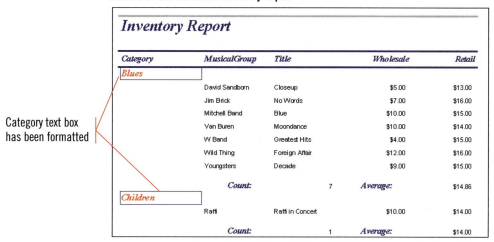

Category text box has been formatted

TABLE D-3: Useful formatting commands

button	button name	description
B	Bold	Toggles bold on or off for the selected control(s)
I	Italic	Toggles italics on or off for the selected control(s)
U	Underline	Toggles underline on or off for the selected control(s)
≣	Align Left	Left-aligns the selected control(s) within its own border
≣	Center	Center-aligns the selected control(s) within its own border
≣	Align Right	Right-aligns the selected control(s) within its own border
⬧	Fill/Back Color	Changes the background color of the selected control(s)
A	Font/Fore Color	Changes the text color of the selected control(s)
⬦	Line/Border Color	Changes the border color of the selected control(s)
⬜	Line/Border Width	Changes the style of the border of the selected control(s)
⬜	Special Effect	Changes the special visual effect of the selected control(s)

Changing Page Layout

In order to fit all of the information on a report on a physical sheet of paper, you may need to change the page layout options such as margins or page orientation. If a report contains a large number of columns, for example, you may want to expand the print area by narrowing the margins. Or, you might want to switch from a portrait (8.5" wide by 11" tall) to a landscape (11" wide by 8.5" tall) paper orientation. Kelsey has created a report called Inventory by Artist Report that doesn't display all of the information properly. You modify the page layout options to provide more room on the paper to help solve this problem.

STEPS

1. **Double-click the Inventory by Artist Report to open it in Print Preview, then click with the ⊕ pointer to zoom in on the report as shown in Figure D-16**

   In examining the report, you see that you need more horizontal space on the paper to display all of the labels and field values properly. One way to provide more horizontal space on the report is to switch from portrait to landscape orientation.

2. **Click the Setup button on the Print Preview toolbar, click the Page tab, click the Landscape option button, then click OK**

   In landscape orientation the paper is wider (11") than tall (8.5"). While this orientation works well for reports with many columns of data, you decide that this report doesn't really need to be printed in landscape orientation, but rather, could fit in portrait orientation with an extra inch of horizontal space. You add the extra inch by narrowing the left and right margins from 1" to 0.5".

3. **Click the Setup button, click the Page tab, click the Portrait option button, click the Margins tab, select 1 in the Left box, type 0.5, select 1 in the Right box, type 0.5, then click OK**

   By narrowing the margins, you have an extra inch of horizontal space to work with Report Design View.

4. **Click the Design View button ⬕ on the Print Preview toolbar, then drag the right edge of the report from the 6.5" mark on the horizontal ruler to the 7.5" mark on the horizontal ruler**

   The horizontal ruler tells you the width of the print area. Because a piece of paper is 8.5" wide in portrait orientation and you have specified 0.5" left and right margins, you can expand the width of the print area to 7.5" to give the existing controls more horizontal space.

5. **Use your moving, resizing, and aligning skills to make Report Design View look like Figure D-17**

   Don't worry if your report doesn't look exactly like Figure D-17, but make sure that all of the labels are wide enough to display the text within them, and be sure to widen the MusicalGroup and Title text boxes so that the field values are not cut off when you preview the report. To increase your productivity, use the [Shift] key to click and select more than one control at a time before you move, resize, or align them.

6. **Click the Save button 🖫, then click the Print Preview button 🔍**

   Your new report should look like Figure D-18. You may need to move back and forth between Report Design View and Print Preview making several adjustments before you are satisfied with your report.

7. **When finished improving the report, click File on the menu bar, click Print, click the Pages option button, type 1 in the From box, type 1 in the To box, and then click OK**

8. **Close the Inventory by Artist Report, close the MediaLoft-D.mdb database, then exit Access**

FIGURE D-16: Initial Inventory by Artist List Report

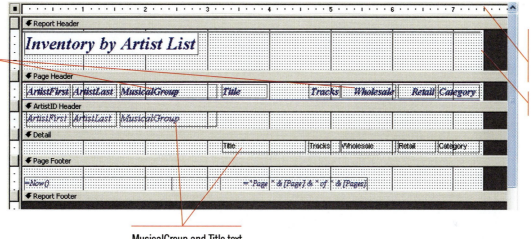

Inventory by Artist List

ArtistFirst	ArtistLast	MusicalG	Title	Tracks	Wholesale	Retail	Category
Kenneth	George	KG					
			KG Live	11	$5.00	$20.00	Rock
			Skyline Fire	10	$14.00	$18.00	NewAge
David	Lantz	Lantz Orc					
			Sacred Roa	12	$6.00	$17.00	Gospel
			Heartsound	14	$7.00	$17.00	Gospel
Leonard	Bernard	Leonard B					
			Favorite Ov	5	$10.00	$15.00	Classical
			Handel's M	11	$6.00	$12.00	Classical

These labels are not displaying properly

Information in MusicalGroup and Title text boxes doesn't display properly

FIGURE D-17: Design View of widened Inventory by Artist Report

Labels are widened to clearly display all text

MusicalGroup and Title text boxes have been widened

7.5" mark on horizontal ruler

Right edge of report

FIGURE D-18: Final Inventory by Artist Report

Inventory by Artist List

ArtistFirst	ArtistLast	MusicalGroup	Title	Tracks	Wholesale	Retail	Category
Kenneth	George	KG					
			KG Live	11	$5.00	$20.00	Rock
			Skyline Firedance	10	$14.00	$18.00	NewAge
David	Lantz	Lantz Orchestra					
			Sacred Road	12	$6.00	$17.00	Gospel
			Heartsounds	14	$7.00	$17.00	Gospel
Leonard	Bernard	Leonard Bernard					
			Favorite Overtures	5	$10.00	$15.00	Classical
			Handel's Messiah	11	$6.00	$12.00	Classical

Report now clearly displays all labels

All text boxes are wide enough to display field values

Practice

▼ CONCEPTS REVIEW

Label each element of the Report Design View window shown in Figure D-19.

FIGURE D-19

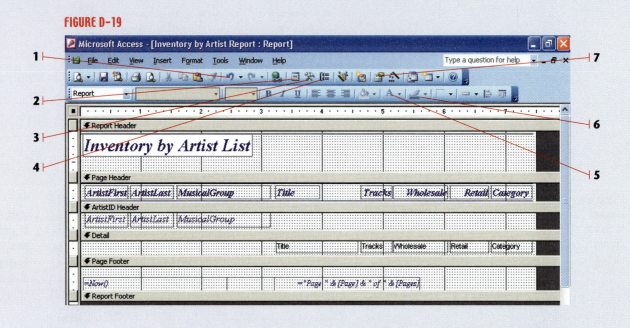

Match each term with the statement that best describes it.

8. **Expression**
9. **Section**
10. **Detail section**
11. **Record Source property**
12. **Formatting**
13. **Grouping**

a. Prints once for every record
b. Determines where a control will display on the report and how often it will print
c. Used to identify which fields and records are passed to the report
d. Enhancing the appearance of information displayed in the report
e. Sorting records *plus* providing a section before and after the group of records
f. A combination of field names, operators, and functions that result in a single value

Select the best answer from the list of choices.

14. Press and hold which key to select more than one control in Report Design View?
  a. [Alt]
  b. [Ctrl]
  c. [Shift]
  d. [Tab]

15. Which type of control is most commonly placed in the Detail section?
  a. Combo box
  b. Label
  c. List box
  d. Text box

16. Which type of control is most commonly placed in the Page Header section?
  a. Bound image
  b. Combo box
  c. Command button
  d. Label

17. A calculated expression is most often placed in which report section?
  a. Detail
  b. Formulas
  c. Group Footer
  d. Report Header

18. Which of the following would be the appropriate expression to count the number of records using the FirstName field?
  a. =Count(FirstName)
  b. =Count[FirstName]
  c. =Count{FirstName}
  d. =Count([FirstName])

19. To align the edges of several controls with respect to one another, you use the alignment commands on the:
  a. Format menu.
  b. Formatting toolbar.
  c. Print Preview toolbar.
  d. Standard toolbar.

20. Which of the following may *not* be changed in the Page Setup dialog box?
  a. Font size
  b. Margins
  c. Paper orientation
  d. Paper size

▼ SKILLS REVIEW

1. Plan a report.

   a. Plan a report to use for tracking members of a ski club. You want to list the member names, their employer, address, dues owed, dues paid, and membership status (Active or Inactive).

   b. Sketch the Report Header, Group Header, and Detail sections of the report by using sample data based on the following information:

- The title of the report should be **Membership Report**.
- The records should be grouped by the Status field so that Active members are listed before Inactive members.
- The Detail section should include information on the person, their employer, address, dues owed, and dues paid.

2. Create a report.

   a. Start Access and open the **Club-D.mdb database** from the drive and folder where your Data Files are stored.

   b. Use the Report Wizard to create a report based on the MEMBERS table.

   c. Include the following fields in the following order for the report: STATUS, FNAME, LNAME, DUESOWED, DUESPAID.

   d. Use STATUS as the grouping field, but do not specify any sort orders.

   e. Use the Stepped layout and Portrait orientation.

   f. Use a Casual style and title the report **Membership Status Report**.

   g. Preview the first page of the new report.

3. Use Group sections.

   a. In Report Design View, open the Sorting and Grouping dialog box, then open the STATUS Footer section using the Sorting and Grouping dialog box.

   b. Close the Sorting and Grouping dialog box.

   c. Preview the first page of the new report.

4. Change the sort order.

   a. In Report Design View, open the Sorting and Grouping dialog box, then add LNAME as a sort field in ascending order immediately below the STATUS field.

   b. Close the Sorting and Grouping dialog box, then preview the first page of the new report.

5. Add a calculation.

   a. In Report Design View, add a text box control to the STATUS Footer section just below the DUESOWED field. Change the label to **Subtotal:** and enter the expression **=Sum([DUESOWED])** in the text box.

   b. Add a text box control to the STATUS Footer section just below the DUESPAID field. Delete the accompanying label, and enter the expression **=SUM([DUESPAID])** in the text box.

   c. Use the property sheet to change the Format property for both of the new calculations to Currency, then close the property sheet.

   d. Click the Label button on the Toolbox toolbar, then click in the Report Header section to add a label control. Modify the label to display your name.

   e. Preview both pages of the report.

6. Align controls.

    a. In Report Design View, right-align the new calculated controls in the STATUS Footer section.

    b. Select the three controls in the STATUS Footer section, then align the bottoms of the controls with respect to one another.

    c. Select the DUESOWED text box in the Detail section, and the =Sum([DUESOWED]) calculated expression in the STATUS Footer section, then right-align the controls with respect to one another.

    d. Select the DUESPAID text box in the Detail section, and the =Sum([DUESPAID]) calculated expression in the STATUS Footer section, then right-align the controls with respect to one another.

7. Format controls.

    a. Select the STATUS text box in the STATUS Header section, change the font size to 12 points, bold and italicize the control, then change the Fill/Back color to bright yellow. The Report Design View should look like Figure D-20.

    b. Save, then preview the report.

8. Change page layout.

    a. Use the Page Setup dialog box to change the top margin of the report to 1.5".

    b. Preview, then print the report.

    c. Close and save the Membership Status Report.

    d. Close the Club-D.mdb database, then exit Access.

FIGURE D-20

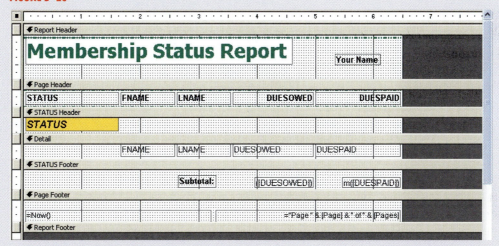

Access 2003

▼ INDEPENDENT CHALLENGE 1

You have been hired to create a report for a physical therapy clinic.

a. Start Access then open the **Therapy-D.mdb database** from the drive and folder where your Data Files are stored.

b. Use the Report Wizard to create a report using all of the fields from the Location Financial Query.

c. View your data by Surveys, group by Street, and sort by PatientLast.

d. Use the Stepped layout, Portrait orientation, and Soft Gray style.

e. Name the report **Location Financial Report**.

f. In Report Design View, open the Street Footer section, then add a text box to the Street Footer section just below the Charges text box in the Detail section.

g. Modify the label to the left of the new text box to display **Subtotal:**

h. Enter an expression in the new text box to sum the Charges field.

i. Right-align the new text box in the Street Footer section and then align the right edges of the new text box in the Street Footer section and the Charges text box in the Detail section with respect to each other.

j. Choose Currency for the Format property of the new text box in the Street Footer section.

k. Click the Label button in the Toolbox toolbar, then click in the Report Header section to add a label control. Modify the label to display your name.

l. Save, then print the first page of the report.

m. Close Location Financial Report, close the Therapy-D.mdb database, then exit Access.

▼ INDEPENDENT CHALLENGE 2

You have been hired to create a report for a physical therapy clinic.

a. Start Access and open the **Therapy-D.mdb database** from the drive and folder where your Data Files are stored.

b. Use the Report Wizard to create a report using all of the fields from the Therapist Satisfaction Query except for the Initials and First fields.

c. View the data by Therapists. Do not add any additional grouping or sorting fields.

d. Use the Block layout, Portrait orientation, and Bold style.

e. Title the report **Physical Therapist Satisfaction Report**, then view the report.

f. In Report Design View, click the Label button in the Toolbox toolbar, then click in the Report Header section to add a label control. Modify the label to display your name.

g. Use the Sorting and Grouping dialog box to group the records by Last. Open the Group Footer section for the Last field.

h. Use the Sorting and Grouping dialog box to further sort the records by PatientLast, then close the Sorting and Grouping dialog box.

i. Add a text box to the Last Footer section below the Courtesy text box in the Detail section. Change the accompanying label to display **Averages:** and enter an expression into the new text box to calculate the average value in the Courtesy field.

j. Add another text box to the Last Footer section below the Knowledge text box in the Detail section. Delete the accompanying label and enter an expression into the new text box to calculate the average in the Knowledge field.

k. Modify the Format property of the two new text boxes in the Last Footer section to be Fixed. Modify the Decimal Places property of the two new text boxes in the Last Footer section to be 1.

l. Resize the new calculated controls so that they are the same size as the Courtesy and Knowledge text boxes in the Detail section.

m. Right-align the two new calculated controls within their own borders.

n. Align the right edge of the text box that calculates the average for the Courtesy field with respect to the Courtesy text box above it. Align the right edge of the text box that calculates the average for the Knowledge field with respect to the Knowledge text box above it.

o. Align the top edges of the new controls in the Last Footer section with respect to each other.

p. Modify the Last label in the Page Header section to read **Therapist**. Be careful to modify the Last label in the Page Header section and not the Last text box in the Detail section.

q. If the report is wider than 6.5" wide, drag the right edge of the report to the left so that the final report is no wider than 6.5".

r. Save, then preview the report. The report should look like Figure D-21.

s. Print then close the Physical Therapist Satisfaction Report.

t. Close the Therapy-D.mdb database, then exit Access.

FIGURE D-21

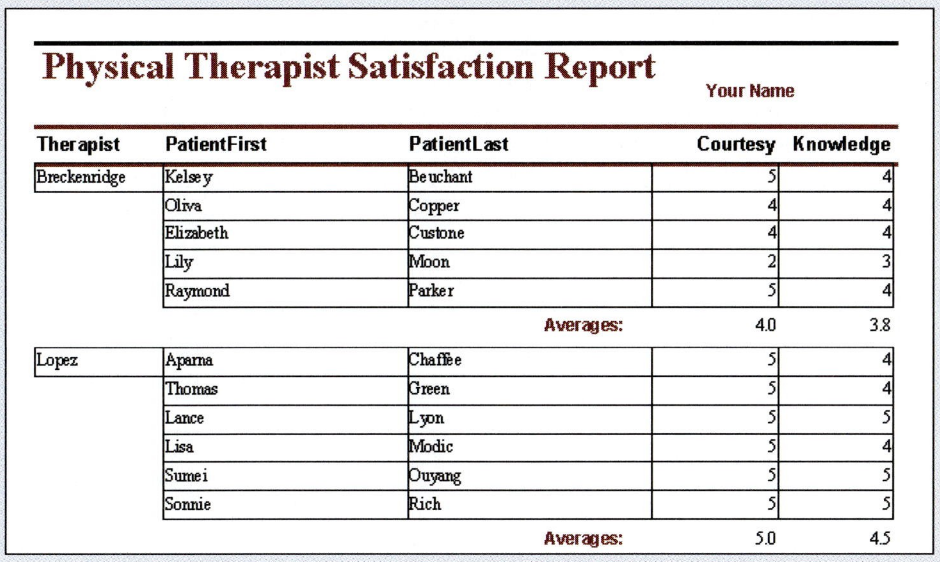

Physical Therapist Satisfaction Report
Your Name

Therapist	PatientFirst	PatientLast	Courtesy	Knowledge
Breckenridge	Kelsey	Beuchant	5	4
	Oliva	Copper	4	4
	Elizabeth	Custone	4	4
	Lily	Moon	2	3
	Raymond	Parker	5	4
		Averages:	4.0	3.8
Lopez	Aparna	Chaffee	5	4
	Thomas	Green	5	4
	Lance	Lyon	5	5
	Lisa	Modic	5	4
	Sumei	Ouyang	5	5
	Sonnie	Rich	5	5
		Averages:	5.0	4.5

▼ INDEPENDENT CHALLENGE 3

You have been hired to modify a report for a physical therapy clinic.

   a. Start Access and open the **Therapy-D.mdb database** from the drive and folder where your Data Files are stored.

   b. Open the Overall Statistics Report in Print Preview, then print the first page so you can examine the problems this report presents because the controls do not have enough horizontal space to display all of the information.

   c. Change the page orientation to landscape, then open Report Design View.

   d. Drag the right edge of the report to the 8" mark on the horizontal ruler.

   e. Click the Label button in the Toolbox toolbar, then click in the Report Header section to add a label control. Modify the label to display your name.

Advanced Challenge Exercise

- Delete the PatientLast label in the Page Header section. Be careful not to delete the PatientLast text box in the Detail section.
- Change the PatientFirst label in the Page Header section to display only the text **Patient**. Be careful to modify the PatientFirst label in the Page Header section and not the PatientFirst text box in the Detail section.
- Change the Font face from Arial to Arial Narrow for the Scheduling, Location, Hours, Courtesy, and Knowledge labels in the Page Header section.
- Use your moving, resizing, and alignment skills so that all of the labels in the Page Header section clearly display all of the text and so that the right edges of these labels are aligned with the right edges of their respective text boxes in the Detail section.

   f. Save, preview, and then print the first page of the report. It should look similar to Figure D-22.

   g. Close the Overall Statistics report, close the Therapy-D.mdb database, then exit Access.

FIGURE D-22

Overall Statistics

Your Name

First	Last	Date	Street	Patient		Scheduling	Location	Hours	Courtesy	Knowledge
Cesar	Lopez									
		10/4/2005	985 North 18th Street	Lance	Lyon	5	4	5	5	5
		12/5/2005	2626 West 74th Street	Sumei	Ouyang	4	4	4	5	5
		2/15/2005	105 South 18th Street	Lisa	Modic	2	4	2	5	4
		7/31/2006	105 South 18th Street	Aparna	Chaffee	5	5	5	5	4
		8/1/2006	985 North 18th Street	Thomas	Green	5	4	4	5	4
		8/2/2006	2626 West 74th Street	Sonnie	Rich	5	5	4	5	5
Douglas	North									
		10/5/2005	985 North 18th Street	Terrance	George	4	4	4	4	4
		2/22/2005	2626 West 74th Street	Lornu	Confetti	1	4	4	4	4
		7/31/2006	105 South 18th Street	Hagrid	Tann	4	3	4	4	4
		8/1/2006	985 North 18th Street	Brook	Black	5	5	5	5	5
		8/1/2006	985 North 18th Street	Karter	Brownline	5	5	4	4	5
		8/1/2006	2626 West 74th Street	Robert	Choe	4	4	5	5	4

▼ INDEPENDENT CHALLENGE 4

You are on the staff of an economic development team whose goal is to encourage tourism in the Baltic Sea region. You have created an Access database called Baltic-D.mdb to track important fields of information for the countries in that region. You have been using the Internet to find information about events and demographics in the area and are entering that information into the database using existing forms. You need to create and then print reports to present to the team.

a. Start Access and open the **Baltic-D.mdb database** from the drive and folder where your Data Files are stored.

b. Connect to the Internet, then go to www.google.com, www.yahoo.com, or another search engine to conduct research for your database. Your goal is to find three upcoming events for Helsinki and Finland and to print the Web pages.

c. Open the Cities form, find the Helsinki record, and enter three events for Helsinki into the Events fields. EventID is an AutoNumber field, so it will automatically increment as you enter the EventName and EventDate information.

Advanced Challenge Exercise

■ Use the Simple Query Wizard to create a query with these fields: City and Country from the Cities table and EventName and EventDate from the Events table. Make the query a Detail query that shows every field of every record and name the query **Baltic Area Festivals**.

■ Use the Report Wizard to create a report based on the Baltic Area Festivals query. Use all of the fields. View the data by Cities, do not add any more grouping levels, and sort the records in ascending order by EventDate.

■ Use an Outline 1 layout, a Portrait orientation, and a Corporate style.

■ Title the report **Baltic Festivals Report**.

■ In Report Design View, click the Label button in the Toolbox toolbar, then click in the Report Header section to add a label control. Modify the label to display your name.

■ Format the report as desired.

■ Save, preview, and print the Baltic Festivals Report, then close it.

d. Close the Baltic-D.mdb database, then exit Access.

▼ VISUAL WORKSHOP

Open the **Club-D.mdb database** from the drive and folder where your Data Files are stored to create the report based on the MEMBERS table. The report is shown in Figure D-23. The Report Wizard, Stepped layout, Portrait orientation, and the Corporate style were used to create this report. Note that the records are grouped by the CITY field and sorted within each group by the LNAME field. A calculated control that counts the number of records is displayed in the City Footer. Add a label with your name to the Report Header section, then save and print the report.

FIGURE D-23

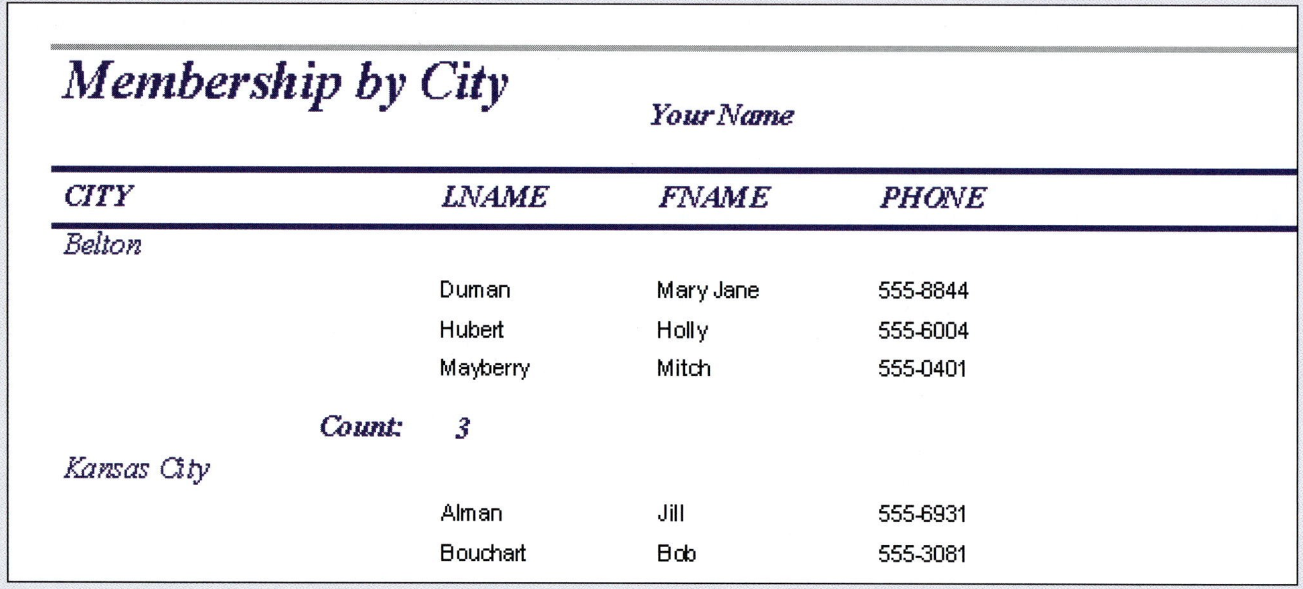

Membership by City

Your Name

CITY	LNAME	FNAME	PHONE
Belton			
	Duman	Mary Jane	555-8844
	Hubert	Holly	555-6004
	Mayberry	Mitch	555-0401
Count: 3			
Kansas City			
	Alman	Jill	555-6931
	Bouchart	Bob	555-3081

Modifying the Database Structure

OBJECTIVES

Examine relational databases

Create related tables

Create one-to-many relationships

Create Lookup fields

Modify Text fields

Modify Number and Currency fields

Modify Date/Time fields

Modify field validation properties

If you have a SAM user profile, you may have access to hands-on instruction, practice, and assessment of the skills covered in this unit. Log in to your SAM account and go to your assignments page to see what your instructor has assigned.

In this unit, you will add a new table to an existing database and link the tables in one-to-many relationships to create a relational database. You will work with fields that have different data types, including Text, Number, Currency, Date/Time, and Yes/No to define the data stored by the database. You will also modify several field properties to format and validate data. Working with Fred Ames, the new coordinator of training at MediaLoft, you created an Access database to track the internal training courses attended by MediaLoft employees. Courses include hands-on computer classes, business seminars, and self-improvement workshops. The database consists of multiple tables that you will link together to create a relational database.

Examining Relational Databases

The purpose of a relational database is to organize and store data in a way that minimizes redundant data yet maximizes the flexibility by which that data may be queried and analyzed. To accomplish these goals, a relational database uses related tables of data rather than a single large table. The Training Department at MediaLoft has attempted to track information about their internal course offerings using a single Access table called Attendance Log, shown in Figure E-1. You see a data redundancy problem because some records duplicate the employee and course information. Therefore, you study the principles of relational database design in order to help the Training Department reorganize these fields into a correctly designed relational database.

DETAILS

To redesign a list into a properly structured relational database, follow these principles:

- **Design each table to contain fields that describe only one subject**

  Currently, the Attendance Log table in Figure E-1 contains three subjects: courses, employees, and attendance data. Putting multiple subjects in a single table creates redundant data. For example, the employee's name must be reentered every time that employee attends a different course. Redundant data causes extra data entry work, a higher rate of data entry inconsistencies and errors, and larger physical storage requirements. Moreover, it limits the user's ability to search for, analyze, and report on the data. These problems are minimized by implementing a properly designed relational database.

- **Identify a primary key field or key field combination for each table**

  A **primary key field** is a field that contains unique information for each record. An Employee Identification or Social Security Number field often serves this purpose in an Employees table. Although using the employee's last name as the primary key field might work in a small database, it is generally a poor choice because it does not accommodate two employees that have the same last name. A **key field combination** is the use of more than one field to uniquely identify each record.

- **Build one-to-many relationships between the tables of your database using a field common to each table**

  To tie the information from one table to another, a field must be common to each table. This common field will be the primary key field on the "one" side of the relationship and the **foreign key field** in the "many" side of the relationship. The primary key field contains a unique entry for each record, but the foreign key field contains the same value in "many" records to create a one-to-many relationship between the tables. Table E-1 describes common examples of one-to-many relationships. Note that the linking field doesn't need to have the same name in both the "one" and "many" tables.

  The new design for the fields of the training database is shown in Figure E-2. One employee may enroll in many courses so the Employees and Enrollments tables have a one-to-many relationship based on the linking EmployeeNo and SSN fields. One course may have many enrollments, so the Courses and Enrollments tables have a one-to-many relationship based on the common CourseID fields.

Clues to Use

Many-to-many relationships

As you are designing your database, you may find that two tables have a **many-to-many** relationship. To join them, you must establish a third table called a **junction table**, which contains two foreign key fields to serve on the "many" side of separate one-to-many relationships with the two original tables. The Employees and Courses tables have a many-to-many relationship because one employee can take many courses and one course may have many employees enrolled in it. The Enrollments table serves as the junction table to link the three tables together.

FIGURE E-1: Attendance Log as a single table

	CourseID	Description	Hours	Prereq	Cost	Last	First	Department	Attended	Passed
▶	Comp1	Computer Concepts	12		$200	Colletti	Shayla	CD	01/29/2006	☑
	Excel1	Introduction to Excel	12	Comp1	$200	Colletti	Shayla	CD	02/12/2006	☑
	Excel2	Intermediate Excel	12	Excel1	$200	Colletti	Shayla	CD	03/07/2006	☑
	ExcelLab	Excel Case Problems	12	Excel2	$200	Colletti	Shayla	CD	03/14/2006	☐
	Internet1	Internet Fundamentals	12	Comp1	$200	Colletti	Shayla	CD	03/14/2006	☑
	Netscape1	Introduction to Netscape	12	Internet1	$200	Colletti	Shayla	CD	04/04/2006	☑
	Outlook1	Introduction to Outlook	12	Comp1	$200	Colletti	Shayla	CD	04/01/2006	☑
	Retail1	Introduction to Retailing	16		$100	Colletti	Shayla	CD	05/07/2006	☑
	Retail2	Store Management	16	Retail1	$100	Colletti	Shayla	CD	05/14/2006	☑
	Word2	Intermediate Word	12	Word1	$200	Colletti	Shayla	CD	02/14/2006	☑
	Word1	Introduction to Word	12	Comp1	$200	Colletti	Shayla	CD	01/18/2006	☑
	Comp1	Computer Concepts	12		$200	Lee	Nancy	Video	01/29/2006	☑
	Access1	Introduction to Access	12	Comp1	$300	Lee	Nancy	Video	02/12/2006	☑
	Internet1	Internet Fundamentals	12	Comp1	$200	Lee	Nancy	Video	03/14/2006	☑
	Netscape1	Introduction to Netscape	12	Internet1	$200	Lee	Nancy	Video	04/04/2006	☑

Duplicate course descriptions

Duplicate employee names

Fields that describe the course

Fields that describe the employee

Fields that describe the enrollment of an employee in a course

FIGURE E-2: Attendance log data split into three related tables

	EmployeeNo	Last	First	Department
▶	115-77-4444	Colletti	Shayla	CD
	134-70-3883	Lee	Nancy	Video
	173-48-5873	Shimada	Jeff	Operations
	222-33-4400	Alber	Lauren	Accounting
	234-56-7800	Rath	Maria	Book
	321-00-8888	Fernandez	Jim	Accounting
	333-33-8887	Dumont	David	Training
	333-44-0099	Hayashi	Jayne	Book
	345-88-0098	Rollo	Miguel	Book

Employees table

	CourseID	Description	Hours	Prereq	Cost
▶	Access1	Introduction to Access	12	Comp1	$300
	Access2	Intermediate Access	24	Access1	$400
	AccessLab	Access Case Problems	12	Access2	$200
	Comp1	Computer Concepts	12		$200
	Excel1	Introduction to Excel	12	Comp1	$200
	Excel2	Intermediate Excel	12	Excel1	$200
	ExcelLab	Excel Case Problems	12	Excel2	$200
	IE1	Introduction to Internet Explorer	12	Internet1	$200
	IE2	Intermediate Internet Explorer	12	Netscape1	$200
	Internet1	Internet Fundamentals	12	Comp1	$200
	Netscape1	Introduction to Netscape	12	Internet1	$200

Courses table

One-to-many link (one employee can enroll many times)

One-to-many link (one course may have many enrollments)

	LogNo	SSN	CourseID	Attended	Passed
▶	1	115-77-4444	Comp1	01/29/2006	☑
	3	134-70-3883	Comp1	01/29/2006	☑
	4	173-48-5873	Comp1	01/29/2006	☑
	5	222-33-4400	Comp1	01/29/2006	☑
	6	234-56-7800	Comp1	01/29/2006	☑
	7	321-00-8888	Comp1	01/29/2006	☑
	8	333-33-8887	Comp1	01/29/2006	☑
	9	333-44-0099	Comp1	01/29/2006	☑
	10	345-88-0098	Comp1	01/29/2006	☑

Enrollments table

TABLE E-1: Common one-to-many relationships

table on "one" side	table on "many" side	linking field	description
Products	Sales	ProductID	A ProductID field must have a unique entry in a Products table, but may be listed many times in a Sales table as many copies of that item are sold
Customers	Sales	CustomerID	A CustomerID field must have a unique entry in a Customers table, but will be listed many times in a Sales table as multiple sales are recorded for the same customer
Employees	Promotions	EmployeeID	An EmployeeID field must have a unique entry in an Employees table, but will be listed many times in a Promotions table as the employee is promoted over time

Creating Related Tables

Once you have developed a valid relational database design, you are ready to define the tables in Access. All characteristics of a table, including field names, data types, field descriptions, field properties, lookup properties, and primary key field designations, are defined in **Table Design View**. Using the new database design, you create the Enrollments table.

STEPS

1. **Start Access, then open the Training-E.mdb database from the drive and folder where your Data Files are stored**

   The Courses and Employees tables already exist in the database. You need to create the Enrollments table.

2. **Click Tables on the Objects bar (if it is not already selected), then click the New button in the Training-E database window**

   The New Table dialog box opens. There are several ways to create a new table. To name and define the fields for a new table, use Table Design View.

3. **Click Design View in the New Table dialog box, then click OK**

   Field names should be as short as possible, but long enough to be descriptive. The field name entered in Table Design View is used as the default name for the field in all later queries, forms, reports, and Web pages.

4. **Type LogNo, press [Enter], click the Data Type list arrow, click AutoNumber, then press [Enter] twice to move to the next row**

   The LogNo field contains a unique number used to identify each record in the Enrollments table (each occurrence of an employee taking a course). The AutoNumber data type, which automatically sequences each new record with the next available integer, works well for this field. Text is the most common data type, but fields that contain dates should have a Date/Time data type, and fields that contain only a value of Yes or No should be defined with a Yes/No data type.

5. **Type the other field names, data types, and descriptions as shown in Figure E-3**

   Field descriptions entered in Table Design View are optional, but are helpful in that they provide further information about the field.

6. **Click LogNo in the Field Name column, then click the Primary Key button on the Table Design toolbar**

   A **key symbol** appears to the left of LogNo to indicate that this field is defined as the primary key field for this table.

7. **Click the Save button on the Table Design toolbar, type Enrollments in the Table Name text box, click OK, then close the table**

   The Enrollments table is now displayed as a table object in the Training-E database window as shown in Figure E-4.

FIGURE E-3: Table Design View for the new Enrollments table

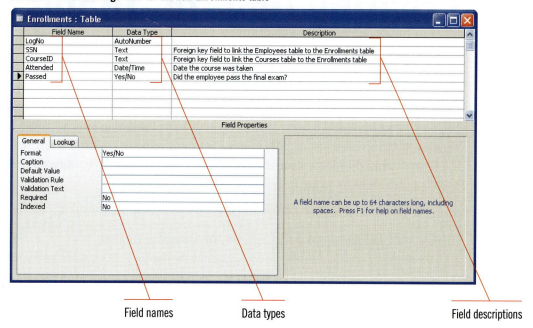

Field names   Data types   Field descriptions

FIGURE E-4: Enrollments table in the Training-E database window

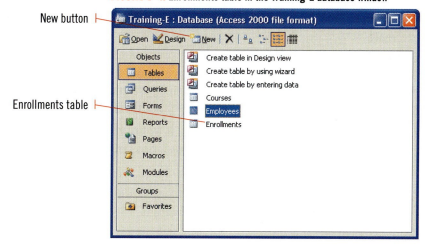

New button

Enrollments table

UNIT E
Access 2003

Creating One-to-Many Relationships

Once the tables have been created, you must link the tables together in appropriate one-to-many relationships before you can build queries, forms, or reports using fields from multiple tables. Your initial database sketch revealed that the SSN field will link the Employees table to the Enrollments table, and that the CourseID field will link the Courses table to the Enrollments table. You define the one-to-many relationships between the tables of the Training-E database.

STEPS

1. **Click the Relationships button on the Database toolbar**

   The Employees and Courses table field lists appear in the Relationships window. The primary key fields are bold.

> **QUICK TIP**
> Drag the table's title bar to move the field list.

2. **Click the Show Table button on the Relationship toolbar, click Enrollments, click Add, then click Close**

   With all three tables visible in the Relationships window, you're ready to link them together.

> **QUICK TIP**
> Drag the bottom border of the field list to display all of the fields.

3. **Scroll the Employees table field list, click EmployeeNo in the Employees table field list, then drag it to the SSN field in the Enrollments table field list**

   Dragging a field from one table to another in the Relationships window links the two tables with the selected fields and opens the Edit Relationships dialog box as shown in Figure E-5. Referential integrity helps ensure data accuracy.

4. **Click the Enforce Referential Integrity check box in the Edit Relationships dialog box, then click Create**

   The **one-to-many line** shows the linkage between the EmployeeNo field of the Employees table and the SSN field of the Enrollments table. The "one" side of the relationship is the unique EmployeeNo value for each record in the Employees table. The "many" side of the relationship is identified by an infinity symbol pointing to the SSN field in the Enrollments table. The CourseID field will link the Courses table to the Enrollments table.

> **TROUBLE**
> Right-click a relationship line, then click Delete if you need to delete a relationship and start over.

5. **Click CourseID in the Courses table field list, drag it to CourseID in the Enrollments table field list, click the Enforce Referential Integrity check box, then click Create**

   The finished Relationships window should look like Figure E-6.

> **QUICK TIP**
> Add your name as a label to the Report Header section in Report Design View if you want your name on the printout.

6. **Click File on the menu bar, click Print Relationships, click the Print button on the Print Preview toolbar, then close the report without saving it**

   A printout of the Relationships window, called the Relationships report, shows how your relational database is designed and includes table names, field names, primary key fields, and one-to-many relationships. This printout is very helpful as you later create queries, forms, and reports that use fields from multiple tables.

7. **Close the Relationships window, then click Yes when prompted to save changes to the layout**

FIGURE E-5: Edit Relationships dialog box

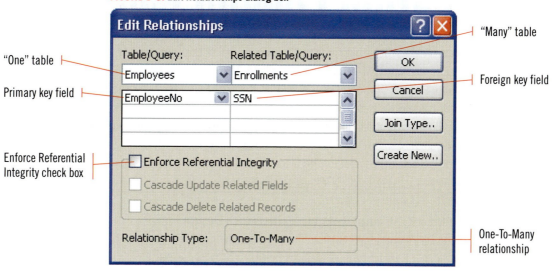

"One" table — Table/Query:

"Many" table

Primary key field — EmployeeNo

Foreign key field

Enforce Referential Integrity check box

One-To-Many relationship

FIGURE E-6: Final Relationships window

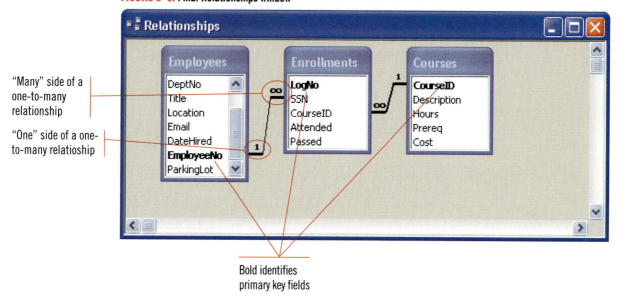

"Many" side of a one-to-many relationship

"One" side of a one-to-many relatioship

Bold identifies primary key fields

Clues to Use

Enforcing referential integrity

Referential integrity is a set of rules that help ensure that no orphan records are entered or created in the database. An **orphan record** is a record in the "many" table that doesn't have a matching entry in the linking field of the "one" table. (For example, an orphan record in the Training database would be a record in the Enrollments table that contains an SSN entry that has no match in the EmployeeNo field of the Employees table, or a record in the Enrollments table that contains a CourseID entry that has no match in the Courses table.) Referential integrity prevents the user from creating orphan records in multiple ways. By enforcing referential integrity you may not enter a value in a foreign key field of the "many" table that does not have a match in the linking field of the "one" table. Referential integrity also prevents you from deleting a record in the "one" table if a matching entry exists in the foreign key field of the "many" table. You should enforce referential integrity on all one-to-many relationships if possible. Unfortunately, if you are working with a database that already contains orphan records, you will not be able to enforce this powerful set of rules.

Creating Lookup Fields

A **Lookup field** is a field that contains Lookup properties. **Lookup properties** are field properties that allow you to supply a drop-down list of values for a field. The values may be stored in another table or entered in the **Row Source** Lookup property of the field itself. Fields that are good candidates for Lookup properties are those that contain a defined set of appropriate values such as State, Gender, or Department. You can set Lookup properties for a field in Table Design View using the **Lookup Wizard**. The ParkingLot field in the Employees table may contain only one of three values: Red, Blue, or Green. You will use the Lookup Wizard to provide these values as a list for this field.

STEPS

1. **Right-click the Employees table, then click Design View**
   You access the Lookup Wizard from the Data Type list for the field for which you want to apply Lookup properties.

2. **Scroll through the fields, click the Text data type for the ParkingLot field, click the Data Type list arrow, then click Lookup Wizard**
   The Lookup Wizard starts and prompts you for information about where the lookup column will get its values.

3. **Click the I will type in the values that I want option button, click Next, click the first cell in the Col1 column, type Red, press [Tab], type Blue, press [Tab], then type Green as shown in Figure E-7**
   These values will populate the lookup value list for the ParkingLot field.

4. **Click Next, then click Finish to accept the default label of ParkingLot and to complete the Lookup Wizard**
   Note that the data type for the ParkingLot field is still Text. The Lookup Wizard is a process for setting Lookup property values for a field, and is not a data type itself.

5. **Click the Lookup tab to observe the new Lookup properties for the ParkingLot field as shown in Figure E-8**
   The Lookup Wizard helped you enter the correct Lookup properties for the ParkingLot field, but you can always enter or edit them directly if you know what values you want to use for each property. The Row Source Lookup property stores the values that are provided in the drop-down list for a Lookup field.

6. **Click the Datasheet View button 🔲 on the Table Design toolbar, click Yes when prompted to save the table, press [Tab] eight times to move to the ParkingLot field, click the ParkingLot list arrow as shown in Figure E-9, then click Blue**
   The ParkingLot field now presents a list of values from which you can select when making an entry in this field.

7. **Close the Employees datasheet**

FIGURE E-7: Entering a Lookup list of values

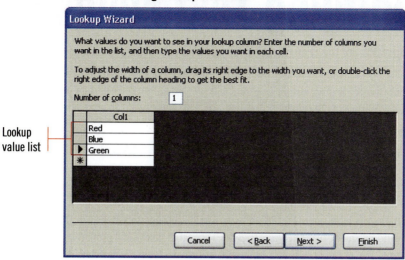

Lookup
value list

FIGURE E-8: Viewing Lookup properties

ParkingLot
field is
selected

Data type
is Text

Lookup tab

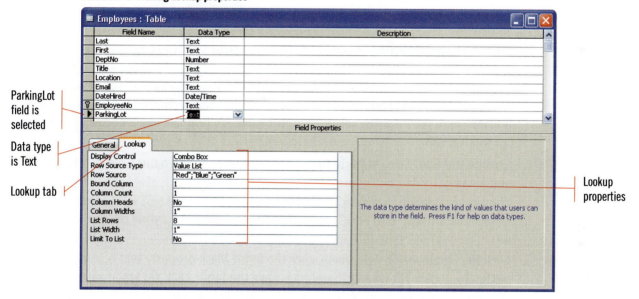

Lookup
properties

FIGURE E-9: Using a Lookup field in a datasheet

		Location	Email	DateHired	EmployeeNo	ParkingLot
⌀	+	San Francisco	nlee@media-loft.com	3/22/1998	134703883	
	+	Corporate	jshimada@media-loft.com	8/20/1998	173485873	Red
	+	Corporate	lalber@media-loft.com	8/6/1998	222334400	Blue
	+	Boston	mrath@media-loft.com	1/3/1997	234567800	Green
	+	Corporate	jfernandez@media-loft.com	7/1/1998	321008888	
	+	Corporate	ddumont@media-loft.com	1/1/1999	333338887	
	+	Seattle	jhayashi@media-loft.com	9/23/1998	333440099	
	+	Kansas City	mrollo@media-loft.com	4/6/1999	345880098	

Modifying Text Fields

Field properties are the characteristics that apply to each field in a table, such as Field Size, Default Value, or Caption. These properties help ensure database accuracy and clarity because they are used to restrict the way data is entered, stored, and displayed. Field properties are modified in Table Design View. See Table E-2 for more information on Text field properties. You decide to make field property changes to several Text fields in the Employees table.

STEPS

1. **If not already selected, click Tables on the Objects bar, right-click the Employees table, then click Design View on the shortcut menu**

   The Employees table opens in Design View. The field properties appear in the lower half of the Table Design View window and display the properties of the selected field. Field properties change depending on the field's data type. For example, when a field with a Text data type is selected, the Field Size property is visible. However, when a field with a Date/Time data type is selected, Access controls the Field Size property, so that property is not displayed. Many field properties are optional, but if they require an entry, Access provides a default value.

2. **Press [↓] to move through each field while viewing the field properties in the lower half of the window**

   A small black triangle in the **field selector button** to the left of the field indicates which field is currently selected.

3. **Click the Last field name, double-click 50 in the Field Size property text box, then type 30**

   Fifty is the default value for the Field Size property for a Text field, but you do not anticipate last name field values to be greater than 30. In general, making the Field Size property for Text fields as small as needed to accommodate the longest entry helps the database be more efficient. Changing the Field Size property for a field that stored two-letter state abbreviations to 2 would also help data accuracy because it would prevent typos such as TXX.

QUICK TIP

Press [F6] to move between field names and field properties in Table Design View.

4. **Change the Field Size property to 30 for the following field names: First, Title, Location, and Email**

   Changing the Field Size property to 30 for each of these text fields in this table will accommodate the longest entry you anticipate for each field. The **Input Mask** property provides a visual guide for users as they enter data. It also helps determine what types of values can be entered into a field.

TROUBLE

If the Input Mask Wizard is not installed on your computer, you can install it now or complete this step by typing 000-00-0000;;_ directly into the Input Mask property for the EmployeeNo field.

5. **Click the EmployeeNo field name, click the Input Mask property text box, click the Build button [...], click Yes when prompted to save the table, click Yes when alerted that some data may be lost (a result of changing the Field Size property from 50 to 30 in the previous steps, but because the entries are less than 30 characters, no data is actually lost), click Social Security Number, then click Finish**

   Table Design View of the Employees table should look like Figure E-10. Notice that the EmployeeNo field is selected and the new Input Mask property is entered. The EmployeeNo field is also the primary key field for the Employees table as evidenced by the key symbol beside the field name.

6. **Click the Save button [💾] on the Table Design toolbar, click the Datasheet View button [📄] on the Table Design toolbar, press [Tab] enough times to move to the EmployeeNo field for the first record, then type 115774444**

   The SSN Input Mask property creates an easy-to-use visual guide to facilitate accurate data entry.

7. **Close the Employees table**

FIGURE E-10: Changing Text field properties

Employees table

EmployeeNo field is selected

Input Mask property

Build button

Short description of selected property

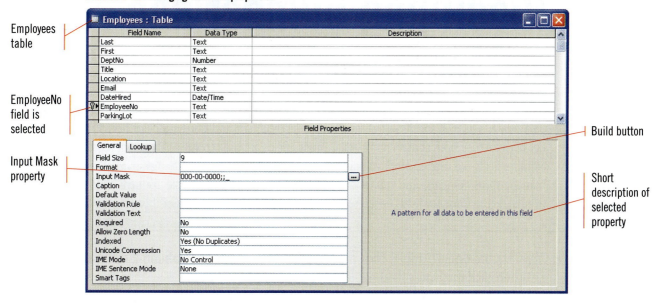

TABLE E-2: Common Text field properties

property	description	sample field	sample property entry
Field Size	Controls how many characters can be entered into the field	State	2
Format	Controls how information will be displayed and printed	State	> (forces all characters to display in uppercase)
Input Mask	Provides a pattern for data to be entered	Phone	(999) 000-0000;1;_
Caption	A label used to describe the field in the first row of a datasheet, form, or report. If the Caption property is not entered, the field name itself is used to label the field.	Emp#	Employee Number
Default Value	Value that is automatically entered in the given field for new records	City	Kansas City
Required	Determines if an entry is required for this field	LastName	Yes

Access 2003

Clues to Use

Input Mask property

The Input Mask property provides a pattern for data to be entered using three parts separated by semicolons. The first part provides a pattern for what type of data can be entered. For example, 9 represents an optional number, 0 a required number, ? an optional letter, and L a required letter. The second part determines whether all displayed characters (such as dashes in a phone number) are stored in the field. For the second part of the input mask, a 0 entry stores all characters such as 555-7722, and a 1 entry stores only the entered data, 5557722. The third part of the input mask determines which character Access uses to guide the user through the mask. Common choices are the asterisk (*), underscore (_), or pound sign (#).

Modifying Number and Currency Fields

Even though some of the properties for Number and Currency fields are the same as for Text fields, each data type has its own specific list of valid properties. Numeric and Currency fields have very similar properties because they both contain numbers. Currency fields are used to store values that represent money, and Number fields are used to store values that represent all other types of numeric values such as quantities, numeric measurements, and numeric scores. The Courses table contains both a Number field (Hours), and a Currency field (Cost). You decide to modify the properties of these two fields.

STEPS

1. **Click the Courses table, click the Design button** in the Training-E database window, **then click the Hours field name**

   The Field Size property for a Number field defaults to Long Integer. See Table E-3 for more information on the options for the Field Size property of a Number field including Long Integer. Access controls the size of Currency fields to control the way numbers are rounded in calculations, so the Field Size property isn't available for Currency fields.

2. **Click Long Integer in the Field Size property text box, click the Field Size list arrow, then click Byte**

   Choosing a Byte value for the Field Size property allows entries from 0 to 255, so it greatly restricts the possible values and the storage requirements for the Hours field.

3. **Click the Cost field name, click Auto in the Decimal Places property text box, click the Decimal Places list arrow, then click 0**

   Your screen should look like Figure E-11. Because all of MediaLoft's courses are priced at a round dollar value, there is no need to display cents in the Cost field.

4. **Click the Save button** on the Table Design toolbar, **then click the Datasheet View button** on the Table Design toolbar

   Because none of the entries in the Hours field is greater than 255, the maximum value allowed by a Number field with a Byte Field Size, you won't lose any data. You want to test the new property changes.

5. **Press [Tab] twice to move to the Hours field for the first record, type 1000, then press [Tab]**

   Because 1000 is larger than the Byte Field Size property will allow (0–255), you are cautioned with an Access error message indicating that the value isn't valid for this field.

6. **Click OK, press [Esc] to remove the inappropriate entry in the Hours field, then press [Tab] twice to move to the Cost field**

   The Cost field is set to display zero digits after the decimal point.

7. **Type 199.75 in the Cost field of the first record, press [Enter], then click $200 in the Access1 record's Cost field**

   Even though the Decimal Places property for the Cost field dictates that entries in the field are formatted to display zero digits after the decimal point, 199.75 is the actual value stored in the field. Modifying the Decimal Places does not change the actual data. Rather, the Decimal Places property only changes the way the data is displayed.

8. **Click the Undo button** on the Table Datasheet toolbar to restore the Cost entry to **$200, then close the Courses table**

FIGURE E-11: Changing Currency and Number field properties

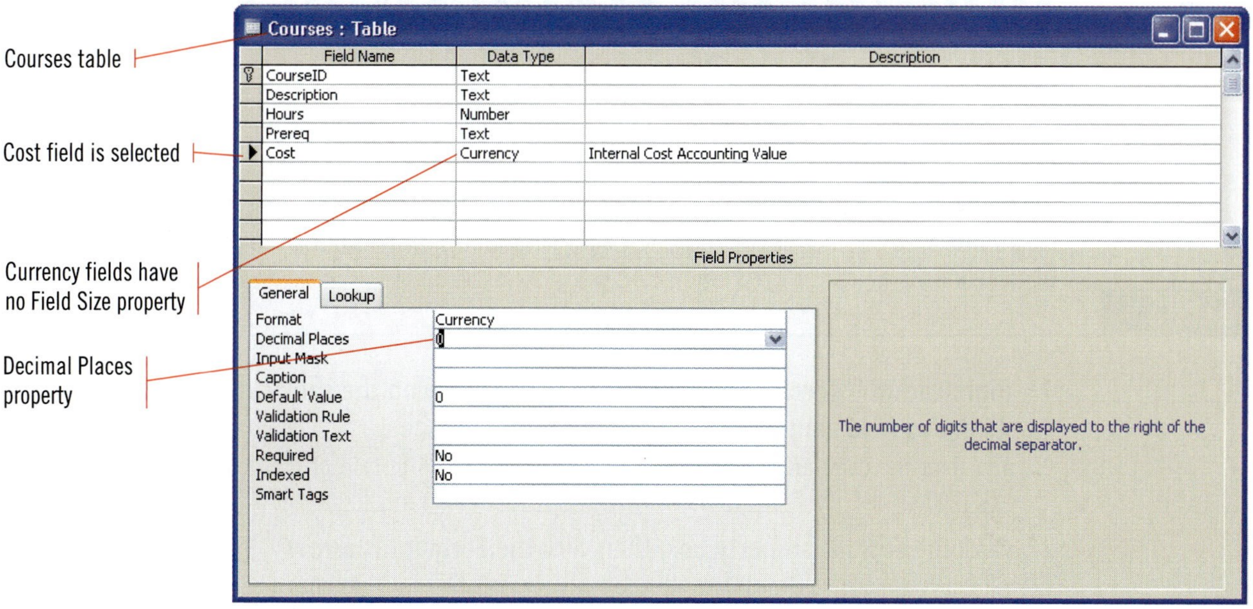

Courses table

Cost field is selected

Currency fields have no Field Size property

Decimal Places property

Courses : Table

	Field Name	Data Type	Description
🔑	CourseID	Text	
	Description	Text	
	Hours	Number	
	Prereq	Text	
▶	Cost	Currency	Internal Cost Accounting Value

Field Properties

General | Lookup

Format	Currency
Decimal Places	0
Input Mask	
Caption	
Default Value	0
Validation Rule	
Validation Text	
Required	No
Indexed	No
Smart Tags	

The number of digits that are displayed to the right of the decimal separator.

TABLE E-3: Common Number field properties

property	description
Field Size	Determines the largest number that can be entered in the field, as well as the type of data (e.g., integer or fraction)
	Byte stores numbers from 0 to 255 (no fractions)
	Integer stores numbers from –32,768 to 32,767 (no fractions)
	Long Integer stores numbers from –2,147,483,648 to 2,147,483,647 (no fractions)
	Single stores numbers (including fractions with six digits to the right of the decimal point) times 10 to the –38th to +38th power
	Double stores numbers (including fractions with over 10 digits to the right of the decimal point) in the range of 10 to the –324th to +324th power
Decimal Places	The number of digits displayed to the right of the decimal point

Modifying Date/Time Fields

Many of a Date/Time field's other properties such as Input Mask, Caption, and Default Value are very similar to fields with a Text or Number data type. Of special interest to a Date/Time field, however, is the **Format** property, which helps you format dates in many ways such as January 25, 2006; 25-Jan-06; or 01/25/2006. You want to change the format of Date/Time fields in the database so that two digits are displayed for the month and day values, and four digits are displayed for the year, for example, 05/31/2006.

STEPS

1. **Right-click the Enrollments table, click Design View on the shortcut menu, then click the Attended field name**

   You want the dates of Enrollments to appear as 01/17/2006 instead of the default presentation of dates, 1/17/2006.

2. **Click the Format property box, then click the Format list arrow**

   Although several predefined Date/Time formats are available, none matches the format you want. To define a custom format, enter symbols that represent how you want the date to appear.

3. **Type mm/dd/yyyy then press [Enter]**

   The updated Format property for the Attended field shown in Figure E-12 forces the date to appear with two digits for the month, two digits for the day, and four digits for the year. The parts of the date are separated by forward slashes.

4. **Click the Save button on the Table Design toolbar**

   The Property Update Options button appears to the left of the property and provides options that help you apply the property change you made to other places that the field appears, such as forms or reports. At this point, however, you haven't built any forms or reports in this database so you don't need to use this feature.

5. **Click the Datasheet View button on the Table Design toolbar**

   You want to test the new Format property for the Attended field so you'll add a new record to see how it works.

6. **Press [Tab] to move to the SSN field, type 115774444, press [Tab], type Comp1, press [Tab], type 1/25/06, press [Tab], then press [Spacebar]**

   Your screen should look like Figure E-13. The new record is entered into the Enrollments table. The Format property for the Attended field makes the entry appear as 01/25/2006 as desired.

FIGURE E-12: Changing Date/Time field properties

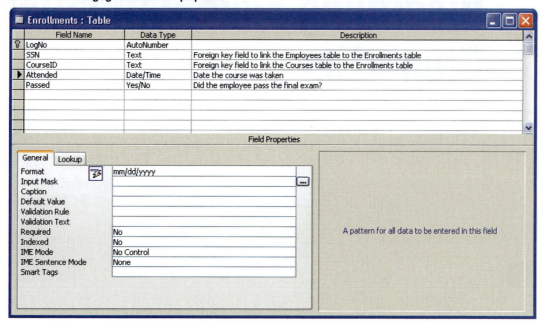

FIGURE E-13: Testing the Format property for the Attended field

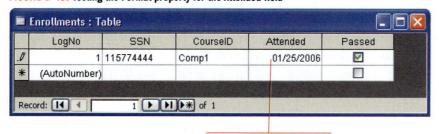

Format property forces the
Attended field to display dates
in a mm/dd/yyyy format

Clues to Use

Smart Tags

The Property Update Options button ⚡ is an Access Smart Tag. **Smart Tags** are buttons that automatically appear under certain conditions. They provide a small menu of options to help you work with the task at hand. Access provides two Smart Tags: the **AutoCorrect Options button** ⚡, which helps you correct typos (or when it appears as the Property Update Options, apply property changes to other areas of the database where a field is used), and the **Error Indicator button** 🔶, which helps identify potential design errors. For example, if you were working in Form Design View and added a text box to the form but did not correctly bind it to an underlying field, the Error Indicator button would appear by that text box to alert you to the problem.

Modifying Field Validation Properties

The Validation Rule and Validation Text field properties can help you prevent unreasonable entries for a field by establishing rules for an entry before it is accepted into the database. The **Validation Rule** property determines if an entry may be accepted. For example, a Validation Rule for a Date/Time field might indicate that valid dates must be on or after 1/1/2006. A Validation Rule for a Currency field might indicate that valid entries must be between $0 and $200. The **Validation Text** property is used to display an explanatory message when a user tries to enter data that isn't accepted by the Validation Rule. MediaLoft started providing in-house courses on January 17, 2004. Therefore, it wouldn't make sense to enter a date in the Attended field prior to 1/17/2004, and you decide to modify the validation properties of the Attended field to prevent the entry of dates prior to 1/17/2004.

STEPS

1. **Click the Design View button on the Table Datasheet toolbar, click the Attended field, click the Validation Rule property box, then type >=1/17/2004**

   This entry forces all dates in the Attended field to be greater than or equal to 1/17/2004. See Table E-4 for more examples of Validation Rule expressions. The Validation Text property provides a helpful message to the user in the event that the entry in the field isn't within the rule entered in the Validation Rule property.

2. **Click the Validation Text box, then type Date must be on or after 1/17/2004**

   The Design View of the Enrollments table should now look like Figure E-14. Once again, Access modified a property to include additional syntax by changing the entry in the Validation Rule property to >=#1/17/2004#. Pound signs (#) are used to surround date criteria.

3. **Click the Save button on the Table Design toolbar, then click Yes when asked to test the existing data with new data integrity rules**

   Because there are no dates in the Attended field earlier than 1/17/2004, there are no date errors in the current data, and the table is saved. You now want to test the Validation Rule and Validation Text properties as they work when entering data in the datasheet.

QUICK TIP
Access assumes that years entered with two digits from 30 to 99 refer to the years 1930 through 1999, and 00 to 29 refers to the years 2000 through 2029. To enter a year before 1930 or after 2029, enter all four digits of the year.

4. **Click the Datasheet View button on the Table Design toolbar, press [Tab] three times to move to Attended field, type 1/1/02, then press [Tab]**

   Because you tried to enter a date that was not true for the Validation Rule property for the Attended field, a dialog box opens and displays the Validation Text entry as shown in Figure E-15.

5. **Click OK to close the validation message**

   You now know that the Validation Rule and Validation Text properties work properly.

6. **Press [Esc] to reject the invalid date entry in the Attended field**

7. **Close the Enrollments table, then close the Training-E.mdb database and exit Access**

FIGURE E-14: Using the validation properties

Attended field is selected

Validation Rule property

Validation Text property

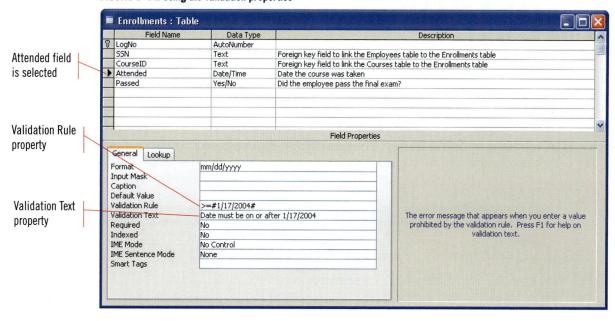

FIGURE E-15: Validation Text message

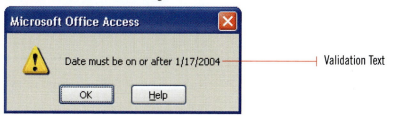

Validation Text

TABLE E-4: Validation Rule expressions

data type	validation rule expression	description
Number or Currency	>0	The number must be positive
Number or Currency	>10 And <100	The number must be between 10 and 100
Number or Currency	10 Or 20 Or 30	The number must be 10, 20, or 30
Text	"IA" Or "NE" Or "MO"	The entry must be IA, NE, or MO
Date/Time	>=#1/1/93#	The date must be on or after 1/1/1993
Date/Time	>#1/1/05# And <#1/1/06#	The date must be between 1/1/2005 and 1/1/2006

Practice

▼ CONCEPTS REVIEW

Identify each element of Table Design View shown in Figure E-16.

FIGURE E-16

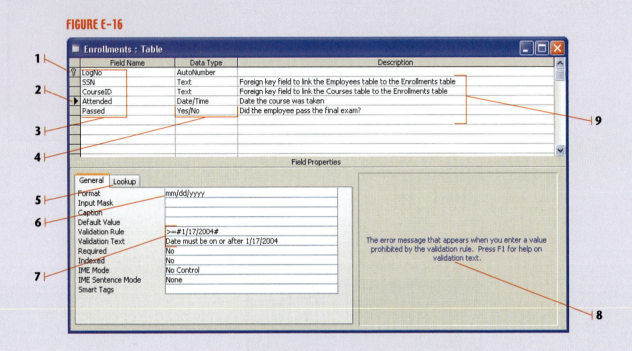

Match each term with the statement that best describes it.

10. Primary key field
11. Validation properties
12. Table Design View
13. Row Source
14. Relational database
15. Input Mask
16. Lookup properties

a. Several tables linked together in one-to-many relationships
b. Field that holds unique information for each record in the table
c. Field properties that help you prevent unreasonable data entries for a field
d. Field properties that allow you to supply a drop down of values for a field
e. Field property that provides a visual guide as you enter data
f. Lookup property that determines where the Lookup field gets its list of values
g. Access window where all characteristics of a table, such as field names and field properties, are defined

Select the best answer from the list of choices.

17. **Which of the following problems most clearly indicates that you need to redesign your database?**
    a. There is duplicated data in the field of several records of a table.
    b. Referential integrity is enforced on table relationships.
    c. Not all fields have Validation Rule properties.
    d. The Input Mask Wizard has not been used.

18. **Which of the following is *not* defined in Table Design View?**
    a. The primary key field
    b. Duplicate data
    c. Field Size properties
    d. Field data types

19. **What is the purpose of enforcing referential integrity?**
    a. To prevent orphan records from being entered
    b. To prevent incorrect entries in the primary key field
    c. To require an entry for each field of each record
    d. To force the application of meaningful validation rules

20. **To create a many-to-many relationship between two tables, you must create:**
    a. Foreign key fields in each table.
    b. Combination primary key fields in each table.
    c. A one-to-many relationship between the two tables with referential integrity enforced.
    d. A junction table.

▼ SKILLS REVIEW

1. **Examine relational databases.**
   a. Write down the fields needed to create an Access relational database to manage the membership information that a philanthropic club, community service organization, or special interest group might track.
   b. Identify those fields that contain duplicate values if all of the fields were stored in a single table.
   c. Group the fields into subject matter tables, and then identify the primary key field for each table.
   d. Pretend that your database will contain two tables: Members and Zipcodes. If you did not identify these two tables earlier, regroup the fields within these two table names, and then identify the primary key field for each table, the foreign key field in the Members table, and how the tables would be related using a one-to-many relationship.

2. **Create related tables.**
   a. Start Access, then click the Create a new file link at the bottom of the Open section of the Getting Started task pane.
   b. Click the Blank database link in the New File task pane. Navigate to the folder where your Data Files are stored, type **Membership-E** in the File name box, then click Create.
   c. Create a new table using Table Design View with the following field names and data types:
   FirstName, Text
   LastName, Text
   Street, Text
   Zip, Text
   Birthdate, Date/Time
   Dues, Currency
   MemberNo, Text
   MemberType, Text
   CharterMember, Yes/No
   d. Specify MemberNo as the primary key field, save the table with the name **Members**, then close it.

    e. Create a new table using Table Design View with the following field names and data types:

       Zip, Text

       City, Text

       State, Text

    f. Identify Zip as the primary key field, save the table as **Zipcodes**, then close it.

    g. Create a new table using Table Design View with the following field names and data types:

       ActivityNo, AutoNumber

       MemberNo, Text

       ActivityDate, Date/Time

       Hours, Number

    h. Identify ActivityNo as the primary key field, save the table as **Activities**, then close it.

3. Create one-to-many relationships.

    a. Open the Relationships window, double-click Activities, double-click Members, then double-click Zipcodes to add all three tables to the Relationships window. Close the Show Table dialog box.

    b. Resize all field lists so that all fields are visible, then drag the Zip field from the Zipcodes table to the Zip field in the Members table to create a one-to-many relationship between the Zipcodes table and Members table using the common Zip field.

    c. Enforce referential integrity for this relationship.

    d. Drag the MemberNo field from the Members table to the MemberNo field in the Activities table to create a one-to-many relationship between the Members and the Activities table using the common MemberNo field.

    e. Enforce referential integrity for this relationship.

    f. Click File on the menu bar, click Print Relationships to create a report of the Relationships window, add your name as a label to the Report Header section if desired, and then print the report.

    g. Close the Relationships report without saving the report, and then close the Relationships window. Save the changes to the Relationships window if prompted.

4. Create Lookup fields.

    a. Open the Members table in Design View, then start the Lookup Wizard for the MemberType field.

    b. Select the option that allows you to enter your own values, enter **Active**, **Inactive**, and **Senior** as the values for the lookup column, and then accept the rest of the Lookup Wizard defaults.

    c. Save the table. In Datasheet View, tab to the MemberType field and click the list arrow to make sure the three values were entered properly for the Lookup field.

    d. Press Esc twice to remove any edits to the first record of the Members table, then close the Members table.

5. Modify Text fields.

    a. Open the Zipcodes table in Design View.

    b. Change the Field Size property of the State field to **2**.

    c. Use the Input Mask Wizard to create an Input Mask property for the Zip field. Choose the Zip Code Input Mask. Accept the other default options provided by the Input Mask Wizard. (*Note*: If the Input Mask Wizard is not installed on your computer, type **00000\-9999;;_** for the Input Mask property for the Zip field.)

    d. Save the Zipcodes table, then close it.

    e. Open the Members table in Design View.

    f. Change the Field Size property of the FirstName, LastName, and Street fields to **30**. Save the changes to the table.

    g. Use the Input Mask Wizard to create the Input Mask property for the Zip field. Choose the Zip Code input mask. Accept the other default options provided by the Input Mask Wizard. (*Note*: If the Input Mask Wizard is not installed on your computer, type **00000\-9999;;_** for the Input Mask property for the Zip field.)

    h. Save the changes, then close the Members table.

6. **Modify Number and Currency fields.**

   a. Open the Members table in Design View.

   b. Change the Decimal Places property of the Dues field to **0**. Save the table then close the Members table.

   c. Open the Activities table in Design View.

   d. Change the Field Size property of the Hours field to **Byte**. Save the table then close the Activities table.

7. **Modify Date/Time fields.**

   a. Open the Members table in Design View.

   b. Change the Format property of the Birthdate field to **mm/dd/yyyy**.

   c. Save the table, then close the Members table.

   d. Open the Activities table in Design View.

   e. Change the Format property of the ActivityDate field to **mm/dd/yyyy**.

   f. Save the table, then close the Activities table.

8. **Modify field validation properties.**

   a. Open the Zipcodes table in Design View.

   b. Click the State field name, click the Validation Rule text box, then type **=IA OR KS OR MO**.

   c. Click the Validation Text box, then type **State must be IA, KS, or MO**. Note that Access automatically added quotation marks to the criteria in the Validation Rule property.

   d. Save the changes then open the Zipcodes table in Datasheet View.

   e. Test the Validation Text and Validation Rule properties by entering a new record with the Zip value of **661112222**, a City value of **Blue Valley**, and a State value of **MN**. Click OK when prompted with the Validation Text message, edit the State value to be **IA**, then close the Zipcodes table.

   f. Close the Membership-E.mdb database and then exit Access.

▼ INDEPENDENT CHALLENGE 1

As the manager of a music store's instrument rental program, you have decided to create a database to track instrument rentals to schoolchildren. The fields you need to track are organized with four tables: Instruments, Rentals, Customers, and Schools.

a. Start Access, then create a new blank database called **Music Store-E** in the folder where your Data Files are stored.

b. Use Table Design View to create the four tables in the Music Store-E database using the information in Table E-5. The primary key field for each table is identified with bold text.

c. Enter **>1/1/04** as the Validation Rule property to the RentalDate field of the Rentals table. This change will only allow dates later than 1/1/04 to be entered into this field.

d. Enter **Dates must be after 1/1/2004** as the Validation Text property to the RentalDate field of the Rentals table. Note that Access added pound signs (#) to the date criteria entered in the Validation Rule as soon as you entered the Validation Text property.

e. Save and close the Rentals table.

TABLE E-5: Fields for tables

table	field name	data type
Customers	FirstName	Text
	LastName	Text
	Street	Text
	City	Text
	State	Text
	Zip	Text
	CustNo	Text
	SchoolNo	Text
Instruments	Description	Text
	SerialNo	Text
	MonthlyFee	Currency
Schools	SchoolName	Text
	SchoolNo	Text
Rentals	**RentalNo**	AutoNumber
	CustNo	Text
	SerialNo	Text
	RentalDate	Date/Time

▼ INDEPENDENT CHALLENGE 1 (CONTINUED)

f. Open the Relationships window, add all four tables to the window in the arrangement shown in Figure E-17, and create one-to-many relationships as shown. Be sure to enforce referential integrity on each relationship.

g. Preview the Relationships report, then print the report making sure that all fields of each table are visible. (If you need your name on the printout, add your name as a label to the Report Header.)

h. Close the Relationships report without saving it. Close the Relationships window, then save the layout if prompted.

i. Close the Music Store-E.mdb database, then exit Access.

FIGURE E-17

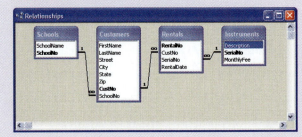

▼ INDEPENDENT CHALLENGE 2

You want to document the books you've read by creating and storing the information in a relational database. You will design the database on paper by identifying the tables, field names, data types, and relationships between the tables.

a. On paper, create three balanced columns by drawing two vertical lines from the top to the bottom of the paper. At the top of the first column write **Table**. At the top of the second column write **Field Name**, and at the top of the third column write **Data Type**.

b. In the middle column, list all of the fields that need to be tracked to record information about the books you've read. You want to track information including the book title, category (such as Biography, Mystery, or Science Fiction), rating (a numeric value from 1–10 that indicates how much you liked the book), date you read the book, author's first name, and author's last name.

c. In the first column, identify the table where this field would be found. (*Hint*: You like to read multiple books from the same author, so you will need to separate the author information into a separate table to avoid duplicate author name entries in the Books table.)

d. Identify the primary key field for each table by circling it. You may have to add a new field to each table if you do not have an existing field that would naturally serve as the primary key field. (*Hint*: Each book has an ISBN—International Standard Book Number—that is a unique number assigned to every book. To uniquely identify each author, use an AuthorNo field. Do not use the AuthorLastName field as the primary key field for the Authors table because it would not uniquely identify authors who have the same last names.)

e. In a third column, identify the appropriate data type for each field.

f. Once all of the field names, table names, and data types are identified for each field, reorder the fields so that the fields for each table are listed together.

g. On a new piece of paper, sketch the field lists for each table as they would appear in the Relationships window of Access. Circle the primary key fields for each table. Include the one-to-many link lines as well as the "one" and "infinity" symbols to identify the "one" and "many" side of the one-to-many relationship. (*Note*: When building a one-to-many relationship between two tables, one field must be common to both tables. To create a common field, you may need to go back to your field lists in Step f and add a foreign key field to the table on the "many" side of the relationship in order to link the tables.)

▼ INDEPENDENT CHALLENGE 3

You want to create a database that documents blood bank donations by the employees of your company. You will design the database on paper including the tables, field names, data types, and relationships. You want to track information such as employee name, employee Social Security number, employee department, employee blood type, date of donation, and the hospital that is earmarked to receive the donation. Also, you'll want to track basic hospital information, such as the hospital name and address.

a. Complete Steps a through g as described in Independent Challenge 2 using the new case information. In this case, you should identify three tables: Employees, Donations, and Hospitals. When creating your field lists for each table, don't forget to always separate personal names into at least two fields, FirstName and LastName, so that you can easily sort, filter, and find data based on either part of a person's name.

b. To help determine how you should create the relationships between the tables, note that one employee can make several donations. One hospital can receive many donations.

Advanced Challenge Exercise

■ Build the database you designed in Access with the name **BloodDrive-E.mdb**. Don't forget to enforce referential integrity on the two one-to-many relationships in this database.

■ Print the Relationships report with your name added as a label to the Report Header section. Close the Relationships report without saving it, and then close the Relationships window and save the layout changes.

■ Add Lookup properties to the blood type field to provide only valid blood type entries of **A-**, **A+**, **B-**, **B+**, **O-**, **O+**, **AB-**, and **AB+** for this field.

■ Close BloodDrive-E.mdb, then exit Access.

▼ INDEPENDENT CHALLENGE 4

You are on the staff of an economic development team whose goal is to encourage tourism in the Baltic Sea region. You have created an Access database called Baltic-E to track important fields of information for the countries in that region and will use the Internet to find information about the area and enter it into existing forms.

a. Start Access, then open the **Baltic-E.mdb** database from the drive and folder where your Data Files are stored.

b. Connect to the Internet, and then go to www.google.com, www.lycos.com, or any general search engine to conduct research for your database. Your goal is to find three upcoming events for Munich, Germany, and to print the Web page(s) that provide this information.

c. Open the Cities form, find the Munich record, and enter three more events for Munich into the Events fields. EventID is an AutoNumber field, so it will automatically increment as you enter the EventName and EventDate information.

d. Open the Cities table in Design View, and then add a field called **MemberStatus** with a Text data type and a Field Size property of **11**. This field will be used to document the city's status with your economic development team.

e. Use the Lookup Wizard to provide the values **Active**, **Inactive**, and **No Interest** for the MemberStatus field. Save the Cities table.

Advanced Challenge Exercise

■ Open the Cities table in Datasheet View. Click the expand button to the left of the Munich, Germany, record to see the related records in the Events subdatasheet. Close the Cities table.

■ Using the Report Wizard, create a report based on all four fields in the Baltic Area Festivals query. View the data by Cities, do not add any more grouping levels, and then sort the records by EventDate.

■ Use a Stepped layout, a Portrait orientation, and a Corporate style.

■ Title the report **Baltic Area Events**, and then apply additional formatting embellishments as desired.

■ In Report Design View, add your name as a label to the Report Header section. Save, print, then close the report.

f. Close the Baltic-E.mdb database and then exit Access.

▼ VISUAL WORKSHOP

Open the **Training-E.mdb** database, and create a new table called **Vendors** using the Table Design View shown in Figure E-18 to determine field names and data types. Make the following property changes: Change the Field Size property of the VState field to **2**, the VZip field to **9**, and VPhone field to **10**. Change the Field size property of the VendorName, VStreet, and VCity fields to **30**. Be sure to specify that the VendorID field is the primary key field. Enter one record into the datasheet with your last name in the VendorName field and print the datasheet.

FIGURE E-18

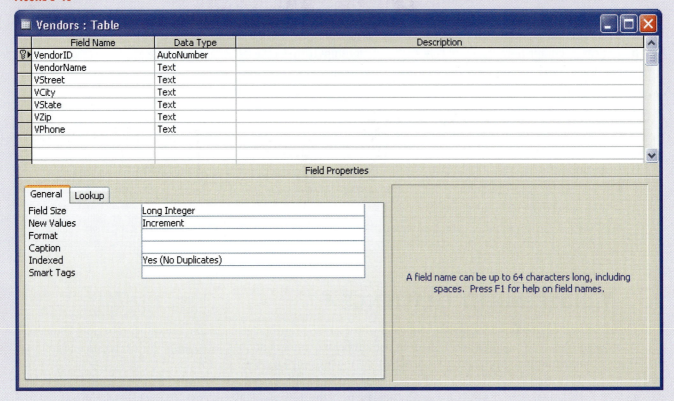

Creating Multiple Table Queries

OBJECTIVES

Build select queries
Sort a query on multiple fields
Develop AND criteria
Develop OR criteria
Create calculated fields
Build summary queries
Build crosstab queries
Build PivotTables and PivotCharts

If you have a SAM user profile, you may have access to hands-on instruction, practice, and assessment of the skills covered in this unit. Log in to your SAM account and go to your assignments page to see what your instructor has assigned.

Queries are database objects that organize fields from one or more tables into a single datasheet. A **select query**, the most common type of query, retrieves fields from related tables and displays records in a datasheet. Select queries are used to select only certain records from a database, and can also sort records, calculate new fields of data, or calculate statistics such as the sum or average of a given field. You can also present data selected by a query in Query PivotTable View or Query PivotChart View. These views display information about summarized groups of records in a crosstabular report or graph. The MediaLoft Training database has been updated so that all three tables (Employees, Enrollments, and Courses) contain data. You help Fred Ames, the coordinator of training, create queries to analyze this information.

Building Select Queries

You can create select queries by using the **Simple Query Wizard** or by building the query in Query Design View. Creating a select query with the Simple Query Wizard is fast and easy, but learning how to use **Query Design View** gives you more flexibility and options regarding the information that you want to select as well as how you want that data presented. When you open (also called "**run**") a query, the fields and records that you have selected for the query are presented as a datasheet in **Query Datasheet View**. Query Datasheet View does not present a duplicate copy of the data stored in the tables. Rather, it displays table data in a new arrangement, sometimes called a **logical view** of the data. If you make any changes to data using a query datasheet, the changes are actually made to the underlying table just as if you were working directly in a table datasheet. Fred asks you to create a query to answer the question, "Who is taking what courses?" You select fields from several tables using Query Design View to display a single datasheet that answers this question.

STEPS

1. **Start Access, then open the Training-F.mdb database from the drive and folder where your Data Files are stored**

2. **Click Queries on the Objects bar, then double-click Create query in Design view**
   The Show Table dialog box opens and lists all the tables in the database. You use the Show Table dialog box to add the tables that contain the fields you want to view in the final query datasheet.

TROUBLE

If you add a table to Query Design View twice by mistake, click the title bar of the extra field list, then press [Delete].

3. **Click Employees, click Add, double-click Enrollments, double-click Courses, then click Close**
   The upper part of Query Design View displays the fields for each of the three selected tables in three small windows called **field lists**. The name of the table associated with each field list is shown in the field list title bar. Primary key fields are bold. To rearrange the field lists in Query Design View, drag the title bar of a field list to move it, or drag the edge of a field list to resize it. Relationships between tables are displayed with **one-to-many join lines** that connect the linking fields, as shown in Figure F-1. The fields that you want the query to display are identified in the **query design grid**, the columns in the lower part of Query Design View.

QUICK TIP

When you drag a field to the query design grid, the existing fields move to the right to accommodate the new field.

4. **Drag the First field in the Employees table field list to the first column of the query design grid**
   The order in which the fields are placed in the query design grid is the order they appear in the datasheet.

5. **Double-click the Last field in the Employees field list, double-click the Registration field in the Enrollments field list, double-click the Description field in the Courses field list, then double-click the Hours field in the Courses field list**
   Query Design View should look like Figure F-2. You may delete a field from the query design grid by clicking the field selector above the field name and pressing [Delete]. Deleting a field from the query design grid removes it from the logical view of this query's datasheet, but does not delete the field from the database. A field is defined and the field's contents are stored in a table object only.

6. **Using the ↓ pointer, click the Hours field selector to select that column of the query design grid, press [Delete], then click the Datasheet View button 🔳 on the Query Design toolbar**
   The resulting datasheet looks like Figure F-3. The datasheet shows the four fields selected in Query Design View, First and Last from the Employees table, Registration from the Enrollments table, and Description from the Classes table. The datasheet displays 153 records that represent the number of times a MediaLoft employee has enrolled in a class. Megan Burik appears in 11 records because she has enrolled in 11 classes.

FIGURE F-1: Query Design View with multiple tables

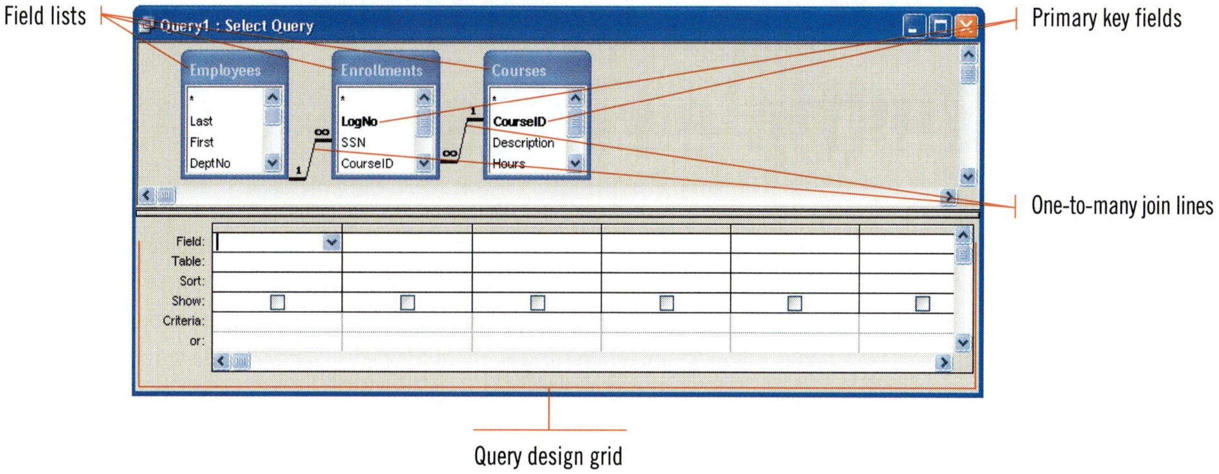

Field lists

Primary key fields

One-to-many join lines

Query design grid

FIGURE F-2: Query Design View with five fields in the query design grid

Datasheet View button

Resize bar

Field selector

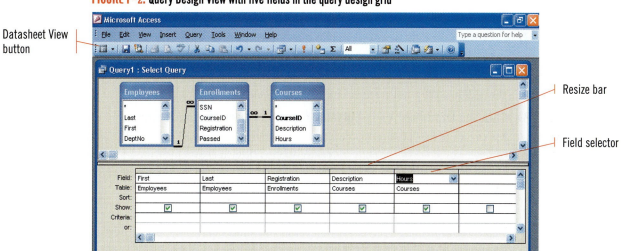

FIGURE F-3: Query datasheet showing related information from three tables

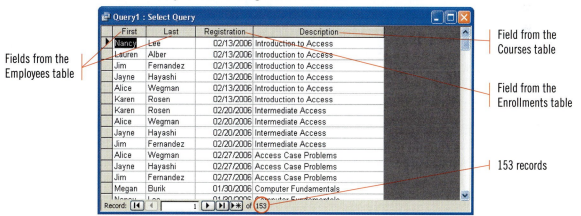

Fields from the Employees table

Field from the Courses table

Field from the Enrollments table

153 records

Clues to Use

Resizing Query Design View

Drag the resize bar up or down to provide more room for the upper (field lists) or lower (query design grid) panes of Query Design View. By dragging the resize bar down, you may have enough room to resize each field list so that you can see all of the field names for each table.

Sorting a Query on Multiple Fields

Sorting refers to reorganizing records in either ascending or descending order based on the values in a field. Queries allow you to specify more than one sort field in Query Design View and evaluate the sort fields from left to right. Therefore, the sort field farthest to the left is the primary sort field. Sort orders defined in Query Design View are saved with the query object. You want to put the records in alphabetical order based on the employee's last name. If the employee attended more than one class, you decide to further sort the records by the registration date of the course.

STEPS

QUICK TIP
You can resize the columns of a datasheet by pointing to the right column border that separates the field names, then dragging ←→ left or right to resize the columns. Double-click ←→ to automatically adjust the column width to fit the widest entry.

1. **Click the Design View button ⊠ on the Query Datasheet toolbar**

   To sort the records by name then by registration date, the Last field must be the primary sort field, and the Registration field the secondary sort field.

2. **Click the Last field Sort cell in the query design grid, click the Sort list arrow, click Ascending, click the Registration field Sort cell in the query design grid, click the Sort list arrow, then click Ascending**

   The resulting query design grid should look like Figure F-4.

3. **Click the Datasheet View button ⊞ on the Query Design toolbar**

   The records of the datasheet are now listed in ascending order based on the values in the Last field, then in chronological order by the entry in the Registration field, as shown in Figure F-5. Maria Abbott attended six classes, but you notice that her name has been incorrectly entered in the database as "Marie." Fix this error in the query datasheet.

4. **Type Maria, then press [↓]**

   Maria's name is pulled from the Employees table six times because she has attended six classes. But because her name is physically stored only once in the database, editing Maria's name in any view changes all other views that use that value as well.

5. **Double-click Fundamentals in the Description field of the third record, type Concepts, then press [↓] to observe the automatic change to Record 8**

   All occurrences of Computer Fundamentals have now been updated to Computer Concepts. A change made to data through a query datasheet automatically updates all other occurrences of that field value. When a query object is saved, it saves **Structured Query Language (SQL)** statements. You can view or work with SQL using Access query objects.

6. **Click the View button list arrow ⊠ ▾ on the Query Datasheet toolbar, then click SQL View**

   The SQL statements determine what fields are selected, how the tables are joined, and how the resulting records will be sorted. Fortunately, you do not have to be able to write or understand SQL to use Access. The easy-to-use Query Design View gives you a way to select and sort data from underlying tables without being an SQL programmer.

7. **Close the SQL window, click Yes when prompted to save the changes, type Employee Registrations in the Query Name text box, then click OK**

   The query is now saved and listed as a query object in the Training-F database window.

FIGURE F-4: Specifying multiple sort orders in Query Design View

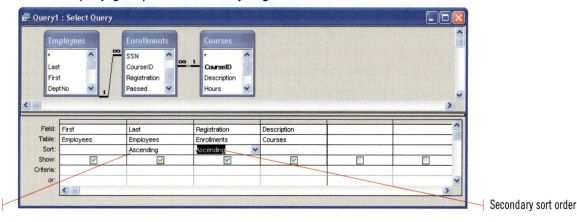

Primary sort order   Secondary sort order

FIGURE F-5: Records sorted by Last, then Registration

Primary sort field   Secondary sort field

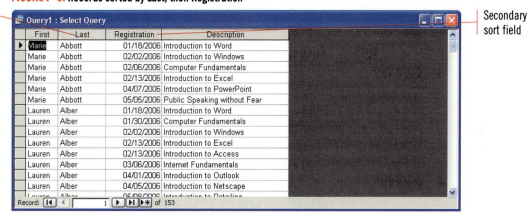

Clues to Use

Specifying a sort order different from the field order in the datasheet

If you had several different employees with the same last name and needed to include a secondary sort on first name but still wanted to display the fields in a first name, last name order, you could use the solution shown in Figure F-6. You can add a field to the query design grid twice and use the Show check box to sort the fields in one order (Last, First, Registration), yet display the fields in the resulting datasheet in another order (First, Last, Registration).

FIGURE F-6: Sorting on a field that is not displayed

Last field is used in query design grid twice

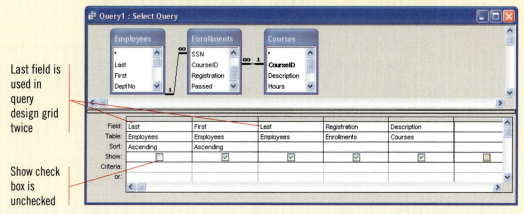

Show check box is unchecked

Access 2003

Developing AND Criteria

You can limit the number of records that appear on the resulting datasheet by entering criteria into Query Design View. **Criteria** are tests, or limiting conditions, for which the record must be true to be selected for a datasheet. To create **AND criteria** enter two or more criteria on the same Criteria row of the query design grid. To create AND criteria for the *same field*, enter the two criteria in the same Criteria cell separated by the AND operator. Fred is looking for a person to assist the Access teacher. To compile a list of potential candidates, you use AND criteria to find all employees who have taken Access courses and who have passed the final exam.

STEPS

1. **Right-click Employee Registrations, click Design View on the shortcut menu, click the View button list arrow on the Query Design toolbar, then click Design View**

   You decide to modify the Employee Registrations query because it already contains most of the data you need. The only additional field you need is the Passed field.

QUICK TIP

Scroll down the Enrollments field list to find the Passed field.

2. **Double-click the Passed field in the Enrollments field list**

   MediaLoft offers several Access courses, so the criteria to find these records must specify that the word "Access" is anywhere in the Description field. You use the asterisk (*), a **wildcard character** that represents any combination of characters, to create this criterion.

QUICK TIP

Criteria are not case sensitive so access, Access, and ACCESS are equivalent criteria entries.

3. **Click the Description field Criteria cell, type *access*, then click the Datasheet View button on the Query Design toolbar**

   The resulting datasheet, as shown in Figure F-7, lists thirteen records that match the criteria. The resulting records all contain the word "access" in some part of the Description field, but because of the placement of the asterisks, it doesn't matter *where* (beginning, middle, or end) Access was found.

4. **Click the Design View button on the Query Datasheet toolbar, click the Passed field Criteria cell, then type yes**

   You added the criterion to display only those records where the Passed field equals Yes as shown in Figure F-8. Access assists you with **criteria syntax**, rules by which criteria need to be entered. Access automatically adds quotation marks around text criteria in Text fields and pound signs (#) around date criteria in Date/Time fields. The criteria in Number, Currency, and Yes/No fields are not surrounded by any characters. In addition, notice that Access added the **Like operator** to the Description field criteria because the wildcard asterisk character was used. See Table F-1 for more information on common Access comparison operators and criteria syntax.

5. **Click on the Query Design toolbar to view the resulting records**

   Criteria added to the same line of the query design grid are AND criteria. When entered on the same line, each criterion must be true for the record to appear in the resulting datasheet. Only nine records contain "access" in the Description field and "yes" in the Passed field.

6. **Click File on the menu bar, click Save As, type Potential Access Assistants in the Save Query 'Employee Registrations' To text box, then click OK**

   The query is saved with the new name, Potential Access Assistants, as a new object in the Training-F database.

7. **Close the Potential Access Assistants datasheet**

FIGURE F-7: Datasheet for Access records

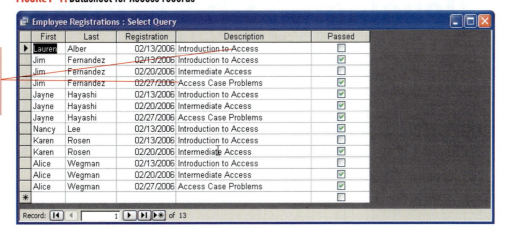

All records contain "Access" somewhere in the Description field

FIGURE F-8: AND criteria

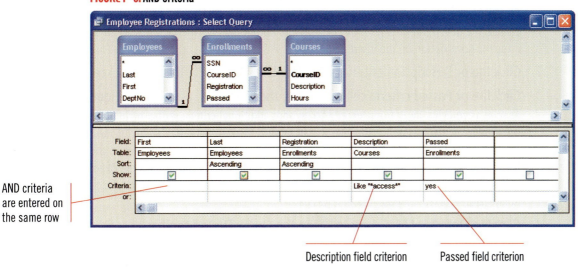

AND criteria are entered on the same row

Description field criterion   Passed field criterion

TABLE F-1: Common comparison operators

operator	description	example	result
>	Greater than	>50	Value exceeds 50
>=	Greater than or equal to	>=50	Value is 50 or greater
<	Less than	<50	Value is less than 50
<=	Less than or equal to	<=50	Value is 50 or less
<>	Not equal to	<>50	Value is any number other than 50
Between...And	Finds values between two numbers or dates	Between #2/2/01# And #2/2/06#	Dates between 2/2/2001 and 2/2/2006, inclusive
In	Finds a value that is one of a list	In ("IA","KS","NE")	Value equals IA or KS or NE
Null	Finds records that have no entry in a particular field	Null	No value has been entered in a field
Is Not Null	Finds records that have any entry in a particular field	Is Not Null	Any value has been entered in a field
Like	Finds records that match the criterion	Like "A*"	Value starts with A
Not	Finds records that do not match the criterion	Not 2	Numbers other than 2

Developing OR Criteria

In a query, all criteria entries define which records will be selected for the resulting datasheet. Whereas AND criteria *narrow* the number of records in the resulting datasheet by requiring that a record be true for multiple criteria, OR criteria *expand* the number of records that will appear in the datasheet because a record needs to be true *for only one* of the criteria rows to be selected. **OR criteria** are entered in the query design grid on different lines (criteria rows). Because each criteria row of the query design grid is evaluated separately, the more OR criteria entries in the query grid, the more records will be selected for the resulting datasheet. Fred is looking for an assistant for the Excel courses. He asks you to modify the Potential Access Assistants query to expand the number of records to include those who have passed either the Access or the Excel courses.

STEPS

1. **Right-click the Potential Access Assistants query, then click Design View on the shortcut menu**

   To add OR criteria, you have to enter criteria in the next available "or" row of the query design grid. By default, the query grid displays nine "or" rows for additional OR criteria, but you can add even more rows using the Rows option on the Insert menu.

2. **Click the or Description criteria cell below Like "*access*", then type *excel***

3. **Click the or Passed criteria cell below Yes, then type yes, as shown in Figure F-9**

   As soon as you click away from *excel*, Access adds additional criteria syntax including quotation marks to surround text criteria as well as the Like operator that is used with criteria that include wildcard asterisk characters. Now, if a record matches *either criteria* row of the criteria grid, it is included in the query's datasheet. Each row is evaluated separately, which is why you must put the Yes criterion for the Passed field in both rows of the query design grid. Otherwise, the second row would specify all records where "excel" is in the description regardless of whether the final test was passed.

4. **Click the Datasheet View button 🔲 on the Query Design toolbar**

   The resulting datasheet displays 28 records, as shown in Figure F-10. All of the records have course Descriptions that contain the word Access or Excel as well as Yes in the Passed field. Also, notice that the sort order (Last, then Registration) is still in effect.

QUICK TIP

To rename an object from the database window, right-click it, then choose Rename on the shortcut menu.

5. **Click File on the menu bar, click Save As, click between Access and Assistants, type or Excel, press [Spacebar], then click OK**

   The Potential Access or Excel Assistants query is saved as a new query object.

6. **Close the Potential Access or Excel Assistants query**

   The Training-F database displays the three queries you created in addition to the two queries that were previously created and stored in the database. Use the Details button 🔲 on the database window toolbar to view more information about each query.

QUICK TIP

When using Details View, click the column headings to sort the objects based on that column.

7. **Click the Details button 🔲 on the database window toolbar to view the date that the queries were created as well as the date that the queries were last modified, then click the List button ⊞ to return to the default database window view**

FIGURE F-9: OR criteria

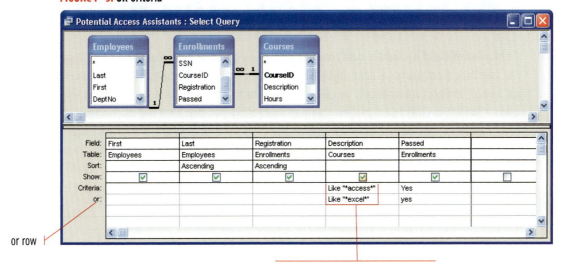

or row

OR criteria are entered on different rows

FIGURE F-10: OR criteria adds more records to the datasheet

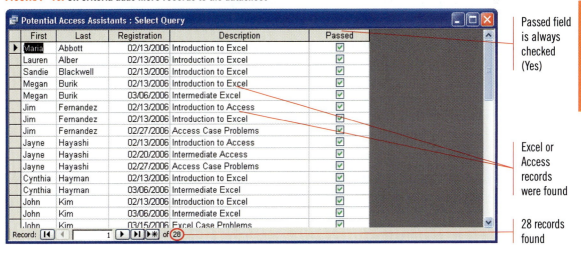

Passed field is always checked (Yes)

Excel or Access records were found

28 records found

Clues to Use

Using wildcard characters in query criteria

To search for a pattern, a wildcard character is used to represent any character in the criteria entry. Use a ? (question mark) to search for any single character and an * (asterisk) to search for any number of characters. Wildcard characters are often used with the Like operator. For example, the criterion Like "10/*/06" would find all dates in October of 2006, and the criterion Like "F*" would find all entries that start with the letter F.

Creating Calculated Fields

A **calculated field** is a field of data that can be created based on the values of other fields. For example, you can calculate the value for a Tax field by multiplying the value of the Sales field by a percentage. To create a calculated field and automatically populate every record with the correct value for that field, define the new calculated field in Query Design View using an expression that describes the calculation. An **expression** is a combination of field names, operators (such as +, –, /, and *), and functions that result in a single value. See Table F-2 for more information on arithmetic operators and Table F-3 for more information on functions. Fred has asked you to report on the hourly cost of each course. To create this information, you'll create a calculated field called HourlyRate that is defined by dividing the Cost field by the Hours field.

STEPS

1. **Click Queries on the Objects bar, double-click Create query in Design view, click Courses in the Show Table dialog box, click Add, then click Close**

   The Courses field list is in the upper pane of the query design window.

2. **Double-click the Description field, double-click the Hours field, then double-click the Cost field**

   A calculated field is created in the Field cell of the design grid by entering a new descriptive field name followed by a colon, then an expression. Field names used in an expression are surrounded by square brackets.

   QUICK TIP
   Right-click an expression, then click Zoom to use the Zoom dialog box for long entries.

3. ▶ **Click the blank Field cell of the fourth column, type HourlyRate:[Cost]/[Hours], then drag the ✛ mouse pointer on the right edge of the fourth column selector to the right to display the entire entry, as shown in Figure F-11**

4. ▶ **Click the Datasheet View button 🔲 on the Query Design toolbar**

   The HourlyRate field calculates correctly, but you do not want to view more than two digits to the right of the decimal point. You can format fields in Query Design View.

   QUICK TIP
   You do not need to show the fields used in the expression (in this case, Hours and Cost) in the query, but displaying them helps you determine if the expression is calculating correctly.

5. **Click the Design View button 🔲 on the Query Datasheet toolbar, right-click the HourlyRate field in the query design grid, then click Properties on the shortcut menu**

   The Field Properties dialog box opens. Because the HourlyRate field represents dollars per hour, you want to format the field with a dollar sign and two digits to the right of the decimal point as provided by the Currency format.

6. **Click the Format box, click the Format list arrow, click Currency, close the property sheet, then click 🔲 to display the records**

   The data shown in the HourlyRate field is now formatted appropriately.

7. **Press [Tab] twice, type 300 in the Introduction to Access Cost field, then press [Enter]**

   The resulting datasheet is shown in Figure F-12. The HourlyRate field recalculated as soon as the Cost field was updated. It is extremely important to create calculated fields in queries rather than define them as new fields in Table Design View because calculated fields always display current data.

8. **Click the Save button 🔲 on the Query Datasheet toolbar, type Hourly Rates in the Save As dialog box, click OK, then close the datasheet**

   The query is saved as an object in the database.

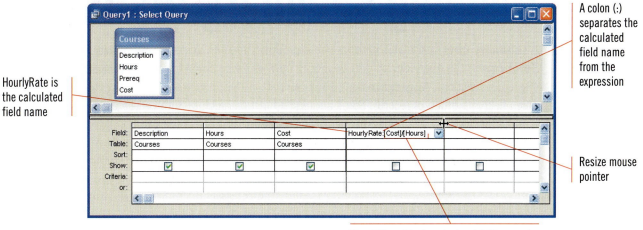

FIGURE F-11: Creating a calculated field

A colon (:) separates the calculated field name from the expression

HourlyRate is the calculated field name

Resize mouse pointer

[Cost]/[Hours] is the calculated field expression

FIGURE F-12: Formatting and testing the calculated field

Updated Cost field automatically updates the calculated HourlyRate field

Currency format

TABLE F-2: Arithmetic operators

operator	description
+	Addition
–	Subtraction
*	Multiplication
/	Division
^	Exponentiation

TABLE F-3: Common functions

function	sample expression and description
DATE	DATE()-[BirthDate] Calculates the number of days between today and the date in the BirthDate field
PMT	PMT([Rate],[Term],[Loan]) Calculates the monthly payment on a loan where the Rate field contains the monthly interest rate, the Term field contains the number of monthly payments, and the Loan field contains the total amount financed
LEFT	LEFT([LastName],2) Returns the first two characters of the entry in the LastName field
RIGHT	RIGHT([Partno],3) Returns the last three characters of the entry in the Partno field
LEN	LEN([Description]) Returns the number of characters in the Description field

Building Summary Queries

A **summary query** calculates statistics about groups of records. To create a summary query, you use the **Total row** in the query design grid to specify how you want to group and calculate the statistics using aggregate functions. **Aggregate functions** calculate a statistic such as a subtotal, count, or average on a given field in a group of records. Some aggregate functions such as Sum can be used only on fields with Number or Currency data types, but others such as Min, Max, or Count can be used on Text fields, too. Table F-4 provides more information on aggregate functions. A key difference between the statistics displayed by a summary query and those displayed by calculated fields is that summary queries provide calculations that describe a *group of records*, whereas calculated fields provide a new field of information for *each record*. The Accounting Department wants to know the total training cost per location. They also want to know how many employees from each location have attended training classes. You will build a summary query to provide these statistics.

STEPS

1. Click **Queries** on the Objects bar, then double-click **Create query in Design view**

2. Double-click **Courses**, double-click **Enrollments**, double-click **Employees**, then click **Close** in the Show Table dialog box

   Even though you won't explicitly use fields from the Enrollments table, you need this table in your query to tie the fields from the Courses and Employees tables together.

3. Double-click the **Location field** in the Employees table, double-click the **Cost field** in the Courses table, then double-click the **Cost field** in the Courses table again

   You added the Cost field to the query grid twice because you want to compute two different summary statistics (subtotal and count) on the data in this field.

4. Click the **Totals button** Σ on the Query Design toolbar

   The Total row is added to the query grid below the Table row. You want to calculate statistics for each location, so the Location field is the Group By field.

5. Click **Group By** for the first Cost field, click the **Group By list arrow**, click **Sum**, click **Group By** for the second Cost field, click the **Group By list arrow**, then click **Count**

   The Totals row tells the query to group the records by the Location field, then sum and count the values in the Cost field as shown in Figure F-13.

6. Click the **Datasheet View button** 🔲 on the Query Design toolbar

   The Boston location had $1,500 of internal charges for the 8 classes its employees attended, as shown in Figure F-14. By counting the Cost field in addition to summing it, you know how many records were combined to reach the total figure of $1,500 for the SumOfCost column. You can sort and filter summary queries, but you cannot enter or edit data in a summary query because each record represents the summary of several records.

7. Click the **Save button** 🔲 on the Query Datasheet toolbar, type **Internal Costs - Your Initials**, click **OK**, click the **Print button** 🖨, then close the datasheet

   The name of the query is automatically placed in the header of the datasheet printout. Therefore, one way to uniquely identify a printout is to include your name or initials in the query name.

FIGURE F-13: Summary Query Design View

Totals button

Total row in query grid

Group the records by the Location field

Sum the Cost field

Count the Cost field

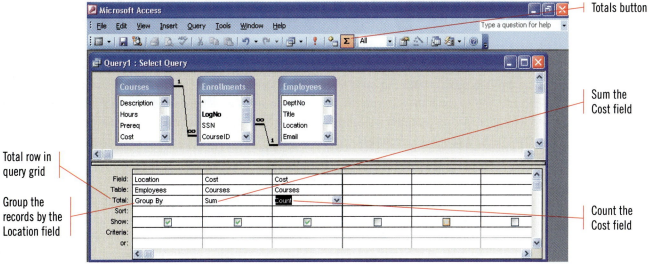

FIGURE F-14: Summarized records

Records are grouped by Location

Cost field is counted for each Location

Cost field is summed for each Location

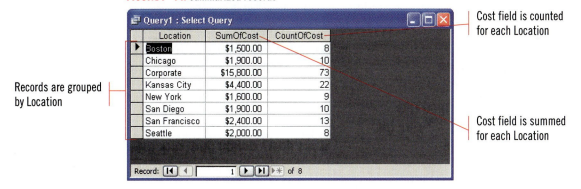

TABLE F-4: Aggregate functions

aggregate function	used to find the
Sum	Total of values in a field
Avg	Average of values in a field
Min	Minimum value in the field
Max	Maximum value in the field
Count	Number of values in a field (not counting null values)
StDev	Standard deviation of values in a field
Var	Variance of values in a field
First	Field value from the first record in a table or query
Last	Field value from the last record in a table or query

Building Crosstab Queries

A **crosstab query** calculates a statistic such as a sum or average by grouping records according to a field in the column heading as well as a field in the row heading. You can use the **Crosstab Query Wizard** to create a crosstab query or you can build the crosstab query from scratch using Query Design View. Fred asks you to continue your analysis of costs by location by summarizing the costs for each course for each location. A crosstab query will work well for this request because you want to summarize information by two fields, Location and (course) Description.

STEPS

TROUBLE
The "Create query by using wizard" shortcut in the database window creates a select query. You must click 🔳 to use the other query wizards.

1. **Click the New button 🔳 on the database window toolbar, click Crosstab Query Wizard in the New Query dialog box, then click OK**

   The first Crosstab Query Wizard question asks you which table or query contains the fields for the crosstab query. The fields for this crosstab query were previously saved in a query called Crosstab Fields.

2. **Click the Queries option button in the View section, click Crosstab Fields in the list of available queries, then click Next**

   The next questions organize how the fields are displayed in the crosstab query datasheet.

3. **Double-click Description to select it as the row-heading field, click Next, click Location for the column heading field, click Next, then click Sum in the Functions list**

   The Sample portion of the Crosstab Query Wizard dialog box presents the Description field as the row heading, the Location field as the column heading, and the summarized Cost field within the body of the crosstab query, as shown in Figure F-15.

4. **Click Next, type Location Crosstab - Your Initials in the query name text box, click the View the Query option button, then click Finish to display the crosstab query, as shown in Figure F-16**

   You can modify a crosstab query to change the row heading field, the column-heading field, or the calculation statistic in Query Design View.

QUICK TIP
Click the Query Type button list arrow 🔳 ▾ on the Query Design toolbar, then click Crosstab Query to change any select query into a crosstab query.

5. **Click the Design View button 🔳 on the Query Datasheet toolbar**

   Note that the Query Type button 🔳 ▾ on the Query Design toolbar displays the crosstab icon and the words "Crosstab Query" are in the title bar of the query itself (versus the more common "Select Query"). The Total row shows that the datasheet is grouped by both the Description and the Location fields. The **Crosstab row** specifies that the Description field will be used as a Row Heading, and that the Location field will be used as a Column Heading.

6. **Click Sum in the Cost field Total cell, click the Sum list arrow, then click Count, as shown in Figure F-17**

   By changing the Sum aggregate function to Count, your crosstab query will now count the number of courses taken for each course description for each location rather than subtotaling the costs.

7. **Click the Datasheet View button 🔳 on the Query Design toolbar, then click the Print button 🔳**

8. **Click the Save button 🔳, then close the crosstab query**

   Crosstab queries appear with a crosstab icon to the left of the query name in the database window.

Clues to Use

Query Wizards

The **Find Duplicates Query Wizard** is used to determine whether a table contains duplicate values in one or more fields. The **Find Unmatched Query Wizard** is used to find records in one table that do not have related records in another table. To use the Find Duplicates, Find Unmatched, or Crosstab Query Wizards, you must click the Queries button on the Objects bar, then click the New button 🔳 on the database window toolbar. You access the Simple Query Wizard, which creates a select query, in the same way, or by clicking the "Create query by using wizard" option in the database window.

FIGURE F-15: Crosstab Query Wizard

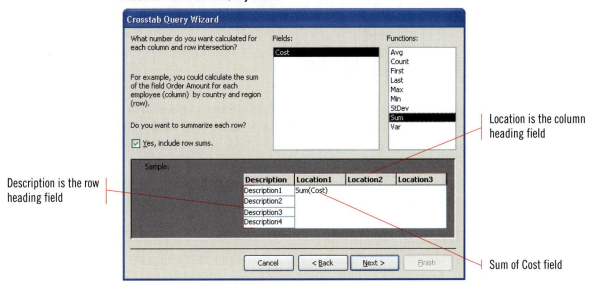

Description is the row heading field

Location is the column heading field

Sum of Cost field

FIGURE F-16: Crosstab datasheet

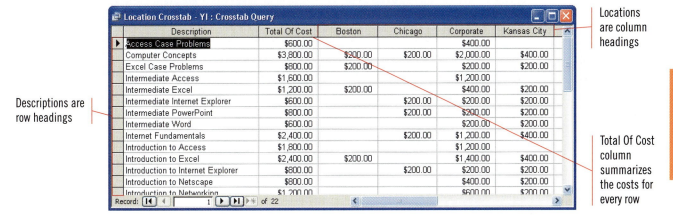

Descriptions are row headings

Locations are column headings

Total Of Cost column summarizes the costs for every row

FIGURE F-17: Query Design View of a crosstab query

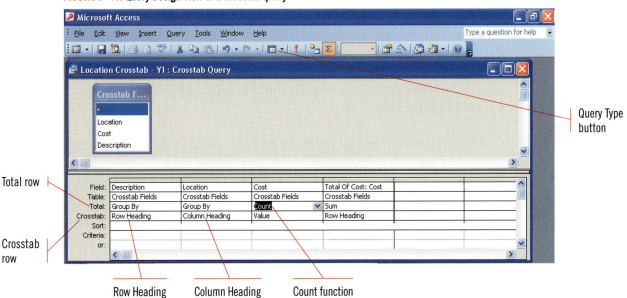

Total row

Crosstab row

Query Type button

Row Heading

Column Heading

Count function

Access 2003

Building PivotTables and PivotCharts

A **PivotTable** calculates a statistic such as a sum or average by grouping records like a crosstab query with the additional benefit of allowing you to filter the presented data. A **PivotChart** is a graphical presentation of the data in the PivotTable. You build a PivotTable using **PivotTable View**. Similarly, you design PivotCharts in **PivotChart View**. The PivotChart and PivotTable Views are bound to one another so that when a change is made in one view, the other is automatically updated as well. You use PivotChart View to graphically present summary information about the courses taken by employees at each location.

STEPS

1. **Double-click the PivotTable Fields query to open its datasheet**

   You can view data of any existing table, query, or form in PivotTable and PivotChart views.

TROUBLE

If the Chart Field List does not appear, click the Field List button to toggle it on.

2. **Click the Design View button list arrow , then click PivotChart View**

   The PivotChart View and Chart Field List appear, as shown in Figure F-18. In PivotChart View, you drag a field from the Chart Field List to a **drop area**, a position on the chart where you want the field to appear. The fields in the **Chart Field List** are the fields in the underlying object, in this case, the PivotTable Fields query. The relationship between drop areas on a PivotChart, PivotTable, and crosstab query are summarized in Table F-5.

TROUBLE

To remove a field, drag it out of the PivotChart window.

3. **Drag Location from the Chart Field List to the Drop Category Fields Here drop area**

   When you successfully drag a field to a drop area, the drop area displays a blue border. Location field values will appear on the x-axis, also called the **category axis**.

TROUBLE

If you cannot see the Series drop area, drag the title bar of the Chart Field List.

4. **Drag Cost from the Chart Field List to the Drop Data Fields Here drop area, drag Last to the Drop Filter Fields Here drop area, then drag CourseID to the Drop Series Fields Here drop area, as shown in Figure F-19**

   Cost field values are now displayed as bars on the chart, and are measured by the numbers displayed on the y-axis, also called the **value axis**. The CourseID field is in the legend, also called the **series**, position for the chart. The Last field is in the filter position for the chart. PivotChart and PivotTable Views are used to present data as well as to analyze data. For example, you can use PivotChart fields to filter for only those records you want to analyze.

QUICK TIP

Click the Show Legend button on the Formatting (PivotTable/PivotChart) toolbar to display the legend below the Series field.

5. **Click the Field List button to toggle it off, click the CourseID list arrow, click the (All) check box to remove all check marks, click the Access1 check box, then click OK in the CourseID filter list**

   The PivotChart is filtered to display only the records for the Access courses. All PivotTable and PivotChart fields (except for the field summarized in the Data area) can be used to filter information. You can also filter data using PivotTable View.

QUICK TIP

The field's list arrow changes from black to blue if used to filter the data.

6. **Click the Design View button list arrow , click PivotTable View, click the CourseID list arrow, click the (All) check box to add all check marks, click OK in the CourseID filter list, click the Last list arrow, click the (All) check box to remove all check marks, click the Abbott check box, then click OK in the Last filter list**

   The PivotTable appears as shown in Figure F-20. The CourseIDs are shown as column headings, and a grand total for each column and row is also displayed.

7. **Click the Save button , print and close the PivotTable, close the Training-F.mdb database, then exit Access**

FIGURE F-18: PivotChart drop areas

Field List button

Filter field area

Data field area

Scale depends on the size of the window

Category field area

Chart Field List

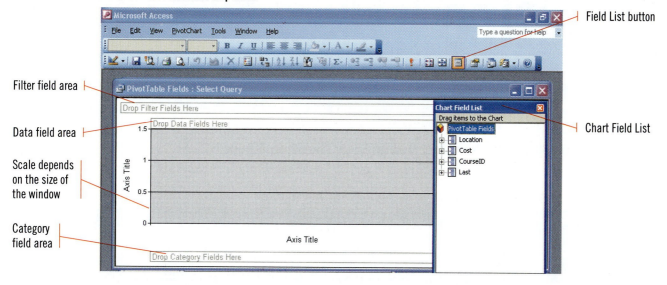

FIGURE F-19: PivotChart View

Last field in the Filter area

Cost field in the Data area

Value axis, y-axis

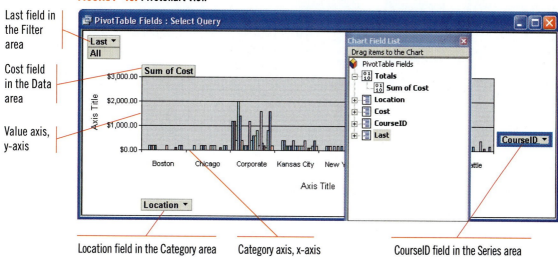

Location field in the Category area

Category axis, x-axis

CourseID field in the Series area

FIGURE F-20: PivotTable View

Field list arrows

Grand Total column

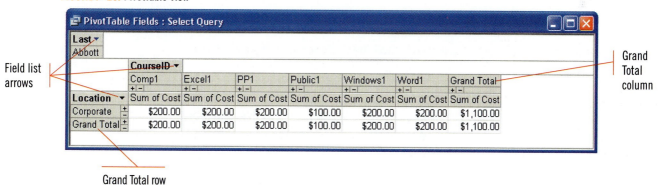

Grand Total row

TABLE F-5: PivotTable and PivotChart drop areas

drop area on PivotTable	drop area on PivotChart	crosstab query field position
Filter Field	Filter Field	(NA)
Row Field	Category Field	Row Heading
Column Field	Series Field	Column Heading
Totals or Detail Field	Data Field	Value

Access 2003

Practice

▼ CONCEPTS REVIEW

Identify each element of the Query Design View shown in Figure F-21.

FIGURE F-21

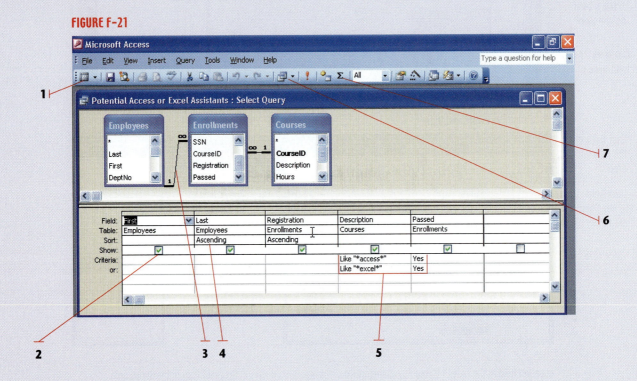

Match each term with the statement that best describes its function.

8. Select query
9. Wildcard character
10. AND criteria
11. Sorting
12. OR criteria

a. Placing the records of a datasheet in a certain order
b. Asterisk (*) or question mark (?) used in query criteria
c. Retrieves fields from related tables and displays records in a datasheet
d. Entered on more than one row of the query design grid
e. Entered on one row of the query design grid

Select the best answer from the list of choices.

13. **The query datasheet can best be described as a:**
    a. Duplication of the data in the underlying table's datasheet.
    b. Logical view of the selected data from an underlying table's datasheet.
    c. Separate file of data.
    d. Second copy of the data in the underlying tables.

14. **Queries may *not* be used to:**
    a. Set the primary key field for a table.
    b. Calculate new fields of data.
    c. Enter or update data.
    d. Sort records.

15. **When you update data in a table that is also displayed in a query datasheet:**
    a. You must also update the data in the query datasheet.
    b. You must relink the query to the table in order for the data to refresh.
    c. The data is automatically updated in the query.
    d. You have the choice whether or not you want to update the data in the query.

16. **Which of the following is *not* an aggregate function available to a summary query?**
    a. Subtotal
    b. Avg
    c. Count
    d. Max

17. **The order in which records in a query are sorted is determined by:**
    a. The order in which the fields are defined in the underlying table.
    b. The alphabetic order of the field names.
    c. The importance of the information in the field.
    d. The left-to-right position of the fields in the query design grid that contain a sort order choice.

18. **The presentation of data in a crosstab query is most similar to:**
    a. Report Print Preview.
    b. PivotTable View.
    c. Table Datasheet View.
    d. PivotChart View.

19. **SQL stands for:**
    a. Standard Query Limits.
    b. Saved Query Links.
    c. Simple Query Layout.
    d. Structured Query Language.

20. **In a crosstab query, which field is the most likely candidate for the Value position?**
    a. FName
    b. Department
    c. Country
    d. Cost

▼ SKILLS REVIEW

1. **Build select queries.**
   a. Start Access and open the **Membership-F.mdb** database from the drive and folder where your Data Files are stored.
   b. Create a new select query in Query Design View using the Members and Zipcodes tables.
   c. Add the following fields to the query design grid in this order:
      FirstName, LastName, and Street from the Members table
      City, State, and Zip from the Zipcodes table
   d. In Datasheet View, replace the LastName value in the first record with your last name.
   e. Save the query as **Address List**, print the datasheet, then close the query.

2. **Sort a query on multiple fields.**
   a. Open the Address List query in Query Design View.
   b. Drag the FirstName field from the Members field list to the right of the LastName field in the query design grid to make the first three fields in the query design grid FirstName, LastName, and FirstName.
   c. Add the ascending sort criteria to the second and third fields in the query design grid, and uncheck the Show check box in the third column. The query is now sorted in ascending order by LastName, then by FirstName, but the order of the fields in the resulting datasheet will still appear as FirstName, LastName.
   d. Use Save As to save the query as **Sorted Address List**, view the datasheet, print the datasheet, then close the query.

3. **Develop AND criteria.**
   a. Open the Address List in Design View.
   b. Type **M*** (the asterisk is a wildcard) in the LastName field criteria cell to choose all people whose last name starts with M. Access assists you with the syntax for this type of criterion and enters Like "M*" in the cell when you click elsewhere in the query design grid.
   c. Enter **KS** as AND criteria for the State field. Be sure to enter the criteria on the same line in the query design grid as the Like "M*" criteria.
   d. View the datasheet. It should select only those people from Kansas with a last name that starts with the letter M.
   e. Enter a new value in the City field of the first record to uniquely identify the printout.
   f. Use Save As to save the query as **Kansas M Members**, print, then close the datasheet.

4. **Develop OR criteria.**
   a. Open the Kansas M Members query in Query Design View.
   b. Enter **M*** in the second criteria row (the or row) of the LastName field.
   c. Enter IA as the criterion in the second criteria row (the or row) of the State field so that those people from IA with a last name that starts with the letter M are added to this query.
   d. Use Save As to save the query as **Kansas or Iowa M Members**, view and print the datasheet, then close the query.

5. **Build calculated fields.**
   a. Create a new select query using Query Design View using only the Members table.
   b. Add the following fields to the query design grid in this order: FirstName, LastName, Birthday.
   c. Create a calculated field called Age in the fourth column of the query design grid by entering the expression:
      Age: (Date()-[Birthday])/365 to determine the number of years old each person is based on the information in the Birthday field.
   d. Sort the query in descending order on the calculated Age field, then view the datasheet.
   e. Return to Query Design View, open the Property sheet for the Age field, then format the Age field with a Standard format and **0** in the Decimal Places property text box.
   f. Save the query with the name **Age Calculation**, view the datasheet, print the datasheet, then close the query.

6. **Build summary queries.**
   a. Create a new select query in Query Design View using the Members and Activities tables.
   b. Add the following fields: FirstName and LastName from the Members table, Hours from the Activities table.
   c. Add the Total row to the query design grid, then change the function for the Hours field from Group By to Sum.
   d. Sort in descending order by Hours.
   e. Save the query as **Total Hours - Your Initials**, view the datasheet, print the datasheet, then close the query.

7. Build crosstab queries.

a. Create a select query with the City and State fields from the Zipcodes table, and the Dues field from the Members table. Save the query as **Crosstab Fields**, then close the query.

b. Click the New button in the database window, click Crosstab Query Wizard in the New Query dialog box, click OK, then base the crosstab query on the Crosstab Fields query.

c. Select City as the row heading, State as the column heading, and sum the Dues field within the crosstab datasheet.

d. Name the query **Dues Crosstab - Your Initials**, then click Finish.

e. View, print, then close the datasheet.

8. Build PivotTables and PivotCharts.

a. Create a select query with the State field from the Zipcodes table, and the CharterMember and Dues fields from the Members table. Save it as **Dues Analysis - Your Initials**.

b. Switch to PivotChart View, open the Chart Field List if it is not already visible, drag the State field to the Drop Category Fields Here drop area, the CharterMember field to the Drop Series Fields Here drop area, and the Dues field to the Drop Data Fields Here drop area.

c. Use the State field to display only the data for the records where the State field value is equal to KS or MO as shown in Figure F-22.

d. Switch to PivotTable View, then print it.

e. Save the changes to the **Dues Analysis - Your Initials** query, close it, close the Membership-F.mdb database, then exit Access.

FIGURE F-22

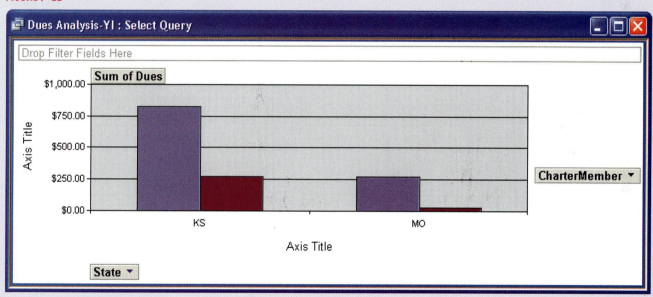

Access 2003

▼ INDEPENDENT CHALLENGE 1

As the manager of a music store's instrument rental program, you have created a database to track instrument rentals to schoolchildren. Now that several rentals have been made, you want to query the database for several different datasheet print-outs to analyze school information.

a. Start Access and open the **Music Store-F.mdb** database from the drive and folder where your Data Files are stored.

b. In Query Design View, create a query with the following fields in the following order:

SchoolName field from the Schools table

RentalDate field from the Rentals table

Description field from the Instruments table

(*Hint*: You need to add the Customers table to this query to make the connection between the Schools table and the Rentals table even though you don't use any fields from the Customers table.)

c. Sort ascending by SchoolName, then ascending by RentalDate.

d. Save the query as **School Rentals**, view the datasheet, replace the current entry in the first record with your elementary school name, then print the datasheet.

e. Modify the School Rentals query by deleting the Description field. Then, use the Totals button to group the records by SchoolName and to Count the RentalDate field. Print the datasheet and use Save As to save the query as **School Count**. Close the datasheet.

f. Use the Crosstab Query Wizard to create a crosstab query based on the School Rentals query. Use Description as the row heading and SchoolName as the column heading. Count the RentalDate field.

g. Save the query as **School Crosstab**, then view, print, and close it.

h. Modify the School Rentals query so that only those schools with the word Elementary in the SchoolName field are displayed. (*Hint*: You have to use wildcard characters in the criteria.)

i. Use Save As to save the query as **Elementary Rentals**, then view, print, and close the datasheet.

j. Close the Music Store-F.mdb database, then exit Access.

▼ INDEPENDENT CHALLENGE 2

As the manager of a music store's instrument rental program, you have created a database to track instrument rentals to schoolchildren. The database has already been used to answer several basic questions, and now that you've shown how easy it is to get the answers using queries, more and more questions are being asked. You will use queries to analyze customer and rental information.

a. Start Access and open the **Music Store-F.mdb** database from the drive and folder where your Data Files are stored.

b. In Query Design View, create a query with the following fields in the following order:

Description and MonthlyFee fields from Instruments table

Zip and City fields from the Customers table

(*Hint*: You will need to add the Rentals table to this query to make the connection between the Customers table and the Instruments table even though you don't need any fields from the Rentals table in this query's datasheet.)

c. Add the Zip field to the first column of the query grid and specify an Ascending sort order for this field. Uncheck the Show check box for the first Zip field so that it will not appear in the datasheet.

d. Specify an Ascending sort order for the Description field.

e. Save the query as **Zip Analysis**.

f. View the datasheet, replace Des Moines with the name of your hometown in the first record's City field, then print and close the datasheet.

g. Modify the Zip Analysis query by adding criteria to find the records where the Description is equal to **viola**.

h. Use Save As to save this query as **Violas**.

Advanced Challenge Exercise

- On a piece of paper, write down how many records the Violas query contains.
- Modify the Violas query with AND criteria that further specify that the City must be **Ankeny**.
- Save this query as **Violas in Ankeny**. On the paper, note how many records the Violas in Ankeny query contains. Briefly explain how AND criteria affected this number.
- Modify the Violas in Ankeny query with OR criteria that find all violas or violins, regardless of where they are located.
- Use Save As to save this query as **Violas or Violins**. On the paper, note how many records the Violas and Violins query contains. Briefly explain how OR criteria affected this number.
- Using the Crosstab Query Wizard, create a crosstab query based on the School Analysis query that uses the Description field for the row headings, the SchoolName field for the column headings, and that Counts the RentalNo field.
- Save the crosstab query as **Crosstab Rentals - Your Initials**, preview the datasheet, then print the datasheet in landscape orientation so that it fits on one page.

i. Close the Music Store-F.mdb database, then exit Access.

Access 2003

▼ INDEPENDENT CHALLENGE 3

As the manager of a music store's instrument rental program, you have created a database to track instrument rentals to schoolchildren. Now that several rentals have been made, you want to query the database to analyze customer and rental information.

   a. Start Access and open the **Music Store-F.mdb** database from the drive and folder where your Data Files are stored.

   b. In Query Design View, create a query with the following fields in the following order:
   FirstName and LastName from the Customers table
   Description and MonthlyFee from the Instruments table
   (*Hint*: You need to add the Rentals table to this query to make the connection between the Customers table and the Instruments table even though you don't need any fields from the Rentals table in this query's datasheet.)

   c. Sort the records in ascending order by the LastName field.

   d. Save the query as **Customer Rentals - Your Initials**, view the datasheet, enter your own last name in the first record's LastName field, then print the datasheet.

   e. In Query Design View, modify the Customer Rentals query by deleting the FirstName and LastName fields. Then, click the Totals button to group the records by Description and to Sum the MonthlyFee field.

   f. Add another MonthlyFee field as a third column to the query design grid, and use the Count function to find the count of rentals within that group.

   g. Sort the records in ascending order by the Description field.

   h. Use Save As to save the query as **Monthly Instrument Income - Your Initials**.

   i. View, print, then close the datasheet.

Advanced Challenge Exercise

   ■ Open the Customer Rentals - Your Initials query in Design View, click the Show Table button on the Query Design toolbar to add the Schools table to the query, then add the SchoolName field as the fifth field in the query design grid.

   ■ Display PivotChart View, then create the PivotChart shown in Figure F-23. The Description field has been used as a filter to show only MonthlyFee data for cellos and violins.

FIGURE F-23

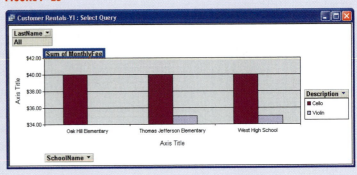

   ■ Click the Show Legend button on the Formatting (PivotTable/PivotChart) toolbar to show the legend box under the Description field in the Series field drop area.

   ■ Print the PivotChart, save and close the Customer Rentals - Your Initials query.

   j. Close the Music Store-F database, then exit Access.

▼ INDEPENDENT CHALLENGE 4

You are on the staff of an economic development team whose goal is to encourage tourism in the Baltic Sea region. You have created an Access database called Baltic-F to track important fields of information for the countries in that region, and are using the Internet to find information about the area that you then enter into existing forms.

a. Start Access and open the **Baltic-F.mdb** database from the drive and folder where your Data Files are stored.

b. Connect to the Internet, then go to www.google.com, www.about.com, or any general search engine to conduct some research for your database. Your goal is to find three upcoming events for Stockholm, Sweden, then print the Web page(s).

c. Open the Cities table datasheet, click the expand button for the Stockholm record to show a subdatasheet of related records from the Events table, and enter the three events you found for Stockholm into the subdatasheet. EventID is an AutoNumber field, so it will automatically increment as you enter the EventName and EventDate information.

d. Using Query Design View, create a select query with the following fields in the following order:
Country and City from the Cities table
EventName and EventDate from the Events table

e. Save the query with the name **Event Info**, then close it.

Advanced Challenge Exercise

■ Use PivotTable View to organize the Event Info information by putting Country in the Filter Fields drop area, City in the Column Fields drop area, EventDate in the Row Fields drop area, and EventName in the Detail Fields drop area.

■ Filter for only the data in Sweden, then print the PivotTable.

f. Save and close the Event Info query, close the Baltic-F.mdb database, then exit Access.

Access 2003

▼ VISUAL WORKSHOP

Open the **Training-F.mdb** database from the drive and folder where your Data Files are stored. In Query Design View create a new select query with the Location field from the Employees table, the Cost and CourseID fields from the Courses table, and the Passed field from the Enrollments table. Display the query in PivotChart View, then create it as shown in Figure F-24. Filter the data for CourseIDs Access1 and Access2 and for the Passed value of Yes. Click the Show Legend button on the Formatting (PivotTable/PivotChart) toolbar to display the legend below the Location field in the Series field area. Save the query with the name **Access PivotChart – Your Initials**, then print it.

FIGURE F-24

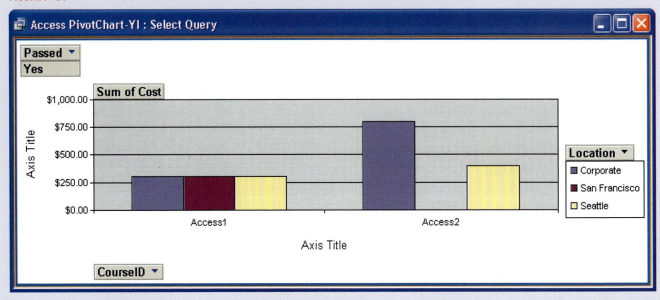

Developing Forms and Subforms

OBJECTIVES

Understand the form/subform relationship

Create subforms using the Form Wizard

Create subforms using queries

Modify subforms

Add a combo box for data entry

Add a combo box to find records

Add option groups

Add command buttons

Add ActiveX controls

SAM

If you have a SAM user profile, you may have access to hands-on instruction, practice, and assessment of the skills covered in this unit. Log in to your SAM account and go to your assignments page to see what your instructor has assigned.

A **form** is a database object designed to make data easy to find, enter, and edit. Forms are created by using **controls** such as labels, text boxes, combo boxes, and command buttons, which make data easier to find, enter, and manipulate than working with data in a datasheet. A form that contains a **subform** allows you to work with related records in an easy-to-use screen arrangement. For example, a form/subform combination would allow you to display customer data as well as all of the orders placed by that customer at the same time. Fred Ames wants to improve the usability of the forms in the MediaLoft training database. You will build and improve forms by working with subforms, combo boxes, option groups, command buttons, and ActiveX controls.

Understanding the Form/Subform Relationship

A **subform** is actually a form within a form. The form that contains the subform is called the **main form**. You add a subform to a main form using a subform control. The subform shows records that are related to the record currently displayed in the main form. Therefore, a form/subform combination is often used to display the records of two tables that are related in a one-to-many relationship. Sometimes a one-to-many relationship is called a **parent/child relationship**, because the "parent" record in the main form is linked to many "child" records displayed in the subform. Well-designed forms/subforms encourage fast, accurate data entry, and shield the data entry person from the complexity of underlying tables and relationships. Creating forms with subforms requires careful planning, so you study form/subform guidelines before creating the forms in Access.

DETAILS

To plan a form/subform:

- **Sketch the layout of the form/subform on paper, identifying which fields belong in the main form and which belong in the subform**

  The sketch in Figure G-1 displays employee information in the main form and enrollment information in the subform to accommodate the one-to-many relationship between the Employees and Enrollments tables. Figure G-2 displays course information in the main form and employee enrollment information in the subform to accommodate the one-to-many relationship between the Courses and Enrollments tables.

- **Decide whether to use the Form Wizard to create the form/subform in one process or whether to create each form separately**

  This decision determines each form's Record Source property value. The **Record Source property** identifies the recordset for the form and may be a table name, a query name, or a Structured Query Language (SQL) statement. Recall that the **recordset** is the data—the fields and records—that will appear on the form. Although building a form/subform using the Form Wizard is fast and easy, this process will insert an SQL statement for the Record Source property value of the form if either the form or subform is based on fields from multiple tables. While the initial form will function well using an SQL statement for the Record Source property, modifying that form's recordset depends upon your SQL skills. For example, later you might want to add a new field to the form or use criteria to limit the number of records that the form displays. Both of these tasks require modifying the recordset.

  If you create the form and subform separately, basing each form on an individual query object, the Record Source property value is the name of the query. Later, if you want to modify the recordset for either form, you simply modify the query that defines the recordset in Query Design View, a relatively simple task compared to that of editing SQL.

  To create each form on an individual query object, you must first build the queries, then build the forms, and then link the subform to the main form. This is obviously a much longer process than building the form/subform combination in one step via the Form Wizard. If you anticipate that you may want to change the recordset for either the form or subform later, however, the extra work may be worth it.

  You decide to use the Form Wizard and then create separate queries and forms to build two form/subform combinations so that you can compare the two processes.

FIGURE G-1: Employees main form with Enrollments subform

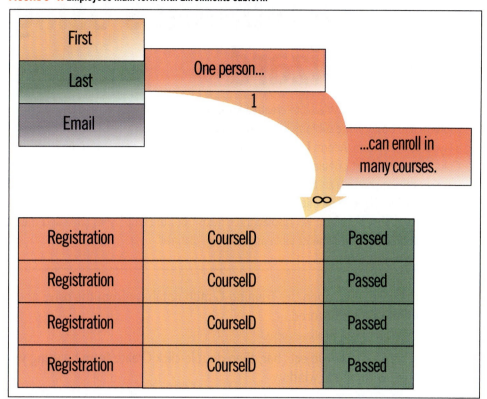

FIGURE G-2: Courses main form with Employee subform

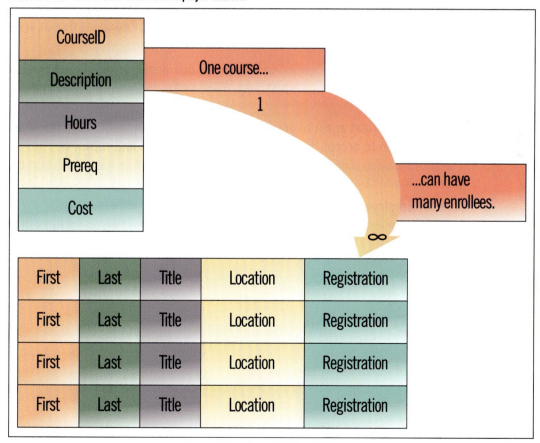

Creating Subforms Using the Form Wizard

When you use the Form Wizard to create a form/subform combination, you create both the main form and subform and position the subform in the main form in one process. The Form Wizard also asks you to choose a layout for each form. A form **layout** is the general way that the data and controls are arranged on the form. Columnar is the most popular layout for a main form, and Datasheet is the most popular layout for a subform, but these choices can be modified by changing the form's **Default View property** in Form Design View. See Table G-1 for a description of form layouts. You decide to create a form/subform using the Form Wizard. The main form will display three fields from the Employees table and the subform will display three fields from the Enrollments table as previously planned.

STEPS

1. **Start Access, then open the Training-G.mdb database from the drive and folder where your Data Files are stored**

   The Training-G.mdb database opens.

2. **Click Forms on the Objects bar, then double-click Create form by using wizard in the Training-G database window**

   The Form Wizard appears and prompts you to select the fields of the form. You need six fields that are stored in three different tables for the final form/subform.

3. **Click the Tables/Queries list arrow, click Table: Employees, double-click First, double-click Last, double-click Email, click the Tables/Queries list arrow, click Table: Enrollments, double-click Registration, double-click CourseID, then double-click Passed, as shown in Figure G-3**

4. **Click Next**

   This Form Wizard question asks how you want to view the data. Because the Employees and Enrollments tables are linked in a one-to-many relationship, the Form Wizard recognizes the opportunity to create a form/subform combination for the selected fields and suggests that arrangement.

   > **QUICK TIP**
   > Use the Standard style when saving a database to a floppy disk. The other styles contain graphics that increase the storage requirements of the form.

5. **Click Next, click Next again to accept the Datasheet layout, click Standard, click Next, then click Finish to accept the default names for the form and subform**

   By default, subforms are created with a Datasheet layout. The Employees form opens and includes the Enrollments subform in Datasheet layout, as shown in Figure G-4.

6. **Close the Employees form**

   The Employees form and the Enrollments subform appear as two new form objects in the Training-G database window.

FIGURE G-3: Form Wizard

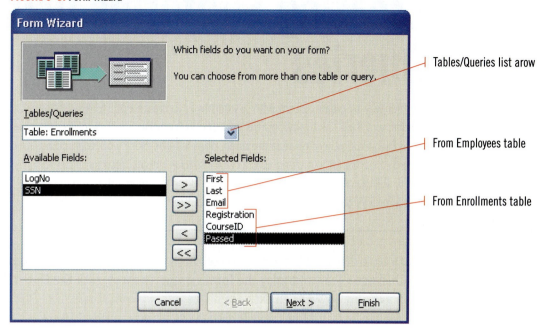

- Tables/Queries list arrow
- From Employees table
- From Enrollments table

FIGURE G-4: Employees main form with Enrollments subform

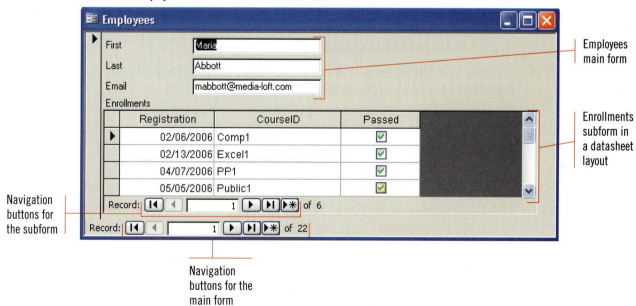

- Employees main form
- Enrollments subform in a datasheet layout
- Navigation buttons for the subform
- Navigation buttons for the main form

TABLE G-1: Form layouts

layout	description
Columnar	Each field appears on a separate row with a label to its left
Tabular	Each field appears as an individual column and each record is presented as a row
Datasheet	Fields and records are displayed as they appear in a table or query datasheet
PivotTable	Fields are organized in a PivotTable arrangement
PivotChart	Fields are organized in a PivotChart arrangement

Creating Subforms Using Queries

Another way to create a form with a subform is to create both forms separately, basing them on individual queries, and then link the two forms together in Form Design View of the main form. Although creating the forms by building them on separate query objects takes more work than doing the same thing using the Form Wizard, the advantage is being able to easily change the recordset of either form by modifying the underlying query. ████████ You decide to create the second form/subform that you previously designed without the help of the Form Wizard. You start by building the subform.

STEPS

TROUBLE

If the property sheet doesn't show the word "Form" in the title bar, click the Form Selector button.

1. **Double-click Create form in Design view, click the Properties button 🖳 on the Form Design toolbar to display the form's property sheet, click the Data tab, click the Record Source list arrow, then click Employee Info**

   The field list for the Employee Info query opens, showing you the fields you can choose for the subform.

2. **Click 🖳 to toggle off the property sheet, double-click the Employee Info field list title bar to select all fields in the list, then drag the selected fields to the form as shown in Figure G-5**

   Now that the subform's fields are selected, you decide to change the Default View property of the subform to Datasheet to match how most subform layouts are organized.

TROUBLE

If you incorrectly drag and position the fields on the form, click Undo 🔄, then try again.

3. **Double-click the Form Selector button to reopen the form's property sheet, click the Format tab, click the Default View list arrow, click Datasheet, click 🖳 to toggle off the property sheet, then click the Datasheet View button 🖳 on the Form Design toolbar**

   The subform displays the selected data in a datasheet presentation.

4. **Click the Save button 🖳 on the Form View toolbar, type Employee Info Subform in the Form Name text box, click OK, then close the form**

   With the Employee Info Subform saved, you're ready to connect it to the main form. The Course Info form has already been created to serve as the main form. Now you need to add the Employee Info Subform to it.

5. **Right-click Course Info, then click Design View on the shortcut menu**

   In the upper portion of the form, the Course Info form displays fields from the Course Info query. The Employee Info Subform will be related to the Course Info main form through the common CourseID field.

6. **Click the Toolbox button 🔧 on the Form Design toolbar to display the Toolbox toolbar (if not already displayed), click the Subform/Subreport button 🖳 on the Toolbox toolbar, then click below the Cost label**

   The SubForm Wizard appears.

TROUBLE

If the SubForm Wizard does not appear, delete the subform control, make sure that the Control Wizards button 🔧 on the Toolbox toolbar is selected, then repeat Step 6.

7. **Click Employee Info Subform in the Use an existing form list box, click Next, click Next to accept CourseID as the linking field, click Finish to accept the default name for the new subform control, click the Form View button 🖳 on the Form Design toolbar, then resize the subform and columns in Form Design View and Form View as shown in Figure G-6**

   The first of 27 courses, Access1, is displayed in the main form. The six employees who completed that course are displayed in the subform.

8. **Save and close the form**

FIGURE G-5: Creating the Employee Info Subform

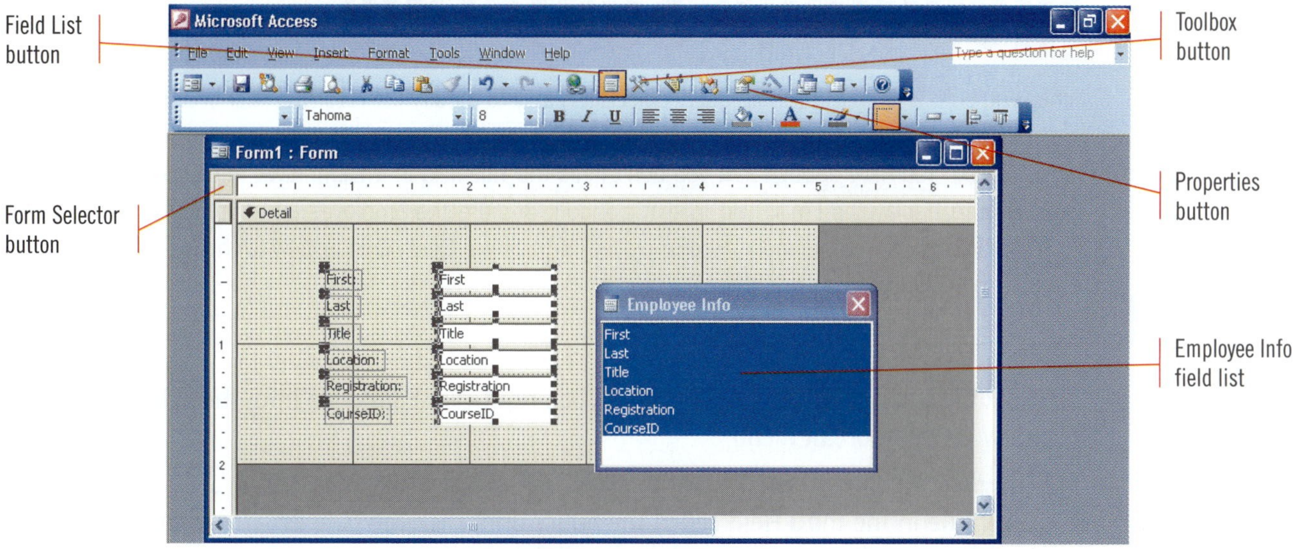

Field List button

Form Selector button

Toolbox button

Properties button

Employee Info field list

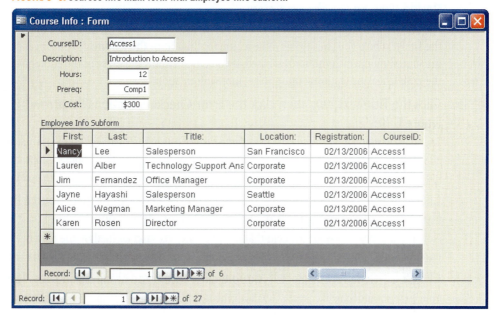

FIGURE G-6: Courses Info main form with Employee Info Subform

Clues to Use

Linking the form and subform

If the form and subform do not appear to be correctly linked, examine the subform's property sheet, paying special attention to the **Link Child Fields** and **Link Master Fields** properties on the Data tab.

These properties tell you which field serves as the link between the main form and subform. The field specified for this property should be present in both queries that underlie the main form and subform.

Modifying Subforms

When you build a form/subform on query objects it is easy to modify the recordset later because modifying the query that is used in the form's Record Source property automatically modifies the recordset that is passed to the form. You have decided that you don't need the Title field in the Employee Info Subform, but rather, would like to display the Email field in that position. Because the Employee Info Subform is based on the Employee Info query, you can modify the Employee Info query in Query Design View to change the fields that are available to the Employee Info Subform.

STEPS

1. **Click the Queries button on the Objects bar, right-click Employee Info, then click Design View on the shortcut menu**

   The Employee Info query opens in Query Design View.

2. **Click Title in the third Field cell in the query grid, click the Title list arrow, then click Email to delete the Title field and add the Email field to this query**

   The Employee Info query should look like Figure G-7.

3. **Click the Save button 🖫 on the Query Design toolbar, then close the query**

   With the Employee Info query modified, the recordset sent to the Employee Info Subform is also automatically modified because the Record Source property of the Employee Info Subform is the Employee Info query.

4. **Click the Forms button on the Objects bar, right-click Employee Info Subform, then click Design View on the shortcut menu**

   Notice that the Title field now displays an **error indicator**, a small green triangle in the upper-left corner of the Title text box. You already know the reason for this error—the Title field is no longer part of the Employee Info query upon which this form is based. If you did not know the cause of the error, however, you could use the Error Checking Options button to get more information.

5. **Click the Title text box, then click the Error Checking Options list arrow ⬦ as shown in Figure G-8**

   The shortcut menu indicates that no field named Title exists in the Field List, and that you could remedy this by either changing the control's Control Source property or the form's Record Source property. You want the text box to display the contents of the Email field, so you'll modify its Control Source property to make this change.

6. **Click Edit the Control's Control Source Property, click the Control Source list arrow, click Email, then click the Properties button 🖻 to close the property sheet**

   Now the text box is bound to a field that is part of the recordset defined by the Employee Info query, so the error indicator has disappeared. The label to the left of the field needs to be modified to describe the new data.

7. **Click the Title label to select it, double-click Title, type Email, then press [Enter]**

   Your form should look like Figure G-9. Both the text box and label are modified to display information about the Email field versus the Title field.

8. **Save and close the Employee Info Subform, then double-click the Course Info form to open it in Form View**

   The Email field information now appears in the subform.

FIGURE G-7: Changing the Employee Info query

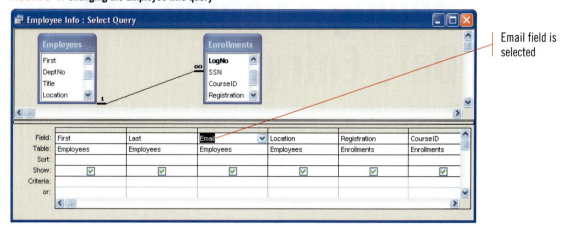

Email field is selected

FIGURE G-8: Using the Error Checking Options button

Error Checking Options button list arrow

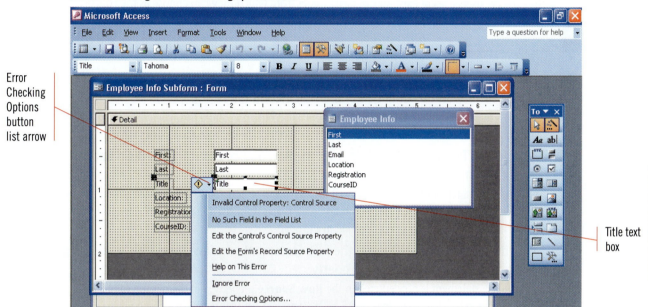

Title text box

FIGURE G-9: Modifying the subform text box and label

Email label has been modified

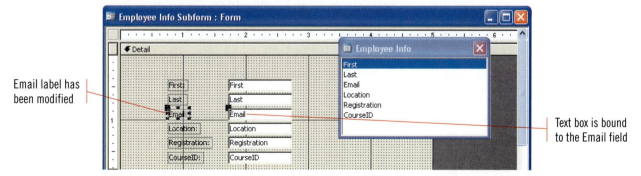

Text box is bound to the Email field

Clues to Use

Error checking options

Access 2003 will check several types of common errors for you in Form and Report Design View. When it finds an error, Access will display the Error Checking Options button to help you resolve the error. The types of errors that Access will check and the ability to turn this feature on and off are found on the Error Checking tab of the Options dialog box. To open the Options dialog box, click Options on the Tools menu.

Adding a Combo Box for Data Entry

Most fields are added to a form as text box controls, but if a finite set of values can be identified for a field, changing the text box to a list box or combo box control should be considered. If you provide the user with a combo box to enter data into a field, a user can select and enter data faster and more accurately than entering data using a text box. Both the **list box** and **combo box** controls provide a list of values from which the user can choose an entry. A combo box also allows the user to type an entry from the keyboard; therefore, it is a "combination" of the list box and text box controls. You can create a combo box by using the **Combo Box Wizard**, or you can change an existing text box or list box into a combo box. You decide to change the Prereq text box (which specifies if a prerequisite course is required) from a text box into a combo box to give users a list of existing CourseID values from which they can choose as the course prerequisite. You also decide to change the Cost text box to a combo box to provide users a list of valid entries for that field.

STEPS

1. Click the Design View button, right-click the Prereq text box in the Detail section of the form, point to Change To, then click Combo Box

   Now that the control has been changed from a text box to a combo box, you are ready to populate the combo box list with values from the CourseID and Description fields from the Courses table.

QUICK TIP

The title bar of the property sheet identifies the name of the control that you are currently working with.

2. Click the Properties button, click the Row Source box, click the Build button, double-click Courses, then click Close

   The SQL Statement window opens and displays a query design grid and a field list you can use to select the fields you want to display in the combo box list. You want the values in the CourseID field to appear in the combo box list, so you'll add this field to the query.

3. Double-click CourseID, close the SQL Statement window, then click Yes when prompted to save the changes to the property

   An SQL statement is now entered in the **Row Source** property that defines the values that are presented in the combo box list. Your final step is to change the Cost text box into a combo box as well. MediaLoft has only four internal charges for its classes, $100, $200, $300, and $400. You want to display these values in the list of a combo box.

4. Right-click the Cost text box, point to Change To on the shortcut menu, then click Combo Box

   With the combo box in place you are ready to populate the combo box list with the appropriate values, $100, $200, $300, and $400. Because these values do not exist in a field in the database, you'll type them directly into the Row Source property. First, however, you must change the Row Source Type property from Table/Query to Value List.

5. Click the Row Source Type text box, click the Row Source Type list arrow, then click Value List

   The Value List option indicates that the combo box gets its values from the list entered in the Row Source property.

TROUBLE

Enter semicolons (;) between the values in the Row Source property.

6. Click the Row Source property text box, type $100; $200; $300; $400, press [Enter], click the Limit to List property list arrow, then click Yes as shown in Figure G-10

   Because you changed the **Limit to List** property to "Yes," the user cannot enter a new entry in this combo box from the keyboard. In other words, the text box part of the combo box has been disabled and the user must select a value from the list.

7. Click to toggle off the property sheet, click the Save button, click the Form View button, click the Cost combo box list arrow, then click $400

   The updated form with two combo boxes should look like Figure G-11.

FIGURE G-10: Modifying the Cost combo box

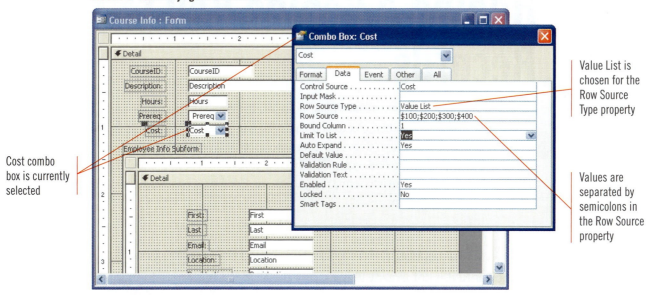

Cost combo box is currently selected

Value List is chosen for the Row Source Type property

Values are separated by semicolons in the Row Source property

FIGURE G-11: Two new combo boxes for data entry

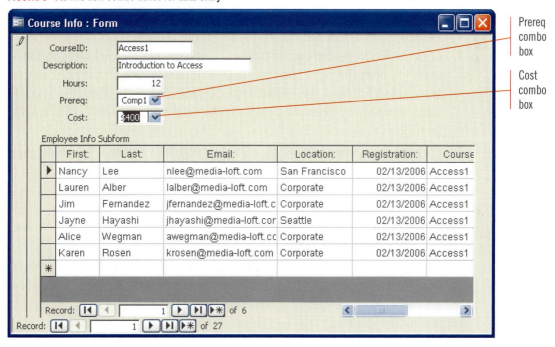

Prereq combo box

Cost combo box

Clues to Use

Choosing between a combo box and a list box

The list box and combo box controls are very similar, but the combo box is more popular for at least two reasons. While both provide a list of values from which the user can choose to make an entry in a field, the combo box also allows the user to make a unique entry from the keyboard. More importantly, however, most users like the drop-down list behavior of the combo box. A list box also provides a list of values, though it displays the list of values from which the user scrolls and selects a choice (the list box has no drop-down action). Some users refer to the combo box as a drop-down list because of the drop-down action.

Adding a Combo Box to Find Records

Most combo boxes are used to enter data; however, the combo box control can also be used to find records. When you use a combo box to find data, you must carefully identify it as a tool used to find and retrieve records so that the user doesn't become confused between the behavior of combo boxes used to enter data and those used to find data. You decide to add a combo box to help quickly locate the desired course on the Course Info form. You will use the Combo Box Wizard to help guide your actions in building this new combo box.

STEPS

1. **Click the Design View button, click the Toolbox button to toggle on the Toolbox toolbar (if it is not already visible), click the Field List button to toggle it off, click the Combo Box button on the Toolbox toolbar, then click on the right side of the main form**

   The Combo Box Wizard opens as shown in Figure G-12. The first question prompts you for the behavior of the combo box. The first option corresponds to how you created the Prereq combo box. The Prereq combo box enters data into the Prereq field by looking up CourseID values from the CourseID field in the Courses table. The second option corresponds to how you created the Cost combo box. The Cost combo box enters data into the Cost field by using a series of values that you entered into the combo box's Value List property. The third option corresponds to what you want to do now—use the combo box to find a record.

2. **Click the Find a record option button, click Next, double-click Description, click Next, use ✛ to drag the right edge of the Description column to the right so that all entries are visible, click Next, type FIND THIS COURSE in the label box, then click Finish**

   The new combo box appears in Form Design View as shown in Figure G-13. You test the combo box in Form View.

3. **Click the Form View button, click the FIND THIS COURSE list arrow, then click Computer Concepts**

   The selection for this combo box determines which record is displayed in the main form. In this case, it displays the Computer Concepts course, which is the fourth record. Now that you've added and tested the combo box successfully, you decide to move it to the Form Header section so that it is in a more logical position as the first control on the form.

4. **Click, click View on the menu bar, click Form Header/Footer, click the FIND THIS COURSE combo box to select it, then use ✋ to move the new combo box and its associated label to the left edge of the Form Header section**

   Save and test your form.

5. **Move and resize the FIND THIS COURSE combo box and label as needed, click the Save button, click, click the FIND THIS COURSE list arrow, then click Internet Fundamentals**

   The new placement of the combo box should look like Figure G-14.

FIGURE G-12: Combo Box Wizard

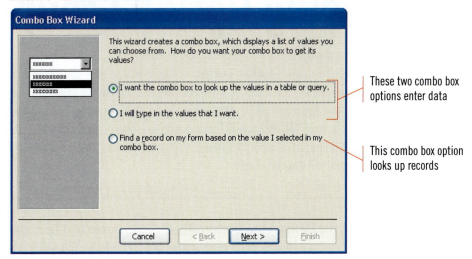

These two combo box options enter data

This combo box option looks up records

FIGURE G-13: New combo box used to find data

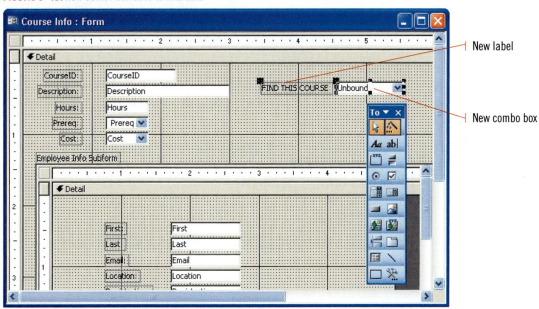

New label

New combo box

FIGURE G-14: Final placement of combo box used to find data

Form Header section

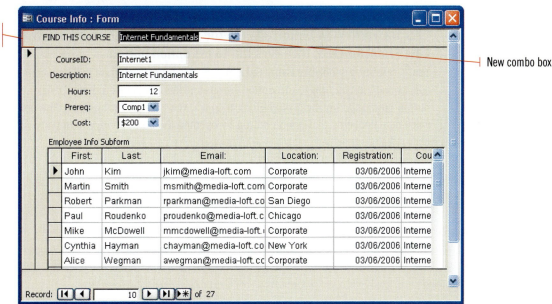

New combo box

UNIT
G

Access 2003

Adding Option Groups

An **option group** is a special type of bound control that is often used when only a few values are available for a field. You place **option button** controls within the option group to determine the value that is selected in the field. Each option button represents a different value that can be entered into the field that is bound to the option group. Option buttons within an option group are mutually exclusive; only one can be chosen at a time. MediaLoft's classes are offered in 6-, 8-, 12-, and 16-hour formats. Because this represents a limited number of options, you decide to use an option group control for the Hours field to further simplify the Courses form.

STEPS

1. **Click the Design View button, click the Hours text box, then press [Delete]**

   Both the Hours text box and its associated label are deleted. You will add the Hours field back to the form as an option group.

2. **Click the Option Group button on the Toolbox, click the Field List button to toggle it on, then drag the Hours field from the field list to the top of the right side of the form**

   The **Option Group Wizard** guides you as you develop an option group. The first question asks about label names for the option buttons.

3. **Type 6 hrs, press [Tab], type 8 hrs, press [Tab], type 12 hrs, press [Tab], type 16 hrs, click Next, click the No, I don't want a default option button, then click Next**

   The next question prompts you for the actual values associated with each option button.

4. **Type 6, press [Tab], type 8, press [Tab], type 12, press [Tab], then type 16 as shown in Figure G-15**

   The rest of the Option Group Wizard questions confirm what field the option group is bound to, the style you want to use for your option buttons, and how you want to label the option group.

5. **Click Next, click Next to accept Hours as the field that the value is stored in, click Next to accept Option buttons controls in an Etched style, then click Finish to accept Hours as the caption for the option group**

   An option group can contain option buttons, check boxes, or toggle button controls. The most common choice, however, is option buttons in an etched style. The Control Source property of the option group identifies the field it is bound to. The **Option Value property** of each option button identifies what value will be placed in the field when that option button is clicked. The new option group and option button controls are shown in Figure G-16.

6. **Click the Form View button, use the FIND THIS COURSE list arrow to find the Access Case Problems class, then click the 16 hrs option button**

   Your screen should look like Figure G-17. You changed the Access Case Problems course from 12 to 16 hrs. To add more option buttons to this option group at a later time, work in Form Design View and use the Option Button button on the Toolbox toolbar to add the new option button to the option group. Modify the value represented by that option button by opening the option button's property sheet and modifying the Option Value property.

Clues to Use

Protecting data

You may not want to allow all users who view a form to change all the data that appears on that form. You can design forms to limit access to certain fields by changing the Enabled and Locked properties of a control. The **Enabled property** specifies whether a control can have the focus in Form View. The **Locked property** specifies whether you can edit data in a control in Form View.

FIGURE G-15: Option Group Wizard

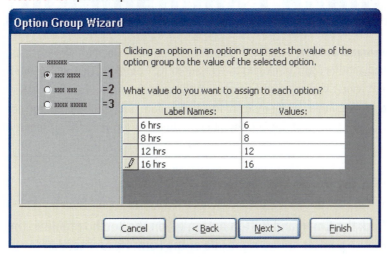

FIGURE G-16: Working with an option group in Form Design View

New option group

Option buttons

Option Group button

Option Button button

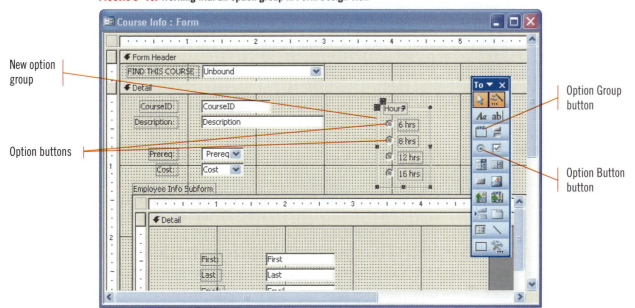

FIGURE G-17: Using an option group

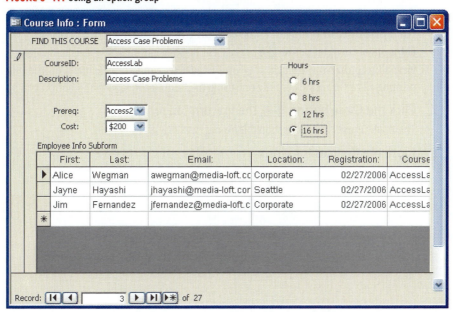

Adding Command Buttons

A **command button** is used to initiate a common action in Form View such as printing the current record, opening another form, or closing the current form. Command buttons are often added to the Form Header or Form Footer sections as the first or last controls on a form. **Sections** determine where controls appear and print. See Table G-2 for more information on form sections. You add a command button to the Form Header section of the Courses Info form to help users print the current record.

STEPS

1. **Click the Design View button**
   You will add the new command button to the right side of the Form Header section.

2. **Click the Command Button button on the Toolbox toolbar, then click with the ⁺☐ mouse pointer on the right side of the Form Header section**
   The Command Button Wizard opens, listing over 30 of the most popular actions for the command button, organized within six categories.

3. **Click Record Operations in the Categories list, click Print Record in the Actions list, click Next, click Next to accept the default picture, type Print Current Record as the button name, then click Finish**
   Your screen should look similar to Figure G-18. By default, the Print button on the Standard toolbar prints every record using the form layout, which creates a long printout. Therefore, adding a command button to print only the current record is very useful.

4. **Click the Form View button to view the new command button, double-click Lee in the first record of the subform, type your last name, then click the Print Record button in the Form Header section**
   Only the current record prints. You can also modify the form so that controls in certain form sections, such as the Form Header, appear on the screen but do not print. The **Display When** property of the Form Header determines when the controls in that section appear on screen and print.

5. **Click , double-click the Form Header section to open its property sheet, click the Format tab, click Always for the Display When property, click the Display When list arrow, click Screen Only, then click the Properties button to toggle off the property sheet**
   Now the Print Record button will appear on the screen when you are working in the form, but will not appear on printouts.

6. **Click the Save button , click , then click the Print Preview button to confirm that the Print button no longer appears on the printout**
   Using either the Print button or the Print Preview button on the Form View toolbar will print or preview all records. Now, though, the Form Header section will not appear on the printout whether you are printing all of the records or only one using the Print Record command button you placed on the form.

7. **Click the Close button , then return to Form View**
   The final Courses Info form should look like Figure G-19.

8. **Close the Courses Info form**

FIGURE G-18: Adding a command button

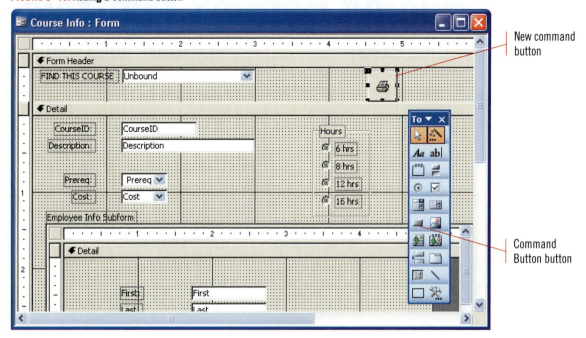

New command button

Command Button button

FIGURE G-19: Final Courses Info form

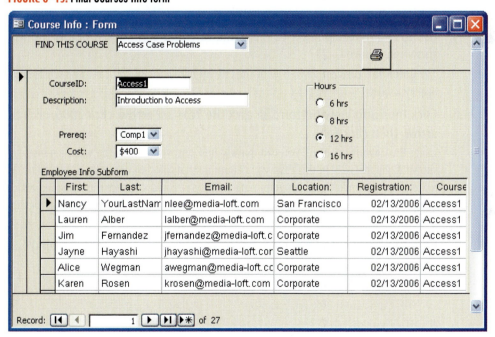

TABLE G-2: Form sections

section	description
Detail	Appears once for every record
Form Header	Appears at the top of the form and often contains command buttons or a label with the title of the form
Form Footer	Appears at the bottom of the form and often contains command buttons or a label with instructions on how to use the form
Page Header	Appears at the top of a printed form with information such as page numbers or dates
Page Footer	Appears at the bottom of a printed form with information such as page numbers or dates

Access 2003

Adding ActiveX Controls

An **ActiveX control** is a control that follows ActiveX standards. **ActiveX standards** are programming standards that were developed by Microsoft to allow developers to more easily share software components and functionality across multiple applications. For example, the same ActiveX control can be used in an Access form, in an Excel workbook, and on a Web page opened in Internet Explorer. The functionality of ActiveX controls covers a wide range of applications such as multimedia players, charting programs, and encryption software. Users of the Enrollments form have asked if you can provide a calendar on the form. You will use the Calendar ActiveX control to add the calendar that they request.

STEPS

1. **Right-click Attendance, then click Design View on the shortcut menu**

   Right now, the form lists six fields in a horizontal arrangement. The ActiveX controls will be placed just below the text boxes in the Detail section.

QUICK TIP

ActiveX controls are also available by clicking the More Controls button on the Toolbox toolbar.

2. **Click Insert on the menu bar, then click ActiveX Control**

   The Insert ActiveX Control dialog box opens as shown in Figure G-20, listing the available ActiveX controls in alphabetical order. The number and type of ActiveX controls will depend on the other programs loaded on your computer.

3. **Press C to move to the ActiveX Controls that start with the letter "C," click Calendar Control 11.0, then click OK**

   The Calendar control is added to the Detail section.

TROUBLE

The Spreadsheet control may be inserted below the Calendar control.

4. **Use the 🖐 mouse pointer to move the calendar control just below the text boxes as shown in Figure G-21**

   The **Calendar control** appears with the current date chosen. You can use the Calendar control to find or display a date.

5. **Click the Form View button 📧, click the Year list arrow, click 2006, click the Month list arrow, then click Feb**

   Using the Calendar control, you can quickly find out what day of the week a particular class started on as shown in Figure G-22. In this case, you determine that the class currently displayed on 2/13/2006 started on a Monday. With additional programming skills, you could connect the Attended text box to the ActiveX Calendar control so that the date clicked in the control was inserted as the value for the Attended field. For now, however, you will use the calendar control for reference purposes.

6. **Click the Save button 🖫, close the Attendance form, close the Training-G.mdb database, then exit Access**

FIGURE G-20: Insert ActiveX Control dialog box

Your list depends on the programs installed on your computer

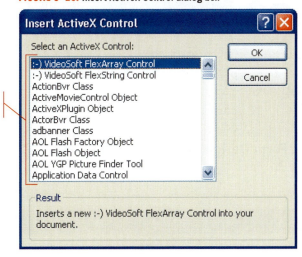

FIGURE G-21: ActiveX Calendar control in Form Design View

Calendar control

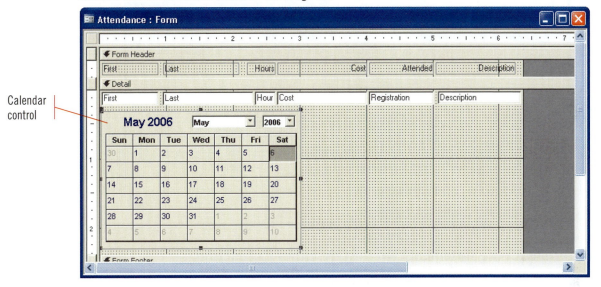

FIGURE G-22: Using the ActiveX Calendar control

Month list arrow

Attended field value

Year list arrow

February 13, 2006

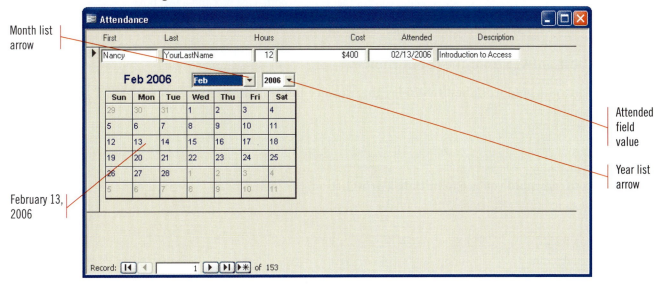

Access 2003

Practice

▼ CONCEPTS REVIEW

Identify each element of the Form Design View shown in Figure G-23.

FIGURE G-23

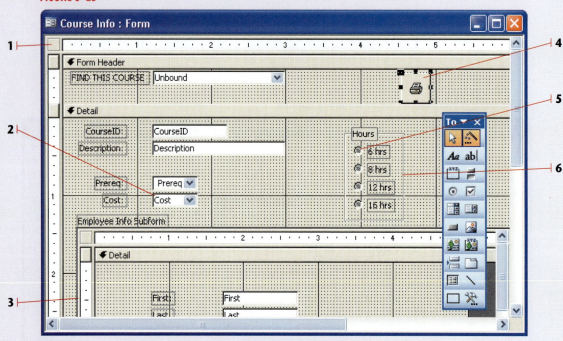

Match each term with the statement that best describes its function.

7. **Combo box**
8. **Command button**
9. **Subform**
10. **Controls**
11. **Option group**

a. Elements you add to a form such as labels, text boxes, and list boxes
b. A control that shows records that are related to one record shown in the main form
c. An unbound control that executes an action when it is clicked
d. A bound control that is really both a list box and a text box
e. A bound control that displays a few mutually exclusive entries for a field

Select the best answer from the list of choices.

12. **Which control would work best to display three choices for a field?**
    a. Text box
    b. Label
    c. Option group
    d. Command button

13. **Which control would you use to initiate a print action?**
    a. Option group
    b. List box
    c. Text box
    d. Command button

14. **Which control would you use to display a drop-down list of 50 states?**
    a. Check box
    b. Field label
    c. List box
    d. Combo box

15. **To view linked records within a form, use a:**
    a. Subform.
    b. List box.
    c. Design template.
    d. Link control.

16. **Which of the following defines what fields and records appear on a form?**
    a. Recordset
    b. Toolbox
    c. Property sheet
    d. ActiveX control

17. **Which is a popular layout for a main form?**
    a. Datasheet
    b. PivotTable
    c. Columnar
    d. Global

18. **Which is a popular layout for a subform?**
    a. Datasheet
    b. PivotTable
    c. Columnar
    d. Global

19. **Which of the following is true of ActiveX controls?**
    a. They always display data from the recordset.
    b. They can be used in many applications.
    c. They are quite limited in scope and functionality.
    d. They are added to a form in Form View.

20. **Which form section would most likely contain a command button?**
    a. Form Header
    b. Page Header
    c. Detail
    d. Page Footer

▼ SKILLS REVIEW

1. **Understand the form/subform relationship.**
   a. Start Access and open the **Membership-G.mdb** database from the drive and folder where your Data Files are stored.
   b. Click the Relationships button on the Database toolbar.
   c. Double-click File on the menu bar, then click Print Relationships.
   d. The Relationships for Membership-G appears as a report in Print Preview. In Report Design View, insert your name as a label in the Report Header section, then print the report.
   e. Close the Relationships report window without saving the report, and then close the Relationships window.
   f. Based on the one-to-many relationships defined in the Membership-G database, sketch two form/subform combinations that you could create.

2. Create subforms using the Form Wizard.

a. Start the Form Wizard.

b. Select all of the fields from both the Activities and the Members tables.

c. View the data by Members, then verify that the Form with subform(s) option button is selected.

d. Accept a Datasheet layout for the subform, a Standard style, name the form **Member Info**, and accept the default title of **Activities Subform** for the subform. View the Member Info form in Form View.

e. Find the record for Lois Market and enter your own first and last names into the FirstName and LastName text boxes.

f. Click File on the menu bar, then click Print. Click the Selected Record(s) option button in the Print dialog box to print only the record that contains your name.

g. Save, then close the Member Info form.

3. Create subforms using queries.

a. Open the Zips in the IA or MO query in Design View, then add the criteria to find only those records from **IA** or **MO** in the State field. View the datasheet to make sure that you have entered the criteria correctly, then save and close the query.

b. Using either the Form Wizard or Form Design View, build a columnar form based on the Zips in the IA or MO query using all fields in the query. Name the form **IA or MO**.

c. Open the IA or MO form in Design View, and add a subform control using the Subform Wizard below the three text boxes in the Detail section of the form.

d. Use the Subform Wizard to specify that the subform will use an existing query, click Next, then select all of the fields in the Dues query for the subform.

e. Allow the Subform Wizard to link the form and subform so that they show Dues for each record in IA or MO using Zip.

f. Accept Dues subform as the subform's name, and then display the form in Form View.

g. Resize the IA or MO form and Dues Subform as necessary to display all of the information clearly. Be sure to resize the datasheet columns so that all of the information in the subform is clearly visible.

h. Find the record for Zip 64105, enter your last name in the LastName field of the first record, and print only that record.

i. Click File on the menu bar, click Save As, name the main form **Zips**, then save and close the form and subform.

4. Modify subforms.

a. Open the Zips in the IA or MO query in Query Design View.

b. Delete the criteria that specifies that only the records with State values of IA or MO appear in the recordset.

c. Use Save As to save the modified query as **All Zips**, then close the query.

d. Open the Zips form in Form Design View.

e. Open the property sheet for the form. Click the Data tab, then change the Record Source property from Zips in IA or MO to **All Zips**.

f. Close the property sheet, save the form, view the form in Form View, then navigate to the record that displays Zip 64145 for Shawnee, Kansas.

g. Change the city to the name of your hometown, print only this record, then close the Zips form.

5. Add a combo box for data entry.

a. Open the Members form in Design View, then right-click the Zip text box and change it to a combo box control.

b. In the property sheet of the new combo box, click the Row Source property, then click the Build button.

c. Select the Zipcodes table only for the query, and then double-click the Zip field to add it as the only column of the query grid.

d. Close the SQL Statement window, and save the changes.

e. Close the property sheet, then save and view the form in Form View.

f. Navigate to the second record, then change the Zip to **64105** using the new combo box.

6. Add a combo box to find records.

a. In Form Design View, open the Form Header section of the Members form.

b. Use the Combo Box Wizard to add a new combo box to the left side of the Form Header section that finds records in the form based on a value you specify.

   c. Select the FirstName and LastName fields, make sure that each column is wide enough to view all values, and label the combo box **Find this Member**.

   d. Save the Members form, then view it in Form View.

   e. Use the Find this Member combo box to find your own record, then print it.

7. Add option groups.

   a. Open the Members form in Design View, then delete the Dues text box and label.

   b. Add the Dues field back to the form as an option group using the Option Group Wizard and below the Birthday text box.

   c. Enter **$25** and **$50** as the label names, then accept $25 as the default choice.

   d. Change the values to **25** and **50** to correspond with the labels.

   e. Store the value in the Dues field, choose Option buttons with an Etched style, type the caption **Annual Dues**, then click Finish.

   f. Save the Members form, display it in Form View, use the combo box to find the record with your name, then change the Annual Dues to **$25**.

8. Add command buttons.

   a. Open the Members form in Design View.

   b. Use the Command Button Wizard to add a command button to the right side of the Form Header section.

   c. Choose the Print Record action from the Record Operations category.

   d. Display the text **Print Current Record** on the button, then name the button **Print**.

   e. Save the form, display it in Form View, then use the combo box to find the record for Christine Collins. The final form should look similar to Figure G-24.

   f. Navigate to the record with your own name, change the month and day of the Birthday entry to your own, then print the record using the new Print Current Record command button.

   g. Save, then close the Members form.

9. Add ActiveX Controls.

   a. Open the Member Info form in Design View, then add a Microsoft Office Spreadsheet 11.0 ActiveX control to the Detail section of the main form.

   b. Resize the spreadsheet control so that about three columns and four rows are visible, then move it just below the CharterMember check box. Move the Activities subform down about 1" so that everything fits on the form.

   c. Save the Member Info form, then view it in Form View. The spreadsheet ActiveX control will be used to calculate the value of the time donated to various activities.

   d. Navigate to the record with your last name. In cell A1 of the spreadsheet, type **8**, the total number of hours you have contributed based on the information in the subform.

   e. In Cell A2 of the spreadsheet, type **12**, the value of one hour of work, to determine your contributions to this club.

   f. In Cell A3 of the spreadsheet, type **=A1*A2**, then press [Enter] to calculate the total value of the hours of time you have donated.

   g. Click File on the menu bar, click Print, then choose the Selected Record(s) option button to print only this record.

   h. Save and close the Member Info form, close the Membership-G.mdb database, then exit Access.

FIGURE G-24

Access 2003

▼ INDEPENDENT CHALLENGE 1

As the manager of a music store's instrument rental program, you have created a database to track instrument rentals to schoolchildren. Now that several rentals have been made, you wish to create a form/subform to facilitate the user's ability to enter a new rental record.

a. Start Access, then open the database **Music Store-G.mdb** from the drive and folder where your Data Files are stored.

b. Using the Form Wizard, create a new form based on all of the fields in the Customers and Rentals tables.

c. View the data by Customers, choose a Datasheet layout for the subform and a Standard style, then accept the default form titles of **Customers** for the main form and **Rentals Subform** for the subform.

d. Add another record to the rental subform for Raquel Bacon by typing **888335** as the SerialNo entry and **5/1/06** as the RentalDate entry.

e. Close the Customers form.

f. You want to add the Description field to the subform information. To do this, start a new query in Query Design View to serve as the record source for the subform.

g. Add the Rentals and Instruments tables to the query, then close the Show Table dialog box.

h. Add all of the fields from the Rentals table and the Description field from the Instruments table to the query, save the query with the name **Rental Description**, view the query datasheet, then close it.

i. Open the Rentals Subform in Design View, then change the Record Source property of the form from Rentals to **Rental Description**.

j. Open the subform's field list, then drag the Description field to just below the RentalDate text box in the Detail section. The field may not line up perfectly with the others but because the Default View of this form is set to Datasheet, this form will appear as a datasheet regardless of the organization of the controls in Form Design View.

k. Close the property sheet, save, then close the Rentals Subform.

l. Open the Customers form. It now contains a new Description field in the subform. Enter your first and last name in the first record of the main form, then use the Selected Records option in the Print dialog box to print only that record. (*Hint*: To open the Print dialog box, click File on the menu bar, then click Print.)

m. Close the Customers form, close the Music Store-G.mdb database, then exit Access.

▼ INDEPENDENT CHALLENGE 2

As the manager of a music store's instrument rental program, you have created a database to track instrument rentals to schoolchildren. You add command buttons to a form to make it easier to use.

a. Start Access then open the database **Music Store-G.mdb** from the drive and folder where your Data Files are stored.

b. Using the Form Wizard, create a form/subform using all the fields of both the Customers and Schools tables.

c. View the data by Schools, use a Datasheet layout for the subform, then choose a Standard style.

d. Accept the default names of **Schools** for the main form and **Customers Subform** for the subform.

e. Resize the subform columns to view all of the data in Form View. Use Form Design View to resize the subform as necessary to display all columns.

f. In Form Design View, open the Form Header section, then drag the top edge of the Detail section down about 0.5" to provide room in the Form Header section for a command button.

g. In Form Design View, add a command button to the middle of the Form Header using the Command Button Wizard. The action should print the current record and display the text **Print School Record**. Name the button **Print**.

Advanced Challenge Exercise

- Add a second command button to the left side of the Form Header section using the Command Button Wizard. The action should add a new record and display the text **Add New School**. Name the button **Add**.
- Add a third command button to the right side of the Form Header section using the Command Button Wizard. The action should close the form and display the text **Close**. Name the button **Close**.
- Select all three command buttons, then use the Top option on the Align submenu of the Format menu to align the top edges of all three controls.
- Open the property sheet for the Form Header and give the Display When property the **Screen Only** value. Close the property sheet, then save the Schools form.
- Display the form in Form View, click the Add New School button, add the name of your high school to the SchoolName field, allow the SchoolNo to increment automatically, then add the information of a friend as the first record within the subform. Note that the CustNo and SchoolNo fields in the subform will be entered automatically.

h. Use the Print School Record button to print only this new school record.

i. Close the Schools form, close the Music Store-G.mdb database, then exit Access.

▼ INDEPENDENT CHALLENGE 3

As the manager of a music store's instrument rental program, you have created a database to track instrument rentals to schoolchildren. Now that the users are becoming accustomed to forms, you add a combo box and option group to make the forms easier to use.

    a. Start Access, then open the database **Music Store-G.mdb**.

    b. Using the Form Wizard, create a form/subform using all the fields of both the Instruments and Rentals tables.

    c. View the data by Instruments, use a Datasheet layout for the subform, and choose a Standard style.

    d. Enter the name **Instruments Main Form** for the main form and **Rentals** for the subform.

    e. In Form Design View of the Instruments Main Form, delete the MonthlyFee text box and label.

    f. Add the MonthlyFee field as an option group to the right side of the main form using the Option Group Wizard.

    g. Enter the Label Names as **$35**, **$40**, **$45**, and **$50**. Do not specify a default option. The corresponding values for the option buttons should be **35**, **40**, **45**, and **50**.

    h. Store the value in the MonthlyFee field. Use Option buttons with an Etched style.

    i. Caption the option group **Monthly Fee**, save the form, then view it in Form View. Resize and move controls as necessary to see all the fields clearly. Move through each of the 30 instrument records in the main form. For those instruments that do not display a $35, $40, or $45 monthly fee value, click the $45 option button. Save and close the Instruments Main Form.

Advanced Challenge Exercise

    ■ In Table Design View of the Instruments table, add a field named **Condition** with a Text data type. This field will record the condition of the instrument as Excellent, Good, Poor, or Fair.

    ■ Start the Lookup Wizard for the Condition field, and choose the "I will type in the values that I want" option button.

    ■ Enter **Excellent**, **Good**, **Fair**, and **Poor** as the four possible values, and accept the name **Condition** as the label for the lookup column. Save and close the Instruments table.

    ■ In Form Design View of the Instruments Main Form, drag the Condition field from the field list area just below the SerialNo text box. On a piece of paper, explain why the Condition field was automatically added as a combo box control rather than a text box control.

    ■ Right-click the Condition combo box and change it into a list box. Resize and move the Condition list box as well as the Rentals subform so that both controls fit on the form without overlapping.

    ■ Save the form then display it in Form View. Move through the records, selecting Excellent as the Condition value choice for the first two records and Good for the third and fourth records. On your paper, comment on the differences between the combo box control and list box control as perceived by the user of the form.

    j. Print only the fourth record (Cello, 1234570) by clicking File on the menu bar, clicking Print, then choosing the Selected Records option button before clicking OK in the Print dialog box.

    k. Close the Instruments Main Form, close the Music Store-G.mdb database, and then exit Access.

INDEPENDENT CHALLENGE 4

You are in the process of organizing your family's photo library. After reviewing the general template sample databases, but not finding any good matches to use for your project, you decide to browse the template gallery featured at the Microsoft Web site to determine if there is a sample database that you can download and use or modify for this purpose.

a. Connect to the Internet, then go to the home page for Access, www.microsoft.com/access.

b. Search for a link to database templates in the Templates Gallery. (You may be able to access templates directly at http://officeupdate.microsoft.com/templategallery/.)

c. Once you are at the Template Gallery, search for database templates.

d. Scroll through the list of available database templates, select the Photograph database, Genealogy database, or any other database template that interests you, then download the template. You may be prompted to accept an end-user license agreement for templates. Read the agreement, then click Accept if you understand and accept the agreement.

e. A file is downloaded to your computer, which you need to double-click to open.

f. Follow the prompts to extract the database.

g. Open the database, explore the objects in the database, enter several records, then print one of them.

h. Close the database, then exit Access.

▼ VISUAL WORKSHOP

Open the **Training-G.mdb** database. Use the Form Wizard to create a new form, as shown in Figure G-25. The First, Last, and Location fields are from the Employees table, the Description field is from the Courses table, and the Registration and Passed fields are from the Enrollments table. View the form by Employees, choose a Datasheet layout for the subform, and choose a Standard style. Name the form **Employee Basic Info**, then name the subform **Test Results**. Add command buttons to the Form Header to print the current record as well as to close the form. Add your name as a label to the Form Header section, then print the first record.

FIGURE G-25

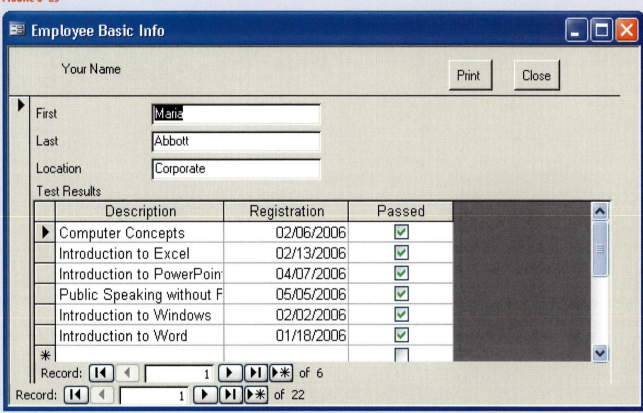

UNIT H
Access 2003

Sharing Information and Improving Reports

OBJECTIVES

Import data

Apply conditional formatting

Add lines

Use the Format Painter and AutoFormats

Create a dynamic Web page

Export data

Compact and repair a database

Back up a database

If you have a SAM user profile, you may have access to hands-on instruction, practice, and assessment of the skills covered in this unit. Log in to your SAM account and go to your assignments page to see what your instructor has assigned.

Although you can print data in forms and datasheets, **reports** give you more control over how data is printed and greater flexibility in presenting summary information. To create a report, you use bound controls such as text boxes to display data, and unbound controls such as lines, graphics, and labels to clarify the data. Another way to share Access information with other people is to export Access data to file formats that others can read such as Excel spreadsheets or Web pages. You will export Access data to various file formats to electronically share Access data with others. You will also create paper reports that use conditional formatting, colors, and lines to clarify the information. Finally, you will learn how to compact, repair, and back up the Training database.

Importing Data

Importing brings data from an external file, such as an Excel spreadsheet or another database, into an existing Access database. The Access import process copies the data from the original source and pastes the data in the Access database. See Table H-1 for more information on the types of data that Access can import. The Accounting Department has requested a quarterly electronic update of data currently stored in the Training-H database. You will create a new database for the Accounting Department, and then import historical cost and attendance information from the Training-H database into it. In addition, you will import data currently stored in an Excel spreadsheet into the new Accounting database.

STEPS

TROUBLE
You can't import from the Training-H database if it is opened in another Access window.

1. **Start Access, click the Create a new file link in the Getting Started task pane, click the Blank database link in the New File task pane, navigate to the drive and folder where your Data Files are stored, type Accounting in the File name text box, then click Create**
   The Accounting database window appears, but no objects are currently in the database.

2. **Click File, point to Get External Data, click Import, navigate to the drive and folder where your Data Files are stored, then double-click Training-H.mdb**
   The Import Objects dialog box opens, as shown in Figure H-1. Any object in the Training-H database can be imported into the Accounting database.

3. **Click the Tables tab (if not already selected), click 1QTR-2006, click Courses, click the Queries tab, click Accounting Info, click the Reports tab, click Accounting Report, then click OK**
   The four selected objects are imported from the Training-H database into the Accounting database.

4. **Click Queries on the Objects bar, then click Tables on the Objects bar to confirm that all four objects were imported successfully**
   The MediaLoft Accounting Department stores department codes in an Excel workbook that also needs to be imported into this database.

5. **Click File on the menu bar, point to Get External Data, click Import, click the Files of type list arrow, click Microsoft Excel, then double-click Deptcodes.xls**
   The Import Spreadsheet Wizard presents the data that you want to import, and then guides you through the rest of the import process.

6. **Make sure the First Row Contains Column Headings check box is checked as shown in Figure H-2, then click Next**
   The column headings in the first row will be the field names when the data is imported as a table into the Accounting database.

7. **Make sure the In a New Table option button is selected, click Next, click Next to accept the default field options, click the Choose my own primary key option button, make sure Code is displayed in the primary key list box, click Next, type Codes in the Import to Table box, click Finish, then click OK**
   The Deptcodes spreadsheet is imported as a table named Codes into the Accounting database.

8. **Explore the imported objects, close all open objects, then close the Accounting database**

FIGURE H-1: Import Objects dialog box

Tables tab is selected

Table objects in Training-H database

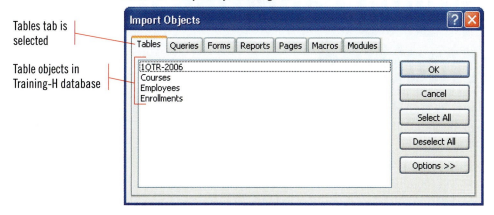

FIGURE H-2: Import Spreadsheet Wizard

Column headings will be field names

Data to import from the spreadsheet

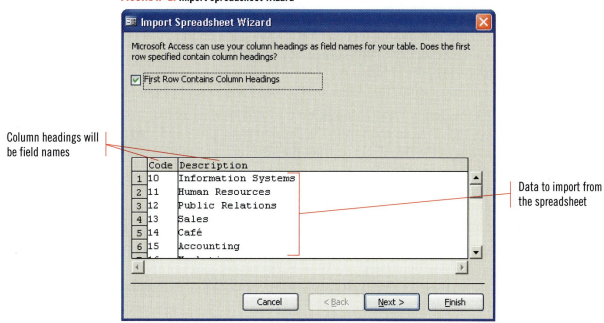

TABLE H-1: Data sources Microsoft Access can import

data source	version or format supported	data source	version or format supported
Microsoft Access database	2.0, 7.0/95, 8.0/97, 9.0/2000, and 10.0/2002	Microsoft Exchange	All versions
Microsoft Access project	9.0/2000, 10.0/2002	Delimited text files	All character sets
dBASE	III, IV, 5, and 7	Fixed-width text files	All character sets
Paradox, Paradox for Windows	3.x, 4.x, 5.0, and 8.0	HTML	1.0 (if a list) 2.0, 3.x (if a table or list)
Microsoft Excel	3.0, 4.0, 5.0, 7.0/95, 8.0/97, 9.0/2000, and 10.0/2002	XML documents	All versions
Lotus 1-2-3	.wks, .wk1, .wk3, and .wk4	SQL tables, Microsoft Visual FoxPro, and other data sources that support ODBC protocol	Open Database Connectivity (ODBC) is a protocol for accessing data in Structured Query Language (SQL) database servers

Applying Conditional Formatting

Conditional formatting allows you to change the appearance of a control on a form or report based on criteria you specify. Conditional formatting helps you highlight important or exceptional data on a form or report. When formatting several controls at the same time, you may find it helpful to group the controls. When you **group controls** it means that a formatting choice you make for any control in the group will be applied to every control in the group. You want to apply conditional formatting to the Attendance by Location report to emphasize those employees that have received more than 200 hours of training. You also want to apply other report formatting techniques such grouping controls and hiding duplicate values.

STEPS

QUICK TIP

Click the Sorting and Grouping button 📑 to view the grouping and sorting fields.

1. **Open the Training-H.mdb database, click Reports on the Objects bar, double-click Location Report, then press [Page Down] and use the Zoom In pointer 🔍 to preview each page of the report**

   The records are grouped by Location and the Hours field is subtotaled for each Location.

TROUBLE

If you cannot see the group selection handles, drag the top edge of the Location Footer section down.

2. **Click the Design View button 📐 on the Print Preview toolbar to switch to Report Design View, click the Last text box in the Detail section, press and hold [Shift], click the First text box in the Detail section, click the Title text box, release [Shift], click Format on the menu bar, then click Group**

   Group selection handles surround the group of three text boxes, so when you click on *any* control in a group, you select *every* control in the group. Clicking a control within a *selected group* still selects just that single control.

QUICK TIP

The title bar of the property sheet indicates that multiple controls have been selected.

3. **Click the Properties button 🖳, click the Format tab, click No in the Hide Duplicates property, click the Hide Duplicates list arrow, click Yes, then click 🖳 to toggle off the property sheet**

   With the **Hide Duplicates** property set to Yes, the First, Last, and Title values will print only once per employee rather than once for each record in the Detail section. This change will help distinguish the records for each employee within each location.

4. **Click the =Sum([Hours]) text box in the Location Footer section, click Format on the menu bar, then click Conditional Formatting**

   The Conditional Formatting dialog box opens.

QUICK TIP

You can add up to three conditional formats for any combination of selected controls.

5. **Click the between list arrow, click greater than, press [Tab], type 200, click the Bold button 🅱 for Condition 1, click the Fill/Back Color button list arrow 🎨 ▾ for Condition 1, then click the yellow box**

   The Conditional Formatting dialog box should look like Figure H-3.

6. **Click OK in the Conditional Formatting dialog box, click the Save button 💾, click the Print Preview button 🔍, then zoom and position the report as shown in Figure H-4**

   Conditional formatting made the Kansas City subtotal appear bold and with a yellow fill color because the value is greater than 200. Default formatting was applied to the subtotal for the New York group because it was not greater than 200.

7. **Click the Design View button 📐, click the Label button 🅰 on the Toolbox toolbar, click the right side of the Report Header section, then type your name**

8. **Save, print, then close the Location Report**

FIGURE H-3: Conditional Formatting dialog box

Default formatting

Condition 1 formatting

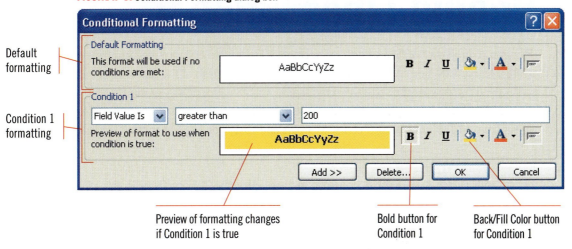

Preview of formatting changes if Condition 1 is true

Bold button for Condition 1

Back/Fill Color button for Condition 1

FIGURE H-4: Location Report with conditional formatting

Duplicate values are hidden

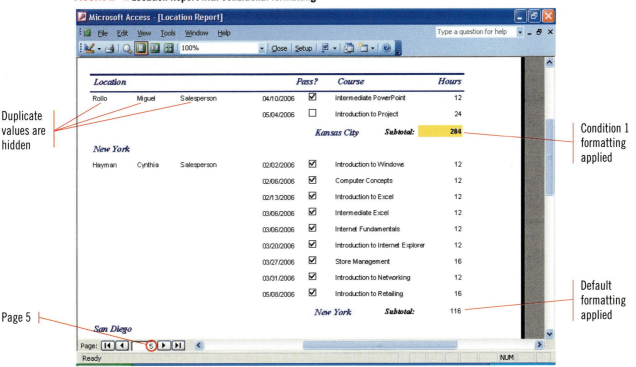

Condition 1 formatting applied

Default formatting applied

Page 5

Adding Lines

Unbound controls such as labels, lines, and rectangles are used to enhance the clarity of a report. When you create a report with the Report Wizard, it often creates line controls at the top or bottom of the report sections to visually separate the sections on the report. You can add, delete, or modify these lines to best suit your needs. ░░░ The Personnel Department has asked you to create a report that lists all of the course registrations, and to subtotal each course by hours and costs. You use line controls to clarify the subtotals.

STEPS

1. **Double-click Create report by using wizard, click the Tables/Queries list arrow, click Query: All Registrations, click the Select All Fields button ▸▸, click Next, click by Employees, click Next, then click Next**

   After determining the grouping field(s), the Report Wizard prompts for the sort field(s).

2. **Click the first sort field list arrow, click Registration to sort the detail records by the registration date of the class, then click the Summary Options button**

   The Summary Options dialog box allows you to include the sum, average, minimum, or maximum value of fields in various sections of the report.

3. **Click the Hours Sum check box, click the Cost Sum check box, click OK, click Next, click the Outline 2 Layout option button, click the Landscape Orientation option button, click Next, click the Formal style, click Next, type Registration Report as the report title, click Finish, then click the Zoom Out pointer 🔍 on the report**

   The wizard created several line and rectangle controls identified in Figure H-5. You want to delete the line between each detail record.

TROUBLE

The easiest place to select the line control in the Detail section is between the Passed check box and Description text box.

4. **Click the Design View button ⬚ on the Print Preview toolbar, click the line control near the top of the Detail section, then press [Delete]**

   You also want to add double lines below the calculations in the Report Footer section to indicate that they are grand totals.

5. **Click the Line button ╲ on the Toolbox toolbar, press and hold [Shift], drag a line from the bottom-left edge of the =Sum([Hours]) text box to the bottom-right edge of the =Sum([Cost]) text box in the Report Footer section, then release [Shift]**

   Copying and pasting lines creates an exact duplicate of the line.

TROUBLE

Be sure to add the lines to the calculations in the Report Footer section, and not the Department Footer section.

6. **Click the Copy button 📋 on the Report Design toolbar, then click the Paste button 📋**

   Design View of the report should look like Figure H-6. Short double lines under the calculations in the Report Footer section indicate grand totals.

7. **Click the Save button 💾, click the Print Preview button 🔍, then click the Last Page Navigation button ▶|**

   The last page of the report should look like Figure H-7. The two lines under the final values indicate that they are grand totals.

FIGURE H-5: First page of Registration Report

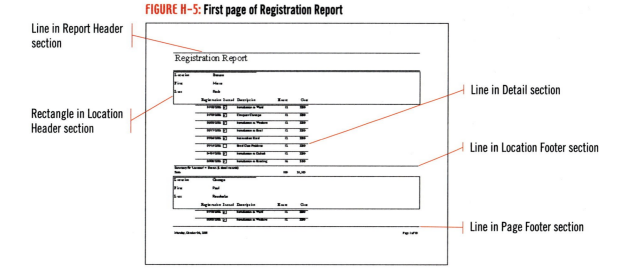

Line in Report Header section

Rectangle in Location Header section

Line in Detail section

Line in Location Footer section

Line in Page Footer section

FIGURE H-6: Registration Report in Design View

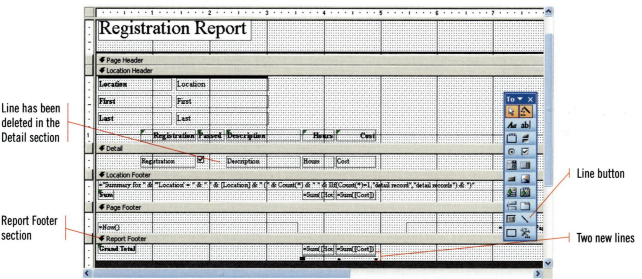

Line has been deleted in the Detail section

Report Footer section

Line button

Two new lines

FIGURE H-7: Last page of Registration Report

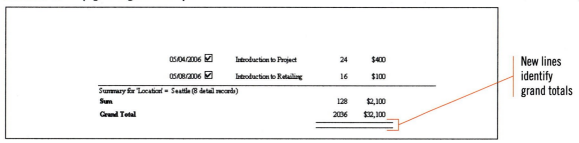

New lines identify grand totals

Access 2003

Clues to Use

Line troubles

Sometimes lines are difficult to find in Report Design View because they are placed against the edge of a section or the edge of other controls. To find lines that are positioned next to the edge of a section, drag the section bar to expand it to expose the line. To draw a perfectly horizontal line, hold [Shift] down while creating or resizing it. Also note that it is easy to accidentally widen a line beyond the report margins, thus creating extra unwanted pages in your printout. To fix this problem, narrow any controls that extend beyond the margins of the printout and drag the right edge of the report to the left. Because the default left and right margins for an 8.5" x 11" sheet of paper are 1" each, a report in portrait orientation must be no wider than 6.5" and a report in landscape orientation must be no wider than 9".

Using the Format Painter and AutoFormats

The **Format Painter** is a tool used to copy multiple formatting properties from one control to another in Form or Report Design View. **AutoFormats** are predefined formats that you apply to a form or report to set all of the formatting enhancements such as font, color, and alignment. Access provides several AutoFormats that you can use or modify, or you can create new ones as well. You will use the Format Painter to change the characteristics of selected labels, then save the report's formatting scheme as a new AutoFormat so that you can apply it to other reports.

STEPS

1. **Click the Design View button, click the Registration label in the Location Header section, click the Font/Fore Color button list arrow, click the blue box in the second row, click the Fill/Back Color button list arrow, click the yellow box in the fourth row, then click the Align Left button**

    Some of the buttons on the Formatting (Form/Report) toolbar such as the **Bold button** and the **Align Left button** appear with a different background color to indicate that they are applied to the selected control. Others, such as the **Font/Fore Color button** and **Fill/Back Color button**, display the last color that was selected. The Format Painter can help you apply multiple formats from one control to another very quickly.

2. **Double-click the Format Painter button on the Report Design toolbar, then click each of the labels in the Location Header section**

    The Format Painter copied all of the formatting properties from the Registration label and pasted those formats to the other labels in the Location Header section, as shown in Figure H-8. You decide to save this set of formatting embellishments as a new AutoFormat so that you can quickly apply them to another report.

    > **QUICK TIP**
    > You can also press [Esc] to release the Format Painter.

3. **Click to turn off the Format Painter, click the AutoFormat button on the Report Design toolbar, click Customize, click the Create a new AutoFormat option button, click OK, type Yellow-Blue, then click OK**

    The AutoFormat dialog box should look like Figure H-9.

4. **Click OK to close the AutoFormat dialog box, save, then close the Registration Report**

    > **TROUBLE**
    > Resize the Email text box in Report Design view as needed.

5. **Double-click Employee Directory to preview the report to see how it is currently formatted, click , click , click Yellow-Blue in the Report AutoFormats list, click OK, click OK when prompted about the Report Header section, then click the Print Preview button**

    Your screen should look like Figure H-10. The AutoFormat you applied changed the formatting properties of labels in the Location Header section.

6. **Click , then click the Save button**

    You decide to delete the Yellow-Blue AutoFormat so that it doesn't remain on this computer.

7. **Click , click Yellow-Blue, click Customize, click the Delete 'Yellow-Blue' option button, click OK, then click Close**

8. **Click the Label button on the Toolbox toolbar, click the right side of the Report Header section, type your name, save, print, then close the Employee Directory report**

FIGURE H-8: Using the Format Painter

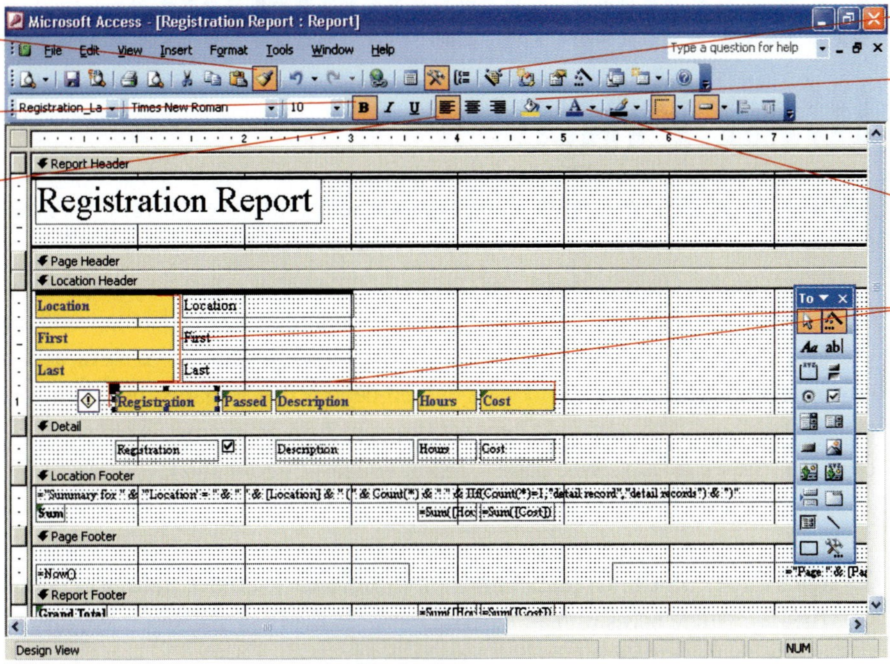

Format Painter button

Bold button

Align Left button

AutoFormat button

Fill/Back Color button

Font/Fore Color button

Labels have been formatted the same way

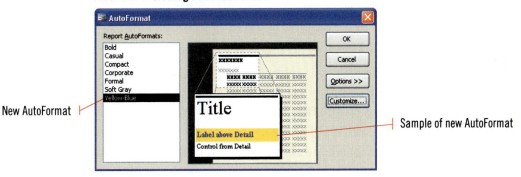

FIGURE H-9: Creating a new AutoFormat

New AutoFormat

Sample of new AutoFormat

FIGURE H-10: Applying the Yellow-Blue AutoFormat to the Employee Directory report

Yellow-Blue AutoFormat changed the controls in the Location Header section

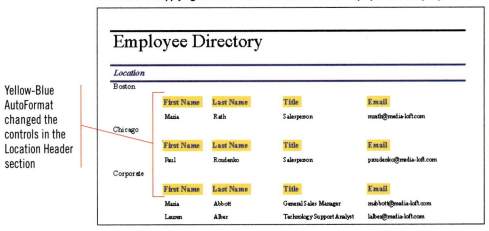

Clues to Use

Creating summary reports

Sometimes you may not want to show all the details of a report, but rather only the summary information that is calculated in the Group Footer section. You can accomplish this by deleting all controls in the Detail section. Calculated controls in a Group Footer section will still calculate properly even if the individual records used within the calculation are not displayed using the Detail section.

Creating a Dynamic Web Page

A **Web page** is a file that is viewed using **browser** software such as Microsoft Internet Explorer. You can use the export capabilities of Access to create static Web pages displaying data that is current as of the moment the Web page was created. **Static** Web pages do not change when the database is updated. You can also use Access to create **dynamic** Web pages that are connected to the database and display up-to-date data. Use the page object to create dynamic Web pages, which are also called **data access pages**. The benefit of converting Access data into any type of Web page is that it makes the information more accessible by merely opening a Web page in a browser program such as Internet Explorer. You use the page object to create a dynamic Web page to report employee information.

STEPS

1. **Click Pages on the Objects bar, then double-click Create data access page by using wizard**
   The Page Wizard opens with an interface similar to the Form and Report Wizards. First, you need to determine what fields you want the Web page to display.

2. **Click the Tables/Queries list arrow, click Table: Employees, click the Select All button >> , then click Next**
   Web pages, like reports, can be used to group and sort records.

3. **Double-click Location to specify it as a grouping field, click Next, then click Next**

   > **TROUBLE**
   > If the Web page opens in Design View, click the Page View button ⊞ to switch to Page View.

4. **Type Employees by Location for the title, click the Open the page option button, then click Finish**
   The Web page opens in **Page View**, a special view within Access that allows you to see how your Web page will appear when opened in Internet Explorer. You modify the structure of a data access page in **Page Design View**.

5. **Click the Expand button + to the left of the Location label to show the fields within that group**
   Your page should look like Figure H-11. On a data access page, the **navigation bars** at the bottom of the Web page not only allow you to move from record to record, they contain buttons to edit, sort, and filter the data. Page View shows you how the Web page will appear from within Internet Explorer.

   > **TROUBLE**
   > If presented with a message about the connection string, read the message, then click OK.

6. **Click the Save button 🖫 on the Page View toolbar, type einfo as the filename, navigate to the drive and folder where your Data Files are stored, then click Save**
   To view the Web page in Internet Explorer, use the **Web Page Preview** view, which opens the page in Internet Explorer.

7. **Click the View button list arrow 🖉 ▾ , then click Web Page Preview**
   Internet Explorer loads and presents the Web page.

   > **TROUBLE**
   > Web pages created through the page object in Access require Internet Explorer version 5.0 or later.

8. **Click the Next button ▶ twice on the Employees-Location navigation toolbar to move to the Corporate location, click + to the left of the Location label, click 8/20/1998 in the DateHired text box, then click the Sort Ascending button ⬆↓ on the Employees Navigation bar**
   The Web page should look like Figure H-12.

9. **Close Internet Explorer, then close the Employees by Location page**

FIGURE H-11: Employees by Location Web page in Page View

Grouping field

Collapse button

Sorting field

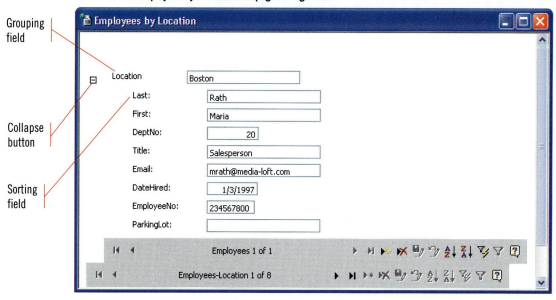

FIGURE H-12: einfo.htm dynamic Web page in Internet Explorer

Internet Explorer

Path to the Web page

DateHired text box

Sort Ascending button on Employees Navigation bar

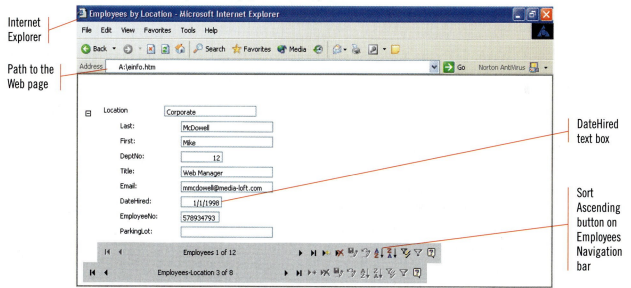

Exporting Data

Exporting quickly converts data from Access to another file format such as an Excel workbook, a Word document, or a static Web page. Exporting copies and pastes data *out of* the database, whereas importing copies and pastes data *into* an Access database. See Table H-2 for more information on the types of data that Access can export. ▓▓▓ You received a request from the Human Resources Department for an electronic copy of the data in the Employees table. You use Access export features to provide this data both as an Excel spreadsheet and as a static Web page.

STEPS

1. **Click Tables on the Objects bar, click Employees, click File on the menu bar, click Export, type EmployeeData as the filename, click the Save as type list arrow, click Microsoft Excel 97-2003, navigate to the drive and folder where your Data Files are stored, then click Export**

   The export process creates the EmployeeData.xls Excel workbook that contains the Employees data.

2. **Click the Start button ⊞ start on the taskbar, point to All Programs, point to Microsoft Office, click Microsoft Office Excel 2003, click the Open button 📂 on the Excel Standard toolbar, navigate to the drive and folder where your Data Files are stored, double-click EmployeeData.xls, then close the task pane if it is open**

   The EmployeeData spreadsheet opens. All of the data has been successfully exported, but some of it is hidden because the columns are too narrow.

3. **Click the Select All button (a blank box above Row 1 and to the left of Column A), double-click the ✚ pointer on the line that separates column heading A and B, then click anywhere on the data**

   With the columns widened, you can clearly see all the data that was exported, as shown in Figure H-13. Field names are exported to Row 1 and the record for the first employee is in Row 2.

4. **Click the Save button 🖫, click File on the menu bar, then click Exit**

   Exporting Access data to other file formats, including static Web pages, is a similar process.

QUICK TIP
If you want to create a *dynamic* Web page that automatically shows current data from the database, create the Web page with the page object rather than the Export option on the File menu.

5. **Click File on the Access menu bar, click Export, type edata as the filename, click the Save as type list arrow, click HTML Documents, navigate to the drive and folder where your Data Files are stored, then click Export**

   The Employees table is saved as an HTML file. **HTML** is short for **HyperText Markup Language**, which defines a set of tags that, when inserted into a text file, give browser software such as Internet Explorer instructions on how to display the file as a Web page. Web pages created using the export feature are *static*; they do not retain any connection to the database and will not display new or updated data after they are created.

6. **Start Internet Explorer, click File on the Internet Explorer menu bar, click Open, click Browse, navigate to the drive and folder where your Data Files are stored, double-click edata.html, then click OK**

   The static edata.html Web page appears as shown in Figure H-14. Static Web pages created through the export process can be successfully viewed using either Microsoft Internet Explorer or Netscape Navigator. Field names are not exported when you export data to a Web page. The first row contains the first record in the database for Megan Burik.

7. **Close Internet Explorer**

FIGURE H-13: EmployeeData.xls spreadsheet

Excel

Select All button

EmployeeData.xls

Field names

FIGURE H-14: edata.html static Web page

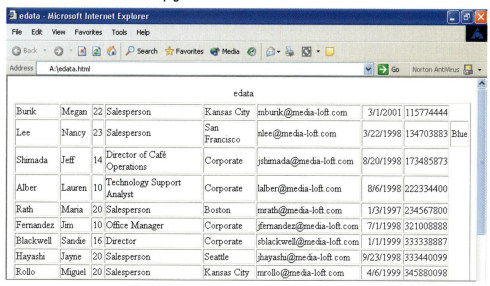

TABLE H-2: Data formats Microsoft Access can export

application	version or format supported	application	version or format supported
Microsoft Access database	2.0, 7.0/95, 8.0/97, 9.0/2000, and 10.0/2002	Lotus 1-2-3	.wk2, .wk1, and .wk3
Microsoft Access project	9.0/2000, 10.0/2002	Delimited text files	All character sets
dBASE	III, IV, 5, and 7	Fixed-width text files	All character sets
Paradox, Paradox for Windows	3.x, 4.x, 5.0, and 8.0	HTML	1.0 (if a list), 2.0, 3.x, and 4.x (if a table or list)
Microsoft Excel	3.0, 4.0, 5.0, 7.0/95, 8.0/97, 9.0/2000, and 10.0/2002	SQL tables, Microsoft Visual FoxPro, and other data sources that support ODBC protocol	Visual FoxPro 3.0, 5.0, and 6.x
Microsoft Active Server Pages	All	XML documents	All

Compacting and Repairing a Database

When you delete data and objects in an Access database, the database can become fragmented and use disk space inefficiently. **Compacting** the database reorganizes the data and objects to improve performance by reusing the space formerly occupied by the deleted objects. The compacting process also repairs damaged databases. You want to compact and repair the Training-H database to make sure that it is running as efficiently as possible.

STEPS

1. **Click Tools on the menu bar, then point to Database Utilities**

   The **Compact and Repair Database** option on the Database Utilities menu allows you to compact and repair an open database, but *if you are working on a floppy disk, do not compact the database*. The compaction process creates a temporary file that is just as large as the database itself. If the floppy disk does not have enough space to build the temporary file, it will not be able to finish the compaction process, and you may corrupt your database beyond repair.

2. **If you are working on your hard drive or a large storage device such as a Zip drive, click Compact and Repair Database**

   If you want to compact and repair the database on a regular basis, you can use the **Compact on Close** feature, which compacts and repairs the database every time it is closed.

3. **Click Tools on the menu bar, click Options, then click the General tab of the Options dialog box**

   The Options dialog box with the Compact on Close option is shown in Figure H-15. By default, the Compact on Close option is not checked for new databases. More information on the default options that you can modify in the Options dialog box is shown in Table H-3.

4. **If you are working on your hard drive or a large storage device such as a Zip drive, click the Compact on Close check box, then click OK**

   The next time you exit the database, Access will automatically compact and repair it before closing the database.

Clues to Use

Object dependencies

Before you delete objects in a database, you may want to view dependencies between database objects. **Object dependencies** identify which objects rely on other objects in your database. For example, a report's record source might depend on the XYZ query, and the XYZ query might depend on one or more tables. Viewing object dependencies helps you avoid deleting an object that affects others. It also helps identify those objects that if deleted, would not affect anything else. This information helps you compact and maintain the database as efficiently as possible. You open the **Object Dependencies task pane** to view object dependencies. Click View on the menu bar, point to Toolbars, then click Task Pane. Click the Task Pane list arrow, then click Object Dependencies. Click the object you want to examine in the database window, click the Show dependency information for the selected object link in the task pane, and then click OK if prompted.

FIGURE H-15: Options dialog box

General tab

Compact on Close

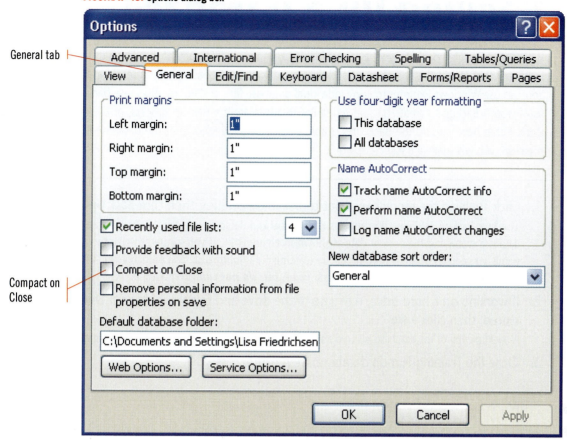

TABLE H-3: Default settings in the Options dialog box

tab	description
View	Determines what items are displayed on the screen such, as the status bar, Startup task pane, new object shortcuts, hidden objects, and system objects; also determines whether an object is opened with a single- or double-click
General	Stores the default print margins, determines the way dates are formatted (with two or four digits), sets the default database folder, and contains default settings for Web, AutoCorrect, and other database features
Edit/Find	Sets the defaults for find/replace, filter by form, and delete confirmation messages
Keyboard	Establishes the default behavior for keystrokes used to enter and edit data
Datasheet	Sets the default color, font, gridlines, cell effects, and other datasheet options
Forms/Reports	Identifies the default form and report templates and other default form and report options
Pages	Sets default page colors and styles and default page folders
Advanced	Stores the default Dynamic Data Exchange (DDE), file format, record locking, and other database-level default options
International	Identifies the defaults for direction of text, alignment, and cursor movement
Error Checking	Identifies which rules are flagged as errors and what color is used for the error indicator
Spelling	Determines which dictionaries are used for the spell check feature, which spell check rules are used, and which AutoCorrect options are applied
Tables/Queries	Stores the default field type and properties for new fields in Table Design View, as well as the default screen elements and query options for Query Design View

Access 2003

Backing Up a Database

If hardware is stolen or destroyed, a recent **backup**, an up-to-date copy of the data files, can minimize the impact of that loss to the business. A good time to back up a database is right after it has been compacted. You can use Windows Explorer to copy individual database files and floppy disks, use backup software such as Microsoft Backup to create backup schedules to automate the backup process, or back up the database from within Access using the Back Up Database utility. Now that the database is compacted and repaired, you will make a backup copy of it.

STEPS

1. **Click Tools on the menu bar, point to Database Utilities, then click Back Up Database**

   The Save Backup As dialog box appears and the backup database is given a default name that includes the database name and the current date as shown in Figure H-16. If you wanted to give the backup a different name, you could change it now. If you are working on a floppy disk, you probably won't have room to save the backup. *If working on a floppy disk, read, but do not complete Step 2.*

2. **If working on a hard drive, navigate to the drive and folder where your Data Files are stored, then click Save**

   A backup copy of the database is saved and you return to the database window in the Training-H database.

3. **Close the Training-H.mdb database, then exit Access**

FIGURE H-16: Save Backup As dialog box

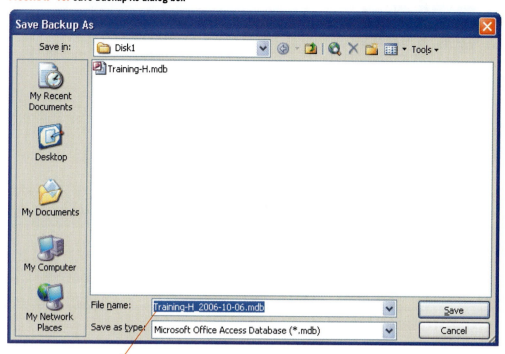

Default backup filename
(your date will differ)

Clues to Use

Backing up an entire folder to floppy disks

If your Data Files are stored in one folder on the hard drive and you want to create a backup to floppy disks, you can do that in one process using Windows Explorer. First, locate the folder that stores your Data Files in the Folders list within Windows Explorer. Right-click the folder, click Send To on the shortcut menu, then click 3½ Floppy (A:). Insert a blank floppy disk into drive A when prompted. If all of the Data Files will not fit on one floppy disk, you will be prompted to insert another floppy disk. One file, however, cannot be larger than a single floppy disk for this backup method to work. If one file is larger than the storage space of a floppy disk, approximately 1.44 MB, you must use backup software such as Microsoft Backup or compression software such as WinZip to compress the files before copying them to a floppy. You can also use a larger storage device such as a Zip, Jaz, or a network drive that accommodates files larger than 1.44 MB. A final option for backing up large files is to upload them to a Web site or attach them to an e-mail that you can access later.

Practice

▼ CONCEPTS REVIEW

Identify each element of the Report Design View shown in Figure H-17.

FIGURE H-17

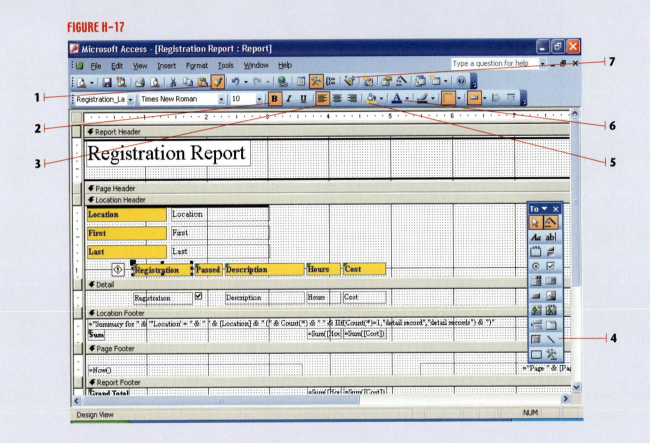

Match each term with the statement that best describes its function.

8. Exporting

9. Compacting

10. Backup

11. Format Painter

12. Importing

a. An up-to-date copy of data files

b. A process to quickly copy data from an external source into an Access database

c. A process that rearranges the data and objects of a database to improve performance and to decrease storage requirements

d. A process to quickly copy data from an Access database to an external file

e. Used to copy formatting properties from one control to another

Select the best answer from the list of choices.

13. **Which control would you use to visually separate groups of records on a report?**
    a. Option group
    b. Image
    c. Bound Object Frame
    d. Line

14. **Which wizard would you use to create a dynamic Web page?**
    a. Page Wizard
    b. Table Wizard
    c. HTML Wizard
    d. Web Wizard

15. **What feature allows you to apply the formatting characteristics of one control to another?**
    a. AutoContent Wizard
    b. AutoFormat
    c. Report Layout Wizard
    d. Format Painter

16. **Which of the following file types cannot be imported into Access?**
    a. Excel
    b. Lotus 1-2-3
    c. Lotus Notes
    d. HTML

17. **If you want to apply the same formatting characteristics to several controls at once, you might consider _____ them.**
    a. AutoFormatting
    b. AutoPainting
    c. Grouping
    d. Exporting

18. **Which feature compacts and repairs the database every time it is closed?**
    a. Compact on Close
    b. Conversion Wizard
    c. Backup Wizard
    d. Repair Wizard

19. **Which Access feature would you use to create a static Web page?**
    a. Web page Wizard
    b. Export
    c. Mailto: HTML
    d. Conversion Wizard

20. **What feature allows you to change the appearance of a control on a form or report based on criteria you specify?**
    a. AutoFormat
    b. Behavioral formatting
    c. Event-driven formatting
    d. Conditional formatting

▼ SKILLS REVIEW

1. **Import data.**
   a. Open the **Membership-H.mdb** database from the drive and folder where your Data Files are stored.
   b. Import the data in the **Prospects.xls** Excel spreadsheet as a table named **Prospects**. The first row contains the column headings, and ContactID should be set as the primary key field.
   c. Open the Prospects table in Datasheet View.
   d. Add your personal information as a new record using **10** as the entry for the ContactID field.
   e. Print the datasheet in landscape orientation, then close the datasheet.

2. **Apply conditional formatting.**
   a. Using the Report Wizard, create a report based on the Member Activity Log using all of the fields in that query.
   b. View the data by Activities, group by MemberNo, sort ascending by ActivityDate, and Sum the Hours field.
   c. Use the Outline 1 Layout, Portrait Orientation, Compact style, type **Member Activity Log** as the report title, then preview the report.
   d. In Report Design View, select the =Sum([Hours]) calculated field in the MemberNo Footer section and use Conditional Formatting to change the text to bold italic, and the Font/Fore color to blue if the field value is greater than or equal to **10**.
   e. Add a label to the Report Footer section with the text **Created by Your Name**.
   f. Group all of the controls in the Report Footer section, then apply italics to the group.
   g. Save, preview, then print the last page of the report.

3. **Add lines.**
   a. Open the Member Activity Log report in Design View, then delete one of the lines above and below the labels in the MemberNo Header section. (*Hint*: There are two lines both above and below the labels in the MemberNo Header section—delete one of them in each position.)
   b. Format the two remaining lines in the MemberNo Header section bright blue. (*Hint*: Use the Line/Border color button on the Formatting (Form/Report) toolbar.)
   c. Delete the text box with the ="Summary for ..." calculation and the line at the top of the MemberNo Footer section.
   d. Draw two short horizontal lines just below the =Sum([Hours]) calculation in the Report Footer section to draw attention to this grand total. (*Hint*: Press and hold [Shift] while creating the line for it to be perfectly horizontal.)
   e. Save the report, then print the last page.

4. **Use the Format Painter and AutoFormats.**
   a. Open the Member Activity Log report in Design View.
   b. Format the MemberNo label in the MemberNo Header section with a bold Arial Narrow 11-point font. Be careful to format the MemberNo label and not the MemberNo text box.
   c. Use the Format Painter to copy that format to the five other labels in the MemberNo Header section (ActivityDate, FirstName, LastName, Dues, and Hours). Be careful to format the labels and not the text boxes in the MemberNo Header section.
   d. Change the color of the Member Activity Log label in the Report Header section to red.
   e. Create a new AutoFormat named **RedTitle** based on the Member Activity Log report.
   f. Add a label with your name to the Report Header section, print the first page of the Member Activity Log report, then save it.
   g. In Design View, apply the Corporate AutoFormat. (*Hint*: Click the report selector button in the upper-left corner of the report to select the entire report before applying an AutoFormat. If an individual section or control is selected when you apply an AutoFormat, it will be applied to only that section or control.)
   h. Use the Customize button in the AutoFormat dialog box to delete the RedTitle style.
   i. Preview, then print the first page of the Member Activity Log report. Save, then close the report.

5. **Create a dynamic Web page.**
   a. Use the Page Wizard to create a Web page based on all of the fields in the Members table.
   b. Group the information by Zip, do not add any sorting orders, title the page **Zip Code Groups**, then open it in Page View.

c. Navigate to the 50266 zip code, then expand the records to show the information for Kristen Larson. Enter your first and last name into the page, as shown in Figure H-18, then save and print that page.

d. Save the data access page with the name **zip.htm** to the drive and folder where your Data Files are stored, then close the page.

FIGURE H-18

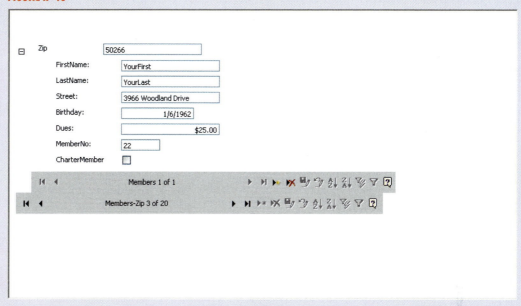

6. Export data.

a. Export the Members table as an HTML Document with the name **members.html** to the drive and folder where your Data Files are stored.

b. Start Internet Explorer, click File on the menu bar, click Open, then click Browse. Find and then double-click the **members.html** Web page, click OK to view it in Internet Explorer, then click Print on the Standard Buttons toolbar to print that page.

c. Close Internet Explorer, then return to the Membership-H database window.

7. Compact and repair a database.

a. If working on a hard drive, compact and repair the database.

b. If working on a hard drive, set the Compact on Close option so that the database automatically compacts and repairs itself every time it is closed.

8. Back up a database.

a. If working on a hard drive, back up the database with the default filename using the Tools menu. Store the backup in the drive and folder where your Data Files are stored.

b. Close the Membership-H.mdb database, then exit Access.

▼ INDEPENDENT CHALLENGE 1

As the manager of a music store's instrument rental program, you created a database to track instrument rentals to schoolchildren. Now that several instruments have been purchased, you often need to print a report listing instruments in inventory. You create a single instrument inventory report based on a parameter query that prompts the user for the type of instrument to be displayed on the report. You conditionally format the report to highlight instruments in poor condition.

a. Start Access, then open the database **Music Store-H.mdb**.

b. Use the Report Wizard to create a report based on the Instruments by Type query. Select all of the fields, group by the Description field, sort in ascending order by the SerialNo field, use a Stepped Layout, use a Portrait Orientation, apply a Corporate style, and title the report **Instruments in Inventory**.

c. Preview the report and type **Cello** when prompted for the type of instrument.

d. Open the report in Design View, then add a label with your name to the Report Header.

e. Select the Condition text box in the Detail section, then use conditional formatting so that when the field value is equal to **Poor**, the text is bold italic, and the Font/Fore Color is red.

f. Save, then preview the report. Enter **Violin** when prompted for the type of instrument.

g. Print the report, then close the Instruments in Inventory report.

h. If working on the hard drive, check the Compact on Close option.

i. Close the Music Store-H.mdb database, then exit Access.

▼ INDEPENDENT CHALLENGE 2

As the manager of a music store's instrument rental program, you have created a database to track instrument rentals to schoolchildren. Now that several instruments have been rented, you need to create a conditionally formatted report that lists which schools have a large number of rentals.

a. Start Access, then open the database **Music Store-H.mdb**.

b. Use the Report Wizard to create a report with the following fields from the following tables:
   Schools: SchoolName
   Instruments: Description, MonthlyFee
   Rentals: RentalDate

c. View the data by Schools, do not add any additional grouping levels, sort in ascending order by RentalDate, and Sum the MonthlyFee field.

d. Use an Outline 1 Layout, Portrait Orientation, Casual style, and title the report **School Summary Report**.

e. Open the report in Design View, then click the =Sum([MonthlyFee]) control in the SchoolNo Footer section.

f. Use Conditional Formatting to specify that the field be Bold and have a bright yellow Fill/Back Color if the sum is greater than or equal to 200.

g. Add a label to the Report Header section with your name, then save the report.

h. Print the first page of the report.

i. Close the School Summary Report, close the Music Store-H.mdb database, then exit Access.

▼ INDEPENDENT CHALLENGE 3

As the manager of a music store's instrument rental program, you have created a database to track instrument rentals to schoolchildren. You need to build both static and dynamic Web pages for this database.

    a. Start Access, then open the database **Music Store-H.mdb**.

    b. Use the Page Wizard to create a data access page with the SchoolName field from the Schools table, the RentalDate field from the Rentals table, and all of the fields in the Instruments table.

    c. Group the records by SchoolName, sort them in ascending order by RentalDate, title the page **School Rentals**, then display it in Page View.

    d. In Design View, click in the Click here and type title text prompt, then type your name.

    e. Save the page as **school.htm** in the folder where your Data Files are stored, then display it in Web Page Preview.

    f. Find the record for the Thomas Jefferson Elementary school, then click the Expand button.

Advanced Challenge Exercise

■ Double-click Excellent in the Condition field for the first instrument, then click the Filter by Selection button in the upper navigation bar to find all instruments rented to this school in excellent condition

■ Navigate to the second instrument with an Excellent condition for the Thomas Jefferson Elementary school, then print that page.

    g. Close Internet Explorer, close the Music Store-H.mdb database, then exit Access.

▼ INDEPENDENT CHALLENGE 4

You are on the staff of an economic development team whose goal is to encourage tourism in the Baltic Sea region. You have created an Access database called Baltic-H to track important fields of information for the countries in that region, and are using the Internet to find information about the area.

a. Start Access and open the **Baltic-H.mdb** database from the drive and folder where your Data Files are stored.

b. Connect to the Internet, then go to www.yahoo.com, www.about.com, or any general search engine to conduct some research for your database. Your goal is to find three upcoming events for Warsaw, Poland, then print the Web page(s).

c. Open the datasheet for the Cities table, then expand the subdatasheet for Warsaw, Poland. Enter the three events for Warsaw in the subdatasheet, then close the Cities table.

d. Use the Report Wizard to build a report based on all of the fields in the Cities table except the CityID, and the EventName and EventDate from the Events table.

e. View the data by Cities, do not add any more grouping levels, sort the records in ascending order by EventDate, use a Block Layout and Portrait Orientation, apply a Bold style, and title the report Baltic Events.

f. Preview the report.

g. In Report Design View, add your name as a label to the Report Header section, then save, print, and close the Baltic Events report.

Advanced Challenge Exercise

- Use Save As to save the report with the name **Baltic Events - Blue**.
- In Report Design View, group and then format the labels in the Page Header section so that all of the text for each label is clearly visible.
- Modify the color of the lines at the top and the bottom of the Page Header section to be bright blue. Modify the text color of the labels in the Report Header section to be bright blue.
- Save, print, and close the Baltic Events - Blue report.

h. Close the Baltic-H.mdb database, then exit Access.

▼ VISUAL WORKSHOP

Open the **Training-H.mdb** database and use the Report Wizard to create the report shown in Figure H-19. Select the First, Last, and Location fields from the Employees table, and the Description and Hours fields from the Courses table. View the data by Employees, do not add any more grouping levels, sort in ascending order by Description, and Sum the Hours. Use the Stepped, Portrait, and Soft Gray style options. Title the report **Employee Education Report**. In Report Design View enter your name as a label in the Report Header section and widen the Description field to display all values clearly. Delete the long calculated field and the Sum label in the EmployeeNo Footer section, and add conditional formatting so that the =Sum([Hours]) field displays in bold with a bright yellow background if the value is greater than or equal to 100. Add a subtotal line above the =Sum([Hours]) field in the EmployeeNo Footer section, and two lines to indicate a grand total below the =Sum([Hours]) field in the Report Footer section. Make other changes as necessary so that the last page of your report looks like Figure H-19.

FIGURE H-19

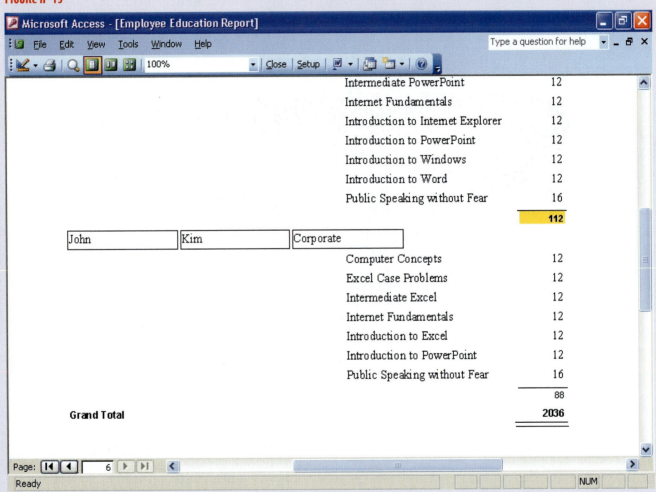

UNIT I
Access 2003

Sharing Access Information with Other Office Programs

OBJECTIVES

Examine Access objects
Set relationships
Import XML data
Link data
Publish data to Word
Analyze data with Excel
Merge data with Word
Export data to XML
Using an Access project with SQL Server

If you have a SAM user profile, you may have access to hands-on instruction, practice, and assessment of the skills covered in this unit. Log in to your SAM account and go to your assignments page to see what your instructor has assigned.

Access is a relational database program that can share data with many other Microsoft Office software products. This capability is important because you may want to use features of one Microsoft Office product with data stored in another type of file. For example, you might want to use Excel's "what-if" analysis and charting features to analyze and chart data that is currently stored in an Access database. Or, you may want to merge records selected by an Access query into a Word document to create a mass mailing. Fortunately, Microsoft provides many tools to share data between Microsoft Office programs. You have developed an Access database that tracks courses, employees, and course attendance for the staff training provided by MediaLoft for Fred Ames, director of training. You will share Access data with other software programs so that each MediaLoft department can have the data they have requested in a format they can use.

Examining Access Objects

To become proficient with Access, you should understand key database terminology, including the name and purpose of the seven Access objects.  You review key Access terminology and the seven Access objects.

Be sure you are familiar with the following database terminology:

- The smallest piece of information in a database is called a **field**, or category of information, such as an employee's name, e-mail address, or department. A **primary key field** is a field that contains unique information for each record, such as an employee's Social Security number. A group of related fields, such as all descriptive information for one employee, is called a **record**. A collection of records for a single subject, such as all of the employee records, is called a **table**.

- When a table is opened, the fields and records are displayed in **Datasheet View**, an arrangement where fields are displayed as columns and records are displayed as rows, as shown in Figure I-1. Several related tables create a **relational database**. Click the **Expand button** ⊞ to the left of a record in a datasheet to see related records from another table.

- Tables are the most important **objects** in an Access database because they contain the data. An Access database can also contain six other object types: **queries**, **forms**, **reports**, **pages**, **macros**, and **modules**. They are summarized in Table I-1.

- Query objects are based on tables. Form, page, and report objects can be based on either tables or queries. You can enter and edit data in four of the objects—tables, queries, pages, and forms—*but the data is physically stored in only one place: tables*. The relationships among database objects are shown in Figure I-2. The macro and module objects can provide additional database productivity and automation features such as **GUI (graphical user interface)** screens and buttons, which mask the complexity of the underlying objects. All of the objects (except for Web pages created by the page object) are stored in one database file that has an **MDB** (Microsoft database) file extension.

TABLE I-1: Access objects

object	purpose
Table	Contains all of the raw data within the database in a spreadsheet-like view called a datasheet
Query	Answers a question a user has about the data in the database, and presents the answer in a datasheet view
Form	Provides an easy-to-use data entry screen that generally shows only one record at a time
Report	Provides a professional printout of data that may contain enhancements such as headers, footers, and calculations on groups of records; mailing labels can also be created from report objects
Page	Creates Web pages from Access objects and provides Web page connectivity features to an Access database
Macro	Stores a collection of keystrokes or commands such as printing several reports or displaying a toolbar when a form opens
Module	Stores Visual Basic for Applications programming code that extends the functions and automated processes of Access

FIGURE I-1: Employees table in Datasheet View

Employees table

Current record

Expand buttons

22 records

FIGURE I-2: Relationships among Access objects

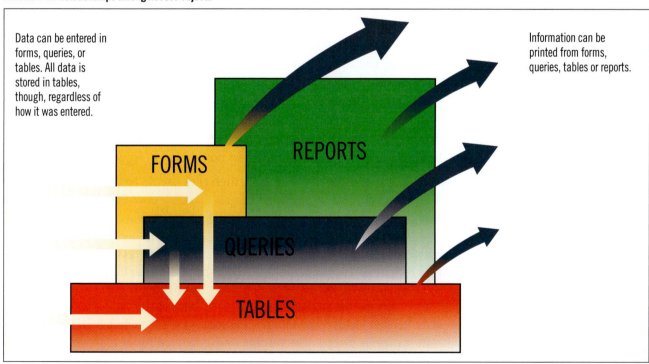

Data can be entered in forms, queries, or tables. All data is stored in tables, though, regardless of how it was entered.

Information can be printed from forms, queries, tables or reports.

REPORTS

FORMS

QUERIES

TABLES

Setting Relationships

An Access database is a **relational database** because tables are related through a common field so that data from multiple tables can be displayed at the same time. The primary benefit of organizing your data into related tables is to minimize redundant data. By minimizing redundant data, you improve the accuracy of the information, and the speed and flexibility with which it can be accessed. The process of designing a database into multiple related tables is called **normalization**, and involves determining appropriate fields, tables, and table relationships. Relationship types are summarized in Table I-2. 🎨 You decide to add an Instructors table to the Training database. You can then relate the Instructors table to the Courses table (one instructor can teach many courses) so that it participates with the rest of the relational database.

STEPS

1. **Start Access, open the Training-I.mdb database from the drive and folder where your Data Files are stored, click Tables on the Objects bar, then double-click the Instructors table**

   Four records have been entered in the Instructors table, but the table has not yet been related to the Courses table. In the Instructors table, the InstructorID field is the **primary key field** and therefore contains unique data for each record. Because each instructor teaches many courses, the Instructors table should be related to the Courses table with a one-to-many relationship. The primary key field always acts as the "one" side of a one-to-many relationship.

2. **Close the Instructors table, right-click the Courses table, then click Design View**

   To link two tables together, a **foreign key field** must be added to the table on the "many" side of a one-to-many relationship to link with the primary key field of the "one" table.

3. **Click the Field Name cell just below Cost, type InstructorID, press [Tab], press N to choose a Number data type, press [Tab], type Foreign Key, as shown in Figure I-3, click the Save button 💾, then close the Courses table**

QUICK TIP

If a table's field list does not appear, click the Show Table button 📇 to add it.

4. **Click the Relationships button 📇 on the Database toolbar**

   The Employees, Enrollments, Courses, and Instructors tables appear in the Relationships window. Primary key fields for each table appear in bold. Right now, the Instructors table is not related to the rest of the tables in the database, but because you added the InstructorID field to the Courses table, a common field exists between the Instructors and Courses tables to create the needed relationship.

5. **Drag the InstructorID field from the Instructors table to the InstructorID field in the Courses table to open the Edit Relationships dialog box shown in Figure I-4**

TROUBLE

If your relationship line doesn't look like Figure I-5, right-click it, click Delete, then redo Steps 5 and 6. If you do not enforce referential integrity, you will not see the "1" and "many" symbols on the link line.

6. **Click the Enforce Referential Integrity check box, then click Create to view the Relationships window, as shown in Figure I-5**

   Checking the **Enforce Referential Integrity** option means that you cannot enter values in the foreign key field unless you first enter them in the primary key field. In this situation, you couldn't enter an InstructorID value in the Courses table that isn't first entered in the InstructorID field of the Instructors table. It also means that you cannot delete records in the "one" table if the "many" table has corresponding related records. This option helps you prevent orphan records from being created in the database. An **orphan** record is a record in the "many" table that has no matching record in the "one" table.

   The **Cascade Update Related Fields** option automatically updates the data in the foreign key field when the matching primary key field is changed. The **Cascade Delete Related Records** option automatically deletes all records in the "many" table if the record with the matching key field in the "one" table is deleted.

7. **Save and close the Relationships window**

FIGURE I-3: Adding the foreign key field to the Courses table in Table Design View

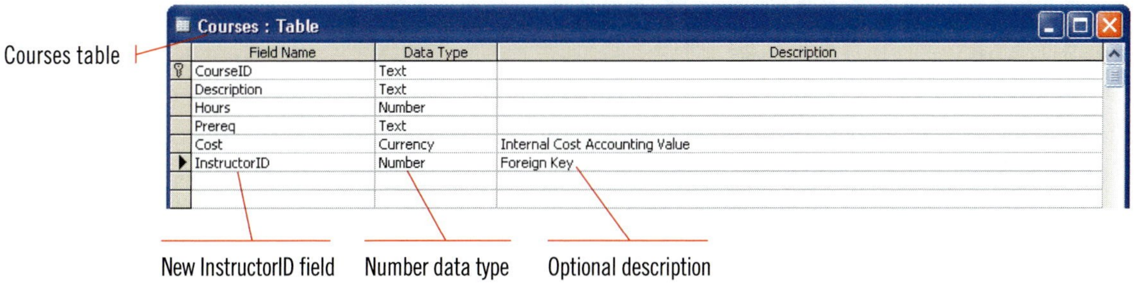

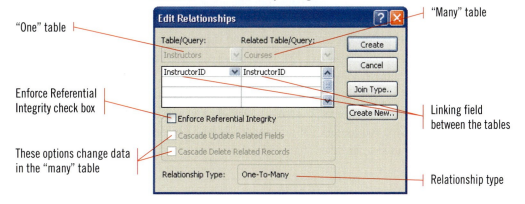

Courses table

New InstructorID field   Number data type   Optional description

FIGURE I-4: Edit Relationships dialog box

"One" table

"Many" table

Enforce Referential
Integrity check box

Linking field
between the tables

These options change data
in the "many" table

Relationship type

FIGURE I-5: Relationships window

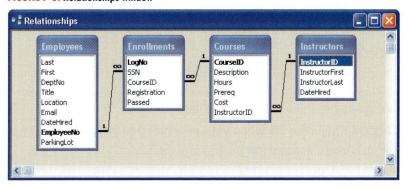

TABLE I-2: Relationship types

relationship	description	examples	notes
One-to-One	A record in Table X has no more than one matching record in a record in Table Y.	A Students table has no more than one matching record in a Graduation table.	This relationship is not common because all fields related this way could be stored in one table.
One-to-Many	A single record in Table X has many records in Table Y.	One item in the Products table can be related to many records in the Sales table.	The one-to-many relationship is the most common relationship type.
Many-to-Many	A record in Table X has many records in Table Y, and a record in Table Y has many records in Table X.	One person in the Employees table can take several courses, and the same course in the Courses table can be taken by several employees.	To create a many-to-many relationship in Access, you must first establish a third table, called a **junction table**, between two original tables; the junction table contains foreign key fields that serve on the "many" side of two separate one-to-many relationships with the two original tables that have a many-to-many relationship.

Importing XML Data

Importing is a process to quickly convert data from an external file into an Access database. You can import data from one Access database to another, or from many other data sources such as files created by Excel, dBase, Paradox, and FoxPro, or text files in an HTML, XML, or delimited text file format. In the past, you might have used a delimited text file to import information from one program to another. A **delimited text file** typically stores one record on each line, with the field values separated by a common character such as a comma, tab, or dash. Now, a more powerful way to share data is by using an XML file. An **XML file** is a text file that contains **Extensible Markup Language (XML)** tags that identify field names and data. XML has become a common method to deliver data from one application to another over the World Wide Web. You may be familiar with **Hypertext Markup Language (HTML)**, which creates Web pages by adding tags to a text file to determine how content such as text and hyperlinks should be formatted and positioned on a Web page. An XML file is similar to an HTML file because each uses **tags**, the programming codes defined by each language that browser software such as Internet Explorer reads to process the content stored within the Web page. Think of an XML file not as a Web page itself, however, but simply as a container for storing and passing data from one computer to another.  Karen Rosen, director of the Human Resources Department, has asked you to track self-study materials for each course in the Training database. This information is stored in an XML file called study.xml.

STEPS

TROUBLE

Import the study.xml file that contains the data rather than the study.xsd file that contains information about the structure of the data.

1. **Click File on the menu bar, point to Get External Data, click Import, navigate to the drive and folder where your Data Files are stored, click the Files of type list arrow, click XML, then double-click study.xml**
   The Import XML dialog box opens.

2. **Click Options**
   The expanded Import XML dialog box is shown in Figure I-6. The upper portion shows the name of the table of data stored within the XML file that can be imported. The options in the lower portion of the dialog box help you determine how the data will be imported.

3. **Click OK, then click OK when you see a message indicating the import is finished**
   The study table is imported into the Training-I database.

4. **Double-click the study table to open its datasheet, then double-click the line that separates field names using the ↔ pointer to resize the columns and show all of the data in each field**
   The study datasheet, with its nine records, is displayed in Figure I-7. All of the data was successfully imported.

5. **Save, then close the study datasheet**

FIGURE I-6: Import XML dialog box

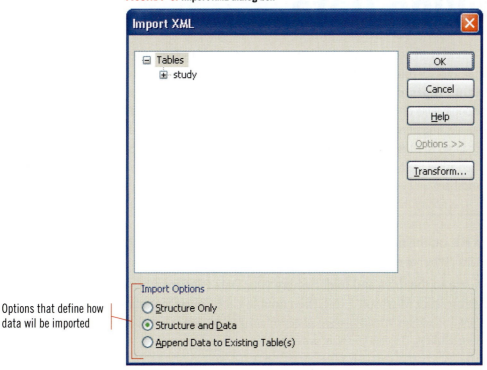

Options that define how
data wil be imported

FIGURE I-7: Datasheet for study table

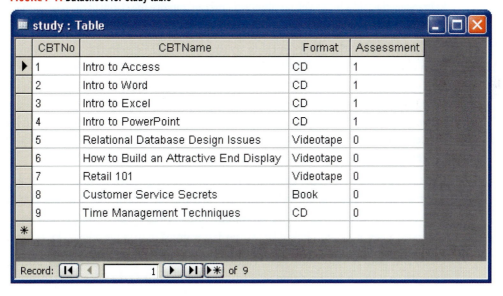

Linking Data

Linking connects an Access database to data in an external file such as another Access, dBase, or Paradox database; an Excel or Lotus 1-2-3 spreadsheet; a text file; an HTML file; an XML file; or other data sources that support **ODBC (open database connectivity)** standards. If you link, data can be entered or edited in either the original file or through the Access database even though the data is only stored in one location—the original file. Importing, in contrast, makes a duplicate copy of the data as a new table in the Access database, so changes to either the original data source or the imported Access copy have no effect on the other. Fred asked the new instructors to make a list of all of their class materials. They created this list in an Excel spreadsheet, and want to maintain it there. You create a link to this data from the Training database.

STEPS

1. **Click File on the menu bar, point to Get External Data, then click Link Tables**

   The Link dialog box opens, listing Access files in the current folder.

2. **Navigate to the drive and folder where your Data Files are stored, click the Files of type list arrow, click Microsoft Excel, then double-click CourseMaterials.xls**

   The Link Spreadsheet Wizard appears, as shown in Figure I-8. Data can be linked from different parts of the Excel spreadsheet. The data you want is on Sheet1.

3. **Click Next, click the First Row Contains Column Headings check box to specify CourseID, Materials, and Type as field names, click Next, type CourseMaterials as the Linked Table Name, click Finish, then click OK**

   The CourseMaterials table appears in the Database window with a linking Excel icon, as shown in Figure I-9. A linked table can and must participate with the rest of a database if a one-to-many relationship between it and another table is created.

4. **Click the Relationships button on the Database toolbar, click the Show Table button, double-click CourseMaterials, then click Close**

   Rearranging the tables in the Relationships window can improve the clarity of the relationships.

   QUICK TIP

   If the relationship type at the bottom of the Edit Relationships dialog box is Indeterminate rather than One-To-Many, click Cancel, then be sure to drag the CourseID field from the *Courses* table to the CourseID field in the *CourseMaterials* table.

5. **Drag the CourseMaterials field list title bar under the Enrollments table, drag the CourseID field in the Courses table to the CourseID field in the CourseMaterials table, then click Create in the Edit Relationships dialog box**

   Your screen should look like Figure I-10. A one-to-many relationship is established between the Courses and CourseMaterials tables, but referential integrity was not enforced and therefore the one and many symbols do not appear on the link line. You cannot establish referential integrity when one of the tables is a linked table, but now that the linked table is related to the rest of the database, it can participate in queries, forms, pages, and reports that use fields from multiple tables.

6. **Click the Save button, close the Relationships window, double-click the CourseMaterials table, click the New Record button on the Table Datasheet toolbar, type Access1, press [Tab], type MediaLoft.mdb, press [Tab], then type File**

   You added a new record to a linked table—the data is stored only in the original Excel workbook.

7. **Close the CourseMaterials table, right-click the Start button start on the taskbar, click Explore, navigate to the drive and folder where your Data Files are stored, double-click the CourseMaterials.xls file to open it in Excel, then press [Page Down]**

   The new Access1 record was added as the last row of the Excel spreadsheet.

8. **Close Excel, then close Windows Explorer**

FIGURE I-8: Link Spreadsheet Wizard dialog box

First row contains field names

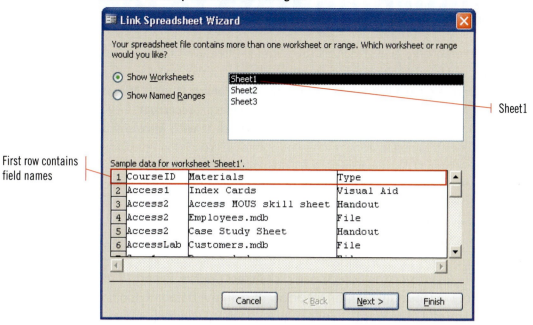

Sheet1

FIGURE I-9: CourseMaterials table is linked from Excel

Linking Excel icon

FIGURE I-10: Relationships window with CourseMaterials table

CourseMaterials field list title bar

One-to-many link line (without enforcing referential integrity)

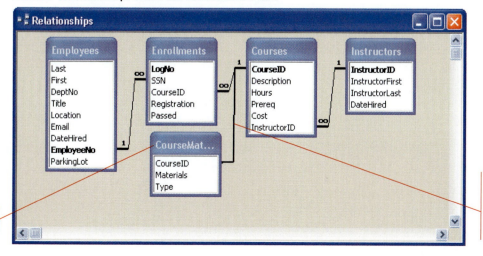

Publishing Data to Word

Word, the word processing program in the Microsoft Office Suite, is a premier software program for entering, editing, and formatting text, especially in long documents. You can copy data from an Access table, query, form, or report into a Word document by using the **Publish It with Microsoft Office Word** feature. Publish It with Microsoft Office Word automatically copies the **recordset** (the fields and records) of a table, query, form, or report object to Word using the **Publish It with Microsoft Office Word button** [W]. Publish It with Microsoft Office Word is one of three OfficeLink tools used to quickly send Access data to another Microsoft Office program. Table I-3 lists the other OfficeLink tools as well as other techniques for copying Access data to other applications. You have been asked to write a report on the demand for Access courses. You will use an OfficeLinks button to send the Microsoft Office report to Word, then you will use Word to add explanatory text to the report.

STEPS

TROUBLE
If a dialog box opens indicating that the file already exists, click Yes to replace the existing file.

1. **Click Reports on the Objects bar, click Access Courses Report (if not already selected), click the OfficeLinks button list arrow [W▾] on the Database toolbar, click Publish It with Microsoft Office Word, then maximize the Word window**

   The records from the Access Courses Report object appear in a Word document in an **RTF (rich text format)** file format, as shown in Figure I-11. The RTF format does not support all advanced Word features, but it does support basic formatting embellishments such as multiple fonts, colors, and font sizes. The RTF file format is commonly used when two different word processing programs need to use the same file.

2. **Type the following:**

   To: Management Committee
   From: your name
   Re: Analysis of Access Courses
   Date: today's date

   The following information shows the recent demand for Access training. The information is sorted by location, and shows that Boston has had the greatest demand for Access courses.

3. **Proofread your document, which should now look like Figure I-12, then click the Print button [🖨] on the Standard toolbar**

   Word's **word wrap** feature determines when a line of text extends into the right margin of the page, and automatically forces the text to the next line without you needing to press Enter. This allows you to enter and edit large paragraphs of text in Word very efficiently.

TROUBLE
If prompted that the file already exists, click Yes to replace the existing file.

4. **Click the Save button [💾] on Word's Standard toolbar to save the Access Courses Report document, then exit Word**

   Files saved through the Publish It with Microsoft Office Word and Analyze It with Microsoft Office Excel feature are saved in the My Documents folder by default for most typical Microsoft Office installations.

FIGURE I-11: Publishing an Access report to Word

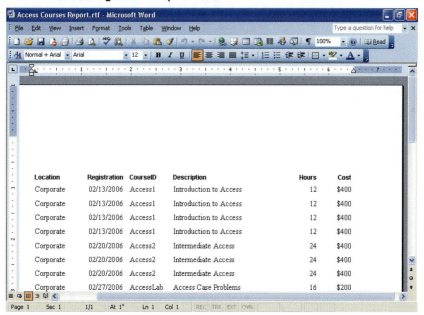

FIGURE I-12: Using Word to enter text

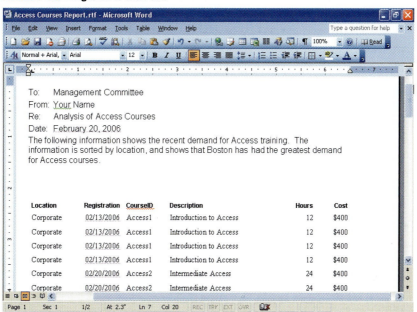

TABLE I-3: Techniques to copy Access data to other applications

technique	button or menu option	description
OfficeLinks	Analyze It with Microsoft Office Excel	Send a selected table, query, form, or report object's records to Excel.
	Publish It with Microsoft Office Word	Send a selected table, query, form, or report object's records to Word.
	Merge It with Microsoft Office Word	Help merge the selected table or query recordset with a Word document.
Office Clipboard	Copy and Paste	Click the Copy button to copy selected data to the Office Clipboard. The Office Clipboard can hold up to 24 different items. Open a Word document or Excel spreadsheet, click where you want to paste the data, then click the Paste button.
Exporting	File on the menu bar, then Export	Copy information from an Access object into a different file format.
Drag and drop	Right-click an empty space on the taskbar, then click Tile Windows Horizontally or Tile Windows Vertically.	With the windows tiled, drag the Access table, query, form, or report object icon from the Access window to the target (Excel or Word) window.

Analyzing Data with Excel

Excel, the spreadsheet software program in the Microsoft Office suite, is an excellent tool for projecting numeric trends into the future. For example, you can analyze the impact of a price increase on budget or income projections by applying several different numbers. This reiterative analysis is sometimes called "what-if" analysis. **What-if analysis** allows you to change values in an Excel worksheet and watch related formulas update instantly. This is a very popular use for Excel. You can use the **Analyze It with Microsoft Office Excel** feature to quickly copy Access data to Excel with the Analyze It with Microsoft Office Excel button ⊠. The Accounting Department asked you to copy some Access data to an Excel spreadsheet so they can analyze how different increases in the cost of the Access classes would affect each of the locations. You have gathered the raw data into a report, called Access Courses Report, and will use Excel to analyze the effect of increased costs.

STEPS

TROUBLE

If a dialog box opens indicating that the file already exists, click Yes to replace the existing file.

1. **Click Reports on the Objects bar, click the Access Courses Report, click the OfficeLinks button list arrow 🗗 ▾ on the Database toolbar, then click Analyze It with Microsoft Office Excel**

   The report data is automatically exported into an Excel workbook, as shown in Figure I-13. When you use the Analyze It with Microsoft Office Excel or Publish It with Microsoft Office Word buttons, the spreadsheet or document you create has the same name as the Access object that was exported, and it is usually saved in the My Documents folder of your C: drive. You can send the recordset of a table, query, form, or report object to Excel using the Analyze It with Microsoft Office Excel button.

2. **Click Cell G1 (Column G, Row 1), type Cost Per Hour, press [Enter], type =F2/E2 (in Cell G2), and then press [Enter]**

   Cell G2 contains a formula that divides the cost in Cell F2 by the hours in Cell E2, or 400/12.

3. **Click Cell G2, then click the Currency Style button 💲 on the Formatting toolbar**

   You can quickly and easily copy Excel formulas to other cells using the **AutoFill** pointer.

4. **Point to the lower-right corner of Cell G2 so that the pointer changes to ✚, then drag down to Cell G14**

   The copied formulas are shown in Figure I-14. The workbook is now ready to perform what-if analysis by changing an assumption value.

5. **Click Cell F2, type 500, and then press [Enter]**

   Your spreadsheet should look like Figure I-15. By changing any value in Column E or F, Excel updates all formulas that depend on those values. In this case, Excel recalculated the formula in Cell G2.

6. **Click the Save button 🖫 on Excel's Standard toolbar to save the Access Courses Report spreadsheet, then exit Excel**

FIGURE I-13: Access Courses Report exported to Excel

Access Courses Report.xls

Cell G1

Cell G2

Cell F2

Cell E2

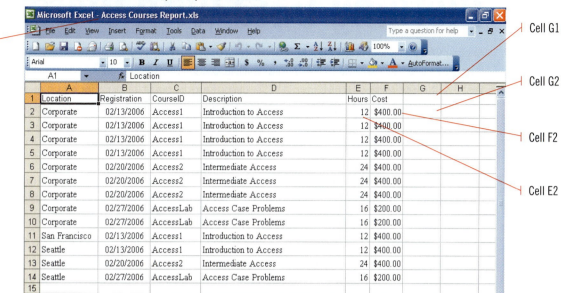

FIGURE I-14: Copying a formula in a spreadsheet

Currency Style button

Cell G14

AutoFill pointer

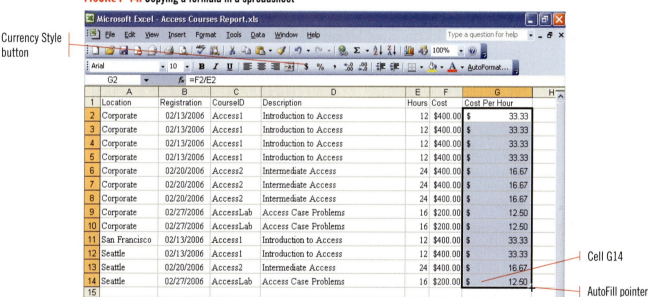

FIGURE I-15: Performing "what-if" analysis

When the value in Cell F2 was changed...

...the formula in Cell G2 automatically recalculated

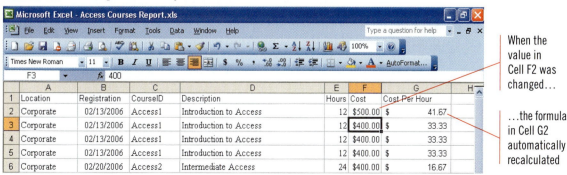

Merging Data with Word

Another OfficeLinks tool called **Merge It with Microsoft Office Word** merges Access records with a Word form letter, label, or envelope to create mass mailing documents. You use the Merge It with Microsoft Office Word button ![icon] to send records from a table, query, form, or report to Word for a mail merge. ![icon] Fred wants to send the MediaLoft employees a letter announcing two new courses. You use the Merge It with Microsoft Office Word feature to customize a standard form letter to each employee.

STEPS

1. **Click Tables on the Objects bar, click Employees, click the OfficeLinks button list arrow ![icon] on the Database toolbar, then click Merge It with Microsoft Office Word**

   The Microsoft Word Mail Merge Wizard starts, requesting information about the merge process.

2. **Click the Create a new document and then link the data to it option button, click OK, maximize the Word window, then type the text shown in Figure I-16**

   Word starts and opens the **Mail Merge task pane** on the right side of the window and the **Mail Merge toolbar** at the top of the window. You can use either or both tools to help you with the mail merge process. Before you merge the Access data with the Word document, though, you must create the **main document**, the document used to determine how the letter and Access data will be combined. This is the standard text that will be consistent for each letter created in the mail merge process as shown in Figure I-16. Once the standard text is entered, you insert the codes that identify where the Access data will be merged with the main document.

3. **Click to the right of To:, press [Tab] to align the insertion point at the same position as Your Name, click the Insert Merge Fields button ![icon] on the Mail Merge toolbar, click First, then click Insert**

   The Insert Merge Field dialog box lists all of the fields in the original data source, the Employees table. You use the Insert Merge Field dialog box to insert **merge fields**, codes that will be replaced with the values in the field that the code represents when the mail merge is processed.

4. **Double-click Last, click Close, click between the First and Last codes, then press [Spacebar] to insert a space between the codes as shown in Figure I-17**

   You must use the Insert Merge Field dialog box to add two merge fields to a Word document—you cannot type them directly from the keyboard. You can, however, insert the same merge field into one letter multiple times. With the main document and merge fields inserted, you are ready to complete the mail merge.

   TROUBLE
   If your final merged document contains a mistake, close it without saving, edit the main document to correct the mistake, and click ![icon] again.

5. **Click the Merge to New Document button ![icon] on the Mail Merge toolbar, then click OK to merge all records**

   The mail merge process combines field values from the Employees table with the main document, creating a letter for each record in the Employees table. The first letter is to Megan Burik, as shown in Figure I-18. "Megan" is the field value for the First field in the first record, and "Burik" is the field value for the Last field in the first record. The status bar of the Word document shows that this document contains 22 pages, one page for each of the 22 records in the Employees table.

6. **Press [Page Down] several times to view several pages of the final merged document**

   Each page is a separate letter to a different employee.

7. **Click File on the menu bar, click Print, click the Current page option button, click OK to print only one page, then close Word without saving any documents**

FIGURE I-16: Creating the main document

Mail Merge toolbar

Insert Merge Fields button

Mail Merge task pane

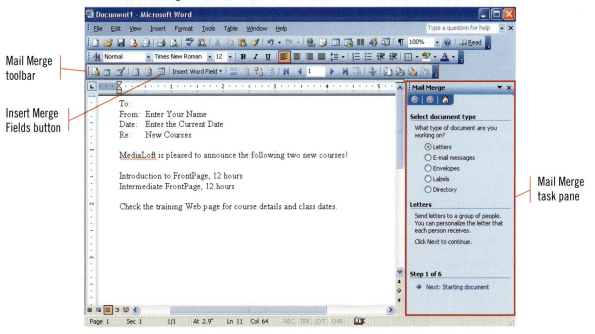

FIGURE I-17: Inserting merge fields

<<First>> merge field

<<Last>> merge field

Merge to New Document button

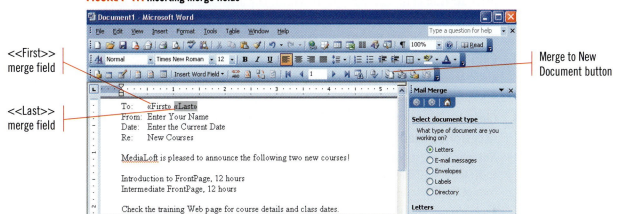

FIGURE I-18: Merged letters

Data merged from the Employees table

22 pages (22 letters)

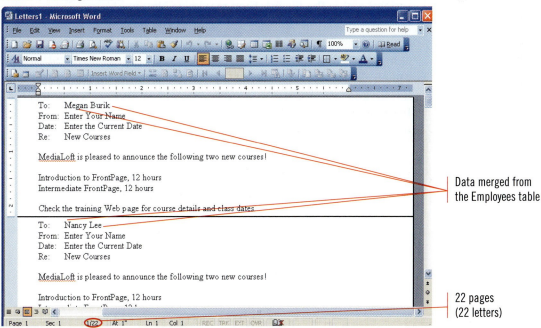

Access 2003

Exporting Data to XML

Exporting is a way to send Access information to another database, spreadsheet, or file format. Exporting is the opposite of importing. You can export data from an Access database to other file types such as those used by Excel, Lotus 1-2-3, dBase, Paradox, and FoxPro, and in several general file formats including HTML, XML, and various text file formats. Unlike linking, data you import or export retains no connection between its original source and the imported or exported copy. The Information Systems Department has requested that you export training activity into an XML file that they will use to develop a Web-based application.

STEPS

1. **Click Queries on the Objects bar, click Accounting History, click File on the menu bar, then click Export**

   The Export dialog box opens, requesting the location and format for the exported information.

2. **Navigate to the drive and folder where your Data Files are stored, type account in the File name text box, click the Save as type list arrow, click XML, then click Export**

   The Export XML dialog box opens, as shown in Figure I-19. The **schema** of the data represents how the tables of the database are related. If you select this check box, Access creates and exports an accompanying **XSD (Extensible Schema Document)** file to store structural information about the database. The **presentation** of the data refers to formatting characteristics such as bold and font size. If you select this check box, Access creates and exports an accompanying **XSL (Extensible Stylesheet Language)** file to store presentation information.

3. **Click OK**

   Access exports the data and its schema to your Data Files folder. To view the XML file, you need to open it in a program that can open text files.

4. **Click the Start button `start` on the taskbar, point to All Programs, point to Accessories, then click Notepad**

   Notepad is a text-editing program that is provided with all versions of Windows. When you want to view an HTML or XML file, Notepad works well because it doesn't insert extra text or codes that could potentially corrupt the file.

5. **Click File on the Notepad menu bar, click Open, navigate to the drive and folder where your Data Files are stored, click the Files of type list arrow, click All Files, double-click account.xml in the file list, then maximize Notepad**

   Your screen should look like Figure I-20. Angle brackets, < and > (also known as the less than and greater than symbols), surround each of the XML tags. These tags are the distinguishing characteristic of markup languages such as HTML and XML. XML data is positioned between two tags, also called the **start tag** and **end tag**. The start tag identifies the field name and is positioned just before the field value. The end tag is positioned just after the field value. End tags are also differentiated from start tags because they contain a slash character, /. Therefore, the XML entry of <Last>Burik</Last> indicates that Burik is the field value for a field named Last.

6. **Close Notepad, then return to Access and close the Training-I.mdb database**

FIGURE I-19: Export XML dialog box

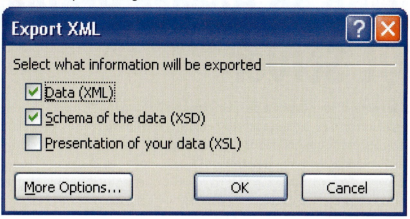

FIGURE I-20: Displaying the contents of an XML file in Notepad

account.xml

Notepad

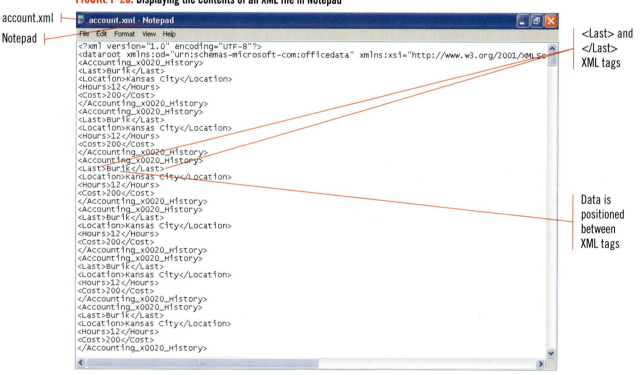

<Last> and
</Last>
XML tags

Data is
positioned
between
XML tags

Using an Access Project with SQL Server

SQL Server is another database program provided by Microsoft. You use SQL Server for databases that are larger, more complex, or have a greater number of users than those typically maintained in Access. If your Access database is growing rapidly, you can **upsize**, or convert your Access database to SQL Server. Microsoft provides the sample **NorthwindCS** database as part of the full Access 2003 installation to illustrate how an Access database can connect to an SQL Server database. The NorthwindCS database is actually an Access **project**, a special Access database file that contains only form and report objects for the end user. The data used by those forms and reports is stored in an SQL Server database that is typically located on a shared file server. In this manner, you can use Access project files connected to an SQL server database to create efficient client/server applications. In this type of **client/server application**, the **client** (your PC) processes forms and reports contained in an Access project stored on your local hard drive. The **server** is a shared file server that all clients may access through a network. The server stores the data that each client uses, analyzes, and updates through their local forms and reports. The Information Systems Department anticipates that the Training database may need to be upsized to SQL Server in the future. You decide to open the sample NorthwindCS database to start learning about client/server computing.

STEPS

QUICK TIP

If the sample databases were not previously installed on your computer, you are prompted to install them.

1. **Click Help on the menu bar, point to Sample Databases, then click Northwind Sample Access Project**

    A dialog box opens for connecting the NorthwindCS ("CS" stands for "Client/Server") project to an SQL Server database.

2. **Click OK**

    The Data Link Properties dialog box opens, as shown in Figure I-21. In this dialog box, you would enter all of the information required to make a successful connection to an SQL Server database such as the server name, database name, and any other information required by the firewall that protects the SQL Server. A **firewall** is a combination of hardware and software that adds a layer of security to corporate data. In its simplest form, a firewall consists of software that requires a valid user name and password before access to information is granted.

3. **Click Cancel**

    Although you can't make the physical connection between the NorthwindCS project and an SQL Server database unless you have access to an SQL Server database on your network, you can still explore the NorthwindCS project.

4. **Click OK on the Northwind Traders welcome window, then click each of the Objects buttons on the Objects bar**

    You see that there are no tables in this file. Rather, this project contains only form, report, macro, and module objects used by the client.

5. **Click Forms on the Objects bar**

    Your screen should look like Figure I-22. Notice that the title bar of the database window indicates that the database is disconnected from an SQL Server. Therefore, you could work in Design View to change or develop forms or reports, but if you tried to view data in Form View or Report Preview, you'd see a message indicating that a connection to the SQL Server database cannot be made and therefore data cannot be displayed.

6. **Close the NorthwindCS project, then exit Access**

FIGURE I-21: Data Link Properties dialog box

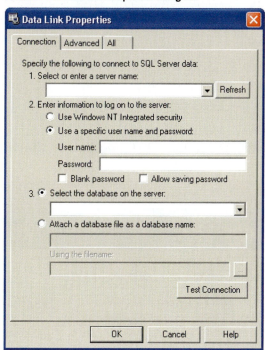

FIGURE I-22: NorthwindCS Project window

NorthwindCS

Project is disconnected

Project file

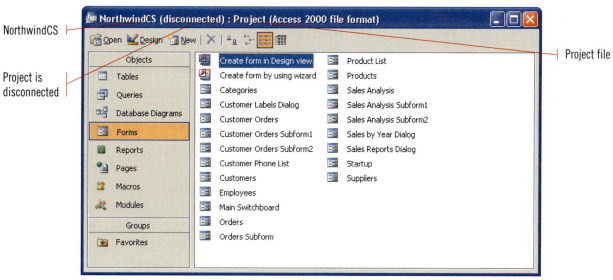

Practice

▼ CONCEPTS REVIEW

Identify each element of the Edit Relationships dialog box as shown in Figure I-23.

FIGURE I-23

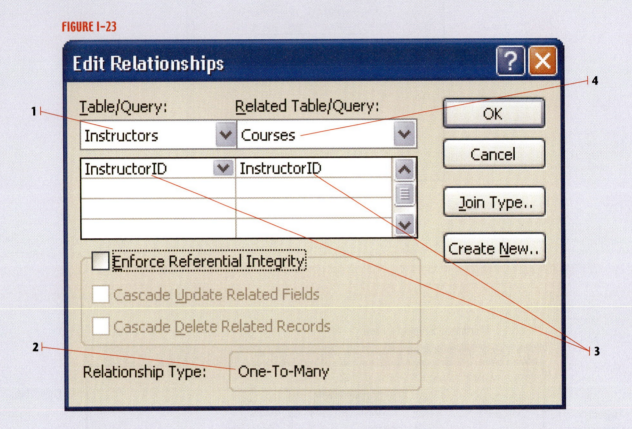

Match each term with the statement that best describes its function.

5. **Normalization**
6. **Foreign key field**
7. **Junction table**
8. **Linking**
9. **What-if analysis**
10. **Primary key field**
11. **Importing**
12. **XML**

a. A field that contains unique information for each record
b. Testing different assumptions in a spreadsheet
c. Used to create a many-to-many relationship
d. The process of designing a relational database
e. The process of converting data from an external source into an Access database
f. A way to connect to data in an external source without copying it
g. A field added to the table on the "many" side of a one-to-many relationship to link with the primary key field of the "one" table
h. A text file that contains tags that identify field names and data

Select the best answer from the list of choices.

13. Which of the following is *not* an Access object?

   a. Report

   b. Spreadsheet

   c. Table

   d. Query

14. Which of the following is *not* part of the normalization process?

   a. Determining the appropriate fields

   b. Identifying the correct number of tables

   c. Creating database hyperlinks

   d. Establishing table relationships

15. Which of the following is *not* true about XML?

   a. It is a popular format for sharing data over the Internet.

   b. An XML file is the same thing as a Web page.

   c. It uses tags to define fields.

   d. An XML file can be opened in Notepad.

16. Which of the following software products would most likely be used to analyze the effect on future sales and profits based on the change to several different assumptions?

   a. Word

   b. PowerPoint

   c. Access

   d. Excel

17. Which of the following is *not* an OfficeLinks button?

   a. Present It with Microsoft Office PowerPoint

   b. Publish It with Microsoft Office Word

   c. Merge It with Microsoft Office Word

   d. Analyze It with Microsoft Office Excel

18. Which is *not* true about enforcing referential integrity?

   a. It helps prevent orphan records.

   b. It prevents you from entering an incorrect value in the primary key field.

   c. It allows you to select the Cascade Update Related Fields option.

   d. It allows you to select the Cascade Delete Related Records option.

19. Which of the following is *not* true about linking?

   a. Linking copies data from one data file to another.

   b. Access can link to data in an Excel spreadsheet.

   c. Access can link to data in an HTML file.

   d. You can edit linked data in Access.

20. During a mail merge, what is the purpose of a main document?

   a. It is the same thing as the final merged document.

   b. It stores all of the data available for the mail merge.

   c. It stores the merge fields that you may insert into letters, envelopes, or labels.

   d. It contains the standard text you that you want each merged letter to display.

▼ SKILLS REVIEW

1. Examine Access objects.

   a. Start Access, then open the **Machinery-I.mdb** database from the drive and folder where your Data Files are stored.

   b. On a separate piece of paper, list the seven Access objects and the number of each type in the Machinery-I database.

   c. Use Table Datasheet View to determine the current number of records in each table. Write down your answers.

   d. Use Table Design View to determine the current number of fields in each table. Write down your answers.

2. Set relationships.

   a. Click the Relationships button on the Database toolbar.

   b. Create a one-to-many relationship between the Products and Inventory Transaction tables using the common ProductID field.

   c. Create a one-to-many relationship between the Purchase Orders and Inventory Transactions tables using the common PurchaseOrderID field. Enforce referential integrity on the relationship.

   d. Create a one-to-many relationship between the Employees and Purchase Orders tables using the common EmployeeNo field. Enforce referential integrity on the relationship.

   e. Move and resize the field lists so that all fields and relationships are visible.

   f. Click File on the menu bar, click Print Relationships, then view the relationships report in Design View.

   g. Add your name as a label to the Report Header section, print the report, then close the report without saving it.

   h. Save the changes to the Relationships window, then close it.

3. Import XML data.

   a. Import the **employ.xml** XML file stored on the drive and folder where your Data Files are stored.

   b. Open the datasheet for the employ table, change the name in the first record to your own, then print it and close the employ table.

4. Link data.

   a. Link to the **Vendors.xls** Excel file stored on the drive and folder where your Data Files are stored.

   b. In the Link Spreadsheet Wizard, specify that the first row contains column headings.

   c. Name the linked table **Vendors**.

   d. Open the datasheet for the Vendors table, change John Deere in the first record to **Your Name's Company**, then close the Vendors datasheet.

   e. Start Excel, then open the **Vendors.xls** file stored on the drive and folder where your Data Files are stored.

   f. Print, then close the Vendors.xls file. Even though you edited the first record to contain your name from within Access, because this data was linked rather than imported to Access, the single copy of the data that is permanently stored in the Vendors.xls file was updated.

5. Publish data to Word.

   a. Send the Every Product We Lease report to Word using the Publish It with Microsoft Office Word button.

   b. Press [Ctrl][Home] to go to the top of the document if the insertion point is not already positioned at the top of the page, press [Enter] twice, then press [Ctrl][Home] to return to the top of the document.

   c. Type the following at the top of the document:

      INTERNAL MEMO

      From: **Your Name**

      To: **Sales Staff**

      Date: **Today's date**

      Do not forget to mention the long lead times on the Back Hoe and Thatcher to customers. We usually do not keep these expensive items in stock.

   d. Proofread the document, save, then print it. Close the document, then exit Word.

6. **Analyze data with Excel.**

   a. Use the Analyze It with Microsoft Office Excel button to send the data in the Products table to Excel.

   b. Click Cell D12, type **=AVERAGE(D2:D11)**, then press [Enter]. This formula calculates the average Unit Price for all values in the range of cells from D2 through D11.

   c. Click Cell A13, type your name, then press [Enter].

   d. Click Cell D7, type **499.75** as the new Unit Price value for the Thatcher, then press [Enter]. Changing the value of the most expensive product should make a big difference in the average price, which automatically recalculated in Cell D12.

   e. Save, print, and close the workbook, then exit Excel.

   f. Open the Products table in Datasheet View in Access, view the Unit Price value for the Thatcher, then close the datasheet.

   g. On a piece of paper, define what it means to import, export, and link data. In your explanation include how edits to linked data differ from those of exported or imported data. Also, identify the process (import, export, or link) used by each of the OfficeLinks buttons.

7. **Merge data with Word.**

   a. Use the Merge It with Microsoft Office Word tool to merge the data from the Employees table to a Word document.

   b. Use the "Create a new document and then link the data to it" option in the Microsoft Word Mail Merge Wizard dialog box.

   c. In the Word document, enter the following standard text to serve as the main document for the mail merge. (*Hint*: Close the Mail Merge task pane to see the full lines of text entered in the main document.)

   Date: **February 9, 2006**
   To:
   From: **Your Name**
   Re: **CPR Training**
   The annual CPR Training session will be held on Friday, February 17, 2006. Please sign up for this important event in the lunchroom. Friends and family over 18 years old are also welcome.

   d. To the right of To:, press [Tab] to position the cursor at the location for the first merge field.

   e. Use the Insert Merge Fields button to add the FirstName and LastName fields to the main document.

   f. Close the Insert Merge Field dialog box and insert a space between the <<FirstName>> and <<LastName>> merge codes.

   g. Use the Merge to New Document button on the Mail Merge toolbar to merge all records.

   h. Print the last page of the merged document, then exit Word without saving any documents.

8. **Export data to XML.**

   a. Export the Products table as an XML file with the name **products.xml** to the drive and folder where your Data Files are stored. Export both the data and schema.

   b. Start Notepad, then open the **products.xml** file in Notepad.

   c. Print products.xml from within Notepad, then close Notepad and close the Machinery-I.mdb database.

9. **Use an Access project with SQL Server.**

   a. Click Help on the menu bar, point to Sample Databases, then click Northwind Sample Access Project.

   b. When prompted to connect to an SQL Server, click OK.

   c. Write down four pieces of information from the Data Link Properties dialog box that you would probably have to supply if you were physically connecting to an SQL Server, then click Cancel.

   d. Click OK on the Northwind welcome window, click the Forms button, then double-click Orders. Click OK when prompted.

   e. In a Word or Notepad document, explain why Access could not display the Orders form in Form View. Use the words client, server, data, Orders form, NorthwindCS, and SQL Server in your answer.

   f. Close the NorthwindCS project, then exit Access.

▼ INDEPENDENT CHALLENGE 1

As the manager of a college women's basketball team, you have created a database called Basketball-I that tracks the players, games, and player statistics. You need to complete the table relationships.

  a. Start Access and open the database **Basketball-I.mdb** from the drive and folder where your Data Files are stored.

  b. Create a one-to-many relationship between the Games table and the Stats table using the common GameNo field. Enforce referential integrity.

  c. Create a one-to-many relationship between the Players and Stats table using the common PlayerNo field. Enforce referential integrity.

  d. Click File on the menu bar, click Print Relationships, and then view the relationships report in Design View.

  e. Add a label to the Report Header section with your name, then close the report without saving it.

  f. Save the changes to the Relationships window, and close it.

Advanced Challenge Exercise

  ■ Open the Players Query in Datasheet View.

  ■ Change the first instance of Lindsey Swift to your name, press [Page Down], then print the first page of the datasheet. On the back of the printout, explain why your name is listed 10 times on this datasheet.

  g. Close the Basketball-I.mdb database, then exit Access.

▼ INDEPENDENT CHALLENGE 2

As the manager of a women's college basketball team, you have created a database called Basketball-I that tracks the players, games, and player statistics. You want to link to an Excel file that contains information on the player's course load. On a form, you also want to create a hyperlink to a Word document.

  a. Start Access and open the database **Basketball-I.mdb** from the drive and folder where your Data Files are stored.

  b. If relationships between the tables have not yet been established, complete Steps b. through f. of Independent Challenge 1.

  c. Use the Publish It with Microsoft Office Word button to send the Player Statistics report to Word.

  d. Press [Enter] three times, then press [Ctrl][Home] to position the insertion point at the top of the document.

  e. Type your name on the first line of the document, then write a paragraph or two that explains the Player Statistics data that follows.

  f. Save, print, and close the Player Statistics document.

  g. Exit Word. Close the Basketball-I.mdb database, then exit Access.

▼ INDEPENDENT CHALLENGE 3

As the manager of a women's college basketball team, you have created a database called Basketball-I that tracks the players, games, and player statistics. You want to export some information in the Basketball-I database to an Excel worksheet to analyze the data.

  a. Start Access and open the database **Basketball-I.mdb** from the drive and folder where your Data Files are stored.

  b. Use the Analyze It with Microsoft Office Excel tool to export the Games table data to Excel.

  c. Click Cell H1, type **Difference**, click Cell H2, type **=E2-F2**, then press [Enter].

  d. Use the AutoFill handle for Cell H2 to copy the formula down the entire column, through Cell H23.

Advanced Challenge Exercise

  ■ Click Cell I2 and type the following formula, **=E2/F2**. This formula helps you further analyze the scores by computing the home score expressed as a percentage of the opponents score.

  ■ Click Cell I2 and then click the Percent Style button on the Excel Formatting toolbar.

  ■ Use the AutoFill handle for Cell I2 to copy the formula down the entire column, through Cell I23.

  e. Click Cell A25, type your name, change the print settings (use the Page Setup option on the File menu) to a landscape orientation, then print the spreadsheet.

  f. Save and close the workbook, then exit Excel. Close the Basketball-I.mdb database, then exit Access.

▼ INDEPENDENT CHALLENGE 4

You are the coordinator for the foreign studies program at your college. You have created a database that documents the primary and secondary languages used by foreign countries. The database also includes a table of common words and phrases, translated into various languages.

a. Start Access, open the **Languages-I.mdb** database from the drive and folder where your Data Files are stored.

b. Open the datasheets for each of the three tables to familiarize yourself with the fields and records. The Language1 and Language2 fields in the Countries table represent the primary and secondary languages for that country.

c. Click the Relationships button and create a one-to-many relationship between the Languages and Countries table using the LanguageID field in the Languages table and the Language1 field in the Countries table. Enforce referential integrity.

d. Create a one-to-many relationship using the between the Languages and Countries tables using the LanguageID field in the Languages table and the Language2 field in the Countries table. Click No when prompted to edit the existing relationship, and enforce referential integrity on the new relationship. The Languages table's field list will appear twice in the Relationships window with Languages_1 as the title for the second field list, as shown in Figure I-24. The Words table is used for reference, and does not have a direct relationship to the other tables.

FIGURE I-24

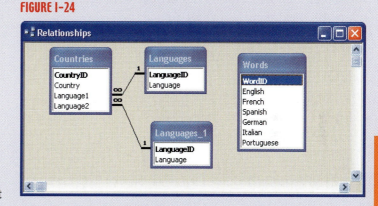

e. Click File on the menu bar, click Print Relationships, then view the relationships report in Design View.

f. Add a label to the Report Header section with your name as the caption, then close the report without saving it.

g. Save and close the Relationships window.

h. Connect to the Internet, and then go to *www.ask.com*, *www.about.com*, or any search engine. Your goal is to find a Web site that translates English to other languages, and to print the home page of that Web site.

i. Add three new words or phrases to the Words table, making sure that the translation is made in all five of the represented languages: French, Spanish, German, Italian, and Portuguese.

j. Print the updated datasheet for the Words table, close the Words table, close the Languages-I.mdb database, then exit Access.

▼ VISUAL WORKSHOP

Start Access and open the **Basketball-I.mdb** database from the drive and folder where your Data Files are stored. Use the Merge It with Microsoft Office Word feature to merge information from the Players table to a form letter. The final page of the merged document is shown in Figure I-25. Notice that the player's first and last names have been merged to the first line, and that the player's first name is merged a second time in the first sentence of the letter. Print the last page of the merged document, then close both documents without saving them.

FIGURE I-25

To: Jamie Johnson
From: Insert Your Name
Date: Insert Current Date
Re: Big 13 Champions!

Congratulations, Jamie, for an outstanding year at State University! Your hard work and team contributions have helped clinch the Big 13 Championship for State University for the third year in a row!

Thank you for your dedication!

Keep the faith,

Coach

Creating Data Access Pages

OBJECTIVES

Understand the World Wide Web

Create Hyperlink fields

Create pages for interactive reporting

Create pages for data entry

Create PivotTables

Create PivotCharts

Add hyperlinks

Publish Web pages to Web servers

If you have a SAM user profile, you may have access to hands-on instruction, practice, and assessment of the skills covered in this unit. Log in to your SAM account and go to your assignments page to see what your instructor has assigned.

The Internet connects a vast amount of information, provides unlimited business opportunities, and supports fast, global communication. Most content provided via the Internet is accessed through a **Web page**, a hyperlinked document that makes the Internet easy to navigate. Web pages and their underlying infrastructure are referred to as the **World Wide Web**. Now, Web page technology has evolved to also include dynamic content. **Dynamic Web pages** are connected to a database, and are re-created with up-to-date data each time the Web page is opened. You can use dynamic Web pages to view, enter, or update data stored in an underlying database. Access 2003 provides the **page** object to create dynamic Web pages. ▧ Fred Ames, coordinator of training, wants to let MediaLoft employees access information stored in the Training database via the company intranet. You will use the Access page object to create dynamic Web pages for this purpose.

Understanding the World Wide Web

Creating Web pages that dynamically interact with an Access database is an exciting process that involves many underlying technologies. Understanding how the Internet, the World Wide Web, and Web pages interact helps you successfully connect a Web page to an underlying Access database. You start by reviewing some of the history and key terminology of the Internet and World Wide Web to better prepare yourself for the task of creating Web pages tied to data stored in an Access database.

Review the following concepts regarding the Internet and the World Wide Web:

- The **Internet** is a worldwide network of computer networks that sends and receives information through a common communications **protocol** (set of rules) called **TCP/IP (Transmission Control Protocol/ Internet Protocol)**.

- The Internet supports many services, including:

  - **E-mail**: Electronic mail
  - **File transfer**: Uploading and downloading files containing anything from text to pictures to music to software programs
  - **Newsgroups**: Similar to e-mail, but messages are posted in a "public mailbox" that is available to any newsgroup subscriber, rather than sent to one individual
  - **World Wide Web (WWW)**: A vast number of linked documents stored on thousands of Web servers that support a wide range of activities including research, education, advertising, entertainment, news, and e-commerce

- The Internet experienced tremendous growth in the past decade partly because of the following three major factors:

  - In the early 1990s, the U.S. government lifted restrictions on commercial Internet traffic, causing explosive growth in electronic commerce activities.
  - Technological breakthroughs in hardware included faster processors and networking media such as fiber optics and satellite transmission.
  - Less-expensive and easier-to-use Internet systems and software were developed for both **clients** (your computer) and **servers** (the computer that "serves" the information to you from the Internet).

- Behind all of these innovations are many amazing people. The World Wide Web was pioneered by a group of scientists who saw the need to easily share real-time information with colleagues, and started linking documents with similar content to one another. Table J-1 introduces more Internet and World Wide Web terminology. Figure J-1 shows how hyperlinks work on a Web page.

FIGURE J-1: Web page with hyperlinks and search boxes

URL

Hyperlinks may be pictures, clip art, or text

Search boxes indicate that the Web page is connected to a database

TABLE J-1: Internet and World Wide Web terminology

term	definition
Web page	A text file that includes Hypertext Markup Language (HTML) tags, which describe how the text, images, and hyperlinks identified within the file should be displayed in a browser.
Web server	A computer that stores and serves Web pages.
Hyperlink	Text (usually underlined), an image, or an icon on a Web page that when clicked, locates and returns another Web page. Hyperlinks can jump to another part of the same Web page, a different page on the same Web server, or to a different Web server in another part of the world.
HTML (Hypertext Markup Language)	A set of symbols (often called **tags**) such as <title> and </title> or <body> and </body> that are inserted into a text file. The tags are used by a browser program such as Internet Explorer to present the information in the text file as a Web page within the browser window. HTML programmers insert these tags directly into text files. Nonprogrammers create HTML Web pages using FrontPage or by converting files such as Word, Excel, and PowerPoint into HTML Web pages.
Browser	Software such as Microsoft's Internet Explorer (IE) or Netscape Navigator used to find and display Web pages.
ISP (Internet service provider)	A company whose purpose is to connect home and business computers to the rest of the Internet. National ISPs include America Online, the Microsoft Network (MSN), and Sprint's EarthLink. Hundreds of regional and local ISPs exist as well.
Modem	Short for *modulate-dem*odulate. A modem is hardware (usually located inside the computer) that converts digital computer signals to analog telephone signals to allow a computer to send and receive information across ordinary telephone lines. New and faster communication technologies such as DSL, satellite systems, and cable modems that can also connect your computer to the Internet without using the existing analog telephone systems are making traditional modems obsolete.
URL (Uniform Resource Locator)	Each resource on the Internet (including Web pages) has an address so that other computers can accurately and consistently locate and view it. For example, http://www.course.com/catalog/ is a URL for the Web page that displays information about Course Technology's products. (Course Technology is the publisher of this textbook). A URL never includes a space.
Domain name	The middle part of a URL, such as www.course.com. The middle part of the domain name is often either the company's name or words that describe the information you find at that site. The last part of the domain name indicates the type of site, such as commercial (com), educational (edu), military (mil), organizational (org), or governmental (gov).
Home page	The home page is the first page displayed on a Web server when you enter only the domain name (and not a longer and more specific URL) into the browser address bar.

Creating Hyperlink Fields

A **Hyperlink field** is a field defined with the Hyperlink data type in Table Design View. The entry in a Hyperlink field can be a **Universal Naming Convention (UNC) path** or a **Uniform Resource Locator (URL) address** used to locate a file on a network. Table J-2 gives more information about networks. URLs may also specify a newsgroup address, an FTP (File Transfer Protocol) server location, an intranet Web page address, or a file on a local area network. You create a Hyperlink field called OnlineResources to store the URL for a Web page that contains up-to-date information on the subject of each class.

STEPS

1. Start Access, open the Training-J.mdb database from the drive and folder where your Data Files are stored, right-click the Courses table, then click Design View on the shortcut menu
   The Courses table opens in Design View, where you can add fields and specify their properties.

2. Click the first empty Field Name cell below InstructorID, type OnlineResources, press [Tab], type h, click the Save button 💾, click the Datasheet View button 🖻, then maximize the datasheet
   The Courses table with the new OnlineResources field opens in Datasheet View.

   > **QUICK TIP**
   > You can omit the first part of the URL (http://) when entering a Web page address into a Hyperlink field.

3. Press [Tab] six times to move to the new OnlineResources field, type www.microsoft.com/office, press [▼], point to the right edge of the OnlineResources field name so that the mouse pointer changes to ↔, then double-click to expand the column
   Your screen should look like Figure J-2. Hyperlink data in a datasheet appears underlined and in bright blue just like most text hyperlinks on Web pages.

   > **QUICK TIP**
   > [Ctrl]['] copies the entry in the field of the previous record to the same field of the current record.

4. Press [Ctrl]['], then press [▼]

5. Point to www.microsoft.com/office in either record so that the pointer changes to 🖑, then click www.microsoft.com/office
   The home page for Microsoft Office opens in the default browser on your computer (in this case, Internet Explorer) as shown in Figure J-3. Web pages are continually updated, so the content of the Web page itself may vary. If you are not already connected to the Internet, your **dialer** (software that helps you dial and connect to your ISP) may appear. Once connected to your ISP, the Microsoft Office Web page should appear.

   > **QUICK TIP**
   > Visited links change to the color purple.

6. Switch to the Courses datasheet, click the OnlineResources field for record 5 (Introduction to Excel), type www.microsoft.com/office, click the OnlineResources field for record 11 (Introduction to Netscape), type www.netscape.com, then press [Enter]

7. Save and close the Courses table, then close any open browser windows

---

Clues to Use

Understanding the Universal Naming Convention

The UNC is another naming convention (in addition to URL) for locating a file on a network. The structure of a UNC is \\servername\foldernames\filename, such as \\jccc\cisdept\forms\grades.html.

UNCs are used for local resources, such as a file stored on a LAN. URL addresses are used for Web pages on the Internet or a company intranet.

FIGURE J-2: Entry in a Hyperlink field

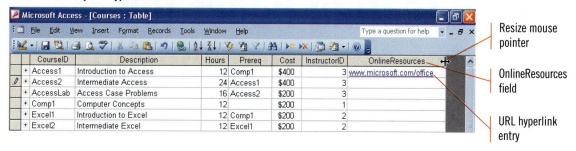

Resize mouse pointer

OnlineResources field

URL hyperlink entry

FIGURE J-3: Office home page

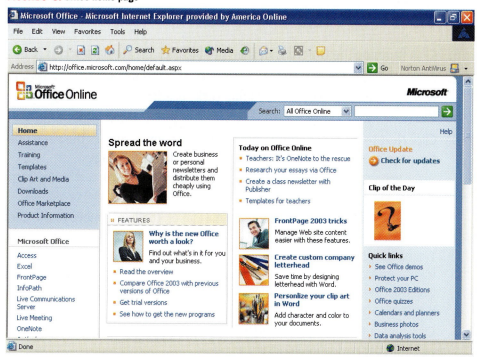

TABLE J-2: Types of networks

type of network	description
LAN (local area network)	Connects local resources such as file servers, computers, and printers by a direct cable; LANs do not cross public thoroughfares such as a street because of distance and legal restrictions on how far and where cables can be pulled.
WAN (wide area network)	Created when a LAN is connected to an existing telecommunications network, such as the phone system, to reach resources across public thoroughfares such as streets, rivers, or great distances
Internet	Largest WAN in the world, spanning the entire globe and connecting many diverse computer architectures
Intranet	WANs that support the same services as the Internet (i.e., e-mail, Web pages, and file transfer), and are built with the same technologies (e.g., TCP/IP communications protocol, HTML Web pages, and browser software), but are designed and secured for the internal purposes of a business

Creating Pages for Interactive Reporting

The **page** object, also called the **data access page (DAP)**, is a special Access object that creates dynamic Web pages used for viewing, entering, editing, and analyzing data stored in a Microsoft Access database. **Dynamic** means that the Web page communicates with the database—the Web page automatically displays the most current data each time it is opened or refreshed by Internet Explorer. Links to existing DAPs appear when you click the Pages button on the Objects bar. Table J-3 describes three major purposes for a DAP. You can also create static Web pages that display Access data by using the export to HTML feature after selecting any table, query, form, or report. **Static** Web pages do not change once they have been created. They can be viewed using any browser. You use the page object to create a Web page for the purpose of creating an interactive report.

STEPS

1. **Click Pages on the Objects bar, then double-click Create data access page by using wizard**

2. **Click the Tables/Queries list arrow, click Query: Attendance Details, click the Select All Fields button >>, click Next, double-click Location to select it as the grouping level field, then click Next**

TROUBLE

Click the Page View button if you are presented with Page Design View instead of Page View.

3. **Click Next to bypass sorting options, type Location Report as the page title, click the Open the page option button, click Finish, then maximize the page**

   Your screen should look like Figure J-4. **Page View** presents the Web page as it will appear within Internet Explorer. You click the **Expand button** to view the detail records within each group.

4. **Click the Next button ▶ twice on the navigation toolbar to move to the Corporate location, then click the Expand button ±**

   Two navigation toolbars are now displayed. The upper navigation toolbar works with the detail records within each location, and the lower navigation toolbar controls the grouping field, Location. The Expand button has become the Collapse button. When clicked, the **Collapse button** hides the detail records within that group.

TROUBLE

You will not see the insertion point inside the Description text box because this Web page cannot be used for data entry.

5. **Click Computer Concepts in the Description field, then click the Filter by Selection button on the upper navigation toolbar**

   Your screen should look like Figure J-5. Being able to expand and collapse detailed information, as well as being able to sort or filter information, makes this presentation of data *interactive*. Because you can view but not enter or edit data on this Web page, it functions as a *report* rather than as a *form*.

6. **Click the Filter Toggle button on the upper navigation toolbar to remove the filter, click the Save button on the Page View toolbar, navigate to the drive and folder where your Data Files are stored, type location in the File name text box, click Save, click No if prompted to change the default folder, then click OK if prompted about the connection string**

   By saving the page, a Web page named location.htm has been saved to the specified drive and folder.

QUICK TIP

Point to a DAP icon to display a ScreenTip that shows the path to the associated Web page.

7. **Close the location data access page**

   The DAP icon named location now appears in the database window, and shows a small linking symbol in the lower-left corner. When you double-click a DAP icon, you open the associated Web page in Page View. You could delete the DAP icon from the Training-J database without disturbing the physical Web page file, but it's much easier to open the Web page in Access (for later modification) if the link to the Web page is available in the database window.

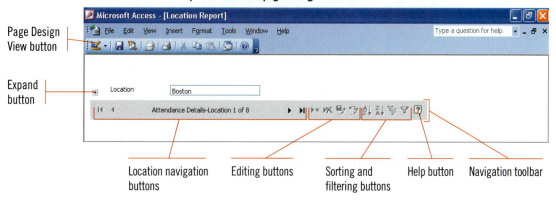

FIGURE J-4: Location Report data access page in Page View

Page Design View button

Expand button

Location navigation buttons

Editing buttons

Sorting and filtering buttons

Help button

Navigation toolbar

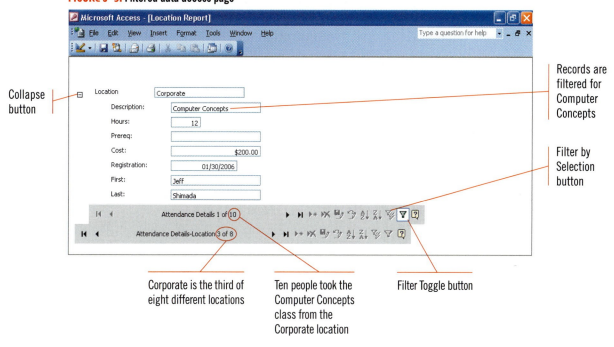

FIGURE J-5: Filtered data access page

Collapse button

Records are filtered for Computer Concepts

Filter by Selection button

Corporate is the third of eight different locations

Ten people took the Computer Concepts class from the Corporate location

Filter Toggle button

TABLE J-3: Purposes for data access pages

purpose	description
Data entry	Web pages that work as forms and can be used to view, add, or edit records
Interactive reporting	Web pages that work as reports and can be used to further sort, group, or filter data
Data analysis	Web pages that work as reports and can be used to analyze data using PivotTables and charts

Creating Pages for Data Entry

Using a DAP for data entry is similar to using an Access form. The big difference, of course, is that a dynamic Web page can be opened with Internet Explorer, whereas a user must have direct access to the actual database file in order to work with a form. Therefore, DAPs not only make a database more accessible, but also add a layer of security because you can allow users to enter and update data without giving them direct access to the actual database file. ▓▓▓▓ The Human Resources Department has offered to help Fred find, enter, and update information on instructors. You create a data access page that works like a form to let the Human Resources Department update data using the Internet Explorer browser.

STEPS

1. **Double-click Create data access page by using wizard, click the Tables/Queries list arrow, click Table: Instructors, click the Select All Fields button** >>, **click Next, then click Finish to accept the rest of the default options**

   The data access page opens in **Page Design View**, as shown in Figure J-6. The **Field List** window, which organizes database objects in a folder hierarchy, may be open. Each item on the Page object is called a control just as it is in Report Design View or Form Design View.

2. **Click the Page View button** 🖳 **on the Page Design toolbar to view the data access page, click the Save button** 💾 **on the Page View toolbar, navigate to the drive and folder where your Data Files are stored, type instruct in the File name text box, then click Save**

   The instruct data access page shows the four records in the Instructors table. You *could* use Page View to enter or edit data, but forms are more flexible data entry tools if you have direct access to the database file. You use DAPs when you want a user to work with Access data who does *not have direct access to the database*, but who does have Internet Explorer.

TROUBLE

If you see #Name? errors on the Web page, click File on the Internet Explorer menu bar, and then click Work Offline.

3. **Click the Design View button list arrow** 🖌️▾, **then click Web Page Preview**

   The instruct.htm file opens in Internet Explorer, as shown in Figure J-7.

TROUBLE

The [Page Up] and [Page Down] keys will not move the focus from record to record when viewing records through a Web page.

4. **Click the New button** ▸* **on the navigation toolbar, type Delores in the InstructorFirst box, press [Tab], type Hanneman in the InstructorLast box, press [Tab], type 9/1/06, click the Previous button** ◂, **then click the Next button** ▸

   Moving between records helps verify that the record for Delores Hanneman was entered successfully. The value for the InstructorID field, 5, was entered automatically because this field is defined in the Training-J database with an AutoNumber data type.

5. **Close Internet Explorer, switch to the Training-J: Database window, click Tables on the Objects bar, then double-click the Instructors table to open it in Datasheet View**

   Your screen should look like Figure J-8. The new record for Delores Hanneman appears in the table. You used a Web page opened in Internet Explorer to dynamically update an underlying Access database.

6. **Close the Instructors datasheet, then close the instruct DAP**

FIGURE J-6: Page Design View

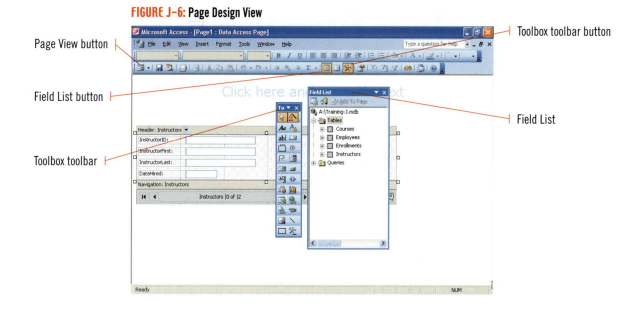

Page View button

Field List button

Toolbox toolbar

Toolbox toolbar button

Field List

FIGURE J-7: instruct.htm Web page opened in Internet Explorer

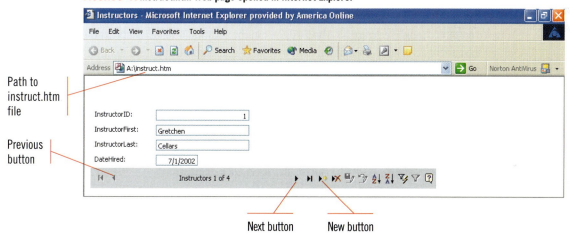

Path to instruct.htm file

Previous button

Next button   New button

FIGURE J-8: Updated Instructors table

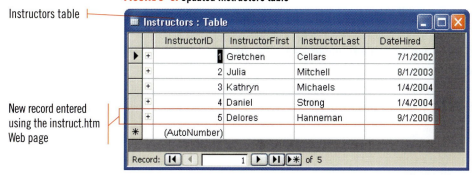

Instructors table

New record entered using the instruct.htm Web page

Creating PivotTables

A **PivotTable** is a presentation of summarized data. Typically, a PivotTable uses one field as the column heading, another field for the row heading, and summarizes a third field in the body of the PivotTable. For example, you could use a PivotTable to subtotal sales by product category and by state. The Sales field would be summarized in the body of the PivotTable and the Category and State fields would be used as column or row headings. Because a PivotTable displays summarized data, you cannot use a PivotTable to edit, delete, or add new data.  You decide to create a data access page with a PivotTable and PivotChart to summarize the internal charges for each class for each MediaLoft location.

QUICK TIP

Although an Access 2003 database may be opened in Access 2002 or Access 2000, the pages that you create can only be modified in Access 2003.

1. **Click Pages on the Objects bar, double-click Create data access page in Design view, click OK if prompted with information about previous versions of Access, then maximize the Design View window (if necessary)**

   Page Design View is very similar to that of Form Design View or Report Design View. Table J-4 summarizes some of the key terminology used in Page Design View.

2. **Click the Queries Expand button ⊞ in the Field List, then drag the Location Charges query into the upper-left area of the Drag fields ... area**

   When you are dragging tables, queries, or fields from the Field List to Page Design View, a blue outline identifies the **drop area**, the area on the page where you can successfully add that item. If the Control Wizards button ⬚ is selected on the Toolbox toolbar, the **Layout Wizard** opens to guide you through the rest of the process.

TROUBLE

If the Layout Wizard dialog box doesn't open, delete the controls that were added to the page, click the Control Wizards button ⬚ on the Toolbox toolbar, then redo Step 2.

3. **Click the PivotTable option button, then click OK**

   Your screen should look like Figure J-9. The fields within the Location Charges query are the column headings within the current PivotTable. To subtotal costs by course and location, you need to move the fields to create the structure for the PivotTable.

4. **Click the PivotTable control so that a hashed border surrounds it**

   A hashed border around the PivotTable indicates that you can now move and work with the individual field within the PivotTable.

5. **Right-click CourseID, click Move to Row Area, right-click Location, click Move to Column Area, right-click any Cost field, point to AutoCalc, then click Sum**

   Now the Cost field is subtotaled within the table according to the CourseID field in the row heading position and the Location field in the column heading position.

6. **Drag the lower-right sizing handle to expand the size of the PivotTable, then click the Page View button 🖼 to view the PivotTable as shown in Figure J-10**

   A PivotTable's major benefit is that it quickly rearranges data so you can analyze it in many ways. For example, you could collapse or expand the details displayed for any CourseID or Location by clicking the Expand and Collapse buttons, or use those fields to filter only the data you want to see.

7. **Click the CourseID list arrow, click the (All) check box to clear all checks, click the AccessLab check box, then click OK**

   The new PivotTable shows that two employees from the Corporate location and one person from Seattle took this class, each at a cost of $200, for a grand total of $600.

QUICK TIP

To make a change to a PivotTable permanent, you must make the change in Page Design View, then save the page.

8. **Click the Save button 🖫, navigate to the drive and folder where your Data Files are stored, type pivot, then click Save**

   The new page link is stored in the Training-J database window and the pivot.htm file is stored in the drive and folder where your Data Files are stored.

FIGURE J-9: PivotTable in Page Design View

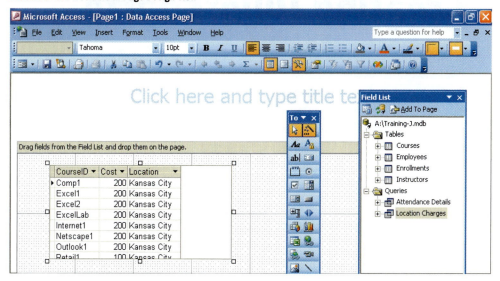

FIGURE J-10: Modified PivotTable in Page View

Location is the column heading field

CourseID is the row heading field

Expand and collapse detail buttons

Cost is the summarized field

Four Access1 classes, for a subtotal of $1,600, were taken by the Corporate location

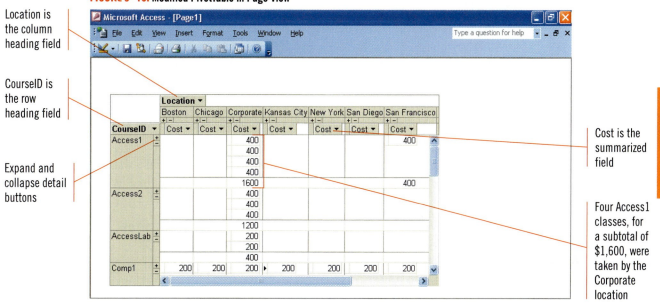

TABLE J-4: Page Design View terminology

term	definition
Field list	List that contains all of the field names that can be added to the page
Toolbox toolbar	Toolbar that contains buttons for the different types of controls that can be added to the page
Control	Each individual element of the page such as labels or text boxes that can be added, deleted, or modified
Bound controls	Controls that display data from an underlying recordset; common bound controls are text boxes, list boxes, and the PivotTable
Unbound controls	Controls that do not display data from an underlying recordset; common unbound controls for a page are labels, lines, and the toolbars
Sections	Areas of the object that contain controls; sections determine where a control will appear on the Web page
Properties	Characteristics that further describe the selected object, section, or control

Creating PivotCharts

A **PivotChart** is a graphical representation of data shown in a PivotTable. You add controls such as a PivotChart to an existing Web page using Page Design View. Page Design View closely resembles Form Design View and Report Design View, but some features of Page Design View are unique to pages. For example, the Field List in Page Design View shows all fields from all tables and queries in the database rather than only one. Also, the Toolbox toolbar contains additional controls as identified in Table J-5. You decide to add a PivotChart to this page to graphically display the data shown in the PivotTable. You will work in Page Design View to create the PivotChart.

STEPS

1. **Click the Design View button, then click the Field List button to close the Field List window**

   To add a PivotChart to the page that is connected to the information presented by the PivotTable, you will use the Office Chart button on the Toolbox toolbar.

2. **Click the Office Chart button on the Toolbox toolbar, click to the right of the PivotTable, then click the Chartspace to open the Commands and Options dialog box as shown in Figure J-11**

   The first thing you must do is select the data source for the chart as presented by the Commands and Options dialog box.

3. **Click PivotTable: PivotTable0 to indicate that the chart's data comes from the existing PivotTable, click the Type tab, click the Stacked Column chart as shown in Figure J-12, then close the Commands and Options dialog box**

   With the chart in place, you will move and resize both the PivotTable and PivotChart to better display the information.

4. **Move and resize the PivotTable and PivotChart so that they equally share the space on the Web page, click the Show/Hide Legend button at the top of the PivotChart control to display the legend, then click the Page View button**

5. **In either the PivotTable or the PivotChart, click the Location list arrow, click the (All) check box to clear it, click the Kansas City check box, then click OK**

   Your final pivot.htm Web page should look like Figure J-13. You can work with the fields on the PivotChart to filter and reorganize the data just as you could with a PivotTable. Because you based the PivotChart on the existing PivotTable, interacting with one of these controls automatically affects the data that is displayed in the other.

6. **Click the Save button**

   Remember, the filters you apply in Page View are temporary. If you wanted this page to be saved with the Kansas City filter applied, you would return to Page Design View, reapply the filter, and save the page while still in Page Design View.

FIGURE J-11: Commands and Options dialog box

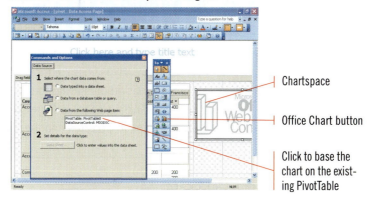

Chartspace

Office Chart button

Click to base the chart on the existing PivotTable

FIGURE J-12: Choosing a chart type

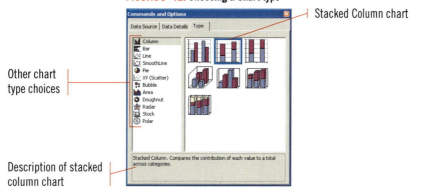

Stacked Column chart

Other chart type choices

Description of stacked column chart

FIGURE J-13: Final PivotTable and PivotChart

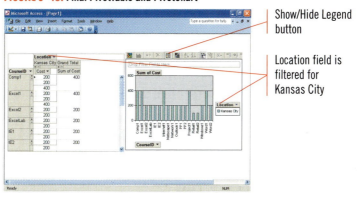

Show/Hide Legend button

Location field is filtered for Kansas City

TABLE J-5: New Controls on the Toolbox toolbar in Page Design View

control	button	used to add a control to a page that...
Bound Span		Binds HTML to a Text or Memo field
Scrolling Text		Displays text that scrolls, or moves, through the control
Expand		Works as a toggle to expand or collapse detail information in grouped records
Record Navigation		Displays a record navigation toolbar
Office PivotTable		Displays a PivotTable
Office Chart		Displays a PivotChart
Office Spreadsheet		Displays a small spreadsheet
Hyperlink		Uses text to link to another Web page, file, or field value
Image Hyperlink		Uses an image to link to another Web page, file, or field value
Movie		Inserts a video clip

Adding Hyperlinks

A **hyperlink** is a label, button, or image that when clicked opens another object, document or graphic file, e-mail message, or World Wide Web page. Hyperlinks are most often used to allow the user to access one Web page from another with a single click, without having to type the URL into the browser address bar for each desired Web page. You add hyperlinks to pages in Page Design View. You want to create a hyperlink between the pivot Web page you just created and the location Web page created earlier.

STEPS

1. **Click the Design View button**

   Hyperlinks are added to pages by using the **Hyperlink control**.

2. **Click the Hyperlink button on the Toolbox toolbar, then click above the PivotTable control**

   The Insert Hyperlink dialog box opens, as shown in Figure J-14. You can create hyperlinks to existing files, Web pages, pages in this database, new pages, or e-mail addresses. You want to create a link to the location.htm Web page.

3. **Click the Page in This Database button, click location in the list, enter Interactive Location Report in the Text to display box, then click OK**

   The pivot Web page now displays a hyperlink to the location page just above the PivotTable. To test the new hyperlink, you'll work with the pivot Web page in Page View.

4. **Click the Save button, click the Page View button list arrow, then click Web Page Preview**

   The pivot Web page now displays a hyperlink to the location page just above the PivotTable, as shown in Figure J-15.

5. **Click the Interactive Location Report hyperlink**

   The location Web page now appears as shown in Figure J-16.

6. **Close Internet Explorer, then switch to the pivot Web page in Design View**

7. **Click in the upper-middle portion of the page, type your name, click to display the page in Page View, click the Location list arrow, click the (All) check box to remove all check marks, click the Seattle check box, then click OK**

   The location Web page now displays only the information for the Seattle location.

8. **Click the Print button, save and close the pivot page, close the Training-J.mdb database, then exit Access**

Clues to Use

Creating a hyperlink from an image

To create an image that works as a hyperlink, click the Image Hyperlink button on the Toolbox toolbar, and then click the page where you want the image to appear. You will be prompted to choose the image you want to use for the hyperlink. You will also be presented the Insert Hyperlink dialog box from which you can choose the Web page, file, or e-mail address you want the image to link to.

FIGURE J-14: Insert Hyperlink dialog box

Text to display box

Page in this Database button

FIGURE J-15: pivot.htm Web page with hyperlink

Hyperlink to location.htm page

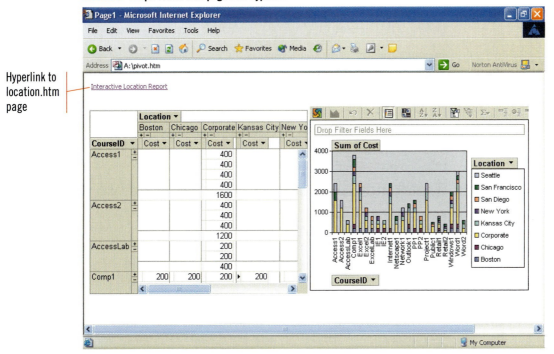

FIGURE J-16: location.htm Web page

Publishing Web Pages to Web Servers

Publishing means to place the Web pages you have created in a location where others can access them. Usually publishing involves moving your Web pages to a **Web server**, a computer devoted to storing and downloading Web pages. Web servers contain **Web folders**, which are special folders dedicated to organizing Web pages. Once your Web page files are stored appropriately, **clients**, computers with appropriate browser and communication software that have access to the Web folder, may download and use those files by entering a URL in the address bar of their browser. Because dynamic access pages can only be viewed successfully using Internet Explorer as the browser, they are most applicable to corporate intranet solutions that control the software that the client computers use. Table J-6 provides more information about how to use Access to create other types of Web pages, both dynamic and static, that work with other browsers. You review the steps necessary to publish the Web pages for use over MediaLoft's intranet.

STEPS

To publish Access Web pages:

- ### Store the Access database in a shared network folder
  On a network, most folders are not available to everyone, so be sure to start with the Access database in a folder that the appropriate people have permission to use. A folder that many people can use is called a **shared network folder** or a **mapped drive**. Access databases are inherently **multiuser**, so that many people can enter and update information at the same time, *provided* they have access to the database. Two people cannot, however, update the same record at the same time, which is referred to as **record locking**.

- ### Use the page object within Access to create dynamic access pages
  Once the database is located in a shared folder, use the page object to create dynamic access pages to enter and edit data, to create interactive reports, and to create data analysis tools, including PivotTables and PivotCharts.

- ### Save the dynamic access pages that you create in a shared Web folder for others to access
  Saving the dynamic access pages that you create in a shared Web folder requires that you have a compatible and secure network infrastructure already in place. Sometimes the process of placing Web pages in shared Web folders is called **publishing**. You can save the database and dynamic access pages in the same shared folder. In large implementations, however, you will want to use different folders, or perhaps entirely different file servers to store the database and Web pages so that you can apply different levels of security and hardware resources.

- ### Give the users the URL or UNC address to access the Web pages
  URLs are used to access Internet Web pages. URLs or UNCs can be used when the file is located on a LAN. Using Internet Explorer, users then enter the URL or UNC into the Internet Explorer address bar to access the dynamic access pages you have created.

- ### Use professional networking resources as necessary
  Setting up a LAN or WAN to serve as a corporate intranet requires many skills. People who build and maintain networks are often called **network administrators**. Those who work with Web servers, Web folders, and supporting Internet technologies are often called **Webmasters**. Figure J-17 illustrates a typical corporate LAN that uses three servers for the purpose of managing the database, Web pages, and other file server activities for a LAN. In this example, the Access database would be located on the database server, the dynamic Web pages that are created using the page object would be stored on the Web server, and the client computers would use Internet Explorer to access these resources through a file server.

FIGURE J-17: Typical local area network used to implement dynamic access pages

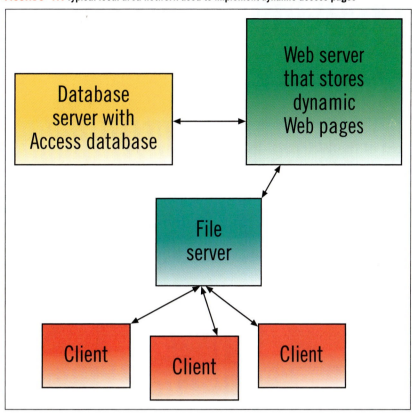

TABLE J-6: Types of Web pages created by Access

to...	do this...
Create DAPs from existing Access forms and reports	Select the form or report, click File on the menu bar, click Save As, then choose data access page in the As list.
Create dynamic Web pages that can be viewed by any browser	Use the Export option on the File menu to create server-generated Web pages from tables, queries, and forms. (Use the **ASP** file type for Microsoft **Active Server Pages**.) Server-generated HTML pages are dynamic (and therefore change as your database changes).
Create static Web pages that can be viewed by any browser	Use the Export option on the File menu to create static Web pages from tables, queries, forms, and reports. The files display a snapshot of the data at the time the static HTML file was created and can be viewed equally well in Internet Explorer and Netscape Navigator.
Open a Web page created by another program in Access	Right-click the file in the Open dialog box, then click Open in Microsoft Access on the shortcut menu.

Access 2003

Clues to Use

The connection between the Web page and database file

Dynamic access pages are connected to the database with path information that specifies the current drive, folder, and filenames for both the Web page and database files. Therefore, if you change the location or name of either the Web page or database file after the Web page is initially created, the link between the two may not work. However, it's not difficult to reestablish the connection. If you open a page in Page View and see the message "The HTML file associated with this link has been moved, renamed, or deleted," click the Update Link button in the error message dialog box, then locate the appropriate Web page associated with that page. If you open a page in Page View or view a Web page in Internet Explorer and see the message "Microsoft Office Web Components could not open the database drive:\path\databasename.mdb," #Name errors on the Web page, or any other errors indicating that the database cannot be found, it means that the database file has been moved or renamed. To correct this, open the page in Page Design View, open the Field List, right-click the name of the database at the top of the Field List, click Connection on the shortcut menu, click the Build button to the right of the database name on the Connection tab, then locate the appropriate database associated with that page.

Practice

▼ CONCEPTS REVIEW

Identify each element of the Web page shown in Figure J-18.

FIGURE J-18

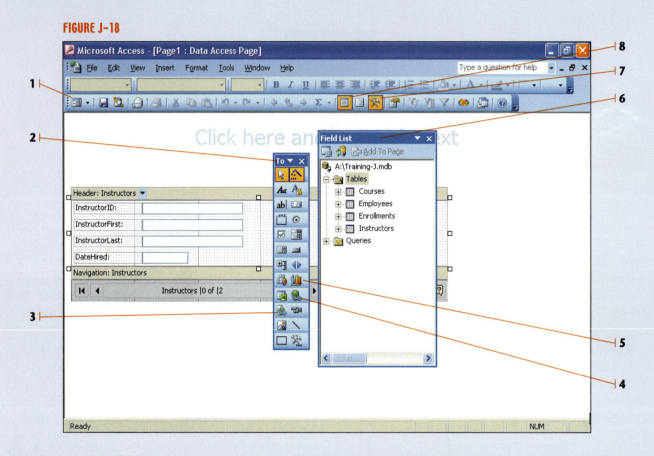

Match each term with the statement that best describes its function.

9. **URL**
10. **HTML**
11. **World Wide Web pages**
12. **Browser**
13. **data access page**
14. **TCP/IP**

a. Software used on a client computer to find and display Web pages

b. Dynamic Web page created by the Access page object

c. Web page address

d. Tags inserted into a text file that browsers read to display Web pages

e. Communications protocol used by the Internet

f. Hyperlinked documents that make the Internet easy to navigate

15. **Which of the following is *not* a valid URL?**
    a. www.jccc.net
    b. www.FBI.GOV
    c. http://www.course.com
    d. http://www.course technology.com

16. **To connect to the Internet through your home computer, you must first connect to a(n):**
    a. ISP.
    b. URL.
    c. Home page.
    d. Webmaster.

17. **Which of the following is *not* a likely entry for a Hyperlink field?**
    a. Path to a file
    b. Web page address
    c. FTP server location
    d. Company name

18. **Which of the following browsers must be used to display data access pages?**
    a. Netscape Navigator
    b. Internet Explorer
    c. America Online's browser
    d. Any current browser will successfully display data access pages

19. **What distinguishes a dynamic Web page from a static Web page?**
    a. The date it was created
    b. The connection it retains with the database
    c. The use of style sheets
    d. The browser used to open the page

20. **Dynamic access pages are best suited for which purpose?**
    a. E-commerce
    b. Discussion threads
    c. Corporate intranet applications
    d. Customer service

21. **The page object in Access creates dynamic access pages that are always:**
    a. Dynamic.
    b. Static.
    c. Used for data entry.
    d. Based on forms.

22. **Which of the following objects *cannot* be converted to a DAP using the Save As option on the File menu?**
    a. Macro
    b. Query
    c. Form
    d. Table

▼ SKILLS REVIEW

1. **Understand the World Wide Web.**
   a. In Word, open the **Web.doc** document, interview four people, and ask them to identify a Web site address where they have recently experienced the following activities. Insert their answers in the first table in the Web.doc document. A response for one person has already been completed as a guide.
      - To sell or purchase a product or service
      - For entertainment
      - To find other Internet resources (search engines)
      - For news, weather, or other informational needs
      - To take a class
   b. Through the same interviews or other research, identify four ISPs in your area, and complete the second table in the Web.doc document with your findings about their costs and basic services.
   c. Type your name at the top of the document, then print it and close Word.

2. **Create Hyperlink fields.**
   a. Start Access, then open the **Machinery-J.mdb** database from the drive and folder where your Data Files are stored.
   b. Open the Products table in Design View.
   c. Add a new field named **HomePage** with a Hyperlink data type.
   d. Save the Products table, open it in Datasheet View, then enter the following home page URLs into the new field for the first six records:
      1) www.toro.com
      2) www.caseih.com
      3) www.snapper.com
      4) www.deere.com
      5) www.troybilt.com
      6) www.stihl.com
   e. Click the link for www.deere.com, then print the first page of the John Deere Web site. If you are not already connected to the Internet, your dialer may appear, prompting you to connect with your chosen ISP. Once connected to your ISP, the John Deere home page should appear.
   f. Close your browser, then close the Products datasheet.

3. **Create pages for interactive reporting.**
   a. Use the Page Wizard to start creating a new data access page.
   b. Select the ProductName and the ReorderLevel fields from the Products table, then select the TransactionDate and UnitPrice fields from the Inventory Transactions table.
   c. Group the records by ProductName, then sort the records in ascending order by TransactionDate.
   d. Type **Product Activity** for the page title, then open the new page in Page View.
   e. Switch to Page Design View, maximize the Design View window, click in the title area of the body of the page, then type the title **your name's Garden Shop Orders**.
   f. Click the Page View button, click the ProductName text box, sort the ProductName in descending order to display the Weed Wacker products, then expand the group and navigate to the second detail record, which has a 6/30/2006 Transaction Date.
   g. Print the Product Activity data access page for this record.
   h. Save the data access page with the name **garden.htm** to the drive and folder where your Data Files are stored, then close the page.

4. Create pages for data entry.

    a. Use the Page Wizard to start creating a new data access page.

    b. Select all of the fields in the Products table.

    c. Do not add any grouping levels, but sort the records in ascending order on ProductName.

    d. Title the page **Products**.

    e. In Design View, click in the title area of the body of the page, then type the title **your name's Products**.

    f. Save the Web page as **products.htm** to the drive and folder where your Data Files are stored, then view the page in Web Page Preview. If you receive #Name? errors on the Web page, click File on the Internet Explorer menu bar, then click Work Offline to toggle off that option.

    g. Find the Mulcher record, change the price of the mulcher from $69.50 to **$79.75**, then print the Web page within Internet Explorer in which you made this change.

    h. Navigate to the next record within Internet Explorer, then back to the Mulcher record to make sure that the price change was saved. Close Internet Explorer.

    i. Open the Products table in the Machinery-J.mdb database, then make sure the Mulcher record now displays $79.75 as the Unit Price. Add your initials to the end of the Serial Number entry for the Mulcher record, then print the Products datasheet in landscape orientation so that it fits on one page.

    j. Close the Products table, then save and close the products.htm data access page.

5. Create PivotTables.

    a. Start a new data access page in Page Design View. Click OK if prompted with a message about different versions of Access.

    b. Open the Field List window if not already visible, then click the Expand button to the left of the Queries folder.

    c. Add the Products Query to the upper-left corner of the Drag fields... area as a PivotTable.

    d. Click the PivotTable control to edit it, then move the ProductName field to the row area. (*Hint*: Remember that the PivotTable control has a hashed border when you are editing it. Also note that you must right-click the field name itself in order to display the shortcut menu that allows you to move that field to the row, column, filter, or detail area of the PivotTable.)

    e. Resize the control so that all three columns are clearly visible.

    f. Click in the title area of the body of the page, type the title **your name's Orders**, then display the page in Page View.

    g. Use the TransactionDate list arrow to select only the **6/30/2006** dates, then print that page, as shown in Figure J-19.

    h. Save the page as **units.htm** to the drive and folder where your Data Files are stored, click OK when prompted about the connection string, then close the page.

FIGURE J-19

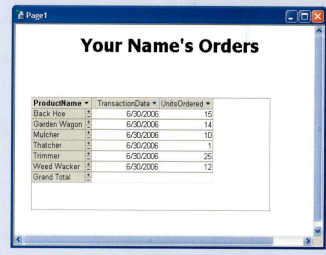

6. **Create PivotCharts.**
   a. Open the **units.htm** data access page in Page Design View.
   b. Open the Toolbox toolbar if it is not already visible.
   c. Use the Office Chart button on the Toolbox toolbar to add an Office Web Component to the right of the PivotTable.
   d. Click the Office Web Component, identify the data source as the PivotTable and the type of chart as a clustered column chart.
   e. On the PivotTable, move the TransactionDate field to the Column area.
   f. In the PivotChart, open the Field List. (*Hint*: The field list for the PivotChart is different from the field list for the entire page. Find the field list for the PivotChart by clicking the Field List button found on the right side of the PivotChart toolbar. The PivotChart toolbar is located at the top of the chart. You will have to widen the PivotChart to display the entire PivotChart toolbar and find the Field List button.)
   g. Drag the UnitsOrdered field from the PivotChart field list to the Drop Data Fields Here area, then close the PivotChart field list.
   h. Resize both the PivotTable and PivotChart to clearly display as much data as possible, and show the legend on the PivotChart.
   i. Display the page in Page View, then filter for Thatchers and Trimmers. Your screen should look like Figure J-20.
   j. Save, print, and then close the units.htm page.

FIGURE J-20

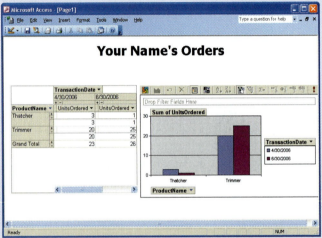

7. **Add hyperlinks.**
   a. Open the **units.htm** data access page in Design View, then use the Hyperlink button on the Toolbox toolbar and the Address text box to add a hyperlink in the lower-left corner of the page to these vendors:
      www.toro.com
      www.snapper.com
   b. The hyperlinks should display the text **Toro** and **Snapper**.
   c. Open the units.htm page in Page View, then test each hyperlink.
   d. Save the units.htm page, then close it.
   e. Close all Internet Explorer windows, close any open page objects within the Machinery-J.mdb database, then exit Access.

8. Publish Web pages to Web servers.

a. Call your ISP and ask for information about the requirements to publish Web pages to their Web server. (If you are not currently connected to the Internet from home, research any ISP of your choice. You may also be able to find this information on the ISP's Web site.)

b. If your ISP does not allow members to publish Web pages, continue researching ISPs until you find one that allows members to publish Web pages.

c. Print or copy the documentation on how to publish Web pages to the ISP's Web server.

d. Open Internet Explorer and type **www.geocities.com** in the Address list box.

e. Follow the links on the Web page to determine how to create your own Web page at the geocities Web site, then print the documentation.

▼ INDEPENDENT CHALLENGE 1

As the manager of a college women's basketball team, you want to enhance the Basketball-J database to include hyperlink field entries for opponents. You also want to develop a Web page to report information on player statistics.

a. Start Access, then open the **Basketball-J.mdb** database from the drive and folder where your Data Files are stored.

b. Open the Games table in Design View, then add a field named **WebSite** with a Hyperlink data type.

c. Save the Games table, then open it in Datasheet View.

d. For the second record, enter **www.creighton.edu** in the WebSite field.

e. For the fifth record, enter **www.drake.edu** in the WebSite field.

f. Click the www.drake.edu link to display the Web page for Drake University, then print the first page.

g. Close the Drake Web page, close the Games table, click Pages on the Objects bar, then start creating a new page using the Page Wizard.

h. Add all of the fields in the Players Query, group the information by the Last field, do not specify any sort fields, then title the page **Player Stats**.

i. In Design View, click in the title text area of the body of the page, then type the title **Iowa State Women's Basketball**. Include your initials in the title if you want them displayed on the printed solution.

j. Save the Web page as **pstats.htm** to the drive and folder where your Data Files are stored, then open the Web Page Preview of the page (which opens the Web page in Internet Explorer).

Advanced Challenge Exercise

- Find and expand the details for the player with the last name of Hile.
- Sort the detail records in descending order on the values in the TotalPts field.
- Print the record for Hile.

k. Close Internet Explorer, save and close the pstats.htm data access page, close the Basketball-J.mdb database, then exit Access.

▼ INDEPENDENT CHALLENGE 2

As the manager of a college women's basketball team, you want to enhance the Basketball-J database by developing a Web page to enter new game information.

   a. Start Access, then open the **Basketball-J.mdb** database from the drive and folder where your Data Files are stored.

   b. Start creating a new data access page using the Page Wizard.

   c. Add all of the fields from the Games table, do not add any grouping levels, sort the records in ascending order by Date, then accept **Games** as the title for the page.

   d. In Design View, click in the title area of the body of the page, then type the title **ISU Games**. Include your initials in the title to include them on the printed solution.

   e. Save the Web page with the name **games.htm** to the drive and folder where your Data Files are stored, then display Web Page Preview to view the Games Web page in Internet Explorer.

   f. Enter the following new record as record 23:

Date:	**3/1/2006**
GameNo:	(The AutoNumber entry for the new record, 23, will be automatically entered.)
Opponent:	**Kansas State**
Mascot:	**Wildcats**
Home-Away:	**H**
Home Score:	**100**
Opponent Score:	**52**
WebSite:	**www.ksu.edu**

   g. Navigate to the first record, then back to the last.

   h. Print this new record, then close Internet Explorer.

   i. Open the datasheet for the Games table to verify the entry in the Basketball-J.mdb database.

   j. Close the Games datasheet, close the games.htm Web page, close the Basketball-J.mdb database, then exit Access.

▼ INDEPENDENT CHALLENGE 3

As the manager of a college women's basketball team, you want to enhance the Basketball-J database by developing a Web page to display player statistical information as a PivotTable.

   a. Start Access, then open the **Basketball-J.mdb** database from the drive and folder where your Data Files are stored.

   b. Start a new data access page in Page Design View. Click OK if prompted with a message about different versions of Access.

   c. Expand the Queries folder in the Field List, then add the Players Query to the data access page as a PivotTable.

   d. Widen the PivotTable control so that all of the seven fields are clearly displayed.

   e. Click in the title area of the data access page, then type the title **Game Stats**. Include your initials in the title to include them on the printed solution.

   f. Select the PivotTable to select it, click it again to edit it, right-click the Opponent field, then choose Move to Row Area on the shortcut menu.

   g. Save the Web page as **gstats.htm** to the drive and folder where your Data Files are stored, then view the page in Web Page Preview so that it loads into Internet Explorer.

   h. Click the Last list arrow in the PivotTable, click the All check box (to clear it), then click the Franco and Tyler check boxes to display only Denise Franco and Morgan Tyler's statistics.

   i. Print this Web page, then close Internet Explorer.

   j. Close the gstats.htm Web page, close the Basketball-J.mdb database, then exit Access.

▼ INDEPENDENT CHALLENGE 4

You are the coordinator of the foreign studies program at your college. You help place students in foreign college study programs that have curriculum and credits that are transferable back to your college. You have started to build a database that documents the primary and secondary language used by the foreign countries for which your college has developed transfer programs. The database also includes a table of common words and phrases, translated into various languages that you use in correspondence with the host colleges.

a. Start Access, then open the **Languages-J.mdb** database from the drive and folder where your Data Files are stored.

b. Open the Words table, observe the field names that represent various languages, then click the Design View button to switch to Table Design View.

c. Add a field to the database that represents a language that doesn't currently exist in the database, then save the table and display its datasheet.

d. Connect to the Internet, then go to www.yahoo.com, www.msn.com, or any general search engine to conduct some research for your database. Your goal is to find a Web page that translates English to the new language that you added to the database, then to print one page of that Web page.

e. Using the features provided by the Web page, translate the existing six words in the English field of the Words table to the new language you added as a field, then print the Words datasheet in landscape mode.

f. Use the Page Wizard to create a Web page with all of the fields in the Words table except for WordID. Do not add any grouping levels, but sort the records in ascending order based on the values in the English field.

g. Title the page **Translations**.

h. In Page Design View, enter the title **Translations** at the top of the page. Include your initials in the title if you want to include them on the printed solution.

i. Save the Web page with the name **trans.htm** to the drive and folder where your Data Files are stored, then display Web Page Preview to view the Translations data access page in Internet Explorer.

j. Navigate to the record for the English word "hello", then print that page, as shown in Figure J-21.

k. Close Internet Explorer, close the trans.htm Web page, close Languages-J.mdb, then exit Access.

FIGURE J-21

Translations		
	Translations	
English:	hello	
French:	bonjour	
Spanish:	hola	
German:	hallo	
Italian:	ciao	
Portuguese:	hello	
Norwegian:	hei	

Words 4 of 6

▼ VISUAL WORKSHOP

As the manager of a college women's basketball team, you need to enhance the **Basketball-J.mdb** database by developing a Web page to display player scoring information as a PivotTable. In Page Design View, use the Scoring query as the basis of the PivotTable. Move the Home-Away field and then the Last field to the Row Area. Figure J-22 shows the final data access page, titled ISU Scoring. Include your initials in the title area if desired. Save the Web page with the name **scoring.htm** to the drive and folder where your Data Files are stored. Open, view, and print the page within Internet Explorer, then close all open applications.

FIGURE J-22

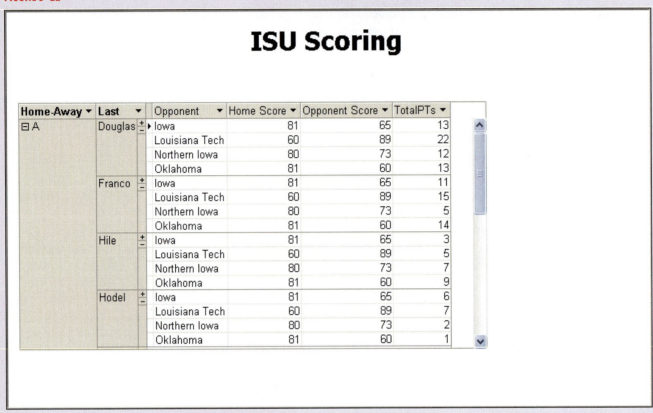

Creating Advanced Queries

OBJECTIVES

Query for top values
Create a parameter query
Modify query properties
Create a make-table query
Create an append query
Create a delete query
Create an update query
Specify join properties
Create find unmatched queries

If you have a SAM user profile, you may have access to hands-on instruction, practice, and assessment of the skills covered in this unit. Log in to your SAM account and go to your assignments page to see what your instructor has assigned.

Queries are database objects that answer questions about the data. The most common query is the **select query**, which selects fields and records that match specific criteria and displays them in a datasheet. Other types of queries, such as top value, parameter, and action queries, are powerful tools for displaying, analyzing, and updating data. An **action query** changes data when it is run. There are four types of action queries: delete, update, append, and make-table. You use advanced queries to help Fred Ames handle the requests for information about data stored in the Training database.

Querying for Top Values

Once a large number of records are entered into a database, it is less common to query for all of the records, and more common to list only the most significant records by choosing a subset of the highest or lowest values from a sorted query. Use the **Top Values** feature in Query Design View to specify a number or percentage of sorted records that you want to display in the query's datasheet. Employee attendance at MediaLoft classes has grown. To help plan future classes, Fred wants to print a datasheet listing the names of the top five classes, sorted by number of students per class. You create a summarized Select Query to find the total number of attendees for each class, then use the Top Values feature to find the five most attended classes.

STEPS

1. **Start Access, open the Training-K.mdb database, click Queries on the Objects bar, then double-click Create query in Design view**

   You need fields from both the Enrollments and Courses tables.

TROUBLE

If you add a table's field list to Query Design View twice by mistake, click the title bar of the extra field list, then press [Delete].

2. **Double-click Enrollments, double-click Courses, then click Close in the Show Table dialog box**

   Query Design View displays the field lists of the two related tables in the upper portion of the query window.

3. **Double-click LogNo in the Enrollments field list, double-click Description in the Courses field list, then click the Datasheet View button on the Query Design toolbar**

   The datasheet shows 153 total records. You want to know how many people took each course. That means you need to group the records by the Description field and count the LogNo field.

QUICK TIP

Click at any time during the query design process to view the datasheet at that point in development.

4. **Click the Design View button , click the Totals button Σ on the Query Design toolbar, click Group By for the LogNo field, click the Group By list arrow, then click Count**

   Sorting helps you further analyze the information and prepare for finding the top values.

5. **Click the LogNo field Sort cell, click the LogNo field Sort list arrow, then click Descending**

   Your screen should look like Figure K-1. Choosing a descending sort order will put the courses with the highest count value (the most attended courses) at the top of the datasheet.

6. **Click the Top Values list arrow on the Query Design toolbar**

   The number or percentage specified in the Top Values list box determines which records will be displayed, starting with the first one on the sorted datasheet. See Table K-1 for more information on how to use the Top Values feature.

7. **Click 5, then click on the Query Design toolbar**

   Your screen should look like Figure K-2. The datasheet shows the five most popular MediaLoft courses. For example, the Computer Concepts course had 19 attendees. If more than one course had 10 attendees (a summarized value of 10 in the CountOfLogNo field), then all courses that tied for fifth place would have been displayed. The LogNo field was automatically renamed CountOfLogNo to indicate that the values within that field are summarized count values.

8. **Click the Save button on the Query Datasheet toolbar, type Top 5 Courses, click OK, then close the datasheet**

   The Top 5 Courses query appears as a query object in the database window. The last Top Value entered (5) is saved with the query.

FIGURE K-1: Designing a summary query for top values

Top Values list arrow

Totals button

Total row

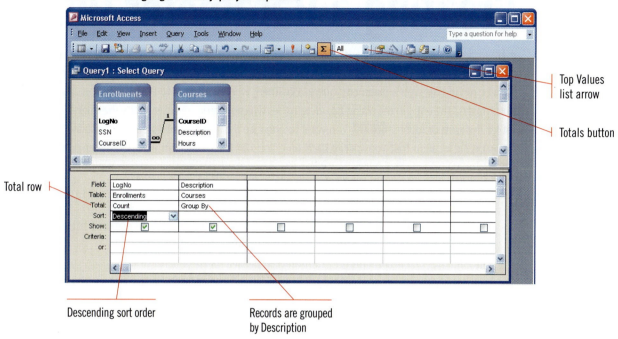

Descending sort order

Records are grouped by Description

FIGURE K-2: Top values datasheet

CountOfLogNo field counts the records within each group

Records are sorted in descending order based on CountOfLogNo field

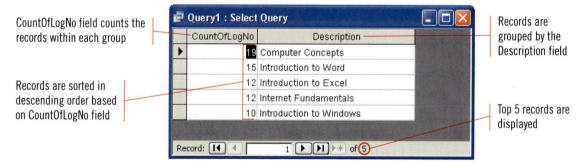

Records are grouped by the Description field

Top 5 records are displayed

TABLE K-1: Top Values options

action	displays
Click 5, or 25, or 100 from the Top Values list	Top 5, 25, or 100 records
Enter a number such as 10 in the Top Values text box	Top 10, or whatever value is entered, records
Click 5% or 25% from the Top Values list	Top 5 percent or 25 percent of records
Enter a percentage, such as 10%, in the Top Values text box	Top 10%, or whatever percentage is entered, of records
Click All	All records

Creating a Parameter Query

A **parameter query** displays a dialog box that prompts you for field criteria. Your entry determines which records will appear on the final datasheet just like criteria entered directly in the query design grid. You can build a form or report based on a parameter query, too. Then, when you open the form or report, the parameter dialog box appears. The entry in the dialog box determines which records are collected by the query to use as the record-set for the form or report. You want to enhance the Top 5 Courses query to display the top five courses for a specific location that you specify each time you run the query. You add parameter prompts to the Top 5 Courses query.

STEPS

1. **Right-click the Top 5 Courses query, click Design View on the shortcut menu, click the Show Table button 🖳, double-click Employees, then click Close**

   The Employees table contains the Location field needed for this query.

2. **Drag the title bar of the Courses field list to the left, then drag the Enrollments field list to the right so that the relationship lines do not cross behind a field list**

   It is not required that you rearrange the field lists of a query, but doing so can help clarify the relationships between them.

> **TROUBLE**
>
> You may have to scroll in the Employees field list to find the Location field.

3. **Double-click the Location field in the Employees field list, click the Top Values list arrow All ▾, click All, then click the Datasheet View button 🖽**

   The query now counts the LogNo field for records grouped by Description as well as Location. Because you only want to query for one location at a time, however, you will add parameter criteria to the Location field.

> **QUICK TIP**
>
> To enter long criteria, right-click the Criteria cell, then click Zoom.

4. **Click the Design View button 🖾, click the Location field Criteria cell, type [Enter location:], then click 🖽**

   Your screen should look like Figure K-3. In Query Design View, parameter criteria must be entered within [square brackets]. The parameter criteria you entered within the square brackets appears as a prompt in the Enter Parameter Value dialog box. The entry you make in the Enter Parameter Value box is used as the final criteria for the field that contains the parameter criteria. You can combine logical operators such as > (greater than) or < (less than) as well as wildcard characters such as * (asterisk) with parameter criteria to create flexible search options. See Table K-2 for more examples of parameter criteria.

> **QUICK TIP**
>
> Query criteria are not case sensitive so "corporate" is the same as "Corporate".

5. **Type Corporate in the Enter location: text box, then click OK**

   Now, only those records with "Corporate" in the Location field are displayed as shown in Figure K-4. The records are still sorted in descending order by the CountOfLogNo field, and they are grouped by both the Description and the Location fields.

6. **Click File on the menu bar, click Save As, type Location Parameter-Your Initials then click OK**

   Because the query name appears in the header of a printed datasheet, adding your name or initials to the query name helps identify the printout.

7. **Click the Print button 🖨, then close the query**

   The new query appears as an object in the database window.

FIGURE K-3: Using parameter criteria for the Location field

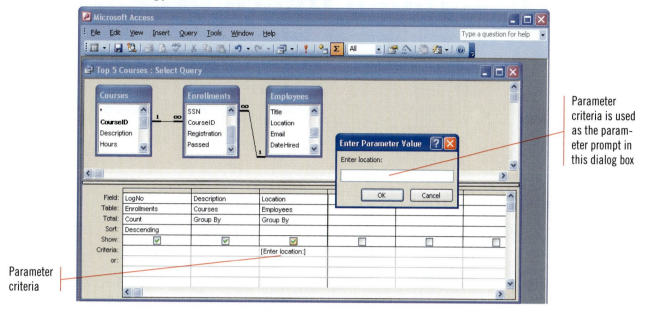

Parameter criteria is used as the parameter prompt in this dialog box

Parameter criteria

FIGURE K-4: Datasheet for records grouped by Description and Location

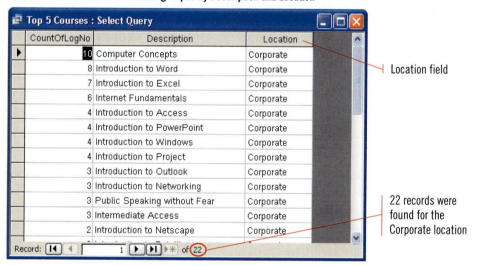

Location field

22 records were found for the Corporate location

TABLE K-2: Examples of parameter criteria

field data type	parameter criteria	description
Date/Time	>=[Enter start date:]	Searches for dates on or after the entered date
Date/Time	>=[Enter start date:] and <=[Enter end date:]	Prompts you for two date entries and searches for dates on or after the first date and on or before the second date
Text	LIKE [Enter the first character of the last name:] & "*"	Searches for any name that begins with the entered character
Text	LIKE "*" & [Enter any character(s) to search by:] & "*"	Searches for words that contain the entered characters anywhere in the field

Modifying Query Properties

Properties are characteristics that define the appearance and behavior of database objects, fields, sections, and controls. You can view the properties for an item by opening its property sheet. Field properties can be changed in either Table Design View or Query Design View. If you change field properties in Query Design View, they are modified for that query only (as opposed to changing the field properties in Table Design View, which affects that field's characteristics throughout the database). Queries themselves also have properties that you may want to modify to better describe or protect the information they present. You modify the query and field properties of the Location Charges query to better describe and present the data.

STEPS

1. **Right-click the Location Charges query, then click Properties**

   The Location Charges Properties dialog box opens, providing information about the query and a text box where you can enter a description for the query.

QUICK TIP

Click the object column headings to sort the objects in ascending or descending order.

2. **Type Lists location, description, hours, and cost, click OK, click the Details button 📖 in the Training-K database window, then maximize the database window**

   Five columns of information about each query object appear, as shown in Figure K-5. The Description property you entered appears in the Description column.

3. **Click the Design button 📐 on the database window toolbar, click the Properties button 📇 on the Query Design toolbar, click to the right of the Employees field list, click Dynaset in the Recordset Type property, click the Recordset Type list arrow, then click Snapshot**

   Your screen should look like Figure K-6. Viewing the query property sheet from within Query Design View gives a complete list of the query's properties. The **Recordset Type** property determines if and how records displayed by a query are locked. **Snapshot** locks the recordset (prevents it from being updated). **Dynaset** is the default value and allows updates to data.

TROUBLE

If the calculated field did not work correctly, return to Design View and make sure that you entered the expression PerHour:[Cost]/ [Hours] correctly.

4. **Click the Datasheet View button 📄, double-click 12 in the Hours field for the first record, then try to type 15**

   Because the query Recordset Type property was set to Snapshot, you can view the records but not update them. Now you want to add a calculated field that calculates the cost per hour of class.

5. **Click 📐, click 📇, click the blank Field cell for the fourth column in the query grid, type PerHour:[Cost]/[Hours], then click 📄**

   The PerHour field was created successfully, but the numbers are not formatted in a way that makes them easy to read. You need to work with the field's property sheet to change the way the numbers are formatted.

QUICK TIP

The title bar of the property sheet always indicates which item's properties are shown.

6. **Click 📐, click the PerHour field in the query grid, click 📇, click the Format text box, click the Format list arrow, click Currency, click the Decimal Places text box, click the Decimal Places list arrow, click 2, then click 📇**

   When you click a property in a property sheet, a short description of the property appears in the status bar. You can press [F1] to open Microsoft Office Access Help for a longer description of the selected property.

7. **Click 📄**

   Your screen should look like Figure K-7. Not only have you created a calculated PerHour field, you have also formatted the field with a currency symbol and two digits to the right of the decimal point using the field's property sheet.

8. **Save, then close the Location Charges query**

FIGURE K-5: Details view of objects in database window

Details button

Column headings

Description property

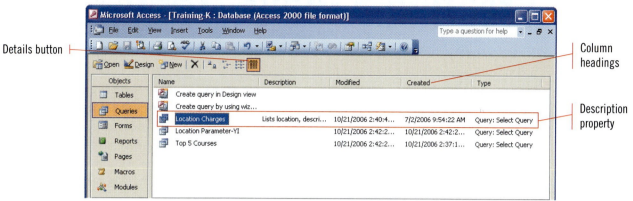

FIGURE K-6: Query property sheet

Properties button

Click here to select the query

Query property sheet

Snapshot selected for Recordset Type property

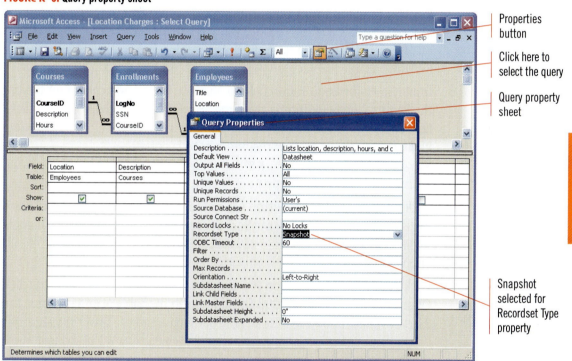

FIGURE K-7: Final datasheet

PerHour calculated field

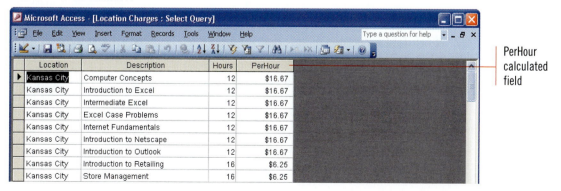

Access 2003

Creating a Make–Table Query

An **action query** changes many records in one process. There are four types of action queries: delete, update, append, and make-table. In order for an action query to complete its action, you must run an action query using the Run button ![icon]. Because you cannot undo this action, it is always a good idea to create a backup of the database before using an action query. See Table K-3 for more information on action queries. A **make-table query** creates a new table of data based on the recordset defined by the query. The make-table query works like an export feature in that it creates a copy of the selected data and pastes it into a new table in a database specified by the query. The location of the new table can be the current or any other Access database. Sometimes a make-table query is used to back up a subset of data. ![palette] You use a make-table query to archive the 1/1/2006 through 3/31/2006 records currently stored in the Enrollments table.

STEPS

1. **Double-click Create query in Design view, double-click Enrollments in the Show Table dialog box, then click Close**

2. **Double-click the * (asterisk) at the top of the Enrollments table's field list**

   Adding the asterisk to the query design grid puts all of the fields in that table in the grid. Later, if fields are added to this table, they will automatically be added to this query because the asterisk represents all fields in the table.

3. **Double-click the Registration field to add it to the second column of the query grid, click the Registration field Criteria cell, type >=1/1/2006 and <=3/31/2006, click the Registration field Show check box to uncheck it, then use the ✛ mouse pointer to widen the Registration column to view the entire criteria entry**

   Your screen should look like Figure K-8. Before changing this select query into a make-table query, it is always a good idea to view the selected data.

4. **Click the Datasheet View button ![icon] on the Query Design toolbar, click any entry in the Registration field, then click the Sort Descending button ![icon] on the Query Datasheet toolbar**

   Sorting the records in descending order based on the values in the Registration field allows you to confirm that no records on or after 4/1/2006 appear in the datasheet.

QUICK TIP
Double-click the Query Type button list arrow to immediately display the entire list of menu options.

5. **Click the Design View button ![icon], click the Query Type list arrow ![icon], click Make-Table Query, type First Quarter 2006 Enrollments in the Table Name text box, then click OK**

   Your screen should look like Figure K-9. The Query Type button displays the Make-Table icon ![icon]. All action query icons include an exclamation point to warn you that data will be changed when you run them. The make-table query is ready, but the new table has not yet been created. Action queries do not change data until you click the Run button ![icon]. Also, Access automatically added pound signs (#) around the date criteria in the Registration field.

6. **Click the Run button ![icon] on the Query Design toolbar, click Yes when prompted that you are about to paste 108 records, then close the query without saving it**

   Once you've made a table of data, you generally do not need to run the same make-table query again and therefore you do not need to save it.

7. **Click Tables on the Objects bar, then double-click First Quarter 2006 Enrollments to view the new table's datasheet**

   All 108 records were pasted into the new table, as shown in Figure K-10. Field properties such as the Input Mask for the SSN field and the Display Control for the Passed field were not copied with the data, but you could modify the fields in Design View of this table to change their appearance just as you could for any other table. (*Note*: –1 is used to designate "yes" and 0 is used to designate "no" when the Display Control property for a Yes/No field is set to Text Box.)

8. **Close the First Quarter 2006 Enrollments table**

FIGURE K-8: Using the asterisk in a query grid

Asterisk in the field list

Asterisk in the query grid

Show check box

Criteria to select first quarter's records

Query Type button

Resize column mouse pointer

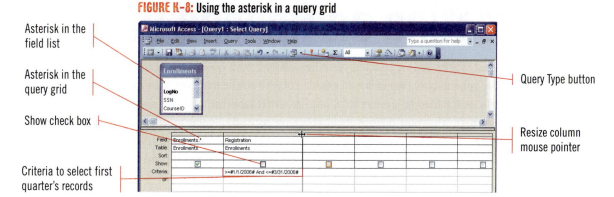

FIGURE K-9: Creating a make-table query

Run button

Make-Table Query is selected

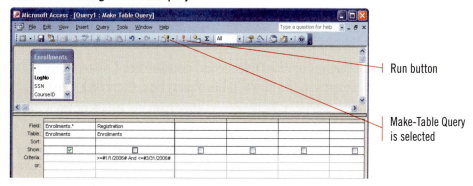

FIGURE K-10: First Quarter 2006 Enrollments datasheet

Input Mask property was not duplicated

First Quarter 2006 Enrollments table

Display Control property was not duplicated

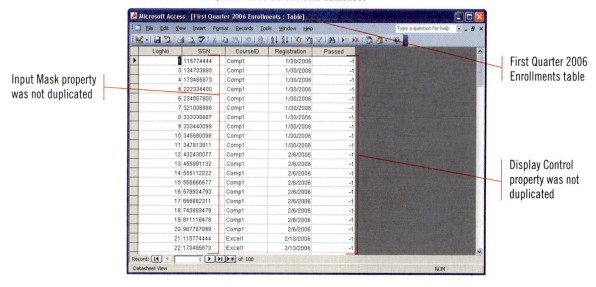

TABLE K-3: Action queries

action query	query icon	description	example
Delete		Deletes a group of records from one or more tables	Remove products that are discontinued or for which there are no orders
Update		Makes global changes to a group of records in one or more tables	Raise prices by 10 percent for all products
Append		Adds a group of records from one or more tables to the end of another table	Append the employee address table from one division of the company to the address table from another division of the company
Make-Table		Creates a new table from data in one or more tables	Export records to another Access database or make a back-up copy of a table

Creating an Append Query

An **append query** adds a selected recordset defined by a query to an existing table called the **target table**. The append query works like an export feature because the records are copied from one location and a duplicate set is pasted to another location. The target table can be in the current database or in any other Access database. The most difficult thing about an append query is making sure that all of the fields you have selected in the append query match fields in the target table where you want to append (paste) them. If the target table has more fields than those you want to append, the append query will append the data in the matching fields and ignore the other fields. If the target table lacks a field defined by the append query, an error message will appear indicating that the query has an unknown field name which will cancel the append action.  You would like to append April's records to the First Quarter 2006 Enrollments table. You use an append query to do this, then rename the table to accurately reflect its contents.

STEPS

1. Click Queries on the Objects bar, double-click Create query in Design view, double-click Enrollments in the Show Table dialog box, then click Close

2. Double-click the Enrollments table's field list title bar, then drag the highlighted fields to the first column of the query design grid

   Double-clicking the title bar of the field list selects all of the fields, allowing you to add all the fields to the query grid very quickly. To successfully complete the append process, you need to identify how each field in the query is connected to an existing field in the target table. Therefore, the technique of adding all of the fields to the query grid by using the asterisk does not work for the append operation because it doesn't break out the individual fields in the query grid.

3. Click the Registration field Criteria cell, type Between 4/1/06 and 4/30/06, widen the Registration field column as needed to view the criteria, then click the Datasheet View button 🔲 on the Query Design toolbar

   The datasheet should show 23 records with an April date in the Registration field. Between...and criteria work the same way as the >= and <= operators you used in the make-table query. **Between...and** criteria select all records between the two dates, including the two dates.

4. Click the Design View button 📐, click the Query Type button list arrow 🔲▾ on the Query Design toolbar, click Append Query, click the Table Name list arrow in the Append dialog box, click First Quarter 2006 Enrollments, then click OK

   Your screen should look like Figure K-11. The Query Type button displays the Append Query icon ➕❗ and the Append To row was added to the query design grid. The Append To row shows how the fields in the query match fields in the target table. The append action is ready to be initiated by clicking the Run button.

5. Click the Run button ❗ on the Query Design toolbar, click Yes to indicate that you want to append 23 rows, then close the query without saving the changes

6. Click Tables on the Objects bar, double-click the First Quarter 2006 Enrollments, click any entry in the Registration field, then click the Sort Descending button 🔽 on the Table Datasheet toolbar

   The April records were appended to the table for a total of 131 records, as shown in Figure K-12.

7. Close the First Quarter 2006 Enrollments datasheet without saving changes, right-click First Quarter 2006 Enrollments in the database window, click Rename on the shortcut menu, type Jan-April 2006, then press [Enter]

   The backup table with Enrollments records from January through April 2006 has been renamed.

FIGURE K-11: Creating an append query

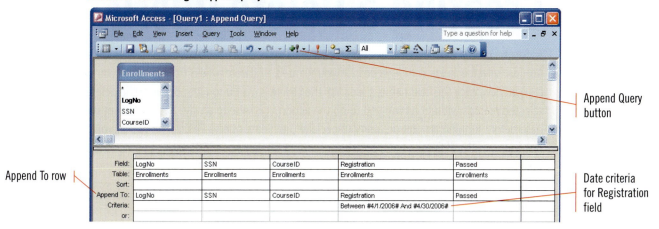

Append Query button

Append To row

Date criteria for Registration field

FIGURE K-12: Updated table with appended records

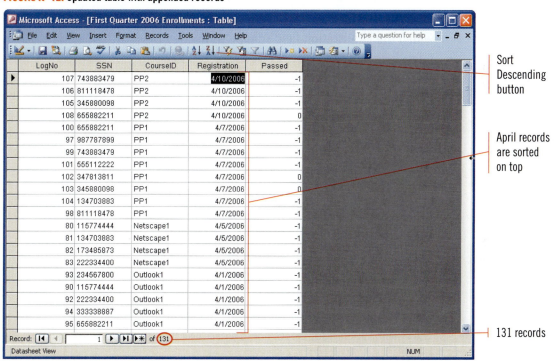

Sort Descending button

April records are sorted on top

131 records

Clues to Use

1900 versus 2000 dates

If you type only two digits of a date, Access assumes that the digits 00 through 29 are for the years 2000 through 2029. If you type 30 through 99, Access assumes the years refer to 1930 through 1999.

If you want to specify years outside these ranges, you must type all four digits of the year.

Creating a Delete Query

A **delete query** deletes a group of records from one or more tables. Delete queries delete entire records, not just selected fields within records. If you wanted to delete a field from a table, you would open Table Design View, click the field name, then click the Delete Rows button 🠆. Because the delete query deletes all selected records without letting you undo the action, it is wise to always have a current backup of the database before running any action query, especially the delete query. 🎨 Now that you have archived the first four months of Enrollments records for 2006 in the Jan-April 2006 table, you want to delete them from the Enrollments table. You use a delete query to accomplish this task.

STEPS

1. Click Queries on the Objects bar, double-click Create query in Design view, double-click Enrollments in the Show Table dialog box, then click Close

2. Double-click the * (asterisk) at the top of the Enrollments table's field list, then double-click the Registration field

   All the fields from the Enrollments table are added to the first column of the query design grid by using the asterisk. The Registration field is added to the second column of the query design grid so you can enter limiting criteria for this field.

3. Click the Registration field Criteria cell, type Between 1/1/2006 and 4/30/2006, then widen the Registration field column as needed to view the criteria

   Before you run a delete query, check the selected records to make sure that you have selected the same 131 records that were added to the Jan-April 2006 table.

4. Click the Datasheet View button 🔲 to confirm that the datasheet has 131 records, click the Design View button ⬔, click the Query Type button list arrow 🔳▾, then click Delete Query

   Your screen should look like Figure K-13. The Query Type button displays the Delete Query icon 🗙, and the Delete row was added to the query design grid. The delete action is ready to be initiated by clicking the Run button 🔴.

5. Click 🔴 on the Query Design toolbar, click Yes to confirm that you want to delete 131 rows, then close the query without saving the changes

6. Click Tables on the Objects bar, then double-click Enrollments

   The records should start in May, as shown in Figure K-14. All records with dates between 1/1/2006 and 4/30/2006 were deleted from the Enrollments table using a delete query.

7. Close the Enrollments datasheet without saving changes

   The default sort order for the records in a datasheet is ascending order based on the values in the primary key field.

FIGURE K-13: Creating a delete query

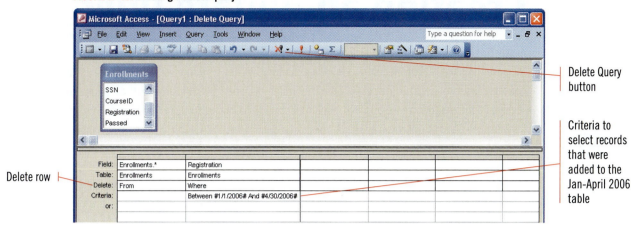

Delete Query button

Criteria to select records that were added to the Jan-April 2006 table

Delete row

FIGURE K-14: Enrollments table after deleting 131 records

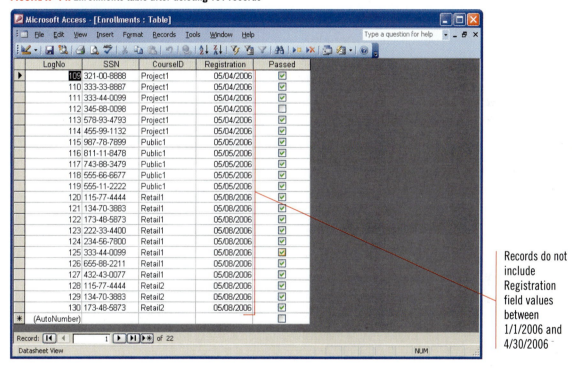

Records do not include Registration field values between 1/1/2006 and 4/30/2006

Clues to Use

Reviewing referential integrity

Referential integrity between two tables may be established (also called enforced) when tables are joined in the Relationships window. Referential integrity applies a set of rules to the relationship that ensures that no orphaned records currently exist, are added to, or are created in the database. Only the table on the "many" side of a one-to-many relationship may contain an orphan record. A table has an **orphan record** when information in the foreign key field of the "many" table doesn't have a matching entry in the primary key field of the "one" table. The term "orphan" comes from the analogy that the "one" table contains **parent records**, and the "many" table contains **child records**. Referential integrity means that a child record cannot be created without a corresponding parent record. Also, referential integrity means that a delete query would not be able to delete records in the "one" (parent) table that has related records in the "many" (child) table.

Creating an Update Query

An **update query** is a type of action query that updates the values in a field. For example, you may want to increase the price of a product in a particular category by 5%. Or you may want to update the value of an area code for a subset of customers. The Training Department upgraded their equipment, and Fred has received approval to increase by 5% the internal cost of all courses. You create an update query to quickly calculate and enter the new values.

STEPS

1. **Click Queries on the Objects bar, double-click Create query in Design view, double-click Courses, then click Close in the Show Table dialog box**

2. **Double-click CourseID from the Courses field list, double-click Description, then double-click Cost**

   Every action query starts as a select query, as reflected in the title bar of the query window. Always look at the datasheet of the select query before initiating any action that changes data to double-check which records will be affected.

3. **Click the Datasheet View button 🔲, note the values in the Cost field, then click the Design View button ⬜**

   After confirming the initial values in the Cost field and identifying the records that will be changed, you're ready to change this select query into an update query.

4. **Click the Query Type button list arrow 🔲▾ on the Query Design toolbar, then click Update Query**

   The Query Type button displays the Update Query icon 🔲 and the Update To: row appears in the query design grid. To update the values in the Cost field by 5% you need to enter the appropriate expression in the Update To cell for the Cost field to multiply the Cost field by 105%.

   > **TROUBLE**
   > Be sure to enter the [Cost]*1.05 update criteria for the Cost field, *not* for the CourseID or Registration fields.

5. **Click the Cost field Update To cell, then type [Cost]*1.05**

   Your screen should look like Figure K-15. The Cost field is not updated until you run the query.

6. **Click the Run button ❗ on the Query Design toolbar, then click Yes to indicate that you want to update 27 rows**

   When you run an action query, Access prompts you with an "Are you sure?" message before actually updating the data. The Undo button cannot undo changes made by action queries. To view the updates to the Cost field, you'll change this query back into a select query, then view the datasheet.

7. **Click Query Type list arrow 🔲▾, click Select Query, then click the Datasheet View button 🔲**

   Your screen should look like Figure K-16.

8. **Close the update query without saving the changes**

   You rarely need to save an update query, because once the data has been updated, you don't need the query object anymore. Also, if you double-click an action query from the database window, you run the query (as opposed to double-clicking a select query, which opens its datasheet). Therefore, don't save any queries that you won't need again, especially action queries that could inadvertently change data.

FIGURE K-15: Creating an update query

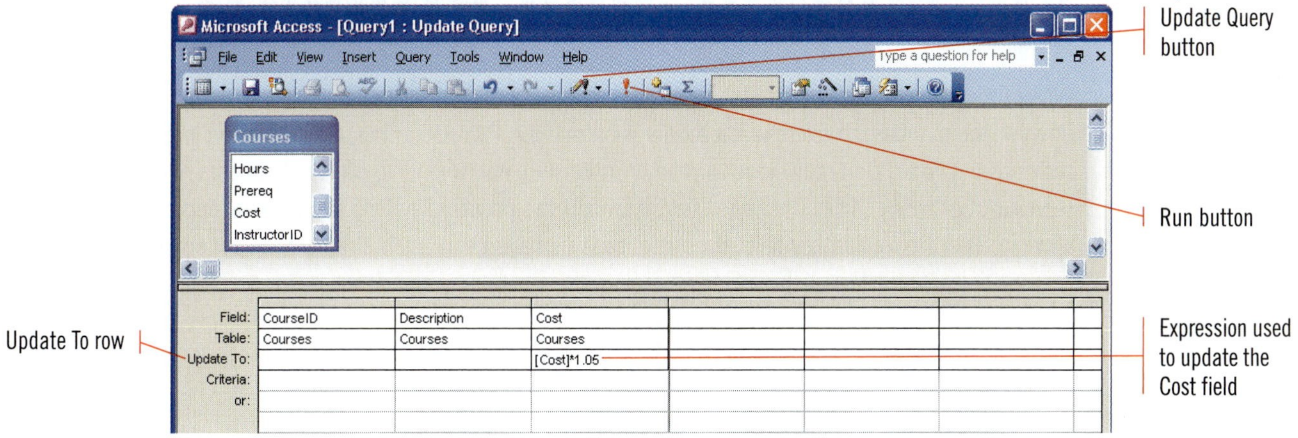

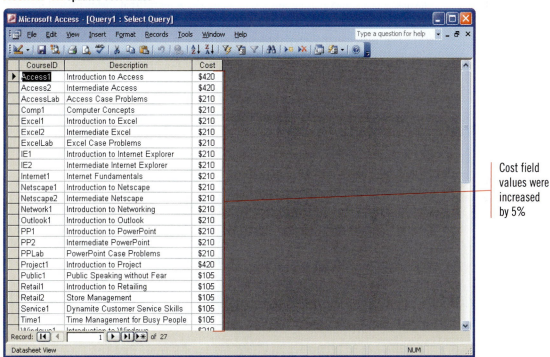

Update Query button

Run button

Update To row

Expression used to update the Cost field

FIGURE K-16: Updated Cost values

Cost field values were increased by 5%

Specifying Join Properties

When more than one table's field list is used in a query, the tables are joined as defined in the Relationships window for the database. If referential integrity is enforced on a relationship, a "1" appears next to the field that serves as the "one" side of the one-to-many relationship, and an infinity sign (∞) appears next to the field that serves as the "many" side. The "one" field is usually the primary key field for its table, and the "many" field is always called the foreign key field. If no relationships have been established, Access automatically creates join lines in Query Design View if the linking fields have the same name and data type in two tables. You can edit table relationships for an individual query in Query Design View by double-clicking the join line. You would like to create a query to find out which courses have never been attended. You use a query and modify the join properties between the Enrollments and Courses table to find this answer.

STEPS

QUICK TIP

Right-click to the right of the field lists, then click Relationships to open the Relationships window.

1. **Double-click Create query in Design view, double-click Courses, double-click Enrollments, then click Close**

   Because the Courses and Enrollments tables have already been related with a one-to-many relationship with referential integrity enforced in the Relationships window, the join line appears, linking the two tables using the CourseID field common to both.

TROUBLE

Double-click the middle portion of the join line, not the "one" or "many" symbols, to open the Join Properties dialog box.

2. **Double-click the one-to-many join line between the field lists**

   The Join Properties dialog box opens and displays the characteristics for the join, as shown in Figure K-17. The dialog box shows that option 1 is chosen, which means that the query will display only records where joined fields from *both* tables are equal. That means that if the Courses table has any records for which there are no matching Enrollments records, those courses would not appear in the resulting datasheet.

3. **Click the 2 option button**

   By choosing option 2, you are specifying that you want to see ALL of the records in the Courses table, even if the Enrollments table does not contain matching records. Because referential integrity is enforced, option 3 would yield the same results as option 1—referential integrity makes it impossible to enter records in the Enrollments table that do not have a corresponding record in the Courses table.

4. **Click OK**

   The join line's appearance changes, as shown in Figure K-18.

5. **Double-click CourseID from the Courses field list, double-click Description from the Courses field list, double-click Registration from the Enrollments field list, then click the Datasheet View button** 🔲

   All courses are now listed in the datasheet, regardless of whether there are any matching Enrollments records. By using a filter, you can quickly isolate those courses.

6. **Click the Access1 Registration field (it is null), then click the Filter by Selection button** 🍷 **on the Query Datasheet toolbar**

   The 23 filtered records represent the courses shown in Figure K-19. They contain a null (nothing) value in the Registration field.

7. **Click the Save button** 💾 **on the Query Datasheet toolbar, type No Enrollments-Your Initials in the Query Name text box, click OK, click the Access1 Registration field, click** 🍷 **to refilter for nulls, click the Print button** 🖨️ **, then close the datasheet without saving it**

FIGURE K-17: Join Properties dialog box

Default join property

Selects all records from the Courses table, even those with no matching records in the Enrollments table

Gives the same results as option 1 because referential integrity is enforced on the relationship

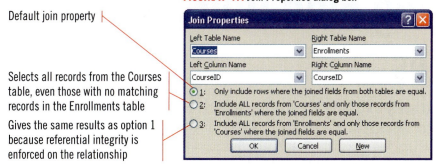

FIGURE K-18: The join line changes when properties are changed

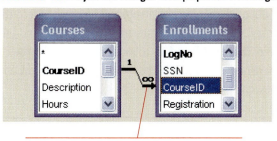

Join line's appearance shows that *all* records from the Courses table will be included in the datasheet

FIGURE K-19: Filtering for courses with no matching Enrollment records

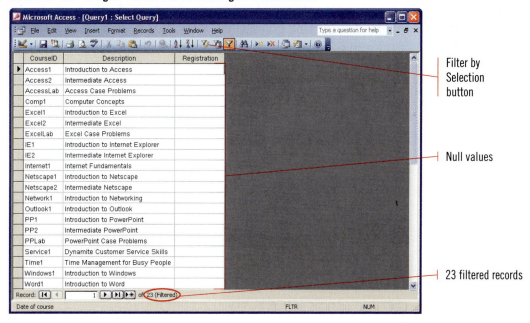

Filter by Selection button

Null values

23 filtered records

Clues to Use

Null and zero-length string values

The term **null** is used to describe a field value that has never been entered. In a datasheet, null values look the same as a zero-length string value, but have a different purpose. A **zero-length string** value is a deliberate entry that contains no characters. You enter a zero-length string by typing two quotation marks ("") with no space between them. A null value, on the other hand, is created by not entering anything in the field. It indicates unknown data. For example, if you were recording e-mail addresses for customers in a Customers table, you would want some way to differentiate the fact that some customers do not have an e-mail address (for which you would want to enter a zero-length string in the Email field), and some customers may have an e-mail address, but you have not yet collected or recorded it (for which you would want to leave a null value in the Email field). By using null and zero-length string values appropriately, you can later query for the records that match one or the other condition. To query for zero-length string values, enter two quotation marks ("") as the criterion. To query for null values, use **Is Null** as the criterion. To query for another value other than a null value, use **Is Not Null** as the criterion.

Creating Find Unmatched Queries

A **find unmatched query** is a query that finds records in one table that does not have matching records in a related table. When referential integrity is enforced on a relationship before data is entered into a database, no one can enter a foreign key field value in the "many" table that doesn't already exist in a record on the "one" side of the relationship. Therefore, with referential integrity enforced, the only unmatched records that could possibly exist in a database are those in the "one" table. Sometimes, though, you inherit a database in which referential integrity was not imposed from the beginning, and unmatched records already exist in the "many" table. You could use your knowledge of join properties and null criteria to find unmatched records, or you could use the **Find Unmatched Query Wizard** to structure the query for you. Fred wonders if there are any employees that have never enrolled in a class. You will use the Find Unmatched Query Wizard to create a query to answer this question.

STEPS

1. **Click the New button on the database window toolbar to open the New Query dialog box**

    The New Query dialog box is the only way to access the Crosstab, Find Duplicates, and Find Unmatched Query Wizards.

2. **Double-click the Find Unmatched Query Wizard, click Table: Employees, then click Next**

    You want to find which employees have not enrolled in a class so the Employees table was selected as the table that contains the records that you want in the query results, and the Enrollments table is selected as the related table.

3. **Click Table: Enrollments, then click Next**

    The next question asks you to identify which field is common to both tables. Because the Employees table is already related to the Enrollments table in the Relationships window via the EmployeeNo field in the Employees table and the SSN field in the Enrollments table, those fields are already selected as the matching fields.

4. **Click Next**

    Now you must select which fields from the Employees table that you want to display in the query datasheet.

5. **Double-click First, double-click Last, then double-click Location as shown in Figure K-20**

    Now you must select which fields from the Employees table that you want to display in the query datasheet.

6. **Click Next, then click Finish**

    The final datasheet is shown in Figure K-21. Four employees have never enrolled in a class. You decide to study the construction of this query in Query Design View.

7. **Click the Design View button, then resize the Query Design View window as shown in Figure K-22**

    This query was created by modifying the join properties of the relationship between the Employees and Enrollments table to show *all* records in the Employees table. One field, SSN, was selected from the Enrollments table. Is Null criteria was entered for the SSN field to select only those employees without matching records in the Enrollments table.

8. **Save and close the Employees Without Matching Enrollments query, then close the Training-K.mdb database**

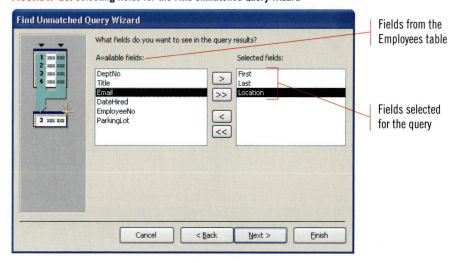

Fields from the Employees table

Fields selected for the query

FIGURE K-21: Employees Without Matching Enrollments query

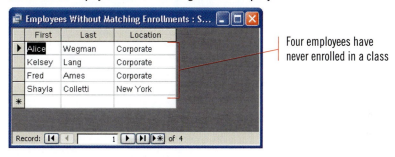

Four employees have never enrolled in a class

FIGURE K-22: Design View of Employees Without Matching Enrollments query

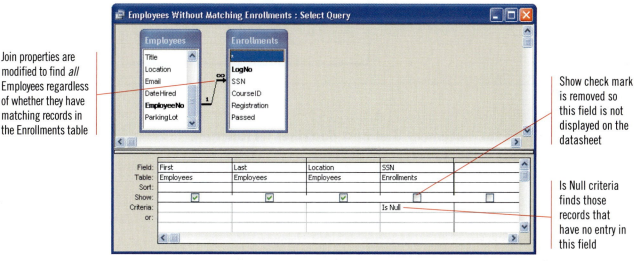

Join properties are modified to find *all* Employees regardless of whether they have matching records in the Enrollments table

Show check mark is removed so this field is not displayed on the datasheet

Is Null criteria finds those records that have no entry in this field

Clues to Use

Find Duplicate Query Wizard

The Find Duplicate Query Wizard is another query wizard that is only available from the New Query dialog box. As you would suspect, the **Find Duplicate Query Wizard** helps you find duplicate values in a field. In particular, it helps you find and correct potential data entry errors. For example, if you suspect that the same customer has been entered with two different names in your Customers table, you could use the Find Duplicate Query Wizard to find records with duplicate values in the Street or Phone field. Once you isolated the records with the same value in one of these fields, you could easily edit or delete incorrect or redundant data.

Practice

▼ CONCEPTS REVIEW

Identify each element of the Query Design View shown in Figure K-23.

FIGURE K-23

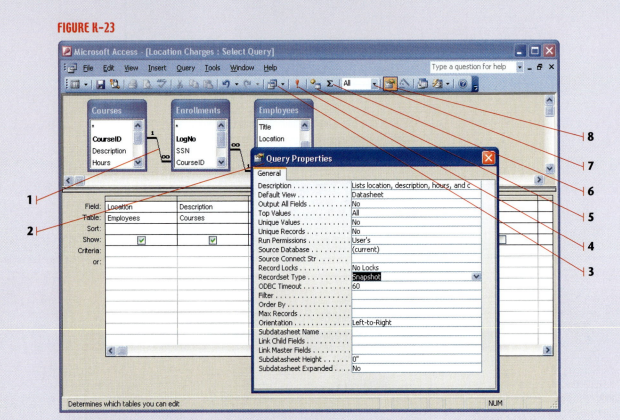

Match each term with the statement that best describes its function.

9. **Top Values query**
10. **Select query**
11. **Action query**
12. **Properties**
13. **Snapshot**
14. **Parameter query**

a. Characteristics that define the appearance and behavior of items within the database

b. Displays only a number or percentage of records from a sorted query

c. Displays a dialog box prompting you for criteria

d. Makes the recordset not updateable

e. Makes changes to data

f. Displays fields and records that match specific criteria in a single datasheet

Select the best answer from the list of choices.

15. Which entry for the Recordset Type query property will *not* allow you to modify the recordset?
    a. Snapshot
    b. No Updates
    c. Referential Integrity
    d. Dynaset (No Nulls)

16. Which of the following is a valid parameter criteria entry in the query design grid?
    a. >=(Type minimum value here:)
    b. >=[Type minimum value here:]
    c. >={Type minimum value here: }
    d. >=Type minimum value here:

17. You *cannot* use the Top Values feature to:
    a. Display a subset of records.
    b. Show the top 30 records.
    c. View the bottom 10 percent of records.
    d. Update a field's value by 10 percent.

18. Which of the following is *not* an action query?
    a. Make-table query
    b. Delete query
    c. Union query
    d. Append query

19. Which of the following precautions should you take before running a delete query?
    a. Check the resulting datasheet to make sure the query selects the right records.
    b. Have a current backup of the database.
    c. Understand the relationships between the records you are about to delete in the database.
    d. All of the above.

20. When querying tables in a one-to-many relationship with referential integrity enforced, which records will appear (by default) on the resulting datasheet?
    a. Only those with matching values in both tables.
    b. All records from the "one" table, and only those with matching values from the "many" side.
    c. All records from the "many" table, and only those with nonmatching values from the "one" side.
    d. All records from both tables will appear at all times.

▼ SKILLS REVIEW

1. **Query for top values.**
   a. Start Access, then open the **Seminar-K.mdb** database from the drive and folder where your Data Files are stored.
   b. Create a new select query with the EventName field from the Events table and the RegistrationFee field from the Registration table.
   c. Add the RegistrationFee field a second time, then click the Totals button on the Query Design toolbar. In the Total row of the query grid, Group By the EventName field, Sum the first RegistrationFee field, then Count the second Registration Fee field.
   d. Sort in descending order by the summed RegistrationFee field.
   e. Enter **2** in the Top Values list box to display the top two seminars in the datasheet.
   f. Save the query as **Top 2 Seminars–Your Initials**, view, print, then close the datasheet.

2. **Create a parameter query.**
   a. Create a new select query with the AttendeeLastName field from the Attendees table, the RegistrationDate field from the Registration table, and the EventName field from the Events table.
   b. Add the parameter criterion **Between [Enter Start Date:] and [Enter End Date:]** in the Criteria cell for the RegistrationDate field.
   c. Specify an ascending sort order on the RegistrationDate field.
   d. Click the Datasheet View button, then enter **5/1/2006** as the start date and **5/31/2006** as the end date in order to find everyone who has attended a seminar in May of the year 2006. You should view 5 records.
   e. Save the query as **May Registration–Your Initials**.

3. **Modify query properties.**
   a. Open the May Registration–Your Initials query in Query Design View, open the property sheet for the query, change the Recordset Type property to Snapshot, then close the Query Properties dialog box.
   b. Right-click the RegistrationDate field, then click Properties on the shortcut menu to open the Field Properties dialog box. Enter **Date of Registration** for the Caption property, change the Format property to Medium Date, then close the Field Properties dialog box.
   c. View the datasheet for records between **5/1/2006** and **5/31/2006**. Print, save, then close the datasheet.

4. **Create a make-table query.**

   a. Create a new select query, and select all the fields from the Registration table by double-clicking the Registration field list's title bar and dragging the selected fields to the query design grid.

   b. Enter **<=3/31/2006** in the Criteria cell for the RegistrationDate field to find those records in which the RegistrationDate is on or before 3/31/2006.

   c. View the datasheet. There should be 16 records.

   d. In Query Design View, change the query into a make-table query that creates a new table in the current database. Give the new table the name **1Qtr2006–Your Initials**.

   e. Run the query to paste 16 rows into the 1Qtr2006–Your Initials table.

   f. Close the make-table query without saving it, click Tables on the Objects bar, open the 1Qtr2006–Your Initials table, view the 16 records, print the datasheet, then close it.

5. **Create an append query.**

   a. Create a new select query, and select all the fields from the Registration table by double-clicking the Registration field list's title bar and dragging the selected fields to the query design grid.

   b. Enter **>=4/1/2006 and <=4/30/2006** in the Criteria cell for the RegistrationDate field to find those records in which the RegistrationDate is in April, 2006.

   c. View the datasheet. There should be one record.

   d. In Query Design View, change the query into an append query that appends to the 1Qtr2006–Your Initials table.

   e. Run the query to append the row into the 1Qtr2006–Your Initials table by clicking the Run button on the Query Design toolbar.

   f. Close the append query without saving it.

   g. Rename the 1Qtr2006–Your Initials table to **Jan-Apr2006 –Your Initials**, open the datasheet (there should be 17 records), print it, then close it.

6. **Create a delete query.**

   a. Create a new select query, and select all the fields from the Registration table by double-clicking the Registration field list's title bar and dragging the selected fields to the query design grid.

   b. Enter **<5/1/2006** in the Criteria cell for the RegistrationDate field to find those records in which the RegistrationDate is before May 1, 2006.

   c. View the datasheet. There should be 17 records.

   d. In Query Design View, change the query into a delete query.

   e. Run the query to delete 17 records from the Registration table.

   f. Close the query without saving it.

   g. Open the Registration table in Datasheet View to confirm that there are only five records, then close it.

Access 2003

7. **Create an update query.**
   a. Create a new select query, and select all the fields from the Registration table by double-clicking the Registration field list's title bar and dragging the selected fields to the query design grid.
   b. View the datasheet. Observe and note the values in the RegistrationFee field. There should be five records.
   c. In Query Design View, change the query to an update query, then enter **[RegistrationFee]+5** in the RegistrationFee field Update To cell in order to increase each value in that field by $5.
   d. Run the query to update the five records.
   e. Using the Query Type button, change the query back to a select query, then view the datasheet to make sure that the RegistrationFee fields were updated properly.
   f. Print, then close the datasheet without saving the query.

8. **Specify join properties.**
   a. Create a new select query with the following fields: AttendeeFirstName and AttendeeLastName from the Attendees table, and EventID and RegistrationFee from the Registration table.
   b. Double-click the link between the Attendees and Registration tables to open the Join Properties dialog box. Click the option button to include *all* records from Attendees and only those records from Registration where the joined fields are equal.
   c. View the datasheet, add your own first and last name as the last record, but do not enter anything in the EventID or RegistrationFee fields for your record.
   d. Apply a filter to find only those names who have never registered for an event.
   e. Save this query as **People To Contact**, refilter for only those who have never registered for an event, then save, print, and close the query.

9. **Create find unmatched queries.**
   a. Start the Find Unmatched Query Wizard.
   b. You want to find the events that have no related records in the Registration table.
   c. The two tables are related by the EventID field, and you want to show all of the fields from the Events table in the query results.
   d. Add your initials to the end of the default query name, **Events Without Matching Registration**, then view the results.
   e. Print the Events Without Matching Registration-YI query, then close the query, close the Seminar-K.mdb database, and exit Access.

▼ INDEPENDENT CHALLENGE 1

As the manager of a college women's basketball team, you want to create several queries using the Basketball-K database.

a. Start Access, then open the **Basketball-K.mdb** database from the drive and folder where your Data Files are stored.

b. Open the Players Query in Query Design View, then enter **Between [Enter start date:] and [Enter end date:]** in the Criteria cell for the Date field.

c. View the datasheet for all of the records between **12/1/2006** and **12/31/2006**. There should be 18 records.

d. Use the Save As option on the File menu to save the query with the name **Parameter Stats–Your Initials**, then print the datasheet.

e. In Query Design View of the Parameter Stats–Your Initials query, sort the records in descending order on the TotalPts field, then use the **25%** Top Values option.

f. View the datasheet for all of the records between **12/1/2006** and **12/31/2006**. There should be five records.

g. Use the Save As option on the File menu to save the query with the name **Parameter Stats–Top 25%–Your Initials**. Print, then close the datasheet.

h. Open the Victories query in Query Design View, then add a new calculated field as the last field with the following field name and expression: **Win%:[Home Score]/[Opponent Score]**.

i. View the datasheet to make sure that the Win% field calculates properly. Because the home score is generally greater than the opponent score, most values will be greater than 1.

Advanced Challenge Exercise

■ In Query Design View, change the Format property of the Win% field to Percent and the Decimal Places property to **0**.

■ View the datasheet as shown in Figure K-24.

j. Use the Save As feature to save the query as **Victories–Your Initials**, print, then close it.

k. Close Basketball-K.mdb database, then exit Access.

FIGURE K-24

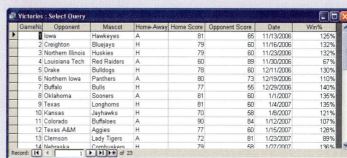

▼ INDEPENDENT CHALLENGE 2

As the manager of a college women's basketball team, you want to enhance the Basketball-K database and need to create several action queries using the Basketball-K database.

   a. Start Access, then open the **Basketball-K.mdb** database from the drive and folder where your Data Files are stored.
   b. Create a new select query, and select all the fields from the Stats table by double-clicking the field list's title bar and dragging the selected fields to the query design grid.
   c. Add criteria to find all of the records with the GameNo field equal to **1**, **2**, or **3**, then view the datasheet. There should be 18 records.
   d. In Query Design View, change the query to a make-table query to paste the records into a table in the current database called **Games123–Your Initials**.
   e. Run the query to paste the 18 rows, then close the query without saving it.
   f. Open the datasheet for the Games123–Your Initials table, then print it.
   g. Create another new select query that includes all of the fields from the Stats table by double-clicking the field list's title bar and dragging the selected fields to the query design grid.
   h. Add criteria to find all of the statistics for those records with the GameNo field equal to 4 or 5, then view the datasheet. There should be 12 records.
   i. In Query Design View, change the query to an append query to append the records to the Games123–Your Initials table.
   j. Run the query to append the 12 rows, then close the query without saving it.
   k. Rename the Games123–Your Initials table to **Games12345–Your Initials**, open the datasheet, then print it. There should be 30 records.
   l. Close the Games12345–Your Initials table, close the Basketball-K.mdb database, then exit Access.

▼ INDEPENDENT CHALLENGE 3

As the manager of a college women's basketball team, you want to query the Basketball-K database to find specific information about each player.

    a. Start Access, then open the **Basketball-K.mdb** database from the drive and folder where your Data Files are stored.

    b. Create a new select query in Query Design View using the Players and Stats tables.

    c. Double-click the linking line to open the Join Properties dialog box, then change the join properties to include *all* records from Players and only those from Stats where the joined fields are equal.

    d. Add the First and Last fields from the Players table, and the Assists fields from the Stats table.

    e. Type **is null** in the Criteria cell for the Assists field, then view the datasheet to find those players who have never recorded an Assist value in the Stats table. There should be seven records.

    f. Add your name as the last record, but do not enter an Assists value for this record.

    g. Print the datasheet, save the query as **Redshirts**, then close the datasheet.

    h. Close Basketball-K.mdb, then exit Access.

▼ INDEPENDENT CHALLENGE 4

Your culinary club is collecting information on international chocolate factories and museums, and has asked you to help build a database to organize the information.

    a. Start Access, then open the **Chocolate-K.mdb** database from the drive and folder where your Data Files are stored.

    b. Open the Places of Interest report, then print it.

    c. Connect to the Internet, then go to a search engine such as www.google.com or www.about.com to search for information about international chocolate factories and museums. Or, you might look for information by going directly to a chocolate company's home page and searching for places to visit. Your goal is to find a Web page with information about an international chocolate factory or museum to add to the existing database, and to print that Web page.

    d. Using the Countries form, add the record you found on the World Wide Web to the database, then close the Countries form.

    e. Open the Places of Interest query in Query Design View, double-click the link line between the Countries and ChocolatePlaces tables, then choose option 2, which includes *all* records from the Countries table.

    f. View, print, then close the Places of Interest query.

Advanced Challenge Exercise

    ■ Open the Places of Interest report in Report Design View, add your name as a label to the header, preview, then print the report. On the printout, circle the record you added to the database. On the printout, circle any countries that do *not* have any related records in the ChocolatePlaces table.

    ■ Close the Places of Interest report.

    g. Close Chocolate-K.mdb, then exit Access.

As the manager of a college women's basketball team, you want to create a query from the **Basketball-K.mdb** database with the fields from the Players, Stats, and Games tables as shown. The query is a parameter query that prompts the user for a start and end date using the Date field from the Games table. Figure K-25 shows the datasheet where the start date of 11/1/2006 and end date of 11/30/2006 are used. Save and name the query **Offense–Your Initials**, then print the datasheet.

FIGURE K-25

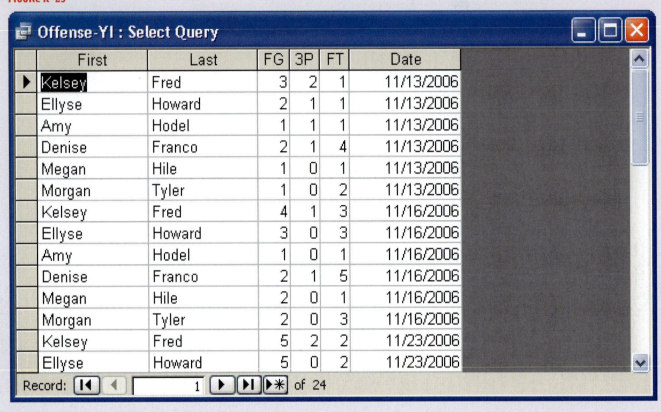

UNIT
L

Access 2003

Creating Advanced Forms and Reports

OBJECTIVES

Add check boxes and toggle buttons

Use conditional formatting in a form

Create custom Help

Add tab controls

Add charts

Modify charts

Add subreport controls

Modify section properties

Use domain functions

If you have a SAM user profile, you may have access to hands-on instruction, practice, and assessment of the skills covered in this unit. Log in to your SAM account and go to your assignments page to see what your instructor has assigned.

Advanced controls such as tab controls, charts, and subreports are powerful communication tools. Conditional formatting allows you to highlight exceptional information within a form or report to more clearly present key information. Using these advanced features to enhance forms and reports improves the value of your database. Fred Ames, coordinator of training at MediaLoft, wants to enhance existing forms and reports to more professionally and clearly present the information. You will use form and report controls such as check boxes, conditional formatting, tab controls, charts, and subreports to help Fred improve the forms and reports in the Training-L database.

Adding Check Boxes and Toggle Buttons

A **check box** is used to display the value of a Yes/No field on a form or report and appears in only one of two ways: checked or unchecked. A check means "Yes", and an unchecked box means "No". It is much easier to answer Yes/No questions on a form by clicking a check box rather than by using a text box control that requires you to type the word "Yes" or "No". A **toggle button** control may also be used to display the value of a Yes/No field. When a toggle button appears indented or pushed in, it means "Yes", and when it appears raised or not pushed in, it means "No". By default, Access represents any field with a Yes/No data type as a check box on a form or report. You would like to improve the visual appeal of the Employee Course Registration form and Registration Subform.

STEPS

1. **Start Access, open the Training-L.mdb database from the drive and folder where your Data Files are stored, click Forms on the Objects bar, then double-click the Employee Course Registration form**

   The form opens in Form View. The Registration Subform is presented as a datasheet.

   TROUBLE

   If the subform appears as a white rectangle, click the Form View button, then click the Design View button to refresh the screen.

2. **Click the Design View button 🖳 on the Form View toolbar, then maximize the Employee Course Enrollment form**

   Your screen should look like Figure L-1. To change the appearance of the controls on the subform, you must change the **Default View** property for the form from Datasheet (which allows no special formatting) to Continuous Forms.

3. **Click the subform to select it, double-click the subform's Form Selector button to open the property sheet, click the Format tab (if not already selected), click Datasheet in the Default View property, click the Default View list arrow, then click Continuous Forms**

4. **Click the Properties button 🔳 on the Form Design toolbar to close it, then click the Form View button 🔳 on the Form Design toolbar**

   Because of the change to the subform's Default View property, the subform displays the records as continuous forms rather than as a datasheet.

5. **Click 🖳 on the Form View toolbar, click the Passed check box on the subform to select it, right-click the Passed check box, point to Change To, then click Toggle Button**

   Table L-1 provides more information on which controls are interchangeable.

6. **Point to the middle-right resize handle on the toggle button, drag the ↔ mouse pointer to the right edge of the form, click the toggle button, type Passed the test?, then click 🔳**

   Your screen should look similar to Figure L-2. Now a pressed toggle button is used to indicate a "Yes" value for the Passed field. An unpressed toggle button represents "No".

7. **Click the Save button 🖳 on the Form View toolbar**

   The changes are saved to the Employee Course Registration form and the Registration Subform.

8. **Close the Employee Course Registration form**

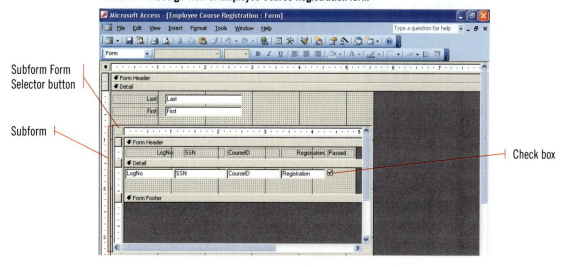

FIGURE L-1: Design View of Employee Course Registration form

Subform Form Selector button

Subform

Check box

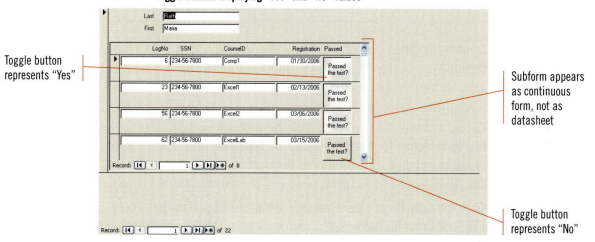

FIGURE L-2: Toggle buttons displaying "Yes" and "No" values

Toggle button represents "Yes"

Subform appears as continuous form, not as datasheet

Toggle button represents "No"

TABLE L-1: Interchangeable bound controls

control	Toolbox toolbar button	can be interchanged with	used most commonly when the field has
Text box	ab	List box, combo box	An unlimited number of choices such as a Price, LastName, or Street field
List box		Text box, combo box	A limited number of predefined values such as a Manager, Department, or State field
Combo box		Text box, list box	A limited number of common values, yet you still need the ability to enter a new value from the keyboard, such as a City field
Check box		Toggle button, option button	Only two values, "Yes" or "No", such as a Veteran field
Option button		Check box, toggle button	A limited number of values, such as "Female" or "Male" for a Gender field; most commonly used with an option group that contains several option buttons, each representing a possible value for the field
Toggle button		Check box, option button	Only two values, "Yes" or "No", and you want the field to look like a button

Using Conditional Formatting in a Form

Conditional Formatting is a set of conditions (rules) that determine how a field on a form or report should be formatted. You use conditional formatting to alert the user to exceptional situations. For example, a conditional formatting rule might evaluate the value in the Country field, and display it in light blue if the value is not equal to "USA" to alert the user that they are working with an international address. Conditional rules can also change the formatting of a control when it has the focus. **Focus** is when a field can receive user input through the keyboard or mouse. By using conditional formatting to indicate which control has the focus, the user may be more productive because the active field is more obvious. The users of the Courses form would like you to modify the form so that they can quickly identify those course attendees with the title of "Salesperson". Additionally, you will use conditional formatting to more clearly show which text box has the focus.

STEPS

TROUBLE
If the subform appears as a white rectangle, click ▣, then click ☒ to refresh the screen.

1. **Double-click the Courses form, view the overall layout of the form and subform, click the Design View button ☒ on the Form View toolbar, then maximize the form**

   The main form provides four fields of information about the course, and the subform represents each person who registered for the course.

2. **Click the subform to select it, click the subform vertical ruler to the left of the Last text box to select all four text boxes in the Detail section of the subform, click Format on the menu bar, then click Conditional Formatting**

   The Conditional Formatting dialog box opens. The first condition will highlight which field has the focus.

3. **Click the Condition 1 Field Value Is list arrow, click Field Has Focus, click the Condition 1 Fill/Back Color list arrow ▒ ▾, then click bright yellow (fourth row, third box from the left)**

   The second condition will highlight which registrants have the title of "Salesperson" with bold, red text. To conditionally format a control based on a value in another field, you use an **expression**, a combination of field names, operators, and values that calculate an answer.

QUICK TIP
You can include up to three conditions in the Conditional Formatting dialog box.

4. **Click Add in the Conditional Formatting dialog box, click the Condition 2 Field Value Is list arrow, click Expression Is, press [Tab], type [Title]="Salesperson", click the Condition 2 Bold button ■, click the Condition 2 Font/Fore Color button ▲ to select red text**

   Your screen should look like Figure L-3. When an expression is used in the Conditional Formatting dialog box, the expression must evaluate to be either "true", which turns the formatting on, or "false", which turns the formatting off.

5. **Click OK, click the Form View button ▣ on the Form Design toolbar, then click Lee (the value in the Last field for the first record) in the subform**

   Your screen should look like Figure L-4. Employees who have the title "Salesperson" appear in bold red. The field with focus has a bright yellow background.

6. **Press [Tab] three times to move the focus to the Salesperson entry for the first record, type Sales Manager, then press [Tab]**

   Your screen should look like Figure L-5. The values in the first record in the subform are no longer red and boldface because the Title field is no longer equal to "Salesperson". Conditional formatting reverts to default formatting if a condition is no longer true.

7. **Save, then close the Courses form**

FIGURE L-3: Conditional Formatting dialog box

Default Formatting section Condition 1

Condition 2

Click here to select all text boxes in the subform

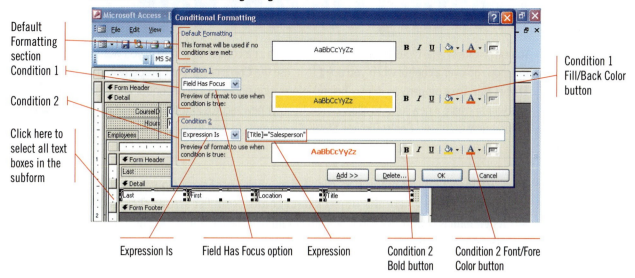

Condition 1 Fill/Back Color button

Condition 2 Font/Fore Color button

Condition 2 Bold button

Expression

Field Has Focus option

Expression Is

FIGURE L-4: Conditional formatting in Form View

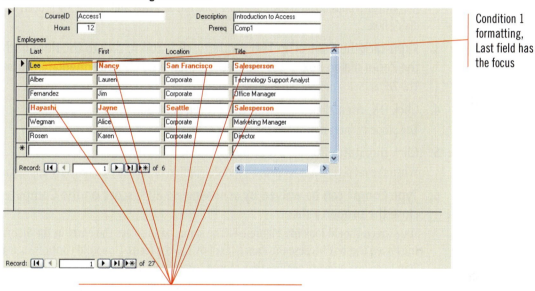

Condition 1 formatting, Last field has the focus

Condition 2 formatting, Title field equals "Salesperson"

FIGURE L-5: Conditional formats change as data is edited

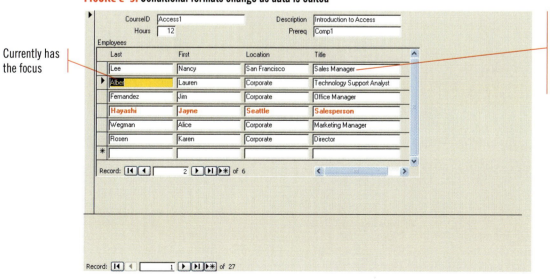

Currently has the focus

Title is no longer "Salesperson" so Condition 2 formats are not applied to the first record

Access 2003

Creating Custom Help

You can create several types of custom Help for a form or a control on a form. If you want to display a textual tip that pops up over a control when you point to it, use the **ControlTip Text** property for that control. Or use the **Status Bar Text** property to display helpful information about a form or control in the status bar. Fred asks you to create a new form to allow others to enter new records into the Courses table. He also wants you to support new users with ControlTip and Status Bar prompts to help them use the new form.

STEPS

1. **Click Insert on the menu bar, click Form, click AutoForm: Columnar, click the Choose the table or query where the object's data comes from list arrow, click Courses, then click OK**

   A new form is created. You can modify the ControlTip Text and Status Bar Text properties for text boxes and other bound controls in Form View.

2. **Click View on the menu bar, click Properties, click the Other tab, click the ControlTip Text property text box, type Introductory classes have a 1 suffix, press [Enter], then point to the CourseID text box**

   A ControlTip pops up, as shown in Figure L-6. You can view and enter long property entries using the Zoom dialog box.

3. **Right-click the ControlTip Text property, click Zoom, click to the right of the word "suffix" in the Zoom dialog box, press [Spacebar], then type and intermediate courses have a 2 suffix**

   The Zoom dialog box should look like Figure L-7.

4. **Click OK, then click Comp1 in the Prereq text box**

   The property sheet now shows the properties for the Prereq text box.

5. **Click the Status Bar Text text box**

   When the property sheet is open, a short description of the selected property appears in the status bar.

6. **Type Comp1 can be waived by achieving an 80% score on the Computers 101 test, then close the property sheet**

   Your screen should look like Figure L-8. The status bar displays the entry in the Status Bar Text property for the Prereq text box because the Prereq text box has the focus. Unbound controls such as labels do not have a Status Bar Text property because they cannot have the focus, but a label can display ControlTip Text. To modify the ControlTip Text property for a label or other unbound control, you must be able to first select the control to access its property sheet. To select an unbound control, you must work in Form Design View.

7. **Click the Save button on the Form View toolbar, type Course Entry in the Form Name text box, click OK, then close the Course Entry form**

FIGURE L-6: Using the ControlTip Text property

ControlTip Text

Other tab

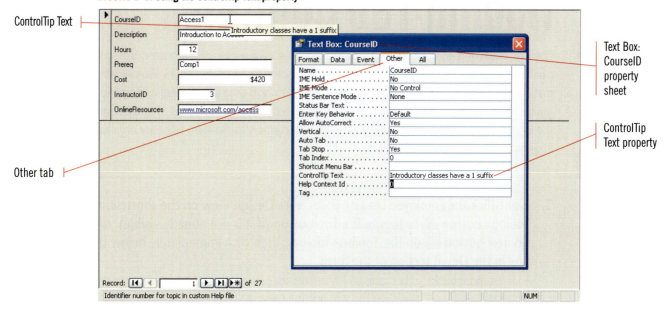

Text Box: CourseID property sheet

ControlTip Text property

FIGURE L-7: Zoom dialog box

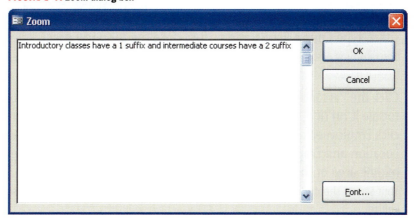

FIGURE L-8: Using the Status Bar Text property

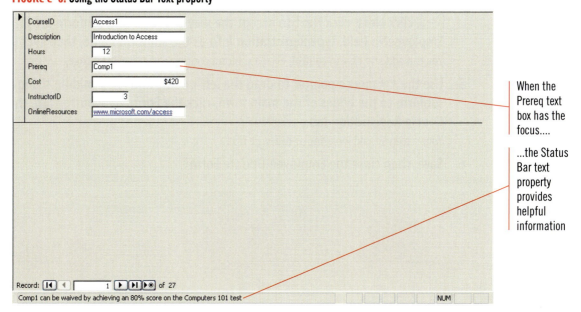

When the Prereq text box has the focus....

...the Status Bar text property provides helpful information

Access 2003

Adding Tab Controls

The **tab control** is an unbound control used to create a three-dimensional aspect to a form so that controls can be organized and displayed by clicking the tabs. Many Access dialog boxes also use tabs to organize information. For example, the property sheet uses tab controls to organize properties identified by property categories: Format, Data, Event, Other, and All. Fred created a form used to update employee data called the Employee Update Form. He asks you to add tab controls to the form to better organize and present the information.

1. **Right-click the Employee Update Form, click Design View on the shortcut menu, click the Toolbox button** 🛠 **to toggle the Toolbox on (if it is not already visible), click the Tab Control button** ⬚ **on the Toolbox toolbar, then click immediately below the First text box in the Detail section of the form**

   Your screen should look like Figure L-9. By default, the tab control is added with two "pages", with the default names of Page17 and Page18 on the tabs because these are the seventeenth and eighteenth controls to be added to the form.

   > **QUICK TIP**
   > To add more pages, right-click the tab control in Form Design View, then click Insert Page on the shortcut menu.

2. **Double-click Page17 to open its property sheet, click the Other tab (if it is not already selected), double-click Page17 in the Name property text box, type Personnel Info, click the Page18 tab on the form, double-click Page18 in the Name text box of the property sheet, type Course Registration, then close the property sheet**

   The tabs now describe the information they will organize, but you still need to add the appropriate controls to each page.

   > **QUICK TIP**
   > The page will become dark gray when you are successfully adding control(s) to that page.

3. **Click the Personnel Info tab, click the Field List button** 🗔 **on the Form Design toolbar to toggle it on (if it is not already visible), click Title in the field list, press and hold [Shift], click EmployeeNo in the field list (you may have to scroll) to select all fields between the Location and EmployeeNo, release [Shift], then drag the highlighted fields to the top middle area of the Personnel Info page**

   Your screen should look similar to Figure L-10. Five fields are added to the Personnel Info page on the tab control.

   > **TROUBLE**
   > The Control Wizards button ⬚ must be selected before you click the Subform/ Subreport button on the Toolbox toolbar in order to use the SubForm Wizard.

4. **Click the Course Registration tab, click the Subform/Subreport button** 🗔 **on the Toolbox toolbar, click the Course Registration page, click Next to use an existing table or query, click the Tables/Queries list arrow, click Enrollments, click the Select All Fields button** >> **, click Next, click Next to accept the way the form and subform are linked via the EmployeeNo field, type Registration Info as the subform name, then click Finish**

   You can add any type of control, even a subform control, to a tab control page.

5. **Use the ↔ mouse pointer to drag the left-middle and right-middle sizing handles of the subform to the edges of the main form, click the Form View button** 🗔 **, then click the Course Registration tab**

   Your screen should look similar to Figure L-11.

6. **Save, then close the Employee Update Form**

FIGURE L-9: Adding a tab control

Tab control with two "pages"

Tab control button

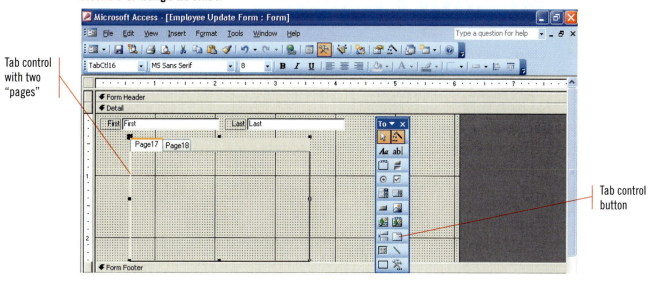

FIGURE L-10: Adding fields to a page on a tab control

Field List button

Course Registration page

Personnel Info page

Field list

Selected fields

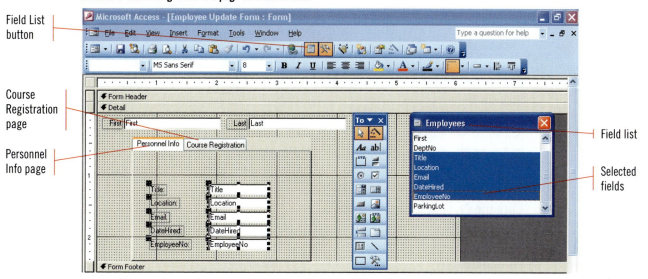

FIGURE L-11: Using a tab control in Form View

Course Registration tab

Registration Info subform

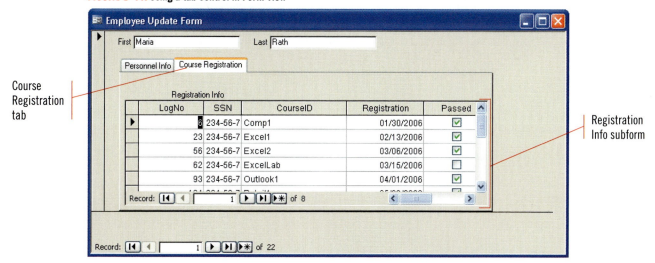

Adding Charts

Charts, also called graphs, are visual representations of numeric data that help users see comparisons, patterns, and trends in data. Charts can be inserted on a form, report, or data access page. Access provides a **Chart Wizard** that helps you with the process of creating the chart. Before using the Chart Wizard, however, you should determine what data you want the graph to show and what chart type you want to use. Table L-2 provides more information on common chart types. Fred created a Location Summary query with two fields: Registration from the Registration table, and Location from the Employees table. Instead of reporting this information as a datasheet of values, he asks you to create a chart to graphically display a count of course registrations for each MediaLoft location.

STEPS

1. Click Reports on the Objects bar, click the New button ⬚ on the database window toolbar, click Chart Wizard, click the Choose the table or query where the object's data comes from list arrow, click Location Summary, then click OK

The Chart Wizard starts and presents the fields in the Location Summary query.

> **QUICK TIP**
>
> Click any chart button to read a description of that chart in the lower-right corner of the Chart Wizard dialog box.

2. Click the Select All Fields button ⬚⬚ , then click Next

The Chart Wizard lists the chart types that you can create, as shown in Figure L-12. The Column Chart is the default chart type.

> **QUICK TIP**
>
> Double-click a button in the Data area to change the way it is summarized.

3. Click Next to accept the column chart selection

The next dialog box determines which fields will be used for the x-axis, data, and series (legend) areas of the chart as shown in Figure L-13. For this chart, each location should be listed on the x-axis and the bars should represent the count of course registrations from each location. The wizard has already positioned the Location field in the Axis position and the CountOfRegistration field in the Data position. No fields are in the Series position. If the fields were in the wrong positions, you could drag them off the chart and then drag the field buttons on the right side of the dialog box to the appropriate positions. Because it appears that the Chart Wizard has already correctly positioned the field you want to use for this chart, you will use the Preview Chart button to determine if those choices are correct.

4. Click the Preview Chart button

A Sample Preview dialog box opens giving you a rough idea of what the final chart will look like. Although all of the Location values do not clearly display on the x-axis because the chart is too small, the chart is structurally correct.

> **TROUBLE**
>
> Depending on the size of your chart, the scale on the y-axis, the labels on the x-axis, or the chart title may appear slightly different.

5. Click Close, click Next, type Total Registration by Location as the title for your chart text box, click the No, don't display a legend option button, then click Finish

The chart opens in Print Preview as shown in Figure L-14. Because there is only one series of bars, you can describe the data in the title of the chart and do not need a legend. The chart is still too small to display all of the Location values on the x-axis, but you can modify a chart in Design View to improve its appearance.

FIGURE L-12: Chart types

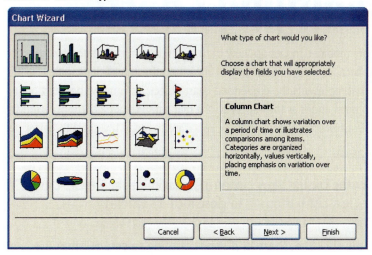

FIGURE L-13: Determining chart layout

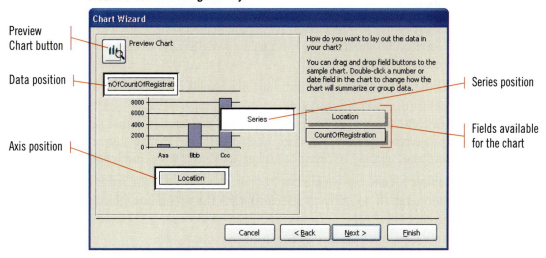

FIGURE L-14: Total Registration by Location chart

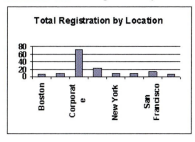

TABLE L-2: Common chart types

chart type	chart icon	used to show most commonly	example
Column		Comparisons of values	Each bar represents the annual sales for a different product for the year 2006
Line		Trends over time	Each point on the line represents monthly sales for one product for the year 2006
Pie		Parts of a whole	Each slice represents total quarterly sales for a company for the year 2006
Area		Cumulative totals	Each section represents monthly sales by representative, stacked to show the cumulative total sales effort for the year 2006

Modifying Charts

Charts are modified in Design View of the form or report that contains the chart. Modifying a chart is challenging because Design View doesn't show you the actual chart values, but instead, displays a chart placeholder that represents the embedded chart object. To modify the chart, you modify the chart placeholder. To view the changes as they apply to the real data you are charting, return to either Form View for a form, or Print Preview for a report. You want to resize the chart to better display the values on the x-axis.

1. **Click the Design View button [icon], maximize the Report Design View window, then click the Field List button [icon] to close it (if it's visible)**

   To make the chart bigger you need to resize the chart object.

2. **Single click the Chart (if it is not already selected), then use the [icon] mouse pointer to drag the lower-right corner of the chart placeholder down and to the right as shown in Figure L-15**

3. **Click the Print Preview button [icon] on the Report Design toolbar to view your changes**

   All eight locations should now be visible on the x-axis. You also decide that you would like to change the bar colors from periwinkle to green.

4. **Click [icon], then double-click the chart placeholder as shown in Figure L-16**

   To edit the items within a chart such as the bar colors, you must double-click it to switch to edit mode. **Edit mode** is used to select and modify individual chart elements such as the title, legend, or axes. If you double-click the *edge* of the chart placeholder, you will open its property sheet instead of opening it in edit mode. The hashed border of the chart placeholder control indicates that the chart is in edit mode.

5. **Double-click any periwinkle bar to open the Format Data Series dialog box, click the Patterns tab (if not already selected), click the green box (third row, fourth column), then click OK**

   The first series of bars changes to green in the chart placeholder.

6. **Click outside the chart to exit Chart edit mode, then click [icon]**

   Your chart should look similar to Figure L-17.

7. **Click File on the menu bar, click Save As, type Location Chart-Your Initials, then click OK**

8. **Click the Print button [icon] on the Print Preview toolbar, then close the Location Chart-Your Initials report**

FIGURE L-15: Resizing a chart in Design View

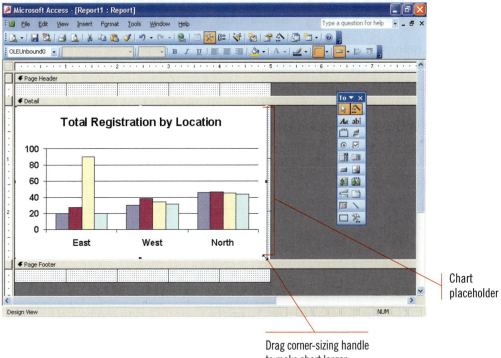

Chart placeholder

Drag corner-sizing handle to make chart larger

FIGURE L-16: Editing a chart in Design View

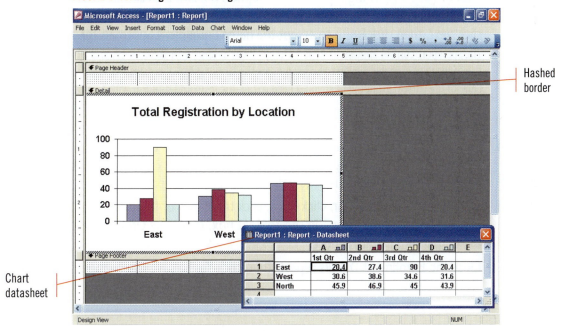

Hashed border

Chart datasheet

FIGURE L-17: Final chart

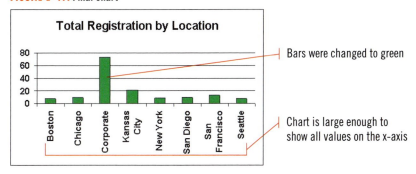

Bars were changed to green

Chart is large enough to show all values on the x-axis

Adding Subreport Controls

A **subreport** control displays a report within another report. The report that contains the subreport control is called the **main report**. You use the subreport control when you want to link two reports together to automate printing. You also use a subreport control when you want to change the order in which information automatically prints. For example, if you want report totals (generally found in the Report Footer section, which prints on the last page) to print on the first page, you could use a subreport to present the grand total information, and place it in the main report's Report Header section, which prints first. ▰▰▰▰ You want to show enrollment subtotals on the first page of the Enrollment Details report in addition to the Group Footer section that they normally display. You decide to use a subreport to accomplish this.

STEPS

1. **Right-click the Enrollment Details report, click Design View on the shortcut menu, then maximize the report**

   You want to add the Enrollment Subtotals report as a subreport to the Report Header section of the Enrollment Details report so that the subtotals print on the first page.

2. **Click the Toolbox button ⚒ on the Report Design toolbar to toggle it on (if it's not already visible), click the Subform/Subreport button ▦ on the Toolbox toolbar, then click toward the left side of the Report Header section**

   The SubReport Wizard opens, as shown in Figure L-18.

3. **Click the Use an existing report or form option button, click Enrollment Subtotals, click Next, scroll and click None when prompted for a field to link the main form to the subform, click Next, then click Finish to accept the name Enrollment Subtotals for the subreport**

   The subreport control appears in Report Design View, as shown in Figure L-19, and automatically expands the size of the Report Footer section to accommodate the large control. If you wanted the subreport to show only the data for the current grouping field you'd need to link the form and subform with a common field. When adding a subreport to the Report Header section, you are merely reordering the way data prints, and automating the printing of two reports at once. Therefore, no link between the main form and subform needs to be established.

4. **Click the Print Preview button 🔍 on the Report Design toolbar**

   Your screen should look like Figure L-20. The Report Header section contains the Enrollment Subtotals report, which will now print on the first page of the Enrollment Details report.

QUICK TIP
If you want your name on the print-out, add it as a label to the Report Header section.

5. **Click File on the menu bar, click Print, click the Pages option button, type 1 in the From: text box, press [Tab], type 1 in the To: text box, then click OK to print the first page of the Enrollment Details report**

6. **Close the Enrollment Details report, then click Yes to save the changes when prompted**

FIGURE L-18: SubReport Wizard

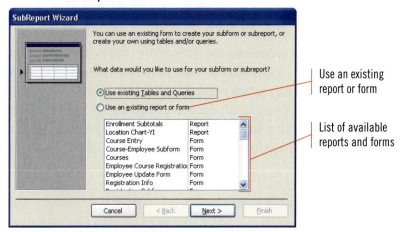

Use an existing report or form

List of available reports and forms

FIGURE L-19: Subreport in Report Design View

Report Header section

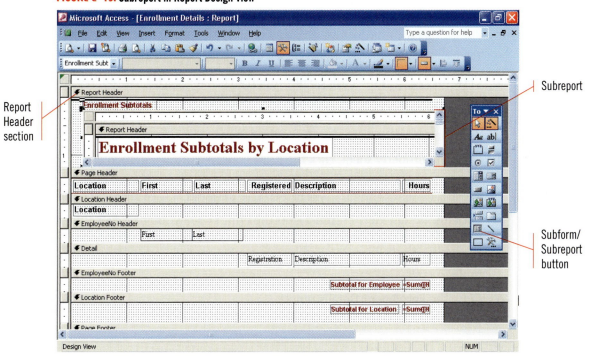

Subreport

Subform/ Subreport button

FIGURE L-20: Subreport in Print Preview

Subreport in Report Header section of main report

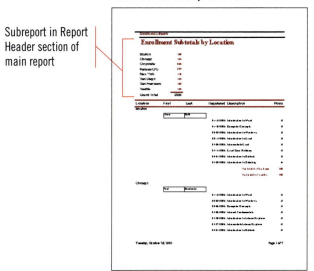

Modifying Section Properties

Report **section properties**, the characteristics that define each section, can be modified to improve report printouts. For example, you may want each new Group Header to print at the top of a new page. Or, you may want to modify section properties to format that section with a background color. Fred wants to change the Enrollment Details report so that the records for each new Location start at the top of a new page. He also wants to highlight Location Header and Location Footer sections by changing their Back Color property. You make these section property changes in Report Design View.

STEPS

1. **Right-click the Enrollment Details report, click Design View on the shortcut menu, double-click the Location Header section to open its property sheet, then click the Format tab in the property sheet (if not already selected)**

   The property sheet for the Location Header section opens, as shown in Figure L-21.

QUICK TIP

For properties with a limited number of choices, double-click the property to select the next available option.

2. **Click None in the Force New Page property, click the Force New Page list arrow, then click Before Section**

   This property change means that before each Location Header prints, the report will move to a new page.

3. **Click 16777215 in the Back Color property, click the Back Color Build button [...], click the light yellow box (first row, second column), then click OK**

   The Location Header section will appear with a light yellow background color in Print Preview, as well as on the printout if a color printer is used.

TROUBLE

If the controls in your report extend beyond the 6.5" mark on the horizontal ruler, a second page is needed to display them. Return to Design View and narrow the width of the report to 6.5" across or less.

4. **Close the property sheet, click the Print Preview button [icon], then view the second page**

   Your screen should look like Figure L-22. By modifying section color properties and starting each group of records at the top of a new page, you have clarified where each new Location starts and stops.

5. **Click the Design View button [icon] on the Print Preview toolbar, click the Label button [Aa] on the Toolbox toolbar, click to the right of the Enrollment Subtotals label in the Report Header section, type your name, then click the Save button [icon] on the Report Design toolbar**

6. **Close the Enrollment Details report**

FIGURE L-21: Specifying section properties in Report Design View

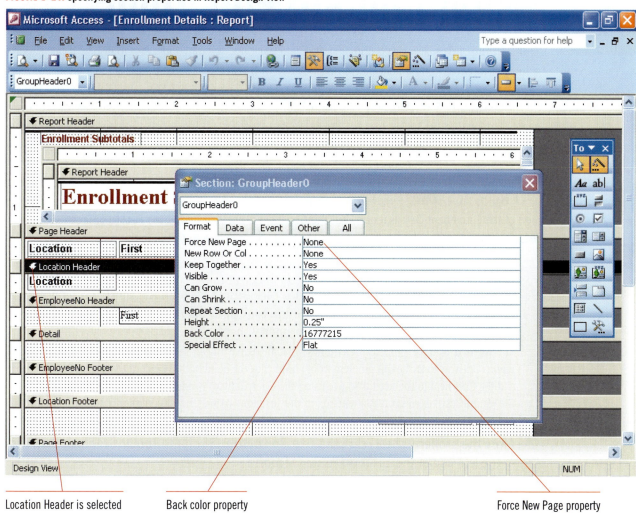

Location Header is selected

Back color property

Force New Page property

FIGURE L-22: Viewing section properties in Print Preview

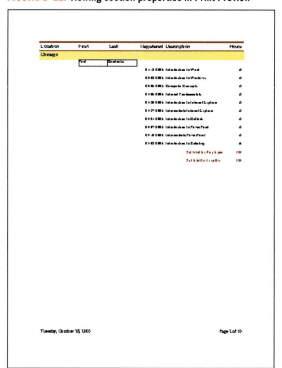

Using Domain Functions

Domain functions, also called domain aggregate functions, are functions used to display a calculation on a form or a report using a field that is not included in the Record Source property for the form or report. Domain functions start with a "D" for "domain" such as DSum, DAvg, DMin, and DMax and do the same calculation as their Sum, Avg, Min, Max, and Count counterparts. Regular functions require only one argument, the field that is to be used for the calculation such as =Sum([Price]). Domain functions have two required arguments, the field that is to be used for the calculation, and the domain name. The **domain** is the recordset (table or query) that contains the field used in the calculation. For example, =DSum("Price","Products") is the expression that uses the DSum function to sum the Price field found in the Products table. Fred wants to include the total cost for each location in the Location Footer section of the Enrollment Details report, but the Cost field is not included in the Record Source for the report. You decide to examine the report and then use a domain function to calculate this data.

STEPS

1. **Right-click the Enrollment Details report, click Design View on the shortcut menu, click the Properties button 🖺 on the Report Design toolbar to open the property sheet for the report, then click the Data tab in the property sheet**

   The **Record Source** property determines what fields have been selected and may be displayed on this report. One way to tackle this problem would be to click the Build button ⋯ for the Record Source property, add the Cost field to the Record Source using the Query Builder window, and use the Sum function to build the =Sum([Cost]) expression in a text box in the Location Footer. Or, you could use a domain function to do the same thing.

2. **Close the property sheet, click the Text Box button ab on the Toolbox toolbar, then click in the left side of the Location Footer section**

   A new text box and accompanying label are added to the Location Footer section.

   QUICK TIP

   The arguments for domain functions are string expressions so they must be enclosed in "quotation marks".

3. **Click Unbound in the new text box in the Location Footer section, then type =DSum("Cost","Courses")**

   The expression sums the Cost field found in the Courses domain.

4. **Double-click the label to the left of the new text box to open the property sheet, click the Format tab (if not already selected), enter Cost Subtotal for Location in the Caption property, close the property sheet, then move and resize the new label and text box so that the entire entry in each control can be read**

   Your screen should look like Figure L-23.

5. **Click the Save button 🖫 on the Report Design toolbar, then click the Print Preview button 🔍**

   The cost subtotal expression should calculate to 5775.

   QUICK TIP

   Align the top edges of all controls in the Location Footer section using the Top option from the Align option of the Format menu.

6. **Click the Design View button 🔧, then format and align the new controls as shown in the final report in Figure L-24**

7. **Click 🖫, click 🔍, click File on the menu bar, click Print, click the Pages option button, type 1 in the From: text box, press [Tab], type 2 in the To: text box, then click OK**

   The first and second pages of the Enrollment Details report are sent to the printer.

8. **Close the Enrollment Details report, close the Training-L.mdb database, then exit Access**

FIGURE L-23: Using the DSum function

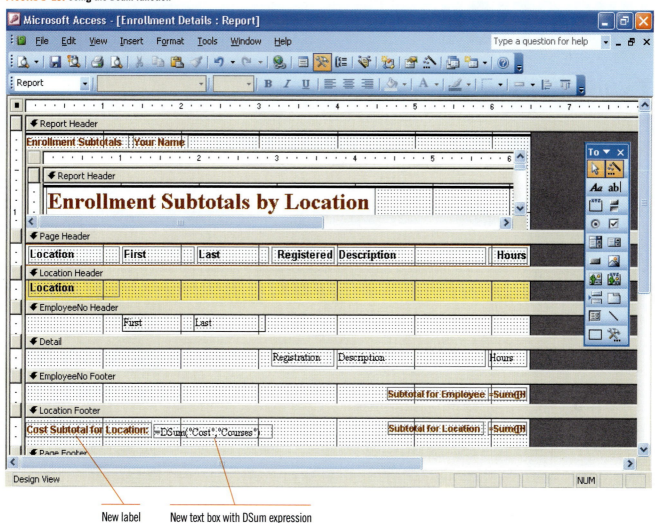

New label   New text box with DSum expression

FIGURE L-24: Viewing the DSum function in Print Preview

Location	First	Last	Registered	Description	Hours
Boston					
	Maria	Rath			
			01/18/2006	Introduction to Word	12
			01/30/2006	Computer Concepts	12
			02/02/2006	Introduction to Windows	12
			02/13/2006	Introduction to Excel	12
			03/06/2006	Intermediate Excel	12
			03/15/2006	Excel Case Problems	12
			04/01/2006	Introduction to Outlook	12
			05/08/2006	Introduction to Retailing	16
				Subtotal for Employee	**100**
				Subtotal for Location	**100**
Cost Subtotal for Location	$5,775.00				

New label   Formatted text box with DSum expression

Practice

▼ CONCEPTS REVIEW

Identify each element of the Report Design View shown in Figure L-25.

FIGURE L-25

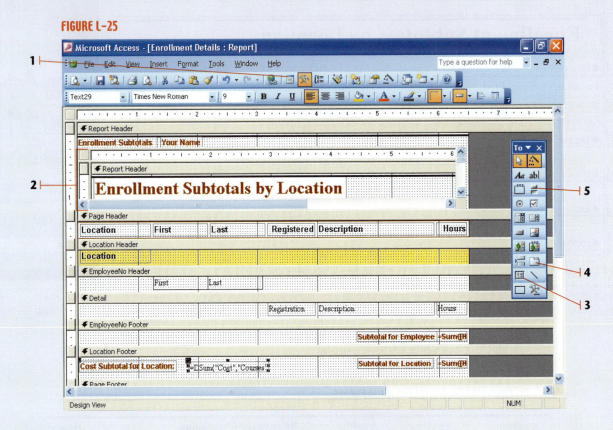

Match each term with the statement that best describes its function.

6. Charts
7. Focus
8. Check box
9. Sections
10. Conditional formatting
11. Tab control

a. Allows you to change the appearance of a control on a form or report based on criteria you specify
b. Visual representations of numeric data
c. The ability to receive user input through the keyboard or mouse
d. Determine where and how controls print on a report
e. A control that is often used to display a Yes/No field on a form
f. An unbound control used to organize a form and give it a three-dimensional look

Select the best answer from the list of choices.

12. Which controls are *not* interchangeable?
    a. Check box and option group
    b. Combo box and list box
    c. Check box and toggle button
    d. Text box and combo box
13. When would you most likely use a toggle button control?
    a. For a Yes/No field
    b. For a Text field
    c. In place of a command button
    d. In place of an unbound label

14. Which control would be the best candidate for a Country field?

a. Toggle button

b. Command button

c. Tab control

d. Combo box

15. Which control property would you use to automatically display text when you point to a control?

a. Popup Text

b. Status Bar Text

c. ControlTip Text

d. Help Text

16. Which type of chart would be the best candidate to show an upward sales trend over several months?

a. Line

b. Area

c. Scatter

d. Pie

17. Which type of control would you use to print two reports together?

a. Main report

b. Report Footer

c. Domain function

d. Subreport

18. Which property would you use to force a new group of records to start printing at the top of the next page?

a. Visible

b. Subreport

c. Force New Page

d. Section Break

19. To modify the colors of chart bars, you must open the chart in:

a. Design mode.

b. Property mode.

c. Edit mode.

d. Chart mode.

20. Domain functions are used to calculate on a field that is not:

a. In the database.

b. Included in the Record Source.

c. Used by a query.

d. Formatted with a Currency format.

▼ SKILLS REVIEW

1. Add check boxes and toggle buttons.

a. Start Access, then open the **RealEstate-L.mdb** database from the drive and folder where your Data Files are stored.

b. Use the AutoForm: Columnar tool to create a form based on the Listings table.

c. In Form Design View, change the check box control bound to the Pool field to a toggle button.

FIGURE L-26

d. Size the toggle button to the width of the Garage text box just above it.

e. Change the Caption of the toggle button to **Pool?**

f. Resize the height of the toggle button to more clearly display the caption if needed.

g. View the form in Form View, and click the Pool? toggle button for the first record, as shown in Figure L-26. Use Form Design View to make modifications as needed.

h. Save the form with the name **Listings Entry Form**.

i. Change the value in the Area field of the first record to your own hometown, then close the form.

2. Use conditional formatting in a form.

a. Open the Listings Entry Form in Design View.

b. Select the Asking text box, then open the Conditional Formatting dialog box.

FIGURE L-27

c. Apply a bold and blue Font/Fore Color for the Condition 1 format when the field value is less than 200000, and apply a bold and red Font/Fore Color for the Condition 2 format when the field value is greater than or equal to 200000, as shown in Figure L-27.

d. Display the form in Form View, then move through the records to make sure that both of the conditions you added in the previous step are applied correctly.

e. Save the form, print only the first record, and close the form.

3. **Create custom Help.**

   a. Open the Listings Entry Form in Design View.

   b. Open the property sheet for the SqFt text box, then select the Other tab.

   c. Type **Square footage not including basement** for the ControlTip Text property. Use the Zoom dialog box to make this long entry, if desired.

   d. Type **As defined by Missouri Realtors Association** for the Status Bar Text property. Use the Zoom dialog box to make this long entry, if desired.

   e. Close the property sheet, save the form, then open the form in Form View.

   f. Click 3400 in the SqFt text box for the first record to make sure that the Status Bar Text property works.

   g. Point to 3400 in the SqFt text box for the first record to make sure that the ControlTip Text property works.

   h. Save, then close the Listings form.

4. **Add tab controls.**

   a. Open the Agency Information form in Design View.

   b. Add a tab control under the City text box.

   c. Modify the first tab name to be **Agents**.

   d. Modify the second tab name to be **Listings**.

   e. Using the SubForm Wizard, add a subform to the Agents page that includes all the fields from the Agent Master List query.

   f. Use the common AgencyNo field to link the main form and subform and accept the default name for the subform.

   g. Using the SubForm Wizard, add a subform to the Listings page that includes all the fields from the Listings Master List query.

   h. Use the common AgencyNo field to link the main form and subform and accept the default name for the subform.

   i. Use Form View and Form Design View to move and resize the tab and subform controls to fill the screen. In Form View, resize the columns of the subforms to maximize the number of columns that can be viewed at any one time.

   j. Navigate to the third agency, Sun and Ski Realtors, and click both tabs. Sun and Ski has two realtors and six listings between the two realtors, as shown in Figure L-28.

   k. Change Sun and Ski Realtors to **Your Last Name Realtors**, then save the Agency Information form.

   l. Print the record with your name as the real estate agency name, then close the Agency Information form.

FIGURE L-28

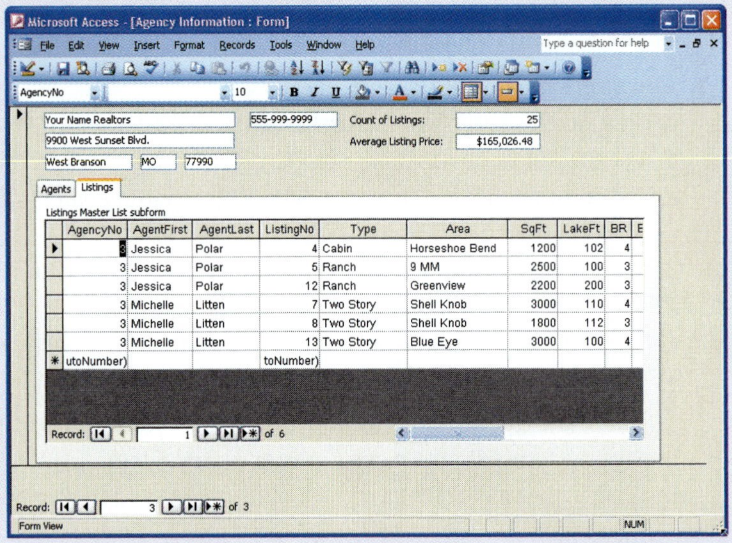

5. **Add charts.**

   a. Use the Chart Wizard to start building a new report. Base the report on the Listings table.

   b. Select Type and Asking as the fields for the chart.

   c. Choose a Column Chart type.

   d. Average the Asking field in the Data area, and use the Type field as the x-axis. (*Hint*: These should be the defaults, but click the Preview Chart button to verify these choices. To average rather than sum the Asking field, double-click the SumOfAsking field, click Avg, then click OK in the Summarize dialog box.)

   e. Type **Average Asking Price** for the chart title, do not show a legend, then display it in Print Preview.

6. **Modify charts.**

   a. Save the report you just created with the Chart Wizard as Average Asking Price, then open it in Design View.

   b. Resize the chart placeholder so that when you view the report in Print Preview, all of the values on the x-axis are clearly displayed.

   c. In Design View, open the chart in edit mode, change the color of the periwinkle series of bars to red.

   d. In Design View, add your name as a label to the Page Header section.

   e. Save the Average Asking Price report, view it in Print Preview, then print and close it.

7. Add subreport controls.

   a. Use the Report Wizard to create a report on all of the fields in the Listings Master List query.

   b. View the data by AgencyNo, then by AgentFirst, AgentLast as suggested by the wizard. Do not add any more grouping levels or sort orders.

   c. Use an Outline 2 layout, a Landscape orientation, and a Soft Gray style.

   d. Type **Listings Report** as the title for the report.

   e. Open Listings Report in Report Design View, then open the Report Footer section by dragging the bottom edge of the report down about one inch.

   f. Use the SubReport Wizard to add a subreport control to the upper-left corner of the Report Footer section.

   g. Use the existing Average Asking Price report for the subreport, and accept the default name for the subreport name.

   h. Move and resize the new subreport as needed to fit in the Report Footer section.

   i. Add your name as a label to the Report Header section of the Listings Report.

   j. Save and preview the report, print the first and last pages, then close the Listings Report.

8. Modify section properties.

   a. Use Report Design View to modify the Listings Report so that a new page is forced just before the AgencyNo Header section prints.

   b. Change the Back Color property of the AgencyNo Header to light blue. (*Hint*: Use the Build button to locate the color on the palette.)

   c. Close the property sheet, save the report, then print the first two pages.

   d. Save, then close the Listings Report.

9. Use domain functions.

   a. Open the Agency Information form in Design View.

   b. Add a new text box to the Detail section, to the right of the AgencyPhone text box.

   c. Use the following expression to calculate the count of real estate listings:

     =DCount("Asking", "Listings")

   d. Add another new text box to the Detail section, just below the previous one.

   e. Use the following expression to calculate the average asking price of all real estate listings:

     =DAvg("Asking", "Listings")

   f. Change the labels to the left of each new text box to **Count of Listings:** and **Average Listing Price:**

   g. Move and resize the new labels and text boxes to clearly display the information in Form View.

   h. Modify the Format property of the new text box that calculates the average listing price to Currency.

   i. Save and preview the form, then print only the third record that includes your name as the real estate company's name.

   j. Close the Agency Information form, close RealEstate-L.mdb, then exit Access.

▼ INDEPENDENT CHALLENGE 1

As the manager of a college women's basketball team, you want to enhance the forms within the Basketball-L.mdb database.

   a. Start Access, then open the database **Basketball-L.mdb** from the drive and folder where your Data Files are stored.

   b. Start creating a form by using the Form Wizard, and select all of the fields in the Players table.

   c. Use a Columnar layout and a Standard style, then type **Player Information** as the title for the form.

   d. Maximize the Player Information form, open it in Design View, then change the Lettered? check box to a toggle button with the text **Varsity Letter?**

   e. Resize the toggle button so that it clearly displays the text and is as wide as the form.

   f. Open the toggle button's property sheet, then type **Must have 200 minutes of playing time to letter** for the ControlTip Text property.

g. In the toggle button's property sheet, type **For the 2005/2006 season** for the Status Bar Text property.

h. Close the property sheet, display the form in Form View, enter your own last name in the first record, then click the toggle button to indicate you've earned a varsity letter.

i. Check to make sure that the ControlTip and Status Bar Text properties work properly for the toggle button, then save the form and print the first record.

j. Change the name in the first record to **Lisa Beem**, close the Player Information form and the Basketball-L.mdb database, then exit Access.

▼ INDEPENDENT CHALLENGE 2

As the manager of a college women's basketball team, you want to enhance the forms within the Basketball-L.mdb database.

a. Start Access, then open the database **Basketball-L.mdb** from the drive and folder where your Data Files are stored.

b. Open the Player Statistics form in Design View, then add a tab control just below the First text box.

c. Modify the first tab name to be **Player Background**.

d. Modify the second tab name to be **Statistics**.

e. Open the field list, then add the Height, PlayerNo, Year, Position, HomeTown, and HomeState fields to the middle of the Player Background page.

FIGURE L-29

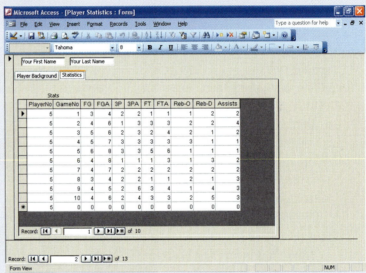

f. Use the SubForm Wizard to add a subform to the Statistics page based on all the fields from the Stats table. Link the main form to the subform by using the common PlayerNo field.

g. Type **Stats** as the name of the subform.

h. Expand the width of the subform control to the existing margins of the form, then view the form in Form View. Keep resizing the subform and tab control in Form Design View as well as narrowing the columns of the subform on the Statistics page in Form View so that all of the columns can be viewed without scrolling.

i. Click the Statistics tab to make sure both tabs work correctly, move to the second record and enter your name in the First and Last text boxes, then print the second record with the Statistics page displayed, as shown in Figure L-29.

Advanced Challenge Exercise

- Use conditional formatting to format the Height text box on the Player Background tab to display a yellow background when the field value is greater than or equal to 72.
- Use conditional formatting to format the Year text box on the Player Background tab to display a green background when the field value is equal to Fr.

j. Save the Player Statistics form. Change the name in the second record to **Gracia Burton**, then print that record.

k. Close the Basketball-L.mdb database, then exit Access.

▼ INDEPENDENT CHALLENGE 3

As the manager of a college women's basketball team, you want to create a chart from the Basketball-L.mdb database to summarize three-point goals.

    a. Start Access, then open the database **Basketball-L.mdb** from the drive and folder where your Data Files are stored.

    b. Start a new report using the Chart Wizard, and base the report on the Stats table.

    c. Select the PlayerNo, three pointers (3P), and three pointers attempted (3PA) fields for the chart.

    d. Select Column Chart for the chart type.

    e. Drag the 3PA field to the Data area of the chart so that both the SumOf3P and SumOf3PA fields are in the Data area, and the PlayerNo field is in the Axis area of the chart.

    f. Type **3 Pointers–Your Initials** for the title of the chart and include the legend.

    g. Save the report with the name **3 Pointers**.

Advanced Challenge Exercise

    ■ In Design View of the 3 Pointers report, open the Report Footer section.

    ■ Use the SubReport Wizard to add a subreport to the Report Footer section.

    ■ Base the subreport on the Players table, and include the PlayerNo, First, and Last fields.

    ■ Use the default name for the subreport.

    h. Preview the 3 Pointers report, move and resize the chart as needed, then save and print it.

    i. Close the 3 Pointers report, close the Basketball-L.mdb database, then exit Access.

 ## ▼ INDEPENDENT CHALLENGE 4

Tab controls appear in many styles and are used on many Web pages to help users navigate a Web site. In this Independent Challenge, surf the Internet to find Web pages that present information organized similarly to how tab controls are used on Access forms.

    a. Connect to the Internet, then go to five large corporate Web sites such as *www.amazon.com*, *www.honda.com*, *www.microsoft.com*, *www.apple.com*, *www.expedia.com*, or others, and explore the navigation aids on the page to determine if any controls work the way tab controls work on a form. Go back to the home page and print only the first page of each of your five choices. On the printout, identify the area of the Web page that worked like tab controls. If you didn't think that the Web page used tab controls, explain why.

    b. Go to *www.atn.com.au* or *www.australia.com*, travel guides to Australia (substitute your own favorite international travel site if desired), and explore the sites to identify tab controls. Print a page of one of the sites that uses a navigation system that works similarly to tab controls. On that printout, identify the area of the Web page that worked like tab controls. If you didn't think that the Web page used tab controls, explain why.

    c. Go to *www.olympic.org* or *www.wimbledon.org*, international sports sites (substitute your own favorite international sports site if desired), and explore the site to identify tab controls. Print a page of one of the sites that uses a navigation system that works similarly to tab controls. On the printout, identify the area of the Web page that worked like tab controls. If you didn't think that the Web page used tab controls, explain why.

    d. Not all Web pages organize their content by using hyperlinks that look like tab controls. On a piece of paper, write a paragraph about the other types of navigation systems (buttons, menus, rollover menus, hyperlinks, maps) you found that help organize and navigate a Web site, and identify which ones you thought worked best and explain why.

▼ VISUAL WORKSHOP

As the manager of a college women's basketball team, you want to create a form that highlights outstanding statistics if either scoring or rebounding totals are equal to or greater than **10** for a player for an individual game. Start Access, then open the **Basketball-L.mdb** database from the drive and folder where your Data Files are stored. Open the Players form in Design View, then use the conditional formatting feature to format the field goals (FG), three-point shots (3P), and free throws (FT) text boxes in the Stats subform to have bold text and a yellow background if the following expression that totals their scoring for that game is true: **2*[FG]+3*[3P]+[FT]>=10**. Conditionally format the offensive rebounds (Reb-O) and defensive rebounds (Reb-D) text boxes to have a bold text and green background if the following expression that totals rebounds is true: **[Reb-O]+[Reb-D]>=5**. Display the record for Gracia Burton, which should look like Figure L-30. Enter your own name in the First and Last text boxes, then print that record.

FIGURE L-30

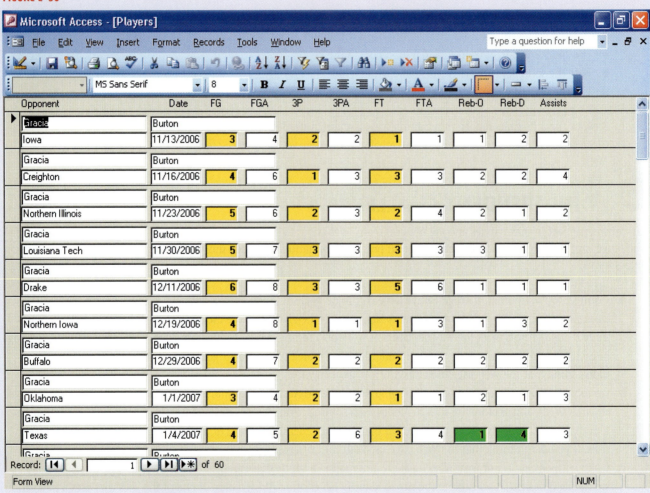

Managing Database Objects

OBJECTIVES

Work with objects

Use the Documenter

Group objects

Modify shortcuts and groups

Create a dialog box

Create a pop-up form

Create a switchboard

Modify a switchboard

If you have a SAM user profile, you may have access to hands-on instruction, practice, and assessment of the skills covered in this unit. Log in to your SAM account and go to your assignments page to see what your instructor has assigned.

As your database grows in size and functionality, the number of objects (especially queries and reports) grows as well. Your ability to find, rename, delete, and document objects, as well as make the database easier to use for others are important skills.  Kristen Fontanelle is the network administrator at MediaLoft corporate headquarters. You have helped Kristen develop a working database to document MediaLoft computer equipment. The number of objects in the database makes it increasingly difficult to find and organize information. You will use Access tools and create navigational forms to manage the growing database and make it easier to use.

Working with Objects

Working with Access objects is similar to working with files in Windows Explorer. For example, you can use the **View buttons** (Large Icons 🔳, Small Icons 🔳, List 🔳, and Details 🔳) on the database window toolbar to arrange the objects in four different ways just as you arrange files within Windows Explorer. Similarly, you can right-click an object within Access to open, copy, delete, or rename it just as you would right-click a file within Windows Explorer. 🎨 You delete, rename, sort, and add descriptions to several queries to make them easier to find.

STEPS

1. **Start Access, open the Technology-M.mdb database from the drive and folder where your Data Files are stored, maximize the database window, click Queries on the Objects bar, then click the Details button 🔳 on the database window toolbar**

   The database window displays five columns of information for each query: Name, Description, Modified (date the object was last changed), Created (date the object was originally created), and Type as shown in Figure M-1. By default, objects are sorted in ascending order by the contents of the Name column, but you can sort the objects by any column by clicking the column heading.

2. **Click the Name column heading to sort the objects in descending order by Name, click the Created column heading to sort the objects in ascending order based on the date they were originally created, then click the Name column heading to sort the objects in ascending order by Name again**

   You use the Description column to further describe the object.

3. **Right-click the Equipment Specs query, then click Properties on the shortcut menu**

   The Equipment Specs Properties dialog box opens.

4. **Enter Includes memory, hard drive, and processor information in the Description text box, then click OK**

   Part of the description appears in the database window and helps identify the selected object. If an object is no longer needed, you should delete it to free up disk space and keep the database window organized.

5. **Right-click the Employees Query, click Delete on the shortcut menu, then click Yes when prompted**

   Although object names can be 64 characters long and can include any combination of letters, numbers, spaces, and special characters except a period (.), exclamation point (!), accent (`), or brackets ([ ]), keep them as short, yet as descriptive, as possible. Short names make objects easier to reference in other places in the database, such as in the Record Source property for a form or report.

6. **Right-click the Human Resources query, click Rename on the shortcut menu, type HR, press [Enter], right-click the Information Systems query, click Rename on the shortcut menu, type IS, then press [Enter]**

   Your final screen should look like Figure M-2. With shorter query names, you can see all of the object names in the database window without resizing the columns.

FIGURE M-1: Viewing object details

View buttons

Name column heading

Details button

Equipment Specs query

Created column heading

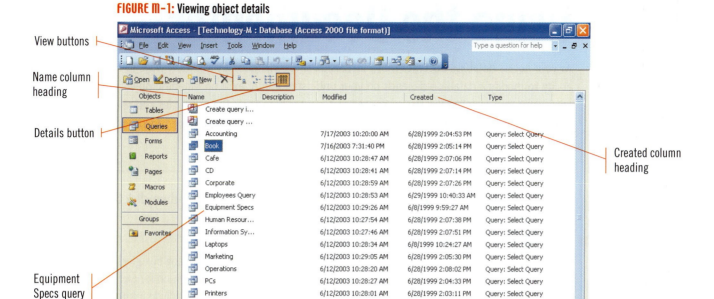

FIGURE M-2: Describing and renaming objects

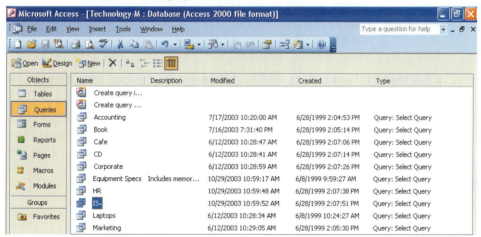

Clues to Use

Updating names with Name AutoCorrect

Name AutoCorrect fixes discrepancies among references to field names, controls on forms and reports, and object names when you change them. For example, if a query includes the field "LastName", but you change that field name to "LName" in Table Design View, the Name AutoCorrect feature will update the field name to "LName" within the query as well. Similarly, if a report is based on a query named "Department Income", and you change the query name to "Dept Inc", the Name AutoCorrect feature will automatically update the Record Source property for the report to "Dept Inc" to match the new query name. However, Name AutoCorrect will not repair references in Visual Basic for Applications code, replicated databases, linked tables, or a number of other database situations. Click Tools on the menu bar in the database window, click Options, and then click the General tab to view the Name AutoCorrect options.

Using the Documenter

As your Access database becomes more successful, users will naturally find new ways to use the data. Your ability to modify a database depends on your understanding of existing database objects. Access provides an analysis feature called the **Documenter** that creates reports on the properties and relationships among the objects in your database. ▒▒▒ You use the Documenter to create paper documentation to support the Technology-M database for other MediaLoft employees.

STEPS

1. **Click Tools on the menu bar, point to Analyze, click Documenter, then click the Tables tab**
   The Documenter dialog box opens, displaying tabs for each object type.

TROUBLE
The choices in the Print Table Definition dialog box reflect those made by the last user.

2. **Click Options in the Documenter dialog box**
   The Print Table Definition dialog box, shown in Figure M-3, opens. This dialog box gives you some control over what type of documentation you will print for the table. The documentation for each object type varies slightly. For example, the documentation on forms and reports would also include information on controls and sections.

3. **Click the Relationships check box to select it, click the Names, Data Types, and Sizes option button, then click OK**
   Be careful before you also print property values for each field because it creates a long printout. You can select or deselect individual objects by clicking check boxes, or you can click the Select All button to quickly select all objects of that type.

4. **Click Select All to select all of the tables, click the Forms tab, click Select All, click OK, then click the 🔍 mouse pointer on the report preview to zoom in**
   Documenter creates a report about all of the table and form objects in the Technology-M.mdb database, and displays it as an Access report as shown in Figure M-4. The first page contains information about the first table in the database, the Assignments table.

5. **Click the Last Page button ▶❘ in the navigation toolbar, then click the Previous Page button ◀**
   The last part of the report contains information about the forms. The properties for each control on the form are listed in two columns. Because most form controls have approximately 50 properties, the documentation to describe a form can be quite long. You can print the report, or send it to a Word document using the OfficeLinks buttons, but you cannot modify a Documenter report in Report Design View or save it as an object within this database.

6. **Click Close on the Print Preview toolbar**

FIGURE M-3: Print Table Definition dialog box

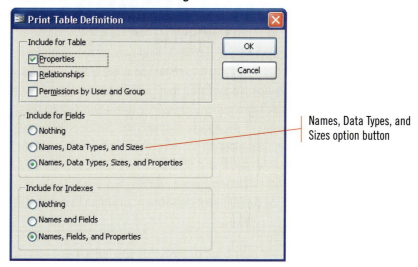

Names, Data Types, and Sizes option button

FIGURE M-4: First page of documentation

Technology-M.mdb database

Assignments table

Field name, type, size

Table relationships

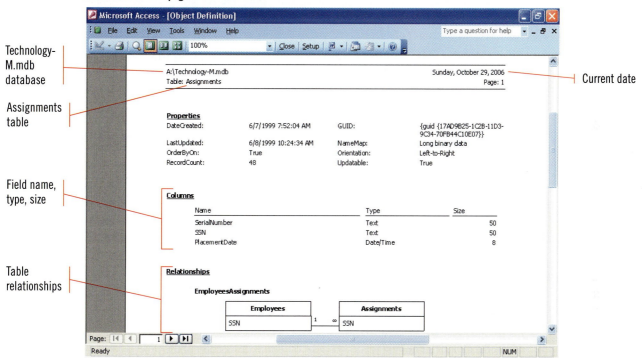

Current date

Clues to Use

Viewing object dependencies

Access 2003 tracks which objects depend on others. For example, a report may be based on a query that may include fields from three tables. Therefore, the report is dependent on the query and the query is dependent on each of the three tables. Knowing object dependencies helps you avoid deleting an object that affects others. To open the **Object Dependencies task pane** to view object dependencies, click File on the menu bar, then click New to open the New File task pane. Click the Task Pane list arrow, then click Object Dependencies. Click the object you want to display dependencies for, then click the show dependency information for the selected object link, and then click OK if prompted. Figure M-5 shows the Object Dependencies task pane for the Employees table. Note that you can view the objects that depend on the Employees table, or switch the view to show which objects the Employees table depends on itself.

FIGURE M-5: Object Dependencies task pane

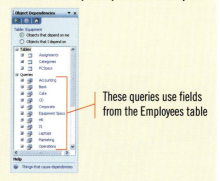

These queries use fields from the Employees table

Grouping Objects

Viewing every object in the database window can be cumbersome when your database contains many objects. Sometimes object naming conventions are used to help identify and organize objects as described in Table M-1. **Groups** are also used to organize objects by subject or purpose. For example, you might create a group for each department so that the forms and reports used by that department are presented as a set. A group consists of **shortcuts** (pointers) to the objects that belong to that group. These shortcuts are used to open the object, but do not affect the original location of the object. More than one shortcut can be created to the same object and placed in several groups. Groups appear in the **Groups bar** below the Objects bar in the database window. You organize the objects in the Technology-M database by creating groups for two different departments: Human Resources (HR) and Accounting.

STEPS

1. **Right-click** Favorites **on the Groups bar, click** New Group **on the shortcut menu, type** HR, **click** OK, **then click** HR **on the Groups bar**

   Your screen should look like Figure M-6. At this point, the HR group doesn't contain any objects. The **Favorites group** is provided for every new Access database and is similar in function to the Favorites folder used in other Microsoft programs.

   TROUBLE
   If the Groups bar is too narrow to display the full name of the group, drag the right edge of the Groups bar to the right to expand it.

2. **Right-click** Favorites **on the Groups bar, click** New Group **on the shortcut menu, type** Accounting, **then click** OK

   After creating the new groups, you are ready to use them to organize other database objects.

3. **Click** Queries **on the Objects bar, drag the** Accounting query **to the** Accounting group, **drag the** Equipment Specs query **to the** Accounting group, **then drag the** HR query **to the** HR group

   Dragging an object to a group icon places a shortcut to that object within that group.

4. **Click** Reports **on the Objects bar, drag the** Accounting report **to the** Accounting group, **drag the** Human Resources report **to the** HR group, **then click the** Accounting group

   Your screen should look like Figure M-7, with three shortcut icons representing two queries and one report in the Accounting group. Because both a query and a report object were named "Accounting", Access added a "1" to the "Accounting" report shortcut to give each shortcut a different name. A shortcut is a pointer to the original object. You can open or design an object by accessing it through a shortcut icon. You also can also create multiple shortcuts to the same object.

   QUICK TIP
   You can resize the Groups or Objects sections by pointing to the top edge of the Objects or Groups button and dragging the ↕ mouse pointer to resize that section of the Objects bar.

5. **Click the** Groups button **on the Groups bar three times**

   Click the Groups button to expand, collapse, or restore this section of the Objects bar.

6. **Click the** Objects button **on the Objects bar three times**

   Displaying all Objects and Groups buttons is a good way to arrange the database window for a new user.

FIGURE M-6: Creating groups

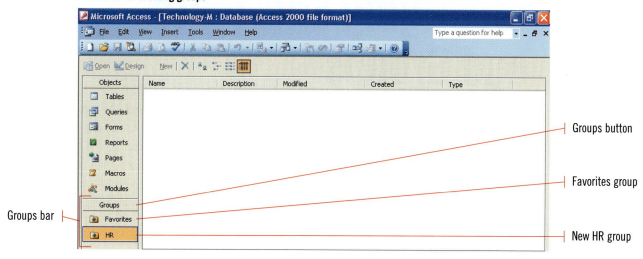

Groups button

Favorites group

New HR group

Groups bar

FIGURE M-7: Dragging objects to groups

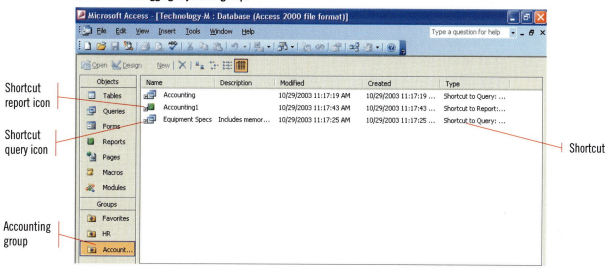

Shortcut
report icon

Shortcut
query icon

Accounting
group

Shortcut

TABLE M-1: Object naming conventions

object type	prefix	object name example
Table	tbl	tblProducts
Query	qry	qrySalesByRegion
Form	frm	frmProducts
Report	rpt	rptSalesByCategory
Macro	mcr	mcrCloseInventory
Module	bas or mdl	basRetirement or mdlCheckCredit

Modifying Shortcuts and Groups

Once groups are created and object shortcuts are added to them, you work with the shortcut as if you were working directly with the original object. Any changes you make to an object by accessing it through a shortcut are saved with the object, just as if you had opened that object without using the shortcut. You can delete, rename, or copy a shortcut by right-clicking it and choosing the appropriate command from the shortcut menu. The biggest difference between working with shortcuts and actual objects is that if you delete a shortcut, you delete only that pointer, which does not affect the original object it references. If you delete an object, however, it is, of course, permanently deleted, and any shortcuts that reference it will no longer function properly. You can also rename or delete entire groups. ⬛ You modify groups and shortcuts to clarify the Technology-M database.

STEPS

1. **Right-click the Accounting1 shortcut in the Accounting group, click Rename on the short-cut menu, type Accounting Report, then press [Enter]**

   A shortcut name does not have to use the same name as the object that it points to, but the shortcuts should be clearly named. The shortcut icon to the left of the shortcut indicates the type of object it represents.

2. **Right-click Accounting on the Groups bar, click Rename Group on the shortcut menu, type Acctg, then press [Enter]**

   The database window should look like Figure M-8.

3. **Right-click Acctg, click New Group on the shortcut menu, type IS in the New Group Name text box, then press [Enter]**

4. **Drag the Equipment Specs shortcut from the Acctg group to the IS group**

   Dragging a shortcut from one group to another creates a copy of that shortcut in both groups. Shortcuts that point to the same object can have the same or different names.

5. **Click IS on the Groups bar, double-click the Equipment Specs shortcut in the IS group to open the query in Datasheet View, double-click 256 in the Memory field for the first record (SerialNo JK123FL3), type 512, then close the datasheet**

   Edits and entries made through a query shortcut work exactly the same as if you had made the change in the original Query Datasheet View. Changes to data from any object view modify data that is physically stored in table objects.

6. **Click Tables on the Objects bar, double-click the PCSpecs table to open its datasheet, click the Find button 🔍 on the Table Datasheet toolbar, type JK123FL3 in the Find What text box, press [Enter], then click Cancel**

   The Memory field for the JK123FL3 record contains the value 512, as shown in Figure M-9.

7. **Close the PCSpecs datasheet**

FIGURE M-8: Modifying shortcuts and groups

Renamed shortcut

Renamed group

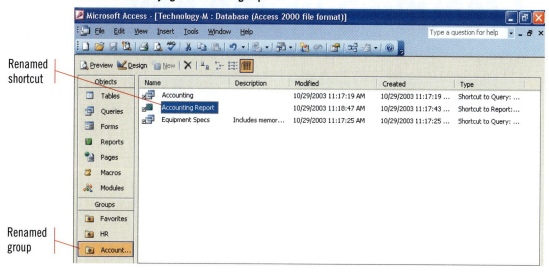

FIGURE M-9: Using shortcuts

JK123FL3

Edit made through shortcut

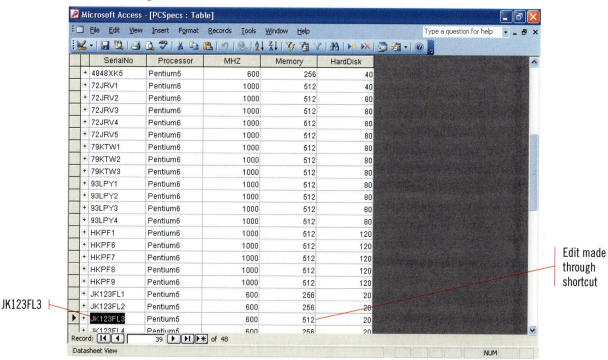

Clues to Use

Speech recognition—interface of the future?

Speech recognition means being able to talk to your computer, and having it respond appropriately to the instruction. For example, to display the query objects in the database window, it would be faster and easier for most people to say "Queries," than to click the Queries button on the Objects bar, especially if your hand wasn't already resting on the mouse. Office 2003 products, including Access 2003, support speech recognition, but you must have a microphone, install the speech recognition software, and train the software to recognize the sound of your unique voice. For more information on speech recognition, open Microsoft Office Access Help to the "About speech recognition" page.

Creating a Dialog Box

A **dialog box** is a special form used to display information or prompt a user for a choice. The purpose of creating a dialog box is to simplify the Access interface. For example, you might create a dialog box to give the user an easy-to-use list of reports to view or print. To make a form look like a dialog box, you modify form properties that affect its appearance and borders. 🎨 You want to create a dialog box to provide an easy way for users from the Accounting Department to print two reports.

STEPS

1. **Click Forms on the Objects bar, then double-click Create form in Design view**

   A dialog box form is not bound to a recordset from an underlying table or query, and therefore doesn't use the form's Record Source property. You place unbound controls on a dialog box such as labels and command buttons to provide the user information and choices.

2. **Click the Toolbox button 🛠 on the Form Design toolbar (if the Toolbox is not already visible), click the Command Button button ▭ on the Toolbox, then click the ⁺▭ mouse pointer in the upper-left corner of the form**

   The **Command Button Wizard** shown in Figure M-10 organizes over 30 of the most common command button actions within six categories.

   > **TROUBLE**
   > Make sure that the Control Wizards button 🔧 is selected on the Toolbox to start the Command Button Wizard.

3. **Click Report Operations in the Categories list, click Preview Report in the Actions list, click Next, click Accounting as the report choice, click Next, click the Text option button, press [Tab], type Equipment List, click Next, type Equip in the button name text box, then click Finish**

   The command button appears in Form Design View, as shown in Figure M-11. The name of the command button appears in the Object box on the Formatting (Form/Report toolbar).

   > **TROUBLE**
   > Every command button must be given a unique name that is referenced in underlying Visual Basic for Applications (VBA) code. Deleting a command button from Design View does not delete the underlying code, so each new button name must be different, even if the button has been deleted.

4. **Click ▭, click ⁺▭ below the first command button, click Report Operations in the Categories list, click Preview Report in the Actions list, click Next, click Accounting Manufacturer, click Next, click the Text option button, press [Tab], type Manufacturer List, click Next, type Mfg, then click Finish**

   With the command buttons in place, you modify form properties to make the form look like a dialog box.

5. **Double-click the Form Selector button to open the form's property sheet, click the Format tab, then double-click the Border Style property to change it from Sizable to Dialog**

   The **Border Style** property determines the appearance of the outside border of the form. The **Dialog** option for the Border Style property indicates that the form will have a thick border and may not be maximized, minimized, or resized. In a dialog box, there is no need for navigation buttons, so you will remove them from this form using the **Navigation Buttons** property.

6. **Double-click the Records Selector property to change it from Yes to No, then double-click the Navigation Buttons property to change it from Yes to No**

7. **Close the property sheet, restore, then resize the form and Form Design window so it is approximately 3" wide by 2" tall, click the Save button 💾, enter Accounting Reports as the form name, click OK, then click the Form View button 🖼**

   The dialog box should look similar to Figure M-12.

8. **Click the Manufacturer List command button**

   Clicking the Manufacturer List command button displays the Accounting Manufacturer report.

9. **Close the Accounting Manufacturer report, then close the Accounting Reports form**

FIGURE M-10: Command Button Wizard

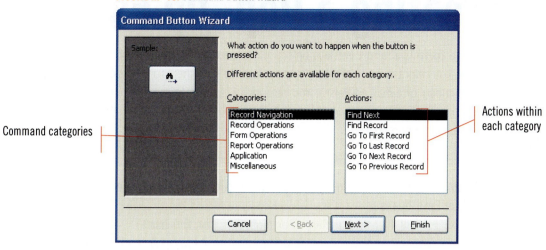

Command categories

Actions within
each category

FIGURE M-11: Adding a command button

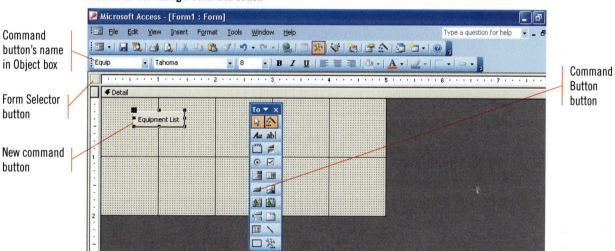

Command
button's name
in Object box

Form Selector
button

New command
button

Command
Button
button

FIGURE M-12: The final dialog box in Form View

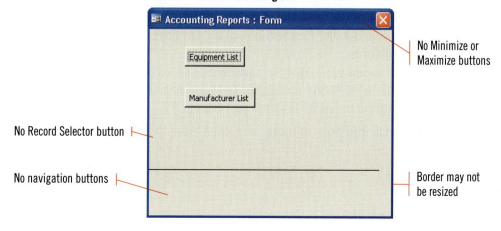

No Minimize or
Maximize buttons

No Record Selector button

No navigation buttons

Border may not
be resized

Creating a Pop-up Form

A **pop-up form** is a form that stays on top of other open forms, even when another form is active. For example, you might want to create a pop-up form to give the user easy access to reference lists such as phone numbers or e-mail addresses. You can open a pop-up form with a command button. You create a pop-up form to access employee e-mail information. You add a command button to the Employees form to open the pop-up form.

STEPS

1. **Double-click Create form by using wizard, click the Tables/Queries list arrow, then click Table: Employees**

   You want to add three fields to the pop-up form, First, Last, and Email.

2. **Double-click First, double-click Last, double-click Email, click Next, click the Tabular option button, click Next, click Standard for the style, click Next, type Email Info for the title of the form, then click Finish**

   The Email Info form opens in Form View, as shown in Figure M-13. You change a form into a pop-up form by changing form properties in Form Design View.

3. **Click the Design View button, double-click the Form Selector button to open the property sheet, click the Other tab, double-click the Pop Up property to change it from No to Yes, close the property sheet, save, then close the form**

   You want to open the Email Info pop-up form with a command button on the Employees form.

4. **Right-click the Employees form, then click Design View on the shortcut menu**

   The Employees form contains four bound fields: Last, First, Department, and Title, as well as a subform that displays the equipment assigned to that employee.

QUICK TIP

If the field list is in the way, drag its title bar to move it or click the Field List button on the Form Design toolbar to toggle it off.

5. **Point to the right edge of the form, then drag the ✛ mouse pointer to the 6.5" mark on the horizontal ruler**

   You want to put the command button in the upper-right corner of the form.

6. **Click the Command Button button on the Toolbox toolbar, click ⁺▢ to the right of the Title text box, click Form Operations in the Categories list, click Open Form in the Actions list, click Next, click the Email Info form, click Next, click Next to accept the "...show all the records" option, click the Text option button, press [Tab], type E-mail Addresses, click Next, type Email as the name of the button, click Finish, then move and resize the new command button as needed**

   Your screen should look similar to Figure M-14.

7. **Click the Form View button, click the Email command button, then move and resize the Email Info window so that your screen looks like Figure M-15**

   Pop-up forms are often used to display reference information. They can be used just like any other form.

8. **Double-click Maria in the First text box of the Employees form, type Mary, then click in the Employees subform**

   The Email Info pop-up form stayed "on top" even though you were working in the Employees form. The change from "Maria" to "Mary" made in the Employees form also appears in the Email Info form because both forms are tied to the underlying Employee table.

9. **Close the Email Info pop-up form, save, then close the Employees form**

FIGURE M-13: Email Info pop-up form

FIGURE M-14: Adding a command button to the Employees form

Form selector button

6.5" mark on the ruler

New command button

Command Button button

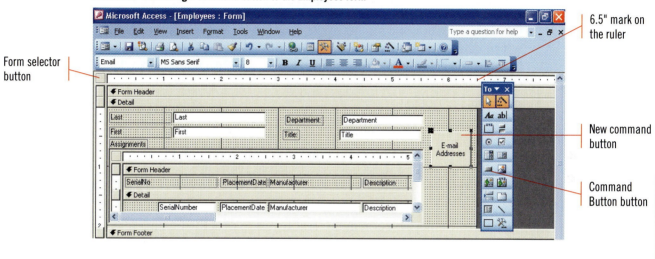

FIGURE M-15: The final form and pop-up form

Employees form

Command button

Subform

Email Info pop-up form

Maria

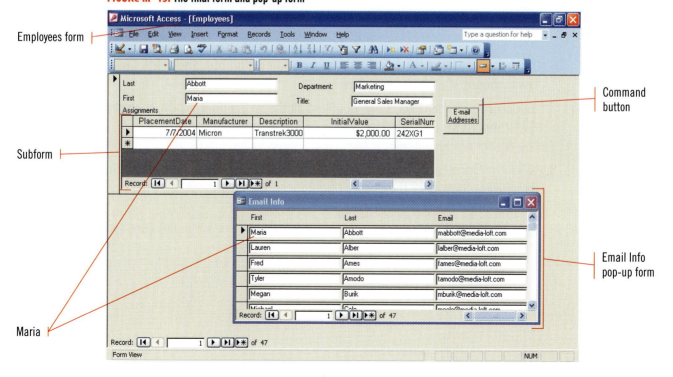

Creating a Switchboard

A **switchboard** is a special Access form that uses command buttons to simplify and secure the database. Switchboards are created and modified by using a special Access tool called the **Switchboard Manager**. Using the Switchboard Manager, you can create sophisticated switchboard forms without having advanced form development skills. ▓▓▓ You create a switchboard form to make the Technology-M database easier to navigate.

TROUBLE ▶

If you need to delete your Switchboard form and start over, you must first delete the Switchboard Items table before you can create the switchboard from scratch.

1. **Click Tools on the menu bar, point to Database Utilities, click Switchboard Manager, then click Yes when prompted to create a switchboard**

   The Switchboard Manager dialog box opens and presents the options for the first switchboard page. A switchboard page may contain no more than eight command buttons, so you may need to create multiple pages and link them together, depending on how many choices you want to provide through the switchboard system. Each new switchboard page you create is listed in the Switchboard Pages list of this dialog box. One switchboard page must be designated as the **default switchboard**, and is the first switchboard in the database used to link to additional switchboard pages as needed. Your first switchboard page will have only two command buttons, so you will add them to the default switchboard page.

2. **Click Edit**

   The Edit Switchboard Page dialog box opens. At this point, the switchboard page does not contain any items.

3. **Click New**

   The Edit Switchboard Item dialog box opens, prompting you for three pieces of information: Text (a label on the switchboard form that identifies the corresponding command button), Command (which corresponds to a database action), and Switchboard (which further defines the command button action).

4. **Type Open Employees Form in the Text text box, click the Command list arrow, click Open Form in Edit Mode, click the Form list arrow, then click Employees**

   The Edit Switchboard Item dialog box should look like Figure M-16.

5. **Click OK to add the first command button to the switchboard, click New, type Accounting Reports in the Text text box, click the Command list arrow, click Open Form in Edit Mode, click the Form list arrow, click Accounting Reports, then click OK**

   The Edit Switchboard Page dialog box should look like Figure M-17. Each entry in this dialog box represents a command button that will appear on the final switchboard.

6. **Click Close to close the Edit Switchboard Page dialog box, then click Close to close the Switchboard Manager dialog box**

7. **Click Forms on the Objects bar, double-click the Switchboard form, then click the Switchboard Restore Window button (if it is maximized)**

   The finished switchboard opens in Form View, as shown in Figure M-18.

8. **Click the Open Employees Form command button on the Switchboard, close the Employees form, click the Accounting Reports command button, then close the Accounting Reports dialog box**

   Switchboard forms provide a fast and easy way to help users work with just those objects they need in a database.

FIGURE M-16: Adding an item to a switchboard page

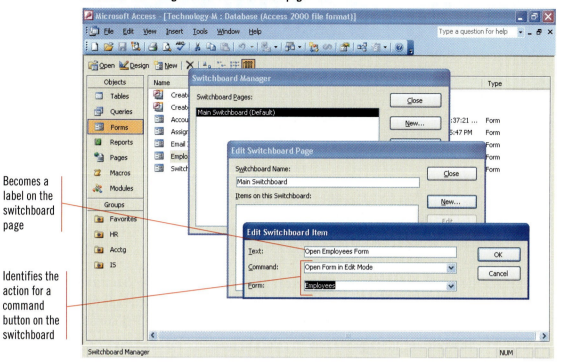

Becomes a label on the switchboard page

Identifies the action for a command button on the switchboard

FIGURE M-17: Edit Switchboard Page dialog box

Two switchboard items

FIGURE M-18: Switchboard form

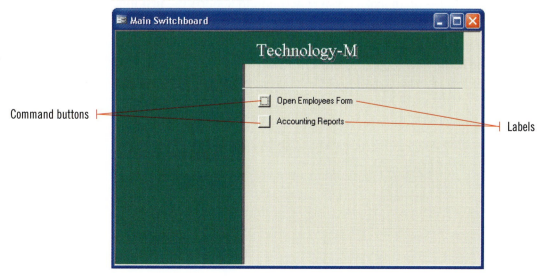

Command buttons

Labels

Modifying a Switchboard

Always use the Switchboard Manager to add, delete, move, and edit the command buttons and labels on a switchboard form. Use Form Design View to make formatting modifications such as changing form colors, adding clip art, or changing the switchboard title. ▓▓▓ Kristen is happy with the initial switchboard form you created, but she would like to improve it by changing the title, colors, and order of the command buttons. You use Form Design View to make the formatting changes and the Switchboard Manager to change the order of the buttons.

STEPS

1. **Click the Design View button ⬐ on the Form View toolbar, then click the teal rectangle on the left of the Detail section**

   The teal areas on the left and top portion of the Switchboard are actually filled rectangles, added to provide color. You can modify them just as you would modify any clip art object.

2. **Click the Fill/Back Color button list arrow ⬐ on the Formatting (Form/Report) toolbar, click the yellow box (fourth row, third column), click the teal rectangle on the top of the Detail section, click ⬐, then click the red box (third row, first column)**

3. **Click the white Technology-M label to select it, point to the edge, use the ✋ mouse pointer to drag the white Technology-M label up, click the gray Technology-M label to select it, then press [Delete]**

   The modified switchboard should look like Figure M-19.

4. **Click the Label button 𝐀𝐚 on the Toolbox toolbar, click the yellow rectangle, type your name, then press [Enter]**

   You use Form Design View to modify colors, clip art, and labels. Notice that the text describing each command button does not appear in Form Design View. This text and other information about the command buttons on the Switchboard form are stored in a table called Switchboard Items.

5. **Click the Save button 🖫 on the Form Design toolbar, close the switchboard, click Tools on the menu bar, point to Database Utilities, click Switchboard Manager, then click Edit**

   You use the Switchboard Manager to add or modify the command buttons on the switchboard, including the text that accompanies command buttons.

6. **Click Accounting Reports, click Edit, click to the left of the A in the Text text box, type Preview, press [Spacebar], then click OK**

   You can change the order of the command buttons from the Edit Switchboard Page dialog box.

7. **Click Move Up to make Preview Accounting Reports the first item in the switchboard, click Close, then click Close**

8. **Double-click the Switchboard form to open it in Form View, click the Print button 🖨 on the Form View toolbar to print the Switchboard, close the switchboard, then exit Access**

   The final switchboard should look like Figure M-20.

FIGURE M-19: Switchboard in Form Design View

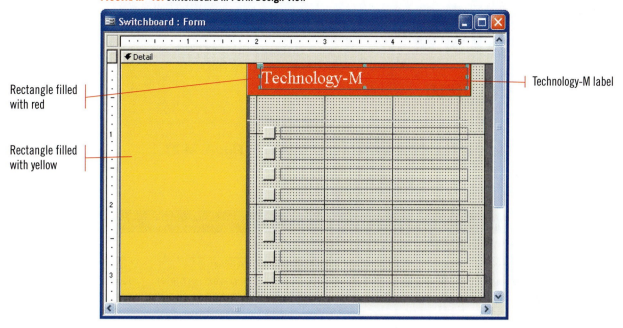

Rectangle filled with red

Rectangle filled with yellow

Technology-M label

FIGURE M-20: Final switchboard

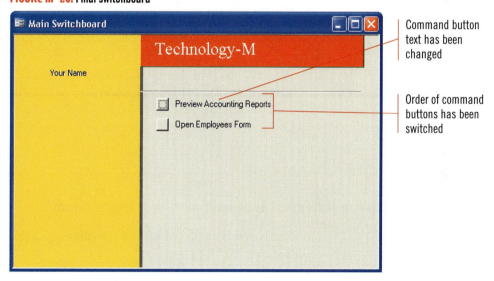

Command button text has been changed

Order of command buttons has been switched

Clues to Use

The Northwind database

Microsoft provides a sample database with Access 2003 called **Northwind.mdb** that illustrates how to use Access switchboards and dialog boxes. To open the Northwind database, click Help on the menu bar, point to Sample Databases, then click the Northwind Sample Database. If this is the first time the database has been opened, you may be prompted to install it. Northwind not only contains sample switchboard forms, but it is a robust relational database that provides many useful sample objects of all types.

Practice

▼ CONCEPTS REVIEW

Identify each element of the database window shown in Figure M-21.

FIGURE M-21

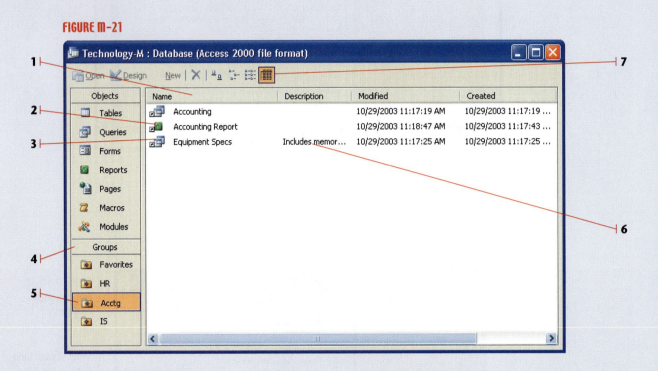

Match each term with the statement that best describes its function.

8. Pop-up form
9. Northwind
10. Name AutoCorrect
11. Documenter
12. Switchboard
13. Shortcut

a. Creates reports on the properties and relationships among the objects in your database

b. Pointer to database objects

c. Stays on top of other open forms, even when another form is active

d. Uses command buttons to simplify access to database objects

e. Sample database used to illustrate many Access features, including switchboards

f. Fixes discrepancies between references to field names, controls on forms and reports, and object names

Select the best answer from the following list of choices.

14. **Which View button do you use to see the date that the object was created?**
    a. Small Icons
    b. List
    c. Details
    d. Date

15. **Which feature helps organize objects in the database window?**
    a. Documenter
    b. Renamer
    c. Groups
    d. Switchboard Manager

16. **If you wanted to add a command button to a switchboard, which view or tool would you use?**
    a. Form Design View
    b. Report Design View
    c. Switchboard Analyzer
    d. Switchboard Manager

17. **Which item would *not* help you organize the Access objects that the Human Resources (HR) Department most often uses?**
    a. A report that lists all HR employees
    b. A switchboard that provides command buttons to the appropriate HR objects
    c. A dialog box with command buttons that reference the most commonly used HR forms and reports
    d. An HR group with shortcuts to the HR objects

18. **Northwind is the name of a sample:**
    a. Database.
    b. Switchboard form.
    c. Dialog box.
    d. Pop-up form.

19. **A dialog box is which type of object?**
    a. Form
    b. Table
    c. Report
    d. Macro

20. **A switchboard is which type of object?**
    a. Form
    b. Table
    c. Report
    d. Macro

21. **If you wanted to modify the text that identifies each command button on the switchboard, which view or tool would you use?**
    a. Form Design View
    b. Table Design View
    c. Documenter
    d. Switchboard Manager

22. **If you wanted to change the clip art on a switchboard, which view or tool would you use?**
    a. Form Design View
    b. Form View
    c. Switchboard Documenter
    d. Switchboard Manager

▼ SKILLS REVIEW

1. **Work with objects.**
   a. Open the **Basketball-M.mdb** database, then maximize the database window.
   b. Click the Details button to view the details, then click Reports on the Objects bar.
   c. Resize the columns to best view the information about each report, then add **Forwards and Guards** to the Description property for the Player Field Goal Stats report.
   d. Click Queries on the Objects bar, then rename Games Query to **Scores**.
   e. Open the Games Summary Report in Design View, open the report property sheet, then check the Record Source property on the Data tab. Because the Games Summary Report was based on the former Games Query object, the new query name, Scores, should appear in the Record Source property if Name AutoCorrect is selected. (*Hint*: Click Tools on the menu bar, click Options, then click the General tab to check the Name AutoCorrect options.)
   f. Close the property sheet, then close the Games Summary Report.

2. Use the Documenter.

   a. Click Tools on the menu bar, point to Analyze, then click Documenter.

   b. Select all tables and the Games Summary Report. Select the Names, Data Types, and Sizes option in the Print Table Definition dialog box.

   c. Watch the status bar to track the progress of the Documenter.

   d. Print the first and last page of the report. Write your name on the printout.

   e. Close the report created by Documenter without saving it.

3. Group objects.

   a. Create a new group named **Forwards**.

   b. Create shortcuts for the Forward Field Goals query and the Forward Field Goal Stats report in the Forwards group.

   c. Create a new group named **Guards**.

   d. Create shortcuts for the Guard Field Goals query and Guard Field Goal Stats report in the Guards group.

4. Modify shortcuts and groups.

   a. Rename the Forward Field Goal Stats report shortcut in the Forwards group to **Forward FG Report**.

   b. Rename the Forward Field Goals query shortcut in the Forwards group to **Forward FG Query**.

   c. Rename the Guard Field Goal Stats report shortcut in the Guards group to **Guard FG Report**.

   d. Rename the Guard Field Goals query shortcut in the Guards group to **Guard FG Query**.

   e. Double-click the Forward FG Query shortcut in the Forwards group, then enter your name to replace Amy Hodel on any record where her name appears.

   f. Print the datasheet, save, then close the Forward Field Goals query.

5. Create a dialog box.

   a. Start a new form in Form Design View.

   b. Add a command button to the upper-left corner of the form using the Command Button Wizard. Select Report Operations from the Categories list, select Preview Report from the Actions list, then select the Games Summary Report.

   c. Type **Preview Games Summary Report** as the text for the button, then type **GamesReport** for the button name.

   d. Add a second command button below the first to preview the Player Field Goal Stats report.

   e. Type **Preview Player FG Stats** as the text for the button, then type **PlayersReport** for the button name.

   f. Below the two buttons, add a label to the form with your name.

   g. In the property sheet for the form, change the Border Style property of the form to Dialog, the Record Selectors property to No, and the Navigation Buttons property to No.

FIGURE M-22

   h. Close the property sheet, restore the form (if it is maximized), resize the form and Form Design View window until it is approximately 3" wide by 3" tall, then save the form as **Team Reports**.

   i. Open the Team Reports form in Form View, test the buttons, then print the form. Your Team Reports form should be similar to Figure M-22.

   j. Close the Team Reports form.

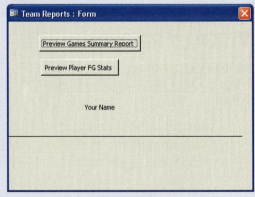

6. Create a pop-up form.

   a. Using the Form Wizard, create a form with the following fields from the Players table: First, Last, and PlayerNo.

   b. Use a Tabular layout, a Standard style, and title the form **Player Popup**.

   c. In Design View of the Player Popup form, resize the First and Last labels and text boxes to about half of their current width.

   d. Move the Last and PlayerNo labels and text boxes next to the First label and text box so that the entire form can be narrowed to no larger than 3" wide. Resize the form to 3" wide.

   e. Open the property sheet for the Player Popup form, change the Pop Up property to Yes, then close the property sheet.

   f. Save, then close the Player Popup form.

▼ SKILLS REVIEW (CONTINUED)

g. Open the Team Reports form in Form Design View, then add a command button to the bottom of the form using the Command Button Wizard.

h. In the Command Button Wizard, select the Form Operations category, the Open Form action, and the Player Popup form to open. The form should be opened to show all of the records.

i. Type **Open Player Pop-up** as the text for the button, then name the button **PlayerPopup**.

j. Save the Team Reports form, then open it in Form View. Click the Open Player Pop-up command button to test it. Test the other buttons as well. The Player Pop-up form should stay on top of all other forms and reports until you close it.

k. Save, then close all open forms and reports.

7. **Create a switchboard.**

a. Start the Switchboard Manager, and click Yes to create a new switchboard.

b. Click Edit to edit the Main Switchboard, then click New to add the first item to it.

c. Type **Select a Team Report** as the Text entry for the first command button, select Open Form in Add Mode for the Command, select Team Reports for the Form, then click OK to add the first command button to the switchboard.

d. Click New to add a second item to the switchboard. Type **Open Player Entry Form** as the Text entry, select Open Form in Add Mode for the Command, select Player Entry Form for the Form, then click OK to add the second command button to the switchboard.

e. Close the Edit Switchboard manager dialog box, then close the Switchboard Manager dialog box. Open the Switchboard form and click both command buttons to make sure they work. Notice that when you open the Player Entry Form in Add Mode (rather than using the Open Form in Edit Mode action within the Switchboard Manager), the navigation buttons indicate that you can only add a new record, and not edit an existing one.

f. Close all open forms, including the Switchboard form.

8. **Modify a switchboard.**

a. Open the Switchboard Manager, then click Edit to edit the Main Switchboard.

b. Click the Open Player Entry Form item, then click Edit.

c. Select Open Form in Edit Mode for the Command, select Player Entry Form for the Form, then click OK.

d. Move the Open Player Entry Form item above the Select a Team Report item, then close the Switchboard Manager.

FIGURE M-23

e. In Form Design View of the Switchboard form, delete both the white and gray Basketball–M labels, add a label with the name of your favorite team's name to the top of the form, then add a label with your own name to the left side of the form. Format the labels with a color and size that makes them easy to read in Form View.

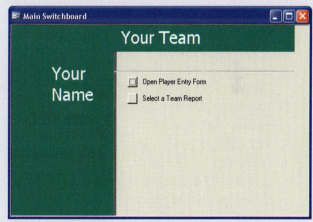

f. View the modified switchboard in Form View, as shown in Figure M-23, then test the buttons. Notice the difference in the Open Player Entry Form button (the Player Entry Form opens in Edit Mode versus Add Mode).

g. Save, print, then close the Switchboard form.

h. Close the Basketball-M.mdb database, then exit Access.

▼ INDEPENDENT CHALLENGE 1

As the manager of a real estate office, you have created a database to track local real estate agencies, agents, and property listings. You want to create a group to organize the database objects used by the realtors. You also want to document the database's relationships.

a. Start Access, then open the database **RealEstate-M.mdb** from the drive and folder where your Data Files are stored.

b. Create a new group named **Agents**.

▼ INDEPENDENT CHALLENGE 1 (CONTINUED)

c. Add the following shortcuts to the Agents group: Agency Information form, Listings Entry Form, Agent List report, and Property List report.

d. Test all of the shortcuts to make sure that they open the object they point to, then close all open objects.

e. Start the Documenter. On the Current Database tab, click the Relationships check box, then click OK.

f. Print the Documenter's report, then close it. Write your name on the printout.

Advanced Challenge Exercise

■ Create a switchboard form with the following four command buttons in the following order:

Text	Command	Form or Report
Open Agency Information Form	Open Form in Edit Mode	Agency Information
Open Listings Entry Form	Open Form in Edit Mode	Listings Entry Form
Open Agent List Report	Open Report	Agent List
Open Property List Report	Open Report	Property List

■ Delete the RealEstate-M labels on the switchboard and insert a label that reads **Your Name's Real Estate Agency**.

■ Save, print, then close the switchboard form.

g. Close the RealEstate-M.mdb database, then exit Access.

▼ INDEPENDENT CHALLENGE 2

As the manager of a real estate office, you have created a database to track local real estate agencies, agents, and property listings. You want to create a new dialog box to make it easier to preview the reports within your database.

a. Start Access, then open the database **RealEstate-M.mdb** from the drive and folder where your Data Files are stored.

b. Start a new form in Form Design View.

c. Using the Command Button Wizard, add a command button to the form. Select Report Operations from the Categories list, select Preview Report from the Actions list, then select the Agent List report.

d. Type **Agent List** as the text for the button, then type **AgentList** for the button name.

e. Using the Command Button Wizard, add a second command button under the first. Select Report Operations from the Categories list, select Preview Report from the Actions list, then select the Property List report.

f. Type **Property List** as the text for the button, then type **PropertyList** for the button name.

g. Using the Command Button Wizard, add a third command button under the second. Select Form Operations from the Categories list, and select Close Form from the Actions list.

h. Use the Exit picture on the button, then type **Close** as the meaningful name for the button.

FIGURE M-24

i. Add a label to the form with your name.

j. Open the property sheet for the form, change Border Style property to Dialog, the Record Selectors property to No, and the Navigation Buttons property to No.

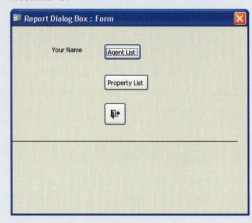

k. Close the property sheet, restore the form (if it is maximized), resize the form and Form Design View window so they are approximately 3" wide by 3" tall, then save the form as **Report Dialog Box**.

l. Open the Report Dialog Box form in Form View, test the buttons, then print the form. It should look similar to Figure M-24.

m. Close the Report Dialog Box form, close the RealEstate-M.mdb database, then exit Access.

▼ INDEPENDENT CHALLENGE 3

As the manager of a real estate office, you have created a database to track local real estate agencies, agents, and property listings. You want to create a pop-up form to provide agent information. You want to add a command button to the Listings Entry Form to open the pop-up form.

a. Start Access, then open the database **RealEstate-M.mdb** from the drive and folder where your Data Files are stored.
b. Use the Form Wizard to create a form with the AgentNo, AgentFirst, AgentLast, and AgentPhone fields from the Agents table.
c. Use a Tabular layout, a Standard style, and type **Agent Popup** for the form title.
d. In Form Design View of the Agent Popup form, resize the AgentNo, AgentFirst, and AgentLast labels and text boxes to about half their current width.
e. Move the AgentFirst, AgentLast, and AgentPhone labels and text boxes next to each other on the left side of the form, then resize the form to no wider than 4.5".
f. Open the property sheet for the form, then change the Pop Up property to Yes.
g. Save, then close the Agent Popup form.
h. In Form Design View of the Listings Entry Form, open the Form Header section about 0.5", then use the Command Button Wizard to create a command button on the right side of the Form Header.
i. Select Form Operations from the Categories list, select Open Form from the Actions list, select the Agent Popup form, and open the form and show all of the records.
j. Type **Agent Popup** as the text for the button, then type **Agents** for the button name.
k. Add a label to the left side of the Form Header with your name.
l. Save the Listings Entry Form, open it in Form View, then click the Agent Popup command button.
m. Move through the records of the Listings Entry Form. The Agent Popup form should stay on top of all other forms.

Advanced Challenge Exercise

- Create a second pop-up form using all of the fields of the Agencies table except for AgencyNo.
- Use a Tabular layout, a Standard style, and title the form **Agency Popup**.
- In Form Design View, resize and move the text boxes so that all of the information can be clearly viewed in Form View.
- Resize the form to be about 5.5" wide by about 3" tall.
- Change the Pop Up property to Yes, then save the form.
- In Design View of the Listings Entry Form, add another command button to open the Agency Popup form and show all of the records.
- Type **Agency Popup** as the text for the button, then type **Agencies** for the button name.
- Move, resize, and align the controls in the Form Header as needed.
- Open the form in Form View, and test both command buttons.

n. Close any open pop-up forms, then print the first record in the Listings Entry form.
o. Close all open forms, close the RealEstate-M.mdb database, then exit Access.

▼ INDEPENDENT CHALLENGE 4

The larger your database becomes, the more important it is to document it properly so that others can also work with it successfully. Some companies require that you use an adopted set of naming standards when you create new fields, objects, and controls so that other database developers can more readily understand and modify a database they have not created. In this Independent Challenge you will search for database naming standards.

a. Connect to the Internet, go *www.google.com*, *www.yahoo.com*, or your own favorite search engine, then search for Web sites with the key words **Access naming conventions**. You might also try searching for the **Leszynski Naming Convention**, **object naming convention**, or **database naming convention**.
b. Find print two different reference pages that describe naming conventions for fields, objects, or controls.
c. Find and print two different discussions of the advantages of adopting a common naming convention for all database development for your company.

▼ VISUAL WORKSHOP

As the manager of a tourism company that promotes travel to European countries, you have created an Access database called **Baltic-M.mdb** that tracks events at various European cities. Create a switchboard form to give the users an easy interface, as shown in Figure M-25. All of the command buttons on the switchboard access a report for the country they reference. Be sure to add your own name as a label to the switchboard, and include any other formatting improvements that you desire. Print the switchboard.

FIGURE M-25

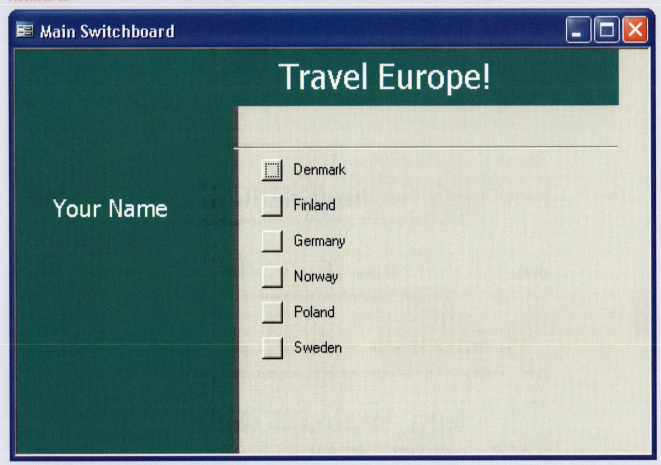

UNIT
N
Access 2003

Creating Macros

OBJECTIVES

Understand macros

Create a macro

Modify actions and arguments

Create a macro group

Set conditional expressions

Work with events

Customize toolbars

Troubleshoot macros

If you have a SAM user profile, you may have access to hands-on instruction, practice, and assessment of the skills covered in this unit. Log in to your SAM account and go to your assignments page to see what your instructor has assigned.

A **macro** is a database object that stores Access actions. When you **run** a macro, you execute the stored set of actions. **Actions** are the tasks that you want the macro to perform. Access provides about 50 actions from which to choose when creating a macro. A repetitive Access task such as printing a report, opening a form, or exporting data is a good candidate for a macro. Automating routine and complex tasks by using macros builds efficiency, accuracy, and flexibility into your database.  Kristen Fontanelle, a network administrator at MediaLoft, has identified several Access tasks that are repeated on a regular basis and has asked you to help her automate these processes with macros.

Understanding Macros

A macro object may contain one or more actions, the tasks that you want Access to perform. Actions are entered in **Macro Design View**, the window in which you build and modify macros. Each action has a specified set of arguments. **Arguments** provide additional information on how to carry out the action. For example, the OpenForm action contains six arguments, including Form Name (identifies which form to open) and View (determines whether the form should be opened in Form View or Design View). After choosing the macro action you want from a list, the associated arguments for that action automatically appear in the lower pane of Macro Design View. You study the major benefits of using macros, macro terminology, and the components of Macro Design View before building your first macro.

DETAILS

The major benefits of using macros include:

- Saving time by automating routine tasks
- Increasing accuracy by ensuring that tasks are executed consistently
- Improving the functionality and ease of use of forms by using macros connected to command buttons
- Ensuring data accuracy in forms by using macros to respond to data entry errors
- Automating data transfers such as exporting data to an Excel workbook
- Creating your own customized environment by using macros to customize toolbars and menus

Macro terminology:

- A **macro** is an Access object that stores a series of actions to perform one or more tasks.
- Each task that you want the macro to perform is called an **action**. Each macro action occupies a single row in Macro Design View.
- **Macro Design View** is the window in which you create a macro, as shown in Figure N-1. See Table N-1 for a description of Macro Design View components.
- **Arguments** are properties of an action that provide additional information on how the action should execute.
- A **macro group** is an Access macro object that stores more than one macro. The macros in a macro group run independently of one another, but are grouped together to organize multiple macros that have similar characteristics. For example, you may want to put all of the macros that print reports in one macro group.
- An **expression** is a combination of values, fields, and operators that result in a value.
- A **conditional expression** is an expression that results in either a true or false answer that determines whether a macro action will execute. For example, if the Country field contains a null value (nothing), you may want the macro to execute an action that sends the user a message to enter a value for that field.
- An **event** is something that happens on a form, window, toolbar, or datasheet—such as the click of a command button or an entry in a field—that can be used to initiate the execution of a macro.

FIGURE N-1: Macro Design View of a macro group

Macro Names button

Current row indicator identifies which action is selected

Arguments for selected action (Close)

Conditions button

Macro columns

Action list arrow

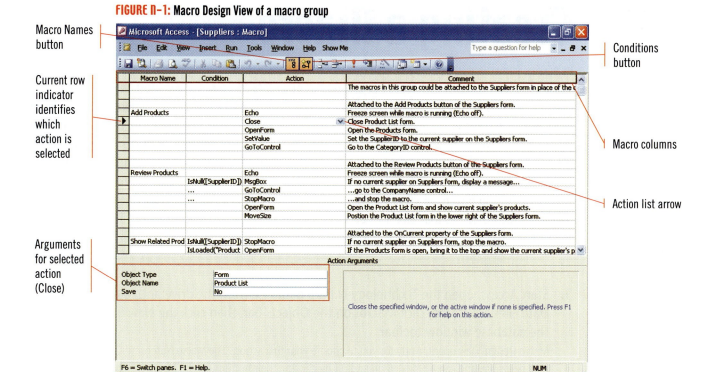

TABLE N-1: Macro Design View components

component	description
Macro Name column	Contains the names of individual macros within a macro group. If the macro object contains only one macro, it isn't necessary to use this column because you can run the macro by referring to the macro by the macro object's name. View this column by clicking the Macro Names button. The Macro Names button works as a toggle to open and close the Macro Name column.
Condition column	Contains conditional expressions that are evaluated either true or false. If true, the macro action on that row is executed. If false, the macro action on that row is skipped. View this column by clicking the Conditions button. The Conditions button works as a toggle to open and close the Condition column.
Action column	Contains the actions, or the tasks, that the macro executes when it runs.
Comment column	Contains optional explanatory text for each row.
Action Arguments pane	Displays the arguments for the selected action.
▶	Indicates which row is currently selected.

Access 2003

Creating a Macro

In Access, you create a macro by choosing a series of actions in Macro Design View that accomplish the job you want to automate. Therefore, to become proficient with Access macros, you must be comfortable with macro actions. Access provides more than 50 macro actions. Some of the most common actions are listed in Table N-2. In some software programs such as Microsoft Word or Microsoft Excel, you create a macro not by using a Macro Design View, but by using a "macro recorder" to save the keystrokes and mouse clicks used to perform a task. Another difference between Access and the other Microsoft Office products is that when you create a macro in Word or Excel, you create Visual Basic for Applications (VBA) statements. In Access, macros do not create VBA code, but after a macro is created, you can convert it to VBA if desired. Kristen observes that time can be saved opening the All Equipment report from the Employees form, so she asks you to create a macro to automate this task.

STEPS

1. **Start Access, open the Technology-N.mdb database from the drive and folder where your Data Files are stored, click Macros on the Objects bar, then click the New button on the database window toolbar**

   Macro Design View opens, ready for you to choose your first action. The Macro Name and Condition columns may be visible, and can be toggled on and off by clicking their buttons on the Macro Design toolbar. They are only needed if you are creating multiple macros in the same macro object or using conditional expressions.

2. **Click the Action list arrow, type o to quickly scroll to the actions that start with the letter "o", then click OpenReport**

   The OpenReport action is chosen for the first line, and the arguments that further define the OpenReport action appear in the Action Arguments pane in the lower half of Macro Design View. The OpenReport action has three required arguments: Report Name, View, and Window Mode. View and Window Mode have default values that may be modified. The Filter Name and Where Condition arguments are optional.

3. **Click the Report Name argument in the Action Arguments pane, click the Report Name list arrow, then click All Equipment**

   All of the report objects in the Technology-N.mdb database appear in the Report Name argument list.

4. **Click the View argument in the Action Arguments pane, click the View list arrow, then click Print Preview**

   Your screen should look like Figure N-2. Macros can be one or many actions long. In this case, the macro is only one action long and has no conditional expressions.

5. **Click the Save button on the Macro Design toolbar, type Preview All Equipment Report in the Macro Name text box, click OK, then close Macro Design View**

   The Technology-N.mdb database window shows the Print All Equipment Report object as a macro object.

6. **Click the Run button on the database window toolbar**

   The All Equipment report opens in Print Preview.

7. **Close the All Equipment preview window**

FIGURE N-2: Macro Design View with OpenReport action

OpenReport action

Report Name argument

View argument

Description of View argument

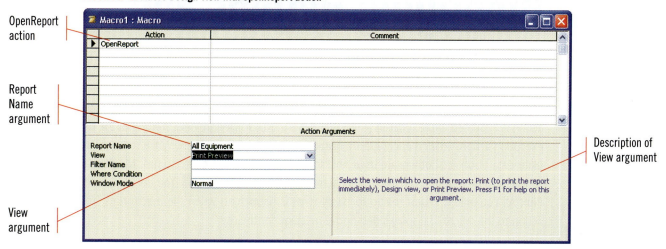

TABLE N-2: Common macro actions

subject area	macro action	description
Handling data in forms	ApplyFilter	Restricts the number of records that appear in the resulting form or report by applying limiting criteria
	FindRecord	Finds the first record that meets the criteria
	GoToControl	Moves the focus (where you are currently typing or clicking) to a specific field or control
	GoToRecord	Makes a specified record the current record
Executing menu options	RunCode	Runs a Visual Basic function (a series of programming statements that do a calculation or comparison and return a value)
	RunCommand	Carries out a specified menu command
	RunMacro	Runs a macro or attaches a macro to a custom menu command
	StopMacro	Stops the currently running macro
Importing/exporting data	TransferDatabase TransferSpreadsheet TransferText	Imports, links, or exports data between the current Microsoft Access database and another database, spreadsheet, or text file
Manipulating objects	Close	Closes a window
	Maximize	Enlarges the active window to fill the Access window
	OpenForm	Opens a form in Form View, Design View, Print Preview, or Datasheet View
	OpenQuery	Opens a select or crosstab query in Datasheet View, Design View, or Print Preview; runs an action query
	OpenReport	Opens a report in Design View or Print Preview, or prints the report
	OpenTable	Opens a table in Datasheet View, Design View, or Print Preview
	PrintOut	Prints the active object, such as a datasheet, report, form, or module
	SetValue	Sets the value of a field, control, or property
Miscellaneous	Beep	Sounds a beep tone through the computer's speaker
	MsgBox	Displays a message box containing a warning or an informational message
	SendKeys	Sends keystrokes directly to Microsoft Access or to an active Windows application

Access 2003

Modifying Actions and Arguments

Macros can contain as many actions as necessary to complete the process that you want to automate. Each action is evaluated in the order in which it appears in Macro Design View, starting at the top. A macro stops executing actions when it encounters a blank row in Macro Design View. While some macro actions manipulate data or objects, others are used only to make the database easier to use. **MsgBox** is a useful macro action because it displays an informational message to the user.  You decide to add an action to the Print All Equipment Report macro to clarify what is happening when the macro runs. You add a MsgBox action to the macro to display a descriptive message for the user.

STEPS

1. Click the Design button 🖼 on the database window toolbar

   The Preview All Equipment Report macro opens in Macro Design View.

2. Click the Action cell for the second row, click the Action list arrow, type m to quickly scroll to the actions that start with the letter "m", then click MsgBox

   Each action has its own arguments that further clarify what the action will do.

QUICK TIP
Press [F1] to display Help text for the action and argument currently selected.

3. Click the Message argument text box in the Action Arguments pane, then type Click the Print button to print this report

   The Message argument determines what text appears in the message box. By default, the Beep argument is set to "Yes" and the Type argument is set to "None".

4. Click the Type argument text box in the Action Arguments pane, read the description in the lower-right corner of Macro Design View, click the Type list arrow, then click Information

   The Type argument determines which icon will appear in the dialog box that is created by the MsgBox action.

5. Click the Title argument text box in the Action Arguments pane, then type To print this report. . .

   Your screen should look like Figure N-3. The Title argument specifies what text will display in the title bar of the resulting dialog box. If you leave the Title argument empty, the title bar of the resulting dialog box will display "Microsoft Office Access."

6. Click the Save button 🖫 on the Macro Design toolbar, then click the Run button ❗ on the Macro Design toolbar

   If your speakers are turned on, you should hear a beep, then the message box should appear, as shown in Figure N-4.

7. Click OK in the dialog box, close the All Equipment report, then close Macro Design View

MsgBox
action is
selected

Arguments
for MsgBox
action

Description
of the Title
argument

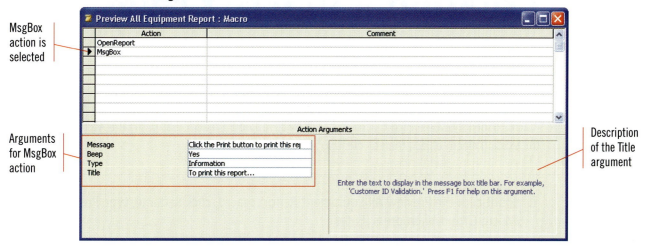

Title argument determines
the text in the title bar

Message argument
determines text

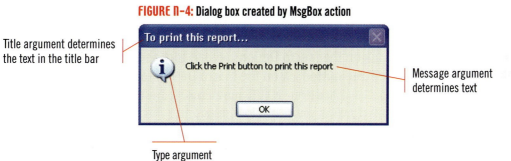

Type argument
determines icon

Access 2003

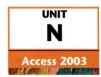
Creating a Macro Group

A **macro group** is a macro object that stores more than one macro. Macro groups are used to organize multiple macros that have similar characteristics, such as all the macros that print reports or all the macros that are used by the same form. When you put several macros in the same macro object to create a macro group, you must enter a unique name for each macro in the Macro Name column of the first action in that macro to identify where each macro starts. You add a macro that prints the Accounting Report to the existing macro object, thereby creating a macro group.

STEPS

1. **Right-click the Preview All Equipment Report macro, click Rename, type Preview Reports Macro Group, then press [Enter]**

   Object names should identify the object contents as clearly as possible.

2. **Right-click the Preview Reports Macro Group, click Design View on the shortcut menu, click the Macro Names button ▧ on the Macro Design toolbar, type Preview All Equipment in the Macro Name column, then press [Enter]**

   An individual macro in a macro group must be given a name in the Macro Name column.

3. **Click the Macro Name cell in the fourth row, type Preview Accounting Report, drag the column divider between the Macro Name and Action columns to the right using the ↔ mouse pointer, then press [Enter]**

   An individual macro in a macro group stops when it encounters a blank row, or when a new macro name is entered in the Macro Name column. Therefore, a blank row between macros is not required, but it helps clarify where macros start and stop even when the Macro Name column is not visible.

4. **Click the Action list arrow, scroll and click OpenReport, click in the Report Name argument in the Action Arguments pane, click the Report Name list arrow, click Accounting, click the View argument, click the View list arrow, then click Print Preview**

   Your screen should look like Figure N-5. One benefit of creating several macros in one macro group is that you can copy and paste actions from one macro to another.

5. **Click the row selector of the MsgBox action of the Preview All Equipment macro, click the Copy button ▤ on the Macro Design toolbar, click the row selector for the fifth row, then click the Paste button ▦ on the Macro Design toolbar**

   Your screen should look like Figure N-6. To run a macro (other than the first macro) from within a macro group in Macro Design View, you use the Tools menu.

6. **Click the Save button ▦, click Tools on the menu bar, point to Macro, click Run Macro, click the Macro Name list arrow in the Run Macro dialog box, click Preview Reports Macro Group.Preview Accounting Report, then click OK**

   Separating a specific macro within a macro group with a period is called dot notation. Dot notation is also used when developing modules with Visual Basic programming code.

7. **Click OK, then close the Accounting report and Macro Design View**

   The Preview Reports Macro Group now contains two macros.

FIGURE N-5: Creating a macro group

Macro names

Record selector button for the second row containing the MsgBox action

Drag the column divider to the right to resize columns

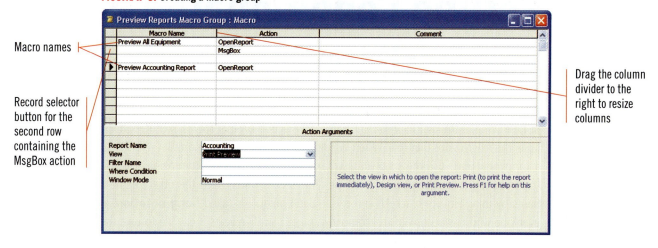

FIGURE N-6: Creating the Print Accounting Report macro

Record selector button for the fifth row

MsgBox action was pasted

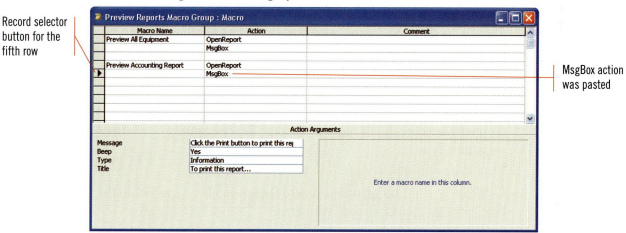

Clues to Use

Assigning a macro to a key combination

You can assign a key combination (such as [Ctrl][L]) to a macro by creating a macro group with the name **AutoKeys**. Enter the key combination in the Macro Names column for the first action of the associated macro. Any key combination assignments you make in the AutoKeys macro override those that Access has already specified.

Therefore, be sure to check the Keyboard Shortcuts information in the Microsoft Access Help system to make sure that the AutoKey assignment that you are creating doesn't override an Access quick keystroke that a user may already be using for another purpose.

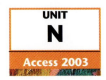

Setting Conditional Expressions

Conditional expressions are entered in the Condition column of Macro Design View. They result in a true or false value. If the condition evaluates true, the action on that row is executed. If the condition evaluates false, the macro skips that row. When building a conditional expression that refers to a value in a control on a form or report, use the following syntax: [Forms]![*formname*]![*controlname*] or [Reports]![*reportname*]! [*controlname*]. Separating the object type (Forms or Reports) from the object name and from the control name by using [square brackets] and exclamation points ! is called **bang notation**. At MediaLoft, everyone who has been with the company longer than five years is eligible to take their old PC equipment home as soon as it has been replaced. You use a conditional macro to help evaluate this information in a form.

STEPS

1. Click the New button on the database window toolbar, click the Conditions button on the Macro Design toolbar (if not already toggled on), right-click the Condition cell in the first row, click Zoom, then type [Forms]![Employees]![DateHired]<Date()-(5*365) in the Zoom dialog box

   The Zoom dialog box should look like Figure N-7. This conditional expression says, "Check the value in the DateHired control on the Employees form and evaluate true if that value is earlier than five years from today. Evaluate false if that value is not earlier than five years ago."

2. Click OK to close the Zoom dialog box, drag the Condition column divider to the right using ✛, click the Action cell for the first row, click the Action list arrow, then scroll and click SetValue

   The SetValue action has two arguments.

3. Click the Item argument text box in the Action Arguments pane, type [Forms]![Employees]![PCProgram], click the Expression text box in the Action Arguments pane, then type Yes

   Your screen should look like Figure N-8.

4. Click the Save button on the Macro Design toolbar, type 5PC in the Macro Name text box, click OK, then close the 5PC macro

   Test the macro using the Employees form.

5. Click Forms on the Objects bar, then double-click the Employees form

   The record for Maria Abbott, hired 3/1/1995, appears. You use the 5PC macro to determine whether the PC Program check box should be checked.

6. Click Tools on the menu bar, point to Macro, click Run Macro, verify that 5PC is in the Macro Name text box, then click OK

   After evaluating the date of this record and determining that this employee has been working at MediaLoft longer than five years, the PC Program check box was automatically checked (set to "Yes"), as shown in Figure N-9.

7. Click 3/1/1995 in the DateHired text box, click the Sort Descending button on the Form View toolbar, click Tools on the menu bar, point to Macro, click Run Macro, verify that 5PC is in the Macro Name text box, then click OK

   Because Fred Ames was not hired more than five years ago, the PC Program check box was not checked (set to "yes") when you ran the macro.

8. Close the Employees form

FIGURE N-7: Zoom dialog box

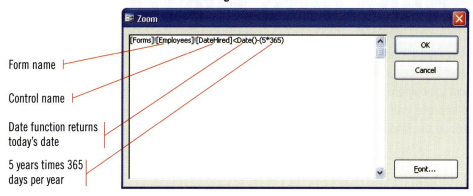

Form name

Control name

Date function returns today's date

5 years times 365 days per year

FIGURE N-8: Creating a conditional expression

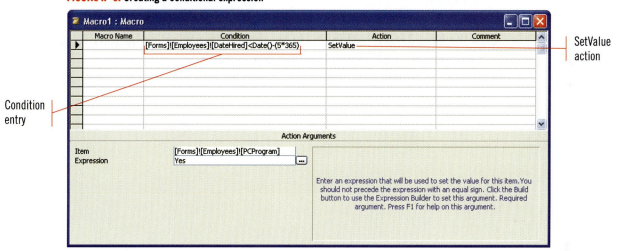

Condition entry

SetValue action

FIGURE N-9: Running the 5PC macro

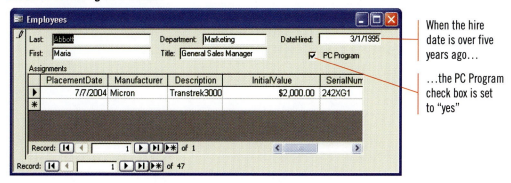

When the hire date is over five years ago…

…the PC Program check box is set to "yes"

Working with Events

An **event** is a specific activity that occurs within the database, such as clicking a command button, editing data, or opening or closing a form. Events can be triggered by the user, or by the database itself. By assigning a macro to an appropriate event, rather than running the macro from the Tools menu, you further automate and improve your database. Now that you have developed the 5PC macro, you will attach it to an event on the Employees form so that you don't have to run the macro for each record.

STEPS

1. **Right-click the Employees form, click Design View on the shortcut menu, then click the Properties button 🖰 to open the property sheet for the form**

   All objects, sections, and controls have a variety of events to which macros can be attached. Most event names are self-explanatory for that item, such as the On Click event (which occurs when that item is clicked).

2. **Click the Event tab, click the On Current list arrow, then click 5PC**

   Your screen should look like Figure N-10. The **On Current** event occurs when focus moves from one record to another, therefore the 5PC macro will automatically run as you move from record to record in the form.

3. **Click 🖰 to close the property sheet, then click the Form View button 🖻 on the Form View toolbar**

   The records are still sorted in descending order based on the DateHired dates.

4. **Click the Next Record button ▶ in the main form navigation buttons at least 15 times while observing the PC Program check box**

   For every DateHired value that is earlier than five years before today's date, the PC Program check box is automatically checked (set to "yes").

5. **Save, then close the Employees form**

Form properties sheet

Properties button

5PC macro assigned to On Current event

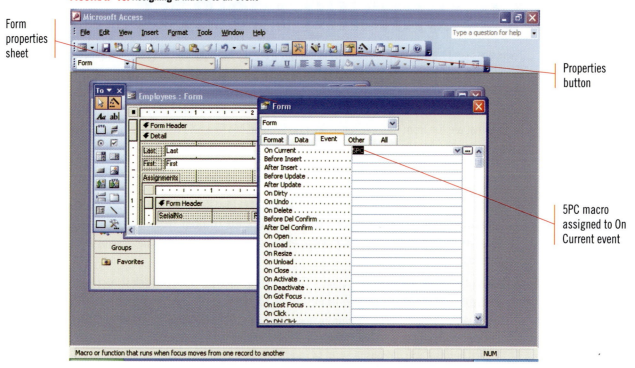

Clues to Use

Assigning a macro to a command button

A common way to run a macro from a form is to first add a command button to the form, and then run the macro from the command button. To do this, add a command button to the form using the Command Button Wizard. Select the Run Macro action from the Miscellaneous category. The selected macro is assigned to the **On Click** event for the command button, and runs when you click the command button in Form View.

Customizing Toolbars

There are many ways to run a macro: by clicking the Run button, by using the Tools menu, by assigning the macro to an event, or by assigning the macro to a toolbar, menu, or shortcut menu. The benefit of assigning a macro to a toolbar button instead of a command button on a form is that the toolbar can be made available to the user at all times, whereas a command button on a form is available only when that specific form is open. Macros that are run from multiple forms are good candidates for custom toolbars. You decide to create a new toolbar for the print macros.

STEPS

1. **Click Macros on the Objects bar, click the Preview Reports Macro Group, click Tools on the menu bar, point to Macro, then click Create Toolbar from Macro**

   The Preview Reports Macro Group toolbar appears on your screen. All of the macros in that group are automatically added to the toolbar.

2. **Drag the Preview Reports Macro Group toolbar title bar to dock it just below the Database toolbar, as shown in Figure N-11**

   Because this toolbar contains buttons for only two macros (the two found in the Preview Reports Macro Group), the entire name of each macro fits comfortably on the toolbar. If you wanted the toolbar to display several buttons, you'd probably want to shorten the text for each button, or use icons in order to fit all of the buttons on the toolbar.

3. **Right-click the Preview Reports Macro Group toolbar, click Customize on the shortcut menu, right-click the Preview All Equipment macro button on the Preview Reports Macro Group toolbar, then point to Change Button Image on the shortcut menu**

   Your screen should look like Figure N-12. The shortcut menu that allows you to modify toolbar button images and text is available only when the Customize dialog box is open.

4. **Click the Shoes icon on the icon palette, right-click the Preview All Equipment macro button again, then click Default Style on the shortcut menu**

   The Default Style for a button displays only the button image, not the text.

5. **Right-click the Preview Accounting Report macro button on the Preview Reports Macro Group toolbar, point to Change Button Image on the shortcut menu, click the Scales icon on the icon palette, right-click the Preview Accounting Report macro button, then click Default Style on the shortcut menu**

   Any image on any toolbar button can be edited to display the shape or color you desire.

6. **Right-click on the Preview Reports Macro Group toolbar, then click Edit Button Image**

   The Button Editor dialog box opens, which allows you to change the appearance of the picture pixel by pixel.

7. **Click the green box on the Colors palette, then click all 11 squares in the left scale, as shown in Figure N-13**

   With enough time and patience, you could create any number of unique button images.

8. **Click OK, then click Close to close the Customize dialog box**

   The new Preview Reports Macro Group toolbar can be turned on or off from anywhere within the database, just like any other toolbar. New buttons can be added or modified at any time.

9. **Point to, then point to on the Preview Reports Macro Group toolbar**

   Each button on the Preview Reports Macro Group toolbar has a ScreenTip like buttons on other toolbars.

FIGURE N-11: Preview Reports Macro Group toolbar

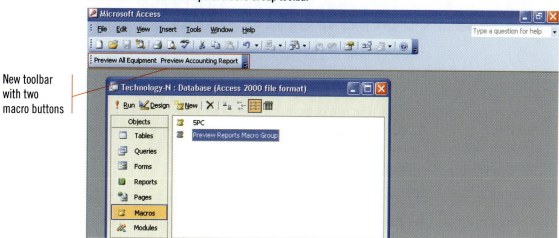

New toolbar with two macro buttons

FIGURE N-12: Customizing a button image

Customize dialog box

Scales icon

Shoes icon

FIGURE N-13: Button Editor dialog box

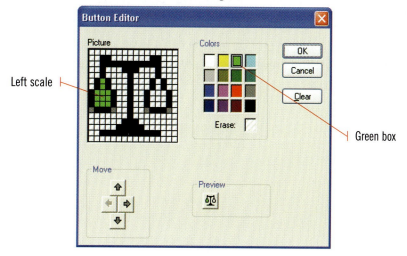

Left scale

Green box

Troubleshooting Macros

When macros don't execute properly, Access supplies several tools to debug them. **Debugging** means determining why the macro doesn't run correctly. It usually involves breaking a dysfunctional macro down into small pieces that can be individually tested. For example, you can **single step** a macro, which means to run it one line (one action) at a time to observe the effect of each specific action in the Macro Single Step dialog box. Another debugging technique is to disable a particular macro action(s) by entering false in the Condition cell for the action(s) that you want to temporarily skip. You use the Preview Reports Macro Group to learn debugging techniques.

STEPS

1. **Right-click Preview Reports Macro Group, click Design View on the shortcut menu, click the Single Step button on the Macro Design toolbar, then click the Run button on the Macro Design toolbar**

   The screen should look like Figure N-14, with the Macro Single Step dialog box open. This dialog box displays information including the name of the macro, whether the current action's condition is true, the action's name, and the action arguments. From the Macro Single Step dialog box you can step into the next macro action, halt execution of the macro, or continue running the macro without single stepping.

2. **Click Step in the Macro Single Step dialog box**

   Stepping into the second action lets the first action execute, and pauses the macro at the second action. The Macro Single Step dialog box now displays information about the second action.

3. **Click Step**

   The second action, the MsgBox action, executes, displaying the message box.

4. **Click OK, then close the All Equipment report**

   You can use the Condition column to temporarily ignore an action while you are debugging a macro.

5. **Click to stop single stepping, click the Conditions button on the Macro Design toolbar, click the Condition cell for the first row, then type False**

   Your screen should look like Figure N-15.

6. **Click the Save button on the Macro Design toolbar, then click**

   Because the Condition value is False for the OpenReport action, it did not execute.

7. **Click OK, double-click False in the Condition cell, then press [Delete]**

   You must delete a value to remove a condition—merely closing the Condition column does not delete or change the values stored in that column. To change the Preview All Equipment macro so that the All Equipment report opens in Print Preview the next time you run this macro, you must delete the False entry for the OpenReport action.

QUICK TIP
If you add your name to the Comment cell for any macro action, it will appear on the printout.

8. **Click File on the menu bar, click Print, then click OK in the Print Macro Definition dialog box**

9. **Save and close the Preview Reports Macro Group, close the Technology-N.mdb database, then exit Access**

FIGURE N-14: Single stepping through a macro

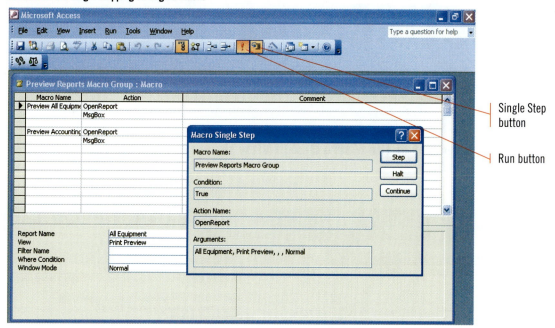

Single Step button

Run button

FIGURE N-15: Using a False condition

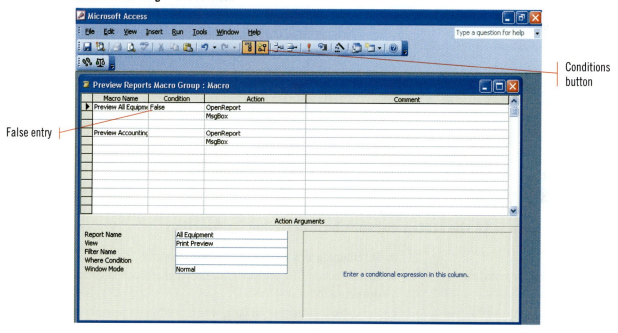

Conditions button

False entry

Clues to Use

Converting a macro to VBA

You can convert an existing Access macro to Visual Basic for Applications (VBA) code by selecting the macro in the database window, then choosing Save As from the File menu. In the Save As dialog box, click Module. The functionality of your macro will be converted to equivalent VBA statements. Those statements are stored in a module object, accessible by clicking the Modules button on the Objects bar in the database window.

Practice

▼ CONCEPTS REVIEW

Identify each element of the Macro Design View shown in Figure N-16.

FIGURE N-16

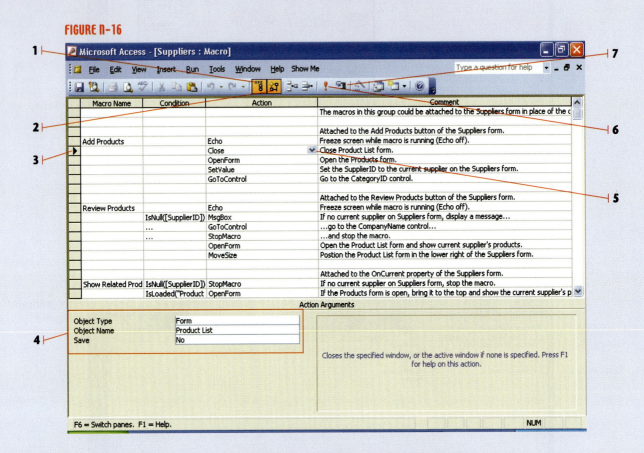

Match each term with the statement that best describes its function.

8. **Macro**
9. **Conditional expression**
10. **Argument**
11. **Debugging**
12. **Action**
13. **Event**

a. Determining why a macro doesn't run properly

b. Specific action that occurs within the database such as clicking a button or opening a form

c. Evaluates as either true or false, which determines whether Access executes that action or not

d. Individual step that you want the Access macro to perform

e. Access object that stores one or more actions that perform one or more tasks

f. Provides additional information to define how an Access action will perform

Select the best answer from the list of choices.

14. Which of the following is *not* a major benefit of using a macro?

    a. To save time by automating routine tasks

    b. To ensure consistency in executing routine or complex tasks

    c. To redesign the relationships among the tables of the database

    d. To make the database more flexible or easy to use

15. Which of the following *best* describes the process of creating an Access macro?

    a. Use the macro recorder to record clicks and keystrokes as you complete a task.

    b. Open Macro Design View and add actions, arguments, and conditions to accomplish the desired task.

    c. Use the Macro Wizard to determine which tasks are done most frequently.

    d. Use the single-step recorder to record clicks and keystrokes as you complete a task.

16. Which of the following would *not* be a way to run a macro?

    a. Double-click the macro action within the Macro Design View window.

    b. Assign the macro to an event of a control on a form.

    c. Add the macro as a button on a toolbar, then click the button.

    d. Click the Run button on the Database window toolbar.

17. Which of the following is *not* a reason to run a macro in single-step mode?

    a. You want to run only a few of the actions of a macro.

    b. You want to observe the effect of each macro action individually.

    c. You want to debug a macro that isn't working properly.

    d. You want to change the arguments of a macro while it runs.

18. Which of the following is *not* a reason to use conditional expressions in a macro?

    a. Conditional expressions allow you to skip over actions when the expression evaluates as false.

    b. More macro actions are available when you are also using conditional expressions.

    c. You can enter "False" in the Conditions column for an action to skip it.

    d. Conditional expressions give the macro more power and flexibility.

19. Which example illustrates the proper syntax to refer to a specific control on a form?

    a. {Forms}!{*formname*}!(*controlname*)

    b. [Forms]![*formname*]![*controlname*])

    c. Forms!*formname.controlname*

    d. (Forms)!(*formname*)!(*controlname*

20. Which event executes every time you move from record to record in a form?

    a. New Record

    b. On Move

    c. Next Record

    d. On Current

▼ SKILLS REVIEW

1. Understand macros.

    a. Start Access, then open the **Basketball-N.mdb** database from the drive and folder where your Data Files are stored.

    b. Open the Print Macro Group in Macro Design View, then record your answers to the following questions on a sheet of paper:

        • How many macros are in this macro group?

        • What are the names of the macros in this macro group?

        • What actions does the first macro in this macro group contain?

        • What arguments does the first action contain? What values were chosen for those arguments?

    c. Close Macro Design View for the Print Macro Group object.

2. **Create a macro.**

   a. Start a new macro in Macro Design View.

   b. Add the OpenQuery action to the first row.

   c. Select Score Delta as the value for the Query Name argument.

   d. Select Datasheet for the View argument.

   e. Select Edit for the Data Mode argument.

   f. Save the macro with the name **View Score Delta**.

   g. Run the macro to make sure it works, close the Score Delta query, then close the View Score Delta macro.

3. **Modify actions and arguments.**

   a. Open the View Score Delta macro in Macro Design View.

   b. Add a MsgBox action in the second row of Macro Design View.

   c. Type **We had a great season!** for the Message argument.

   d. Select Yes for the Beep argument.

   e. Select Warning! for the Type argument.

   f. Type **Iowa State Cyclones** for the Title argument.

   g. Save the macro, then run it to make sure the MsgBox action works as intended.

   h. Click OK in the dialog box created by the MsgBox action, then close the Score Delta query and the View Score Delta macro.

4. **Create a macro group.**

   a. Rename the View Score Delta macro, changing it to **Query Macro Group**.

   b. Open Query Macro Group in Macro Design View.

   c. Open the Macro Name column, then enter **View Score Delta** as the name for the first macro.

   d. Start another macro by typing **View Forward FG** in the Macro Name cell of the fourth row.

   e. Add an OpenQuery action for the first action of the View Forward FG macro.

   f. Select Forward Field Goals for the Query Name argument of the OpenQuery action, and use the default entries for the other two arguments.

   g. Add a MsgBox action for the second action of the View Forward FG macro.

   h. Type **Forward Field Goals** as the Message argument for the MsgBox action.

   i. Select Yes for the Beep argument of the MsgBox action.

   j. Select Critical for the Type argument of the MsgBox action.

   k. Type **Big 12 Conference** for the Title argument of the MsgBox action, then save the macro.

   l. Run the View Forward FG macro from the Tools menu.

   m. Click OK, close the query datasheet, then close the Query Macro Group.

5. **Set conditional expressions.**

   a. Start a new macro in Macro Design View.

   b. Open the Condition column.

   c. Enter the following condition in the Condition cell of the first row: **[Forms]![Game Summary Form]![Home Score]>[Opponent Score]**. (*Hint*: Use the Zoom dialog box or widen the column to more clearly view the entry.)

   d. Add the SetValue action to the first row.

   e. Type the following entry in the Item argument value for the SetValue action: **[Forms]![Game Summary Form]![Victory]**.

   f. Type **Yes** for the Expression argument for the SetValue action.

   g. Save the macro with the name **Victory Calculator**, then close Macro Design View.

6. **Work with events.**

   a. Open the Game Summary Form in Form Design View.

   b. Open the property sheet for the form.

   c. Assign the Victory Calculator macro to the On Current event of the form.

   d. Close the property sheet, save the form, then open the Game Summary Form in Form View.

e. Navigate through the first four records. The Victory check box should be marked for the first three records, but not the fourth.

f. Add your name as a label in the Form Header section to identify your printouts, print the third and fourth records, then close the Game Summary Form.

7. Customize toolbars.

a. Convert the Print Macro Group into buttons on a toolbar.

b. Dock the toolbar with the three text buttons just below the Database toolbar in the database window.

c. Open the Customize (toolbars) dialog box.

d. Change the button image for each of the three macros to the question mark icon and a default style (image only).

e. Edit the button images so that the second macro question mark button is red (instead of yellow) and the third is blue (instead of yellow).

f. Close the Customize dialog box, then point to each icon to make sure that the ScreenTip relates to the three macro names in the Print Macro Group as shown in Figure N-17.

FIGURE N-17

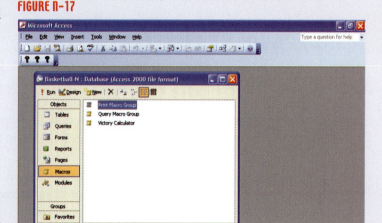

8. Troubleshoot macros.

a. Open the Print Macro Group in Macro Design View.

b. Click the Single Step button on the Macro Design toolbar, then click the Run button on the Macro Design toolbar.

c. Click Step twice to step through the two actions of this macro, then click OK in the resulting message box.

d. Open the Condition column if it's not already open.

e. Enter the value **False** as a condition to the first row, the OpenReport action of the Game Stats macro.

f. Save the macro, then single step through the macro again.

g. This time the Games Summary report should *not* be printed. Click OK when prompted with the information created by the MsgBox action.

h. Delete the False condition in the first row, save the macro, then click the Single Step button to toggle it off.

i. Click File on the menu bar, click Print, click OK in the Print Macro Definition dialog box, then close Macro Design View.

j. Close the Basketball-N.mdb database, then exit Access.

▼ INDEPENDENT CHALLENGE 1

As the manager of a doctor's clinic, you have created an Access database called Patients-N.mdb to track insurance claim reimbursements. You will use macros to help automate the database.

a. Start Access, then open the database **Patients-N.mdb** from the drive and folder where your Data Files are stored.

b. Open Macro Design View of the CPT Form Open macro. (CPT stands for Current Procedural Terminology, which is a code that describes a medical procedure.) If the Single Step button is toggled on, click it to toggle it off.

c. On a separate sheet of paper, identify the macro actions, arguments for each action, and values for each argument.

d. In two or three sentences, explain in your own words what tasks this macro automates.

e. Close the CPT Form Open macro.

f. Open the Claim Entry Form in Form Design View. Maximize the window.

g. In the footer of the Claim Entry Form are several command buttons. (*Hint*: Scroll the main form to see these buttons.) Open the property sheet of the Add CPT Code button, then click the Event tab.

h. On your paper, write the event to which the CPT Form Open macro is assigned.

i. Open the Claim Entry Form in Form View, then click the Add CPT Code button in the form footer.

▼ INDEPENDENT CHALLENGE 1 (CONTINUED)

j. On your paper, write the current record number that is displayed for you.

k. Scroll up the CPT form, then find the record for CPT Code 99243. Write the RBRVS value for this record, then close the CPT form and Claim Entry form. (RBRVS stands for Resource Based Relative Value System, a measurement of relative value between medical procedures.)

l. Close the Patients-N.mdb database, then exit Access.

▼ INDEPENDENT CHALLENGE 2

As the manager of a doctor's clinic, you have created an Access database called Patients-N.mdb to track insurance claim reimbursements. You will use macros to help automate the database.

a. Start Access, then open the database **Patients-N.mdb** from the drive and folder where your Data Files are stored.

b. Start a new macro in Macro Design View, then open the Macro Name column. If the Single Step button is toggled on, click it to toggle it off.

c. Type **Preview DOS Denied** as the first macro name, then add the OpenReport macro action in the first row.

d. Select Date of Service Report Denied for the Report Name argument, then select Print Preview for the View argument of the OpenReport action.

e. In the third row, type **Preview DOS Fixed** as a new macro name, then add the OpenReport macro action in the third row.

f. Select Date of Service Report Fixed for the ReportName argument, then select Print Preview for the View argument of the second OpenReport action.

g. Save the object with the name **Preview Group**, close Macro Design View, then click the Preview Group macro object to select it.

h. Run the Preview DOS Denied macro to test it, then close Print Preview.

i. Run the Preview DOS Fixed macro to test it, then close Print Preview.

Advanced Challenge Exercise

- In Preview Group, create two more macros, one that previews the Monthly Claims Report Denied report and the other that previews the Monthly Claims Report Fixed report. Name the two macros **Preview MCR Denied** and **Preview MCR Fixed**.
- Test each macro, then save and close Macro Design View for the Preview Group.
- Convert the Preview Group macro group into a toolbar.
- Change the image of each button to an icon. Use smiley face icons for the "Fixed" reports and sad face icons for the "Denied" reports. Note that even if you use the same icon for two buttons, the ScreenTip that appears for each button when you point to it shows the name of the macro, helping differentiate the buttons.

j. Print the Preview Group macro using the Print Macro Definition dialog box.

k. Close the Patients-N.mdb database, then exit Access.

▼ INDEPENDENT CHALLENGE 3

As the manager of a doctor's clinic, you have created an Access database called Patients-N.mdb to track insurance claim reimbursements. You will use macros to help automate the database.

a. Start Access, then open the **Patients-N.mdb** database from the drive and folder where your Data Files are stored.

b. Start a new macro in Macro Design View, then open the Condition column. If the Single Step button is toggled on, click it to toggle it off.

c. Enter the following in the Condition cell of the first row: **[Forms]![CPT Form]![RBRVS]=0**.

d. Select the SetValue action for the first row.

e. Enter the following as the Item argument value for the SetValue action: **[Forms]![CPT Form]![Research]**.

f. Type **Yes** as the Expression argument value for the SetValue action.

▼ INDEPENDENT CHALLENGE 3 (CONTINUED)

g. Save the macro with the name **Value Research**, close Macro Design View, then click the Value Research macro object to select it.

h. Click File on the menu bar, click Print, then click OK in the Print Macro Definition dialog box.

i. Open the CPT Form in Form Design View, and open the property sheet for the form.

j. Assign the Value Research macro to the On Current event of the form.

k. Close the property sheet, save the form, then open the CPT Form in Form View.

l. Use the Next Record button to move quickly through all 64 records in the form. Notice that the macro places a check mark in the Research check box only when the RBRVS value is equal to zero.

Advanced Challenge Exercise

■ Open the Claim Entry Form in Form Design View.

■ Select the Add CPT Code command button in the Form Footer section, then open the property sheet.

■ Click the Event tab to observe the 12 events that are associated with the command button.

■ Using the information provided by the status bar when you click a property or Microsoft Office Access Help, write a short description for six events used by the command button. Which one do you think is used most often? Explain why you chose that event.

m. Save and close the CPT Form, then close the Patients-N.mdb database.

▼ INDEPENDENT CHALLENGE 4

Your culinary club is collecting information on international chocolate factories, museums, and stores, and has asked you to help build a database to organize the information. You collect some information on the World Wide Web to enter into the database, then tie the forms together with macros attached to command buttons.

a. Go to www.godiva.com. Your goal is to determine if there is a Godiva store in Toronto, Ontario, Canada, where some members of your group will be visiting.

b. Click the Boutique Locator link on the Godiva home page to locate the Godiva Boutique stores in Toronto, Ontario, Canada. (Web sites change often. You may need to search for Godiva Boutique stores using a search box or site map.)

c. Once you find the page that lists the Godiva store locations in Toronto, Canada, select that information on the Web page, then print the selection.

d. Open the **Chocolate-N.mdb** database from the drive and folder where your Data Files are stored, then open the Countries form in Form View.

e. Click the New Record button for the main form, then type **Canada** in the Country text box.

f. In the subform for the Canada record, enter **Godiva Boutique** in the Name field, **S** in the Type field (S for store), the address information that you found on the Web site in the Street field, **Toronto** in the City field, and **Ontario** in the StateProvince field.

g. Open Macro Design View for a new macro, then add the PrintOut action to the first row. If the Single Step button is toggled on, click it to toggle it off. Modify the Print Range argument to Selection, save the macro with the name **PrintRecord**, then close it.

h. In Form Design View of the Countries form, add a label with your name to the left section of the Form Header section, then add a command button to the right section. If the Command Button Wizard starts, click Cancel.

i. In the property sheet for the Command button, select the PrintRecord macro for the On Click property on the Event tab. You attached the PrintRecord macro to the On Click property for this command button. Therefore, when the command button is clicked in Form View, the PrintRecord macro should run.

j. Double-click the text on the command button, then type **Print Current Record**.

k. Save the form, then view it in Form View.

l. Find the Canada record, then click the Print Current Record command button. Only that record should print.

m. Close the Countries form, then exit Access.

▼ VISUAL WORKSHOP

As the manager of a doctor's clinic, you have created an Access database called **Patients-N.mdb** to track insurance claim reimbursements. Develop a new macro called **Query Group** with the actions and argument values shown in Figure N-18 and Table N-3. Run both macros to test them, and debug them if necessary. Print the macro by clicking File on the menu bar. Click Print, and then click OK in the Print Macro Definition dialog box.

TABLE N-3

macro name	action	argument	argument value
Denied	OpenQuery	Query Name	Monthly Query – Denied
		View	Datasheet
		Data Mode	Edit
	Maximize		
	MsgBox	Message	These claims were denied
		Beep	Yes
		Type	Information
		Title	Denied
Fixed	OpenQuery	Query Name	Monthly Query – Fixed
		View	Datasheet
		Data Mode	Edit
	Maximize		
	MsgBox	Message	These claims were fixed
		Beep	Yes
		Type	Information
		Title	Fixed

FIGURE N-18

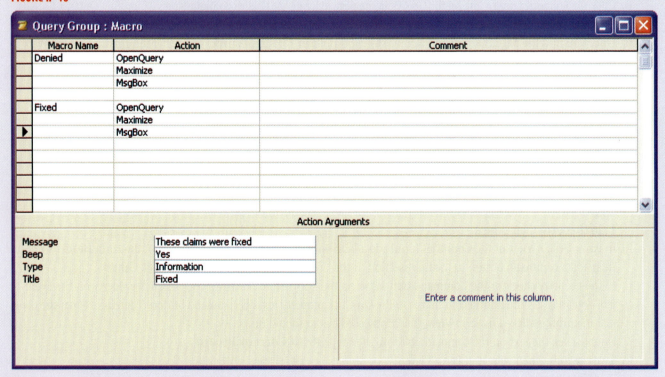

UNIT
O
Access 2003

Creating Modules and VBA

OBJECTIVES

Understand modules and VBA
Compare macros and modules
Create functions
Use If statements
Document procedures
Create class modules
Create sub procedures
Troubleshoot modules

If you have a SAM user profile, you may have access to hands-on instruction, practice, and assessment of the skills covered in this unit. Log in to your SAM account and go to your assignments page to see what your instructor has assigned.

Access is a robust and easy-to-use relational database program. With Access, users can quickly create reports and forms using user-friendly tools such as wizards and Design Views that previously took programmers hours to build. You may, however, want to automate a task or create a new function that goes beyond the capabilities of the built-in Access tools. Within each program of the Microsoft Office suite, a programming language called **Visual Basic for Applications (VBA)** is provided to help you extend the capabilities of each program. In Access, VBA is stored within modules.  You want to learn about VBA and create modules to enhance the capabilities of the Technology-O database.

Understanding Modules and VBA

A **module** is an Access object that stores Visual Basic for Applications (VBA) programming code. VBA is written in the **Visual Basic Editor Code window** (**Code window**), shown in Figure O-1. The components and text colors of the Code window are described in Table O-1. An Access database has two kinds of modules: **class modules**, which contain VBA code used only within a form or report, and store the code within the form or report object itself; and **standard modules**, which contain global code that can be executed from anywhere in the database. Standard modules are displayed as module objects in the database window when you click the Modules button on the Objects bar. You ask some questions about VBA.

The following questions and answers introduce the basics of Access modules:

- **What does a module contain?**

  A module contains VBA programming code organized in procedures. A procedure contains several lines of code, each of which is called a **statement**. Modules may also contain **comments**, text that helps explain and document the code.

- **What is a procedure?**

  A **procedure** is a series of VBA statements that perform an operation or calculate an answer. There are two types of procedures: functions and subs. **Declaration statements** precede procedure statements and help set rules for how the statements in the module are processed.

- **What is a function?**

  A **function** is a procedure that returns a value. Access supplies many built-in statistical, financial, and date functions, such as Sum, Pmt, and Now, that can be used in an expression in a query, form, or report to calculate a value. You might want to create a new function, however, to help perform calculations unique to your database. For example, you might create a new function called StockOptions to calculate the date an employee is eligible for stock options within your company.

- **What is a sub?**

  A **sub** (also called **sub procedure**) performs a series of VBA statements, but does not return a value and cannot be used in an expression like a function procedure. You use subs to manipulate controls and objects. They are generally executed when an event occurs, such as when a command button is clicked or a form is opened.

- **What are arguments?**

  Arguments are constants, variables, or expressions passed to a procedure (usually a function procedure) that the procedure needs in order to execute. For example, the full syntax for the Sum function is Sum(*expr*), where *expr* represents the argument for the Sum function, the item that is being summed. In VBA, arguments are declared in the first line of the procedure. They are specified immediately after a procedure's name and are enclosed in parentheses. Multiple arguments are separated by commas. For example, in the first VBA statement used to create the StockOptions function, Function StockOptions(*Salary,StartDate*), two arguments are declared, Salary, and StartDate.

- **What is an object?**

  In VBA, an **object** is any item that can be identified or manipulated, including the traditional Access objects (table, query, form, report, page, macro, module), and smaller pieces of the traditional objects including controls, sections, and existing procedures.

- **What is a method?**

  A **method** is an action that *an object can perform*. Procedures are often written to invoke methods in response to user actions. For example, you could invoke the GoToPage method when the user clicks a command button on a form to move the focus to a specific control on the second page of a form.

FIGURE O-1: Visual Basic Editor Code window for a standard module

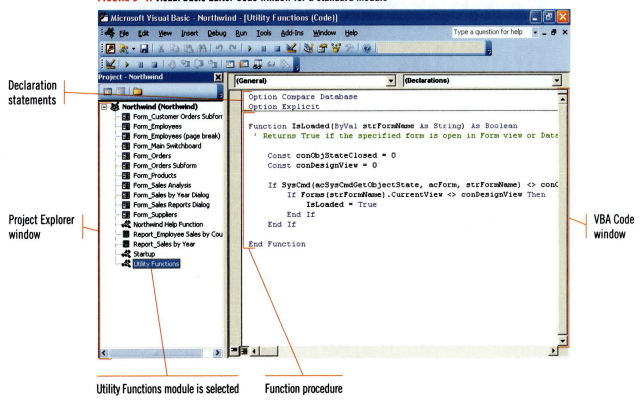

Declaration statements

Project Explorer window

VBA Code window

Utility Functions module is selected

Function procedure

TABLE O-1: Components and text colors for the Visual Basic window

component or color	description
Visual Basic window	Comprises the entire Microsoft Visual Basic program window that contains smaller windows, including the Code window and Project Explorer window
Code window	Contains the VBA for the project selected in the Project Explorer window
Project Explorer window	Displays a hierarchical list of the projects in the database; a project can be a module itself, or an object that contains class modules, such as a form or report
Procedure View button	Shows the statements that belong only to the current procedure
Full Module View button	Shows all the lines of VBA (all of the procedures) in the current module
Declaration statements	Include statements that apply to every procedure in the module, such as declarations for variables, constants, user-defined data types, and external procedures in a dynamic link library
Object list	In a class module, lists the objects associated with the current form or report
Procedure list	In a standard module, lists the procedures in that module; in a class module, lists events (such as Click or Dblclick)
Blue	Indicates keyword text—blue words are reserved by VBA and are already assigned specific meanings
Black	Indicates normal text—black words are the unique VBA code developed by the user
Red	Indicates syntax error text—a line of code in red indicates that it will not execute correctly because there is a syntax error (perhaps a missing parenthesis or a spelling error)
Green	Indicates comment text—any text after an apostrophe is considered documentation, and is therefore ignored in the execution of the procedure

Comparing Macros and Modules

Both macros and modules help run your database more efficiently and effectively. Creating either a macro or a module requires some understanding of programming concepts, an ability to follow a process through its steps, and patience. Some tasks can be accomplished by using either an Access macro or with VBA, and there are guidelines to help guide your choice of which tool is best for the task. You learn how Access macros and modules compare by asking more questions.

The following questions and answers provide guidelines for using macros and modules:

- **For what types of tasks are macros best suited?**

  Macros are an easy way to handle repetitive, simple tasks such as opening and closing forms, showing and hiding toolbars, and printing reports. Any process that can be automated through a macro action is probably easier to create using macro actions than by writing equivalent VBA statements.

- **Which is easier to create, a macro or a module, and why?**

  Macros are generally easier to create because you don't have to know any programming syntax. The hardest part of creating a macro is choosing the correct action (Access presents a limited list of about 50 actions from which you must choose). But once the action is chosen, the arguments associated with that action are displayed automatically in the Action Arguments pane, eliminating the need to learn any special programming syntax. To create a module, however, you must know a robust programming language, VBA, as well as the correct **syntax** (rules) for each VBA statement. In a nutshell, macros are simpler to create but VBA is far more powerful.

- **When must I use a macro?**

  You must use macros to make global, shortcut key assignments. You can also use an automatic macro that executes when the database first opens.

- **When must I use a module?**

  - You must use modules to create unique functions. Macros cannot create functions. For instance, you might want to create a function called Commission that calculates the appropriate commission on a sale using your company's unique commission formula.

  - Access error messages can be confusing to the user. But using VBA procedures, you can detect the error when it occurs and display your own message. Macros cannot be used to detect errors.

  - You can't use a macro to accomplish many tasks outside Access, but VBA code stored in modules works with other products in the Microsoft Office suite.

  - VBA code can contain nested If statements, Case statements, and other programming logic which makes them much more powerful and flexible than macros. Some of the most common VBA keywords, including If...Then, are shown in Table O-2. VBA keywords appear blue in the Code window. The only logic available to a macro is whether or not to execute a macro action based on whether an expression entered in the Condition column evaluates true or false.

  - VBA code may declare **variables**, which are used to store data that can be used, modified, or displayed during the execution of the procedure. Macros cannot declare variables.

  - Class modules, like the one shown in Figure O-2, are stored as part of the form or report object in which they are created. If you develop forms and reports in one database and copy them to another, class module VBA automatically travels with the object that stores it.

FIGURE O-2: Code window for a class module

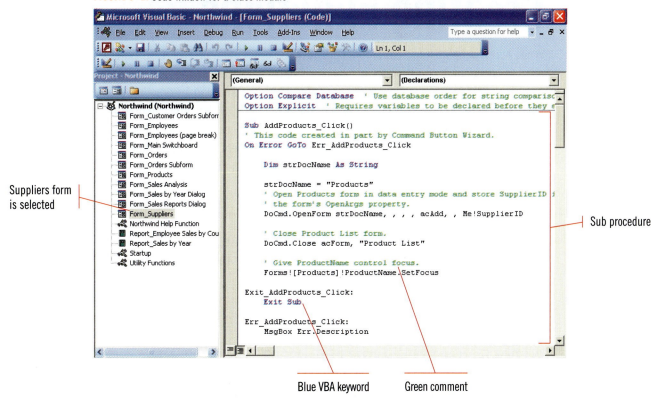

Suppliers form is selected

Sub procedure

Blue VBA keyword

Green comment

TABLE O-2: Common VBA keywords

statement	explanation
Function	Declares the name and arguments that create a new function procedure
End Function	When defining a new function, the End Function statement is required as the last statement to mark the end of the VBA code that defines the function
Sub	Declares the name for a new sub procedure; **Private Sub** indicates that the sub is accessible only to other procedures in the module where it is declared
End Sub	When defining a new sub, the End Sub statement is required as the last statement to mark the end of the VBA code that defines the sub
If...Then	Executes code (the code follows the Then statement) when the value of an expression is true (the expression follows the If statement)
End If	When creating an If...Then statement, the End If statement is required as the last statement
Const	Declares the name and value of a **constant**, an item that retains a constant value throughout the execution of the code
Option Compare Database	A declaration statement that determines the way string values (text) will be sorted
Option Explicit	A declaration statement that specifies that you must explicitly declare all variables used in all procedures; if you attempt to use an undeclared variable name, an error occurs at **compile time**, the period during which source code is translated to executable code
Dim	Declares a **variable**, a named storage location that contains data that can be modified during program execution
On Error GoTo	Upon error in the execution of a procedure, the On Error GoTo statement specifies the location (the statement) where the procedure should continue
Select Case	Executes one of several groups of statements called a **Case** depending on the value of an expression; use the Select Case statement as an alternative to using **ElseIf** in **If...Then...Else** statements when comparing one expression to several different values
End Select	When defining a new Select Case group of statements, the End Select statement is required as the last statement to mark the end of the VBA code

Creating Functions

While Access supplies hundreds of functions such as Sum, Count, Ilf, First, Last, Date, and Hour, you might need to create a new function to calculate a value based on the unique business rules used by your company. You would store the VBA used to create new function in a standard module so that it can be used in any query, form, or report in the database. MediaLoft has implemented a program that allows employees to purchase computer equipment when it is replaced. Equipment that is less than a year old will be sold to employees at 75% of its initial value, and equipment that is more than a year old will be sold at 50% of its initial value. You use VBA to create a new function called EmployeePrice that will determine the employee purchase price of replaced computer equipment.

STEPS

QUICK TIP

The Option Explicit statement automatically appears if the Require Variable Declaration option is checked. To view the default settings, click Options on the Tools menu.

1. **Start Access, open the Technology-O.mdb database, click Modules on the Objects bar, click the New button 🖾 on the database window toolbar, then maximize the Code window and the Visual Basic window**

   Access automatically inserts the Option Compare Database declaration statement. This statement is used to determine the way string values (text) will be sorted. Your new function won't sort text, but leaving the statement in the Code window doesn't create any problems.

2. **Type Function EmployeePrice(StartingValue), then press [Enter]**

   This statement creates a new function, EmployeePrice, and states that it contains one argument, StartingValue. VBA automatically adds the **End Function** statement, a required statement to mark the end of the code that defines the new function. Because both Function and End Function are VBA keywords, they are blue. The insertion point is positioned between the statements so that you can further define how the new EmployeePrice function will calculate using more VBA statements.

QUICK TIP

If the Project Explorer window organizes objects within folders, click the Toggle Folders button 🗀 to remove the folder view.

3. **Press [Tab], type EmployeePrice = StartingValue * 0.5, then press [Enter]**

   Your screen should look like Figure O-3. The second statement explains how the EmployeePrice function will calculate. The function will return a value that is calculated by multiplying the StartingValue by 0.5. It is not necessary to indent statements, but indenting code between matching Function/End Function, Sub/End Sub, or If/End If statements enhances the program's readability. Also, it is not necessary to enter spaces around the equal sign and an asterisk used as a multiplication sign, but when you press [Enter], Access adds spaces as appropriate to enhance the readability of the statement.

4. **Click the Save button 🖫 on the Standard toolbar, type Functions in the Save As dialog box, then click OK**

   Now that the function is created, it can be used in a query, form, or report.

5. **Close the Visual Basic window, click Queries on the Objects bar, right-click the Employee Pricing query, then click Design View on the shortcut menu**

   You can use the new function, EmployeePrice, in a query, form, or report.

QUICK TIP

Field names used in expressions are not case sensitive, but they must exactly match the spelling of the field name as originally defined in Table Design View.

6. **Click the blank Field cell to the right of the InitialValue field, type Price:EmployeePrice ([InitialValue]), click the Datasheet View button 🖩 on the Query Design toolbar, then maximize the datasheet**

   Your screen should look like Figure O-4. In this query, you created a new field called Price that used the EmployeePrice function. The value in the InitialValue field was used for the StartingValue argument. The InitialValue field was multiplied by 0.5 to create the new Price field.

7. **Save the Employee Pricing query, then close the datasheet**

Toggle Folders button

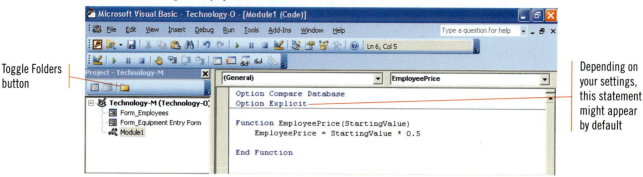

Depending on your settings, this statement might appear by default

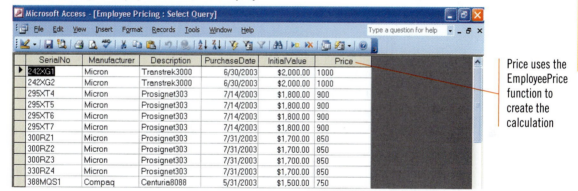

Price uses the EmployeePrice function to create the calculation

Access 2003

Using If Statements

If...Then...Else logic allows you to test logical conditions and execute statements only if the conditions are true. If...Then...Else code can be composed of one or several statements, depending on how many conditions you want to test, how many possible answers you want to provide, and what you want the code to do based on the results of the tests. You need to add an If statement to the EmployeePrice function to test the age of the equipment, and then calculate the answer based on that age. Right now, the calculation multiplies the StartingValue argument by 50%. You want to modify it so that if the equipment is less than one year old, the function multiplies the StartingValue argument by 75%.

STEPS

1. **Click Modules on the Objects bar, right-click the Functions module, then click Design View**

   The Functions Code window with the EmployeePrice function opens. To determine the age of the equipment, the EmployeePrice function needs another argument, the purchase date of the equipment.

2. **Click just before the right parenthesis in the Function statement, type , (a comma), press [Spacebar], then type PurchaseDate**

   The new function now contains two arguments. The statement is:

   ```
   Function EmployeePrice(StartingValue, PurchaseDate)
   ```

   Now that another argument has been established, the argument can be used in the function.

   > **QUICK TIP**
   >
   > Indentation doesn't affect the way the function works, but does make the code easier to read.

3. **Click to the right of the right parenthesis in the Function statement, press [Enter], press [Tab], type If (Now() – PurchaseDate) >365 Then, then press [Enter]**

   The expression compares whether today's date, represented by the Access function Now(), minus the PurchaseDate argument value is greater than 365 days. If true, this indicates that the equipment is older than one year.

4. **Indent, then enter the rest of the statements exactly as shown in Figure O-5**

   The Else statement will be executed only if the expression is false (if the equipment is less than 365 days old). The End If statement is needed to mark the end of the If block of code.

   > **QUICK TIP**
   >
   > If you get a compile or syntax error, open the Visual Basic window, check your function against Figure O-5, then correct any errors.

5. **Click the Save button 🖫 on the Standard toolbar, close the Visual Basic window, click Queries on the Objects bar, right-click the Employee Pricing query, then click Design View on the shortcut menu**

   Now that you've modified the EmployeePrice function to include two arguments, you need to modify the expression in the query in order for it to calculate the correct answer.

6. **Right-click the Price field in the query design grid, click Zoom on the shortcut menu, click between the right square bracket and right parenthesis, then type ,[PurchaseDate]**

   Your Zoom dialog box should look like Figure O-6. Both of the arguments used to calculate the EmployeePrice function are field names, so they must be typed exactly as shown, and surrounded by square brackets. Commas separate multiple arguments in the function.

7. **Click OK in the Zoom dialog box, then click the Datasheet View button 🔲 on the Query Design toolbar**

8. **Click any entry in the PurchaseDate field, then click the Sort Ascending button 📊 on the Query Datasheet toolbar**

   The EmployeePrice function now calculates two ways, depending on the age of the equipment determined by the date in the PurchaseDate field, as shown in Figure O-7. The new calculated Price field is based on the current date on your computer, so your results may vary.

9. **Save, then close the Employee Pricing query**

FIGURE O-5: Using an If...Then...Else statement

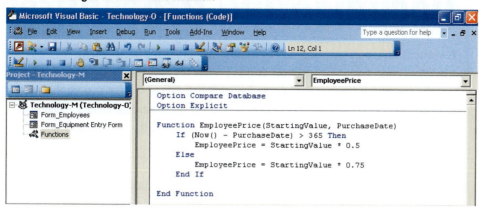

FIGURE O-6: Modifying the expression

FIGURE O-7: Price field is calculated two ways based on the If statement

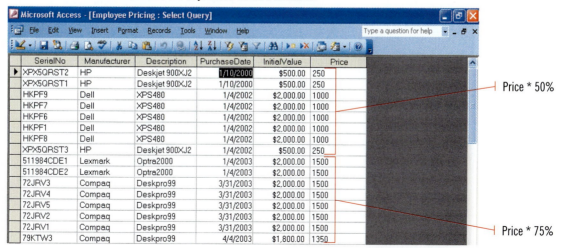

Documenting Procedures

Comment lines are statements in the code that document the code, and do not affect how the code runs. At any future time, if you want to read or modify existing code, you can write the modifications much more quickly if the code is properly documented. Comment lines start with an apostrophe, and are green in the Code window. You decide to document the EmployeePrice function in the Functions module with descriptive comments. This will make it easier for you and others to follow the purpose and logic of the function later.

STEPS

1. **Click Modules on the Objects bar, right-click the Functions module, then click Design View**
   The Code window for the Functions module opens.

2. **Click to the left of the Function statement, press [Enter], press [↑], type 'This function is called EmployeePrice and has two arguments, then press [Enter]**
   As soon as you move to another statement, the comment statement becomes green in the Code window.

3. **Type 'Created by Your Name on Today's Date, then press [Enter]**
   Your screen should look like Figure O-8. You also can place comments at the end of a line by entering an apostrophe to mark that the next part of the statement is a comment. Closing the Project Explorer window gives you more room for the Code window. (You use the **Project Explorer window** to switch between open projects, objects that can contain VBA code. The utility project contains VBA code that helps Access with certain activities such as presenting the Zoom dialog box. It automatically appears in the Project Explorer window when you use the Access features that utilize this code.)

4. **Click the Close button on the Project Explorer window, click to the right of Then at the end of the If statement, press [Spacebar], then type 'Now() is today's date**
   This comment explains that the Now() function is today's date. All comments are green, regardless of whether they are on their own line or at the end of an existing line.

5. **Click to the right of 0.5, press [Spacebar], then type 'If > 1 yr, value is 50%**

6. **Click to the right of 0.75, press [Spacebar], then type 'If < 1 yr, value is 75%, then press [↓]**
   Your screen should look like Figure O-9. Table O-3 provides more information about the Standard toolbar buttons in the Visual Basic window.

7. **Click the Save button on the Standard toolbar, click File on the menu bar, click Print, then click OK**

8. **Click File on the menu bar, then click Close and Return to Microsoft Office Access**

FIGURE O-8: Adding comments to the Code window

Project Explorer Close button

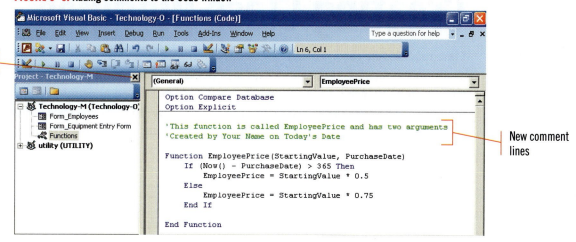

New comment lines

FIGURE O-9: Adding comments at the end of a statement

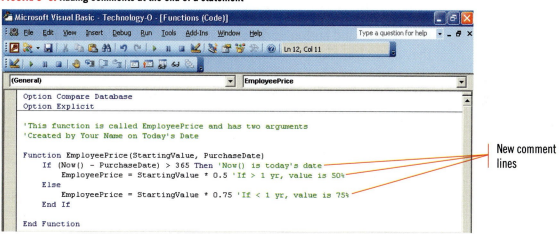

New comment lines

TABLE O-3: Standard toolbar buttons in the Visual Basic window

button name	button	description
View Microsoft Office Access		Toggles between the Access and the active Visual Basic window
Insert Module		Opens a new module or class module Code window, or inserts a new procedure in the current Code window
Run Sub/UserForm		Runs the current procedure if the insertion point is in a procedure, or runs the UserForm if it is active
Break		Stops the execution of a program while it's running, and switches to **break mode**, the temporary suspension of program execution in which you can examine, debug, reset, step through, or continue program execution
Reset		Resets the procedure
Project Explorer		Displays the Project Explorer, which displays a hierarchical list of the currently open projects (set of modules) and their contents
Object Browser		Displays the **Object Browser**, which lists the defined modules and procedures as well as available methods, properties, events, constants, and other items that you can use in the code

Creating Class Modules

Class modules are contained and executed within specific forms and reports. Class modules most commonly contain sub procedures and execute in response to an **event**, which is a specific action that occurs on or to an object, and is usually the result of a user action. Clicking a command button, editing data, or closing a form are examples of events. You do not always have to know VBA code to create class modules. The Command Button Wizard, for example, creates sub procedures stored in class modules. You use the Command Button Wizard to create four command buttons on the Equipment Entry Form. You examine the sub procedures in this form to better understand class modules.

STEPS

1. **Click Forms on the Objects bar, right-click the Equipment Entry Form, click Design View on the shortcut menu, then maximize the form**

   The form has three command buttons. Each command button is connected to a sub procedure that is executed when the button is clicked (when the On Click event of the command button occurs). These procedures are stored in a class module within the form. Each time you use the Command Button Wizard, you add a new sub procedure to the class module.

2. **Click the Command Button button on the Toolbox toolbar, click below the Print this record command button, click Form Operations in the Categories list, click Close Form in the Actions list, click Next, then click Next**

   The "meaningful name" that you give the button in the Command Button Wizard is extremely important. The name you enter in this dialog box is used to name the sub procedure in the underlying class module.

3. **Type CloseForm, then click Finish**

   To see the VBA that is stored in this form's class module, you need to open the Code window.

4. **Click the Code button on the Form Design toolbar, then scroll to the bottom of the window**

   The Code window for the Equipment Entry Form class module appears, as shown in Figure O-10. The names of the subs, AddNewRecordButton_Click, DeleteThisRecordButton_Click, PrintThisRecordButton_Click, and CloseForm_Click, correspond to the four command buttons on the form. The _Click suffix identifies which event will cause the sub to execute. When a procedure runs in response to an event, it is sometimes called an **event handler procedure**. Notice that the "meaningful name" you entered in the Command Button Wizard in Step 2 is used in the VBA statement that creates the name of the procedure. Another way to build class modules is to work with event properties directly from a control's property sheet.

5. **Close the Visual Basic window, then click the Properties button**

   Notice that [Event Procedure] is listed in the On Click property. This entry connects the CloseForm_Click() procedure to this command button. To create an event handler procedure associated with another event, you can use the property sheet and Build button to help create the appropriate procedure name.

   TROUBLE
   If prompted with the Choose Builder dialog box, click Code Builder, then click OK.

6. **Click the On Got Focus property, click the Build button, then click OK**

   The class module Code window opens, as shown in Figure O-11. Because you entered the Code window through a specific event (On Got Focus) of a specific command button (CloseForm), the Code window knew what control name and event name to use for the new procedure, CloseForm_GotFocus. The Code window also automatically supplied the last VBA statement for the procedure, the End Sub statement. The rest of the sub's statements, however, would require that you type them in yourself.

7. **Select the Private Sub CloseForm_GotFocus() statement and the End Sub statement, press [Delete], close the Visual Basic window, then save and close the Equipment Entry Form**

FIGURE O-10: Examining the CloseForm_Click procedure

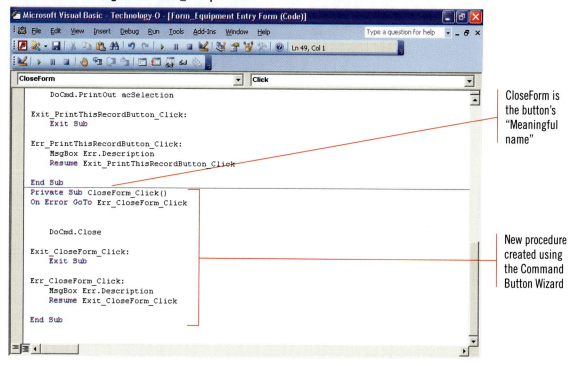

CloseForm is the button's "Meaningful name"

New procedure created using the Command Button Wizard

FIGURE O-11: Examining the CloseForm_GotFocus procedure

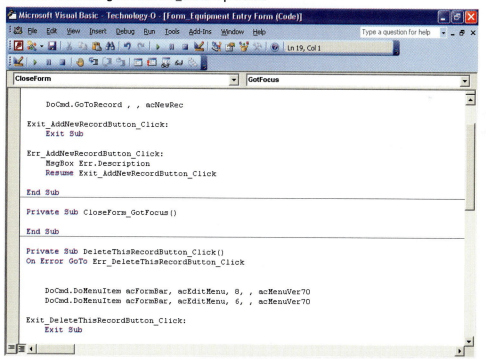

Creating Sub Procedures

While it is easy to create sub procedures using a wizard, not all subs can be created this way. The Command Button Wizard, for example, always attaches its code to the **On Click** event of a command button. You might want to create a sub that executes based on another event, such as double-click, or one that is assigned to a control other than a command button. You would like to add built-in documentation to a form that the user can access by clicking the form. To accomplish this, you write a sub procedure in a form class module.

STEPS

1. **Right-click the Equipment Entry Form, click Design View on the shortcut menu, then click the Properties button** 📧 **on the Form Design toolbar to open the property sheet (if it's not already visible)**

2. **Click the Event tab, click the On Dbl Click text box, click the Build button** ⎣···⎦**, then click OK**
   The class module opens with two new statements to identify the first and last lines of the new procedure. The name of the new sub is Form_DblClick. The name of the new sub references both the specific object and the specific event you chose in the property sheet.

3. **Type MsgBox ("Created by Your Name on Today's Date") as the single statement for the Form_DblClick sub, then click the Save button** 🖫 **on the Standard toolbar**
   Your screen should look like Figure O-12.

4. **Close the Visual Basic window, close the property sheet, click the Form View button** 🖼 **on the Form Design toolbar, then double-click the record selector to the left of the record**
   The MsgBox statement in the Form_DblClick sub creates the dialog box, as shown in Figure O-13.

5. **Click OK in the message box, click the Close Form command button, then click Yes if prompted to save the form**
   VBA is as robust and powerful as Access itself. It takes years of experience to appreciate the vast number of objects, events, methods, and properties that are available. With only modest programming skills, however, you can create basic sub procedures.

FIGURE O-12: Creating the Form_DblClick procedure

Object list

Procedure list

New event procedure

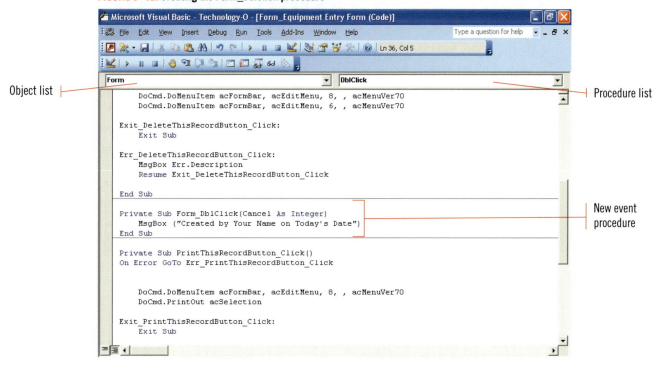

FIGURE O-13: Executing the MsgBox statement

Record selector

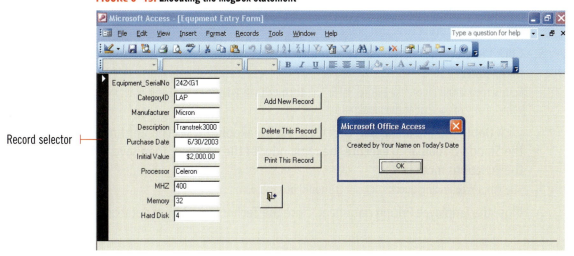

Access 2003

Troubleshooting Modules

You might encounter three types of errors as your code runs, and Access provides several techniques to help you **debug** (find and resolve) these errors. **Compile-time errors** occur as a result of incorrectly constructed code. For example, you may have forgotten to write an End If statement following an If clause, or you may have a **syntax error**, such as a missing parenthesis. This type of error is the easiest type to identify because your code will turn red as soon as it detects a syntax error. **Run-time errors** occur after the code starts to run, and include attempting an illegal operation such as dividing by zero or moving focus to a control that doesn't exist. When you encounter a run-time error, VBA will stop executing your procedure at the line in which the error occurred and highlight that line with a yellow background. **Logic errors** are the most difficult to troubleshoot because they occur when the code runs without problems, but the procedure still doesn't produce the desired result. You study debugging techniques using the Functions module.

STEPS

1. **Click Modules on the Objects bar, right-click Functions, click Design View, click to the right of the End If statement, type your name, then press [↓]**

   Because entering your name is not a valid way to start a VBA statement it becomes red.

2. **Click OK in the Compile error message box, delete your name, then click anywhere in another statement**

   Another VBA debugging tool is to set a **breakpoint**, a bookmark that suspends execution of the procedure at that statement to allow the user to examine what is happening.

> **QUICK TIP**
> Click the gray bar to the left of a statement to toggle breakpoints on and off.

3. **Click anywhere in the If statement, click Debug on the menu bar, then click Toggle Breakpoint**

   Your screen should look like Figure O-14.

> **TROUBLE**
> You may need to drag the top edge of the Immediate window up from the bottom of the screen to view it.

4. **Click the View Microsoft Office Access button 🖉 on the Standard toolbar, click Queries on the Objects bar, then double-click Employee Pricing**

   When the Employee Pricing query opens, it immediately runs the EmployeePrice function. Because you set a breakpoint at the If statement, that statement is highlighted, as shown in Figure O-15, indicating that the code has been suspended at that point.

> **QUICK TIP**
> Pointing to an argument in the Code window displays a ScreenTip with the argument's current value.

5. **Click View on the menu bar, click Immediate Window, type ? PurchaseDate, then press [Enter]**

   Your screen should look like Figure O-16. The **Immediate window** is an area where you can determine the value of any argument at the breakpoint.

6. **Click Debug on the menu bar, click Clear All Breakpoints, click the Continue button ▶ on the Standard toolbar to execute the remainder of the function, then save, print, and close the Functions module**

   The Employee Pricing query's datasheet should be visible.

7. **Close the Employee Pricing datasheet, close the Technology-O.mdb database, then exit Access**

Clues to Use

Using Visual Basic screen prompts

When you enter a Visual Basic keyword such as MsgBox, shown in Figure O-17, Visual Basic prompts appear to help you complete the statement. In the MsgBox function syntax, the bold italic words are the **named arguments** (required arguments). Arguments enclosed in brackets are optional. (Do not type the brackets in your Visual Basic code.) Therefore, for the MsgBox function, the only argument you must provide is the Prompt argument, which consists of the text you want the dialog box to display.

FIGURE O-17: MsgBox prompt

```
MsgBox (
MsgBox(Prompt, [Buttons As VbMsgBoxStyle = vbOKOnly], [Title], [HelpFile], [Context])
As VbMsgBoxResult
```

FIGURE O-14: Setting a breakpoint

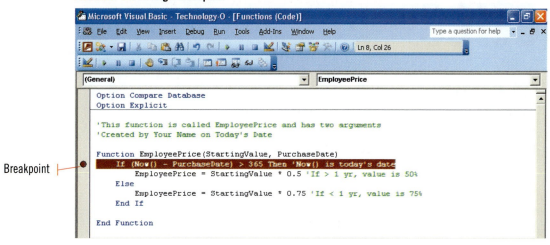

Breakpoint

FIGURE O-15: Stopping execution at a breakpoint

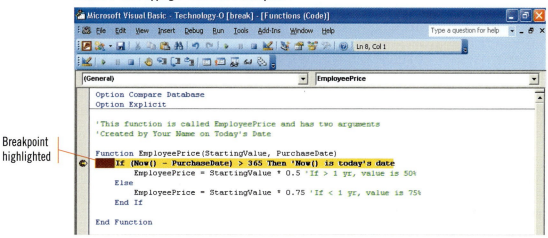

Breakpoint highlighted

FIGURE O-16: Using the Immediate window

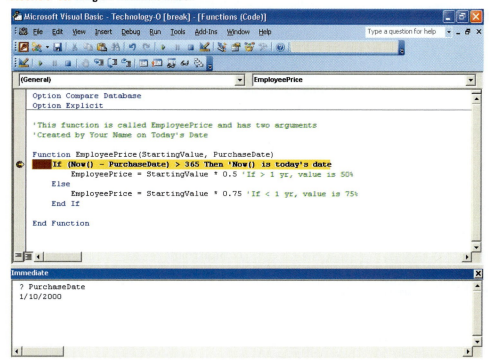

Practice

▼ CONCEPTS REVIEW

Identify each element of the Visual Basic window shown in Figure O-18.

FIGURE O-18

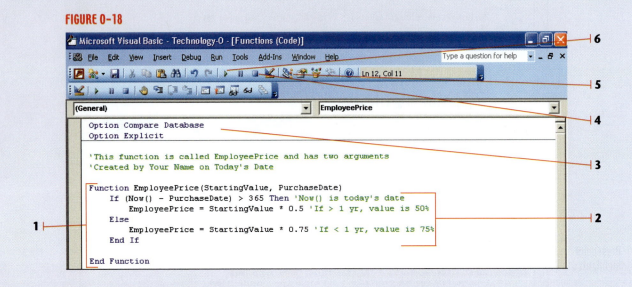

Match each term with the statement that best describes its function.

7. Visual Basic for Applications (VBA)
8. Module
9. Arguments
10. Function
11. Debugging
12. Breakpoint
13. Procedure
14. If...Then...Else statement
15. Class modules

a. Allows you to test a logical condition and execute commands only if the condition is true
b. The programming language used in Access modules
c. A line of code that automatically suspends execution of the procedure
d. A procedure that returns a value
e. Constants, variables, or expressions passed to a procedure to further define how it should execute
f. Stored as part of the form or report object in which they are created
g. The Access object where VBA code is stored
h. A series of VBA statements that perform an operation or calculate a value
i. A process to find and resolve programming errors

Select the best answer from the list of choices.

16. A module contains VBA programming code organized in units called:
    a. Procedures.
    b. Arguments.
    c. Breakpoints.
    d. Macros.
17. Which type of procedure returns a value?
    a. Sub
    b. Sub procedure
    c. Function
    d. Class module

18. Which of the following is *not* a reason to use modules rather than macros?

a. Modules are used to create unique functions.

b. Modules contain code that can work with other Microsoft Office software programs.

c. Modules are usually easier to write than macros.

d. Modules can contain procedures that mask error messages.

19. Which of the following is *not* a type of VBA error?

a. Class action

b. Run time

c. Logic

d. Compile time

20. Which of the following is a specific action that occurs on or to an object, and is usually the result of a user action?

a. Argument

b. Event

c. Function

d. Sub

▼ SKILLS REVIEW

1. Understand modules.

a. Start Access, then open the **Basketball-O.mdb** database from the drive and folder where your Data Files are stored.

b. Open the Code window for the Shot Statistics module.

c. Record your answers to the following questions on a sheet of paper.

- What is the name of the function defined in this module?
- What are the names of the arguments defined in this module?
- What is the purpose of the If statement?
- What is the purpose of the End Function statement?
- Why is the End Function statement in blue?
- Why are some of the lines indented?

2. Compare macros and modules.

a. If not already opened, open the Code window for the Shot Statistics module.

b. Record your answers to the following questions on a sheet of paper.

- Why was a module rather than a macro used to create this function?
- Why is code written in the Shot Statistics Code window generally more difficult to create than a macro?
- Identify each of the keywords or keyword phrases, and explain the purpose for each.

3. Create functions.

a. If not already opened, open the Code window for the Shot Statistics module.

b. Create a function called Contribution below the End Function statement of the TotalShotPercentage function by typing the VBA statements shown in Figure O-19.

c. Save the Shot Statistics module, then close the Visual Basic window.

d. Use Query Design View to create a new query using the First and Last fields from the Players table and all of the fields from the Stats table.

FIGURE O-19

```
Function Contribution(fg, threept, ft, offreb, defreb, assists)
    Contribution = (fg * 2 + threept * 3 + ft + offreb * 2 + defreb + assists * 2)
End Function
```

e. Create a calculated field named **Rank** in the first available column by carefully typing the Contribution function as follows:

Rank: Int(Contribution([FG], [3P], [FT], [RebO], [RebD], [Assists]))

(*Note*: The Int function converts the result to an integer rather than text for later sorting purposes.)

f. Sort the query in ascending order on the GameNo field.

▼ SKILLS REVIEW (CONTINUED)

g. View the datasheet, as shown in Figure O-20, change PlayerNo 21 to your first and last name, then print the first page of the datasheet in landscape orientation.

h. Save the query with the name **Rankings**, then close the Rankings datasheet.

4. Use If statements.

a. Open the Code window for the Shot Statistics module, click to the right of the Function Contribution statement, press [Enter], then modify the function with the statements shown in Figure O-21. The new function tests to see whether the player contributed any points (field goals plus three pointers plus free throws), and if not, divides their total contribution by 2. It also tests to see whether the player had any rebounds (rebounds on offense plus rebounds on defense), and if not, divides their total contribution by 3. (*Hint*: You can use copy and paste to copy repeating statements, then edit for the differences.)

b. Save the Shot Statistics module, then close the Visual Basic window.

c. Open the Rankings datasheet, then print the first page in landscape orientation. You should see the Rank calculated value go down for those players who did not score any points or who did not have any rebounds.

d. Close the datasheet.

5. Document procedures.

a. Open the Code window for the Shot Statistic module, and edit the Contribution function to include the five comment statements and blank lines as shown in Figure O-22.

b. Save the changes to the Shot Statistics module, print the module, then close the Visual Basic window.

6. Examine class modules.

a. Open the Player Entry Form in Form Design View.

b. On the right side of the form, select the Command Button that is named PrintCurrentRecord and displays a printer icon.

c. Open the property sheet for the button, click the Event tab, click the On Click property, then click the Build button to open the class module.

d. Edit the comment on the last line to show your name and the current date; save and print the module, then close the Visual Basic window.

FIGURE O-20

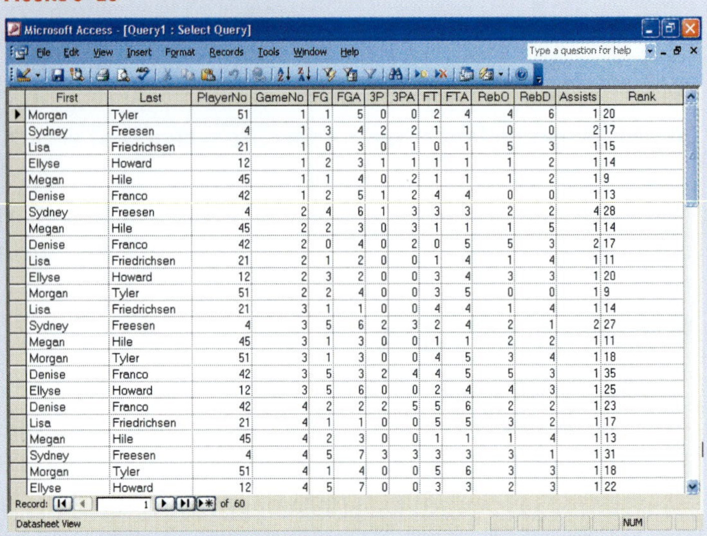

First	Last	PlayerNo	GameNo	FG	FGA	3P	3PA	FT	FTA	RebO	RebD	Assists	Rank
Morgan	Tyler	51	1	1	5	0	0	2	4	4	6	1	20
Sydney	Freesen	4	1	3	4	2	2	1	1	0	0	2	17
Lisa	Friedrichsen	21	1	0	3	0	1	0	1	5	3	1	15
Ellyse	Howard	12	1	2	3	1	1	1	1	1	2	1	14
Megan	Hile	45	1	1	4	0	2	1	1	1	2	1	9
Denise	Franco	42	1	2	5	1	2	4	4	0	0	1	13
Sydney	Freesen	4	2	4	6	1	3	3	3	2	2	4	28
Megan	Hile	45	2	2	3	0	3	1	1	1	5	1	14
Denise	Franco	42	2	0	4	0	2	0	5	5	3	2	17
Lisa	Friedrichsen	21	2	1	2	0	0	1	4	1	4	1	11
Ellyse	Howard	12	2	3	2	0	0	3	4	3	3	1	20
Morgan	Tyler	51	2	2	4	0	0	3	5	0	0	1	9
Lisa	Friedrichsen	21	3	1	1	0	0	4	4	1	4	1	14
Sydney	Freesen	4	3	5	6	2	3	2	4	2	1	2	27
Megan	Hile	45	3	1	3	0	0	1	1	2	2	1	11
Morgan	Tyler	51	3	1	3	0	0	4	5	3	4	1	18
Denise	Franco	42	3	5	3	2	4	4	5	5	3	1	35
Ellyse	Howard	12	3	5	6	0	0	2	4	4	3	1	25
Denise	Franco	42	4	2	2	2	5	5	6	2	2	1	23
Lisa	Friedrichsen	21	4	1	1	0	0	5	5	3	2	1	17
Megan	Hile	45	4	2	3	0	0	1	1	1	4	1	13
Sydney	Freesen	4	4	5	7	3	3	3	3	3	1	1	31
Morgan	Tyler	51	4	1	4	0	0	5	6	3	3	1	18
Ellyse	Howard	12	4	5	7	0	0	3	3	2	3	1	22

FIGURE O-21

```
Function Contribution(fg, threept, ft, offreb, defreb, assists)
   If fg + threept + ft = 0 Then
      Contribution = (offreb * 2 + defreb + assists * 2) / 2
   ElseIf offreb + defreb = 0 Then
      Contribution = (fg * 2 + threept * 3 + ft + assists * 2) / 3
   Else
      Contribution = (fg * 2 + threept * 3 + ft + offreb * 2 + defreb + assists * 2)
   End If
End Function
```

FIGURE O-22

```
Function Contribution(fg, threept, ft, offreb, defreb, assists)

'If no field goals, 3 pointers, or free throws were made
   If fg + threept + ft = 0 Then

'Then the Contribution statistic should be divided by 2
      Contribution = (offreb * 2 + defreb + assists * 2) / 2

'If no offensive or defensive rebounds were grabbed
   ElseIf offreb + defreb = 0 Then
      Contribution = (fg * 2 + threept * 3 + ft + assists * 2) / 3

'Then the Contribution statistic should be divided by 3
   Else
      Contribution = (fg * 2 + threept * 3 + ft + offreb * 2 + defreb + assists * 2)
   End If
End Function

'This function was created by Your Name on today's date
```

7. **Create sub procedures.**

   a. Open the Player Entry Form in Form Design View, if it's not already opened.

   b. Open the property sheet for the form, click the Event tab, click the On Mouse Move property text box, click the Build button, click Code Builder, then click OK.

   c. Enter the following statement between the Private Sub and End Sub statements:

   ```
   [First].ForeColor = 255
   ```

   d. Enter a comment below this statement as follows:

   ```
   'When the mouse moves, the First text box will become red.
   ```

   e. Save, then close the Visual Basic window.

   f. Close the property sheet, save, then open the Player Entry Form in Form View.

   g. Move the mouse beyond the edge of the Detail section of the form. The color of the First text box should turn red.

   h. Save, then close the Player Entry Form.

8. **Troubleshoot modules.**

   a. Open the Code window for the Shot Statistics module.

   b. Click anywhere in the If fg + threept + ft = 0 statement.

   c. Click Debug on the menu bar, then click the Toggle Breakpoint option to set a breakpoint at this statement.

   d. Save and close the Visual Basic window, then return to Microsoft Access.

   e. Click Queries on the Objects bar, then double-click the Rankings query. This action will use the Contribution function, which will stop and highlight the statement where you set a breakpoint.

   f. Click View on the menu bar, click Immediate Window (if not already visible), type **?fg**, then press [Enter]. On a piece of paper, write down the current value of the fg variable.

   g. Type **?offreb**, then press [Enter]. On a piece of paper, write down the current value of the offreb variable.

   h. Click Debug on the menu bar, click Clear All Breakpoints, then click the Continue button on the Standard toolbar.

   i. Return to the Rankings query in Datasheet View. Using both Query Design View and Query Datasheet View, answer the following questions:
   - When calculating the Rank field, what field is used for the fg argument?
   - When calculating the Rank field, what field is used for the offreb argument?
   - What is the value of the fg argument for the first record ?
   - What is the value of the offreb argument for the first record?

   j. Close the Rankings query, close the Basketball-O.mdb database, then exit Access.

▼ INDEPENDENT CHALLENGE 1

As the manager of a doctor's clinic, you have created an Access database called Patients-O.mdb to track insurance claim reimbursements and general patient health. You want to modify an existing function within this database.

   a. Start Access, then open the **Patients-O.mdb** database from the drive and folder where your Data Files are stored.

   b. Open the Body Mass Index (BMI) module in Design View, then record your answers to the following questions on another sheet of paper:
   - What is the name of the function in the module?
   - What are the function arguments?
   - How many comments are in the function?

   c. Edit the BMI function by adding a comment at the end of the code with your name and today's date.

   d. Edit the BMI function by adding a comment above the Function statement with the following information:

   ```
   'A healthy BMI is in the range of 21-24.
   ```

e. Edit the BMI function by adding an If clause that checks to make sure the height argument is not equal to 0. The final BMI function code should look like Figure O-23.

f. Save and print the module, then close the Visual Basic window.

g. Double-click the BMI Query to open its datasheet, then test the If statement by entering **0** in the Height field for the first record for Sara Johnson. When you press [Tab] to move to the Weight field, the bmicalc field should recalculate to 0.

h. Edit the first record to contain your first and last name, print, save, then close the BMI Query datasheet.

i. Close the Patients-O.mdb database, then exit Access.

FIGURE O-23

```
'This function calculates BMI, body mass index.
'A high BMI indicates an unhealthy weight to height ratio.
'A healthy BMI is in the range of 21-24.
   Function BMI(weight, height)
        If height = 0 Then
             BMI = 0
        Else
             BMI = (weight * 0.4536) / (height * 0.0254) ^ 2
        End If
   End Function
'Your Name and today's date.
```

▼ INDEPENDENT CHALLENGE 2

As the manager of a doctor's clinic, you have created an Access database called Patients-O.mdb to track insurance claim reimbursements. You want to study the existing sub procedures stored as class modules in the Claim Entry Form.

a. Start Access, then open the **Patients-O.mdb** database from the drive and folder where your Data Files are stored.

b. Open the Claim Entry Form in Form Design View.

c. Click the Code button on the Form Design toolbar, then record your answers to the following questions on another sheet of paper:
- What are the names of the sub procedures in this class module?
- What Access functions are used in the PtFirstName_AfterUpdate sub?
- How many arguments do the functions in the PtFirstName_AfterUpdate sub have?
- What do the functions in the PtFirstName_AfterUpdate sub do? (*Hint*: You may have to use the Visual Basic Help system if you are not familiar with the functions.)
- What is the purpose of the On Error command? (*Hint*: Use the Visual Basic Help system if you are not familiar with this command.)

Advanced Challenge Exercise

- Open the Claim Entry Form in Form Design View, then add a command button to the right of the Form Footer section of the main form using the Command Button Wizard. The new command button will be used to delete a record.
- Use the Delete Record picture for the button, and the meaningful button name of **DeleteRecordButton**.
- Open the Code window for the form, and then add a comment with your name to the procedure that contains the VBA code that is executed when the DeleteRecordButton is clicked.
- Select all of the VBA statements that constitute the procedure for the DeleteRecordButton, including the comment with your name, then use the Selection option in the Print dialog box to print only that procedure.

d. Close the Visual Basic window, save and close the Claim Entry Form, then close the Patients-O.mdb database.

e. Exit Access.

▼ INDEPENDENT CHALLENGE 3

As the manager of a doctor's clinic, you have created an Access database called Patients-O.mdb to track insurance claim reimbursements that are fixed (paid at a predetermined fixed rate) or denied (not paid by the insurance company). You want to enhance the database with a class module.

a. Start Access, then open the **Patients-O.mdb** database from the drive and folder where your Data Files are stored.

b. Open the CPT Form in Form Design View.

c. Expand the width of the CPT Form to about the 5" mark on the horizontal ruler.

d. Use the Command Button Wizard to add a command button in the Form Header section. Choose the Add New Record action from the Record Operations category.

e. Enter **Add Record** as the text on the button, then name the button **AddRecordButton**.

f. Use the Command Button Wizard to add a command button in the Form Header section to the right of the existing Add Record button. (*Hint*: Move and resize controls as necessary to put two command buttons in the Form Header section.)

g. Choose the Delete Record action from the Record Operations category.

h. Enter **Delete Record** as the text on the button, and name the button **DeleteRecordButton**.

i. Save and view the CPT Form in Form View, then click the Add Record command button.

j. Add a new record (it will be record number 65) with a CPTCode value of **999** and an RBRVS value of **1.5**.

k. To make sure that the Delete Record button works, click the new record you just entered, click the Delete Record command button, then click Yes to confirm the deletion.

Advanced Challenge Exercise

- In Form Design View, click the Delete Record command button, then press the [Delete] key.
- Click the Code button on the Standard toolbar to examine the class module associated with this form, then record your answers to the following questions on another sheet of paper:
- How many subs exist in this class module and what are their names?
- What was the effect of deleting the command button in Form Design view on the associated Visual Basic code?

l. Add a comment as the last line of code in the Code window with your name and the current date, save, print, then close the Visual Basic window.

m. Save and close the CPT Form, close the Patients-O.mdb database, then exit Access.

▼ INDEPENDENT CHALLENGE 4

Learning a programming language is sometimes compared to learning a foreign language. But have you ever wondered how it would feel to learn a new software program or programming language if English wasn't your primary language, or if you had some other type of accessibility challenge? Advances in technology are helping to break down many barriers to those with vision, hearing, mobility, cognitive, and language impairments. In this exercise, you explore the Microsoft Web site for resources to address these issues.

a. Go to www.microsoft.com/enable, then print that page. Explore the Web site.

b. Go back to www.microsoft.com/enable, click the Guides by Disability link, then click the Language & Speech Impairments link.

c. After exploring the Web site (you may want to print some pages as well, but be careful as some articles are quite long), write a one-page, double-spaced paper describing some of the things that you learned about how Microsoft products accommodate people with language and speech impairments.

d. Go back to www.microsoft.com/enable, click the Worldwide Sites link near the top of the window, then explore the sites for other languages such as Chinese and Japanese. You may be prompted to install a language pack in order to display these languages. Write down the languages for which the Microsoft Accessibility Web site is available.

▼ VISUAL WORKSHOP

As the manager of a college basketball team, you are helping the coach build meaningful statistics to compare the relative value of the players in each game. The coach has stated that one offensive rebound is worth as much to the team as two defensive rebounds, and would like you to use this rule to develop a "rebounding impact statistic" for each game. Open the **Basketball-O.mdb** database and use Figure O-24 to develop a new function called **ReboundImpact** in a new module called **Rebound Statistic** to calculate this statistic. Include your name and the current date as a comment in the last row of the function. Print the function.

FIGURE O-24

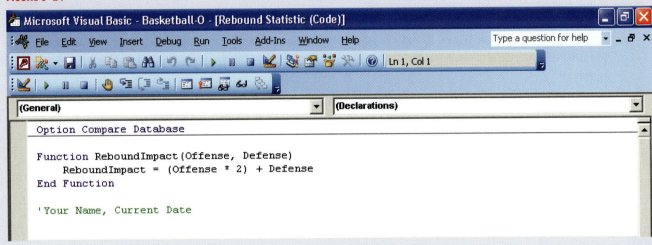

Managing the Database

OBJECTIVES

Convert databases
Set passwords
Change startup options
Encode a database
Analyze performance
Split a database
Replicate a database
Synchronize a database

If you have a SAM user profile, you may have access to hands-on instruction, practice, and assessment of the skills covered in this unit. Log in to your SAM account and go to your assignments page to see what your instructor has assigned.

Access databases are unlike the other Microsoft Office files in that they are typically used by more people and for much longer than Word documents or Excel spreadsheets. Therefore, spending a few hours to secure a database and improve its performance is a good investment. **Database administration** involves the task of making the database faster, easier, more secure, and more reliable. You work with Kristen Fontanelle, network administrator at MediaLoft, to examine several administrative issues such as setting passwords, changing startup options, and analyzing database performance to protect, improve, and enhance her database.

Converting Databases

When you **convert** a database you change the file into one that can be opened in another version of Access. In Access 2003, the default file format for a new database is Access 2000, as evidenced by the text in the database window title bar. This means that you can open an Access 2000 database in Access 2000, 2002 (also called XP), or 2003 without converting the database. While Microsoft Word and Microsoft Excel have enjoyed this type of backward and forward compatibility in previous versions, Access 2002 was the first version of Access that created an Access 2000 database, which meant it could be shared with Access 2000 users without first going through a conversion tool. If you want to open an Access 2000 database in Access 97, however, you need to convert it to an Access 97 database first. ▰▰▰ The Training Department has asked you to convert the Technology-P.mdb database to a version that they can open and use in Access 97 for a training class.

STEPS

1. **Start Access, then open the Technology-P.mdb database from the drive and folder where your Data Files are stored**

   To convert a database, you must make sure that no other users are currently working in it. Because you are the sole user of this database, you can start the conversion process.

2. **Click Tools on the menu bar, point to Database Utilities, point to Convert Database, then click To Access 97 File Format**

   The Convert Database Into dialog box opens, prompting you for the name of the database.

3. **Make sure the Save In list references the drive and folder where your Data Files are stored, then type Technology 97 in the File name text box**

   Your screen should look like Figure P-1. Because both Access 2000 and Access 97 databases have the same **.mdb** file extension, it is helpful to identify the version of Access in the filename if you are going to be working with both file types on the same computer.

4. **Click Save in the Convert Database Into dialog box, then click OK when prompted about the Access 97 File Format**

   As Access converts the database, you can follow the progress on the status bar. When the conversion is finished, and the Technology97.mdb database is created, you return to your original Access 2000 file, Technology-P.mdb.

5. **Right-click the Start button ⊞ start on the taskbar, click Explore on the shortcut menu, then scroll and locate your Data Files in the Folders list**

6. **Click View on the menu bar, then click Details**

   Your screen should look similar to Figure P-2. By viewing file details, the Name, Size, Type, and Modified columns display the name, size in KB, file type, and date the file was last modified. Notice that the list includes Technology97, the database that was just created by converting the Technology-P.mdb Access 2000 database to an Access 97 version database. The filename Technology-P.mdb appears twice, though, both with an .mdb and an .ldb extension. The **.ldb** file is a temporary file that keeps track of record-locking information when the database is open. It helps coordinate the multiuser capabilities of an Access database so that several people can read and update the same database at the same time. The .ldb file may already be closed if your Data Files are stored on the hard drive.

7. **Close Windows Explorer**

FIGURE P-1: Convert Database Into dialog box

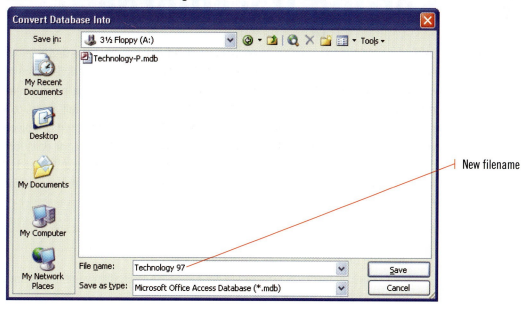

New filename

FIGURE P-2: Using Windows Explorer to view files

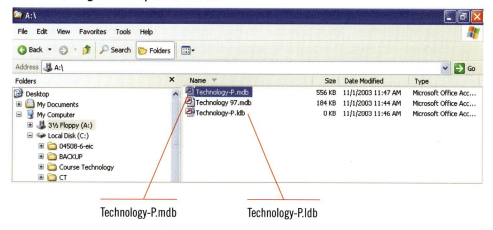

Technology-P.mdb   Technology-P.ldb

Clues to Use

Converting from Access 2000 to Access 2002–2003

Microsoft Office Access 2003 provides some new features such as smart tags (which help you update properties and find errors), the ability to view object dependency information, better backup tools, and expanded XML support. *Access database files* themselves, however, have not dramatically changed from the Access 2000 to the Access 2002–2003 file format. Therefore, use the default Access 2000 file format for new databases created in Access 2003 unless your database is extremely large (a 2002–2003 file format performs better if the database is very large), or if you are planning extensive future programming projects. By using the 2000 file format, you preserve seamless forward and backward compatibility with Access 2000 and 2002 software users.

Setting Passwords

UNIT P
Access 2003

Setting passwords is a common strategy to secure information. You can set three types of passwords on an Access database: database, security account (also called user-level), and Visual Basic for Applications (VBA) passwords. If you set a **database password**, all users must enter that password before they are allowed to open the database, but once they open the database, they have full access to it. **Security account passwords** are applied to **workgroups**, files that determine the user(s), objects, and permissions to which the user(s) of that workgroup are granted (such as read, delete, or edit) for specific objects in the database. **VBA passwords** prevent unauthorized users from modifying VBA code. Other ways to secure an Access database are listed in Table P-1. You apply a database password to the Technology-P.mdb database to further secure the information.

STEPS

QUICK TIP

It's always a good idea to back up a database before creating a database password.

1. **Click File on the menu bar, then click Close**

   The Technology-P.mdb database closes, but the Access application window remains open. To set a database password, you must open it in Exclusive mode.

2. **Click the Open button ⧉ on the Database toolbar, navigate to the drive and folder where your Data Files are stored, click Technology-P.mdb, click the Open list arrow in the Open dialog box, then click Open Exclusive**

   Exclusive mode means that you are the only person who has the database open, and others cannot open the file during this time.

3. **Click Tools on the menu bar, point to Security, then click Set Database Password**

   The Set Database Password dialog box opens, as shown in Figure P-3. If you lose or forget your password, it can't be recovered. For security reasons, your password will not appear as you type; for each keystroke, an asterisk will appear. Therefore, you must enter the exact same password in both the Password and Verify text boxes to make sure you haven't made a typing error. Passwords are case sensitive, so Cyclones and cyclones are different.

QUICK TIP

Check to make sure the Caps Lock light is not on before entering a password.

4. **Type cyclones in the Password text box, press [Tab], type cyclones in the Verify text box, then click OK**

   Passwords should be easy to remember, but not as obvious as your name, the word "password," the name of the database, or the name of the company.

5. **Click File on the menu bar, then click Close**

   Of course, it's important to test the new password.

6. **Click ⧉ on the Database toolbar, navigate to the drive and folder where your Data Files are stored, then double-click Technology-P.mdb**

   The Password Required dialog box opens, as shown in Figure P-4.

7. **Type cyclones, then click OK**

   The Technology-P.mdb database opens, giving you full access to all of the objects. To remove a password, you must exclusively open a database, just as you did when you set a database password.

8. **Click File on the menu bar, click Close, click ⧉ on the Database toolbar, click Technology-P.mdb, click the Open list arrow in the Open dialog box, click Open Exclusive, type cyclones in the Password Required dialog box, then click OK**

9. **Click Tools on the menu bar, point to Security, click Unset Database Password, type cyclones, then click OK**

FIGURE P-3: Set Database Password dialog box

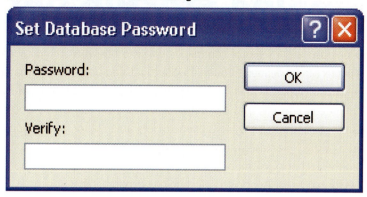

FIGURE P-4: Password Required dialog box

TABLE P-1: Methods to secure an Access database

method	description
Password	Restricts access to the database, and can be set at the database, workgroup, or VBA level
Encoding	Makes the data indecipherable to other programs
Startup options	Hides or disables certain functions when the database is opened
Show/hide objects	Shows or hides objects in the database window; a simple way to prevent users from unintentionally deleting objects is to hide them in the database window by checking the Hidden property in the object's property sheet
Split a database	Separates the back-end data from the front-end objects (such as forms and reports) into two databases that work together; splitting a database allows you to give each user access to only those front-end objects they need as well as add additional security measures to the back-end database that contains the data

Clues to Use

Creating workgroups

The most extensive way to secure an Access database is to use the **Workgroup Administrator** to create workgroups that define the specific users and object permissions to which the users have access. To start the Workgroup Administrator, click Tools on the menu bar, point to Security, then click Workgroup Administrator.

Using Workgroup Administrator, you can grant or deny permissions to any object in the database to any group or individual that is defined within the workgroup information file. Microsoft refers to a database that is protected with workgroup-level security as a **secure database**.

Changing Startup Options

Startup options are a series of commands that execute when the database is opened. Many common startup options can be defined through the Startup dialog box, such as what form and menu bar to display when the database opens. Other startup options require that a **command-line option**, a special series of characters added to the end of the path to the file (for example, C:\My Documents\MediaLoft.mdb /excl), executes a command when the file is opened. See Table P-2 for information on several startup command-line options.  Because you know that most users immediately open the Employees form as soon as they open the Technology-P.mdb database, you decide to use the Startup dialog box to specify that the Employees form opens as soon as the Technology-P.mdb database opens.

STEPS

1. **Click Tools on the menu bar, then click Startup**

   The Startup dialog box opens, as shown in Figure P-5.

2. **Click the Display Form/Page list arrow, then click Employees**

   In addition to specifying which form will open when the Technology-P.mdb database opens, the Startup dialog box provides several other options to customize and secure the database.

3. **Click in the Application Title text box, type MediaLoft Computer Assets, click the Allow Toolbar/Menu Changes check box to clear the check box, then click OK**

   Clearing the Allow Toolbar/Menu Changes check box will not allow users to customize or change the view of toolbars or menus in any way. Provided the correct toolbars appear on each window, not allowing the users to change them can simplify, secure, and improve the usability of the database. The text entered in the Application Title text box appears in the Access title bar.

4. **Close the Technology-P.mdb database, click the Open button 📂 on the Database toolbar, navigate to the drive and folder where your Data Files are stored, then double-click Technology-P.mdb**

   The Technology-P.mdb database opens, followed by the Employees form, as shown in Figure P-6.

5. **Close the Employees form, then double-click View on the menu bar**

   The Toolbars option is no longer available because you disabled toolbar changes in the Startup dialog box.

> **QUICK TIP**
> Press and hold [Shift] while opening a database to bypass the startup options.

6. **Right-click the Database toolbar**

   No shortcut menus are available from any toolbar because you disabled toolbar changes in the Startup dialog box.

FIGURE P-5: Startup dialog box

Application Title text box

Display Form/Page list arrow

Allow Toolbar/Menu Changes check box

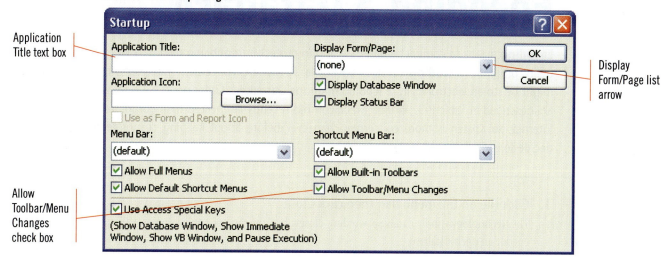

FIGURE P-6: Using startup options

Application title bar

Employees form automatically opens

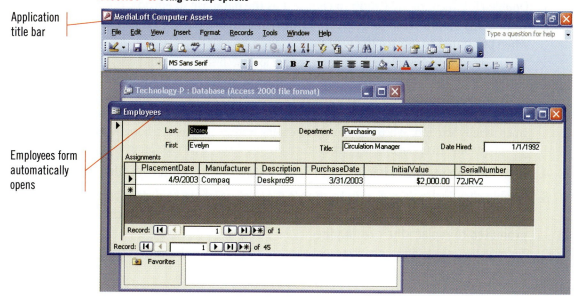

TABLE P-2: Startup command-line options

option	effect
/excl	Opens the database for exclusive access
/ro	Opens the database for read-only access
/pwd *password*	Opens the database using the specified *password*
/repair	Repairs the database (In Access 2000 and 2002, compacting the database also repairs it. If you choose the Compact on Close command, you don't need the /repair option.)
/convert *target database*	Converts a previous version of a database to an Access 2000 database with the *target database* name
/x *macro*	Starts Access and runs specified *macro*
/nostartup	Starts Access without displaying the task pane
/wrkgrp *workgroup information file*	Starts Access using the specified *workgroup information file*

Encoding a Database

Encoding means to compact a database and to protect it from being read by a word processor or text utility program. **Decoding** reverses encoding. If you are concerned that your Access database file might be stolen electronically, encoding might be warranted. Other potential threats to your database are described in Table P-3. ▓▓▓ MediaLoft has recently connected their corporate file servers to the Internet, so Kristen is more concerned than ever before about keeping corporate data secure. You decide to encode the database.

STEPS

QUICK TIP
It's always a good idea to back up a database before encoding it.

1. **Click File on the menu bar, then click Close**

   The Technology-P.mdb database window closes, but the Access application is still running. You cannot encode an open database.

2. **Click Tools on the menu bar, point to Security, click Encode/Decode Database, then navigate to the drive and folder where your Data Files are stored**

   The Encode/Decode Database dialog box opens, as shown in Figure P-7.

3. **Double-click Technology-P.mdb to choose it as the database to encode, double-click Technology-P.mdb again to choose it as the name for the encoded database, then click Yes when prompted to replace the existing file**

   You can encode a database file to the same filename or to a new filename. In either case, a back-up copy of the database on a separate disk protects your file should the encoding process be unsuccessful (unlikely but possible) or the equipment malfunctions during the encoding process. To users authorized to open the file, an encoded database works in exactly the same way as the original file; it is not restricted until you create workgroup security accounts. Whether or not you are using workgroup accounts, however, encoding still helps protect data when it is sent over network connections. You decode a database using the same steps.

4. **Click Tools on the menu bar, point to Security, then click Encode/Decode Database**

5. **Double-click Technology-P.mdb to choose it as the database to decode, double-click Technology-P.mdb again as the name for the decoded database, then click Yes when prompted to replace the existing file**

   The status bar presents information about the progress of the encoding or decoding process. The database returns to its original decoded format.

FIGURE P-7: Encode/Decode Database dialog box

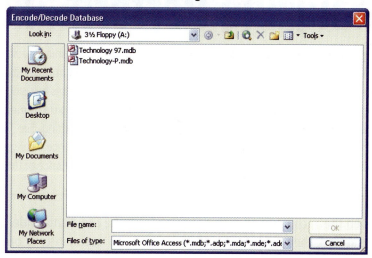

TABLE P-3: Database threats

incident	what can happen	appropriate actions
Virus	Viruses can cause a vast number of damaging actions, ranging from profane messages to destruction of files	Purchase the leading virus-checking software for each machine, and keep it updated
Power outage	Power problems such as **brown-outs** (dips in power often causing lights to dim) and **spikes** (surges in power) can cause damage to the hardware, which may render the computer useless	Purchase a **UPS** (Uninterruptible Power Supply) to maintain constant power to the file server (if networked) Purchase a **surge protector** (power strip with surge protection) for each end user
Theft or intentional damage	Computer thieves or other scoundrels steal or vandalize computer equipment	Place the file server in a room that can be locked after hours Use network drives for user data files, and back them up on a daily basis Use off-site storage for backups Set database passwords and encode the database so that files that are stolen cannot be used Use computer locks for equipment that is at risk, especially laptops

Clues to Use

Creating an MDE file

An Access **.mde** file is a special copy of the database that prevents others from opening or editing form, report, or module objects in Design View. You can still enter data and use the MDE file just like the original database MDB file, but an MDE file gives you a way to distribute the database without revealing the development work you put into the forms, reports, and modules. An MDE file is also much smaller and runs faster than a regular database MDB file. To create an MDE file, close all open databases, but leave Access running. Click Tools on the menu bar, point to Database Utilities, and then click the Make MDE File option. Then enter the names of the original database and the MDE file.

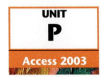

Analyzing Performance

Access provides a tool called the **Performance Analyzer** that studies the structure and size of your database and makes a variety of recommendations on how you could improve its performance. With adequate time and Access skills, you can alleviate many performance bottlenecks by using software tools and additional programming techniques to improve database performance. With extra money, however, you can often purchase faster processors and more memory to accomplish the same thing. See Table P-4 for tips on optimizing the performance of your computer. You use the Performance Analyzer to see whether Access provides any recommendations on how to easily maintain peak performance of the Technology-P.mdb database.

STEPS

1. **Open the Technology-P.mdb database from the drive and folder where your Data Files are stored, then close the Employees form that automatically opens**

2. **Click Tools on the menu bar, point to Analyze, click Performance, then click the Forms tab**
   The Performance Analyzer dialog box opens, as shown in Figure P-8. You can choose to analyze selected tables, forms, other objects, or the entire database.

3. **Click the All Object Types tab, click Select All, then click OK**
   The Performance Analyzer examines each object and presents the results in a dialog box, as shown in Figure P-9. The key shows that the analyzer gives four levels of advice regarding performance: recommendations, suggestions, ideas, and items that were fixed.

4. **Click Table 'Assignments': Change data type of field 'SSN' from 'Text' to 'Long Integer' in the Analysis Results list**
   The lightbulb icon tells you that this is an idea. The Analysis Notes section of the Performance Analyzer dialog box gives you additional information regarding that specific item. In this case, the idea is to change the data type of the field SSN from Text to Number (with a Long Integer field size). While this might not be an appropriate action for an SSN field, the three fields in the PCSpecs table—Memory, HardDisk, and MHz—all represent numeric values that could be changed from Text to Number with the suggested field size. All of the Performance Analyzer's ideas should be considered, but they are not as important as recommendations and suggestions.

5. **Click Close to close the Performance Analyzer dialog box**

FIGURE P-8: Performance Analyzer dialog box

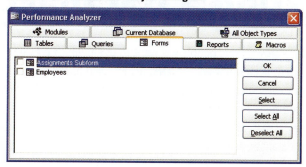

FIGURE P-9: Performance Analyzer results

Icon key

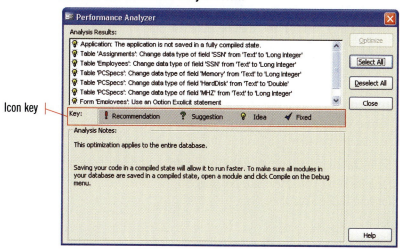

TABLE P-4: Tips for optimizing performance

degree of difficulty	tip
Easy	To free up memory and other computer resources, close all applications that you don't currently need
Easy	If they can be run safely on an "as-needed" basis, eliminate memory-resident programs such as complex screen savers, e-mail alert programs, and virus checkers
Easy	If you are the only person using a database, open it in Exclusive mode
Easy	Use the Compact on Close feature to regularly compact and repair your database
Easy	Convert the database to an Access 2002 database
Moderate	Add more memory to your computer; once the database is open, memory is generally the single most important determinant of overall performance
Moderate	If others don't need to share the database, load it on your local hard drive instead of the network's file server (but be sure to back up local drives regularly, too)
Moderate	Split the database so that the data is stored on the file server, but other database objects are stored on your local (faster) hard drive
Moderate to difficult	If using disk compression software, stop doing so or move the database to an uncompressed drive
Moderate to difficult	Run Performance Analyzer on a regular basis, examining and appropriately acting on each recommendation, suggestion, and idea
Moderate to difficult	Make sure that all PCs are running the latest versions of Windows and Access; this may involve purchasing more software or upgrading hardware to properly support these robust software products

Splitting a Database

As your database grows, more people will want to use it, which creates the need for higher levels of database connectivity. **Local area networks (LANs)** are installed to link multiple PCs together so they can share hardware and software resources. Once a LAN is installed, a shared database can be moved to a **file server**, a centrally located computer from which every user can access the database by using the network. The more users share the same database, however, the slower it responds. The **Database Splitter** feature improves the performance of a database shared among several users by allowing you to split the database into two files: the **back-end database**, which contains the actual table objects and is stored on the file server, and the **front-end database**, which contains the other database objects (forms, reports, so forth), and links to the back-end database tables. You copy the front-end database for as many users as needed because the front-end database must be located on each user's PC. You can also customize the objects (queries, forms, reports) each front-end database contains. Therefore, front-end databases not only improve performance, but also add a level of customization and security. You use the Database Splitter to split the Technology-P.mdb database into two databases in preparation for the new LAN being installed in the Information Systems Department.

STEPS

QUICK TIP

It's always a good idea to back up a database before splitting it.

1. **Click Tools on the menu bar, point to Database Utilities, then click Database Splitter**

   The Database Splitter dialog box opens, and provides additional information on the process and benefits of splitting a database, as shown in Figure P-10.

2. **Click Split Database, then navigate to the drive and folder where your Data Files are stored**

   The Create Back-end Database dialog box suggests the name Technology-P_be.mdb ("be" stands for "back-end") for your back-end database.

3. **Click Split**

   The status bar provides information about the split process.

4. **Click OK when prompted that the split was successful**

   The Technology-P.mdb database has become the front-end database, with all database objects intact except for the table objects. Technology-P.mdb no longer contains any table objects, but rather, contains links to the Technology-P_be.mdb database that stores the actual data, as shown in Figure P-11.

5. **Click Forms on the Objects bar, double-click the Employees form, then type Cosgrove in the Last text box**

   Even though the data is physically stored in the Technology-P_be.mdb database, the other objects in the Technology-P.mdb database can access this data through the linked tables, and the forms can be used to edit and enter data just as they could before.

6. **Close the Employees form, click Tables on the Objects bar, right-click Equipment, click Design View, then click Yes when warned that some properties cannot be modified**

7. **Press [F6] to move the focus to the Field Size property for the SerialNo field, then press [▼] to move through the properties while viewing the right side of the Field Properties pane**

   Most field properties cannot be modified in a linked table, including those that affect the actual size or structure of the data being stored. Properties that do not affect the physical data, but only how it appears to the user, such as Format and Input Mask, may be modified in a linked table.

8. **Close the Equipment table, then close the Technology-P.mdb database**

FIGURE P-10: Database Splitter dialog box

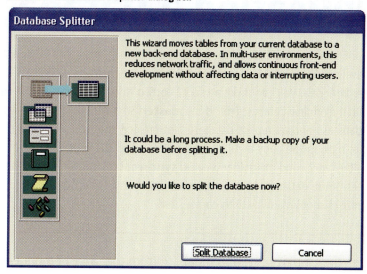

FIGURE P-11: Tables are linked in the front-end database

Linked table icons

Clues to Use

Client/Server computing

Splitting a database into a front-end and back-end database that work together is an excellent example of client/server computing. **Client/Server computing** can be defined as two or more information systems cooperatively processing to solve a problem. In most implementations, the **client** is defined as the user's PC and the **server** is defined as the shared file server, mini, or mainframe computer. The server usually handles corporate-wide computing activities such as data storage and management, security, and connectivity to other networks. Within Access, client computers generally handle those tasks specific to each user, such as storing all of the queries, forms, and reports used by that particular user. Effectively managing a vast client/server network in which many front-end databases link to a single back-end database is a tremendous task, but the performance and security benefits are worth the effort.

Replicating a Database

If you want to copy a database to another computer, such as a home PC or a laptop computer that you use when traveling, Access provides a way to help you keep the copied database synchronized with the original database. In Access, you can make a special copy of the database (called a **replica**) that can be synchronized with the original database (called the **master**) so that updates to one will be applied to the other. The master database and all replica database files created from the master are called the **replica set**. The process of making the copy is called **replication**, and the process of reconciling and updating changes between the replica and the master is called **synchronization**. Kristen wants to take a copy of the Employees-P.mdb database on a laptop to work with it off-site. You replicate the database so that you can synchronize changes made by both copies later.

STEPS

QUICK TIP

It's always a good idea to back up a database before replicating it.

1. **Open the Employees-P.mdb database from the drive and folder where your Data Files are stored**

   The Employees-P.mdb database contains two tables, Courses and Employees.

2. **Click Tools on the menu bar, point to Replication, then click Create Replica**

   A dialog box informs you that you can't replicate an open database.

3. **Click Yes, click Yes (if prompted to install this feature), click Yes when prompted to make a backup of the database before converting it to a Design Master, click OK when Access suggests Replica of Employees-P.mdb as the replica name, then click OK when prompted that the replica has been created**

   As stated by the dialog box, only the Design Master can accept changes to the database structure, but data can be modified in either the replica or the database. The Employees-P.mdb database, now a Design Master, looks like Figure P-12.

4. **Close the Employees-P.mdb database**

Design master

Replica icons

Clues to Use

Using a Briefcase folder

By default, the desktop displays a single Briefcase icon called "My Briefcase." A **Briefcase** is actually a special type of folder designed to help users with two computers to keep the files that are used on both computers updated. If there is no Briefcase folder on the desktop, you can easily create as many new Briefcase folders as you need. Copying an Access database to a Briefcase folder is another method to replicate it.

Synchronizing a Database

Synchronization is the process of updating the records and objects in each member of the replica set. You can synchronize a replica set from within Access or by using the buttons on a Briefcase window toolbar. You will open the Replica of Employees-P.mdb database and edit a record. Then you will synchronize it with the master to see how a replica set is kept up-to-date.

STEPS

1. **Open the Replica of Employees-P.mdb database from the drive and folder where your Data Files are stored**

   Your screen should look like Figure P-13. The replica icons by the database objects look the same for the Design Master and the replica, but the database window title bar indicates whether the database is a Design Master or replica.

2. **Double-click Employees, then type Rivers as the entry for the Last field of the first record**

   A replica database can be used to enter or edit data, but not to change the structure of the table in Table Design View.

3. **Close the Employees datasheet, then close the Replica of Employees-P.mdb database**

4. **Open the Employees-P.mdb database from the drive and folder where your Data Files are stored**

5. **Double-click Employees**

   Right now, Nancy Lee is listed in the first record because the two databases have not yet been synchronized.

6. **Close the Employees table, click Tools on the menu bar, point to Replication, then click Synchronize Now**

   The Synchronize Database 'Employees-P' dialog box opens, as shown in Figure P-14.

7. **Click OK, click Yes, then click Yes (if prompted to install this feature), click OK when prompted that the synchronization is finished, then double-click Employees**

   Nancy Lee has now been updated to Nancy Rivers.

8. **Close the Employees datasheet, close the Employees-P.mdb database, then exit Access**

FIGURE P-13: Replica of Employees-P is a replica database

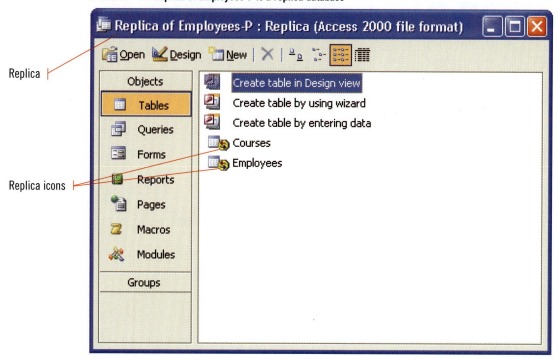

Replica

Replica icons

FIGURE P-14: Synchronize Database 'Employees-P' dialog box

Clues to Use

Using the Briefcase with a laptop computer

You might use the Briefcase to replicate a database when a master database is stored on a file server and the replica is stored on the hard drive of a laptop computer. When you are in the office, your laptop computer is connected to the network through a docking station, so you would use the master database just like all of the other users. When you are in the field, however, you would work on the replica stored in a Briefcase folder on the laptop's hard drive. When you return to the office, you could use the Briefcase update features to resynchronize the master on the hard drive and replica database on your laptop.

Practice

▼ CONCEPTS REVIEW

Identify each element of the Startup dialog box in Figure P-15.

FIGURE P-15

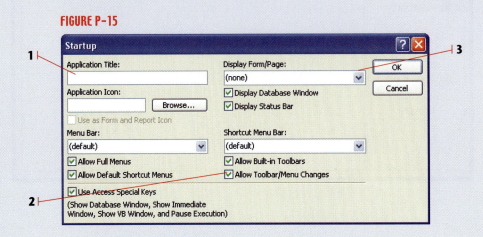

Match each term with the statement that best describes its function.

4. **Exclusive mode**
5. **Database Splitter**
6. **Encoding**
7. **Performance Analyzer**
8. **Synchronization**

a. Means that no other users will have access to the database file while it's open

b. Scrambles data so that it is indecipherable when opened by another program

c. Studies the structure and size of your database, and makes a variety of recommendations on how you can improve its speed

d. Breaks the database into two files to improve performance. One database contains the tables and the other contains the rest of the objects with links to the tables.

e. Updates the files in a replica set so that they all have the same information

Select the best answer from the list of choices.

9. **Changing a database file into one that can be opened in Access 97 is called:**
   a. Splitting.
   b. Analyzing.
   c. Encrypting.
   d. Converting.

10. **Which is *not* a type of password that can be set on an Access database?**
   a. Security account
   b. Database
   c. Object
   d. Visual Basic for Applications

11. **Which of the following determines the users, objects, and permissions to which the users are granted?**
   a. Passwords
   b. Briefcase names
   c. Permission logs
   d. Workgroups

12. **Which character precedes a command-line option?**
   a. /
   b. @
   c. !
   d. ^

▼ SKILLS REVIEW

1. Convert a database.

   a. Start Access, then open the **Basketball-P.mdb** database from the drive and folder where your Data Files are stored.

   b. Click Tools on the menu bar, point to Database Utilities, point to Convert Database, then click To Access 97 File Format.

   c. Navigate to the drive and folder where your Data Files are stored, enter **Basketball97** as the filename, click Save in the Convert Database Into dialog box, then click OK when prompted.

   d. Start Windows Explorer, navigate to the drive and folder where your Data Files are stored, then check to make sure that both the Basketball-P.mdb and Basketball97.mdb databases are present. You may see a Basketball-P.ldb file, because Basketball-P.mdb is currently open.

   e. Close Explorer.

2. Set passwords.

   a. Close the Basketball-P.mdb database, but leave Access open.

   b. Open the **Basketball-P.mdb** database in Exclusive mode.

   c. Set a database password to **big12**. (*Hint:* Check to make sure the Caps Lock light is not on because passwords are case sensitive).

   d. Close the Basketball-P.mdb database, but leave Access open.

   e. Reopen the **Basketball-P.mdb** database in Exclusive mode. Type **big12** as the password.

   f. Unset the database password.

   g. On a piece of paper, explain why it was necessary for you to open the database in Exclusive mode in Steps b and e.

3. Change startup options.

   a. Open the Startup dialog box.

   b. Type **Iowa State Cyclones** in the Application Title text box, click the Display Form/Page list arrow, click the Game Summary Form, clear the Allow Toolbar/Menu Changes check box, then click OK. Notice the change in the Access title bar.

   c. Close the Basketball-P.mdb database, but leave Access open.

   d. Open the **Basketball-P.mdb** database to check the startup options.

   e. Close the Game Summary Form that automatically opened when the database was opened.

   f. Right-click the Database toolbar to make sure that you are unable to change or modify any of the toolbars.

   g. On a piece of paper, identify one reason for changing each of the three startup options modified in Step b.

   h. Close the Basketball-P.mdb database, but leave Access open.

4. Encode a database.

   a. To encode the database, click Tools on the menu bar, point to Security, then click Encode/Decode Database.

   b. Navigate to the drive and folder where your Data Files are stored, click **Basketball-P.mdb**, then click OK.

   c. In the Encode Database As dialog box, click **Basketball-P.mdb**, then click Save.

   d. Click Yes when asked to replace the existing Basketball-P.mdb file.

   e. To decode the database, click Tools on the menu bar, point to Security, then click Encode/Decode Database.

   f. In the Encode/Decode Database dialog box, click **Basketball-P.mdb**, then click OK.

   g. In the Decode Database As dialog box, click **Basketball-P.mdb**, click Save, then click Yes.

   h. On a piece of paper, identify two database threats for which encoding could be used to protect the database.

5. Analyze performance.

   a. Open **Basketball-P.mdb**, then close the Game Summary Form.

   b. Click Tools on the menu bar, point to Analyze, then click Performance.

   c. Click the All Object Types tab, click Select All, then click OK.

   d. Click the Analysis Results item, then read the Analysis notes.

   e. On a piece of paper, explain whether or not you would apply the idea given, and why.

   f. Close the Performance Analyzer dialog box.

6. Split a database.

   a. Click Tools on the menu bar, point to Database Utilities, then click Database Splitter.

   b. Click Split Database, make sure that the Save in list shows the drive and folder where your Data Files are stored, then click Split to accept the default name of **Basketball-P_be.mdb** as the filename.

   c. Click OK when prompted that the database was successfully split.

▼ SKILLS REVIEW (CONTINUED)

d. On a sheet of paper, identify two reasons for splitting a database.

e. On the paper, identify the back-end and front-end database filenames, then explain what these databases contain.

f. On the paper, explain what the table icons in the front-end database look like and what they represent.

g. Close the Basketball-P.mdb database.

7. Replicate a database.

a. Open the **Team-P.mdb** database from the drive and folder where your Data Files are stored.

b. Create a replica of the Team-P.mdb database using the default filename. Do not make a backup copy of the Design Master when prompted.

c. In the Players table of the Team-P.mdb database, modify the record for PlayerNo 4 to have your own first and last name.

8. Synchronize a database.

a. Close the Players table, then synchronize the Design Master with the replica.

b. Close the Team-P.mdb database, then open the replica.

c. Open the Players table. It should display your name in the first record.

d. Close the replica, then exit Access.

▼ INDEPENDENT CHALLENGE 1

As the manager of a doctor's clinic, you have created an Access database called Patients-P.mdb to track insurance claims. You want to set a database password on this file, and also encode the database.

a. Start Access. Open **Patients-P.mdb** in Exclusive mode from the Drive and Folder where your Data Files are stored.

b. Click Tools, point to Security, then click Set Database Password.

c. Enter **health** in the Password text box as well as the Verify text box, then click OK.

d. Close the Patients-P.mdb database, but leave Access running.

e. To encode the database, click Tools, point to Security, then click Encode/Decode Database.

f. In the Encode/Decode Database dialog box, click **Patients-P.mdb**, then click OK.

g. Enter **health** as the password, then click OK.

h. In the Encode Database As dialog box, click **Patients-P.mdb**, click Save, click Yes to replace the existing file, then click OK.

i. Exit Access.

▼ INDEPENDENT CHALLENGE 2

As the manager of a doctor's clinic, you have created an Access database called Patients-P.mdb to track insurance claims. You want to change the startup options.

a. Start Access, then open the database **Patients-P.mdb** from the drive and folder where your Data Files are stored.

b. If prompted for a password (if you completed Independent Challenge 1, the file will be password protected), enter **health**, then click OK.

FIGURE P-16

c. To set startup options, click Tools on the menu, then click Startup.

d. In the Startup dialog box, enter **Drs. Aaron and Kelsey** in the Application Title text box, choose the Claim Entry Form as the choice for the Display Form/Page option, clear the Allow Toolbar/Menu Changes check box as shown in Figure P-16, then click OK.

e. Close the Patients-P.mdb database.

f. Open the **Patients-P.mdb** database to test the startup options. Enter **health** as the password if prompted, then click OK.

▼ INDEPENDENT CHALLENGE 2 (CONTINUED)

g. Close the Claim Entry Form, then right-click the toolbar to make sure that toolbars cannot be modified. Check to make sure that Drs. Aaron and Kelsey appears in the title bar of the Access window.

Advanced Challenge Exercise

■ On a piece of paper, list the options shown in the Startup dialog box and write a sentence that describes what each option is used for. Use Microsoft Access Help to support your research.

h. Close the Patients-P.mdb database, then exit Access.

▼ INDEPENDENT CHALLENGE 3

As the manager of a doctor's clinic, you have created an Access database called Patients-P.mdb to track insurance claims. You want to create a replica set.

a. Open Windows Explorer, locate the **Patients-P.mdb** database from the drive and folder where your Data Files are stored, then copy the database to the desktop. Close Explorer.

b. Start Access, then open the **Patients-P.mdb** database stored on your desktop using the Open Exclusive option. If a password is set on the Patients-P.mdb database, you must remove it before you can use the database to create a replica set. If you were not prompted for a password, skip the next step.

c. Enter **health** as the password, close the Claim Entry Form if it automatically opened, click Tools, point to Security, click Unset Database Password, enter **health**, then click OK.

d. Create a replica of Patients-P.mdb with the default replica name. Make a backup copy of the Design Master when prompted.

e. Close any forms that may have been opened at startup, open the Doctors table in the Patients-P.mdb Design Master, then enter your own information as a new record in the PodFirstName (your first name initial), PodLastName (your last name), and PodCode (your first and last name initials, which must be unique from the other records because it is the key field) fields.

f. Close the Doctors datasheet and close the Patients-P.mdb database.

g. Open the **Replica of Patients-P.mdb** database.

h. Close any forms that may have been opened at startup, then double-click the Doctors table to open its datasheet.

i. Add a friend's name as a new record in the table, making sure that you enter unique initials in the PodCode field.

j. Close the Doctors datasheet, then resynchronize the databases.

k. Open the Doctors datasheet in the Replica of Patients-P.mdb database. Both your name as well as the name of your friend should be listed in the datasheet.

l. Close the Replica of Patients-P.mdb database, then open the **Patients-P.mdb** database.

m. Open the Doctors datasheet. Both your name as well as the name of your friend should be listed in the datasheet. Print the Doctors datasheet.

n. Close the Doctors datasheet, close the Patients-P.mdb database, then close Access.

▼ INDEPENDENT CHALLENGE 4

Microsoft provides extra information, templates, files, and ideas at a Web site called Tools on the Web. In this exercise, you'll explore the Tools on the Web services.

a. Start Access, but do not open any databases.

b. Click Help on the menu bar, then click Microsoft Office Online.

c. Explore the site at your own pace. You may want to print some articles, but be careful as some articles are quite long. Your goal is to find the available Access templates. You may find them from the Templates link.

d. Browse through the available templates until you find one that uses an Access database. (*Hint*: You may want to search Templates for the word "Access".) Follow the instructions to download, extract, and open the sample database.

e. Explore the database.

f. On a piece of paper, write a couple sentences critiquing the tables, forms, and reports in the database. For tables, consider whether they contain the right number of fields. For forms, critique their design and ease-of-use. For reports, consider if they report the information you would need in the manner in which you would like to see it.

▼ INDEPENDENT CHALLENGE 4 (CONTINUED)

g. Use the Performance Analyzer to study each object. Determine if there are any recommendations, suggestions, or ideas that might help you improve the database. On your paper, explain each recommendation, suggestion, or idea that was presented.

h. Close the database.

Advanced Challenge Exercise

- Return to the Microsoft Office Web site. Find the Office Worldwide Web page (*Hint*: It may be at *www.microsoft.com/office/worldwide.mspx*), then explore the Web pages for other regions and countries such as Poland and Spain. Print the first page of the Spain Web page, then click the Back button on your browser toolbar.
- Click the China link. Notice what characters your browser uses to represent the Chinese language.
- Print the first page of the Chinese Web page (in whatever form it is in), then click the Back button on your browser toolbar.
- Explore as many country sites as you like. Explore the More International Downloads link below the list of countries on the Welcome to Office Worldwide Web page.
- Write a one-page, double-spaced paper describing some of the things you learned.

i. Close Access and any other open windows.

▼ VISUAL WORKSHOP

As the manager of a doctor's clinic, you have created an Access database called **Patients-P.mdb** to track insurance claims. Use the Performance Analyzer to generate the results shown in Figure P-17 by analyzing all object types.

FIGURE P-17

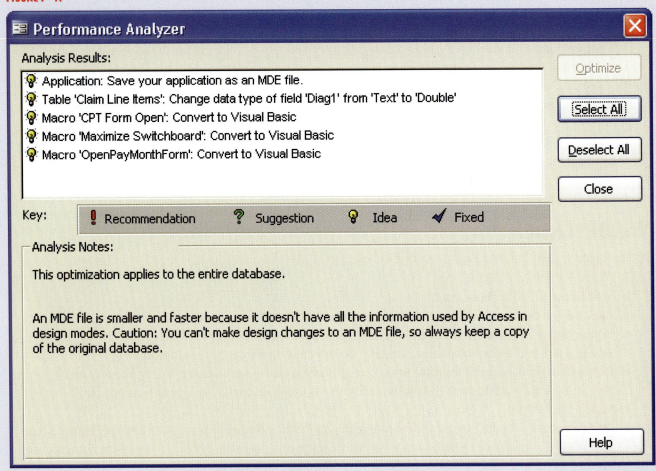

Glossary

Access database file All of the objects (tables, queries, forms, reports, macros, modules) created in an Access database are stored in one file with an .mdb extension.

Action A task that you want a macro to perform.

Action query A query that makes changes to underlying data. There are four types of action queries: delete, update, append, and make-table.

ActiveX control A control that follows ActiveX standards.

ActiveX standards Programming standards developed by Microsoft to allow developers to more easily share software components and functionality across multiple applications.

Aggregate function A function such as Sum, Avg, and Count used in a summary query to calculate information about a group of records.

Align Left Button you click to align selected text or controls along a left margin.

Alignment Commands used in Form or Report Design View to either left-, center-, or right-align a value within its control, or to align the top, bottom, right, or left edge of the control with respect to other controls.

Analyze it with Microsoft Office Excel An OfficeLink feature that allows you to quickly copy Access data to Excel.

AND criteria Criteria placed in the same row of the query design grid. All criteria on the same row must be true for a record to appear on the resulting datasheet.

AND query A query that contains AND criteria—two or more criteria present on the same row of the query design grid. Both criteria must be true for the record to appear on the resulting datasheet.

Append query An action query that appends records to another table.

Argument For a macro, arguments are additional information for each action of a macro that further clarifies how the action is to execute. For a module, arguments are constants, variables, or expressions that are passed to a procedure and are required for it to execute.

Arithmetic operator Plus (+), minus (–), multiply (*), divide (/), or exponentiation (^) character used in a mathematical calculation.

Ascending order A sequence in which information is placed in alphabetical order or arranged from smallest to largest.

Asterisk Wildcard character that represents any group of characters.

AutoCorrect Options button Smart Tag that helps you correct typos or, when it appears as Property Update Options, helps you apply property changes to other areas of the database where a field is used.

AutoFill A pointer that you use in Microsoft Office Excel to quickly and easily copy Excel formulas to other cells.

AutoForm Tool to quickly create a form that displays all of the fields of the selected record source.

AutoFormat Predefined format that you can apply to a form or report to set the background picture, font, color, and alignment formatting choices.

AutoKeys A special name reserved for the macro group object that contains key combinations (such as [Ctrl] [L]) that are used to run associated macros.

AutoNumber A field data type in which Access enters a sequential integer for each record added into the datasheet. Numbers cannot be reused even if the record is deleted.

Avg function Built-in Access function used to calculate the average of the values in a given field.

Back-end database When a database has been split using the Database Splitter, a back-end database is created that contains all of the data and is stored on a computer accessible by all users (that computer is usually the file server in a LAN).

Backup An up-to-date copy of the database.

Bang notation Syntax used to separate parts of an object (the parts are separated by an exclamation point, hence "bang") in the VBA programming language.

Between...and Query criterion that selects all records between two values, including the two values.

Border Style A form property that determines the appearance of the borders around a form.

Bound control A control used in either a form or report to display data from the underlying record source; also used to edit and enter new data in a form.

Bound object frame A bound control used to show OLE data, such as a picture on a form or report.

Break mode The temporary suspension of program execution in which you can examine, debug, reset, step through, or continue executing the program.

Breakpoint A bookmark set in VBA code that temporarily suspends execution of a procedure so that the user can examine what is happening.

Briefcase A Windows program used to help synchronize two computers that regularly use the same files.

Brown-out A dip in power that often causes lights to dim.

Browser Software, such as Microsoft Internet Explorer, used to find, download, view, and use Web pages.

Calculated control A control that uses information from existing controls to calculate new data, such as subtotals, dates, or page numbers; used in either a form or report.

Calculated field A field created in Query Design View that results from an expression of existing fields, Access functions, and arithmetic operators. For example, the entry Profit: [RetailPrice]-[WholesalePrice] in the field cell of the query design grid creates a calculated field called Profit that is the difference between the values in the RetailPrice and WholesalePrice fields.

Calculation A new value that is created by entering an expression in a text box on a form or report.

Calendar control An ActiveX control that shows the current date selected on a small calendar. You can use this control to find or display a date in the past or future.

Caption A field property used to override the technical field name with an easy-to-read caption entry when the field name appears on datasheets, forms, and reports.

Cascade Delete Related Records An option that can be applied to referential integrity, and which automatically deletes all records in the "many" table if the record with the matching key field in the "one" table is deleted.

Cascade Update Related Fields An option that can be applied to referential integrity and which means that data in the foreign key field of the "many" table will automatically change when primary key fields values in the "one" table are changed.

Case In VBA, a group of statements.

Category axis On a PivotChart, the horizontal axis. Also called the x-axis.

Category field On a PivotChart, the field that supplies the values for the horizontal axis. Analogous to the Row Field on a PivotTable and the Row Heading field for a crosstab query.

Chart Visual representation of numeric data that helps a user see comparisons, patterns, and trends in data.

Chart Field List A list of the fields in the underlying record source for a PivotChart.

Chart Wizard Access wizard that steps you through the process of creating charts within forms and reports.

Check box Bound control used to display "yes" or "no" answers for a field. If the box is "checked" it indicates "yes" information in a form or report.

Child record In a pair of tables that have a one-to-many relationship, the "many" table contains the child records.

Class module A module used only within a particular form or report object, and therefore is stored within the form or report object.

Client In Internet terminology, this is your computer. In a client/server application, your computer, or the one typically used to manage a user interface such as forms.

Client/server applications An application that uses both a server (typically used to manage data and communications process) and clients (typically used to manage the user interface such as forms) for one application.

Collapse button A button that looks like a minus sign (–) to the left of a record displayed in a datasheet and that when clicked, collapses the subdatasheet that is displayed.

Column Field On a PivotTable, the field that supplies values for each column. Analogous to the Series field in a PivotChart and the Column Heading field of a crosstab query.

Combo box A bound control used to display a list of possible entries for a field in which you can also type an entry from the keyboard. It is a "combination" of the list box and text box controls.

Combo Box Wizard A bound control used to display a list of possible entries for a field in which you can also type an entry from the keyboard. It is a "combination" of the list box and text box controls.

Command button An unbound control used to provide an easy way to initiate an action or run a macro.

Command Button Wizard A wizard that steps you through the process of creating a command button.

Command-line option A special series of characters added to the end of the path to the database file that starts with a forward slash and modifies the way that the database is opened.

Comment line A VBA statement that does not execute any actions but is used to clarify or document other statements. Comment lines appear in green in the VBA Code window and start with a single apostrophe.

Compact and Repair Database Option on the Database Utilities menu allows you to compact and repair an open database.

Compact on Close Feature found on the General tab of the Options dialog box which compacts and repairs your database each time you close it.

Compacting Rearranging the data and objects on the storage medium so space formerly occupied by deleted objects is eliminated. Compacting a database doesn't change the data, but reduces the overall size of the database.

Comparison operators Characters such as > and < that allow you to find or filter data based on specific criteria.

Compile time The period during which source code is translated to executable code.

Compile time error A VBA error that occurs because of incorrectly constructed VBA code.

Conditional expression An expression that results in either a "true" or "false" answer that determines whether a macro action will execute or not.

Conditional formatting Formatting that is based on specified criteria. For example, a text box may be conditionally formatted to display its value in red if the value is a negative number.

Constant In VBA, an item that retains a constant value throughout the execution of the code.

Control Any element such as a label, text box, line, or combo box, on a form or report. Controls can be bound, unbound, or calculated.

ControlTip Text property Property of a control that determines the text displayed in tip that pops up when you point to that control with the mouse.

Convert To change a database file into one that can be opened by an earlier version of Access.

Count Aggregate function that calculates the number of values in a field (not counting null values).

Criteria Entries (rules and limiting conditions) that determine which records are displayed when finding or filtering records in a datasheet or form, or when building a query.

Criteria syntax Rules by which criteria need to be entered in Query Design View.

Crosstab query A query that presents data in a cross-tabular layout (fields are used for both column and row headings), similar to PivotTables in other database and spreadsheet products.

Crosstab Query Wizard A wizard used to create crosstab queries and which helps identify fields that will be used for row and column headings, and fields that will be summarized within the datasheet.

Crosstab row A row in the query design grid used to specify the column and row headings and values for the crosstab query.

Currency A field data type used for monetary values.

Current record box *See* Record selector box.

Current record symbol A black triangle symbol that appears in the record selector box to the left of the record that has the focus in either a datasheet or a form.

DAP *See* page.

Data The unique information you enter into the fields of the records.

Data access page (DAP) *See* page.

Data field On a PivotChart, the field that supplies the values that are summarized as bars or lines within the PivotChart. Analogous to the Totals or Details field on a PivotTable and a Value field in a crosstab query.

Data type A required property for each field that defines the type of data that can be entered in each field. Valid data types include AutoNumber, Text, Number, Currency, Date/Time, OLE Object, and Memo.

Database A collection of tables associated with a general topic (for example, sales of products to customers).

Database administration The task of making a database faster, easier, more secure, and more reliable.

Database password A password that is required to open a database.

Database Splitter An Access feature that improves the performance of a shared database by allowing you to split it into multiple files.

Database toolbar Toolbar that contains buttons for common tasks that affect the entire database or are common to all database objects.

Database window The window that includes common elements such as the Access title bar, menu bar, and toolbar.

Database window toolbar Toolbar that contains buttons used to open, modify, create, delete, and view objects.

Database Wizard An Access wizard that creates a sample database file for a general purpose such as inventory control, event tracking, or expenses. The objects created by the Database Wizard can be used and modified.

Datasheet A spreadsheet-like grid that displays fields as columns, and records as rows.

Datasheet View A view that lists the records of the object in a datasheet. Table, query, and most form objects have a Datasheet View.

Date function Built-in Access function used to display the current date on a form or report.

Date/Time A field data type used for date and time data.

Debug To determine why a macro doesn't run properly.

Decimal Places A field property that determines the number of digits that should be displayed to the right of the decimal point (for Number or Currency fields).

Declaration statement A VBA statement that precedes procedure statements and helps set rules for how the statements in the module are processed.

Decode To reverse the encoding process.

Default Switchboard The first switchboard in the database and the one used to link to additional switchboard pages.

Default Value A field property that provides a default value, automatically entered for a given field when a new record is created.

Default View A form property that determines whether a subform automatically opens in Datasheet or Continuous Forms view.

Delete query An action query that deletes records based on an expression.

Delimited text file A file with only text (no formatting) that typically stores one record on each line with field values separated by a common character such as a comma, tab, or dash.

Design grid *See* Query design grid.

Design View A view in which the structure of the object can be manipulated. Every Access object has a Design View.

Detail section The section of a form or report that contains the controls that are printed for each record in the underlying query or table.

Dialer Software that helps you dial and connect to your Internet Service Provider.

Dialog box A special form that displays information or prompts a user for a choice.

Dialog property option An option for the Border Style form property that adds a thick border to the form and prevents the form from being maximized, minimized, or resized.

Display When A control property that determines whether the control will appear only on the screen, only when printed, or at all times.

Documenter An Access feature that creates reports on the properties and relationships among the objects in your database.

Domain The recordset (table or query) that contains the field used in a domain function calculation.

Domain function A function used to display a calculation on a form or a report using a field that is not included in the Record Source property for the form or report. Also called domain aggregate function.

Domain name The middle part of a URL, such as "course" in www.course.com.

Drop area A position on a PivotChart or PivotTable where you can drag and place a field. Drop areas on a PivotTable include the Filter field, Row field, Column field, and Totals or Detail field. Drop areas on a PivotChart include the Filter field, Category field, Series field, and Data field.

Dynamic Web page A Web page automatically updated with the latest changes to the database each time it is opened. Web pages created by the page object are dynamic.

Dynaset A type of recordset displayed within a query's datasheet that allows you to update all fields except for those on the "one" side of a one-to-many relationship.

E-mail Electronic mail.

Edit mode The mode in which Access assumes you are trying to edit a particular field, so keystrokes such as [Ctrl][End], [Ctrl][Home], [▲] and [▼] move the insertion point within the field.

Edit record symbol A pencil symbol that appears in the record selector box to the left of the record that is currently being edited in either a datasheet or a form.

Enabled Control property that determines whether the control can have the focus in Form View.

Encode To make the database objects and data within the database indecipherable to other programs.

End function A required VBA statement that marks the end of the code that defines a new function.

End tag In markup languages such as HTML and XML, an end tag marks the end of data.

Enforce Referential Integrity An option that can be applied to a one-to-many relationship. When applied, it ensures that no orphan records are entered or created in the database by making sure that the "one" side of a linking relationship (CustomerNumber in a Customer table) is entered before that same value can be entered in the "many" side of the relationship (CustomerNumber in a Sales table).

Error Indicator button Smart Tag that helps identify potential design errors in Report or Form Design View.

Event Something that happens within a database (such as the click of a command button or the entry of a field) that can be used to initiate the execution of a macro. Events are associated with toolbars, objects, and controls, and can be viewed by examining that item's property sheet.

Event handler procedure A procedure that runs in response to an event.

Excel *See* Microsoft Office Excel.

Exclusive mode A mode in which only one person has a database open, and others cannot open the file during this time.

Expand button A button that looks like a plus sign (+) to the left of a record displayed in a datasheet view, and that when clicked, will show related records in a subdatasheet.

Exporting A process to quickly convert data from Access to another file format such as an Excel workbook, a Word document, or a static Web page.

Expression A combination of values, functions, and operators that calculates to a single value. Access expressions start with an equal sign and are placed in a text box in either Form Design View or Report Design View.

Extensible Markup Language A set of tags and codes that allow one application to deliver data to another application using Web pages.

Extensible Schema Document A file format that stores structural information about a database. It accompanies and helps describe the data in an XML file.

Extensible Stylesheet Language A file format that stores presentation (formatting characteristics) about data. It accompanies and helps describe the data in an XML file.

Favorites group A group on the Groups bar that organizes frequently used objects.

Field The smallest piece of information in a database, for example, the customer's name, city, or phone number.

Field list A list of the available fields in the table or query that the list represents.

Field names The names given to each field in Table Design or Table Datasheet View.

Field Properties pane The lower half of Table Design View that shows you the properties for the currently selected field.

Field property *See* Properties.

Field selector button The button to the left of a field in Table Design View that indicates which field is currently selected. Also the thin gray bar above each field in the query grid.

Field Size A field property that determines the largest number that can be entered in a field (for Number or Currency fields) or the number of characters that can be entered in a field (for Text fields).

File transfer Uploading and downloading files containing anything from text to pictures to music to software programs.

Fill/Back Color Button on the Formatting toolbar that you click to change the background color of a selected object or area.

Filter A temporary view of a subset of records. A filter can be saved as a query object if you wish to apply the same filter later without re-creating it.

Filter field On a PivotTable or PivotChart, the field in the upper-left corner, but neither a row nor column heading.

Filter window A window that appears when you click the Filter By Form button when viewing data in a datasheet or in a form window. The Filter window allows you to define the filter criteria.

Find A command used to locate specific data within a field.

Find Duplicates Query Wizard A wizard used to create a query that determines whether a table contains duplicate values in one or more fields.

Find unmatched query A query that finds records in one table that does not have matching records in a related table.

Find Unmatched Query Wizard A wizard used to create a query that finds records in one table that doesn't have related records in another table.

Firewall A combination of hardware and software that adds a layer of security to corporate data. In its simplest form, a firewall consists of software that requires a valid user name and password before access to information is granted.

First Aggregate function that returns the field value from the first record in a table or query.

Fit (print option) An option that automatically adjusts a preview to display all pages in a report.

Focus The property that indicates which field would be edited if you were to start typing.

Font/Fore Color Button on the Formatting toolbar that you click to change the foreground color of a selected object or text.

Foreign key field In a one-to-many relationship between two tables, the foreign key field is the field in the "many" table that links the table to the primary key field in the "one" table.

Form An Access object that provides an easy-to-use data entry screen that generally shows only one record at a time.

Form Design toolbar When working in Form Design View, the toolbar that appears with buttons that help you modify a form's controls.

Form Design View The view of a form in which you add, delete, and modify the form's properties, sections, and controls.

Form Footer A section that appears at the bottom of the screen in Form View for each record, but prints only once at the end of all records when the form is printed.

Form Header A section that appears at the top of the screen in Form View for each record, but prints only once at the top of all records when the form is printed.

Form View View of a form object that displays data from the underlying recordset and allows you to enter and update data.

Form Wizard An Access wizard that helps you create a form.

Format Field property that controls how information will be displayed and printed.

Format Painter A tool that you can use within Form Design View and Report Design View to copy formatting characteristics from one control, and paint them on another.

Formatting Enhancing the appearance of the information through font, size, and color changes.

Front-end database When a database has been split using the Database Splitter, a front-end database is created that contains links back to the data stored in the back-end database as well as any objects needed by the user. The front-end database is stored on the user's computer, which is also called the client computer.

Function A special, predefined formula that provides a shortcut for a commonly used calculation, for example, SUM or COUNT.

Glossary terms Words in the Access Help system that are shown as blue hyperlinks and display the word's definition when clicked.

Graphic image *See* Image.

Graphical user interface An interface that comprises buttons, lists, graphical elements, and other controls that can be controlled using the mouse rather than just the keyboard.

Group A collection of objects.

Group Footer A section of the report that contains controls that print once at the end of each group of records.

Group Header A section of the report that contains controls that print once at the beginning of each group of records.

Group selection handles Selection handles that surround grouped controls.

Grouping To sort records in a particular order, plus provide a section before and after each group of records.

Grouping controls Allow you to identify several controls as a group to quickly and easily apply the same formatting properties to them.

Grouping records In a report, to sort records based on the contents of a field, plus provide a group header section that precedes the group of records and provide a group footer section that follows the group of records.

Groups bar Located just below the Objects bar in the database window, the Groups bar displays the Favorites and any user-created groups, which in turn contain shortcuts to objects. Groups are used to organize the database objects into logical sets.

Groups button Button on the Groups bar that expands or collapses that section of the database window.

GUI *See* Graphical user interface.

Handles *See* Sizing handles.

Hide Duplicates Control property that when set to "Yes," hides duplicate values for the same field from record to record in the Detail section.

Home page The first page displayed when you enter a new URL in your browser.

HTML HyperText Markup Language, a set of codes inserted into a text file that browser software such as Internet Explorer can use to determine the way text, hyperlinks, images, and other elements appear on a Web page.

Hyperlink A field data type that stores World Wide Web addresses. A hyperlink can also be a control on a form that when clicked, opens another database object, external file, or external Web page.

Hyperlink control The tool you use to add a hyperlink to an Access object.

HyperText Markup Language *See* HTML.

If...Then...Else A series of VBA statements that allow you to test for a logical condition and execute one set of commands if the condition is true and another if the condition is false.

Image A nontextual piece of information such as a picture, piece of clip art, drawn object, or graph. Because images are graphical (and not numbers or letters), they are sometimes referred to as graphical images.

Image control A control used to store a single piece of clip art, a photo, or a logo on a form or report.

Immediate window In the VBA Code window, the area where you can determine the value of any argument at the breakpoint.

Importing A process to quickly convert data from an external source, such as Excel or another database application, into an Access database.

Input Mask Field property that provides a visual guide for users as they enter data.

Insert Merge Field A Word dialog box that lists all of the fields you can use to merge into the main document to create a customized mass mailing.

Internet A worldwide network of computer networks that sends and receives information such as Web pages and e-mail through a common protocol called TCP/IP.

Internet Service Provider A company that connects your computer to the Internet.

Intranet A wide area network uses the same technologies as the Internet (TCP/IP protocol, e-mail, Web pages), but is built for the internal purposes of a company.

Is Not Null Criterion that finds all records in which any entry has been made in the field.

Is Null Criterion that finds all records in which no entry has been made in the field.

ISP *See* Internet Service Provider.

Junction table A table created to establish separate one-to-many relationships to two tables that have a many-to-many relationship.

Key field *See* Primary key field.

Key field combination Two or more fields that as a group contain unique information for each record.

Key field symbol *See* Key symbol.

Key symbol In Table Design View, the symbol that appears as a miniature key in the field indicator box to the left of the field name. It identifies the field that contains unique information for each record.

Label An unbound control that displays static text on forms and reports.

LAN *See* Local area network.

Last Aggregate function that returns the field value from the last record in a table or query.

Layout The general arrangement in which a form will display the fields in the underlying recordset. Layout types include Columnar, Tabular, Datasheet, Chart, and PivotTable. Columnar is most popular for a form, and Datasheet is most popular for a subform.

Layout Wizard A tool that helps you create PivotTables and PivotCharts.

.ldb The file extension for a temporary file that keeps track of record locking information when an Access database is open.

Left function Access function that returns a specified number of characters starting with the left side of a value in a Text field.

Like operator An Access comparison operator that allows queries to find records that match criteria that include a wildcard character.

Limit to List Combo box control property that allows you to limit the entries made by that control to those provided by the combo box list.

Line control An unbound control used to draw lines on a form or report that divide it into logical groupings.

Link Child Fields A subform property that determines which field will serve as the "many" link between the subform and main form.

Link Master Fields A subform property that determines which field will serve as the "one" link between the main form and the subform.

Linking To connect an Access database to an external file such as another Access, dBase, or Paradox database; an Excel spreadsheet, or a text file.

List box A bound control that displays a list of possible choices for the user. Used mainly on forms.

Local area network A network that connects local resources such as files servers, user computers, and printers by a direct cable.

Locked property A control property specifies whether you can edit data in a control in Form View.

Logic error An error that occurs when code runs without problems, but the procedure still doesn't produce the desired result.

Logical view The datasheet of a query is sometimes called a logical view of the data because it is not a copy of the data, but rather, a selected view of data from the underlying tables.

Lookup A reference table or list of values used to populate the values of a field.

Lookup field A field that has lookup properties. Lookup properties are used to create a drop-down list of values to populate the field.

Lookup properties Field properties that allow you to supply a drop-down list of values for a field.

Lookup Wizard A wizard used in Table Design View that allows one field to "look up" values from another table or entered list. For example, you might use the Lookup Wizard to specify that the CustomerNumber field in the Sales table display the CustomerName field entry from the Customers table.

Macro An Access object that stores a collection of keystrokes or commands such as those for printing several reports in a row or providing a toolbar when a form opens.

Macro Design View An Access view you use to create macros and list macro actions in the order you want them to run.

Macro Group An Access macro object that contains more than one macro.

Mail Merge task pane A tool that appears in Word to help you with the mail merge process.

Mail Merge toolbar A Word toolbar that assists in the process of a mail merge.

Main document A Word document that contains the standard text that will be used for each letter in a mass mailing.

Main form A form that contains a subform control.

Main report A report that contains a subreport control.

Make-table query An action query that creates a new table.

Many-to-many relationship The relationship between two tables in an Access database in which one record of one table relates to many records in the other table and vice versa. You cannot directly create a many-to-many relationship between two tables in Access. To relate two tables with such a relationship, you must establish a third table called a junction table that creates separate one-to-many relationships with the two original tables.

Mapped drive A network folder that many people can use.

Master The original Access database file that is copied to the Briefcase.

Max Aggregate function that returns the maximum value in the field.

.mdb The file extension for Access databases.

.mde file A special copy of a database that prevents others from opening or editing form, report, or module objects in Design View.

Memo A field data type used for lengthy text such as comments or notes. It can hold up to 64,000 characters of information.

Menu bar Contains menu options appropriate for the current view of the database.

Merge fields The variable pieces of data that are merged from an Access database into a Word main document during a mail merge process.

Merge It with Microsoft Office Word An OfficeLink feature that allows you to quickly merge Access database records with a Word document for mass mailing purposes.

Method An action that an object can perform.

Microsoft Office Excel The spreadsheet program in the Microsoft Office suite.

Microsoft Office Word The word processing program in the Microsoft Office suite.

Min Aggregate function that returns the minimum value in the field.

Modem Hardware that converts digital computer signals to analog telephone signals. Short for modulate-demodulate.

Module An Access object that stores Visual Basic programming code that extends the functions of automated Access processes.

MsgBox A macro action that displays an informational message.

Multiuser A quality that allows many people to enter and update information at the same time. Access databases are inherently multiuser.

Name AutoCorrect A feature that fixes discrepancies among references to field names, controls on forms and reports, and object names when you change them.

Name property Property of a text box that gives the text box a meaningful name.

Named argument In VBA, a value that provides information to an action, event, method, procedure, property, or function.

Navigation bar A bar containing buttons that let you move from one record to another. On a data access page, the navigation bars also contain buttons to edit, sort, and filter data.

Navigation buttons Buttons in the lower-left corner of a datasheet or form that allow you to quickly navigate between the records in the underlying object as well as add a new record.

Navigation Buttons property A form property that determines whether navigation buttons appear on the form.

Navigation mode A mode in which Access assumes that you are trying to move between the fields and records of the datasheet (rather than edit a specific field's contents), so keystrokes such as [Ctrl][Home] and [Ctrl][End] move you to the first and last field of the datasheet.

Navigation toolbar Toolbar at the lower-left corner of Datasheet View, Form View, or a Web page that helps you navigate between records.

Network administrator Person who builds and maintains a network.

New Record button Button you click to add records to a database.

Newsgroups Similar to e-mail, but messages are posted in a "public mailbox" that is available to any subscriber, rather than sent to one individual.

Normalization The process of creating a relational database that involves determining the appropriate fields, tables, and table relationships.

Northwind.mdb A sample database provided with Microsoft Office Access 2003.

NorthwindCS A sample Access database that illustrates how an Access database can connect to an SQL Server database.

Notepad A free Windows accessory text-editing program.

Null The state of "nothingness" in a field. Any entry such as 0 in a numeric field or a space in a text field is not null. It is common to search for empty fields by using the Null criteria in a filter or query. The Is Not Null criteria find all records where there is an entry of any kind.

Number A field data type used for numeric information used in calculations, such as quantities.

Object A table, query, form, report, page, macro, or module in an Access database. In VBA, an item that can be identified or manipulated, including the traditional Access objects, such as a table, query, or form, and smaller parts of these objects, such as controls, sections, and procedures.

Object Browser The part of the VBA Code window that lists the defined modules and procedures as well as available methods, properties, events, constants, and other items that you can use in the code.

Object buttons Buttons on the Objects bar that provide access to the different types of objects (tables, queries, forms, reports, macros, modules) in the current database.

Object Dependencies task pane A task pane that identifies which objects in a database depend on other objects.

Objects button Button on the Objects bar that expands or collapses that section of the database window.

ODBC *See* Open Database Connectivity.

OfficeLinks Three tools within Access (Publish It with Microsoft Office Word, Publish It with Microsoft Office Excel, and Merge It with Microsoft Office Word) that allow you to quickly send data from an Access database to another Microsoft Office software product.

OLE Object A field data type that stores pointers that tie files, such as pictures, sound clips, or spreadsheets, created in other programs to a record.

On Click An event property that causes a macro to run when a command button is clicked.

On Current An event property that occurs when a macro moves the focus from one record to another.

One-to-many line The line that appears in Query Design View or the Relationships window and shows which field is duplicated between two tables to serve as the linking field. The one-to-many line displays a "1" next to the field that serves as the "one" side of the

relationship and displays an infinity symbol next to the field that serves as the "many" side of the relationship when referential integrity is specified for the relationship. Also called the one-to-many join line.

One-to-many relationship The relationship between two tables in an Access database in which a common field links the tables together. The linking field is usually the primary key field in the "one" table of the relationship and the foreign key field in the "many" table of the relationship.

Open Database Connectivity Standards that allow data sources to share data with one another.

Option button A bound control used to display a limited list of mutually exclusive choices for a field such as "female" or "male" for a gender field in a form or report.

Option group A bound control placed on a form that is used to group together several option buttons that provide a limited number of values for a field.

Option Group Wizard An Access wizard that guides the process of developing an option group with option buttons.

Option Value property Property of an option button that identifies the numeric value that will be placed in the field to which the associated option group is bound.

OR criteria Criteria placed on different rows of the query design grid. A record will appear in the resulting datasheet if it is true for any single row.

OR query A query that contains OR criteria—two or more criteria present on different rows in the query design grid. A record will appear on the resulting datasheet if it is true for either criteria.

Orphan record A record in a "many" table that doesn't have a linking field entry in the "one" table. Orphan records can be avoided by using referential integrity.

Page An Access object that creates Web pages from Access objects as well as provides Web page connectivity features to an Access database. Also called data access page.

Page Design View A view that allows you to modify the structure of a data access page.

Page Footer A section of a form or report that contains controls that print once at the bottom of each page.

Page function Built-in Access function used to display the current page number on a report.

Page Header A section of a form or report that contains controls that print once at the top of each page. On the first page of the report, the Page Header section prints below the Report Header section.

Page View A view that allows you to see how your dynamic Web page will appear when opened in Internet Explorer.

Parameter query A query that displays a dialog box prompting you for criteria each time you run it.

Parent record In a pair of tables that have a one-to-many relationship, the "one" table contains the parent records.

Parent/Child relationship The relationship between the main form and subform. The main form acts as the parent, displaying the information about the "one" side of a one-to-many relationship between the forms. The subform acts as the "child," displaying as many records as exist in the "many" side of the one-to-many relationship.

Performance Analyzer An Access feature that studies the size and structure of your database and makes a variety of recommendations on how you could improve its performance.

Personalized menus/toolbars The menus and toolbars that modify themselves to reflect those features that you use most often.

PivotChart A graphical presentation of the data in a PivotTable.

PivotChart View The view in which you build a PivotChart.

PivotTable An arrangement of data that uses one field as a column heading, another as a row heading, and summarizes a third field, typically a Number field, in the body.

PivotTable List A control on a Web page that summarizes data by columns and rows to make it easy to analyze.

PivotTable View The view in which you build a PivotTable.

PivotTable Wizard Form creation tool that provides a series of steps to create a summarized arrangement of data in a PivotTable arrangement.

Pixel One pixel is the measurement of one picture element on the screen.

Pop-up form A special type of form that stays on top of other open forms, even when another form is active.

Pound sign Wildcard that stands for a single-number digit.

Primary key field A field that contains unique information for each record. A primary key field cannot contain a null entry.

Primary sort field In a query grid, the leftmost field that includes sort criteria. It determines the order in which the records will appear and can be specified "ascending" or "descending."

Private Sub A type of VBA statement that declares the name for a new sub procedure; indicates that the sub is accessible only to other procedures in the module where it is declared.

Procedure A series of VBA programming statements that perform an operation or calculate an answer. There are two types of procedures: functions and subs.

Project A special Access file that contains no data, but rather, form and report objects. The data for the database is typically located on a file/server to which the project file is linked.

Project Explorer window The window you use to switch between open projects, objects that can contain VBA code.

Properties Characteristics that further define the field (if field properties), control (if control properties), section (if section properties), or object (if object properties).

Property sheet A window that displays an exhaustive list of properties for the chosen control, section, or object within the Form Design View or Report Design View.

Protocol A set of rules.

Publish It with Microsoft Office Excel An OfficeLink feature that allows you to quickly copy a query, form, or report object to Excel.

Publish It with Microsoft Office Word An OfficeLink feature that allows you to quickly copy a query, form, or report object to Word.

Publishing Saving Web files to Web folders on a server.

Query An Access object that provides a spreadsheet-like view of the data, similar to that in tables. It may provide the user with a subset of fields and/or records from one or more tables. Queries are created when the user has a "question" about the data in the database.

Query Datasheet View The view of a query that shows the selected fields and records as a datasheet.

Query design grid The bottom pane of the Query Design View window in which you specify the fields, sort order, and limiting criteria for the query.

Query Design View The window in which you develop queries by specifying the fields, sort order, and limiting criteria that determine which fields and records are displayed in the resulting datasheet.

Query grid *See* Query design grid.

Question mark Wildcard character that stands for any single character.

Raw data *See* Data.

Record A group of related fields, such as all demographic information for one customer.

Record locking A feature of Access databases that prevents two users from updating the same record at the same time.

Record number box *See* Specific record box.

Record selector box The small square to the left of a record in a datasheet that marks the current record or the edit record symbol when the record has the focus or is being edited.

Record Source In a form or report, the property that determines which table or query object contains the fields and records that the form or report will display. It is the most important property of the form or report object. A bound control on a form or report also has a Record Source property. In this case, the Record Source property identifies the field to which the control is bound.

Recordset The value of the Record Source property.

Recordset Type A query property that determines if and how records displayed by a query are locked.

Rectangle control An unbound control used to draw rectangles on the form that divide the other form controls into logical groupings.

Referential integrity Ensures that no orphan records are entered or created in the database by making sure that the "one" side of a linking relationship (CustomerNumber in a Customer table) is entered before that same value can be entered in the "many" side of the relationship (CustomerNumber in a Sales table).

Relational database A database in which more than one table, such as the customer, sales, and inventory tables, can share information. The term "relational database" comes from the fact that the tables are linked or "related" with a common field of information. An Access database is relational.

Relational database software Software such as Access that is used to manage data organized in a relational database.

Replica The copy of the Access database file that is stored in the Briefcase.

Replica set Both the original (master) and replicated (replica) database file. There may be more than one replica in a replica set, but there is only one master.

Replication The process of making replicas of a master database file using the Briefcase.

Report An Access object that creates a professional printout of data that may contain such enhancements as headers, footers, and calculations on groups of records.

Report Design View View of a report in which you add, delete, and edit the report's properties, sections, and controls.

Report Footer On a report, a section that contains controls that print once at the end of the last page of the report.

Report Header On a report, a section that contains controls that print once at the top of the first page of the report.

Report section properties Properties that determine what information appears in different report sections and how it is formatted.

Report Wizard An Access wizard that helps you create a report.

Required A field property that determines if an entry is required for a field.

Rich text format A file format that does not support all advanced Word features, but does support basic formatting embellishments such as font types and colors.

Row field On a PivotTable, the field that supplies values for the row headings. Analogous to the Category field on a PivotChart and a Row Heading field on a crosstab query.

Row selector The small square to the left of a field in Table Design View or the Tab Order dialog box.

Row Source The Lookup property that defines the list of values for the Lookup field.

RTF *See* Rich text format.

Rulers Vertical and horizontal guides that appear in Form and Report Design View to help you position controls.

Run To open a query and view the fields and records that you have selected for the query presented as a datasheet. Also to execute a stored set of actions, called a macro.

Run-time error An error that occurs after code starts to run, and includes attempting an illegal operation such as dividing by zero or moving focus to a control that doesn't exist.

Schema A pictorial representation of how the tables of the database are related. Access presents the database schema in the Relationships window.

ScreenTip A descriptive message that appears when you point to a toolbar button.

Secondary sort field In a query grid, the second field from the left that includes sort criteria. It determines the order in which the records will appear if there is a "tie" on the primary sort field. (For example, the primary sort field might be the State field. If two records both contained the data "IA" in that field, the secondary sort field, which might be the City field, would determine the order of the IA records in the resulting datasheet.)

Section A location of a form or report that contains controls. The section in which a control is placed determines where and how often the control prints.

Secure database A database that is protected with workgroup-level security.

Security account password A password applied to workgroups and is used to determine which objects each workgroup has access to and at what level.

Select query The most common type of query that retrieves data from one or more linked tables and displays the results in a datasheet.

Series On a PivotChart, the area that is also called the legend.

Series field On a PivotChart, the field that supplies the values for the legend. Analogous to the Column field in a PivotTable and the Column Heading field of a crosstab query.

Server In Internet terminology, this would be the computer that serves the information to you from the Internet, for example, a Web page or an e-mail message. In a client/server application, a shared file server is one that all clients may access through a network. The server stores the data that each client uses, analyzes, and updates through their local forms and reports.

Shared network folder A network folder that many people can use.

Shortcut A pointer to an object. You can use a shortcut to open an object without affecting the original location of the object.

Simple Query Wizard A wizard used to create a select query.

Single step To run a macro one line at a time, and observe the effect of each line as it is executed.

Sizing handles Small squares at each corner of a selected control in Access. Dragging a handle resizes the control. Also known as handles.

Smart Tags Buttons that provide a small menu of options and automatically appear when certain conditions are present to help you work with the task at hand, such as correcting errors. For example, the AutoCorrect Options button, which helps you correct typos and update properties, as well as the Error Indicator button, which helps identify potential design errors in Form and Report Design View, are Smart Tags.

Snapshot A type of recordset displayed within a query's datasheet that does not allow you to update any field.

Sort Reorder records in either ascending or descending order based on the values of a particular field.

Source document Original paper document, such as an employment application or medical history form, upon which data are recorded.

Specific record box Part of a box in the lower-left corner in Datasheet view and Form view of the Navigation buttons and which indicates the current record number. You can click in the specific record box, then type a record number to quickly move to that record. Also called the current record box or record number box.

Speech recognition A feature that allows you to speak directly to your computer and have it respond to your commands.

Spike A surge in power.

Split To organize a database so that the data is stored on the file server, but other database objects are stored on your local (faster) hard drive.

SQL *See* Structured Query Language (SQL).

SQL Server A database program provided by Microsoft for databases that are larger and more complex than those managed by Access.

Standard module A module stored as objects within the database window. Standard modules can be executed from anywhere within the database.

Start tag In markup languages such as HTML and XML, a start tag is used to mark the beginning of data.

Startup option A series of commands that execute when a database is opened.

Statement A line of VBA code.

Static Web page Web pages created by exporting a query or report to HTML from an Access database are static because they never change after they are created.

Status bar The bar at the bottom of the Access window that provides informational messages and other status information (such as whether the Num Lock is active).

Status Bar Text property Property of a control that determines what text displays in the status bar when that control has the focus.

StDev Aggregate function that returns the standard deviation of values in a field.

Structured Query Language (SQL) A standard programming language for selecting and manipulating data stored in a relational database.

Sub A procedure that performs a series of VBA statements but does not return a value nor can be used in an expression. You create subs to manipulate controls and objects.

Sub procedure *See* Sub.

Subform A form placed within a form that shows related records from another table or query. A subform generally displays many records at a time in a datasheet arrangement.

Subreport A report placed as a control within another report.

Sum Aggregate function that returns the total of values in a field.

Summary query A query used to calculate and display information about records grouped together.

Surge protector A power strip with surge protection.

Switchboard A special type of form that uses command buttons to simplify and secure access to database objects.

Switchboard Manager An Access feature that simplifies the creation and maintenance of switchboard forms.

Synchronization The process of reconciling and updating changes between the master and replicas of a replica set.

Syntax The technical rules that govern a language or program.

Syntax error A VBA error which occurs because of a typing error or misspelling. Syntax errors are highlighted in the Code window in red.

Tab control An unbound control used to create a three-dimensional aspect to a form so that other controls can be organized and shown in Form View by clicking the "tabs."

Tab order The sequence in which the controls on the form receive the focus when the user presses [Tab] or [Enter] in Form view.

Table A collection of records for a single subject, such as all of the customer records.

Table Datasheet toolbar The toolbar that appears when you are viewing a table's datasheet.

Table Design View The view in which you can add, delete, or modify fields and their associated properties.

Table Wizard An interactive tool used to create a new table from a list of sample tables and sample fields.

Tag A programming code defined by markup language that browser software such as Internet Explorer reads to process the content stored within a Web page.

Target table A table to which an append query adds a record set.

TCP/IP *See* Transmission Control Protocol/Internet Protocol.

Text A field data type that allows text information or combinations of text and numbers such as a street address. By default, it is 50 characters but can be changed. The maximum length of a text field is 255 characters.

Text box A common control used on forms and reports to display data bound to an underlying field. A text box can also show calculated controls such as subtotals and dates.

Title bar Contains the program name (Microsoft Office Access 2003) or filename of the database.

Toggle button A bound control used to indicate "yes" or "no" answers for a field. If the button is "pressed" it displays "yes" information.

Toolbox toolbar The toolbar that has common controls that you can add to a report or form when working in Report Design View or Form Design View.

Top values A feature within Query Design view that allows you to limit the number of records in the resulting datasheet to a value or percentage of the total.

Total row Row in the query design grid used to specify how records should be grouped and summarized with aggregate functions.

Totals or Detail Field On a PivotTable, the field that supplies the data that is summarized in the body of the report. Analogous to the Data field in a PivotChart and the Value field in a crosstab query.

Transmission Control Protocol/Internet Protocol The set of common communications protocol that Internet uses to send and receive information.

Unbound control A control that does not change from record to record and exists only to clarify or enhance the appearance of the form, using elements such as labels, lines, and clip art.

Unbound object frame An unbound control that is used to display clip art, a sound clip, or other multimedia content and that doesn't change as you navigate from record to record on a form or report.

UNC *See* Universal Naming Convention.

Undo button Button that allows you to undo your last action.

Uniform Resource Locator A Web page address that allows other computers to find that Web page.

Uninterruptible Power Supply A device that allows a computer to maintain constant power.

Universal Naming Convention The address you give a file on a local area network.

Unmatched record *See* orphan record.

Update query An action query that updates data based on an expression.

UPS *See* Uninterruptible Power Supply.

Upsize To convert an Access database to an SQL Server database.

URL *See* Uniform Resource Locator.

Validation Rule A field property that helps eliminate unreasonable entries by establishing criteria for an entry before it is accepted into the database.

Validation Text A field property that determines what message will appear if a user attempts to make a field entry that does not pass the validation rule for that field.

Value axis On a PivotChart, the vertical axis. Also called the y-axis.

Var Aggregate function that returns the variance of values in a field.

Variable A named storage location that can contain data that can be modified during program execution.

VBA (Visual Basic for Applications) The Access programming language that is very similar to Visual Basic and which is stored within module objects.

VBA password A password that prevents unauthorized users from modifying VBA code.

View buttons Four buttons in the database window that determine how the object icons are displayed (as Large Icons, Small Icons, List, and Details).

Visual Basic Editor Code window (Code window) The window you use to write Visual Basic programming code.

WAN *See* Wide area network.

Web folder Special folder dedicated to organizing Web pages.

Web page A file that is viewed using browser software such as Microsoft Internet Explorer.

Web Page Preview Viewing a Web page created by a data access page in Internet Explorer.

Web server A computer that stores and serves Web pages to clients.

Webmaster Person who builds and maintains a Web server.

What-if analysis A reiterative analysis, usually performed in Excel, where you change values in a workbook and watch related calculated formulas update instantly.

Wide area network A network created when a LAN is connected to an existing telecommunications network.

Wildcards Special characters used in criteria to find, filter, and query data. The asterisk (*) stands for any group of characters. For example, the criteria I* in a State field criterion cell would find all records where the state entry was IA, ID, IL, IN, or Iowa. The question mark (?) wildcard stands for only one character.

Word *See* Microsoft Office Word.

Word wrap A Word feature that determines when a line of text extends into the right margin of the page, and automatically forces text to the next line without you needing to press Enter.

Workgroup A description of users, objects, and permissions to which those users have access to the objects stored as a file.

Workgroup Administrator An Access tool for creating workgroups that define the specific users and object permissions to which the users have access.

World Wide Web A global network of networks that use Web servers, Web pages, browser software, and other common technologies to share documents across the world.

XML *See* Extensible Markup Language.

XML file A text file that contains Extensible Markup Language (XML) tags that identify fields and contain data.

XSD *See* Extensible Schema Document.

XSL *See* Extensible Stylesheet Language.

Yes/No A field data type that stores only one of two values, "Yes" or "No."

Zero-length string A value with a deliberate entry that contains no characters. You enter a zero-length string by typing two quotation marks ("") with no space between them.

Zoom pointers Mouse pointers displayed in Print Preview that allow you to change the zoom magnification of a printout.

Index

Import XML dialog box, ACCESS I-6, ACCESS I-7

importing data, ACCESS H-2–3
  XML data, ACCESS I-6–7

In operator, ACCESS F-7

inactive programs, WINDOWS XP A-10

Input Mask property, ACCESS E-10, ACCESS E-11

Insert ActiveX Control dialog box, ACCESS G-18, ACCESS G-19

Insert Hyperlink dialog box, ACCESS J-14, ACCESS J-15

Insert Module button, ACCESS O-11

Intellimouse, WINDOWS XP A-5

Internet, ACCESS J-2, ACCESS J-3, WINDOWS XP A-2
  accessing from desktop, WINDOWS XP A-3

Internet Explorer, WINDOWS XP A-3

Internet Service Providers (ISPs), ACCESS J-3

Is Not Null criterion, ACCESS B-17

Is Not Null operator, ACCESS F-7

Is Null criterion, ACCESS B-17

ISPs (Internet Service Providers), ACCESS J-3

Italic button, ACCESS D-15

►J

join(s), properties, ACCESS K-16–17

Join Properties dialog box, ACCESS K-16, ACCESS K-17

►K

key field(s), ACCESS A-4

key field combinations, ACCESS E-2

key symbol, ACCESS B-6, ACCESS B-7, ACCESS E-4

keyboard navigation indicators, WINDOWS XP A-10

keyboard shortcuts, WINDOWS XP A-10, WINDOWS XP A-12
  Edit mode, ACCESS A-15
  menus, WINDOWS XP A-11
  Navigation mode, ACCESS A-11

keywords, VBA, ACCESS O-5

►L

labels, ACCESS C-3
  modifying, ACCESS C-8–9

LANs (local area networks), ACCESS J-5, ACCESS P-12

laptop computers, using Briefcase, ACCESS P-17

Large Icon view, ACCESS A-9

Last function, ACCESS F-13

layout, forms, ACCESS G-4, ACCESS G-5

LEFT function, ACCESS F-11

legends, displaying, ACCESS F-16

LEN function, ACCESS F-11

less than operator (<), ACCESS B-17, ACCESS F-7

less than or equal to operator (<=), ACCESS B-17, ACCESS F-7

Like operator, ACCESS F-6, ACCESS F-7

Limit to List property, ACCESS G-10

line(s)
  adding to reports, ACCESS H-6–7
  problems, ACCESS H-7

Line and rectangle control, ACCESS C-3

Line button, WINDOWS XP B-5

line charts, ACCESS L-11

Line/Border Color button, ACCESS D-15

Line/Border Width button, ACCESS D-15

Link Spreadsheet Wizard, ACCESS I-8, ACCESS I-9

linking
  data, ACCESS I-8–9
  forms and subforms, ACCESS G-7

list arrow, filtering data, ACCESS F-16

list boxes, ACCESS C-3, ACCESS G-10, ACCESS G-11, ACCESS L-3, WINDOWS XP A-13

List view, ACCESS A-9

Local area networks (LANs), ACCESS J-5

local area networks (LANs), ACCESS P-12

Locked property, ACCESS G-14

Log Off command, WINDOWS XP A-19

logic errors, ACCESS O-16

logical view, ACCESS F-2

Look In option, Find and Replace dialog box, ACCESS B-12

Lookup fields, ACCESS E-8–9

Lookup properties, ACCESS E-8, ACCESS E-9

Lookup Wizard, ACCESS E-8

Lookup Wizard data type, ACCESS B-3

►M

macro(s), ACCESS A-4, ACCESS A-5, ACCESS I-2, ACCESS N-1–17
  actions. See macro actions
  arguments. See macro arguments
  assigning to command buttons, ACCESS N-13
  assigning to key combinations, ACCESS N-9
  conditional expressions, ACCESS N-10–11
  converting to VBA, ACCESS N-17
  creating, ACCESS N-4–5
  customizing toolbars, ACCESS N-14–15
  events, ACCESS N-12–13
  modules compared, ACCESS O-4–5
  running, ACCESS N-1
  terminology, ACCESS N-2
  troubleshooting, ACCESS N-16–17

macro actions, ACCESS N-1, ACCESS N-2, ACCESS N-5
  modifying, ACCESS N-6, ACCESS N-7

macro arguments, ACCESS N-2
  modifying, ACCESS N-6, ACCESS N-7

Macro Design View, ACCESS N-2, ACCESS N-3

macro groups, ACCESS N-2, ACCESS N-8–9

Macro Name column, Macro Design View, ACCESS N-3

Magnifier button, WINDOWS XP B-5

Mail Merge task pane, ACCESS I-14

Mail Merge toolbar, ACCESS I-14

main document, ACCESS I-14, ACCESS I-15

main form, ACCESS G-2

main report, ACCESS L-14

make-table queries, ACCESS K-8–9

many-to-many relationships, ACCESS E-2, ACCESS I-5

mapped drives, ACCESS J-16

master, replicating databases, ACCESS P-14

Match Case option, Find and Replace dialog box, ACCESS B-12

Match option, Find and Replace dialog box, ACCESS B-12